PEACE AND *Conflict* STUDIES

DAVID P. BARASH
CHARLES P. WEBEL

SAGE Publications
International Educational and Professional Publisher
Thousand Oaks ■ London ■ New Delhi

For information:

Sage Publications, Inc.
2455 Teller Road
Thousand Oaks, California 91320
E-mail: order@sagepub.com

Sage Publications Ltd.
6 Bonhill Street
London EC2A 4PU
United Kingdom

Sage Publications India Pvt. Ltd.
M-32 Market
Greater Kailash I
New Delhi 110 048 India

Printed in the United States of America

Library of Congress Cataloging-in-Publication Data

Barash, David P.
    Peace and conflict studies / David P. Barash, Charles P. Webel.
        p. cm.
    Includes bibliographical references and index.
    ISBN 0-7619-2507-4 (cloth : alk. paper)
    1. Peace.   2. War.   3. Arms control.   4. Conflict management.
I. Webel, Charles.   II. Title.
    JZ5538 .B37 2002
    303.6′6—dc21

                                                        2001007985

This book is printed on acid-free paper.

04 05 10 9 8 7 6 5 4 3 2

Acquisitions Editor:	Jim Brace-Thompson
Editorial Assistant:	Karen Ehrmann
Production Editor:	Sanford Robinson
Copy Editor:	Kate Peterson
Typesetter:	Graphicraft, Hong Kong
Indexer:	Teri Greenberg
Cover Designer:	Michelle Lee

Contents

Preface

Welcome to *Peace and Conflict Studies*.

In this book, we have sought to emphasize important themes and readability rather than immersion in the technical literature. We have also been relatively generous with historical material, to supplement and if possible deepen the reader's appreciation of current issues, such as civil wars involving nationalism and "ethnic cleansing," nuclear proliferation, international law, terrorism, world poverty, and pressing environmental concerns.

It is a cliché—often trotted out at graduation ceremonies—that "you (i.e., the graduating students) have reached a crossroad," requiring important, life-defining choices. Well, all of us—that is, human beings—have in fact reached such a crossroad, although perhaps humanity is always approaching one choice point or another. Our global situation seems constructed of equal parts danger and opportunity: opportunity because the world is no longer hostage to the paralyzing effects of the debilitating U.S.-Soviet conflict formerly known as the Cold War, but also danger because the risk of mass destruction still looms. There is also an array of additional threats to our species and our planet: sometimes overt and violent, sometimes covert and insidious.

Our interest in this project goes beyond mere scholarship, pedagogy, or even our (presumably) enlightened self-interest as world citizens. Thus, we are personally committed to the social and political goals of *Peace and Conflict Studies*. The field itself differs from most other human sciences in that it is value oriented, and unabashedly so. Accordingly, we wish to be up front about our own values, which are frankly antiwar, antiviolence, antinuclear, antiauthoritarian, antiestablishment, proenvironment, pro-human rights, pro-social justice, propeace, and politically progressive. At the same time, we believe that emotional and political efforts at personal and social transformation are most effective if they build on serious intellectual efforts, including an attempt to understand all sides of complex debates.

We also acknowledge that—to our chagrin—a scholarly account of such material as poverty, environmental threats, the denial of human rights, and especially war necessarily involves a degree of detached writing that can never capture the vitality of the subject matter, not to mention the ineffable horrors and terror of violence and war. We can only plead that we have done our best.

We also wish to say a bit about the making of this book. Its first edition was called *Introduction to Peace Studies* and was written by David Barash. The book eventually went out of print, and Charles Webel contacted David about a second edition. David and Charles agreed to rewrite it as a work for a new century. The text you have in your hands is their joint product, with Charles principally responsible for revising the first half (Parts I and II) and David for the second half (Parts III and IV).

As is often the case with coauthored books, there are some unresolved, and probably unresolvable, issues connected with this work. In this case, although we agree on almost every matter discussed in this book—which is remarkable given the range and number of topics covered—we are not in complete accord about the "end of the Cold War" or the "dangers of the new technologies." But we most emphatically agree that these important matters should be researched, discussed, and debated—as should all the vital and often controversial topics discussed in this book.

While the present book was in press, the World Trade Center in New York City and the Pentagon in Washington, D.C., were attacked, resulting in about 3,000 deaths and unleashing enormous grief, confusion, and anger. These horrifying events, although to some degree unique, also share features with many other acts of warfare and collective violence throughout history; if anything, they make peace and conflict studies all the more relevant, especially to citizens of the United States, who have not experienced such carnage on their own soil since the Civil War.

In the aftermath, it seems more important than ever to inquire deeply into the causes of all forms of violence, whether state sponsored or not, as well as to ask about suitable responses, not only by sovereign states but also via the institutions of international law; in addition, persons concerned about peace must question seriously the morality as well as the efficacy of framing "security" in strictly military terms. Furthermore, these terrible events have emphasized the role of emotional, economic, religious, and historical factors, along with the degree to which East-West antagonisms may be eclipsed by North-South disparities and conflicts, as we enter the 21st century.

Peace has never been more important, or complicated.

We thank and applaud you for pursuing peace and conflict studies and encourage you to pursue your interest in understanding and promoting peace long after you have finished reading this book.

May peace be with you all.

DAVID P. BARASH
Seattle,
Washington

CHARLES P. WEBEL
Berkeley,
California

Acknowledgments _____

Our greatest debt is to the many scholars and activists who have struggled for a more peaceful world including—but not limited to—those who have explicitly labored in the newly developing field of peace and conflict studies. We want to take this opportunity to thank them and also to urge them to keep up what is undeniably "good work"! We also want to explicitly thank Chadwick Alger of Ohio State University for useful, specific suggestions; Jim Brace-Thompson of Sage Publications for seeing merit in the project; Sanford Robinson and Karen Ehrmann for helping bring it to fruition; as well as the reviewers of an earlier version of this book.

A United Nations peacekeeping soldier, with a group of local children, conducts a security patrol in Dili, East Timor. (Photo courtesy of UN/DPI)

PART I

The Promise of Peace, the Problems of War

Only the dead have seen the end of war.

—Plato as cited by General Douglas MacArthur

At the dawn of the 21st century, human beings are faced with many problems: an increasingly polluted and otherwise threatened planet composed of finite resources whose limits may soon be reached; gross maldistribution of wealth, which prevents the overwhelming majority of human beings from realizing their potential and ensures that vast numbers die prematurely; and regrettable patterns of social and political injustice, in which racism, sexism, and other forms of unfairness abound, and in which representative government is relatively rare and torture and other forms of oppression, distressingly common. And this is only a partial list.

Yet, despite all of these difficulties, the remarkable fact is that enormous sums of money and vast resources of material, time, and energy are expended, not in solving what we might call the "problems of peace," but rather in threatening and actually making war on one another. Although it seems unlikely that human beings will ever achieve anything approaching heaven on earth, it does seem reasonable to hope—and perhaps even to demand—that we will someday behave far more responsibly and establish a global society based on the needs of the entire planet and the beings who inhabit it, a planetary society that is just and sustainable, and not characterized by major outbreaks of violence.

In this book, we explore some of the needs, prospects, and obstacles involved in achieving such a world. After some introductory remarks on the meanings of peace, we proceed to an examination of war—its causes, prevention, and alternatives. This issue reflects what is perhaps humanity's most serious challenge, because behind the threat of war—especially of a global nuclear and/or biochemical war—lies the prospect that human beings may end their civilization, and perhaps all life on earth. This challenge is also the primary reason for this book, and for the special urgency of establishing an enduring system of peace.

Part I looks specifically at the promise of peace and the problems of war. Although war and peace are not polar opposites, there is nonetheless a fundamental tension between them, two differing visions of the way people interact with one another. Part II considers war and its apparent causes, and Part III looks at possible routes toward preventing and abolishing war. Part IV turns to deeper aspects of peace, examining the outlines of our dilemma and considering some solutions, including the creation of positive structures of peace—steps that go beyond the mere prevention of war. Throughout the entire book, we hope to challenge you, the reader, not only intellectually but also in many other dimensions of your life.

1 The Meanings of Peace

We need an essentially new way of thinking if mankind is to survive. Men must radically change their attitudes toward each other and their views of the future. Force must no longer be an instrument of politics. . . . Today, we do not have much time left; it is up to our generation to succeed in thinking differently. If we fail, the days of civilized humanity are numbered.

—Albert Einstein

This text is based on a number of assumptions. War is one of humanity's most pressing problems; peace is almost always preferable to war; and moreover, peace can and must include not only the absence of war but also the establishment of positive, life-affirming, and life-enhancing values and social structures. We also assume, with regret, that there are no simple solutions to the problems of war; most aspects of the war-peace dilemma are complex, interconnected, and poorly understood. On the other hand, much can be gained by exploring the various dimensions of war and peace, including the possibility of achieving a more just and sustainable world—a way of living that can nurture life itself and of which all humans can be proud.

Throughout this book, we maintain that there is good reason for such hope, not simply as an article of faith, but based on the realistic premise that human beings are capable of understanding the global situation and of recognizing their own specieswide best interests. Humans can behave rationally, creatively, and with compassion. Positive steps can be taken that will diminish our species' reliance on violence in attempting to settle disputes and that will facilitate the development of a more just and truly peaceful world.

Most people think they know what *peace* means. But in fact, different people often have very different understandings of this seemingly simple word. And although most people would agree that some form of peace—whatever it means—is desirable, there are often vigorous, even violent, disagreements over how to obtain it.

Some Historical Views of Peace

In some cases, the word *peace* has an undesirable connotation. The Roman poet Tacitus spoke of making a desert and calling it "peace," an unwanted place of sterility and emptiness. Similarly, although nearly everyone desires "peace of mind," the temporary "peace" that comes from drug-based withdrawal from social reality, the peacefulness of sleep, or the undesired "peace" of a coma or even of death may not seem so desirable. To be *pacified* (derived ultimately from the Latin word for peace, *pax*) often means to be lulled into a false and misleading quietude. Indeed, *appeasement*—buying off a would-be aggressor (such as Neville Chamberlain's appeasement of Hitler shortly before Hitler's commencement of World War II), thereby achieving a short-lived "peace" by making concessions to a potential war maker—has a very bad name indeed. By contrast, even the most peace loving among us recognize the merits of certain martial and aggressive attitudes, acts, and metaphors, especially when they refer to something other than direct military engagements: Lyndon Johnson's "war on poverty," for example, or the medical "war on cancer" and "battle against AIDS."

Some Eastern Concepts of Peace

The foregoing is not simply a matter of playing with words. Fighting, striving, and engaging in various forms of conflict and combat (especially when they are successful) are widely associated with vigor, energy, and other positive virtues. Nonetheless, it is no exaggeration to claim that peace may be (with happiness) the most longed-for human condition.

The Chinese philosopher Lao-tzu (sixth century B.C.E.), founder of Taoism and author of *Tao De Ching*, emphasized that military force is not the "Tao," or "Way," for human beings to follow. He frequently referred to peaceful images of water or wind—both of them soft and yielding, yet ultimately triumphant over such hard substances as rock or iron. The teachings of K'ung-Fu-tzu (or Confucius, approximately 551–479 B.C.E.) are often thought by most Westerners to revolve exclusively around respect for tradition, including elders and ancestors. But Confucius did not hold to these ideas because he valued obedience and order as virtues in themselves; rather, he maintained that the attainment of peace was the ultimate human goal and that peace came from social harmony and equilibrium. His best-known collection of writings, the *Analects,* also emphasizes the doctrine of *jen* (empathy), founded on a kind of hierarchical Golden Rule: Treat your subordinates as you would like to be treated by your superiors.

The writings of another renowned ancient Chinese philosopher and religious leader, Mo-tzu (468–401 B.C.E.), took a more radical perspective. He argued against war and in favor of all-embracing love as a universal human virtue and the highest earthly goal, yet one that is within the grasp of each of us. Mo-tzu said, "Those who love others will also be loved in return. Do good to others and others will do good to you. Hate people and be hated by them. Hurt them and they will hurt you. What is hard about that?"[1]

In what is now India, the Buddhist monarch Aśoka (third century B.C.E.) was renowned for abandoning his successful military campaigns in mid-career, and he devoted himself to the religious conversion of his adversaries by nonviolent means of persuasion. The great Indian text, the Hindu epic *Mahabharata* (written about 200 B.C.E.), contains as perhaps its most important segment the *Bhagavad Gita.* This is a mythic account of a vicious civil war in ancient India, in which one of the principal warriors, Arjuna, is reluctant to fight because many of his friends and relatives are on the opposing side. Arjuna is ultimately persuaded to engage in combat by the god Krishna, who convinces Arjuna that he must fight, not out of hatred or hope for personal gain, but out of selfless duty. Although the *Gita* can and has been interpreted as supporting caste loyalty and the obligation to kill when bidden by a superior party to do so, it also inspired the great 20th-century Indian leader Mohandas Gandhi as an allegory for the de-emphasis of individual self in the pursuit of higher goals. (The *Gita* was also cited by the "father of the atomic bomb," J. Robert Oppenheimer, when he described the first atomic explosion as a contemporary incarnation of Krishna: "I am become Death, the Destroyer of Worlds.")

Some Judeo-Christian Concepts of Peace

Peace per se is not prominent in the Old Testament. The God (Yahweh) of Abraham, Moses, and David is frequently portrayed as rather bellicose, even bloodthirsty, and the ancient Israelites were often merciless warriors. Exceptions to this norm exist, however, such as the prophet Isaiah, who praised the reign of peace and described war not as a reward or a route to success, but rather as a punishment to be inflicted on those who have failed God.

Under the influence of Isaiah and later Hebrew prophets—and despite the ostensibly defensive violence of the Maccabees and Zealots (who opposed Roman rule in Palestine)—Jewish tradition has tended to strongly endorse peacefulness, in contrast with the warrior traditions of some of the Christian and Islamic societies within which most Jews have lived. On the other hand, it can also be argued that with the emergence of Israel as a militarily threatened—and threatening—state, this tradition has been substantially changed. In fact, Jewish, Christian, and Islamic traditions all have bellicose components and elements in their history. A key question is whether these martial activities—often quite persistent and widespread—are part of a pattern of faithfulness to, or a deviation from, their underlying religious worldview.

A deep irony underlies the concept of peace in these three great Western religious systems. Christianity, for example, gave rise to one of the great warrior traditions in the world, and yet it is unique among Western religions in the degree to which it was founded upon a message of peace, love, and nonviolence. "My peace I give unto you," declares Jesus according to the New Testament, along with "the peace of God, which passeth all understanding." Although definitions of peace often vary, and hypocrisy is not infrequent, most human beings share a positive presumption in favor of peace, in accord with the stated aspirations of these great religions.

Positive Versus Negative Peace

An important distinction should be made between what may be called *negative peace* and *positive peace*. Negative peace simply denotes the absence of war. It is a condition in which no active, organized military violence is taking place. The noted 20th-century French intellectual Raymond Aron was thinking of negative peace when he defined peace as a condition of "more or less lasting suspension of rivalry between political units."[2]

Aron's is the most common understanding of peace in the context of international relations, and it epitomizes the (neo-)*realist* view of matters of war and peace. This view suggests that peace is found whenever war or other direct forms of organized state violence are absent. From this perspective, then, the peace proclamations of pharaonic Egypt, the *Philanthropa*, were actually statements of a negative peace, expressions of benevolence from a stronger party toward those who were weaker. The *pax* of Roman times really indicated nothing more than the absence of overt interstate violence, typically a condition of nonresistance or even acquiescence enforced by legal arrangements and the military might of the Roman legions. The negative peace of the *Pax* Romana was created and maintained through social and political repression of the people who lived under Roman law.

An alternative view to this "realist" (or *Realpolitik*) perspective is one that emphasizes the importance of positive peace (and that has been particularly advanced by the Norwegian peace researcher Johan Galtung). Positive peace is more than the mere absence of war or even the absence of interstate violence. It refers to a social condition in which exploitation is minimized or eliminated, and in which there is neither overt violence nor the more subtle phenomenon of underlying *structural violence*.

The Role of Structural Violence

One commonly understood meaning of violence is that it is physical and readily apparent through observable bodily injury and/or the infliction of pain. But as Galtung notes, it is important to recognize the existence of another form of violence, one that is more indirect and insidious than observable physical violence. This structural violence is typically built into the very structure of social, cultural, and economic institutions. (For example, both ancient Egypt and imperial Rome practiced slavery and were highly despotic, although they were technically in states of negative peace for long periods of time.)

Structural violence usually has the effect of denying people important rights, such as economic well-being; social, political, and sexual equality; a sense of personal fulfillment and self-worth; and so on. When people starve to death, or even go hungry, a kind of violence is taking place. Similarly, when humans suffer from diseases that are preventable, when they are denied decent education, affordable housing, opportunities to work, play, raise a family, and freedom of expression and peaceful assembly, a kind of violence is occurring, even if no bullets are shot or clubs wielded. A society commits violence against its members when it forcibly stunts their development and undermines their well-being, whether because of religion, ethnicity, gender, age, sexual preference, or some other social reason. Structural violence is a serious form of social oppression. And it is regrettably widespread and often unacknowledged.

Under conditions of structural violence, many people who behave as "good citizens," and who think of themselves as peace-loving people, may, according to Galtung, participate in "settings within which individuals may do enormous amounts of harm to other human beings without ever intending to do so, just performing their regular duties as a job defined in the structure."[3] Reviewing the role of "normal" people, such as Adolf Eichmann, who participated in the Holocaust during World War II, the noted philosopher Hannah Arendt referred to the "banality of evil" to emphasize that routine, workaday behavior by otherwise normal and decent people can contribute to mass murder, social oppression, and structural violence.

Structural violence, including hunger, political repression, and psychological alienation, often is unnoticed and works slowly to erode humanistic values and impoverish human lives. By contrast, direct violence generally works much faster and is more visible and dramatic. In cases of overt violence, even those people not specifically involved in the conflict may be inclined to take sides. News coverage of these events is often intense (as in the O. J. Simpson and Rodney King episodes, not to mention the Persian Gulf War and the war in Kosovo). And because the outcome is often quite visible and undeniable (e.g., the forcible extraction of Iraq's forces from Kuwait and of Serbia's troops from Kosovo and the violent removal of

Chinese citizens from Tiananmen Square by Red Army troops), the viewer is more likely to pay attention to this tangible violence than to the underlying structural factors that may have led to the conflict.

Achieving Positive Peace

Despite the prevalence of structural violence, many cultural and spiritual traditions have identified political and social goals that are closer to positive peace than to negative peace. The ancient Greek concept of *eireinei* (English *irenic*) denotes harmony and justice as well as peace. Similarly, the Arabic *salaam* and the Hebrew *shalom* connote not only the absence of violence but also the presence of well-being, wholeness, and harmony within oneself, a community, and among all nations and peoples. The Sanskrit word *shanti* refers not only to peace but also to spiritual tranquility, an integration of outward and inward modes of being, just as the Chinese noun *ping* denotes harmony and the achievement of unity from diversity. In Russian, the word *mir* means peace, a village community, and the entire world.

Attention to negative peace, or the simple absence of war, usually results in a diplomatic emphasis on peacekeeping or peace restoring (if a war has already broken out). By contrast, positive peace focuses on peace building, the establishment of nonexploitative social structures, and a determination to work toward that goal even when a war is not ongoing or imminent. Negative peace is thus a more conservative goal, as it seeks to keep things the way they are (if a war is not actually taking place), whereas positive peace is more active and bolder, implying the creation of something that does not currently exist.

Unfortunately, wars between nations in the contemporary world are ongoing in many places (roughly 30 a year) and imminent in many others. Moreover, just as there is disagreement about how best to avoid a war—that is, about how to achieve a negative peace—even among decision makers who may be well-intentioned, there is at least as much disagreement about the best routes toward positive peace. Positive peace is more difficult to articulate, and possibly more difficult to achieve, than negative peace. And although there is relatively little debate now about the desired end point in the pursuit of negative peace (most people agree that war in general is a bad thing, but may disagree about the justification for any particular war), when it comes to positive peace, there is substantial disagreement about specific goals and the means to achieve them. Some theorists have argued, for example, that peace should exist only as a negative symbol (the avoidance of war), because once defined as a specific ideal system to be achieved, peace becomes something to strive for, even perhaps to the point of going to war. As Quincy Wright, one of the 20th century's preeminent researchers into the causes of war, put it:

Wars have been fought for the sanctity of treaties, for the preservation of law, for the achievement of justice, for the promotion of religion, even to end war and to secure peace. When peace assumes a positive form, therefore, it ceases to be peace. Peace requires that no end should justify violence as a means to its attainment.[4]

Other notable figures, on the other hand, have maintained that a free society may justify—or even require—occasional violence. Thomas Jefferson, for example, wrote in 1787 that "the tree of liberty must be refreshed from time to time with the blood of patriots and tyrants." This apparent paradox —violence as a precondition for the attainment of nonviolence, or peace— is a recurring theme in the study of and quest for peace.

There are other ways, however, in which peace can assume a positive form. And these are more than mere cliches: for example, cooperation, harmony, equity, justice, and love. Supporters of positive peace uniformly agree that a repressive society, even if it is not at war, should be considered "at peace" only in a very narrow sense. In addition, a nation "at peace" that tolerates outbreaks of domestic violence on a widespread level, despite an absence of violent conflicts with other nations, is really not at peace with itself.

Social Justice

Having recognized the importance and underdeveloped nature of positive peace, it is now time to give further attention to a related notion: social justice. Although almost everyone today agrees that a "just society" is desirable, widespread disagreement continues to exist as to what, exactly, a just society would look like. For example, whereas capitalists and individualists tend to privilege economic freedom (from state intervention) and individual liberty—often at the cost of mass poverty, malnutrition, and homelessness —socialists and collectivists tend to value economic and social security— sometimes at the price of individual political freedoms. Also, many Western individualists assert that nations with capitalist economies and democratic political systems seldom if ever go to war with one another, whereas many non-Western and dissident Western critics of capitalism claim that capitalism by its very expansionistic nature is inherently predatory and militaristic.

Social Justice and War

Social injustices, such as economic exploitation and political autocracy, are important not only as contributors to structural violence but also as major factors in the outbreak of wars. Perhaps ironically, although the

United States of America was originally created from a war of independence from Great Britain in the late 18th century, by the end of the 20th century the United States had become widely perceived in the "lesser developed countries" as both an antirevolutionary force and the "policeman of the world." However, for most American citizens, as well as for privileged Europeans and other economic elites in less affluent societies, the military, cultural, and political hegemony of the United States at the beginning of this millennium is welcomed as the guarantor of their wealth, power, and status. For them, peace means the continuation of things as they now are, with the additional hope that overt violence will be minimized or prevented altogether. For others—perhaps for a majority of the world's present population—dramatic social and economic change from the status quo is desired. And for some of the most militant among them, peace is something to kill and die for if it can bring about greater social justice and economic equity. As a Central American peasant is reported to have said, "I am for peace, but not peace with hunger." And the great 18th-century French philosopher Denis Diderot was convinced that a world of justice and plenty would mean a world free from tyranny and war. Hence, in his treatise, the *Encyclopedia*, Diderot hoped to establish peace by disseminating globally all of humanity's accumulated scientific and technical knowledge, from beekeeping and leather tanning to iron forging.

Similar efforts continue today, although few advocates of economic and social development and equity claim that the problem of war can be solved simply by spreading knowledge or even by keeping everyone's belly full. At the beginning of this millennium, it is indeed disquieting that in a time of unprecedented affluence in many Western nations, and of the increasing global dissemination of Western (particularly American) economic and cultural ideals, the inhabitants of this planet continue to dissipate their resources and lives fighting among themselves, or preparing to do so, for an increased share of earth's abundance. While there is nothing new in the human experience about this recourse to war and political violence, what is new, as we shall see, is the omnicidal risk involved in these potentially cataclysmic squabbles.

The Peace-War Continuum

"War is not sharply distinguished from peace," according to Quincy Wright. Moreover, "Progress of war and peace between a pair of states may be represented by a curve: the curve descends toward war as tensions, military preparations, and limited hostilities culminate in total conflict; and it rises toward peace as tensions relax, arms budgets decline, disputes are settled, trade increases, and cooperative activities develop."[5]

Many people, if pressed, would agree that with respect to overt and direct violence, war and peace are two ends of a continuum, with only a vague and uncertain transition between the two. But the fact that two things may lack precise boundaries does not mean that they are indistinguishable. For example, at dawn, night grades almost imperceptibly into day, and vice versa at dusk. Yet when two things are very distinct, we say that "they are as different as night and day." The transition from war to peace may frequently be similarly imprecise (although the move from peace to war may be all too clear and dramatic, as was evident at the beginning of World War II, both in Europe and in the Pacific), but the characteristics of either state of affairs are often quite apparent.

Consider, for example, that the U.S. involvement in Vietnam and the rest of Southeast Asia began in the early 1950s with economic and military aid to French forces seeking to retain their colonial possessions in that part of the world. It progressed to include the deployment of relatively small numbers of "technical advisers" in the early 1960s to what was then called South Vietnam. Larger numbers of American "advisers" were eventually sent to South Vietnam, accompanied by combat troops in "small numbers," followed by limited and then massive bombing of all of Vietnam (and its neighbors Laos and Cambodia), and then massive escalation of the war. Finally, even though more than 500,000 American troops were committed to propping up a notoriously corrupt and autocratic South Vietnamese government engaged in a civil war with its own people and with what was then called North Vietnam, and more than 50,000 Americans died and perhaps as many as two million Vietnamese, the United States never formally declared war. Yet there was no doubt that a state of war existed.

There is an increasing tendency—especially since the Vietnam War—for nations to fight wars without formal declarations announcing their beginnings or solemn peace ceremonies and treaties signaling their end. The Korean War, for example, which began in 1950, has never really "ended" and was never officially declared, either (although there has been a prolonged cease-fire between North and South Korea lasting a half-century). And one of the most destructive wars of the second half of the 20th century, the conflict between Iran and Iraq in the 1980s, which produced casualties that may well have numbered in the millions (and during which Iraq used biological and/or chemical weapons), was never declared. In fact, most of the world's armed conflicts involve revolutionary, counterrevolutionary, genocidal, and/or terrorist violence with no declarations of war whatsoever (as in East Timor, Kashmir, Sudan, Congo [Zaire], Rwanda, Burundi and much of the rest of central Africa, and the former Yugoslavia and several independent nations spawned from the former Soviet Union, as well as El Salvador, Nicaragua, Guatemala, Afghanistan, Angola, and Cambodia).

The reluctance of most governments to declare war, as opposed to their willingness to fight or promote wars, may also be due to the fact that although wars continue to be fought and to break out, most citizens and politicians are not proud of that fact. And despite the potential for theoretical arguments over the precise transition points between different stages of conflicts, most people know at a gut level what is meant by war. There is also little doubt that given the choice, most human beings prefer peace to war.

The Desirability of Peace Versus Justifications for Wars

Given the positive response that most people have to the word *peace*, it is fair to question why for almost all human cultures and for most of our history we have never attained it. In fact, for many centuries, war has been considered acceptable, even honorable, by large numbers of people and most governments. How can one explain the conundrum that the same human beings who say they want peace will nonetheless kill other human beings, sometimes ruthlessly and indiscriminately, to obtain it and to protect their own "vital interests" and "national security"? What justifications are provided for violent conflicts and what are the motivations that underlie decisions made by leaders who make war?

War in U.S. History

Thomas Jefferson is reported to have written that in the United States "peace is our passion," and American citizens like to think of themselves, as do most citizens in most nations, as peace-loving people. But the fact is that the United States has not been especially peaceful, either before its war of independence from Great Britain (ask the Native American peoples) or since the founding of the American republic at the end of the 18th century. Like most nation-states, whenever the United States employs organized, state-sanctioned violence against other countries, its leaders seek to convince its citizens and other peoples that such actions are justified. Moreover, more than any other advanced industrial society, the United States is rife with symbols of war and the tools of violence. Guns and other weapons, for example, retain an almost hallowed place in American folklore (and in American homes): the Kentucky long rifles that opened the frontier, the Winchester repeating rifle that "won the West," the Colt 45 revolver, the "great equalizer," and the "winning weapon" (including "Little Man" and "Big Boy," the atomic bombs dropped on Japan during World War II), not to mention the "peacekeeper" (MX) long-range, nuclear-tipped ballistic missiles.

According to Benjamin Franklin, "There never was a good war or a bad peace." But Franklin also reputedly warned that "even peace can be purchased at too high a price." And indeed, U.S. history is often taught as a chronology of wars, including the War of Independence, the War of 1812, the Mexican-American War, the Civil War, the Spanish-American War, World War I, World War II, the Korean War, the Vietnam War, the Persian Gulf War, the "war against terror[ism]," and so on. But what is less known (or publicized) is that the United States has "intervened" militarily on more than 130 separate occasions, including multiple incursions into China, Mexico, Panama, Nicaragua, Honduras, Columbia, Afghanistan, Turkey, the Dominican Republic, Japan, Argentina, Cuba, Haiti, Hawaii (when it was an independent kingdom), Samoa, Fiji, Uruguay, Guatemala, Lebanon, Sumatra, the former Soviet Union, and Grenada, and single incursions into Puerto Rico, Sudan, Brazil, Chile, Morocco, Egypt, Taiwan, Peru, the Philippines, Cambodia, Laos, Syria, and the Ivory Coast. In many cases, these were relatively brief invasions, or air attacks, officially intended to protect alleged U.S. economic and/or security interests or to help maintain compliant governments. Since the early 1990s, there has been increasing lip service paid to the defense of "human rights" and the "prevention of genocide" as justifications for military actions, both unilaterally by the United States and multilaterally by international organizations, such as the United Nations, and by military alliances, such as the North Atlantic Treaty Organization (NATO). But for people caught up in such violence, especially for unarmed civilians, who make up a majority of the casualties during such incursions, it was still war.

Although the United States (as does virtually every nation) cherishes its avowed commitment to peace, and also the constitutional separation of military from civilian rule, it has also chosen a number of its presidents from among its generals: Washington, Jackson, Grant, and Eisenhower. Some of its leaders who became presidents have even espoused the desirability of war: Just before 1900, for example, Theodore Roosevelt urged his countrymen not to shrink from acquiring world empire, by war if need be. He wrote that U.S. citizens should value and exercise "the great fighting masterful virtues" and accept its imperial responsibilities in Hawaii, Puerto Rico, the Philippines, and Cuba, lest "bolder and stronger peoples . . . pass us by, and . . . win for themselves the domination of the world."[6]

Biological Justifications for Wars

Theodore Roosevelt spoke from an ancient tradition. War has long been the ultimate arbiter of human disputes and a way of achieving glory, both for individuals and for entire peoples and nations. Ares, the Greek god of war (Mars was his Roman equivalent), was a major deity, whereas Irene, the Greek goddess of peace, was a minor figure at best. According to Heraklitos, the presocratic philosopher, "War (or strife) is the father of all things." And an influential 19th- and 20th-century intellectual movement, social Darwinism, maintained that war was not only rewarding, virtuous, and manly but also biologically appropriate. Social Darwinism attempted to apply (or misapply) the evolutionary concept of natural selection to human political and social activities by providing a biological rationale for national conquests, imperialism, military dictatorships, and the subjugation of "weaker" by "stronger" peoples. But in fact, social Darwinism is not scientifically valid, since natural selection and thus the process of organic evolution favor living things that are most successful reproductively, not necessarily those that are the most aggressive. Moreover, there is no objective basis for assuming that just because something is true in the biological world, it is therefore socially desirable, ethically defensible, or even characteristic of the human world. AIDS and typhoid fever, for example, are both "natural" and "organic," yet virtually all people agree that neither is desirable.

Social and Political Justifications for Wars

Some influential Western philosophers, including Hobbes and Hegel, have at times expressed views that seem to deem war as not merely natural but as beneficial to humanity because, in Hegel's words (which are also a critique of Immanuel Kant's pathbreaking essay "Perpetual Peace"), "war prevents a corruption of nations which a perpetual, let alone an eternal peace would produce."[7]

Although this view may be in disrepute today, throughout most of the "civilized" world the fact is that wars have often shaken up the existing (and often unjust) sociopolitical order and have resulted in many changes, not all of them for the worse. Through revolutionary wars and wars of national liberation, many peoples have won their independence from colonial powers, both by overthrowing despotic governments and by repulsing the efforts of other powers to force them back into subjugation. In some cases, however, revolutionary struggles have resulted in newer forms of autocracy, as in the Iranian revolution of 1979, in which the despotic pro-Western shah was overthrown, only to be replaced by the despotic Islamic Fundamentalist Ayatollah Khomeini. Still, revolts against oppression should not automatically be condemned because they sometimes go astray after the insurrectionary groups have seized state power.

Consider the case of Cuba. In the aftermath of the Cuban Revolution of 1959, despite more than 40 years of an American embargo of Cuban imports and exports, infant mortality in Cuba has declined to the lowest in Latin America; life expectancy increased from 55 years in 1959 to 73 years in 1984; health care was nationalized and made available to all Cuban citizens at no or little cost; literacy exceeded 95%; and although prostitution, begging, and homelessness returned to Cuba in the 1990s (almost entirely for economic reasons due to the embargo and to the loss of support from the former Soviet Union), Cuba still has far fewer of these problems than virtually all other countries in Latin America. While Cuba is far from an earthly paradise, and certain individual rights and civil liberties are not yet widely practiced, the case of Cuba indicates that violent revolutions can sometimes result in generally improved living conditions for many people. Moreover, although Western governments (especially the United States) criticize and impose sanctions on governments they detest (such as those in Cuba and Iraq), and may even overtly or covertly try to overthrow those governments, such efforts may result in worsened conditions for the great majority of the populace in the targeted "rogue nations" (as in Iraq since 1991).

Thus, wars, especially those fought to throw off the shackles of despotic indigenous regimes or the sometimes less visible controls of imperial global powers, may at times serve the enticing ends of enhancing, at least for a short period of time, national self-determination and political liberty. Indigenous peoples, no less than those in advanced technological societies, also tend to "rally 'round the flag" in times of perceived military danger, and this sense of patriotic fervor and national unity is usually achieved at the cost of projecting a stereotyped, and often dehumanized, image of "the enemy." Indeed, domestic political elites often employ the unifying effect of war and the threat of war to distract their citizenry from domestic problems and scandals in order to increase electoral support for their own campaigns.

Political Ideologies and Militarism

The noted British historian Michael Howard has introduced the term *bellicist* to refer to cultures "almost universal in the past, far from extinct in our own day, in which the settling of contentious issues by armed conflict is regarded as natural, inevitable and right." For example, Howard continues, bellicism during World War I "accounts not only for the demonstrations of passionate joy that greeted the outbreak of war but sustained the peoples of Europe uncomplainingly through years of hardship and suffering."[8]

While this account may overstate the "peoples of Europe's" toleration of horrific loss of life (tens of millions of people died violently in Europe between 1914 and 1918, many of them civilians), it does point to the fact that many people are inclined (or manipulated) to identify perceived adversaries as bellicist, while claiming that they (and their governments) are peace loving, if not pacifist (a term of opprobrium hurled by many political leaders against opponents they wish to caricature as weak). During the 20th century, far more people, mostly civilians, died violently as a result of wars than in any other century. Not coincidentally, certain political ideologies, notably Fascism and Nazism, have openly glorified war, not only as a means to alleged national political goals but also as a desirable end in itself.

Some Conservative Viewpoints

In contrast with more liberal and progressive political worldviews, conservatism has long tended to look upon war more favorably. Nonetheless, even most conservative ideologies have espoused a view of peace and war prevention. The mainstream Anglo-American conservative tradition, for example, traces its roots to a rather pessimistic, even bellicose, view of human nature. One of the philosophical founders of this tradition, the great 17th-century English philosopher Thomas Hobbes, warned that because of humanity's ostensibly inherent, competitive, and sinful nature, life for humans in what Hobbes termed "the state of nature" consisted of *bellum omnium contra omnes* (the war of everyone against everyone). For Hobbes, this "natural state" of war required people who wished to avoid the fate of violent death to impose on themselves an autocratic governmental authority (called "Leviathan" by Hobbes).

More than 2,000 years earlier, Socrates had also argued against democracy and popular sovereignty, though for very different reasons. Socrates claimed that the great majority of Athenian citizens were inclined to being misled and duped by political and religious demagogues and hence could not be trusted to make rational decisions (an assembly of Socrates' peers in fact condemned him to death for "impiety" and "misleading the young"). So, in Plato's *Republic*, Socrates is depicted as arguing that only philosopher-kings should rule, rather than the people as a whole. Plato also concluded from the Peloponnesian War (which lasted for decades and which effectively ended the Golden Age of Athenian Greece) that (city-)states must be hierarchically and stringently organized if they were to survive in a violent, unruly world in which war seemed an unavoidable fact of life.

The mainstream Western conservative tradition also suggests that strong moral and governmental controls over individual conduct are necessary if social order and peace are to be secured. To many conservatives, wars usually occur because we are, at bottom, predatory and aggressive animals by nature, and also because social order and political stability constantly threaten to break down. Since social organizations are regarded by most conservatives as basically unstable and often irrational, peace, security, and stability can be safeguarded only by strong laws and the efficacious use of force and punishment.

For Hobbes, and for many in the mainstream Western conservative tradition, virtually nothing justifies the overthrow of a monarch or duly elected political authority. From this perspective, the "state of nature" is so dangerous and abhorrent that the people make a *social contract* with political authority, whereby they cede to the leviathan their allegiance (and forgo their right to rebel) in return for protection against real and alleged enemies, foreign and domestic. This is a contract whose purpose is to minimize the risk of *anarchy* (lack of order) within a nation-state. Possibly ironically, however, Hobbes also noted that states interacted with other nations in what was essentially a comparably anarchic situation. "The state of Commonwealths considered in themselves is natural, that is to say, hostile," declared Hobbes in *The Citizen*, and so "neither if they cease from fighting, is it therefore to be called peace; but rather a breathing time."[9]

According to mainstream Western conservative political ideology, if power is properly and securely held and wielded, there should be little reason for war or insurrection, except perhaps for occasional brief wars to adjust the "international state system," that is, for what has come to be called (legitimate) "reasons of state." War may be acceptable, even laudable, if it serves to prevent civic and moral breakdown. For example, the Roman historian Livy (59 B.C.E. to A.D. 17) reported approvingly in *The Early History of Rome* that the Roman Senate had "ordered an immediate raising of troops and a general mobilization on the largest possible scale" in the hope that the revolutionary proposals that some Roman tribunes were bringing forth might be forgotten in the bustle and excitement of three imminent military campaigns against Rome's perceived enemies. The Roman general Vegetius is first credited with having coined the phrase *vis pacem, para bellum* (if you wish peace, prepare for war). And in more recent times, the doctrines of "balance of power," "peace through strength," "national security," and "Realpolitik" have continued this line of conservative political thought.

Probably the most articulate spokesperson for conservative political theory in the English-speaking world was the 18th-century orator and statesman Edmund Burke. Burke articulated mainstream Anglo-American conservative political doctrine by stressing the primacy of "community" and "tradition," the importance of preserving existing institutional order, and skepticism about the perfectability of human societies and individual persons. This philosophy has long been motivated by a lack of trust in the rational potential of autonomous individual citizens and by a deep suspicion of democracy. For most mainstream conservatives, the traditions inherited from past generations must be respected. Social cohesion and political stability are seen to come from reverence for, and deference to, established authority (which is one reason why K'ung-Fu-tzu, or Confucius, is also considered to be a conservative social thinker). Authority per se, and typically patriarchy and authoritarianism as well, are typically valued over equality, spontaneity, and change. According to Burke, society is a partnership "not only between those who are living, but between those who are living, those who are dead, and those who are to be born."[10]

Social hierarchies have also been generally admired by most mainstream conservative political theorists. Hierarchical social and political relations are claimed by conservatives to provide a citizenry with necessary reference points and stability. In the 19th and 20th centuries, however, with the overthrow of hereditary monarchy in most of Europe, mainstream Western conservatism shifted its focus away from a prior veneration of established political authorities and began instead to concentrate more on the advocacy of "rugged individualism," and "free enterprise and free markets," unimpeded by "state interference." This is an ironic inversion of the classical Greco-Roman privileging of community and society over individualism. Many contemporary Anglo-American conservative thinkers in particular have also become ambivalent about the state, generally opposing big government (except in the realm of military expenditures and in support of what has been called "the prison-industrial complex"), yet also revering patriotism and loyalty to the state.

Not surprisingly, most conservatives have long been especially concerned about the alleged threats of disorder and subversion being imported from abroad. Writing about the most important political event of his day, the French Revolution, Burke observed, "It is a war between the partisans of the ancient, civil, moral, and political order of Europe [the monarchy] against a set of fanatical and ambitious atheists which means to change them all." Burke continued, "As I understood the matter, we were at war, not with its [the French Revolution's] conduct, but with its existence, convinced that its existence and its hostility were the same."[11]

Some Liberal Viewpoints

Most Anglo-American political liberals have valued highly the autonomous individual, free from political and ecclesiastical authority. Major liberal theorists in the Anglo-American tradition include John Locke, Thomas Jefferson, Jeremy Bentham, John Stuart Mill, John Maynard Keynes, John Kenneth Galbraith, and John Rawls. According to the mainstream liberal tradition in the English-speaking world, political and legal equality are more desirable than social hierarchy. The classical liberalism of the early 18th century (represented most keenly by Jefferson, Bentham, and J. S. Mill) was opposed to monarchism and in favor of free-market entrepreneurship. This early defense of capitalism by classical liberals may come as a surprise to many contemporary conservatives, who have associated liberalism with advocacy of the welfare state. But the two leading theorists and defenders of capitalist economics, Adam Smith and David Ricardo, were considered the leading liberals of their day. The liberal theorist Norman Angell even claimed in 1913 that capitalists were necessarily opposed to war because "the capitalist has no country, and he knows . . . that arms and conquests and juggling with frontiers serve no ends of his and may very well defeat them, through the great destruction that such wars will generate."[12]

Another major strand in Western liberal political thought addresses the issue of peace from an economic perspective. In *The Spirit of Laws*, the 18th-century French political philosopher Montesquieu proposed that international trade and commerce would naturally tend to promote peace: "Two

nations which trade with each other become reciprocally dependent; if it is to the advantage of one to buy, it is to the advantage of the other to sell; and all unions are founded on mutual needs." (This foreshadows the widespread view of many liberal theorists in the 1990s that democracies do not go to war against each other in large measure because their economic interests would be severely undermined by international conflicts.) Montesquieu also argued that trade leads to an improvement in manners and basic civility: "It is almost a general rule that wherever there are tender matters, there is commerce, and wherever there is commerce, there are tender matters."[13] And in a similar vein, J. S. Mill claimed that "it is commerce which is rapidly rendering war obsolete, by strengthening and multiplying the personal interests which act in natural opposition to it."[14]

Mill's and Montesquieu's view soon became a part of the liberal antiwar credo: By expanding commerce and spreading free-market capitalism around the world, as well as by promoting democracy and harnessing public opinion, war could be made obsolete. The leaders of the so-called Manchester school of British economic theory, Richard Cobden and John Bright, for example, in the mid- to late 19th century opposed foreign interventionism by the British crown and maintained that maximum free trade between peoples would serve to make war not only unnecessary but also impossible. As the process of economic globalization gathered steam at the beginning of the 21st century, its supporters have argued that increased trade and economic interdependence would contribute not only to enhanced wealth for most nations but also to peace. The opponents of globalization disagree vehemently with these claims.

In a reversal of theoretical roles, however, 20th-century liberals, especially in the United States, placed greater emphasis on social responsibility and community than have the conservative champions of free enterprise and possessive individualism, except possibly in the area of civil liberties, where liberals defend individual rights and freedom and most conservatives consider traditional social units, such as the family, church, and state, to have a higher priority.

With regard to the establishment of peace and the reasons for wars, Anglo-American liberals have often decried the excessive power of nation-states and their often imperious leaders. However, most liberals were also caught off-guard by the rise of fascist, racist, and xenophobic movements in 20th-century central Europe (which, perhaps ironically, was also the birth-place of many liberal and progressive ideas, social movements, and political parties), especially in Austria, Germany, and Italy. In those countries particularly, a combination of right-wing populism, virulent nationalism, and xenophobic ethnocentrism led directly to political authoritarianism and militarist campaigns against perceived threats to the established political orders. With their optimistic view of human nature, most liberals have had great difficulty understanding how this could take place within advanced

industrial societies with long-standing democratic traditions and humanistic cultural values.

After World War II, conservatives generally saw the rise of Communism in the former Soviet Union and in "Red China" as the chief peril to the free world, and they were prepared to use any military and propaganda means necessary to "defeat world Communism." By contrast, most Western liberals were less rhetorically aggressive in promoting the "war against Communism," while nonetheless continuing to allocate massive expenditures to military and espionage activities aimed at defeating left-wing governments, many of which were more nationalist than "communist inspired." Both liberals and conservatives applauded in triumphalist ways the apparent end of Soviet Marxism and the breakup of the former Soviet Union in 1991. Still, compared with conservatives, Anglo-American liberals tend to be more favorably disposed to arms control agreements with the Russians and other perceived threats to national security, and they place more hope in the peacemaking and peacekeeping roles of international organizations, such as the United Nations, than do most conservatives, who tend to be quite skeptical of any supranational institutions.

Liberals have on occasion supported specific wars. The Spanish civil war from 1936 to 1939, for example, was initially seen by virtually all Western progressives as an unambiguously just war, the defense of a popularly elected (socialist) government against attack by reactionary forces aided by fascist dictatorships in Germany and Italy. America's entry into World War II occurred under the administration of perhaps the most liberal American president of the 20th century, Franklin Delano Roosevelt. Many liberals associated with the Kennedy and Johnson administrations initially supported America's war in Southeast Asia. And virtually all prominent liberal congressional figures in the United States also were in favor of American involvement in both the Persian Gulf War and the war in Kosovo. At the same time, the rationale for American involvement in wars of the 1990s shifted from its previous anticommunist rhetoric to a defense of human rights in the face of potentially genocidal *ethnic cleansing*, a term most frequently employed to depict the actions by ethnic Serbs in Bosnia against Bosnian Muslims and Croats.

Liberals have typically been more ambivalent about war than most conservatives, and typically require a "better rationale" for military action. Nonetheless, by the beginning of the 21st century, traditional liberal and conservative perspectives on war and peace have become even more fractionated. Some conservatives, for example, have embraced an isolationist approach to international relations, while others, especially in the United States, favor selective military interventions in order to maintain and enhance the global military and economic preeminence of the United States ("the indispensable nation," in the words of American secretary of state Madeleine Albright). And some liberals favor military intervention for humanitarian purposes, while others oppose any military incursion into another country.

Some Progressive or Radical Leftist Viewpoints

Virtually all political movements of the far right (and even some moderate right-wing or conservative parties) have rarely if ever professed peace as an important national political goal; most left-wing (progressive and/or radical) thinkers and parties have traditionally claimed a strong association with world peace (although, as we have just seen, many of the less radical, more liberal members of progressive political movements and parties have frequently approved of war under certain conditions). The most explicit and best-known example of a radical left-wing (or Communist) leader supporting war is Mao Tse-tung, who wrote,

> Political power grows out of the barrel of a gun. . . . All things grow out of the barrel of a gun. . . . Some people ridicule us as advocates of the "omnipotence of war." Yes, we are advocates of the omnipotence of revolutionary war; that is good, not bad. . . . We are advocates of the abolition of war, we do not want war; but war can only be abolished through war, and in order to get rid of the gun it is necessary to take up the gun.[15]

Mao's apparently paradoxical rationale for war (as the best means to abolish war) is the quintessential Realpolitik perspective, one that justifies organized violence (war) as the best means to end class violence and social oppression. Ironically, whereas the purported goals of left-wing revolutionary wars differ from the espoused aims of right-wing military campaigns, people from all political perspectives have justified the use of organized state violence as a defensible (if sometimes regrettable) means of attaining allegedly higher political, social, and economic goals, such as freedom and national security. This *Machiavellism*, according to the noted political theorist Friedrich Meinecke, often cuts across and transcends political ideologies.

Within left-wing political traditions, stemming from Karl Marx and continuing through Lenin, Mao, and Che Guevara to the present, there is a further justification for the selective use of revolutionary violence (and even of terror) against established regimes. This is found in the ostensibly humanistic social goals of such violence: the emancipation of workers and other oppressed peoples from capitalist domination and exploitation, and the construction of socialism (leading eventually perhaps to a classless, or "communist," society) both domestically and globally. This radical political tradition is often in opposition to another viewpoint, namely, an antimilitarist, socialist-pacifist tradition, represented in the 20th-century European progressive movements by Rosa Luxemburg, Karl Liebknecht, and Bertrand

Russell and in the United States by Eugene V. Debs, Norman Thomas, Emma Goldman, and A. J. Muste. For Muste in particular, religious considerations loomed large, such as the necessity of personal, faith-based "witness" against war. Muste is particularly well-known for his insistence that "there is no way to peace; peace is the way" and that "wars will end when men refuse to fight."

Prior to World War I, European pacifists and socialists had hoped that *worker solidarity* would prevent the outbreak of war. But the war that erupted between 1914 and 1918 was an enormous blow to the optimism of many socialist-pacifists, especially since overwhelming majorities in European Socialist and Social Democratic Parties elected to support their governments in their war efforts (with such notable exceptions as Rosa Luxemburg and Karl Liebknecht), rather than to organize massive antiwar protests and demonstrations. And 85 years later, in 1999, many members of the European Left—especially those with important political offices in England and Germany—enthusiastically supported NATO's bombing campaigns in Serbia and Kosovo, despite the protests of many more pacifistically inclined members of their own political parties (such as the Labour, Social Democratic, and Green Parties).

In summary, radical leftists and other political progressives have long advocated opposition to war in general, although many have believed that the abolition of war, and the prevention of genocide, can be accomplished only via war. With the fall of the Soviet Union, and the end of the 20th-century Cold War, many progressives have tended to become more involved in local, often environmentally related movements, rather than in the mass antiwar and antinuclear movements with which they had been closely identified between 1950 and 1990. Whether this continues to be the case in the first part of this millennium remains to be seen.

Is War Inevitable?

Many 19th-century liberals viewed war as a deplorable interruption in the linear progression of our species to a better, more peaceful world. Even today, many liberal views of the causes of wars emphasize the role of misperceptions and cognitive errors (rather than human iniquity on the part of political leaders who initiate wars). War is, in this view, a blunder, the consequence of human fallibility: If decision makers would only operate in a more realistic manner, most wars could be prevented.

In contrast, there is another, sterner tradition, traditionally associated with conservative viewpoints. The emphasis here is on innate human weakness, sin, and/or the allegedly unalterable fact of "evil" in human nature. According to one of the most important conservative politicians of the 20th century, Winston Churchill, "The story of the human race is war." From this perspective, wars do not in general occur because one side, presumably the one that is more peace loving, misunderstands the other. Rather, wars are usually forced on otherwise rational and peace-loving national leaders because their "vital interests" have been assaulted, or because they realistically perceive an impending threat to their "national security," and hence must defend themselves and others against those who would do them harm. According to this view, the defense of liberty requires a political willingness by national statesmen to go to war if need be.

Regardless of one's thinking about the ultimate, underlying causes of wars, the belief that war is inevitable carries a great danger (and in fact the 1991 Seville "Statement on War and Violence," by a group of notable sociologists, refutes the notion that war and violence lie "in our genes" and are hence inescapable features of the human condition). Consider, for instance, the idea of a *self-fulfilling prophecy*, in which something that is not necessarily true may become true if enough people believe it will occur. Thus, if one believes that another person or country is an enemy, and acts on this assumption, the belief may create a new reality. Similarly, if war is deemed inevitable and societies therefore prepare to fight against each other—by drafting an army, procuring and deploying weapons systems that threaten their neighbors, and/or engaging in bellicose foreign policy—war may well result. Such a war may then be cited as "proof" that war was inevitable from the start. Moreover, it may be used to justify similar bellicose behavior in the future (as was often the case during the Cold War of the late 20th century).

It is also important to remember that many social practices once common and widely viewed by many as inevitable—such as slavery and dueling—are virtually unknown today. If opponents of slavery and dueling had simply conceded the inevitability (if undesirability) of this ancient social practice, they would not have struggled to end it. Nonetheless, it must be acknowledged that ending slavery and dueling may well have been easy compared with ending war, since these social changes were often feasible without regard to what other nation-states, especially the most heavily armed, were doing. A state that renounces war as a means of settling international conflicts may find itself vulnerable to demands and threats made by other, better-armed nations, particularly by nuclear states. In short, unlike the case of slavery in the United States, an end to war cannot be simply declared by a Lincoln-like "emancipation proclamation," which is then unilaterally implemented. An end to war in this millennium seems to require a global will to do so.

Can Nations Change?

There are, however, some reasons for guarded optimism. For example, history provides many examples of societies changing dramatically from warlike to peaceful tendencies. During the early Middle Ages, the Swiss were among Europe's most bellicose people, fighting successfully against the French in northern Italy, and for their own independence against the Holy Roman Empire. But Switzerland hasn't participated in an external war since 1515, when it was defeated by France and adopted a policy of permanent neutrality. Today, Switzerland's vaunted "neutrality" (most keenly compromised during World War II due to the support by many Swiss for Nazi Germany) is undergirded by a large, well-equipped modern army and by a civilian defense network of underground shelters designed to shield virtually the entire population of the country from a nuclear or biochemical attack.

Japan has also changed notably over the centuries. It gave birth to one of the world's great warrior traditions, the code of *bushido* and the very aggressive *samurai*. Within several decades after European firearms reached Japan via Portuguese traders (in 1542), Japanese musketry was among the most advanced in the world. But a century later, guns were virtually absent from all of Japan. And when Commodore Matthew Perry "opened" Japan (for Western trade) in 1853, Japanese warfare was technologically medieval.

The process of Japan's transformation had been remarkable. The 16th-century shogun Tokugawa, upon being victorious over his rivals, centralized all firearms manufacture and arranged for all gunpowder weapons gradually to be destroyed, without replacement. His decision was not based on a wholehearted devotion to peace; rather, it reflected the samurais' great distaste for muskets and cannons, which threatened to ruin the cult of the warrior/nobleman. Despite the reasons for this "conversion," the Japanese example is still inspiring, since it demonstrates that militarism can be curtailed, and whole societies reorganized along more peaceful lines, once the authorities (and in democracies, the citizenry) consider such changes to be in their best interest.

It should also be noted, however, that demilitarization can be reversed, as was the case in Japan during the latter half of the 19th century. After Perry's visit to Japan in 1853, Japan modernized very rapidly and initiated successful wars against China (1894) and Russia (1904–1905). But Japan's increasingly aggressive and warlike ventures, including its attacks on China and much of the rest of Asia in the late 1930s and on the United States in 1941 at Pearl Harbor, culminated in its defeat and the atomic devastation of Hiroshima and Nagasaki in 1945. Since the end of the Second World War, Japan has kept a military force that is considerably smaller than comparably affluent nations (in part because it has been "protected by America's nuclear umbrella") and has instead devoted its energies to its economy (although there is some current discussion of Japan increasing its military role).

Germany has been similarly variable in its war/peace behavior. About one third of all people living on German soil perished during the devastating Thirty Years' War (1618–1648), many of them civilian noncombatants. The principalities and kingdoms in the German-speaking world then went on to become the philosophical, musical, and scientific centers of central Europe, although militarism did flourish in Prussia, the most influential of the German states. Beginning around 1860, with the wars of German unification, the newly constituted nation of Germany became increasingly militarized, a process culminating in Germany's military aggression during World War I and World War II, and in its total defeat by the Allies in 1945. Since the end of the Second World War, Germany (like Japan) has been comparatively demilitarized (although it participated directly in NATO's military strikes against Serbia in 1999, much to the consternation of Germany's considerable antiwar movement).

Peaceful traditions can be ruptured by war, just as peaceful societies can become militarized. For example, despite long-standing Jewish advocacy of peace and nonviolence, modern-day Israel expends about 30% of its gross national product on its military, and Israel has been involved in four wars (1948, 1956, 1967, and 1974), as well as many military incursions into Lebanon, during its brief existence. On the other hand, nations that had previously been rent by war and domestic violence can renounce those behaviors, as did Costa Rica when it abandoned its maintenance of a national standing army.

War can thus become a national habit, and militarism, a way of life. But so can peace. Long-standing traditions of war and conflict may, with sufficient popular support, give way to traditions of nonbellicose alliance. Great Britain and France, for example, which were bitter opponents for hundreds of years and had fought many devastating wars against each other, were close allies for much of the 20th century, as were other longtime enemies, such as the United States and Great Britain. Kenneth Boulding, one of the founders of peace studies, has pointed out that a zone of "stable peace" has spread to include most of Western Europe (though notably not in the Balkans or in Northern Ireland and the Basque region of Spain), North America, and Oceania (Australia and New Zealand). Within this zone, war is deemed unlikely to break out between democratically governed nation-states.

However one judges the desirability of peace or the legitimacy of (at least some) wars, it should be clear that peace and war exist on a continuum of violent/nonviolent national behaviors and that they constantly fluctuate. Neither should be taken for granted, and neither is humanity's "natural state." The human condition—whether to wage war or to strive to build an enduring peace—is for us to decide.

The Nature and Functions of Conflict

We end this chapter with a brief discussion of various ways of conceptualizing conflict. The word *rivalry*, for example, originated with the Latin *rivus* (river or stream). Rivals were literally "those who use a stream in common."

Competitors, by contrast, are those who seek to obtain something that is present in limited supply, such as water, food, mates, or status. But the word *enemy* derives from the Latin *in* (not) plus *amicus* (friendly), and it implies a state of active hostility. Rivals necessarily compete, if there is a scarcity of a sought-after resource—this much is unavoidable—but they do not have to be enemies. The word *conflict*, on the other hand, derives from the Latin *confligere*, which means literally "to strike together." It is impossible for two physical objects, such as two billiard balls, to occupy the same space. They conflict, and if either is in motion, the conflict will be resolved by a new position for both of them.

Within the human realm, conflict occurs when different social groups are rivals or otherwise in competition. Such conflicts can have many different outcomes: one side changed, one side eliminated, both sides changed, neither side changed, or (rarely) both sides eliminated. Conflicts can be resolved in many ways: by violence, by the issues changing over time, or by mutual agreement.

A Final Note on the Meanings of Peace

It should be emphasized that neither the study nor the pursuit of peace ignores the importance of conflict. Neither does the burgeoning field of peace and conflict studies aim to abolish conflict, any more than its practitioners expect to eliminate rivalry or competition in a world of finite resources and imperfect human conduct. (Analogously, the field of medicine does not realistically seek to eliminate all bacteria or viruses from the world.) Peace and conflict studies does, where possible, seek to develop new avenues for cooperation, as well as to reduce significantly (and eventually to eliminate) violence, especially organized and increasingly destructive state-sanctioned violence. It is this violence, by any definition the polar opposite of peace, that has so blemished human history and that—with the advent of nuclear weapons, biochemical weapons, and other weapons of global destruction—now threatens the future of all life on this planet. And it is the horrors of such violence, as well the glorious and perhaps even realistic hope of peace (both negative and positive), that makes peace and conflict studies especially frustrating, fascinating, and essential.

Notes

1. Mo-tzu. *The Writings of Mo-tzu*, XV.
2. Raymond Aron. 1966. *Peace and War*. New York: Doubleday.
3. Johan Galtung. 1985. "Twenty Five Years of Peace Research: Ten Challenges and Responses." *Journal of Peace Research* 22: 414–431.

4. Quincy Wright. 1964. *A Study of War.* Chicago: University of Chicago Press.

5. Quincy Wright. 1968. "War." In D. S. Sills, ed., *International Encyclopedia of the Social Sciences.* New York: Macmillan.

6. Theodore Roosevelt. 1910. *The Strenuous Life and Other Essays.* New York: Review of Reviews.

7. G. W. F. Hegel. 1942. *Philosophy of Right.* T. M. Knox, trans. Oxford, UK: Clarendon.

8. Michael Howard. 1986. *The Causes of Wars.* Cambridge, MA: Harvard University Press.

9. Thomas Hobbes. 1949. *The Citizen.* New York: Appleton-Century-Crofts.

10. Edmund Burke. 1961. *Reflections on the Revolution in France.* New York: Doubleday.

11. Ibid.

12. Norman Angell. 1913. *The Great Illusion.* London: Heinemann.

13. C. L. Montesquieu. 1977. *The Spirit of Laws.* David Carrithers, trans. Berkeley: University of California Press.

14. John Stuart Mill. 1958. *Considerations on Representative Government.* New York: Liberal Arts Press.

15. Mao Tse-tung. 1966. *Basic Tactics.* Stuart R. Schram, trans. New York: Praeger.

2 Peace Movements

War is a defeat for humanity. Only in peace and through peace can respect for human dignity and its inalienable rights be guaranteed.

—Pope John Paul II, World Day of Peace, January 1, 2000

Just as there have been wars, and changes in war making throughout history, there have also been peace and efforts toward peacemaking. If one judged such matters by the number of years spent at war versus those at peace, or even by the total number of wartime deaths versus peacetime deaths, one would be tempted to conclude that the peacemakers are far ahead. However, if we consider that virtually any war is an odious tarnishing of the human record, we must agree that the work of peacemaking is not only unfinished but woefully unsatisfactory. By many measures, wars have become more serious, making the work of the peacemaker all the more urgent. There have been, nonetheless, numerous efforts at peace, raising many possibilities and opportunities, some long-standing and others quite recent. There have also been hints of success; although paradoxically, whereas the toll of war can be tallied, it is impossible to assess how many wars—or how much destruction during wars—have been prevented by the efforts of various peace movements.

Popular Attitudes Toward Peace

One difficulty faced by would-be peacemakers is that although most people claim to be in favor of peace, the great majority seems to be far more interested in war. The new emphasis on peace culture as witnessed in the UN

AUTHOR'S NOTE: This chapter was written with the assistance of Larry J. Fisk.

Decade for a Culture of Peace and Nonviolence (2000–2010) is designed to magnify interest in matters of peace. At present, all too many people find peace boring, and war, exciting. We can readily identify a war novel, a war movie, a war song, a war painting, or a war toy; by contrast, how many of us can identify clearly a *peace* novel, movie, song, painting, or toy? When war is mentioned on the daily newscasts, people prick up their ears; when peace is mentioned, people are more likely to yawn.

On the other hand, a distinct peace culture exists in the form of antiwar poetry (notably the works of Wilfred Owen and Siegfried Sassoon after World War I), novels (such as *All Quiet on the Western Front* and *Catch-22*), films (including *Platoon, Gandhi, The War Game,* and *Saving Private Ryan*), and the words and music of Sting ("Russians," "Fragile," and "They Dance Alone") and John Lennon's "Imagine." Opposition to war, interestingly, seems easier to express than commitment to peace. Thus, not surprisingly, most peace movements have been fundamentally antiwar movements.

_____ The Semantics of Peace and Peace Movements

Human beings tend to use a variety of different terms to identify things in which they are particularly interested. The Inuit peoples of the far north, for example, have 11 different words for what in English is known simply as "snow," and the Bedouins have a hundred distinct words for "camel," depending on an animal's age, sex, health, and temperament. Similarly, we assign titles to all our different wars, for example, the Punic Wars, the War of the Roses, the Seven Years' War, the Balkan Wars. By contrast, *peace* is a generic term, used only in the singular, even though the "peace" that obtained, say, in Europe between World Wars I and II differed markedly from that of the 1950s, or the period just after the defeat of Napoleon. Perhaps when our interest in peace equals our interest in war, we shall begin to identify not only "wars" but also "peaces," as something more meaningful than simply the intervals between wars.

Peace entails more than the absence of war. However, there seems little doubt that historically—and only marginally less so at present—the defining characteristic of peace movements has been their antiwar stance. Efforts to achieve ecological balance, economic fairness, and human rights are crucially important, and they certainly belong within the purview of peace and conflict studies, but they are only just beginning to be integrated into what has generally been meant by a peace movement.

At the present stage of human development (technological no less than moral), even some advocates of so-called political realism are increasingly recognizing that war is not always a viable instrument of national policy. Accordingly, there are virtually no "war movements"—at least, none that would identify themselves as such! Instead, a wide variety of doctrines and organizations espouse various (often contradictory) ways of achieving peace. Advocates of "peace through strength," for example, claim that it is in the interest of peace that states must maintain large military forces, along with a willingness to employ them if necessary. For the present, however, we shall consider "peace movements" as they are more traditionally identified, that is, as sources of popular opposition to war and to militarism. As such they can be seen as representing one aspect of the more practical and results-oriented side of the academic discipline known as peace and conflict studies.

Most 21st-century students of peace and war will agree that war has reached its nadir: It has become less useful and less desirable than ever before. Virtually every modern war has been unacceptably wasteful, destructive, and cruel. Moreover, in many cases, the state initiating a given war has not achieved its aims. For example, during the 20th century, many aggressors were either defeated or stymied in their goals: the Central Powers in World War I, the Axis in World War II, North Korea in the Korean War, Pakistan in the India-Pakistan Wars, Iraq in its war with Iran and its venture into Kuwait and the resulting Gulf War, as well as Serbia in Bosnia and Kosovo. The most recent trend, however, is to diffuse "blame," with relatively few clear-cut aggressors or innocent victims; moreover, these wars ended, most commonly, in stalemate. But there have also been some politically successful wars, notably some wars of national liberation, such as those for independence in Indonesia, Algeria, and Kenya, as well as the North Atlantic Treaty Organization's (NATO) war against Serbia. The Vietnam War can also be seen as a successful war of unification for the Vietnamese, with distinctly anticolonial overtones as well, since it represented the culmination of struggles with France, Japan, and last, the United States.

Historical and Current Perceptions of War

Although many contemporary readers may be surprised, until recently war has not generally been recognized as a serious human problem, nor has it been widely or deeply deplored. Indeed, war has not even been considered particularly unseemly. Rather, it has been accepted as an instrument of statesmanship, to be used under appropriate circumstances. Several factors seem to be involved in the recent public perception that war is a problem and that peace is not only a desirable goal but one that is—or must be—attainable:

1. *The potential for global destruction.* The development of increasingly destructive weapons, including various forms of conventional explosives, chemical and biological substances, and most especially nuclear weapons, has given all people a stake in the permanent abandonment of armed hostilities. Peace has come to be increasingly important; some might say, essential.

2. *The social, economic, and environmental toll.* The enormous economic, social, and environmental costs of war and war preparations have induced many people to call for the reduction of the role of the military in daily life, even in the absence of the actual threat of war. Peace has become domestically desirable, if not imperative.

3. *The evolution of the earth into a "global village."* The increased means and speed of communications and transportation have enhanced the interconnections among human beings: economically, socially, and emotionally. More than ever before, people are directly affected by the experiences of others. Peace on the planet Earth has become indivisible: There is no real peace so long as war is raging anywhere.

4. *The increase in political involvement.* With the growth in literacy and the spread of more democratic forms of government, many people are more likely than ever before to accept personal responsibility for the actions of their country. To an extent not seen in the past, war is no longer considered a visitation of some god, or an acceptable consequence of a monarch's whim. Likewise, peace is increasingly seen as everyone's business, something that is attainable, if enough people want it and are willing to work for it.

Before 1914, states were relatively unashamed to acknowledge their own offensive goals in starting a war. But since 1945 in particular, brazen aggression has become more and more rare. Some states now feel obliged to proclaim their *defensive* motivations, and even if their *behavior* is not dramatically different, this difference in emphasis may well be meaningful. Prior to 1947, for example, the United States had a War Department; its name was subsequently changed to the Defense Department. Indeed, the military branch of government of virtually every state in the world employs the word *defense*, rather than *war*. Perhaps the switch is merely cosmetic. But even so, it reflects a significant change of attitude: Defense is acceptable, offensive war is not.

Some Conceptualizations of Peace

Not content with something as apparently irrational and destructive as war, many people through history have opposed it. Still, one of the problems with peace plans is that, almost invariably, they are far less specific and detailed—and typically, less workable—than a military staff's plans for war.

For centuries, leaders and citizens alike have spoken out strongly against war. Whereas many have urged a "war against war" or a "national campaign to make war obsolete," the truth is that such campaigns have only rarely gone beyond the level of well-meaning exhortation. And peace campaigns, even the best organized and most generously funded, have rarely come close to rivaling the organization and funding behind even the smallest or most confined wars.

Religious and Renaissance Traditions

The Dutch theologian Erasmus, writing early in the 15th century, was one of the most prominent Renaissance Christian scholars to condemn the institution of war. He recoiled at the "mad uproar, the furious shock of battle, and the wholesale butchery, the cruel face of the killers and the killed, the slaughtered lying in heaps, the fields running with gore, the rivers dyed with human blood." Erasmus' views went counter to the prevailing climate of opinion, which tolerated and frequently even reveled in warfare as good and noble, so long as it met the necessary requirements of a "just war." Erasmus even went so far as to heap scorn on military leaders, as "Military idiots, thick-headed lords . . . not even human except in appearance." Although a religious thinker, Erasmus provided perhaps the first substantial humanistic effort in the West to question the divine right of kings to engage in war. "Among the soldiers," he pointed out, "the one who has conducted himself with the most savagery is the one who is thought worthy to be captain in the next war."[1]

Many religious traditions have had a clear conception of peace, although relatively few have specifically elevated peace to central position in their dogma or practice. A notable exception, within Christianity, is the Society of Friends (also known as the Quakers), established by George Fox in the mid-17th century. Quakers have maintained a tradition of peacemaking and, notably, opposition to military conscription and resistance to taxes for military purposes, which continues to this day. Numerous attempts have also been made to design systems of world government, in the hopes of making war less likely.

Democratic Theory

Political leaders, especially in democratic societies, have persistently maintained that democracy is inherently favorable to peace. In 1951, U.S. senator Robert Taft wrote: "History shows that when the people have the opportunity to speak they as a rule decide for peace if possible. It shows that arbitrary rulers are more inclined to favor war than are the people at any time."[2] In fact, political rhetoric notwithstanding, the evidence is overwhelming that democracies are no more peaceful than other forms of government, although they are unlikely to go to war against each other. Over the past 200 years, bigger democratic nations have been almost as likely as dictatorships to find themselves at war, against nations not commonly viewed as democratic.

A complex relationship seems to exist between social/political ideologies and the perceived desirability and feasibility of peace. Probably most individuals have formally opposed war, but this opposition has been largely personal, sometimes religious, and often narrowly focused. Peace movements, by contrast, have been organized opposition movements, derived overwhelmingly from the political left. On occasion, however (notably, in recent times, with the opposition to the Vietnam War and to nuclear weapons), they have enjoyed substantial support from the political center and from those lacking in clear ideological affiliation.

A Brief History of Peace Movements

An important distinction must be made between the peace proposals of specific individuals and the history of peace movements in general. Mass-mobilized peace movements as we understand them today are relatively recent developments, dating from the early 19th century. But they draw on a vast reservoir of popular discontent with war and have been nourished, in large part, by a belief in *universalism*, a cosmopolitan ethic that sees shared humanity and a common interest in peace underlying and uniting political and ethnic distinctions between peoples.

Perhaps the first organization specifically devoted to achieving lasting peace was the Amphictyonic League, organized among a number of city-states in ancient Greece; the members agreed not to attack one another, or to cut off one another's water supply. The Olympic Games also served a peace-making function in ancient Greece. Every four years, any ongoing hostilities were halted by a one-month truce, during which Greeks were prohibited from bearing arms or making war and instead supported the athletic competition at Olympus.

Religious Peace Movements

The early Christian church was largely pacifist. During the first few centuries A.D., Christians were persecuted by the Roman Empire for refusing to serve in the Roman legions. Renunciation of arms was inspired by the teachings of Jesus, notably as presented in the Sermon on the Mount. In addition, early Christian writing rejected service in the Roman legions as "idolatry." Pacifism also seemed especially appropriate to many early Christians because it involved renunciation of the secular world, in anticipation of the Second Coming of Christ. Subsequently, with the conversion of Emperor Constantine, Christianity also experienced a dramatic conversion, toward a state-supportive view of the legitimacy of war and of military service. Earlier pacifist views came to be considered heresy by the so-called Christian realists, who believed that the Second Coming was not imminent and that therefore Christians must come to terms with the world of power and politics, that is, the world of "Caesar," as in the biblical injunction to "render unto Caesar that which is Caesar's." Christian realists, including Augustine, the founder of Just War theory, granted a certain legitimacy to the secular world of military force.

During the Middle Ages, the Roman Catholic Church made some efforts to limit war, at least among Christians. The "Truce of God" forbade warfare on Sundays and certain other holidays (the word *holiday* originally referred to "holy day"), and the "Peace of God" forbade fighting in certain holy places while also granting immunity to specific persons, such as priests and nuns. (However, the Church also promoted the Crusades, and supported the prosecution of so-called just wars, even among Christians.) Traditions of absolute pacifism nonetheless reemerged during the Middle Ages, most of which carried a strong antistate flavor as well: The Waldensians of the 12th century and the Anabaptists of the 16th century were notable in this regard, and they were aggressively persecuted by both Church and state. Nonetheless, vigorous, if small-scale sects such as the Quakers, Mennonites, and the Brethren—sometimes known as the "prophetic minorities"—maintained religiously oriented peace traditions. Much of their activity was centered on individual statements of religious and ethical conscience, an individual refusal to participate in war often referred to as "personal witness."

Secular Peace Movements

By contrast, secular peace movements, as we know them today, are less than two centuries old. Numerous organizations sprang up during the 19th century. The New York and Massachusetts Peace Societies, for example, were both founded in 1815, and the following year The Society for the Promotion of a Permanent and Universal Peace" was established by the Quakers. Soon thereafter, other organizations were founded on both sides of the Atlantic, including The American Peace Society and the Universal Peace Union in 1866. Many international peace conferences were held during the mid-19th century, including gatherings in London (1843), Brussels (1848), Paris (1849), and Frankfurt (1850).

These efforts received some attention from governments, but were largely political fringe events. Other than legitimizing the concept of peace, and spreading hope among those attending, they had virtually no concrete political successes. Later, the Hague Peace Conferences (circa 1890s–1909 and its May 1999 centenary) had more influence with government leaders, generating widespread expectations among many citizens as well. Although measurable successes have been rare, it can be argued that by placing the concept of international peacemaking on the world agenda and keeping it there, international peace meetings helped set the stage for such achievements as the establishment of the League of Nations after World War I and the United Nations after World War II. They also helped generate a growing international mood in which war was seen as uncivilized, and recourse to war became increasingly unpopular.

Probably the first organized efforts by any peace group to *prevent* a war took place in the United States, prior to the Mexican-American War (1845). Although the effort failed, peace groups did succeed in getting the antagonists to negotiate their differences, and a propeace viewpoint was forcefully expressed. During that war, Henry David Thoreau was jailed for refusing to pay a poll tax, which, in his judgment, indirectly supported that conflict. His essay *Civil Disobedience* has been enormously influential ever since. In it, Thoreau argued that citizens of a democracy have a higher obligation than to the policies of their government. He maintained that the conscientious citizen is obliged to do what is right and to refuse personal participation in wrongdoing—even if the wrongdoing is sanctioned by the legal authority of government, and even if defiance leads to government retribution. The idea of civil disobedience has been greatly enlarged upon by modern practitioners of nonviolence.

Within the past 100 years, the dominant periods of peace movement activism within the United States, and the primary theme of each, can be identified as follows:

1890–1914: Alarm about modern armaments such as accurate, breech-loading artillery, machine guns, heavily armed naval vessels

1916–1921: Opposition to World War I and to Western interventionism in the Soviet civil war

1920s: A variety of movements based on revulsion to World War I

1930–1939: Concern about a second world war and anxiety about the risks of aerial bombardment

1957–1963: Opposition to nuclear weapons, notably atmospheric nuclear testing with its resulting fallout

1965–1972: Opposition to the Vietnam War

1980–1985: Opposition to nuclear weapons, military bellicosity, and the growing danger of nuclear war; support of a nuclear freeze

1986–1990: Opposition to military involvement in Central America, concern regarding underground testing, deployment of "new generation" weapons, and the militarization of space

1991–1999: Concerns centering around military use of depleted uranium, child soldiers, and proliferation of small arms; greater emphasis on humanitarian intervention in intrastate wars, enhanced role of international organizations (United Nations, NATO, International Criminal Court)

2000–present: Transnational mobilization; "culture of peace"; networks on war prevention; nuclear arms and land mine abolition; opposition to proliferation of nuclear, chemical, and biological weapons; potential nuclear and biochemical blackmail or terrorism; space-based weapons; genocide and "ethnic cleansing"; support of nonviolent conflict resolution and human rights in peace and security

The worldwide antiwar movement was probably at its peak after World War I. This was because despite mutual distrust among the great powers of the time, and the long history of military and economic competitiveness that preceded that war, prior to World War I the European antagonists had no grudges or antagonisms that justified the immense slaughter that ensued. Neither side was obviously aligned on the side of "good" or "evil," and indeed, the First World War appears to have been largely a consequence of blunders, on both sides. Hence, it has widely been labeled "the war nobody wanted." The popular Anglo-American understanding of "pacifism" derives largely from opposition to World War I and the widespread movement against conscription that it stimulated. People who considered themselves peace loving, but who supported President Wilson's "war to end all wars," began calling themselves internationalists; they placed their long-term hopes on international agreements between states. By contrast, strict pacifists were (and still are) associated with a firm personal refusal to fight in *any* war, a stance that typically is based on individual religious and/or moral convictions.

In the United States, the antiwar movement of 1917 was eventually aborted by wholesale arrests, brutal police raids (most notorious were the Palmer Raids in 1919, named for the attorney general at the time), and vigilante mobs. Many leaders were given long prison terms or expelled from the country.

Peace Movements in Historical Context

Historically, periods of war have tended to be followed by periods in which peace is espoused with particular vigor. This is apparently due in part to potential adversaries' simple physical, economic, and social exhaustion, as well as to the literal inability of devastated societies to mobilize the resources—emotional and material—necessary to prosecute a lengthy war. The Greek historian Herodotus, called the "father of history" for his masterful treatment of the Greco-Persian Wars (500–479 B.C.E.), pointed out that "in peace, children bury their parents; war violates the order of nature and causes parents to bury their children."[3] Insofar as such experiences are what psychologists describe as *aversive stimuli*—events, such as corporal punishment, that are supposed to have the effect of reducing one's inclination to repeat the immediately preceding behavior—most people are especially likely to favor peace after they have buried their children, that is, in the immediate aftermath of war.

For example, after the Peloponnesian War, Greece experienced an upwelling of pacifist sentiment. Again, following the chaotic civil and imperial wars toward the end of the Roman Republic, a widespread popular yearning for peace contributed to the consolidation of the Roman Empire. The Truce of God and Peace of God, orchestrated by the Catholic Church in the early Middle Ages, were stimulated in large part by the loss of life following coastal raids by Vikings, bloody squabbles among feudal lords, and inland assaults from steppe-dwelling nomads. Later in the Middle Ages, the Crusades, as well as the various wars among dynastic rivals, including the murderous Hundred Years' War between England and France, partially induced the pacifism of humanists such as Erasmus, as well as numerous suggestions for doctrines of international law.

The Thirty Years' War ended in 1648 with the establishment of the modern state system; statesmen were motivated in part by recognition of how devastating the most recent war had been. But the new system of states did not prevent war, at least not for long. One hundred fifty years later, the ruinous Napoleonic Wars led not only to the so-called Holy Alliance and the "balance-of-power peace" of mid-19th-century Europe but also to an increased interest in international prohibitions on war and in the various and scattered peace conferences of that century. The wars of nationalism, especially the Franco-Prussian War (1871), led to renewed popular concern with the structure of international law. And, of course, the horrors of World War I were directly responsible for creation of the League of Nations and various disarmament efforts during the 1920s and 1930s, just as World War II led to the establishment of the United Nations as well as renewed interest in world government. The threat of global thermonuclear war, which intensified during the U.S.-Soviet Cold War, was responsible for unprecedented concern about limiting and, if possible, abolishing a whole class of weapons. Such "nuclear abolitionism" is now a much less prominent concern for both the public and politicians than it was during the Gorbachev era (1985–1991) and before.

Unlike World War I, popular support for World War II was much more widespread. To some extent, in fact, World War II legitimized war in the minds of many and led to a lull in peace movement activity. In part, the Second World War was widely viewed as having occurred because the Western democracies had been unwilling to confront Germany and Japan strongly enough and early enough (the so-called "lessons of Munich"). In addition, because the aggressive militarism of Germany and Japan had represented such a threat to the West, pacifism became widely discredited as a way of coping with international "evil." Moreover, during the decades following World War II, anticolonial liberation movements gave further credence to the legitimacy of organized violence, so long as it was for a "good cause," while the growth of Stalinism in the USSR and Maoism in China served to justify militarism on the part of the United States and its NATO allies.

The resurgence of peace movement concerns during the 1950s and 1960s was due largely to growing popular anxiety about nuclear weapons, as well as opposition to specific wars, as in Korea and—to a much greater extent—Vietnam. The peace movement also was influenced by activity in the so-called Third World, notably the nonviolence of Gandhi and antinuclear awareness promoted by the *hibakusha,* Japanese survivors of Hiroshima and Nagasaki.

A Typology of Peace Movements

Peace movements may coalesce in opposition to a specific war (the Vietnam War, intervention in El Salvador, Nicaragua, Iraq, and Kosovo), to a particular weapon or weapons system (cruise missiles, neutron bombs, the MX missile, chemical weapons, land mines), to an aspect of the war system (conscription, war taxes, sanctions), or to the prevailing socioeconomic system (capitalism, globalization). Or they may be opposed to the institution of war more generally (the position of absolute pacifism). Peace movements may be divided into three categories:

1. Movements to eliminate war in general

2. Movements to stop particular aspects of war

3. Movements to stop particular wars

It is easier to stop specific wars than to stop war in general; hence, efforts to banish war altogether are also most likely to be associated with efforts to reshape public opinion and to establish firm structures of positive peace. Such efforts are also more likely to persist, in contrast with opposition to particular wars or to specific means of waging war, which typically end along with the war in question or with the banning (or deployment) of the contested weapons.

Movements to eliminate war generally have spawned secular groups such as the Peace Pledge Union in England and the Women's International League for Peace and Freedom (WILPF), as well as various religious organizations and traditions, such as the Fellowship of Reconciliation (FOR), Pax Christi, the Quakers, and numerous advocates of nonviolence. Movements to stop particular aspects of war have included opposition to poison gas, to specific weapons delivery systems (Euromissiles, the MX missile, and the B-1 bomber), to nuclear weapons themselves (SANE, the Freeze campaign, the British Campaign for Nuclear Disarmament and European Nuclear Disarmament), and to conscription (War Resisters League), as well as campaigns in support of converting military industries to civilian production (the Ploughshares Fund). Movements to stop particular wars have included widespread mobilization to oppose the Vietnam War, notably in the United States (often known at that time as the "Mobilization," or the "Mobe"), and to U.S. intervention in Nicaragua and El Salvador.

The following list, modified from Nigel Young's pioneering work on these matters, suggests a more detailed typology of peace movements, identifying some of the major traditions, and an example of each:[4]

Tradition	Example(s)
Religious pacifism	Conscientious objection: Society of Friends (Quakers), Pax Christi (Catholic), Fellowship of Reconciliation
Liberal internationalism	UN associations, national peace councils, world disarmament campaigns
Anticonscription	War Resister's League, Amnesty International
Socialist internationalism	No exact contemporary equivalents, but very active until World War I, including the International Workers of the World ("Wobblies")
Feminist antimilitarism	Women for Peace, Women's International League for Peace and Freedom
Ecological pacifism	Greenpeace, Green Party (especially in Germany)
Communist internationalism	World Peace Council
Nuclear pacifism	Europe: CND (Campaign for Nuclear Disarmament), END (European Nuclear Disarmament); U.S.: SANE/Freeze, Physicians for Social Responsibility, and many others

Note that liberal internationalism has sometimes been called *pacificism*, as distinct from *pacifism* Although the former seeks to prevent war, it does not entirely renounce it as an instrument of policy in extreme circumstances. Note, too, that this is necessarily a very incomplete list. It does not, for example, include groups opposed to specific weapons, of which there have been many (Live Without Trident, Coalition Against the MX, the movement to ban land mines, etc.). Numerous other organizations could also be identified within any one of these traditions; moreover, the traditions often overlap, both conceptually and in terms of membership.

The Communist Role

Even in the years just prior to the end of the Soviet regime (1991), the USSR attempted to influence peace movement directions, largely through its

World Peace Council, with headquarters in Helsinki, and through various other peace councils located in other countries. Certain international petitions, such as the Stockholm Peace Appeal of 1950—which accumulated millions of signatures in support of the abolition of nuclear weapons as well as universal disarmament—received major sponsorship from the former USSR. Many international peace and antiwar conferences were supported by and/or held in the former Soviet Union, which officially promoted nuclear disarmament (especially under Gorbachev), and until 2000 held to a policy of "no first use" of nuclear weapons.

The Soviet Union was also favorably disposed toward the antimissile demonstrations in Europe during the early 1980s. However, of the millions of people who opposed these missiles, and nuclear weapons more generally, communists comprised a very small fraction. Within the United States, the influence of the U.S. Communist Party within labor unions, as well as in civil rights and peace movement activities, was negligible. Nonetheless, government leaders in the West often sought to portray peace movements in particular as communist dominated or, at minimum, communist influenced. Such accusations greatly exaggerated the strength of the Communist Party, immensely understated the depth of grassroots, nonideological antiwar sentiment, and also revealed the desperation of Western governments to destroy the credibility of indigenous movements critical of their own policies.

The guarded but nevertheless serious support of presidents and UN secretaries-general for movements such as the Hague Appeal for Peace and Justice and in opposition to the World Trade Organization is evidence of a new era in which the Communist scare no longer has the same currency.

Interconnections Between Peace and Other Social Movements

Although peace activists have tended to align themselves with specific organizations, there are numerous and important interconnections between them and between certain peace traditions and other popular social movements. For example, feminist antimilitarism, which emerged in the early years of the 20th century, was strongly infused with energy and leadership from the women's suffrage movement. Opposition to nuclear power—in the late 1960s and throughout much of the 1970s—contributed to broader antinuclear sentiment in the 1980s. Many people active in feminist, socialist, gay and lesbian rights, religious nonviolent, and other social justice movements participate in peace movement activities as well. Environmental organizations, such as Greenpeace and Friends of the Earth, have found themselves increasingly involved in antinuclear protests. Such groups express their antiwar, and particularly antinuclear, concerns because of the threat of environmental destruction, which they perceive as arising from nuclear war and also from ongoing radioactive contamination emanating from nuclear weapons facilities, even while "nuclear peace" prevails.

Other groups, which focus primarily on economic justice, have found themselves increasingly drawn to the peace movement agenda due to their recognition of the economic costs of military expenditures. Although military spending does create jobs, many people are coming to recognize that comparable spending in the civilian economy generates even more jobs while often addressing critical social needs. The era of avowedly conservative U.S. government policies, ushered in with the election of Ronald Reagan, and followed by George Bush, resulted in massive federal budget deficits, a hesitancy to raise taxes, and belt-tightening with respect to social expenditures. At the time, American activist groups became more aware of the *opportunity costs* of military spending, that is, the degree to which military expenditure diminishes a country's opportunity to invest that money in ways that are socially more productive. With the end of the Cold War and unprecedented and unforeseen budget surpluses beginning under President Bill Clinton, new rallying cries emerged for many Western progressives as the 21st century opened: opposition to military spending, an enhanced call for economic conversion, environmental protection, humanitarian intervention, and increased social services for enlarged domestic peace and justice. Those who believed that the end of Cold War rivalry and the achievement of budget surpluses would result in the end of the peace movement were not proven to be correct. (At the same time, those who believed that these developments would result in greater domestic investment—the much hoped-for "peace dividend"—were also disappointed.) A more accurate portrayal of peace movement life is one of a brief hiatus followed by regeneration around revised issues.

Current Peace Movements

Modern peace movements—both in the United States and worldwide—tend to be somewhat periodic and generational (they rise and fall), pluralistic (i.e., influenced by a variety of traditions and motivated by a range of concerns, and tactically diverse (they employ a variety of techniques). Some peace movement activities, for example, are closely associated with feminists, such as the Greenham Commons women's camps, formed in Britain to protest deployment of U.S. ground-launched cruise missiles. Others are allied with environmentalists, such as Greenpeace and Friends of the Earth. In addition, occasional coalitions are formed between peace movement activists and gay rights activists, as well as opponents of nuclear power. In the mid-1960s, against the advice of some of his associates—who feared possible dilution of the domestic focus of his work and the alienation of some supporters—the Reverend Martin Luther King, Jr., came out forcefully in

opposition to the war in Vietnam, arguing that the struggle for civil rights
was inextricably linked to a halt in unjust and destructive warfare.

The United States

Despite these interconnections between peace and other social justice movements, however, the contemporary peace movement in the United States
has often been accused of being excessively a movement of middle-class
white people. The reenergized antinuclear movement of the 1980s made
efforts to reach out to progressive social justice groups organized by the
poor and by people of color, to broaden its appeal and deepen its commitment to social justice. Nevertheless, antinuclear protesters—the Freeze
campaign, supporters of a comprehensive test ban, opponents of Star Wars[5]
—as well as feminists and environmental activists were largely drawn from
the relatively well-educated and well-to-do sectors of American society.
By contrast, opposition to U.S. intervention in Central America and to
apartheid in South Africa, as well as support for civil and gay rights, seemed
derived from a wider socioeconomic cross section of society. Organizations
such as CISPES (Committee in Solidarity with the People of El Salvador), and
others seeking more peace-affirming policies toward Nicaragua, regularly
underwent FBI harassment, but nonetheless persevered and grew. Contemporary American oppositional movements—to sanctions against Iraq, to the
School of the Americas, to the bombing of Iraq or Serbia—also appear to
have undergone similar scrutiny by the federal government. These varied
activities and the coalition building around them, which extended to the
Hague Appeal worldwide, may augur well for a widening of peace movements in the United States.

Peace movements (and left-of-center movements within the United States
in general) have tended to focus largely on one issue at a time, as earlier concerns are abandoned and the latest issue—cynics would say, the most recent
fad—attract most of the energy and outrage. Thus, in the late 1950s, it was
opposition to McCarthyism; in the early 1960s, protests against atmospheric
testing and fallout shelters and in favor of arms control; in the mid-1960s,
the civil rights movement; in the late 1960s, opposition to the Vietnam War;
in the early 1970s, defense of the environment; in the late 1970s, affirmation
of feminism and human rights generally; in the early to mid-1980s, abolition
of nuclear weapons and nuclear war fighting; in the late 1980s and early
1990s, protests against South African apartheid and U.S. interventionism in
Central America; and in the late 1990s and early 2000s, support of humanitarian intervention, economic conversion, and strategic nonviolence
through various social movements, along with opposition to economically
oppressive and environmentally destructive "globalization."

To some extent, it can be argued that these shifting priorities were
appropriate, reflecting changing global threats to peace. It should come as

no surprise that the Reagan administration, for example, with its verbal bellicosity and cavalier attitude toward nuclear war, generated the most vigorous antinuclear peace movement in U.S. history.

Often, however, peace movements have been motivated by a surge of popular anxiety regarding a perceived threat that quickly subsides, even though the underlying problem remains as serious as ever. For example, the antinuclear movement of 1958–1963 diminished rapidly after the Partial Test Ban Treaty was signed, although nuclear testing and the nuclear arms race simply went underground, increasing the number of such tests—and the intensity of the arms race itself—rather than diminishing either. In other cases, peace movements that were narrowly focused around opposition to something specific tended to disband—perhaps appropriately—when "their issue" was resolved. A good example is the resistance to the war in Vietnam, which ended when U.S. ground forces eventually withdrew. European opposition to the deployment of nuclear missiles by NATO sparked a virtual firestorm of antinuclear protest during the early 1980s. With the signing of the INF (Intermediate Range Nuclear Forces) Treaty of 1988, which banned the deployment by both NATO and the Soviet Union of such missiles, the European antinuclear movement became much more quiet.

At the same time, by exposing the absurdities of various war-fighting, war-surviving, and war-winning doctrines, the antinuclear movement succeeded in delegitimizing nuclear weapons to such a degree that even the Reagan administration found itself proclaiming that "a nuclear war can never be won and must never be fought" and rescinding (at least for public consumption) its earlier bellicosity and pronuclear stance. In this way, the path of the U.S. antinuclear movement has been similar to that of the environmental movement of the early 1970s, many of whose goals and ways of thinking have progressed from radical to mainstream.

Europe

Several important peace movement traditions have also developed in Europe. One is the Green Party (*Die Gruenen*), which originated in what was then West Germany. In the reunified Germany, the Greens have gained political prominence, forming part of a coalition government with the Social Democrats. The Green movement gave rise to other Green Parties throughout Europe and began spreading to the United States as well. The movement's underlying philosophy is a synthesis of ecology, feminism, political decentralization, community and workplace democracy, antiauthoritarianism, and antimilitarism. The movement is based on grassroots coalitions of local groups, most of which remain largely autonomous. Counter-culture politics are strongly established in the Federal Republic of Germany, perhaps in part due to the role of Germany in World War II, the large number of conscientious objectors opposed to military service, and the denazification struggles of the 1990s. In addition, between 1945 and 1989, Germany had suffered a divided homeland (as a result of the Cold War) and was highly vulnerable as the likely battlefield and initial victim of any "theater" nuclear war on the European continent.

European and American peace movements have long been dominated by direct opposition to war, and this trend continued through the last decades of the 20th century. As indicated above, anticonscription advocates, especially the Berlin Appeal, became popular in both East and West Germany. Nearly 20% of those eligible for military service applied for conscientious objector status in West Germany, while the evangelical Lutheran churches of the German Democratic Republic (East Germany) also helped consolidate antimilitary sentiment. These church groups were particularly influential in organizing opposition to the former East German government, resulting in the dramatic events of late 1989 and 1990, when it (and other East European governments under Soviet influence) was toppled, and the hated Berlin Wall dismantled.

Also in Europe, the Campaign for Nuclear Disarmament (CND) was founded in 1958, stimulated initially by British opposition to nuclear testing. During the 1980s, largely in response to the intensification of the Cold War during the early Thatcher and Reagan years, the CND expanded dramatically as a broad-based, populist movement. CND membership was about 3,000 in 1979; by 1984 it exceeded 100,000. In 1981, massive street demonstrations involving tens, sometimes hundreds, of thousands of people convulsed the cities of Bonn, Brussels, Athens, London, Rome, Madrid, and Amsterdam, largely in opposition to NATO's nuclear weapons policies. These demonstrations were part of a peace movement revitalization that united antinuclear protesters with antinuclear power activists. They included the women's and ecological movements, gay and lesbian rights supporters, and socialists and internationalists of a variety of orientations, including supporters of the United Nations, a sprinkling of pro-Kremlin peace fronts, and advocates of world government.

Another peace movement goal, the establishment of nuclear-free zones, has long enjoyed substantial popular and political support, in such forms as the Nordic Nuclear Free Zone (the Scandinavian countries) and the Balkans Nuclear Free Zone (Greece, Bulgaria, Romania). In the 1980s, this geographic approach to nuclear abolitionism spread to other regions, including Africa, the Middle East, and notably, the South Pacific, where continued French nuclear testing and U.S. insistence on nuclear weapon bases combined to generate an increasingly unified antinuclear stance among indigenous Polynesian peoples.

Many issues remain unresolved, however, and are still troublesome. The lack of a massive peace movement in France, the "top down" experience of the peace movement in the former USSR (which has colored its responses to post-Soviet Russian militarist actions, especially vis-à-vis Chechnya), and the repression of anything approaching truly independent peace movement efforts in Turkey constitute some ongoing difficulties.

Beyond Europe to the World

The late 1990s witnessed an unprecedented and largely unanticipated organizational success of a major international conference known as the Hague Appeal (originating in the Netherlands). It ushered in a new era of peace movement activity, based on worldwide networking. This conference signaled the initial success of transnational mobilization for support on 50 issues as part of the long-term "Appeal for Peace and Justice for the Twenty-First Century." The appeal focused on four themes: the root causes of war/culture of peace; international humanitarian and human rights law and institutions; prevention, resolution, and transformation of violent conflict; and disarmament and human security. The conference and its follow-up networking have been particularly successful in attracting young people, including strong representations from Asia and Africa.

Peace movements throughout the world have also been successful in marshaling global support on issues related to the banning of land mines, led by the American Nobel Peace Prize winner Jody Williams, Britain's late Princess Diana, and Canada's foreign affairs minister, Lloyd Axworthy, and the resulting "Ottawa Process." The land mine ban signaled a route forward via cooperation between peace movements and sympathetic governments (Cambodia, Netherlands, Sweden, and Canada, to name but a few). Others joined in successfully holding at bay a multilateral agreement on investment (MAI) and protested the role of the World Trade Organization, both of which have been charged with protecting the interests of multinational corporations at the expense of workers' rights and the environment. Much of the success of these activities can be credited to international mobilization, the linking of otherwise disconnected groups (e.g., labor and environmental activists), and skilled use of the Internet.

_____ Some Internal Debates Within Peace Movements

Peace movements, as we have seen, are not homogeneous. They have fluctuated substantially over time, as well as in goals. They have periodically been galvanized by opposition to especially atrocious wars (Vietnam) or weapons (poison gas, nuclear, depleted uranium-tipped shells), only to recede somewhat when the war is terminated (Vietnam, end of the Cold War) or especially provocative actions have been removed (above-ground nuclear testing, Euromissiles, etc.). One observer of the European peace movement during the 1980s suggested that peace movements were like whales, which periodically break the surface then disappear under the waves. "When the whale disappears in a dive, those on the right believe the movement no longer exists. Supporters of the movement, on the other hand, see the leaping whale and claim it can fly."[6] The truth is somewhere in between.

In addition to their fickleness, peace movements are notorious for their ideological heterogeneity and occasional combativeness. Paradoxically, peace activists fight a lot, at least with each other! (Not actual violence, mind you, but often with substantial verbal and conceptual aggressiveness.) Aside from the distinct orientations of different groups and the diverse personal agendas of the individuals constituting these groups, certain sources of debate and tension have persisted within "the movement," which is actually much more plural than singular. In part, this may be because movements advocating social change tend to attract adherents who are antiestablishment, strong-willed, and inclined to rebel against authority. In any event, here are some of the major controversies that have caused substantial splitting within peace movements but have also contributed to the vibrancy that comes from vigorous internal debate.

State-Centeredness

Supporters of this position claim that since states are the primary actors on the international war-peace arena, it is essential to reform the way states behave toward one another—for example, by encouraging trade, democracy, disarmament conferences, and agreements on the rules of war; the abolition of certain weapons; and the establishment of international agencies such as the League of Nations and the United Nations. On the other hand, critics of the state-centered approach claim that focusing on the behavior of states merely perpetuates such behavior by exacerbating rather than alleviating nationalist biases. They think that states are the problem, not the solution, and that, accordingly, genuine solutions must be less state centered.

This argument leads to an important debate regarding the merits of nonalignment. In Europe especially, public opinion tends to favor the peace movement's perspective with regard to nuclear weapons, yet also identifies itself strongly with the NATO alliance. Accordingly, some European peace activists have argued that an antinuclear, anti-NATO stance would alienate public opinion that would otherwise support major initiatives in denuclearization and demilitarization generally. Others maintain that by adhering to the Western alliance, peace groups buttressed the Cold War and undermined their own prospects for ultimate success. Following the breakup of the Warsaw Pact in the 1990s, NATO's move to fill the Eastern European strategic vacuum and employ its military muscle in Iraq and Kosovo prompted new divisions in the peace movement. Some praise the international cooperation implicit in NATO's new interventionist role as a welcome challenge to state sovereignty and superpower policing of the world. Others see the same actions as an extension of Western hegemony and of inordinate American influence.

The Use of Military Force

Within the European peace movement, the same internal divisions over NATO's role arose over bombing raids in Iraq and Serbia. Some defended military action as a means of assisting humanitarian causes, such as defense of the Kosovars. Opponents of any use of military force (*absolute pacifists*) disagree with those we might call *relative pacifists*, or *pacificists*, who believe that a "good" or permissible war or military action (such as that in Kosovo, the Gulf War, the Spanish Civil War, or World War II) may still be possible, but who often oppose specific wars, as in Vietnam or Central America. Even with so-called "good" wars, the question must be posed: Is the "evil" to be overcome (Slobodan Milosevic's ethnic cleansing, Saddam Hussein's alleged weapons of mass destruction, Nazism in World War II, slavery in the Civil War) greater than the "evil" of the war that was waged to overcome the malignancy? (An analogy with cancer may be apt, since cures for this disease are often as devastating as the illness.)

A similar debate attends the use of smaller military forces. Was the "liberation" of Grenada worth the loss of life that resulted from the 1983 invasion of that island by the United States? And did the removal of Panama's former dictator (and CIA hireling) Manuel Noriega warrant another American invasion in 1989? Did American Marines move too quickly into Somalia and then conduct a too hasty retreat when American lives were threatened by local tribal warlords? Some self-styled realists argue that under certain conditions, the use of force is appropriate; others—equally realistic—maintain that violence is ultimately self-defeating. Absolute pacifists typically object to the idea of ever institutionalizing a worldwide military force, even one designed for peacekeeping. Others worry more about the potential for despotism. Still others, as noted above, regret the absence of such an international force.

Centralization Versus Grassroots Organization

One antiwar tradition favors the development of strong leadership and central authority. The other prefers local, grassroots organizing. Within the antinuclear movement, the former has included such organizations as SANE, the Union of Concerned Scientists, and the Council for a Livable World. Grassroots activities, by contrast, have characterized the nuclear freeze movement, and the Mobilization for Survival. The merger of SANE and Freeze in 1987 presaged an integration of these approaches along with a new organizational philosophy. The centralized organizational umbrella supplied by the United Nations, as well as the Hague Appeal for Peace and

Justice for the Twenty-First Century, reflect this new organizational philosophy, which involves intensive consultation with and within hundreds of
civil society and peace movement organizations.

It is unclear whether peace movements have historically had greater success
when they were composed primarily of large numbers of people mobilized
as "objects" or of relatively fewer but more strongly motivated individuals,
who see themselves as "subjects" of their own intense actions and protests.
Thus, the peace movement mobilization of one million people in New York
City in June 1982 had an undeniable impact on the Reagan administration,
but so did the handful of Buddhist monks, who, a decade or so earlier,
immolated themselves to protest the Vietnam War.

Single-Issue Versus Broader Social Agendas

Many groups have opposed specific aspects of war (weapons such as
the MX missile, Trident submarines, neutron bombs, and cruise missiles in
Europe; conscription; war taxes; or specific wars, as in Vietnam, Iraq, and
Kosovo), whereas others have emphasized the importance of broadening
their agenda to embrace economic aspects of social justice (employment at
decent wages, medical care, affordable housing, and child care), environmental concerns (wildlife conservation, clean air and water, preservation of
open space, renewable energy sources, protection of tropical forests, and
mitigation of the greenhouse effect), support for gay rights, and opposition
to racism and sexism in the United States and apartheid in South Africa.

In some cases, peace movements have become closely associated with a
single political party, such as Labour in Britain or the Communist Party in
Italy. Supporters of the single-issue approach emphasize that by concentrat-
ing on a small number of manageable concerns, they are more likely to have
a demonstrable effect, which will also provide them with successes upon
which to build. Supporters of a broader agenda counter with the argument
that specific issues come and go and that the peace movement can actually
be weakened whenever a single issue is resolved, no matter what the outcome. In addition, peace advocates are increasingly aware of the importance
of pointing out the linkages between various "single issue" considerations.
For example, the Freeze campaign in the United States during the 1980s
received relatively little support from African Americans, at least in part
because the U.S. underclass was more concerned with immediate issues
of economic and social justice. On the other hand, greater political success
was achieved when this movement combined calls for jobs with antiwar
programs; there is a natural linkage here, since a military economy actually
creates fewer jobs than would similar expenditures in the domestic sector.

Single-issue politics offers the advantage of bringing sharp, substantial
pressure to bear on a narrow point. However, such thrusts are also susceptible to being turned aside by mainstream opposition. Broad, programmatic,

consensus-building blueprints for social change, by contrast, bring pressure across a much wider societal front, but with less visible impact in any one area.

Practicality Versus Idealism

How high should peace movements aim? Is there danger that by setting their sights too high, they will make "the best an enemy of the good"? On the other hand, don't peace movements have an obligation to be above normal politics, which bills itself as the "art of the possible"? At times of unique danger and opportunity, perhaps peace movements should, as some peace advocates put it, "be realistic—demand the impossible." Thus, there can be a disadvantage in being too timorous: "Realism" on the part of the U.S. Freeze campaign, for example, appeared like a step backward to many in the European peace movement, who had long demanded substantial *reductions* in nuclear weapons.

Another dilemma of practicality versus idealism may be observed in Germany, where the Green Party has enjoyed such electoral success that at the turn of this century the elected Green Party members became insiders rather than protestors on the outside. Earlier, the party had generated two factions within the Green movement: the "Fundis" ("fundamentalists"), who held out for ideal goals such as the total abolition of nuclear weapons and a refusal to form coalitions with more conservative parties, and the "Realos" ("realists"), who were willing to make certain practical concessions in the interest of achieving immediate, although incomplete, political goals. There can be substantial tension here, between "doing what can be done" and "attempting to do what needs to be done."

A useful—although often unfavorable—view of peace movements is that they serve as grit in the cogwheels of the world's war machines, preventing them from running smoothly, and perhaps eventually causing them to break down altogether. Another analogy—and a more positive one—compares peace movements to bread yeast, helping dough to rise. Perhaps states are by their nature and structure unqualified to promote creative transformations and are dependent on changes that emerge only from civil society, including peace movements. In any case, peace movement activists remain divided as to whether they ought to compromise their principles in the interests of real but ambiguous "progress," such as support for conventional modernization of military forces or increased use of smart weapons, in return for denuclearization and minimized civilian casualties.

Civil Disobedience

Supporters of civil disobedience maintain that when the government is engaging in ethically unacceptable behavior—often counter to the tenets of international law—it is acceptable and even essential to oppose these practices, even if opposition of this sort involves breaking domestic law. Opponents of civil disobedience worry about the morality and consequences of law-breaking, and also about the possibility that such acts may alienate the majority of the citizenry and ultimately prove counterproductive. This is actually part of a broader debate about tactics, especially between those who advocate grassroots activism "in the streets," by as many people as possible, and those who favor a more top-down approach that focuses on working within the political system to influence decision makers. In turn, the debate about tactics is part of an even larger issue: whether to *oppose* war through the electoral process, by writing, speaking, organizing and attending meetings, and passing resolutions, or actively to *resist* it, by strikes, tax resistance, closing down meetings, and nonviolent civil disobedience, or even by violent confrontations.

An Assessment of Peace Movements

Although this book clearly supports peace movements, they have not always contributed positively to peace. In some cases, public opinion has been mobilized by peace movement efforts, but it has also been alienated by them. In some cases, wars have been made more unpopular by peace movements, but in others they may have actually been prolonged. Peace movement efforts nearly always have unseen, latent consequences as well as visible, immediate ones. This makes it difficult to pronounce a specific peace campaign—or the movement as a whole—a success or failure.

Some Criticisms of Peace Movements

In the famous Oxford Peace Union Pledge during the 1930s, many students in England declared that they would not "fight for king and country," which in turn may have emboldened Hitler by suggesting that his aggressive designs might not be resisted. Similarly, it can be argued that the other vigorous European peace movements of the 1930s not only may have made Nazi and fascist aggression more likely but may have partially diminished the degree of Allied preparedness when war finally did come.

More generally, peace movements, by excessive wishful thinking, may sometimes blind their fellow citizens to the provocative and dangerous behavior of others. "Nothing is more promotive of war," writes peace researcher Quincy Wright, "than diversion of the attention of the prospective victims from the aggressor's preparations."[7] As we shall see, however, there are many contributing reasons for wars; of these, the occasional counterproductive effects of peace movements are quite insignificant. Few things are more disruptive of peace, we might conclude, than blaming well-intentioned peace movements for the war-prone behavior of states and their leadership.

Nonetheless, peace movements often have a difficult time. During war, they are typically denounced and often banned or even attacked as un-patriotic, cowardly, or traitorous for giving "aid and comfort to the enemy." And during times of peace, they often are hard-pressed to make a dent in public complacency. A sociopsychological view of peace movement activism puts special emphasis on the personal needs presumably being met by such activity: such as "acting out" youthful rebellion, opposing author-ity as a predictable "age appropriate" stage in personal development, and exercising the opportunity of behaving outrageously while still relatively free of social or family responsibilities. This line of argument can readily be overused, especially by right-wing critics eager to discredit peace movement activism. But it would also be a mistake to ignore the diverse personal moti-vations of peace movement activists. Current peace movement activists in fact represent a rather wide cross section of ages; many are peace movement veterans, some of whom may have "dropped out" for a while, to develop careers or to start families, only to return when the issues appear especially acute, when time allows (the children are grown, retirement is at hand), or when their conscience beckons.

Another question arises: How vociferous should peace activists be in criticizing their own governments? Most devotees of peace studies point out that world peace, demilitarization, and an end to violence are not *zero-sum games*, in which one side must lose if the other wins. Rather, all sides stand to come out ahead if a peace agenda is actually realized.

Increasingly, peace movement goals include modifying the behavior of all global players: the United States, Russia, all the NATO allies, China, North and South Korea, Serbia and Kosovo, India and Pakistan, Israel and its Arab neighbors, and so on. It is a fact of life, however, that citizens are usually most able to influence the polities of which they are members: for U.S. citizens, this is the government of the United States, just as for Russians it is the Russian government, and so on. In most cases, governments are all too happy to have their citizens—whether members of a peace movement or not—criticize and demonstrate against rival foreign powers. But in doing so, they are unlikely to have much impact on the conduct of their own governments.

To some degree, peace movement activists accept the proposition that human beings all share important common bonds and are therefore mutu-ally responsible for whatever happens on this, their shared planet. But they also operate on the reasonable assumption that people—especially those fortunate enough to be living in a democracy—have a special responsibility to evaluate critically and, if necessary, to seek to reform the behavior of their own government. In this respect, citizens of the United States have much to do.

Maintaining the Momentum of Peace Movements

It is all too easy for peace activists to fall victim to personal fatigue, despair, and cynicism. But, in fact, peace workers worldwide have already accomplished a great deal. In the 20th century, for example, conscientious objection became widely recognized in most Western countries as a basic legal right, although exercising that right was sometimes perilous. It is interesting to note that within peace movements themselves, even anticon-scription was not universally accepted as an appropriate goal. Historically, a segment of socialist antiwar activists actually applauded conscription, hoping it would create a "people's army," whereas others feared that it would simply contribute to an "army against the people." The Vietnam War was terminated in large part because of American discontent with the war, fueled by immense pressure from the domestic peace movement. Similarly, in the 1980s and 1990s, nuclear weapons underwent a rapid process of dele-gitimization, much to the dismay of militarists and cold warriors. Such arguments were especially poignant and frustrating in the context of Western bombing of Serbia and Iraq at the close of the 20th century: These highly aggressive and war-making activities were immensely destructive, and yet, they were justified as being in support of peace and the delegitimation of violence! Not surprisingly, peace advocates of good conscience found themselves on both sides of these conflicts (as did people supporting a right-wing, militarist perspective).

It remains to be seen whether contemporary peace movements can sustain their momentum when immediate, readily perceived threats do not exist, and when governments modulate their rhetoric but not their policies, or co-opt various peace movement agendas by showy but relatively trivial concessions.

More specifically, it is uncertain whether antiwar sentiment in the United States will outlast specific crises in the Balkans, Africa, Asia, and Central America, and whether the antinuclear movement will continue to be prominent when and if national policies become less controversial, or if such policies lead to significant reductions in strategic nuclear forces. The point is that when a movement focuses narrowly on a specific weapon, it can readily be co-opted or left feeling empty-handed and uninspired, even when it has been politically successful.

Accordingly, contemporary peace movements may well profit by developing alternative foreign policy concepts, alternative defense strategies, a positive view of social goals, broader motivations beyond single-issue rallying points, a workable model of a disarmed (or, at least, substantially demilitarized) economy, and staying power. In addition, successful peace movements will have to be realistic in confronting the power of the state while also, when possible, breaking out of a strictly state-centered model of politics.

The overriding goal of many peace movement activists is not so much the elimination of states as their transformation. Specifically, demilitarization could serve not only as a goal but also as a method of such change. And demilitarization, as such, is independent of specific weapons or specific "hot spots" around the world. The peace movement of the 1980s and 1990s called for the denuclearization of military policy as well as the demilitarization of defense policy. It called into question the fundamental rationality of "national security" based on military means alone. In addition, it called not only for widespread participation, but also for empowerment of ordinary citizens. The early-21st-century peace movement appears to have a full agenda based on the developments of the last two decades of the 20th century.

Peace movements are sometimes depicted as quixotic, hopeless quests, peopled by refugees from the 1960s and 1980s. This view of the 1960s participants was held especially by many in the "me generation" that followed. Twenty-first-century peace activists—with their interests in conflict resolution, mediation, human rights, and global security—have made comparable criticisms of 1980s priorities and those who developed them.

Yet evidence abounds that the movements of the past, with all their peculiarities, often influenced national policy, and nearly always for the better. Both supporters and opponents of the war in Vietnam, for example, agree that the United States terminated its involvement in that conflict because of an ebbing of political will to continue prosecuting the war. In addition, there seems little doubt that the Reagan administration, during its latter years, grew increasingly less pronuclear due to peace movement pressure that was widespread, vocal, and highly visible. National policy in New Zealand was also strongly influenced by peace movement sentiment in that country. The result was a ban on all nuclear facilities, including visits by nuclear-armed or nuclear-powered naval vessels, much to the consternation of the American government.

Moreover, history offers many examples of successful movements that initially appeared to be facing impossible odds: support for women's suffrage; opposition to monarchy; opposition to dueling as a means of settling personal disputes; and opposition to the institution of slavery, which was an ancient and firmly rooted practice, at one time virtually worldwide and considered by many to be an immutable and irrevocable part of human society. In the 20th century, few people would have imagined that India would win its independence from Britain through a campaign of militant but nonviolent protest, that decades-old fascist dictatorships in Spain and Portugal would give way to modern parliamentary democracies, that bloody tyrannies in the Philippines or Haiti could have been overthrown peacefully, that the Soviet Union would renounce its Stalinist heritage and institute massive democratic restructuring (*perestroika*) and political/ideological openness (*glasnost*), that the "captive nations" of Eastern Europe would throw off their shackles and emerge as fledgling democracies eager to embrace free-market economic reforms, or that the apartheid regime of South Africa would end, and with remarkably little bloodshed, given its violent past and formerly oppressive governments. Maybe sometime in the future, people will look back wonderingly at the latter part of the 20th century and early years of the 21st century, noting with amazement that in such a war-prone world, persistent, widespread peace movements could mount so successful a campaign against war itself.

A Final Note on Peace Movements

In recent times, successful peace movements have led to such tangible events as independence for India, the civil rights movement in the United States, an end to above-ground nuclear testing, and the democratization of Eastern Europe, among others. It remains to be seen whether a successful 21st-century movement for peace—both negative and positive—will be similarly constituted, or similarly rewarded. The alternative is to continue "business as usual" in a world of war, injustice, and deprivation. Many people have long recognized that this old way is unacceptable, a perception that has become even more widespread with the advent of weapons of mass destruction. Yet progress toward a different and more peaceful world has been painfully slow. With the demise of the USSR, it now seems that we have been, as Matthew Arnold put it,[8]

> Wandering between two worlds, one dead,
> The other powerless to be born.

The special hope of peace movements is that they might serve as midwives for this newer world, providing it with the impetus and power to be born at last. Just as birth may be difficult, often painful, even dangerous, we have seen that the course of peace movements has not run altogether smoothly, nor have peace movements been unidirectional or universally welcomed. But just as birth is natural and necessary if life is to continue, it seems equally certain that peace is necessary (whether or not it is natural) and that peace movements may contribute mightily toward success.

Notes

1.   Desiderius Erasmus. 1967. "Dulce Bellum Inexpertis." In M. M. Phillips, ed., *Erasmus and His Times*. Cambridge, UK: Cambridge University Press.

2.   Quoted in K. Waltz. 1959. *Man, the State, and War*. New York: Columbia University Press.

3. Herodotus. 1910. *History*. G. Rawlinson, trans. New York: E. P. Dutton.

4. Modified from Nigel Young. 1984. "Why Peace Movements Fail." *Social Alternatives* 4: 9–16.

5. "Star Wars" was the term used by the mass media to describe the Reagan administration's proposal—called the Strategic Defense Initiative (SDI) in the early and mid-1980s—to develop a new ostensibly defensive antimissile system. The system became known as Star Wars, after the popular movie, because it was presumably intended to destroy missiles from space. A more contemporary version of SDI, or Star Wars, is National or Ballistic Missile Defense, as championed by the second Bush administration.

6. Philip P. Everts. 1989. "Where the Peace Movement Goes When It Disappears." *Bulletin of the Atomic Scientists* 45: 26–30.

7. Quincy Wright. 1964. *A Study of War*. Chicago: University of Chicago Press.

8. Matthew Arnold. 1934. "Stanzas From the Grande Chartreuse." *Essays and Poems of Matthew Arnold*. New York: Harcourt Brace Jovanovich.

3 The Meanings of Wars

Man's body is so small, yet his capacity for suffering is so immense.

—Rabindranath Tagore

Most human activities—buying and selling, sowing and reaping, loving, learning, eating, sleeping, worshiping—take place with a minimum of overt conflict, and certainly without anything even remotely like war. Warfare nonetheless has a special importance for human beings, particularly since the invention of nuclear weapons in 1945, which raised the very real possibility that war could extinguish human civilization and, possibly, life on earth. Peace researcher Quincy Wright began his *A Study of War* by noting that

> to different people war may have very different meanings. To some it is a plague which ought to be eliminated; to some, a mistake which should be avoided; to others, a crime which ought to be punished; to still others, it is an anachronism which no longer serves any purpose. On the other hand, there are some who take a more receptive attitude toward war and regard it as an adventure which may be interesting, an instrument which may be useful, a procedure which may be legitimate and appropriate, or a condition of existence for which one must be prepared.[1]

If wars are to be understood, and ultimately overcome, we must first agree as to what they are. In this text, we will consider "hot" wars; that is, overt violent conflicts between governments or rival groups hoping to establish governments. In recent times, an official declaration of war has been relatively rare; nonetheless, in many cases, "wars" can still easily be recognized, not only between different nation-states but also civil wars and so-called wars of liberation. We shall largely exclude feuds, disputes, or cases of banditry, as well as trade wars, propaganda wars, or "cold" wars, except insofar as these have a bearing on hot wars.

Defining Wars

Many people have tried to compile data on wars throughout history, both to help identify the issue and to test various empirical hypotheses about the causes of wars. However, researchers have not always been able to agree which armed struggles deserve to be included in such a compilation. There is little doubt, for example, that World Wars I and II are major examples, but what about the War of the Bavarian Succession (1778–1779)? In this "war," fully armed Prussian and Austrian troops marched while drums rolled, but not a shot was fired. War was declared, but no one died. By contrast, consider the Korean War, in which more than two million people (military and civilian) were killed: The United States was a major protagonist, and yet war was never declared. (In fact, neither was peace. This conflict is still officially unresolved, with an ongoing armed truce.) Instead, it was officially known as a United Nations "peace action." Or consider the Vietnam War, in which once again, no official state of war was ever acknowledged.

Quincy Wright considered a war to have taken place either when it was formally declared or when a certain number of troops were involved; he suggested 50,000 as a baseline. Lewis Richardson, another pioneering peace researcher, sought to define wars by the number of deaths incurred. J. D. Singer and M. Small have focused on a minimum of 1,000 combat-related fatalities. Whatever the technicalities involved, most people might agree that war can be described in much the same way as a jurist's observation about pornography: "I may not be able to define it, but I know it when I see it."

Similarly, there can be debate over exactly when a given war began. The United States entered World War II in December 1941, after the Japanese attack on Pearl Harbor, just as the Soviet Union had entered the war six months earlier, after it had been attacked by Germany in June. Most historians, however (and virtually all Europeans), consider that World War II began with Hitler's invasion of Poland in 1939, after which France and Britain declared war on Germany. On the other hand, some would argue that World War II began with Italy's invasion of Ethiopia (1935), or even earlier, with Japan's initial incursion into China (1931). And some historians have even maintained that in fact World War II began when World War I ended, with the Treaty of Versailles (1919), which created great resentment among the German people, leading ultimately to a resumption of armed hostilities 20 years later.

Psychologically, the essence of war is found in the intensely hostile attitudes among two or more contending groups. Economically, war often involves the emergency diversion of major resources from civilian to military pursuits. Sociologically, it frequently results in a rigid structuring of society, with prominence given to military functions. Perhaps the most famous definition of war, however, speaks to its political significance. Karl von Clausewitz (1780–1831), a Prussian army officer best known for the treatise *On War*, defined it as "an act of violence intended to compel our opponents to fulfill our will." He further emphasized that war was "the continuation of politics by other means," by which he meant war should not simply reflect senseless fury; rather, it should be an orchestrated action, with a particular political goal in mind. Very often, that political goal is the preservation of the power of those statesmen and other elites who orchestrate and hope to benefit from a particular war. It is the victors among warring elites who, ex post facto, will normally declare the war to have been "good" and/or "just." The losers and victims of wars, naturally, have a different view of the matter.

In the past few centuries, several prominent Prussian leaders advocated the brusque use of force, including war if necessary, to achieve desired ends. Frederick II, also known as Frederick the Great, king of Prussia from 1740 to 1786, wrote that diplomacy without armaments is like music without instruments. In the same vein, Otto von Bismarck, architect of German unification during the late 19th century, announced to his Parliament, "It is not by speeches and resolutions that the great questions of the time are decided . . . but by iron and blood."

The Frequency and Intensity of Wars

By some measures, wars have been relatively infrequent. Based on the number of nation-states existing since 1815, there have been between 16,000 and 20,000 nation-years, and during this time, war has occupied about 4% of the possible total. The 20th century was in comparison with most previous centuries a very warlike one. And yet modern warfare, even with its enormous devastation, was directly responsible for fewer than about 2% of all deaths occurring during the past century. Note, however, that there have also been many indirect casualties of war, since wars and the preparations for wars divert resources that might be directed against other causes of death, such as disease and starvation (in Iraq since 1991, for example, the number of civilian casualties due to these factors—initiated during the devastating Gulf War and aggravated by sanctions imposed on Iraq by the United Nations under prodding by the United States—has far exceeded the number of military and civilian deaths that occurred during the Gulf War itself). The extraordinary horror and impact of wars derive from their extraordinary violence and the scale and intensity of needless human suffering that occur because of that violence.

Scholars estimate that between the years 1500 and 1942 there was an average of nearly one formally declared war per year. This estimate does not count armed revolutions, of which between 1900 and 1965 there were approximately 350, an average of 5 or more per year. According to Lewis Richardson, there were at least 59 million deaths from human violence between 1820 and 1946, of which fewer than 10 million were attributable to individual and small-group violence; the remainder were due to wars.

Indirect Killing

In addition to the direct casualties, war kills indirectly, particularly by disease among armed forces personnel as well as by starvation as a result of disrupted food production and distribution services. For example, more than 8 million soldiers and 1 million civilians died during World War I, with approximately 18 million additional people dying during the influenza epidemic of 1918. Historically, in fact, more soldiers have died of diseases and of exposure than from enemy fire: More than eight times as many French soldiers died from cholera during the Crimean War than from battle. Similarly, of Napoleon's forces that invaded Russia in 1812, many more died from the cold and pneumonia than from Russian military resistance. During the Thirty Years' War, the armies of Gustavus and Wallenstein, facing each other outside Nuremberg in 1632, lost 18,000 men to typhus and scurvy, then separated without a shot having been fired.

In modern times, deaths due to disease have become less prominent during times of war, as a result of improved medical technology. At the same time, advances in military technology have made wars themselves more deadly, especially for nearby civilians: Military deaths were roughly the same in World Wars I and II (about 17 million in each war), but civilian deaths in World War II (approximately 35 million) were about seven times greater than in World War I. In the past, civilians often suffered horribly during wars, notably during the Thirty Years' War, when an estimated one third of the German population was killed, and during the sacking of fallen cities, such as Carthage at the end of its long wars with Rome. But through most of human history, war casualties were overwhelmingly concentrated among military forces. With advances in military technology, not only have casualties generally increased, but the ratio of civilian to military deaths also rose to unprecedented levels during the 20th century. In the event of nuclear or a biochemical war, either deliberate or "accidental," the casualties could well include essentially all the civilian population on both sides, and possibly billions of "bystanders" in other countries as well.

The Waste of War

The sheer wastefulness of war has been appalling, even with conventional (nonnuclear) weapons. During the Battle of the Somme (1916) in World War I, for example, the British sought to pierce the German lines, gaining a mere 120 square miles, at a cost of 420,000 men while the Germans lost 445,000. At the Battle of Ypres (1917), the British advanced 45 square miles, in the process losing 370,000 men. During World War I alone, Europe lost virtually an entire generation of young men. Here is F. Scott Fitzgerald's description of the Somme battlefield:

> See that little stream—we could walk to it in two minutes. It took the British a month to walk to it—a whole empire walking very slowly, dying in front and pushing forward behind. And another empire walked very slowly backward, a few inches a day, leaving the dead like a million bloody rugs.[2]

Numbers can be numbing. For example, of the 2,900,000 men and women who served in the U.S. armed forces during the Vietnam War (average age 19), 300,000 were wounded and 55,000 were killed. Yet these figures convey very little of the war's significance or of its horror, both for those who served and for the country at large—especially for the people of Vietnam. They also ignore the war's devastating socioeconomic consequences for Vietnam, Laos, and Cambodia, as well as for the United States, where it had profound social effects, including widespread alienation of millions of young people and massive antiwar demonstrations around the country. There were also political consequences, not all of them negative, including a hesitancy to engage U.S. servicemen and servicewomen in foreign conflicts (the "Vietnam syndrome"). In Vietnam itself, the economy and natural environment were devastated, and several million Vietnamese were killed.

Incidentally, it is deceptively easy to present a sanitized summary, often in statistical form, of incalculable carnage and misery, thereby synopsizing ineffable horrors in a few well-chosen words. In this book, we plead guilty to this form of euphemism and linguistic sanitation, offering only the excuse that the demands of space (and cost) do not permit the reproduction of photos that could reveal the atrocity of warfare infinitely better than an edited text.

Historical Trends in War

Some Numerical Trends

The following list of (admittedly bloodless) facts and figures should give some idea of how war has evolved over the past half-millennium. Consider, for example, these trends:

1. *An increase in the human, environmental, and economic costs of war, and in the number of civilian casualties.*   More than three hundred years ago, the Thirty Years' War laid waste to much of what is today Germany; World War II did the same to a large part of Europe, including the western USSR, as well as Japan and much of Southeast Asia and China. The 20th century also witnessed the initiation of large-scale attacks on civilian shipping, especially with the use of submarines. Attacks on noncombatants became particularly pronounced with the use of air bombardment—of Ethiopians by Italy; of Spanish Loyalists by German and Italian "volunteers" during the Spanish Civil War; of Chinese by Japan; of Poles, Dutch, and English by Germany; of Finns by the USSR; of Japanese and Germans by the United States and Britain during World War II; and of Iraq and Serbia by the United States and its North Atlantic Treaty Organization (NATO) allies during the 1990s. The ratio of civilian to military casualties at Hamburg, Dresden, Hiroshima, and Nagasaki was on the order of thousands to one.

2. *An increase in the geographic areas involved in the actual battles.*   In ancient times, battles typically took place in, and were named for, cities or mountain passes: the Battle of Thermopylae, Waterloo, Gettysburg. By World War I, battles had expanded to encompass entire rivers: the Battle of the Marne, the Somme, the Isonzo. During World War II, many battles had expanded yet more, to whole countries or oceans: the Battle of Britain, the Battle of the Atlantic; on land, the tides of battle swept across the entire continent of Europe, as well as across much of northern Africa, East Asia, and the Pacific Ocean. Following this tradition, World War III would almost certainly be global.

3. *An increase in the length of battles, in the number of battles fought per year during the course of a war, and in the number of battles per war.*   The average European war of the 16th century comprised fewer than 2 major battles; the 17th century, 4; the 18th and 19th centuries, around 20; and until the last decade of the 20th century, more than 30. Battles once commonly lasted a few hours or an afternoon, and typically did not take place during the winter months or at night; contemporary battles may last for weeks and occur at any time of day or night and any time of the year.

4. *A decrease in the average length of wars, and in the ratio of years spent at war to years spent at peace.*   Although their battles tend to be longer, modern wars tend to be briefer but more intense than earlier ones, such as the Hundred Years' War or the Thirty Years' War. During the 16th and 17th centuries, the major European powers spent about 65% of their time in a formal state of war; this percentage has decreased steadily to 38% in the 18th century; 28% in the 19th century, and 18% in the 20th. On the other hand, if undeclared "wars," such as colonial expeditions and various armed interventions, are counted, these figures increase dramatically. The United

States—which prides itself (legitimately or not) on its peacefulness—has in fact experienced only 20 years since 1789 when its armed forces have not been seeing action somewhere around the globe.

5. *An increase in both the absolute size of armies and in their size relative to the total population in the number (both absolute and relative) actually mobilized during war, in the number of combatants engaged in battle, and in the number of civilians involved in war preparation and conduct.* European armies during the 16th century were largely made up of mercenaries and rarely exceeded 20,000. Seventeenth-century armies commonly numbered about 50,000, which translated into approximately 3 soldiers per 1,000 population (about the same proportion as during the Roman Empire). The 18th-century armies of Frederick the Great (Prussia) and Lord Marlborough (England) approached 100,000, and those of Louis XIV (France) reached nearly 200,000. During the 19th century, by contrast, Napoleon fielded as many as 200,000 men *for a single battle.* And in the world wars of the 20th century, armies were measured in the millions.

6. *A decrease in the casualty rate among combatants—that is, a lower proportion of those actually involved in a battle being injured.* In the Middle Ages, for example, the defeated side, typically the one that broke and ran, would be cut down by the victors, often losing as many as 50% of their fighting men. By modern standards, however, the actual numbers in question were small: thousands or, at most, tens of thousands involved in combat, as opposed to modern armies numbering in the hundreds of thousands. Up to the 16th century, about 25% of combatants died; by the 17th century, this proportion was about 20%, dwindling to 15% in the 18th century, 10% in the 19th, and 6% in the 20th. This is partly because with modern technology, a larger proportion of "combatants" are engaged in support and supply rather than actual fighting. In addition, the proportion of combat injuries leading to death had decreased because of better medical care for the wounded. And disease, once a major scourge during wartime, now causes fewer combat fatalities (although the sequelae of combat may kill many civilians, as in Iraq since 1991). On the other hand, the proportion of the civilian population in the armed services has increased, and since the number and duration of battles has increased as well, the percentage of the national population dying in war has also gone up. In France, for example, approximately 11 out of every 1,000 deaths during the 17th century were due to military service; in the 18th century, this number had increased to 27; by the 19th century, 30; and in the 20th, 63.

7. *An increase in the speed at which wars spread to additional belligerents, in the number of belligerents involved in a given war, and in the area covered.* During the 15th and 16th centuries, each war had, on average, just slightly more than two collective participants. By the 20th century, the number of

states involved had jumped to five. As to geographic area, consider that the Thirty Years' War took place in central Europe, the War of the Spanish Succession in Holland, the Napoleonic Wars throughout Europe and parts of the Near East, and World Wars I and II throughout the world. (By the same token, the Seven Years' War, although it was fought during the 18th century, has claim to being a world war in its own right, with fighting in Europe, India, and North America, as well as in the Caribbean.)

Considering the increase in world population and in the number of independent nation-states, no clear-cut evidence exists that war is increasing, measured either as the number of wars occurring during a given time period or as the number of states at war per year. The frequency of wars has in fact been increasing, but about at the same pace as the increase in number of nation-states. In recent times, there have actually been somewhat fewer wars than in the past, with longer periods of peace in between. On the other hand, when wars have occurred in modern times, they have been more bloody overall than in the past, both in the actual number of deaths and in the proportion of the population affected. So we are having fewer, shorter wars, but they have become more intense and more lethal.

These generalizations apply only to international wars. Historically, civil wars have tended to be the most costly of all in terms of lives lost: the War of the Roses (England) during the 15th century; the Huguenot wars (France) during the 16th century; the Thirty Years' War (Germany) during the 17th century; the War Between the States (U.S.) and the Tai'ping Rebellion (China) in the 19th century; and the Spanish, Chinese, Nigerian, Yugoslavian (Bosnia and Kosovo), Russian (Chechnya), Sudanese, Ethiopian, and central African civil wars of the 20th century, to name just a few. In such cases, one nation bears virtually the entire cost of war, which tends to produce very high casualties, probably because large numbers of relatively untrained soldiers typically are involved, and because the struggle may occur over wide areas with few prepared defenses.

8. *Since World War II, an increase in the frequency of so-called low-intensity conflicts (LICs), in which the United States and the former Soviet Union, especially, became indirectly involved in Third World conflicts, revolutions, and counterrevolutions.* Both the United States and the former Soviet Union—although the United States to a greater degree—tended to consider that their "national interests" included the outcome of struggles taking place virtually anywhere on the globe. Often, they interpreted strictly indigenous conflicts, especially those reflecting revolutionary nationalism, as evidence of meddling by the other side and regarded the nations involved, therefore, as pawns in the East-West conflict. Moreover, as war has become potentially more destructive and more likely to engulf nuclear powers, military strategy has focused increasingly on fighting comparatively limited wars—

for example, U.S. support for the contras in Nicaragua, or the mujahideen in Afghanistan—that are perceived as less threatening to the major powers but that nonetheless allow them to carry on their rivalry, on someone else's soil. The U.S. experience in the Vietnam War (and quite possibly, the Russian experiences in Afghanistan and Chechnya) also sensitized government leaders to the difficulties of conducting wars that are expensive, in terms of money as well as lives, and that do not enjoy strong public support. As a result, one might expect increased interest in the 21st century by the nuclear powers in orchestrating LICs that are comparatively low profile, and hence, less controversial and domestically disruptive.

At the same time, it must be emphasized that the phrase "low-intensity conflict" is very much a euphemism, dangerously misleading as to the death and misery it may produce. Similar euphemisms would include the "police action" in Korea (1950–1953) and Vietnam (1962–1974), "peacekeeping" in the Dominican Republic (1965), and the "rescue operation" in Grenada (1983). To many defense strategists in the United States, who by the late 1980s were especially committed to the concept, an LIC is really a war, typically in the Third World, in which the number of U.S. combatants and casualties is kept low; for those directly affected, by contrast, the damage can be staggering. For example, consider the death toll in Nicaragua during the U.S.-sponsored contra war of the 1980s: more than 29,000. To gain a better perspective on this, imagine that Nicaragua's population (3.5 million) were that of the United States (about 285 million). In that case, a comparable cost to the United States would be more than 2 million lives. Proportionately, the Nicaraguan death toll in this "low-intensity war" exceeded all U.S. losses in all the wars of our history, from the Revolutionary War to Vietnam.

Trends in Style and in Citizen Participation

There have been other trends. A major one involves the declining role of personal honor and glory, as well as the end of the so-called code of chivalry and the former relative immunity of civilian noncombatants from military attack. The Battle of Crécy (1356), for example, at which English longbowmen soundly defeated a much larger contingent of heavily armored French knights, is considered one of the major turning points in military history. Following that battle, the victorious Prince of Wales hosted a formal banquet to honor the captured king of France and his son Philip. According to a contemporary historian, the gracious victor offered the following toast:

In my opinion . . . you have this day acquired such high renown for prowess, that you have surpassed all the best knights on your side. I do not, dear sir, say this to flatter you, for all those of our side who have seen and observed the actions of each party, have unanimously allowed this to be your due, and decree you the prize and garland for it.

The account continues:

> At the end of this speech there were murmurs of praise heard from every one; and the French said, the prince had spoken nobly and truly, and that he would be one of the most gallant princes in Christendom, if God should grant him life to pursue his career of glory.[3]

Although such sensitivity and courtesy still linger on occasion, as with the respectful treatment sometimes accorded captive officers, modern war has become increasingly more brusque and less mannered.

Warfare among hunter-gatherer bands, in comparison, only rarely involved slaughter, and often resembled disorganized skirmishes. In other cases, preindustrial warfare was often highly ritualized and organized; nonetheless, the emphasis was typically on individual accomplishments, especially prestige and revenge. Premodern war frequently had little to do with the acquisition of property or anything resembling modern-day political "power." For these warriors, the idea of conquest was virtually unknown.

Over time, however, as political organization grew more complex, and as military power brought tangible gains to the victors—and the absence of such power brought defeat and subjugation to the vanquished—very important changes developed in the relationship of civilians to the military. In the past, entire societies were only rarely organized for war. Raiding parties would be formed on specific occasions, but otherwise, the population was civilian. Eventually, various forms of local militias were established, to defend grain storehouses, cattle and sheep, and so on. Although the Romans had full-time legionnaires, for centuries, military forces generally were limited by the financial capabilities of the empire. During the late Middle Ages and early Renaissance, the walled cities of Italy were defended by the *condottierri*, or mercenaries under contract from the civilian leaders of each city. Eventually, as each city-state found itself increasingly pressured to compete with neighboring military forces, these arrangements became fixed. And in the mid-17th century, following the Thirty Years' War, the modern system of armed nation-states was established in Europe.

Following the Italian wars of the 15th century, in which French armies were eventually expelled from the Italian peninsula, the political theorist Niccoló Machiavelli emphasized that citizen-soldiers were preferable to mercenaries. Nonetheless, the major European states generally maintained a distinct class separation between warrior and nonwarrior, with the former coming from the two extremes of society: War *making* became the province of the upper class, which supplied the officers, while actual war *waging* was done by the lower class, which provided most of the soldiers. In Prussia, for example, the aristocratic *Junkers* monopolized the upper echelons of warfare, while the lower ranks were filled with conscripts and, occasionally, volunteers.

Until the 20th century, the great majority of the human population was relatively uninvolved in wars. During the 18th century, for example, war was the sport of kings, who engaged in statesmanship via warfare and the threat of war. Accordingly, many wars were precipitated by disputes over who was to rule after a reigning monarch died, especially if there were no heirs: the War of the Spanish Succession, the War of the Austrian Succession, and so on.

The *Levée en Masse*

When the monarchical powers of Europe sought to invade France and reestablish the Bourbon monarchy after the French Revolution, the beleaguered French government introduced something new: universal conscription, or the so-called *levée en masse*. The following decree was issued by the Parisian National Convention in 1793:

> From this moment until that in which our enemies shall have been driven from the territory of the Republic, all Frenchmen are permanently requisitioned for service in the armies. The young men shall fight; the married men shall forge weapons and transport supplies; the women will make tents and clothes and serve in hospitals . . . and old men will be brought to the public squares to arouse the courage of the soldiers, while preaching the unity of the Republic and hatred against Kings. . . . The public buildings shall be turned into barracks, the public squares into munition factories. . . . All firearms of suitable caliber shall be turned over to the troops: the interior will be policed with shotguns and cold steel. All saddle horses shall be seized for the cavalry; all draft horses not employed in cultivation shall draw the artillery and supply wagons.[4]

In fact, France did not actually become as thoroughly militarized as this decree suggests. And some forms of conscription had existed before the 19th century, although this usually took place on a much smaller scale, such as the so-called press gangs that would descend upon hapless young men and forcibly enlist them in the armed forces. Nonetheless, the *levée en masse* introduced a new twist into modern war making: an entire nation in arms. With it, the new French revolutionary government was able to field by far the largest armies ever known, to defeat the invading powers, and then, under Napoleon, to come close to conquering much of Europe. It was risky for monarchies at the time to arm their populace, but Napoleon's opponents eventually learned to fight fire with fire, and by the end of the Napoleonic Wars (1815), most major European governments had established national armies whose ranks were filled with their own conscripted citizens.

An important effect of the *levée en masse* was to devalue the lives of individual troops. "You cannot defeat me," Napoleon once boasted to Austria's famed diplomat, Count Metternich, "I spend 30,000 men a month." In fact, out of a total population of less than 29 million, France lost what was at that time an unparalleled number of soldiers, 1.7 million, during the Revolutionary and Napoleonic Wars. (The trend of increasing militarization continued among the warlike powers of Europe into modern times; by the end of World War II, for example, two thirds of all German men age 18–45 were in the armed forces.)

The Napoleonic era also initiated another trend with special importance for today: the existence of guerrilla warfare. Resistance and "terrorist" fighters had existed since antiquity; best known, perhaps, were the *zealots*, dagger-wielding Jewish opponents of Roman rule in biblical Palestine. But the concept of guerrilla warfare as an organized if rather informal uprising on a national scale originated with the Spanish resistance to Napoleon. In fact, during the five years of French occupation, Spanish guerrillas (aided by English forces in Portugal) accounted for as many French casualties as Napoleon's forces suffered during their ill-fated Russian campaign.

Technological Trends

Even if the over six billion people currently on the earth used only clubs or bows and arrows in organized conflict with one other, war would still be an important and tragic issue in human affairs. What makes war an especially pressing concern, of course, is that people have been extraordinarily inventive in developing fast, efficient, and devastating means of destroying other people (as well as animals, plants, buildings, and land), with ever-increasing ease and at ever-increasing distances. We can identify three major eras of weaponry: (1) the earliest period (lasting from the entire preindustrial period), based primarily on muscle power; (2) an intermediate period (from approximately the Renaissance until the first half of the 20th century in the West and still the case in most of the rest of the world), powered by chemicals, especially gunpowder, as well as steam and internal combustion engines; and (3) the most recent period, the second half of the 20th century, dominated by the threat of nuclear weapons and other weapons of potential mass destruction (especially biochemical weapons). It is the "advance" from stone ax to hydrogen bomb that gives particular urgency to peace and that impels us to understand the instruments of war so as to appreciate the need for developing alternative, nonweapon "instruments" of peace.

Muscle-Power Weapons

Preindustrial peoples developed stone axes and clubs in the middle Pleistocene (200,000 years ago), and throwing spears and bows and arrows in the upper Pleistocene (about 35,000 years ago). There is no evidence, however, that *weapons*—as opposed to hunting implements—were invented before the Neolithic era, about 13,000 years ago. And for thousands of years, the primary weapons of war—spears, swords, bows and arrows—changed relatively little. Indeed, there is no evidence that the weapons used against other people were any different from those designed for use when hunting animals.

But with the accumulation of agricultural surplus, ancient city-states developed, and these in turn became susceptible to attack. Accordingly, by about 5000 B.C.E., the numerous cities of Mesopotamia (modern-day Iraq) had begun surrounding themselves with complex, walled fortifications. Attackers would besiege a city, often using battering rams or catapults to destroy its walls, or they would simply try to starve its residents into submission. The defenders would use arrows, boiling water and oil, hot coals, and so on to repel the attackers.

Bronze weapons and armor first appeared in Mesopotamia, around 3500 B.C.E., when the first city-states were formed. Iron came later, around 1200 B.C.E. Initially, all fighting was done on foot, but by about 1800 B.C.E., horses were being employed to draw war chariots carrying at least one driver and one bowman. Horsemanship developed increasingly, especially among the nomadic steppe dwellers. By around 700 B.C.E., spurred by the invention of stirrups by Mongol nomads, warriors discovered how to shoot arrows while riding quickly astride a horse, and to wield sword and lance at high speed. Armored cavalry was introduced into combat around A.D. 100–300, along with the heavy warhorse. The best defense against a cavalry charge was the pikeman, a foot soldier armed with a very long spear, the butt of which was fixed into the ground and the sharp end pointed at an onrushing horseman. Soldiery consisted largely of archers for long-distance barrage (about 200 yards), cavalry with lance or swords, foot soldiers wielding swords or clubs, and pikemen. Those who could afford it wore relatively heavy armor.

The Phoenicians and Greeks specialized in the use of ships in war, initially as transport vehicles. Other ships were then designed to ram the transport vessels, thereby disabling them. During the 9th and 10th centuries, the Vikings successfully used ships for surprise raids along the ocean coasts and rivers. Initially, progress in naval design was comparatively slow: The relatively clumsy galleons of the Spanish Armada, for example, would not have been terribly out of place among the warships commanded by Lord Horatio Nelson at Trafalgar 150 years later. However, such ships were ultimately superseded by sleeker, longer, and more heavily armed battleships; these ships dominated naval battles until the late 19th century, when ironclads replaced the older wooden hulls, and steam engines and then diesel power replaced sails.

Firearms and Other Modern Developments

On land, although the crossbow and longbow increased the range and penetrating power of arrows, the overall conduct of war remained fundamentally unchanged until the 14th century, when gunpowder arrived in Europe from China. Catapults were eventually replaced by cannons, and swords and bows and arrows gave way to muskets and bullets. In 1453, for example, the Ottoman Turks successfully captured Constantinople, using cannons to breach that city's walls. Because such cannons were virtually immobile, as well as very inefficient, however, they were literally forged on the spot, during the prolonged siege.

Small arms became generally available by the 1550s, thereby gradually offsetting the superiority of nomads (and cavalry in general) on the battlefield. Small arms also eliminated the aristocrat's advantage in war, since a bullet—inexpensive to produce and easy for any trained soldier to load and fire—could penetrate expensive armor and also stop a well-trained, carefully bred horse. Early firearms, however, were very inaccurate; in fact, they were generally not fired at a specific target, but rather discharged in the general direction of the enemy. In addition, they were quite difficult to reload: Early musketeers required extensive training in the many movements required to prepare their weapon for refiring. With the invention of the detachable bayonet, pikemen finally became obsolete. And with improvements in hand-held firearms, armor and cavalry also became further outmoded, leading to other changes in the style and substance of warfare. When the flintlock replaced the matchlock, for example, the rate of fire was multiplied three-fold. As a result, a larger front could be occupied, resulting in a greater risk of troops being encircled and/or outflanked. The size of armies therefore increased, from about 70,000 at the beginning of Louis XIV's reign, to more than 200,000 at the end. Simplification of training and standardization of weaponry made soldiers easier to produce and therefore more expendable.

Even after the military value of cavalry was virtually nullified by the invention of accurate rifles, though, it is interesting to note that the cavalryman had such a dashing image that many nations continued to maintain cavalry, well into the 20th century. (The last recorded cavalry charges took place in 1939, when Polish cavalrymen charged—suicidally—against invading German armored divisions.)

King Gustavus Adolphus of Sweden introduced light muskets and small, mobile field artillery in the early 17th century, revolutionizing the European battlefield. Nonetheless, from the mid-17th until the late 18th century, European warfare was often a highly choreographed encounter, almost like a ritual game. The soldiers had become highly trained professionals, many of whom were considered too valuable to lose in combat. Commanders would maneuver for advantage, and one side or the other would typically then surrender, sometimes with very few shots having been fired. This rather genteel conception of war was altered not only by the advent of national armies in the late 18th and early 19th centuries but also by the invention of rifles. Industrial technology also contributed significantly to the changing character of war. For example, by the mid-19th century, breech-loading rifles replaced the older, muzzle-loading varieties. This not only allowed quicker reloading because the soldier did not have to ram powder and lead down the muzzle of his gun, but it also enabled each soldier to fire repeatedly while lying on the ground. The new rifles helped Prussia in a period of only six weeks to defeat a much larger foe, Austria, in the Austro-Prussian War of 1866.

Transportation and Communication Advances

The invention of the breech-loading rifle is significant not only in itself but also in signifying a general and continuing trend: the use of technology to achieve greater range, accuracy, and firepower. Two other technological advantages contributed to that Prussian victory, and also changed the face of modern war: railroads and the telegraph. And in turn, the newfound and crucial reliance on railroads and telegraphs during the mid- to late 19th century reflects the importance of technological developments in both transportation and communication. Railroads enabled very rapid mobilization of troops, from reserve status to front-line units. Quick, efficient transportation also permitted each side to concentrate its forces in a small area, thereby achieving the kind of local superiority needed for a tactical breakthrough.

At the same time, the use of communications technology—first telegraph and later, radio—permitted single commanders to control vast forces. At one time, commanders actually engaged in the fighting; Alexander the Great, for example, placed himself at the forefront of his battles, wearing a conspicuous, plumed helmet, and Napoleon watched the fighting at Waterloo from astride his horse. In such cases, it was very difficult for a commander to obtain information as to the progress of a battle and thus to plan the disposition of his troops. And it was usually impossible for him to maintain close and effective control over their behavior. Orders were typically sent by runners, who might be intercepted or disbelieved, and who would often arrive too late to be effective. With advances in the technology of transportation and communication, however, commanders could employ much larger armies than ever before. For example, von Moltke, the Prussian commander, directed the entire campaign against Austria without leaving Berlin. Technology, especially railroads, also permitted Prussia to win an even more surprising and decisive victory, this time over France in the Franco-Prussian

War. Within two weeks after the declaration of war, in 1870, the Prussians had sent more than a million troops to the front, as compared to the French force of little more than 300,000. Decisive innovations in technology, however, are carefully watched and rapidly emulated. Soon, all major European nations had breech-loading rifles, efficient railroads, telegraph systems, and so on.

On the other hand, whereas effective technology typically spreads rapidly, it has generally taken much longer for these innovations to be incorporated into actual tactics or strategy. Military leaders are commonly accused of being so conservative as to be self-defeating: It is often said, for example, that generals are always ready to refight the last war. For instance, many military experts expected that World War I would be fought quickly and decisively, as the Franco-Prussian War had been; instead, the machine gun gave a large advantage to the defense, and the struggle bogged down into interminable trench warfare, with enormous casualties and no quick and decisive victory. The invention of the tank finally hastened the end of that war, by providing a means for penetrating the entrenchments.

Modern Weaponry

Before 1939, it was assumed by many strategic thinkers that World War II would largely be a replay of the static trench warfare of World War I; instead, the German Army used quick-moving armored forces closely coordinated with air strikes, in a new style of rapidly penetrating battle known as the *Blitzkrieg*, or "lightning war," which again benefited the offense. In contrast with trench warfare, there were relatively few casualties in the Nazi conquest of Poland, the Low Countries (Holland and Belgium), and even France. The major loss of life in the European theater during the Second World War occurred during prolonged fighting on the eastern front, where the Soviet Union suffered more than 20 million casualties, and Germany sustained nearly 90% of its wartime losses.

Toxic gas was used extensively by both sides during World War I. Japan employed chemical weapons against unprepared Chinese forces during the 1930s; Italy did the same in Ethiopia. Subsequently, advances in CBW (chemical and biological warfare) have raised new fears about the potentially devastating consequences of future wars, along with their possible use by "terrorists" (as in the 1995 attack on the Tokyo subway system by Aum Shinrikyo, a religious cult). Iraqi forces apparently used chemical weapons (mustard gases) in their war with Iran during the 1980s, as well as against Kurdish rebels inside Iraq itself, in both cases violating international law. Iraq may also have been planning to use such weapons against both Israel and the allies during the Gulf War. And there may well be biochemical attacks on civilians in the United States and elsewhere during the ongoing "war against terrorism" being conducted around the world.

There have been many innovations in war-fighting technology within the past hundred years: breech-loading artillery, land mines, grenades, torpedoes, machine guns, tanks, chemical warfare, powered ships (first steam, later diesel), iron-hulled ships, submarines, and aircraft, including fighters and bombers. Also, advances in rocketry have permitted swift, stealthy, and accurate attacks on distant targets. In general, technological trends have enhanced the capacity to wage war from a distance. The Battle of Leyte Gulf, during World War II, for example, was the greatest naval engagement of all time: In five days, Japan lost four aircraft carriers, three battleships, six heavy cruisers, and 11 destroyers, all destroyed by torpedoes launched by submarines or by bombs dropped by airplanes; there were no direct encounters between the surface vessels of the two sides.

Other developments in conventional weaponry involve improved armor plating for tanks and ships, as well as highly accurate *precision-guided munitions*—relatively inexpensive, highly accurate rocket-propelled devices that can be fired by small groups of soldiers and that endanger costly targets, such as tanks or aircraft. Many military analysts believe that the future will see further development of highly lethal munitions and robots, used on an increasingly automated, even electronic, battlefield. These trends have culminated in what is probably the most important technological development in war making, the invention and high-speed delivery of nuclear weapons.

Has Technology Made War Obsolete?

In the age of nuclear and biochemical weapons, some people claim that the very destructiveness of these devices has made war obsolete. It is interesting to note, however, that this suggestion is not new, nor is it unique to contemporary weapons of mass destruction: Throughout history, people have regularly claimed that the latest advances in weaponry (the most recent "winning weapons"), by their very deadliness, will somehow prevent war. War has become unthinkable, it has often been claimed, because of its very destructiveness. And then comes the next war. (This brings to mind Mark Twain's comment: "It is easy to stop smoking; I've done it many times.")

Following the invention of the bayonet, for example, an English editor wrote in 1715 that "perhaps Heaven hath in Judgment inflicted the Cruelty of this invention on purpose to fright Men into Amity and Peace, and into an Abhorrence of the Tumult and Inhumanity of War." Similarly, Alfred Nobel hoped that his new invention, dynamite, would make war impossible. In 1911, an Englishman, Norman Angell, wrote a best-selling book, *The Great Illusion*, in which he argued that because of the economic interconnectedness of nations, as well as the increased destructiveness of modern military forces, war had finally become impossible. The "great illusion" was that no one could rationally conceive of or wage war in the 20th century;

ironically, World War I began just three years after the publication of Angell's book. And in that conflict, the invention of the machine gun made neither people nor war obsolete. Rather, it led to the deaths of hundreds of thousands, often in just a single battle, such as the Battle of the Somme.

Since the dawn of the nuclear age in 1945, some observers of the global military scene (such as John Mueller in his book *Retreat From Doomsday*[5]) have once again suggested that since war has become unacceptably destructive—to a would-be aggressor and even to a "victor," if one could be imagined following a nuclear winter—the likelihood of war has actually decreased. Although this line of reasoning may appear somewhat comforting, it is also seriously flawed. Let us grant that nuclear war, because of its potential for global annihilation, is in a sense its own deterrent. States possessing nuclear weapons (especially the nuclear superpowers) may well be very cautious in any conflict with other nuclear weapons states. But at the same time, theories of mutual nuclear deterrence seem to have produced the expectation that because of the seriousness of nuclear war, each side can count on the other to refrain from anything resembling a nuclear provocation, which in turn makes the world yet more "safe for conventional war." In addition, there is the great danger that in a nuclear confrontation, each side will presume that the other will be deterred by the prospect of annihilation, and therefore, each may expect the other to back down, while remaining determined to stand firm itself. Moreover, nuclear weapons carry with them an inherent ambiguity: Since the consequences of using them are so extreme, the threat to do so lacks credibility. As a result, although technological "progress" in war making has undeniably made war—especially nuclear war—horrifically destructive, it remains uncertain whether such developments have actually made war any less likely. In fact, because of the increased likelihood of "accidental" local (or *theater*) nuclear wars, as well as the proliferation of nuclear devices after the dissolution of the Soviet Union, it may well be true that a nuclear conflict or accident is more, not less, likely in this century than in the previous one.

Perhaps most disturbing of all, the fact remains that human beings, including decision makers, are influenced by many things beyond a cool, rational calculation of their perceived best interests. Wars have been initiated for many reasons, often including mistaken judgment or faulty information. And when war takes place, the combatants make use of whatever weapons they have. Never in the history of human warfare has an effective weapon been invented, and then allowed to rust without at some time being used.

Historically, the impact of "war is obsolete" reasoning has also been ironic: It has not so much discouraged governments from waging war as diminished whatever hesitation scientists, engineers, and industrialists might otherwise have had about lending their talents to the production of ever more destructive weapons. Even the liberal view of the perfectibility of human nature helped justify science's contribution to the manufacture of cannons, no less than steam engines or new techniques of manufacturing metal alloys. And from the late 1980s until the present, many scientists similarly justify their participation in "Star Wars" (Strategic Defense Initiative/ National Missile Defense-related) research.

Some strategic thinkers even claim that since nuclear weapons states are necessarily advanced technologically, they also possess the qualities of judgment that virtually ensure that such horrible weapons will never be used. Aside from the hidden racism that underlies such assertions—the implication that unlike Caucasians, darker-skinned societies lack the intellect or moral rigor to restrain themselves—the fact remains that the only state that has actually used nuclear weapons against other people is the same state whose technological sophistication enabled it to invent nuclear weapons: the United States of America. In the late 18th century, the historian Edward Gibbon argued that powerful weapons could be invented only by advanced civilizations and that such civilizations, because of their advancement, wouldn't allow force to be the arbiter of disputes. Then came the Napoleonic Wars.

Total War

One of the most important changes in modern war has been the combination of (1) increased destructiveness of the weapons and (2) decreased selectivity as to their targets. The weapons, in short, have become more deadly, while at the same time, they have been increasingly directed toward civilians. Traditionally, noncombatants have been granted immunity during war—in theory, if not always in practice. In his book *Sentimental Journey Through France and Italy*, English author Laurence Sterne recounted how, in the 18th century, he went to France, entirely omitting the fact that at the time England and France were fighting the Seven Years' War. There was a time when states would engage in war without the lives of all their citizens poisoned, corrupted, or otherwise focused by the conflict. In 1808, for example, with the Napoleonic Wars raging, the French Institute conferred its gold medal on Sir Humphry Davy, an Englishman, who blithely crossed the English Channel to accept his award to the enthusiastic cheers of the great scientists of France. However, this separation between civilian and military, between the lives of the people and the behavior of their states, has changed dramatically with the "hardening" of political boundaries as well as the advent of what has come to be called *total war*.

The Home Front

Although to some extent, military forces have long been raised by taxing the population at large, armies had largely supported themselves once they were in the field, either by foraging, purchasing, or pillaging. With the advent of immense national armies that employed advanced technology and that were unable to provide for themselves, it became necessary for the home front to be mobilized to provide the immense amounts of food, clothing, and munitions needed. As entire populations were enlisted in the war effort, it became more and more difficult to distinguish between combatants and noncombatants: After all, it was argued, how can the enemy be limited to the person who pulls a trigger, ignoring those who build the bombs, guns, ships, and other articles of war? Furthermore, why shouldn't war also be waged against those who make the clothing used in military uniforms, or even those who grow the food, without which no military force can be maintained?

During the Russian retreat before Napoleon's invading French army, partisans destroyed crops and other civilian articles that might be useful to the invader. And toward the end of the War Between the States, the Union's General Sherman marched destructively through Georgia, punishing the civilians in that part of the Confederacy no less than the rebel military. Total war was therefore not unknown by the 20th century; civilians, moreover, have in many cases suffered greatly after their side was militarily defeated, especially if their city was sacked. What was new in 20th-century total war, however, was the organized use of military force directly and explicitly against an opponent's homeland in order to win the war.

Total war became institutionalized during World War I, with the first use of the term *home front* and the direct and deliberate targeting of the people maintaining that front, the civilians. Italy had actually initiated military bombing during its 1911 campaign in Libya, but Germany's use of zeppelins to bomb London was the first major attack on a home front. To appreciate some of the ambivalence among some bombers that this tactic raised, consider the following letter from Captain Peter Strasser, chief of Germany's naval airship division, to his mother:

> We who strike the enemy where his heart beats have been slandered as "baby-killers" and "murderers of women." . . . What we do is repugnant to us too, but necessary. Very necessary. Nowadays there is no such animal as a non-combatant; modern warfare is total warfare. A soldier cannot function at the front without the factory worker, the farmer and all the other providers behind him. You and I, mother, have discussed this subject, and I know you understand what I say. My men are brave and honorable. Their cause is holy, so how can they sin while doing their duty? If what we do is frightful, then may frightfulness be Germany's salvation.[6]

Loosening of Restraints

The tendency toward total war at that time was widespread, and certainly not limited to Germany. For example, the British naval blockade of Germany during World War I caused great suffering and widespread malnutrition, leading to an estimated 800,000 civilian deaths above the normal mortality figures. As one critic puts it, "One consequence [of industrialization] was to loosen the restraints upon war. With the growing material power to make war, what was needed was more politeness, more art, more wit in the conduct of international relations. What came was more grossness."[7]

What also came, as a result of national commitment to total war, was an inability on the part of the belligerents to call a halt to the carnage. Thus, for example, the disputes leading up to World War I were in their own way no more serious than those of the 18th century, which were resolved with much less bloodshed. What happened, in part, was that

the techniques of war had completely overpowered the ability of governments to limit their commitment to it. The axiom that force can only be overcome by greater force drove them to make war total, and the scale of the sacrifices they then had to demand of their citizens required that the purposes of the war must also be great. . . . When the people's willingness to go on making sacrifices has been sustained in every country by hate propaganda that depicts the war as a moral crusade against fathomless evil—then governments cannot just stop the fighting, sort out the petty and obscure Balkan quarrel that triggered it, swap around a few colonies and trade routes, and thank the surviving soldiers and send them home. Total war requires the goal of total victory, and so the propaganda has become the truth: the future of the nation (or at least the survival of the regime) really does depend on victory, no matter what the war's origins were.[8]

Strategic Bombing

The invention of airplanes, and with it the possibility of long-range, strategic bombing, opened up yet another phase in the march of total war. Following the horrors of trench warfare in World War I, some military analysts initially welcomed the possibility of attacking an enemy's homeland as a means of guaranteeing that future wars would be short and, on balance, less destructive than in the recent past. Foremost among these theorists was the Italian Air Force general Guido Douhet (1869–1930), who emphasized that air power, applied directly to an enemy's industry and to the workforce that sustained its war effort, would destroy that side's "will to resist" and break its morale, resulting in a relatively quick and painless victory:

A complete breakdown of the social structure cannot but take place in a country being subjected to . . . merciless pounding from the air. The time would soon come when, to put an end to horror and suffering, the people themselves, driven by the instinct of self-preservation, would rise up and demand an end to the war.[9]

In pursuit of total war, during the 1930s and continuing through World War II, numerous civilian targets were attacked. German bombers targeted Rotterdam (Holland) as well as Coventry and London (Britain), while British and American strategic bombers eventually retaliated and then exceeded the initial German bombings, conducting large-scale raids against many German urban areas, including, notably, the firebombings of Hamburg and Dresden. In the Far East, U.S. bombers attacked Japanese civilian targets, culminating in firebombings of Tokyo and the use of atomic bombs against the cities of Hiroshima and Nagasaki.

With the exception of these latter two cases, there is no evidence that the national will to resist was ever seriously shaken by total war; on the contrary, national will was typically hardened by such attacks (as in Iraq and Serbia), even as the civilian casualty toll mounted. It is estimated, for example, that German bombs killed 60,000 British civilians during World War II and that Allied bombs killed more than 300,000 Germans and 500,000 Japanese. Perhaps most troubling of all, today many decision makers and others take civilian casualties for granted, although perhaps we have not yet reached Shakespeare's prediction in *Julius Caesar*:

> Blood and destruction shall be so in use
> And dreadful objects so familiar,
> That mothers shall but smile when they behold
> Their infants quartered with the hands of war. (III, i)

_____ Wars, Empires, Colonialism, and National Liberation

To some extent, the history of war *is* the history of civilization, or more accurately, a history of failures in our struggle to be civilized. The earliest peace treaties known are clay tablets dating from about 3000 B.C.E. and that result from wars among the city-states of the Tigris and Euphrates valley. The rise and fall of empires and states have been marked—if not specifically caused—by a pattern of military successes followed eventually by defeats. Empires that rose by the sword generally died by the sword.

Some Ancient Empires

In the ancient Near East, for example, the Sumerian empire was established around 2500 B.C.E., and replaced by that of Sargan of Akkad, which in turn ended around 2000 B.C.E. Hammurabi then forged a Babylonian empire, which lasted about 200 years, until it was conquered by the Mitanni and the Assyrians around 1400 B.C.E. Egypt began uniting in approximately 3000 B.C.E., whereupon it spread via conquest and contacted the Mitanni, signing a nonaggression pact with them and with the Hittites around 1400 B.C.E. But the Assyrians eventually conquered Egypt as they did the Babylonians. In turn, the Assyrian capital of Nineveh was destroyed by the revivified Egyptians and Medes in 612 B.C.E.

Next to rise to prominence were the Persians, who conquered Babylon in 538 B.C.E. The Persian empire under Darius I in the fifth century B.C.E. extended from what is now southern Russia to southern Egypt, and from the Danube to the Indus Rivers. But the Greeks held off the Persians, and following their rather unexpected victory, Athenian Greece entered into its Golden Age, 500–400 B.C.E. However, this period of prosperity and cultural creativity was shattered by the devastating Peloponnesian War between Sparta and Athens, and the Greeks never regained their civic and military glory.

Ultimately, the Greeks were defeated by the Macedonians under Philip. Philip's son, Alexander the Great, enabled the Greeks to conquer Egypt and virtually everything previously held by the Persians. Meanwhile, Rome developed as a major force, conquering Macedonia and Greece and defeating its rival Carthage in the Punic Wars by the third century B.C.E. The ensuing *Pax* Romana lasted about 500 years, but the western Roman Empire ceased to exist after A.D. 476, because of successful attacks by such "barbarians" as the Huns, Visigoths, and Vandals. The eastern (Byzantine) part of the Roman Empire later came under attack by Muslim Saracens and ultimately fell to the Turks in 1453. Before this, Islamic forces had conquered Egypt, northern Africa, Palestine, and Spain and were engaged in periodic wars with the Christian Crusaders.

Medieval to Modern Empires

Muslim armies, however, were stopped in their advance into Europe at Tours, in modern-day France, by forces under the leadership of Charles Martel. Charlemagne, Martel's grandson, was subsequently crowned Holy Roman Emperor by the pope, in the forlorn hope of rekindling the power of ancient Rome. Several centuries later, in the 12th century, Genghis Khan, leader of nomadic Mongol herdsmen from central Asia, established the largest land empire ever known, and although Khan's army was never conclusively defeated, the Mongol empire eventually gave way as well, largely because the various subjugated peoples retained their cultural identity even as they assimilated certain Mongol traditions as well.

As the Mongol and Islamic empires receded in influence, others gained prominence, each relying heavily on military power, and each relatively short-lived. Thus, the Italian city-states, as well as Spain, Portugal, and the Netherlands, have all had their experience as major world powers, especially through their trading activities, secured by naval power. England and France contested the spoils of the New and Old Worlds for centuries, essentially to a draw. Napoleon, and, in more recent times, Hitler, have attempted to conquer large parts of the known world, and although they succeeded briefly (at least in continental Europe), their imperial ambitions were defeated by countervailing military force. From the 18th to the early 20th centuries, Britain was the supreme world power, but the British Empire has also declined, in large measure hastened by the bloodletting and economic costs of World Wars I and II. Neither the "thousand-year Reich" (Hitler's imperial design for Germany) nor the "greater east Asia co-prosperity sphere" (Japan's euphemism for its imperial sway over Asia) succeeded for more than a few years. World War I brought about the end of most European monarchism and of four empires. World War II left the United States and the Soviet Union as the two preeminent global powers; soon thereafter, the Cold War was initiated between them. The end of European colonialism in the 20th century was hastened by numerous wars of national liberation.

Wars and Social Change

Although wars have been crucial to many of the major political changes on the world scene, paradoxically, they have often also served to prevent significant social and economic changes. In this sense, the threat of war has helped maintain the status quo. The *Pax* Romana, during the period of Roman hegemony, was due largely to the ability of Rome to act essentially as (Western) world police. The same was true, but to a lesser extent, during the so-called *Pax* Britannica, from the late 18th century to the early 20th century. Following World War II, the United States attempted to forge a kind of *Pax* Americana; some would claim it succeeded. But it may well be the case that the only kind of peace likely to be truly lasting and socially significant will have to be something as yet unknown in modern times, a *Pax* mundi—that is, a global peace associated not with an individual nation but with the entire world.

Owing largely to their advantage in technology, the major European powers—and to a lesser extent, the United States and the former Soviet Union—have been able to conquer, or at least to dominate militarily and politically, large areas of the globe. In the early stages of European colonial expansion, indigenous peoples such as the American Indians, Africans, and Chinese had numerical superiority, but they lacked modern firearms and often the necessary social and political organization to resist effectively. Cortez, for example, conquered 8 million Aztecs with 400 men with muskets, 16 horses, and three cannons. Pizzaro was similarly successful in Peru, and Clive in India. Commodore Perry "opened" Japan with a handful of naval vessels. An Englishman, Hillaire Belloc, offered this sardonic commentary on the crucial role of technology in 19th-century British imperial conquest:

Whatever happens we have got
The Maxim gun, and they have not.

But just as American Indians eventually obtained rifles (especially during the late 19th century), antijunta rebels in El Salvador during the 1980s
captured large amounts of military hardware, provided initially by the
United States to the repressive, neocolonial Salvadoran government. And
much of Saddam Hussein's Iraqi arsenal, as well as the arms controlled by
the anti-Soviet mujahideen in Afghanistan, came by way of their eventual
enemies.

Revolutionary nationalism, especially in the form of guerrilla warfare,
has been very successful, particularly since World War II, in evicting the
weakened European powers from such regions as eastern Africa, Algeria,
Vietnam, and Indonesia. By contrast, revolutionary forces have only rarely
triumphed over locally based, nationalist governments, except when those
governments were corrupt and generally out of touch with their citizenry, as
happened in Russia in 1917, China in 1949, Cuba in 1959, and Nicaragua
and Iran in 1979.

Terrorism and Counterterrorism

In September 2001, during the first year of the new millennium, the cities of
New York and Washington, D.C., were attacked by what most political and
military leaders in the West have described as "terrorist" groups. The loss of
life in a single day due to these attacks (about 3,000 civilians) was exceeded
in American history only by battles during the Civil War. However, many
bombing attacks on urban centers during World War II resulted in far
greater casualties to noncombatants in other countries. Raids on Hamburg,
Dresden, and Tokyo caused tens of thousands of deaths, not to mention the
atomic bombings of Hiroshima and Nagasaki, each of which resulted in at
least 100,000 dead and wounded noncombatants. What may be unprecedented is that the attacks of September 2001 were perpetrated by foreign
"terrorists" on American soil, that U.S. civilian airplanes were transformed
into weapons of mass destruction, that the United States was not in a
declared state of war at the time, that the identity of the perpetrators was
unknown, and that although the leadership of certain countries (notably
Afghanistan) was perceived in many Western circles to be sympathetic to the
attacks, the actual perpetrators were probably non-state actors.

Terrorism is a vexing term. Any actual or threatened attack against civilian noncombatants may be considered an act of "terrorism." In this sense,
terrorism is as old as human history. "Terrorists" are people who may feel
militarily unable to confront their perceived enemies directly and who
accordingly use violence, or the threat of violence, against noncombatants
to achieve their political aims. "Terrorism" is also a contemporary variant

of what has been described as guerrilla warfare, dating back at least to the anticolonialist and anti-imperialist struggles for national liberation conducted in North America and Western Europe during the late 18th and early 19th centuries against the British and French Empires.

Placing terrorist in quotation marks may be jarring for some readers, who consider the designation self-evident. We do so, however, not to minimize the horror of such acts but to emphasize the value of qualifying righteous indignation by the recognition that often one person's "terrorist" is another's "freedom fighter." Thus, who is or is not a terrorist and what may or may not be acts of terrorism depend largely on the perspective of the person or group using these terms.

Prior to the U.S. Civil War, militant abolitionists such as John Brown were considered terrorists. During the 1940s, Menachim Begin—who subsequently became prime minister of Israel and a close ally of the United States—headed a militant Zionist group known as the Irgun; this organization conducted numerous acts of violence, primarily against British-occupied Palestine, which included the notorious bombing of the King David Hotel, a civilian target. Yasser Arafat, head of the Palestine Liberation Organization, has similarly been denounced (in the West and in Israel) as a terrorist; among Palestinians, he is widely regarded as a heroic leader. The government of Pakistan, which criticized "terror attacks" on the United States as "un-Islamic," has long sponsored violent agitators in Kashmir, who are considered terrorists by the government of India. The Irish Republican Army is widely regarded in Great Britain as a terrorist organization, yet many Irish Catholics consider this group to be laudably patriotic, and much of its funding has come from donations raised in the United States.

After the attacks on the World Trade Center in New York City and the Pentagon in Washington, D.C., many Americans evidently agreed with pronouncements by many senior politicians that the United States was "at war" with "terrorism." Yet, to many disempowered people in other regions, "Americans are the worst terrorists in the world" (according to Osama bin Laden in a 1998 TV interview with the American Broadcasting Company). Following the attacks, President George W. Bush announced that the United States "would make no distinction between terrorists and the countries that harbor them." For many frustrated, impoverished, infuriated people—who view the United States as a terrorist country—attacks on American civilians were justified in precisely this way: making no distinction between a "terrorist state" and the citizens who aid and abet that state.

There are also levels of terrorism. These range from threats to individual security experienced by civilians whose airplanes have been hijacked to the global existential threat posed by the very existence of nuclear and other weapons of mass destruction. Accordingly, at present there exist *state* and *state-sponsored* terrorism in addition to terrorist groups, as well as government-created *counter-* and *antiterrorist* agencies and operations. What seems particularly novel, and terrorizing, about this state of affairs in the early 21st century are the global scope of terrorist and counterterrorist operations, and the suddenness and lethality of such actions. In addition, whereas people often demand swift and decisive response from their government in the face of violent events of this sort, the perpetrators are typically elusive and often difficult to identify, much less to punish or apprehend.

Any war against terrorism will likely be part of an increasingly recognized 21st-century pattern: so-called asymmetric warfare. In this circumstance, large, wealthy, heavily armed, and technologically sophisticated countries and their military forces find themselves aligned against small, poor, lightly armed, low-tech opponents, who are often willing to die for their cause. Although the latter can typically be defeated in straightforward "set-piece battles," the former—in part because of the openness of their civil societies as well as the fact that they offer a "target rich" environment—are likely to remain vulnerable.

In this regard, another major concern is the "law of unintended consequences," whereby actions (especially violent ones) often bring about results that are unpredictable as well as undesirable. This can apply to those responding to terrorism no less than to the perpetrators. Thus, violent retribution by the leaders of a victimized country runs the risk of not only killing additional innocent civilians but also of generating yet more attacks, in a potentially endless cycle of violence. (This problem is exacerbated when, as already noted, terrorist perpetrators are difficult to identify and target.) In the specific case of the events unleashed following the attacks of September 2001, there is great danger that a U.S.-led "crusade" against terrorism will be seen as a war directed against Islam, which could in turn destabilize certain moderate regimes, resulting in governments that are yet more extremist and violence prone. Given that Pakistan, for example, is a nuclear weapon state, such concerns seem especially cogent.

Historically, terrorists have sought not only to cause death, injury, and terror itself but often to induce their victims to strike back; the more bloody and indiscriminating the retaliation, the more perceived benefit derived by the terrorists themselves. Thus, a violent response tends not only to delegitimize the respondent morally, it also plays into the hands of the original perpetrators, by recruiting others, newly victimized, to their cause.

A peace-oriented perspective condemns not only terrorist attacks but also any violent response to them. It is tempting to conclude that under such circumstances, violence is always counterproductive. Nonetheless, an alternative view also deserves respect. Consider a country that refuses to respond forcefully after large numbers of its citizens are attacked: It must be acknowledged that well-meaning, well-informed people honestly disagree as to whether such a policy might actually encourage more attacks, resulting in reduced overall security. Although vengeance is not highly regarded by most civilized persons, justice is.

Accordingly, the best response to such terrible events is often maddeningly unclear, and should not be made precipitously, in the heat of the moment. One course of action might be for international organizations such as the United Nations and the International Court of Justice to be empowered to bring to justice the perpetrators of such crimes against humanity as acts of terrorism involving the mass murder of civilians. In any event, any policy—military, diplomatic, and/or economic—must be chosen with the greatest care and with the utmost respect for human life. No one has a monopoly on wisdom.

A Final Note on War

Today's armed conflicts, as previously noted, rarely involve a formal declaration of war, probably because, in general, diplomatic formalities are less prominent, and war is increasingly considered an illegitimate way to settle grievances. However, wars—often under such euphemisms as "police actions"—are still taking place, causing immense destruction and misery. Moreover, the threat of war remains very great, with its likely consequences more severe and potentially far-reaching than ever.

Even "small" conventional wars can be devastating: For example, the Six-Day War between Israel and its Arab opponents in 1967 resulted in 21,000 battle-related deaths, far greater than the rate of killing per day that occurred during the Korean War. And between 1980 and 1988, the war between Iran and Iraq, generally considered a minor conflagration on the world scene, may have claimed more than a million lives. Between 1991 and 2000, wars and "ethnic cleansing" in Rwanda, Burundi, Iraq, East Timor, and in many parts of the former Soviet Union and Yugoslavia claimed millions of civilian casualties. A little-publicized civil war in Sudan, between an Islamic government in the northern part of that country and Christian and animist secessionists in the south, has claimed perhaps two million lives, both from direct fighting and from subsequent disease and mass starvation. In absolute terms, military expenditures are now higher than ever before, exacting an enormous toll on civilian economies, although relative to such measures as gross national product, military expenditures are relatively stable since the economies of many nation states (especially the United States and Western Europe) have also been growing.

Although human life may not have become cheap, the history of war in the 20th century shows that it certainly is *not* considered to be priceless. It also shows that some lives are valued more than others, especially those of white, Western male soldiers and decision makers when they choose to perform military "operations" on other peoples. Moreover, a great danger lurks in a very special kind of calamity—nuclear or chemical-biological war

—that could be catastrophic not only for all humans but also, perhaps, for all life on earth.

Notes

1. Quincy Wright. 1964. *A Study of War*. Chicago: University of Chicago Press.

2. F. Scott Fitzgerald. 1934. *Tender Is the Night*. New York: Scribner.

3. John Froissart. [1336] 1901. *Chronicles of England, France, Spain and the Adjoining Countries From the Latter Part of the Reign of Edward II to the Coronation of Henry IV*. New York: Colonial Press.

4. From J. F. C. Fuller. 1961. *The Conduct of War, 1789–1939*. London: Eyre and Spottiswode.

5. John Mueller. 1989. *Retreat From Doomsday*. New York: Basic Books.

6. From A. Norma. 1969. *The Great Air War*. New York: Macmillan.

7. John C. Nef. 1950. *War and Human Progress*. Cambridge, MA: Harvard University Press.

8. Gwynne Dyer. 1985. *War*. New York: Crown.

9. Guido Douhet. 1942. *The Command of the Air*. New York: Coward-McCann.

4 The Special Significance of Nuclear Weapons

The splitting of the atom has changed everything but our way of thinking, and hence we drift toward unparalled catastrophe.

—Albert Einstein

Albert Einstein once noted that, as a child, he had been taught that modern times began with the fall of the Roman Empire. But everything changed with the atomic bombings of Hiroshima and Nagasaki: Now, Einstein observed, we must say that modern times began in 1945.

There is indeed something special about nuclear weapons. They represent a dramatic discontinuity in human history, and they offer the possibility of an even more dramatic break: a canceling of the past, an end to the present, and a negating of the future. As destructive and dangerous as conventional warfare has been—and continues to be—it clearly takes a back seat to the sheer terror and horrific consequences of nuclear war.

At least four factors must be understood if one is to grasp the nature of nuclear war and the urgency as well as the prospects of preventing it: (1) the weapons (bombs and warheads) themselves and their effects; (2) "delivery systems" (the means by which nuclear weapons are to be fired at their targets); (3) "strategic doctrine," which is concerned with the plans and strategies for the use of nuclear weapons; and (4) the problem of nuclear proliferation.

The Nature of Nuclear Weapons

Nuclear weapons derive their explosive power from the conversion of matter into energy. This conversion takes place according to the well-known equation, $E = mc^2$, in which E is the amount of energy released, m = the mass to be converted into energy, and c = the speed of light. Since the speed of light is itself a very large number, and is squared in the equation, the resulting energy release is truly enormous. Nuclear fusion drives the sun and the stars; prior to 1945, the explosive power of nuclear energy had never been released by humans.

The power of nuclear weapons exceeds that of most conventional explosives by approximately a factor of one million. Herein rests the underlying significance of nuclear weapons and nuclear war: Something radically new, qualitatively different from previous human experience has been introduced into the world of war and into strategic thinking about conflicts.

Atomic bombs result from *nuclear fission*, the splitting of large, unstable atoms, most commonly uranium-235 (a radioactive isotope of the element uranium) or plutonium-239 (another radioactive element, one that is essentially man-made). When enough fissionable material is gathered together in one place, and exposed to a barrage of neutrons, some of the unstable nuclei are split, releasing energy as well as additional neutrons. These neutrons, in turn, split the nuclei of other atoms, releasing yet more energy and also more neutrons, which continue to split additional nuclei in a chain reaction that accelerates geometrically, and thus, at extraordinary speed. The material has reached *critical mass* when each nucleus, after being split (or "fissioned"), releases enough neutrons to split approximately two nearby nuclei. As a result, an immense amount of energy can be released in a very short time. For example, in 0.00000058 seconds, 2^{57} nuclei (approximately 2 followed by 24 zeros) will have been split, releasing the energy equivalent to 100,000 tons of TNT.

Atomic, or fission, explosions are typically measured in *kilotons* (KT), that is, the equivalent energy that would be released by the detonation of thousands of tons of TNT. Thus, a 12-KT atomic explosion—the size that destroyed the Japanese city of Hiroshima—releases the same amount of energy as would be released if 12,000 tons of TNT were to detonate.

The first nuclear weapons were based on fission. Most nuclear weapons today, however, are *fusion*, or *thermonuclear*, devices. They derive much of their energy from the squeezing together of very small atoms, notably deuterium and tritium, two isotopes of hydrogen. In the process, the element helium is produced, and through the conversion of mass into energy, vast amounts of energy are released. When plutonium, for example, is split, the total mass of the fission products that are formed—such as iron, cobalt, and manganese—is slightly less than that of the parent nucleus with which the process started. Similarly, the total mass of the helium nuclei produced by fusion is slightly less than the mass of the hydrogen isotopes with which a fusion reaction begins. This mass has not been "lost." Rather, it has been converted into energy.

Fusion is more efficient than fission in that more energy per starting mass is released. But fusion is also more difficult to initiate than fission, since great heat and pressure are required literally to squeeze the hydrogen nuclei together. Therefore, fusion explosions—or "hydrogen bombs," as they are often known—start with a relatively small "atomic" explosion, which serves as a trigger to initiate the much more powerful fusion reaction. This requirement of great heat and pressure is why fusion reactions are also known as *thermo*nuclear explosions. Fusion explosions are also typically boosted with an additional fission component, as the energy released by the fusion is captured by a lower-grade form of uranium, usually U-238, which is induced to split as well. So the typical thermonuclear (H-bomb or hydrogen bomb) explosion is fission-fusion-fission, all occurring in a minuscule fraction of a second. The energy released in such detonations can extend into the range of *megatons* (Mt), equivalent to millions of tons of TNT. Although nuclear explosives are often referred to as *bombs*, they are in fact more likely to be carried by a missile, in which case they are known as *warheads*. In addition, nuclear weapons are often designated as either *tactical* or *strategic*. The former usually refers to weapons that are intended for use on a battlefield; the latter are normally intended for use against an adversary's (usually distant) homeland.

The Effects of Nuclear Weapons

Given that nuclear weapons have only twice been exploded in wartime (both in 1945, at Hiroshima and Nagasaki), it may seem strange that they should command so much attention. The reason is simple, and related primarily to their effects: Nuclear explosions are extraordinarily powerful and devastating. Consider this account of the first atomic bomb test, at Alamogordo, New Mexico, in July 1945:

> No man-made phenomenon of such tremendous power had ever occurred before. The lighting effects beggared description. The whole country was lighted by a searing light with the intensity many times that of the midday sun. It was golden, purple, violet, gray and blue. It lighted every peak, crevasse and mountain range with a clarity and beauty that cannot be described but must be seen to be imagined. It was the beauty the great poets dream about but describe most poorly and inadequately. Thirty seconds after the explosion came . . . to be followed almost immediately by the strong, sustained, awesome roar which warned of doomsday and made us feel that we puny things were blasphemous to dare tamper with the forces heretofore reserved to the Almighty. Words are inadequate tools for the job of acquainting those not present with the physical, mental and psychological effects. It had to be witnessed to be realized.[1]

For insight into the effects of a nuclear explosion on the world as we live in it, however, it is more useful to consider eyewitness accounts of the actual use of atomic weapons, such as this one describing the impact on Nagasaki:

> For some 1,000 yards, or three-fifths of a mile, in all directions from the epicenter . . . it was as if a malevolent god had suddenly focused a gigantic blowtorch on a small section of our planet. Within that perimeter, nearly all unprotected living organisms . . . perished instantly. Flowers, trees, grass, plants, all shriveled and died. Wood burst into flames. Metal beams . . . began to bubble, and the soft gooey masses twisted into grotesque shapes. Stones were pulverized, and for a second every last bit of air was burned away. The people exposed within that doomed section neither knew nor felt anything, and their blackened, unrecognizable forms dropped silently where they stood.[2]

Former Soviet chairman Nikita Khrushchev once was reported to have said that following a nuclear war, the survivors would envy the dead.

Nagasaki and Hiroshima were both hit with atomic bombs, carrying the explosive power of about 20 KT and 12 KT, respectively. These are very small compared with the bombs and warheads now available: Hydrogen bombs have been produced and deployed in the multimegaton range. Since 1 Mt is equivalent in energy to 1 million tons of TNT, it follows that a 9-megaton bomb is slightly less than 1,000 times more powerful than the one that destroyed Hiroshima. Most bombs and warheads in the strategic arsenal of the United States and Russia are about 100-500 KT, or approximately 8 to 40 times more powerful than the Hiroshima explosion. In 1990, the total U.S. strategic arsenal was about 3,200 Mt; by comparison, the entire explosive force detonated (by both sides) during World War II was approximately 3 Mt.

Immediate Effects of Nuclear Weapons

Most estimates of nuclear war fatalities are lower than they should be, because the relevant effects are generally considered separately. In reality, all would occur simultaneously: People would be trapped in collapsing buildings (blast), which would then likely burn (heat), while the survivors would also have to contend with radiation. Infections are a serious complication of burns, and radiation reduces the body's ability to ward off infection. Many victims would likely be burned and irradiated and might also suffer from crushing or piercing injuries. In addition, most hospitals and medical personnel are located in major cities, which would almost certainly be targeted and destroyed, and pharmaceuticals would be almost entirely unavailable. Fire fighting would also be virtually impossible, because streets would be impassably blocked with the debris of collapsed buildings, water pressure would be nonexistent because of the rupture of pipes, and potential fire-fighters would likely be dead or contending with their own personal tragedies.

Of the approximately 200,000 fatalities resulting from the bombing at Hiroshima, about 50% were due to burns, while about 30% were due to lethal doses of radiation. Another 75,000 people eventually perished due to the atomic bombing of Nagasaki. Although technical knowledge of this sort is important, such sanitized data are grossly inadequate for conveying the full horror of nuclear war—even the very small nuclear attack that took place in August 1945. Another kind of knowledge, more personal and visceral, may be more meaningful.

There are harrowing accounts of people with empty eyesockets whose eyeballs were literally melted, of infants attempting to nurse at the corpses of dead mothers, of burn victims with their skin hanging in loose strips, and of family members trying to rescue relatives who had been trapped under collapsed and burning buildings. One survivor gives this account:

> The sight of the soldiers was more dreadful than the dead people. . . .
> I came upon . . . many, burned from the hips up . . . where the skin had peeled, their flesh was wet and mushy. . . . And they had no faces! Their eyes, noses, and mouths had been burned away, and it looked like their ears had melted off. It was hard to tell front from back.[3]

Even for those not physically injured, the psychological effects of such an immense and sudden disaster were overwhelming for most survivors. A Hiroshima physician describes some survivors leaving the city:

> Those who were able walked silently toward the suburbs in the distant hills, their spirits broken, their initiative gone. . . . They were so broken and confused that they moved and behaved like automatons . . . a people who walked in the realm of dreams. . . . A spiritless people had forsaken a destroyed city.[4]

The Hiroshima and Nagasaki bombs were very small by today's standards; moreover, at that time there was an "outside world "from which aid eventually reached the survivors. In the event of full-fledged war today between nuclear superpowers, the experience would be many times worse, with virtually no prospect of recovery.

The Effects of Nuclear Weapons on Social, Economic, and Political Organization

In addition to the radioactive fallout that would follow nuclear explosions, a major midrange effect of nuclear war would be its impact on social, economic, and political organizations. Food storage regions would likely be destroyed or inaccessible; cities would be devastated, with rescue, fire fighting, and medical services largely unavailable; transportation might well cease altogether. Electricity-generating plants would almost certainly be destroyed, along with oil refineries. Most sources of power—for communication, transportation, manufacturing, agriculture—would be eliminated, perhaps permanently. A simple barter system would probably replace traditional money-based economies for any possible survivors. As economist John Kenneth Galbraith has emphasized, communism and capitalism might well be indistinguishable in the ashes. Diseases such as cholera would spread rapidly, with sanitation and public hygiene virtually eliminated, and billions of insects and trillions of bacteria would multiply in the rotting, unburied corpses.

Shortly before he was assassinated in 1979, Lord Mountbatten gave a speech in which he asked:

And when it is all over, what will the world be like? Our . . . great buildings, our homes will exist no more. The thousands of years it took to develop our civilization will have been in vain. Our works of art will be lost. Radio, television, newspapers will disappear. There will be no means of transport. There will be no hospitals. No help can be expected for the few mutilated survivors . . .—there will be no neighboring towns left, no neighbors . . . there will be no hope.[5]

By contrast, many nuclear strategists calculated that nuclear war might be survivable, at least for some people and with appropriate precautions, such as (in the early 1960s) blast and/or fallout shelters, and (in the 1980s) crisis relocation plans, which were intended to organize the evacuation of the citizenry from high-risk areas to other regions, thought to be untargeted. Such thinking was especially prominent among those nuclear strategists who fretted that "excessive" anxiety about the effects of nuclear war might erode U.S. willingness to stand up to its possible adversaries. They worried also about the possibility that antinuclear anxiety would diminish the credibility of the stated U.S. intention to resort to nuclear weapons under certain circumstances, such as an invasion of Western Europe. In addition, some conservative politicians have been long concerned that nuclear fears might undermine a continuing commitment by the United States to ever-more weaponry, and undercut the "better dead than red" mentality, which has been prevalent among many Cold Warriors.

By the 1990s, however, such thinking had become increasingly difficult to defend, largely as a result of the widespread publicity concerning the horrific prompt and intermediate effects of nuclear war, as well as revelations concerning their likely long-term effects. The peace movement, both in the United States and worldwide, can take substantial credit for awakening many government leaders to the unacceptable consequences of nuclear war, as epitomized in the belated observation by President Reagan that a "nuclear war can never be won and must never be fought."

Long-Term Consequences of Nuclear Weapons

Undoubtedly, the most serious possible long-term consequence of war between nuclear superpowers, in addition to significant ozone depletion and resulting dangerous increases in ultraviolet radiation, would be the phenomenon of *nuclear winter*. This refers to the cooling and darkening of the planetary environment that most atmospheric scientists believe would result from a widespread nuclear war. The basic concept of nuclear winter is as follows: A nuclear war would produce not only immense amounts of dust but—far more important—enormous fires, which in turn would generate huge quantities of smoke and soot. Rising into the upper atmosphere, this material would absorb incoming heat and light from the sun, thereby making the earth cold and dark.

Some estimates show that nuclear winter could be triggered by the detonation of as "little" as 100 Mt, a tiny fraction of the world's arsenals. The effects would be worldwide and catastrophic: Temperatures could plummet as much as 50° F, which would result in extreme freezing over widespread areas and total disruption of agriculture and natural ecosystems, as well as perhaps making fresh water unavailable for people, plants, and/or animals for prolonged periods of time. Certainly, such an event would greatly complicate the problems of survival in what is sometimes, in a sanitized way, referred to as the "postattack environment."

The nuclear winter scenario has generated considerable controversy, as specialists have questioned some of its assumptions, such as how much smoke would actually be produced, how it would be distributed globally, and how intense and how persistent the climatic darkening and freezing would therefore be. There is also debate over the possible modulating effect of the oceans and the effect of increased cloud cover, as well as questions as to what proportion of the targeted cities would actually burn. Thus far, however, most of the conclusions reached by scientists studying the issue have proven to be quite robust, although the prospect of nuclear winter is, fortunately, still only theoretical.

Alternative Scenarios Regarding the Effects of Nuclear War

Numerous studies have been conducted on the likely effects of nuclear war. The findings vary, depending on the assumptions made. However, even a small-scale nuclear war (between regional nuclear powers) undeniably would be a human and environmental catastrophe unknown in human history, and a full-scale nuclear war between nuclear superpowers would dwarf any disaster that has occurred on earth in many millions of years.

Tens of millions of people would die immediately, perhaps hundreds of millions or even billions. The worldwide effects, even making minimal assumptions regarding nuclear winter, would also be catastrophic. The disruption of agriculture, trade, medical, and hygienic facilities would result in the deaths of hundreds of millions more and the debilitation of most of the remaining survivors. Some specialists agree, however, that the human species might persevere, especially in parts of the Southern Hemisphere, and perhaps in small, desperate bands in isolated areas elsewhere.

These assurances give scant comfort. The grotesque and utterly unacceptable consequences of nuclear war are a major motivating force for people concerned with the maintenance of peace and the prevention of war, especially nuclear war. Nuclear hawks accuse peace movement adherents of exaggerating the likely horrors of nuclear war, in order to increase popular revulsion against these weapons and to make governments especially cautious about ever employing them. Peace movement activists and scholars reply that, if so, this tendency to dramatize has been a justifiable response to the dangerously cavalier attitude of government officials—especially during the Reagan administration—toward the prospect of nuclear war.

It might be useful to contrast the likely results of being wrong, in either direction. Thus, what if the effects of nuclear war have been overestimated? In this case, the United States might find itself unduly wary of asserting military power, with the possible consequence of "losing" some geopolitical confrontations. In the words of Assistant Secretary of Defense Richard Perle, an influential hawk in the Reagan administration, "I've always worried less about what would happen in an actual nuclear exchange than about the effect that the nuclear balance has on our willingness to take risks in local situations."[6]

Alternatively, what if those who minimize the effects of nuclear war are wrong? Virtually everyone gives lip service to the fact that nuclear war would be terrible. However, the intensity with which people will seek to avoid nuclear war, and hence, the willingness of policymakers to forgo possible short-term gains in order to prevent a potential nuclear holocaust, will vary with their judgment of just how terrible nuclear war would be. Those who consider that it would be an overwhelming and utterly unacceptable disaster are less likely to precipitate, or to persevere, in policies or confrontations that might conceivably result in such a disaster. Those who, by contrast, take a more sanguine and perhaps minimizing attitude, will be more liable to practice *brinkmanship*. If the nuclear hawks are wrong, then the consequence of being too willing to undergo nuclear war might be catastrophic for the United States, and for the planet as well.

At present, and despite a growing consensus that nuclear war is an unacceptable option, some aspects of nuclear strategy depend on the willingness of governments to employ nuclear weapons, or at least, on the belief by an adversary that such willingness exists. Hence, one comes across such statements as the observation by Henry Kissinger that nuclear diplomacy "requires strong nerves" and that, accordingly, the United States should "leave no doubt about our readiness and our ability to face a final showdown."[7]

During the early years of the Reagan administration, for example, official pronouncements appeared to minimize the likely consequences of nuclear war. In 1982, Deputy Undersecretary of Defense T. K. Jones claimed that "everybody's going to make it if there are enough shovels to go around. . . . Dig a hole, cover it with a couple of doors and then throw three feet of dirt on top. It's the dirt that does it."[8] Other pronouncements of this sort, combined with a massive and unprecedented military buildup of both conventional and nuclear weapons, stimulated renewed interest in—and anxiety about—the effects of nuclear war.

By the late 1990s, antinuclear peace movement activities had succeeded, at least in making it unacceptable for politicians and strategic planners to speak lightly of precipitating a nuclear holocaust. Toward the latter years of the Reagan and Bush (Senior) administrations, official pronouncements on this topic became much more circumspect, which is testimony to the impact of a populace and a peace movement that had become increasingly antinuclear because of these administrations' policies. Nonetheless, there appear to have been remarkably few changes in U.S. nuclear procurement policies, or in the actual operational plans for using nuclear weapons.

Nuclear Delivery Systems

The technology—and the peace/war implications—of delivering nuclear weapons to their targets are almost as important as that of the weapons themselves. The strategic nuclear forces of both the United States and Russia are based on a *triad* of three distinct components: long-range bombers, land-based intercontinental missiles, and missile-carrying submarines, as well as cruise missiles. The other nuclear powers—China, France, Great Britain, India, Pakistan, and Israel—each employ one, or at most two, "legs" of such a triad.

Bombers

Bombers were originally intended to attack targets by dropping gravity bombs. That role has to some extent been superseded by the use of bombers as "launch platforms" for a variety of air-to-land and cruise missiles. More recently, however, interest has been revived in using bombers as "penetrating aircraft," as in *stealth bombers*, this time having them fly very low, thereby ducking under radar detection. The wars conducted by the North Atlantic Treaty Organization (NATO) over Serbia and Kosovo, and by the United States and its allies over Iraq and Kuwait, made heavy usage of high-altitude conventional bombing, which resulted in very few (or no) casualties for the fliers and significant casualties for civilians and soldiers who happened to be in the path of "precision-guided" and/or "errant" munitions.

Intercontinental Ballistic Missiles

Ballistic missiles are rockets. They travel very rapidly, reaching speeds of greater than 10,000 mph, and during intercontinental flight they actually leave the earth's atmosphere, to reenter before striking their targets. Intercontinental ballistic missiles, or ICBMs, are located underground, in steel- and concrete-reinforced silos. The United States maintains about 1,000 ICBMs (as with all such weapons for all countries, the exact numbers keep changing, when older models are phased out and new ones brought into service). Russia and, increasingly, China have invested especially heavily in ICBMs.

Most ICBMs are *MIRVed*, which means that they are equipped with multiple, independently targeted reentry vehicles. A single MIRVed missile can be equipped with 10 or more warheads, each of which can be aimed at a different target. Fifty MX missiles in the active U.S. arsenal, for example, can destroy 500 distinct targets, each with a warhead of between 350 KT (nearly 30 times the power of the Hiroshima bomb) and 2 Mt. Russian missiles tend to be larger than their U.S. counterparts, a fact that has caused great consternation to some in the United States and that has been used to buttress claims that the United States was "behind" in ICBMs, thereby helping to generate support for additional missile programs. But in fact, the smaller size of U.S. ICBMs was an indication of the *superiority*, not inferiority, of U.S. missile technology. According to the physics of nuclear explosions, the accuracy of a warhead is far more important than its explosive size: A small increase in accuracy is equivalent—in the probability of destroying a given "hardened" target—to a very large increase in total explosive force. The U.S. arsenal has achieved very high degrees of accuracy; as a result, it has been possible to decrease the megatonnage and also to employ ICBMs that are significantly smaller than the first, relatively bulky missiles. It would take approximately 30 minutes for ICBMs fired by one nuclear superpower to devastate the other, and much less time for regional nuclear powers to obliterate one another.

Submarine-Launched Ballistic Missiles

Nuclear submarines can be nuclear in two senses: They are typically propelled by nuclear power plants, and they also carry nuclear missiles, known as SLBM*s*, for submarine-launched ballistic missiles. These missiles are designed to be fired while the submarine remains submerged. The particular advantage of strategic submarines is that, unlike bombers or ICBMs, they cannot be targeted by an adversary once they are on deep-ocean patrol. In terms of strategic doctrine, they have therefore long been considered an ideal deterrent weapon, in that they offer the prospect of a secure retaliatory force. However, SLBMs have certain disadvantages, notably the fact that it is often quite difficult to communicate with deeply submerged submarines.

Strategic submarines carry many SLBMs; the U.S. *Trident* submarine, for example, carries 24 missiles. Like ICBMs, SLBMs tend to be MIRVed, although the United States has progressed farther than Russia in this regard. When it comes to strategic submarines, the United States also enjoys an immense geographic advantage over Russia because of its extensive, ice-free ocean coastlines. The United States is also acknowledged to have a substantial lead in submarine technology, including antisubmarine warfare.

Cruise Missiles

Since the early 1990s, cruise missiles have become increasingly prominent, and they have become in a sense the fourth leg of America's triad. Cruise missiles are pilotless jet aircraft that travel comparatively slowly (about the speed of sound) but close to the ground and are therefore difficult for radar to detect. They are also relatively inexpensive to produce. Equipped with modern navigational and homing devices, they are also becoming extremely accurate. In addition, cruise missiles are quite small, perhaps 20 feet long. Thus, once they have been deployed in large numbers, verification of their elimination at any time in the future, even if countries possessing them muster the political will to do so, becomes extremely difficult if not impossible. Cruise missiles can be armed with conventional or nuclear warheads, and at present there is no way to distinguish the two kinds from a distance. Cruise missiles with conventional warheads were used by the United States against Iraq during the Gulf War.

Strategic Doctrine: Deterrence

Strategic doctrine refers to the plans that purportedly underlie the accumulation of nuclear weapons, the justifications for their existence, and the expectations as to their use. The major component of U.S. strategic doctrine is alleged to be *deterrence*, the idea that nuclear war will be prevented by the threat that any attacker would suffer unacceptable retaliation. Realizing this, the would-be attacker would therefore be deterred. Deterrence as such is not unique to nuclear weapons. What is unique to nuclear deterrence, however, is the consequence of failure, and the fact that, heretofore, military forces that ostensibly provided deterrence also did double duty in providing defense, should deterrence fail. For centuries, for example, the Roman legions defended Rome and its colonies by deterring would-be attackers, but when attacks nonetheless occurred, the legions were also available to defend Rome. In the nuclear age, despite efforts at achieving strategic defense, the fact remains that the offense is all-powerful (despite hopes by some that the National Missile Defense [NMD] program might lessen the dominance of offense); if nuclear deterrence between nuclear superpowers should fail, there would be no effective defense. Shortly after World War II, American strategic analyst Bernard Brodie recognized the qualitative change in deterrence ushered in by nuclear weapons:

> The first and most vital step in any American security program for the age of atomic bombs is to take measures to guarantee . . . in case of attack the possibility of retaliation in kind. The writer . . . is not . . . concerned about who will *win* the next war in which atomic bombs have been used. Thus far the chief purpose of our military establishment has been to win wars. From now on its chief purpose must be to avert them. It can have almost no other useful purpose.[9]

Deterrence theory has been modified and adjusted many times, varying with the state of U.S.-Russian relations and weaponry. However, the basic premise of deterrence has remained that no Great Power would use nuclear weapons against the other so long as the victim retains the ability to cause unacceptable damage to the attacker. In such thinking, the initial attack is referred to as a *first strike*, and a *first-strike capability* is generally taken to mean the ability to conduct a first strike that will render the victim unable to retaliate.

According to deterrence theory, therefore, it behooves each country to maintain a *second-strike capability,* the capacity to absorb a first strike and still retaliate. If one side has a second-strike capability, then the other, by definition, lacks a first-strike capability. The result is considered to be *strategic stability*, a situation in which neither side can profit by striking first; thus, war should not occur. This, of course, is not peace at all, but rather a kind of suspended animation in which overt warfare is merely postponed.

Skeletons in the Closet of Deterrence

Deterrence theory is not as cut-and-dried, or even as reliable, as its proponents might wish. A number of factors—or "skeletons in the closet"—have consistently undermined the presumed goal of strategic nuclear stability based on mutual deterrence.

Skeleton 1: How much is enough?   No simple rule of thumb or straightforward quantitative measure can assure national leaders that they have accumulated enough retaliatory force to deter an adversary. Indeed, if one side is willing to be annihilated in a counterattack, then it cannot be deterred.

And if one side is convinced of the other's implacable hostility, then no amount of weaponry can ever be "enough." So long as money is made by accumulating weapons, so long as prestige and careers are served by designing, producing, and deploying new "generations" of nuclear forces, there will be continuing insistence on yet more weapons. Finally, insofar as nuclear weapons also in part serve symbolic, psychological needs, such as conveying legitimacy to otherwise insecure leaders and countries—thereby ostensibly demonstrating the scientific and technological accomplishments of a nation—then, once again, there is no rational way to put a cap on the optimum size of one's arsenal.

Nonetheless, in the early 1960s, then defense secretary Robert McNamara attempted to establish a reasonable criterion that would enable the United States to make some assessment of its deterrent needs, thereby—it was hoped—avoiding a never-ending accumulation of nuclear arms. It was estimated that approximately 400 Mt would destroy roughly one quarter of the Soviet population and two thirds of its industry. Beyond that amount, a process of diminishing returns sets in, such that (as Winston Churchill commented with regard to strategic bombing in World War II), additional explosions simply "made the rubble bounce." Since then, strategic planners have further declared that to be "prudent," each leg of the strategic triad should be able to deliver 400 Mt. However, because of the many factors that drive the nuclear arms race—and to some extent, arms races in general—the arsenals of both the United States and Russia have expanded to many times this amount.

Skeleton 2: Credibility. A second major difficulty of deterrence theory is the problem inherent in basing security on the threat to do something that is grossly self-destructive, and therefore lacking in credibility. Thus, granted that one side would be irrational to attack a nuclear-armed opponent that had a second-strike capability, the victim would be equally irrational to reply with nuclear weapons. Not only would retaliation be useless, but it would almost certainly be counterproductive, adding to worldwide destruction (through fallout, ozone depletion, nuclear winter, etc.) while also raising the possibility of yet another attack from the aggressor's remaining nuclear forces. In addition, given the ethical issues raised by a willingness to commit mass murder on the largest scale in human history, there might be additional reason to doubt a nuclear state's willingness to do so.

The problem caused by the inherent incredibility of nuclear deterrence is magnified yet more when deterrence is extended to cover not only nuclear attacks against the United States but also attacks against America's NATO allies in Europe, oil supplies in the Persian Gulf (the so-called Carter Doctrine), and the states of Israel, Japan, South Korea, and so on, including the contested "state" of Taiwan. *Extended deterrence* implies that the United States will respond, with nuclear weapons if necessary, to situations in which perceived vital U.S. interests are engaged but that fall short of actual attacks against U.S. territory. To enhance the credibility of this doctrine, the United States has developed theories and weaponry for the fighting of so-called limited nuclear wars, under the assumption that if the threat of World War III is not believable, the threat to initiate limited use of nuclear weapons might suffice.

"One cannot fashion a credible deterrent out of an incredible action," wrote former defense secretary McNamara. "Thus, security for the United States and its allies can only arise from the possession of a range of graduated deterrents, each of them fully credible in its own context."[10] Such thinking led, in turn, to the notion of "flexible response," according to which NATO should possess a range of military options, including a diversity of nuclear responses short of all-out nuclear war.

There are, however, serious problems with doctrines of limited war fighting. First, to be credible, such doctrines must be based on weapons and tactics that are in fact usable: generally, missiles, bombs, and warheads that are smaller and highly accurate and that produce relatively less *collateral damage* (the killing of civilians and the destruction of their property). So in order to be effective, which in the case of nuclear weapons means in order *not to be used*, these weapons must be made *more usable*. But this poses a major paradox, and one that may someday be catastrophic: The more usable, hence credible, they are, the more likely they are actually to be used. And numerous studies have shown that in the event of nuclear war between nuclear superpowers, no matter how small and controlled the opening shots, the confrontation is very likely to escalate to an all-out strategic exchange, with catastrophic consequences for all involved. Moreover, even without such escalation, a limited nuclear war, in Europe or between regional nuclear powers (such as India and Pakistan), for example, would appear quite unlimited to the Europeans or South Asians, for whose benefit the war was ostensibly being fought. As a result of all this, even limited nuclear war— hence, nuclear deterrence—may be seen as lacking in credibility after all.

Skeleton 3: Vulnerability.   As we have seen, deterrence entails the possession of a second-strike capability. This in turn requires that the nuclear weapons of each side remain invulnerable to attack, or at least, that the probability of them being destroyed in a first strike be very low. Over time, however, as nuclear missiles have become increasingly accurate, concerns have been raised about the growing vulnerability of these weapons. Such alleged vulnerability has been enhanced by the development of so-called *counterforce* doctrines, policies that favor the targeting of an adversary's weapons rather than population centers. Although counterforce appears less unethical than its alternative, *countervalue* targeting (or the deliberate targeting of civilian populations in cities), it also raises concerns that the other side may be planning a first strike since, in theory at least, a successful counterforce attack would preclude retaliation.

There are, in fact, other justifications for so-called counterforce targeting. These include the following:

1. The supposed greater morality of aiming at weapons rather than people.

2. A desire to limit the opponent's ability to cause further damage, by destroying weapons that could theoretically be used in a second wave of attacks.

3. The presumption by some hawkish strategists that the Russians (and "rogue" nations) value their weapons more than their population; hence, they would be more deterred by threats to the former than to the latter.

4. The persistence of a rather absent-minded but well-established military tradition of "target practice," wherein accuracy has been stressed as a virtue.

5. The fact that deterrence, by threatening the destruction of the opponent's cities, requires fewer nuclear weapons and less technology than is needed to threaten the opponent's military assets. The latter are more difficult to hit; thus, a counterforce strategy permits an expanded role for both the military and the nuclear weapons industry. Whereas there are only about 100 Russian cities, for example, with a population over 100,000, U.S. strategic analysts have been able to identify many thousands of Russian (and Chinese) missile silos, military depots, and other potential counterforce targets.

Whatever its origin, the result of counterforce strategy is the perception of vulnerability, which in turn leads to strategic instability. On the one hand, the side possessing a first-strike capability may be tempted to make such an attack, especially under conditions of crisis, when war seems likely and perhaps inevitable. On the other hand, the vulnerable side might well calculate that since its opponent has the ability to strike a devastating first blow, it should preempt such an attack by striking first. This is also more likely during an international crisis. (There is virtually no limit to this chain of reasoning: Side A, fearing that side B is about to preempt in this way, may be tempted to pre-preempt, leading side B, which anticipates such a pre-preemption, to consider pre-pre-preempting, and so forth.)

The phenomenon of MIRVing has added further to concerns about vulnerability to a first strike, for the following reason: With all missiles armed with only a single warhead, it would take a missile to destroy a missile. (Actually, it would take more than one, since the attacker, because of possible malfunctions and misses, would have to use at least two warheads to have any confidence of destroying an opposing missile.) But if each missile is armed with, say, 10 warheads, then an attacker could destroy—in theory—10 of the other side's missiles (and 100 warheads) while only expending one of its own. To "cover" each victim missile with two warheads would still require only two attacking missiles; in return, there would be a relatively high probability of destroying 10 of the opponent's missiles.

The result is very dangerous in that it threatens to undermine deterrence. Deterrence rests on creating a situation in which neither side would be tempted to shoot first; MIRVing, combined with accuracy, leads to *crisis instability*, in which, during conditions of crisis—when each fears that the other may gain an advantage by making a preemptive attack—either side may be tempted to strike first. It is the *perception* of vulnerability that could be destabilizing, and all nuclear states seem determined to deploy new missiles that are ever more accurate.

Skeleton 4: Human psychology. Deterrence theory assumes optimal "rationality" in decision makers, or at least that those with their fingers on the nuclear triggers will remain calm and cognitively unimpaired under extremely stressful conditions. It also assumes that leaders will always retain control over their nuclear forces and that, moreover, they will always retain control over their emotions as well, making decisions based solely on the basis of a cool calculation of the costs and benefits associated with each course of action. Deterrence theory maintains that each side will scare the other with the prospect of the most hideous, unimaginable consequences and that the persons thus terrified will then behave with the utmost in cool, precise instrumental rationality. Ironically, virtually everything we know about human psychology suggests precisely the opposite outcome: Intense fear under highly stressful conditions is incompatible with careful cognition.

Deterrence theory also ignores the fact that, even without intense fear, many people often behave in ways that are irrational, vengeful, and even spiteful and self-destructive (i.e., hurtful to themselves as well as others). Moreover, they may be the victims of insufficient or faulty information, or of various other perceptual distortions that cause them to make incorrect judgments as to the intentions of others, the probabilities of various alternative courses of action, and so on. It requires no arcane strategic wisdom to know that people often act out of anger, despair, insanity, stubbornness, revenge, and/or dogmatic conviction. And finally, in certain situations—such as when either side is convinced that war is inevitable, or when the pressures to avoid losing face are especially intense—an irrational act, even a lethal one, may appear quite "rational," or otherwise appropriate—even unavoidable.

How a Nuclear War Could Start

There are many possible scenarios (imagined sequences of interactions) according to which nuclear war could occur. Here are some examples:

Bolt out of the blue.   Although most laypeople imagine a surprise, middle-of-the-night attack, most experts agree that a so-called bolt out of the blue, or BOOB, attack is the least likely scenario of all. Neither side would come out ahead, and unless other factors are operating, deterrence should prevent any such calculated madness. On the other hand, strategic analysts worry constantly that one side may be tempted to attack preemptively if it becomes convinced that its perceived adversary's weapons could be destroyed in a surprise first strike. More realistic scenarios for BOOB attacks generally depend on some combination of the various other scenarios discussed below.

A game of "chicken."   A popular but risky game played by teenagers and captured memorably in the 1950s James Dean movie *Rebel Without a Cause* was to play "chicken" in automobiles. Two drivers would drive toward a cliff at high speed, straddling the white line. The first one to swerve lost; the one who persevered was the winner. In a game of chicken, therefore, the goal is to induce the opponent to swerve, and not to do so oneself.

The most dramatic example of nuclear chicken occurred during the Cuban Missile Crisis in 1962, when the Soviet Union attempted to install medium-range nuclear missiles in Cuba, hoping to deter the United States from invading Cuba and to "balance" the American deployment of nuclear-tipped missiles in Turkey (bordering the former Soviet Union) and Great Britain. The United States demanded that the missiles be withdrawn; the Soviets refused. After considering and rejecting various options—including a conventional attack on the missile sites, an invasion of Cuba, and a preemptive nuclear strike against the Soviet Union—President John F. Kennedy decided on a naval blockade (designated at the time as a "quarantine"). The situation was exceedingly tense, and President Kennedy subsequently stated that he thought the chance of nuclear war had been between one in two and one in three. Premier Khrushchev eventually ordered Soviet naval vessels to turn back, and an accommodation was reached in which the Soviet missile site was dismantled and the United States promised not to invade Cuba. (An unofficial part of the deal was that the United States would quietly decommission its medium-range missiles in Turkey, something it had already planned to do before the Cuban Missile Crisis.)

As then secretary of state Dean Rusk put it, "We were eyeball to eyeball, and the other guy blinked." Or in other words, the Soviets turned aside in that game of nuclear chicken. They may have been induced to do so, at least in part by the fact that at that time the USSR was militarily inferior to the United States, both in conventional forces in the Caribbean and in nuclear arms as well. However, the United States and Russia now appear equally capable of destroying each other completely, and the rest of the world as well, and neither side is likely to accept the ignominy of being the one to swerve. In contests of nuclear chicken, when each side insists that the other one turn aside, the result is likely to be "fried chicken."

Escalated conventional war. Military forces of the United States and Russia have not engaged in direct hostilities since the United States—along with the other Western powers—tried unsuccessfully to undo the Bolshevik Revolution. It is quite possible (some would say, likely) that such restraint has been due to the shared possession of nuclear weapons. Nonetheless, each side has been engaged in conventional fighting—the Soviets, for example, in Hungary (1956), Czechoslovakia (1968), and Afghanistan (1979–1988), and the Russians in Chechnya (1996–present), and the United States in Korea (1950–1953), Vietnam (1962–1974), Beirut (1982), Grenada (1983), Panama (1989), the Persian Gulf (1990–1991), the former Yugoslavia (1999), and Afghanistan, to mention just a few cases.

The United States has seriously considered the use of nuclear weapons many times, from 1946, when President Truman threatened to employ nuclear weapons unless Stalin withdrew his forces from Iran (which he did), to 1968, when American generals considered the possible use of nuclear weapons to help lift the siege of Khe Sanh in Vietnam. The United States under former president George Bush (Senior) may also have contemplated using nuclear weapons against Iraq during the Gulf War. Thus far, such threats and confrontations have been resolved short of nuclear war, but there is no assurance that this can continue indefinitely.

There is also an ongoing threat that, during conventional warfare, nuclear weapons will be used in a last-ditch effort to win the war, or simply to prevent one's homeland from being overrun. Nearly 20 years after leaving the Defense Department, Robert McNamara warned that

> we face a future in which . . . we must contemplate continuing confrontation between East and West. Any one of these confrontations can escalate . . . into military conflict. And that conflict will be between blocs that possess fifty thousand nuclear warheads—warheads that are deployed on the battlefields and integrated into the war plans. . . . In the tense atmosphere of a crisis, each side will feel pressure to delegate authority to fire nuclear war weapons to battlefield commanders. As the likelihood of attack increases, these commanders will face a desperate dilemma: use them or lose them.[11]

Proxy wars. Both the United States and the former Soviet Union have supported other nations that have in some ways functioned as proxies for the two nuclear superpowers. When a nuclear state offers security guarantees to such a third party, the possibility exists that nuclear weapons might be employed if the ally is losing. Or at least, the "protector" feels the need to threaten such use, which could elicit a comparable threat from the other side, leading to nuclear chicken. Early in the 1973 October War between Israel and the Arab states, for example, Israeli forces were doing poorly, and Israel may well have been on the verge of employing its own (as yet undeclared) nuclear arsenal. The former USSR began military preparations—reportedly suggesting the possible use of nuclear weapons—as a guarantee to the Arabs, which in turn led the United States to order a worldwide nuclear alert. The October War was eventually concluded by the successful Israeli use of conventional weapons (assisted by massive U.S. military aid, especially tank ammunition), but not until both superpowers again came close to being drawn into the fray. When the Israelis had eventually turned the tide and threatened to overrun Cairo, the Soviets mobilized forces in support of Egypt, whereupon the United States again instituted a nuclear alert. The crisis was eventually defused by the United Nations.

Nuclear accidents. An accidental nuclear detonation has never officially taken place, although both Russia and the United States may have come close. In several cases, the conventional explosive that is part of a nuclear weapon has detonated, scattering large amounts of radioactive material. Furthermore, nuclear-armed bombers and submarines have crashed, exploded, and/or sunk. Given the chaos that would doubtless follow an accidental nuclear explosion, it is always possible that such an event would lead to retaliation. A full-fledged nuclear detonation would dwarf such accidents as those that occurred at Three Mile Island (U.S.) and Chernobyl (Ukraine, in the former Soviet Union) nuclear power plants. Moreover, if a nuclear explosion occurred during a time of international tension, the consequences may well be extremely grave for all parties.

Unauthorized use and "loose nukes." Both the United States and Russia have until the late 1990s kept relatively tight, centralized control over their nuclear weapons, in an effort to make certain that they will be employed only if appropriate orders are given by the highest level of political leadership. Numerous fail-safe devices are incorporated into U.S. weapons design, and until the 1990s it was widely assumed that comparable controls existed on the Russians' part as well. However, there is no guarantee that something could not go wrong, and as a result, someone relatively low in military/political rank could wind up starting a nuclear war.

Since the collapse of the Soviet Union in 1991, the danger of "loose nukes" not subject to stringent command and control procedures has grown in magnitude. Adding to the uncertainty is the distinct possibility that fissionable materials could be stolen, and then fabricated into nuclear weapons, or even that small nuclear bombs or warheads could be sold to interested buyers. It is often rumored that nuclear weapons formerly under Soviet hands are for sale to the highest bidder. It has also been suggested that, given the economic and social decline of post-Soviet Russia, formerly well-paid weapons designers have become willing to sell their expertise to the highest bidder. It is also widely acknowledged that Israel commandeered a shipload of enriched uranium in the late 1960s. It is also conceivable that governments or terrorist groups could steal ready-made bombs or warheads while they are in transit or in storage depots. Or governments could purchase ready-made nuclear weapons: Libya, for example, attempted unsuccessfully to buy nuclear bombs from China.

Irrational use.   It can readily be argued that *any* use of nuclear weapons constitutes irrational use. Beyond this, however, the possibility also exists that those persons exercising the highest political authority may themselves go insane or behave irrationally. Many famous leaders throughout history were severely emotionally disturbed and/or experienced psychotic episodes: Caligula, Nero, and probably Adolf Hitler and Joseph Stalin as well. Woodrow Wilson and Dwight Eisenhower suffered serious strokes while in office, which compromised their ability to perform their duties and to think clearly. During the final days before resigning his presidency in 1974, Richard Nixon is said to have acted irrationally, possibly due in large measure to the stress of the Watergate investigations. No precedent and no set of guidelines currently exist for countermanding the orders of a sitting president, no matter how dangerous or unwise such orders might be, and the use of nuclear weapons could legally be ordered without a formal declaration of war by Congress, and even without any prior consultation. In other nuclear states, including Russia, China, India, Pakistan, and Israel, the possibility of unnerved political decision makers, or "rogue officers," authorizing the use of nuclear and/or other weapons of mass destruction is at least as high as in the United States.

False alarms.   Perhaps the most chilling—because the most likely—scenario for nuclear war involves failure in the C^3I (command, control, communications, and intelligence) systems of a nuclear state. Before the nuclear age, countries worried about being the victims of a surprise attack, as happened to the United States at Pearl Harbor and to the Soviet Union when Germany suddenly invaded it in June 1941. In the era of nuclear weapons, a danger even greater than surprise attack, paradoxically, is that one side—thinking it is under attack—may "retaliate" when in fact it had not actually been attacked at all.

The leadership of all nuclear states is essentially hostage to the correct functioning of their warning systems. And during times of international stress or crisis, this connection may be especially perilous. Thus, there have been many false alarms: According to the Senate Armed Services Committee, there were 151 "serious" nuclear false alarms and 3,703 lesser alerts during a (presumably representative) period between January 1979 and July 1980. In the past, radar signals bouncing off the newly risen moon have been taken for enemy missiles, migrating geese have been similarly misinterpreted, and a fire in a Siberian natural gas pipeline set off a satellite sensor, which identified it as the exhausts of a Soviet missile launch. In 1980, a practice war-games tape was erroneously read by military computers as an actual attack, and faulty microchips have several times generated unnecessary alerts.

Because the extreme destructive power of nuclear weapons is combined with exceedingly high speed and short warning times—literally, a matter of minutes—there would be great pressure on decision makers to know quickly whether such an attack is under way, and if so, to respond immediately. In addition, as nuclear delivery systems became increasingly accurate, counterforce weapons have made it more and more feasible (at least in theory) for the attacking side to demolish the victim's nuclear forces. And as that feasibility increases, reports of such an attack become more believable. The result is to put great pressure on a prospective victim to "use it or lose it," with a resulting increased risk of severe miscalculation and premature launch. The hot line between the White House and the Kremlin—installed after the Cuban Missile Crisis—and the crisis control centers are supposed to reduce the danger that similar false alarms will lead to nuclear war by miscalculation. But it remains unclear what sort of communication would reassure a side that believes it is being attacked and feels that it must respond immediately.

Launch on warning.   Nuclear deterrence depends, essentially, on the other side believing that if attacked, the victim will retaliate. But as we have also seen, nuclear deterrence must deal with the problem of *credibility*: Having suffered immense destruction in an initial attack, an attacked nation has literally nothing to be gained by retaliating, and, moreover, a great deal to lose, if the attacker responds to the victim's retaliation by firing yet more missiles. In addition, the great speed and increasing accuracy of strategic missiles have led some strategic analysts to conclude that, at least in theory, an opponent could target a large proportion of the victim's land-based missiles. So it has been argued that to shore up the credibility of nuclear deterrence, it will always be necessary to employ a system known as *launch on warning*, in which the decision to launch is made upon warning of an attack, rather than waiting until the attacker's warheads have literally begun exploding on U.S. soil. Moreover, to bolster the credibility that the victim will actually make such a retaliation, launch on warning is also often taken to mean that the "decision" to launch will be removed from human beings and placed in the hands of computers, preprogrammed to launch when advised of an impending attack. There have been numerous reports of near launches based on computer, satellite sensors, and/or human mistakes. And with the increased reliance on computer systems (which are never perfect), and the decreased control by Moscow of the nuclear weapons in the former Soviet Union, the danger of nuclear retaliation to "avenge" a real or perceived attack on either side has not decreased since the end of the Cold War.

Launch on warning, the supremely "logical" consequence of nuclear deterrence theory itself, thus carries immense dangers. First, it drastically

reduces the time span in which a decision must be made—perhaps the most
fateful decision in the history of the world. Second, it places the fate of earth
in the hands of potentially fallible sensor and warning systems. And third, it
makes us all dependent on the correct functioning of computers. It is widely
acknowledged that Russian, Chinese, Indian, and Pakistani computer systems are less efficient than those computers used by the Pentagon, which
themselves are hardly fail-safe.

Has Deterrence Worked?

Many strategic analysts would say, "Of course." They would claim that
because there has been no nuclear or conventional war between nuclear
states, the reason for this has been the fact of nuclear deterrence. Some
would also claim that the fall of the Soviet Union and the "defeat of Communism" were also brought about by the West's "robust" nuclear deterrent,
which allegedly prevented the former Soviet Union from invading Western
Europe.

Others, however, would argue that the absence of a war between the
United States and its NATO allies, on the one hand, and the former Soviet
Union and its Warsaw Pact allies, on the other hand, was not primarily due
to nuclear deterrence but to other factors, such as the absence of any wars
between America and Russia prior to the advent of the nuclear age and to
internal domestic considerations within each country. In any event, should
"deterrence fail," there will likely be no strategists or historians left to
debate the reasons for its failure.

Nuclear Proliferation _____

We have focused on the two nuclear superpowers because between them the
United States and Russia still account for over 90% of the world's nuclear
weapons. In addition, the United States and Russia are primarily responsible for the qualitative as well as the quantitative dimensions of the nuclear
arms race. We have accordingly focused on what has been called *vertical
proliferation*, the accumulation of weapons and delivery systems by the
nuclear superpowers. However, there is substantial reason to be concerned
about *horizontal proliferation* as well, the acquisition of nuclear weapons
by other, previously nonnuclear countries, especially with long-standing traditions of hostility between them (such as India and Pakistan).

But there is also another view, probably a minority one: Since nuclear
weapons, in the hands of the Great Powers, have ostensibly helped "keep the
peace," then these same weapons, widely proliferated, might conceivably
be a stabilizing influence on world affairs. (After all, if the U.S. and Russian
publics are supposed to believe that nuclear weapons are good for them,

then why wouldn't nuclear weapons be equally good for, say, Iran, Nigeria, Iraq, Brazil, or Argentina?) This is the so-called porcupine theory, that a world composed of many nuclear-armed states would be a safe one because each state would carefully avoid antagonizing its neighbors, just as porcupines walk in relative safety through the forest.

Perhaps even more significant than *how* to "go nuclear" is the question of *whether* to do so. Thus, numerous countries that could readily go nuclear have not done so—Sweden, Canada, Germany, Japan, Australia, the Netherlands, Switzerland—while Pakistan and India, with much less developed economic and technological bases, have joined the nuclear club, leaving other nations, such as South and North Korea, Taiwan, Libya, Iraq, and Iran, as possible future entrants to the nuclear "club."

Among the existing nuclear powers, the proliferation path has been much like a chain of dominoes: The United States initiated a nuclear weapons program out of fear of being beaten to the punch by Germany during World War II and to intimidate the Soviet Union; the Soviet Union followed suit, in response to the U.S. nuclear monopoly; China went nuclear largely because of the USSR; India developed nuclear weapons primarily because of China; and Pakistan has developed a small nuclear arsenal in response to India. And Israel furtively became a nuclear power ostensibly to deter conventional and chemical attacks from its Arab neighbors.

In some of these cases, states went nuclear after they discovered that the nuclear superpowers could not be counted on to provide a "nuclear guarantee"—that is, to risk nuclear war on their behalf. Nuclear states cannot really be blamed for hesitating to run such a grave a risk as nuclear war, even on behalf of an ally. The problem is closely intertwined with that of state sovereignty: States insist on their absolute sovereignty and freedom of action in a world that is increasingly interdependent, and in which *globalization* is the latest buzzword.

There is also another, more general motivation behind would-be proliferators: pride. Britain and France, for example, had little strategic motivation for developing their own nuclear arsenals, but both countries in the 1950s and 1960s were contending with the dismantling of their overseas empires, and with the psychological stress of having to forgo their previous position as "Great Powers." If it possesses nuclear weapons, a state is virtually guaranteed a place in world councils, and it should not be surprising that many leaders in less economically advanced nations believe that their country, their people, and their culture deserve the same recognition that more affluent societies have arrogated to themselves. Many legitimate reasons for opposing nuclear proliferation exist, including the following:

1. As more people and organizations have their "finger on the button," it becomes more likely that someone, somewhere, will for some reason press it.

2. In many less economically developed countries, political power is held by military dictators and political autocrats who are not accountable to their citizenry, who have obtained power without democratic checks and balances, and who may be psychologically unstable.

3. Countries with a limited technological base may be hesitant to invest heavily in various "fail-safe" protective devices, thereby increasing the danger of accidental detonations, unauthorized use, and/or war by false alarm.

4. According to standard deterrence theory, states with a very small nuclear arsenal may actually be more at risk of preemptive attack than those having an ability to absorb such an attack and then retaliate.

5. Many would-be proliferators are currently engaged in active or smoldering hostilities directly on their borders. This is especially the case in the republics in and near the former Soviet Union. Terrorist groups might well make use of nuclear weapons if they obtained them, or engage in nuclear blackmail.

The existing nuclear powers have a shared interest in restricting nuclear proliferation, and they have established an international framework toward that end, the Nonproliferation Treaty (which, regrettably, not all the nuclear powers have signed). However, today's nuclear powers are ill-situated to criticize other countries for seeking to obtain nuclear weapons so long as they continue to add to and modernize their own vast arsenals: "Do as I say," they appear to be pronouncing, "not as I do."

Other Proliferation Problems

In addition to the problem of nuclear proliferation, attention has begun to focus on other, related issues, notably, the proliferation of chemical and/or biological warfare capabilities, of conventional weapons with near-nuclear effects, and of ballistic missile technology.

Chemical weapons have been called the "poor man's atomic bomb," and in fact, the manufacture of highly toxic chemical munitions is relatively easy and inexpensive. Iraq used such weapons against Iran, and also against its own Kurdish rebels, and may have attempted to use them during the Gulf War; Libya—assisted by a German chemical firm—has been accused by the United States of constructing a chemical warfare facility. France, Russia, and the United States have maintained large chemical weapons stockpiles until very recently. Of these, the U.S. arsenal has probably been the most sophisticated, consisting of "binary" chemicals, two subcomponents that are not lethal in themselves but become highly toxic when combined immediately prior to use. The major holders of these weapons have indicated their intention of destroying their chemical arsenals, but not all have done so. Furthermore, in the final years of the Clinton administration, official U.S. doctrine came to include the implied threat that the United States might employ nuclear weapons in response to nonnuclear—chemical and/or biological—attacks against its interests. This has been matched by the declaration of the Russian government under Putin that Russia might use nuclear weapons to defend itself against a nonnuclear attack, a significant change in policy from its avowed "no first use" doctrine of the latter half of the 20th century.

A Final Note on Nuclear Weapons

There is an ancient Chinese proverb: "Unless we change direction, we shall end up where we are headed." The proliferation of nuclear weapons and of other weapons of mass destruction—both vertically and horizontally—poses the most serious imaginable threat to human beings and to the planet. As we have emphasized, a world that is truly at peace must be more than one not actively at war. It is our planet, our lives, and we have the right, even the duty, to aim high. And yet, when it comes to nuclear weapons, the narrow goal of simply preventing war is so essential that it seems satisfactory as an end in itself. Given the extraordinary dangers of nuclear war, however, mere prevention—from day to day, year to year—is not sufficient; we must aim for a higher degree of confidence. Undoubtedly, any satisfactory solution to the nuclear dilemma must be political, and not just technological. But at the same time, peace in the nuclear age utterly demands the elimination of the nuclear threat itself. In the long run, nothing less will do.

Notes

1. Quoted in L. Groves. 1962. *Now It Can Be Told*. New York: Harper & Row.
2. Frank Chinnock. 1969. *Nagasaki: The Forgotten Bomb*. New York: World.
3. From John Hersey. 1946. *Hiroshima*. New York: Modern Library.
4. From M. Hachiya. 1955. *Hiroshima Diary*. Chapel Hill: University of North Carolina Press.
5. From a speech delivered by Lord Mountbatten in Strasbourg, France, 1979.
6. Quoted in Robert Scheer. 1982. *With Enough Shovels*. New York: Random House.
7. Henry Kissinger. 1957. *Nuclear Weapons and Foreign Policy*. New York: Norton.
8. Quoted in Scheer, *With Enough Shovels*.

9.   Bernard Brodie. 1946. *The Absolute Weapon*. New York: Harcourt Brace Jovanovich.

10.   Robert McNamara. 1968. *The Essence of Security*. New York: Harper & Row.

11.   Robert McNamara. 1986. *Blundering Into Disaster: Surviving the First Century of the Nuclear Age*. New York: Pantheon.

The second hijacked plane is seen as it is about to hit the second tower of the World Trade Center in New York City on Tuesday, Sept. 11, 2001. (Photo by Dan Joyce/Corbis SABA)

PART II

The Reasons for Wars

The central reality of our time is that the advent of globalization and the revolution in information technology have magnified both the creative and destructive potential of every individual, tribe, and nation on our planet.

—President Bill Clinton

In Part I, we presented an overview of peace and war. The absence of war is a necessary but not a sufficient condition for the realization of peace. It is insufficient because a life without war can nonetheless also be lacking in peace. But at the same time, the prevention of war is necessary if any meaningful peace is ever to be achieved. Real peace simply cannot coexist with war. And so our hopes for peace, and our work toward it, must take account of war; in particular, we must turn to the reasons for wars, if our suggestions, means, and goals are to enjoy any realistic prospect of success.

For too long, students of peace—in their legitimate eagerness to embrace a new and more peaceful world—have abandoned the understanding of war and other forms of violent human conflict to their "hardheaded," "realistic" colleagues in the more traditional academic disciplines of political science and international relations. As a result of this division of responsibility, while centers for strategic studies and the like engage in the planning and legitimation of war and other acts of government-initiated violence, many people in peace and conflict studies and in peace movements spend too much time trying to conceptualize peace while avoiding the very real problems of war and violence. In doing so, they have run the risk of becoming increasingly marginalized, not only in academic circles but also with respect to their potential influence in the real world. This is not to propose that peace and conflict studies students and teachers should become handmaidens of the academic war establishment, whether cold or hot; rather, they should get to know their "enemy." And that enemy, more than anything else, is war.

As we have discussed, "war" does not exist, but rather, individual wars exist, just as the species *Homo sapiens* does not, per se, exist; rather, there are individual people. Furthermore, it is far easier to understand individual people than to encompass the complexity and diversity of the more than six billion souls who constitute the human species. Just as we can make useful generalizations about the human species, however, we can do the same about the "species" of violent human conflict known as war.

In doing so, it is helpful to distinguish between the *real* or *underlying reasons* (or what in much of the relevant literature has been referred to as the *causes*)—of a particular war—and the *ostensible reasons* (or pretexts) for such wars. The former refer to the underlying factors that actually give rise to the war; the latter, to the propagandistic excuses frequently enunciated by governments to justify their actions. We are primarily concerned in this part of the book with the reasons for wars, insofar as they can be identified. Then in Part III of this book, we assess various suggestions for preventing war. Nonetheless, the task is daunting. Indeed, trying to specify the reasons for war generally, that is, the motives that led decision makers to make war or even just the causes of any one war (i.e., the structural forces and long-term factors that form the background within which leaders make decisions), is a bit like the story of the blind men and the elephant by the 19th-century American, John Saxe:

> It was six men from Industan, to learning much inclined,
> Who went to see the elephant (though all of them
>   were blind)
> That each by observation might satisfy his mind. . . .

Not surprisingly, each one felt a different part, so that the one touching the legs thought they were tree trunks, the one touching the tail thought it was a snake, etc.

And so, at the end, they disputed loud and long,
Each in his opinion stiff and strong,
Though each was partly in the right, and all of them were
    wrong.[1]

In reviewing the various proposed reasons for wars, we shall proceed from the most reductionistic interpretations to the most inclusive. Thus, we begin with an examination of the reasons for wars at the personal level, move through a consideration of wars among small groups of preindustrial and nontechnological peoples, to the functioning of large, advanced social units and nation-states. Then we examine decision making by national leaders, assess the role of social and economic factors, and finally, we summarize the reasons for wars. Although we shall necessarily consider these explanations one at a time, let us try to avoid the blind-men's blunder, by recognizing at the outset that war, like an elephant, is a complex and integrated phenomenon, which to be understood must be taken in its entirety, and with a hefty dose of humility.

Consider, for example, that someone has just died. We might ask, "What was the cause of death?" And perhaps we are told, "He died of disease." "What kind of disease?" "Heart disease." "What was the nature of the heart disease?" "Hardening of the arteries leading to a massive stroke—that is, a coronary thrombosis." And if we then inquire, "What was the cause of that?" we are likely to get any number of answers: He had poor dietary habits, he had a genetic predisposition to high cholesterol levels, he didn't get regular medical care, he was under a great deal of stress, he smoked too much and didn't get enough exercise, and so forth. One of these might be the precipitating factor, but it is most likely that several of them, taken in combination, were ultimately responsible. The social, psychological, and historical reasons for wars can be at least as complex as the physical causes of one person's death.

We should also keep in mind the logical distinction between *necessary* and *sufficient* conditions. Thus, for war to occur, it may be necessary for human beings to exist in societies, but it certainly is not sufficient—there are human societies that have apparently never known war. Similarly, it may be necessary for

individuals to be motivated so as to participate in the preparations and conduct of war, but once again, this is not sufficient—
people often get angry, but this does not necessarily mean that
their country goes to war as a result. Moreover, wars often occur
without very much personal anger being involved.

Every scholar of peace and war, it appears, has a different
framework for understanding the reasons for organized human
violence. Peace researcher Quincy Wright, for example, identified four major factors: idealistic, psychological, political, and
legalistic, arguing that

> individuals and masses have been moved to war (1) because
> of enthusiasm for ideals expressed in the impersonal symbols
> of a religion, a nation, an empire, a civilization, or human-
> ity, the blessings of which it is thought may be secured or
> spread by coercion of the recalcitrant [idealistic]; or (2)
> because of the hope to escape from conditions which they
> find unsatisfactory, inconvenient, perplexing, unprofitable,
> intolerable, dangerous, or merely boring [psychological].
> Conditions of this kind have produced unrest and have
> facilitated the acceptance of ideals and violent methods
> for achieving them. Governments and organized factions
> have initiated war (3) because in a particular situation war
> appeared to them a necessary or convenient means to carry
> out a foreign policy, to establish, maintain, or expand the
> power of a government, party, or class within the state; to
> maintain or expand the power of the state in relation to
> other states; or to reorganize the community of nations
> [political]; or (4) because incidents have occurred or cir-
> cumstances have arisen which they thought violated law
> and impaired rights and for which war was the normal or
> expected remedy according to the jural standards of the
> time [legalistic].[2]

Although there is disagreement as to the most useful way to
categorize the reasons for wars, there is consensus that every
war—just like every human being—must have progenitors. Efforts
at identifying warmongering culprits, as individuals rather than
impersonal forces, have been especially frequent in the aftermath
of every major war. One scholar described the chronology of
such culprit-hunting as follows:

> In the eighteenth century many philosophers thought that
> the ambitions of absolute monarchs were the main cause of

war: pull down the mighty, and wars would become rare. Another theory contended that many wars came from the Anglo-French rivalry for colonies and commerce: restrain that quest, and peace would be more easily preserved. The wars following the French Revolution fostered an idea that popular revolutions were becoming the main cause of international war. In the nineteenth century, monarchs who sought to unite their troubled country by a glorious foreign war were widely seen as culprits. At the end of that century the capitalists' chase for markets or investment outlets became a popular villain. The First World War convinced many writers that armaments races and arms salesmen had become the villains, and both world wars fostered the idea that militarist regimes were the main disturbers of the peace.[3]

Similarly, the Vietnam War—to take just one example—was said to have been caused by

the desire of American capitalists for markets and investment outlets, by the pressures for markets and investment outlets, by the pressures of American military suppliers, by the American hostility to communism, by the crusading ambitions of Moscow and Peking, the aggressive nationalism or communism of Hanoi, the corruption or aggression of Saigon, or the headlong clash of other aims.[4]

Clearly, for the Vietnam War—or for just about any other war—a host of different causes can be identified, many of which might be operating simultaneously, some of which may involve individuals, and others, more frustrating and faceless considerations. In their yearning for Truth, however, many people are dissatisfied with complex, multifactorial explanations. For example, it is tempting to say that the country that initiates a war is the one that "started" it, and therefore, the one that "caused" it—that is, the culprit. But the real world is only rarely this simple. For example, England declared war on Napoleon's France in 1803, but this was at least in part because France had invaded Switzerland, to which England at that time felt committed. When the United States "started" the War of 1812 with Britain, it was at least partly in response to the impressment of American sailors by British naval forces. (It was also in part because of U.S. imperialistic designs on British Canada.) And although nearly everyone considers that Nazi Germany initiated the European part of

World War II, the fact remains that Britain and France first declared war on Germany, not the other way around, but only after Germany invaded Poland in 1939.

Wars, in short, often occur as a result of preexisting antagonisms that lead to provocations, so that the underlying reasons for a war may lie further back in time. And of course, those provocations are themselves the result of yet earlier factors. The German invasion of Poland, for example, was itself "caused" in part by Britain and France's earlier appeasement of Hitler, which convinced the German leader that aggression against Poland would go unpunished. Meanwhile, Hitler's aggressive and expansionist policies were also "caused," at least in part, not only by his own personal idiosyncrasies but also by German anger over the terms of the Treaty of Versailles, which ended World War I. And so it has gone.

The dominant Western conception of causality requires that for every effect (including war), there must be a preexisting cause. It also suggests that this cause should be clear-cut, direct, and linear. Even if we grant the legitimacy of cause-and-effect, however, there is no reason why reasons—especially the reasons for something so complicated as war—should not be diffuse, indirect, curvilinear, and multifaceted. In short, war is, to borrow the psychoanalytic term, "overdetermined"; it has multiple reasons for its existence, both in general and in specific violent conflicts.

But this is not to claim that a search for the reason (or reasons) for war is a waste of time, even though the results can sometimes be misleading. Out of that search can come a deeper appreciation of the conundrum that is war. Moreover, our judgment as to the reasons for war will have great influence on our preferred methods for preventing specific wars, and our hopes for eliminating war altogether.

Notes _____

1. John Saxe. 1892. "The Blind Men and the Elephant." *The Poetical Works of John Godfrey Saxe*. Boston: Houghton.

2. Quincy Wright. 1966. "Analysis of the Causes of War." In R. Falk and S. Mendlovitz, eds., *Toward a Theory of War Prevention*. New York: World Law Fund.

3. Geoffrey Blainey. 1973. *The Causes of War*. New York: Free Press.

4. Ibid.

5 The Individual Level

A *weapon is an enemy even to its owner.*

—Turkish proverb

Wars require the organized activity of large numbers of people. But even the facts of complex organization and massive numbers do not eliminate the personal involvement and responsibility of individuals. To some degree, individual people acquiesce to war, prepare for it, and often participate in it, either passively (by permitting it to occur) or actively (by providing material assistance or actually doing the fighting). If many individuals didn't allow, encourage, or engage in them, wars wouldn't happen. Hence, without denying the importance of other dimensions—which we shall explore in subsequent chapters—our search for the reasons for wars might commence by looking to the inclinations and behavior of individual people.

The preamble to the constitution of the United Nations Educational, Scientific, and Cultural Organization (UNESCO) states that "wars begin in the minds of men" (and we must add, women as well, although possibly to a somewhat lesser extent). It takes no great stretch of imagination to charge the human psyche with prime responsibility for the initiation of war. Former senator J. William Fulbright emphasized the personal dimension of war making (and thus, war preventing) when he wrote:

> The first, indispensable step toward the realization of a new concept of community in the world is the acquisition of a new dimension of self-understanding. We have got to understand . . . why it is, psychologically and biologically, that men and nations fight; why it is . . . , that they always find *something* to fight about.[1]

When we concern ourselves with peace and war, we normally talk about the actions of large social units, often entire countries. But at least in part, when we say that a social unit "acts" in a particular way, what we really mean is that many individuals within those units act in such a manner. Thus, we say that the state acts, often meaning that the people within it—especially decision makers in the government—act.

First, we examine four major perspectives on the reasons for wars by focusing on the level of the individual person: instinct theory, sociobiology (and evolutionary psychology), Freudian and post-Freudian psychoanalysis, and the postulation of innate human depravity. These perspectives, while differing in significant ways, share an emphasis on the role of inborn, biological factors. Then, after considering some criticisms of these "human nature" approaches, we consider a variety of other factors believed to operate at the individual level, all of which involve greater attention to the role of learning and other social experiences.

Aggression, Drives, and Instincts

Many thinkers have assumed human beings to be instinctively aggressive. A particularly influential version of instinctivist theory has developed around presumed biological traits of the human species. Thus, one of the most influential U.S. textbooks on international relations begins as follows: "The drives to live, to propagate, and to dominate are common to all men."[2]

According to such notions, human warfare can be traced to our biological heritage, attributable directly to genetic, hormonal, neurobiological, and/or evolutionary mechanisms, including a tendency to form dominance hierarchies, to defend territories, and to behave aggressively toward others. Much emphasis is placed on the existence of comparable behavior patterns among certain animals, and the presumption that the behavior of animals reflects underlying principles that hold for the human species as well.

The Lorenzian Approach

Perhaps the most influential exponent of this perspective was the Nobel Prize-winning Austrian ethologist (student of the biology of animal behavior), Konrad Lorenz. Lorenz helped conceptualize a view of instinctive behavior according to which animals are endowed with certain behaviors, called "fixed action patterns," whose actual physical performance is genetically fixed and unvarying from one individual to another. In his book *On Aggression*, Lorenz argued that certain "species preserving" aspects of aggression applied to human beings as well. They include the following:

1. Providing an opportunity for competition within a species, after which the most fit will emerge to produce the next generation.

2. Achieving spacing and population control, to minimize the disadvantages of overpopulation.

3. Establishing a means whereby the pair-bond can be strengthened, as by shared aggression of a mated pair against competitors.

Lorenz was not concerned with extolling human aggression, but with understanding it. He noted that, in moderate amounts, aggression may well be functional and healthy, but at the same time, he deplored its occurrence in excess, especially when combined with what he called "militant enthusiasm," the tendency of people to lose their normal inhibitions against violence when united with others similarly motivated. Lorenz also emphasized that animals that have lethal natural weapons, such as wolves or hawks, also tend to possess innate inhibitions against employing such weapons against members of the same species. By contrast, animals such as rabbits, doves, or human beings—not naturally equipped with lethal weapons—lack such inhibitions. According to this line of thought, the human condition is especially perilous because while we have developed the ability, by technological means, to kill our fellow humans, quickly, easily, and in great numbers, our biological evolution remains far behind our technological progress. We continue to lack genetically based mechanisms to keep our newfound lethality in check.

The Lorenzian approach, which tends to "extrapolate war from human instinct," is in some ways a caricature of biological (ethological) views. According what might be called the *classical ethological approach*, aggression is genetically controlled behavior, such that the actual behavior patterns are rigidly stereotyped, invariant, and independent of learning. In this perspective, aggression can also emerge spontaneously; that is, individuals have a *need* to discharge this drive by behaving aggressively.

Lorenz suggests that one way to deal with our instinctive penchant for aggression and militant enthusiasm is by rechanneling this biological energy in socially useful (or at least, nondestructive) forms of competition, such as athletics, the exploration of space, or medical research. Nonetheless, Lorenz is led to a pessimistic assessment of the human future:

An unprejudiced observer from another planet, looking down on man as he is today, in his hand the atom bomb, the product of his intelligence, in his heart the aggressive drive inherited from his anthropoid ancestors, which this same intelligence cannot control, would not prophesy long life for the species.[3]

Other members of the "war in our genes" school have also contributed to the instinctivist approach. "Was my response to Pearl Harbor innate or conditioned?" asked the writer Robert Ardrey:

Was it something I had been born with or something I had been taught? Was it truly a command of genetic origin, an inheritance from the experience and natural selection of thousands of generations of my human and hominid ancestors?[4]

In this book and in his earlier work, *African Genesis*, Ardrey clearly associates himself with the Lorenzian view, arguing that since human beings evolved from anthropoid apes that hunted at least occasionally, and were probably at least somewhat carnivorous, then we must be genetically aggressive as well.

Is War in Our Genes?

Although biology may well provide valuable insights into the current human condition, such simplistic extrapolations from animal to human can also be dangerously misleading. For example, it is no more valid to argue that human beings are naturally murderous because baboons sometimes kill other baboons than it is to conclude that human beings are naturally vegetarians because gorillas exclusively eat plants or that humans can fly because birds have wings.

There is a danger that by accepting war as part of "human nature," one thereby justifies war itself, in part by diminishing the human responsibility to behave more peacefully. If war is "in our genes," then presumably we cannot act otherwise, so we should not be blamed for what we do; maybe, then, we shouldn't even bother trying to do anything about our warlike inclinations. At minimum—and perhaps, at its most pernicious—such biological fatalism supports a pessimistic perspective on the human condition, one that provides an excuse for the maintenance of large military forces and leads to profound distrust of others, especially those who look different from ourselves. There is, indeed, evidence that people who are generally promilitary tend to be disproportionate believers in the doctrine that war is somehow etched in our DNA.

To address (and scientifically to refute) biological determinism, a group of prominent behavioral scientists from 12 nations met in 1986 in Seville, Spain, and agreed on the "Seville Statement," which has since been endorsed by the American Psychological Association and the American Anthropological Association, and other scholarly organizations. Some excerpts from this statement are as follows:

- It is scientifically incorrect to say that we have inherited a tendency to make war from our animal ancestors. Warfare is a peculiarly human phenomenon and does not occur in other animals. War is biologically possible, but it is not inevitable, as evidenced by its variation in occurrence and nature over time and space.
- It is scientifically incorrect to say that war or any other violent behavior is genetically programmed into our human nature. Except for rare

pathologies, the genes do not produce individuals necessarily predisposed to violence. Neither do they determine the opposite.

- It is scientifically incorrect to say that in the course of human evolution there has been a selection for aggressive behavior more than for other kinds of behavior. In all well-studied species, status within the group is achieved by the ability to cooperate and to fulfill social functions relevant to the structure of that group.

- It is scientifically incorrect to say that humans have a "violent brain." While we do have a neural apparatus to act violently, there is nothing in our neurophysiology that compels us to.

- It is scientifically incorrect to say that war is caused by "instinct" or any single motivation. The technology of modern war has exaggerated traits associated with violence both in the training of actual combatants and in the preparation of support for war in the general population.

- We conclude that biology does not condemn humanity to war, and that humanity can be freed from the bondage of biological pessimism. Violence is neither in our evolutionary legacy nor in our genes. The same species . . . [that] invented war is capable of inventing peace.

Sociobiology and Evolutionary Psychology

A more sophisticated version of instinctivism is associated with the discipline of sociobiology, whose best-known practitioner has been the entomologist Edward O. Wilson. The mainstream sociobiological approach, which in the 1990s was somewhat superseded by an even more recent discipline known as evolutionary psychology, differs from instinctivism in that it places new emphasis on evolution as a process rather than a historical event. That is, sociobiologists and evolutionary psychologists are particularly concerned with the *adaptive significance* of behavior, or the way in which particular behavior patterns are maintained and promoted in a population because they contribute to the reproductive success of individuals (not species) that possess these traits.

A sociobiological or evolutionary psychological view of human war examines such phenomena as ecological competition (for food, nesting sites, etc.), male-male competition (for dominance in the pecking order and for mates), and the role of kinship patterns in directing aggressive behavior in particular ways. Among many species, for example, males tend to be larger, showier, and more aggressive than females. In addition, biological differences between males and females mean, among other things, one male can successfully fertilize many females. Sexual differences of this sort, in turn, convey a reproductive payoff (enhanced evolutionary fitness) to individuals —especially males—who succeed in defeating their rivals, whether in symbolic display or outright combat. Consistent with this theory, men tend to be more aggressive than women (especially outside the family), and more likely to be involved in public violence of all sorts, including war. Another important tenet of sociobiological theory is the role of genetic relatedness: Individuals who share genes probably will behave benevolently (altruistically) toward each other, because such behavior tends to contribute to the success of genes predisposing toward such behavior; conversely, a low probability of genetic relatedness is likely to be associated with aggressiveness. Consistent with this theory, appeals to patriotism often involve what anthropologists call *fictive kinship*, calling on citizens to stand up for the motherland, fatherland, Uncle Sam, "brothers and sisters," and so forth.

As for competition, it has been defined by Wilson as "the active demand by two or more individuals . . . for a common resource or requirement that is actually or potentially limiting."[5] Many studies have pointed to the role of primitive war in gaining access to mates, animal protein, and social prestige, such that warfare among preindustrial or nontechnological peoples, which in the past appeared to be irrational and nonadaptive, is now increasingly seen to possess an internal logic of its own—although not necessarily a logic that is consciously appreciated by the participants.

Sociobiologists and evolutionary psychologists tend to back away from the simplistic "either/or" dichotomy of instinctivism, on the one hand, or social constructionism, on the other hand. It is misleading to ask, as Robert Ardrey has done, whether a given behavior is instinctive or learned, since all behavior results from the interaction of genetic potential with experience, both nature and nurture. "In order to be adaptive," writes Wilson,

> it is enough that aggressive patterns be evoked only under certain conditions of stress such as those that might arise during food shortages and periodic high population densities. It also does not matter whether the aggression is wholly innate or is acquired part or wholly by learning. We are now sophisticated enough to know that the capacity to learn certain behaviors is itself a genetically controlled and therefore evolved trait.[6]

Finally, another important evolutionary perspective, represented notably by anthropologist Robert Bigelow, considers war to have had a prominent role in the early evolution of the human species. Conceivably, proto-human warrior bands were a major selective force in our own early evolution, with successful bands killing off those that were less successful. Large brains could well have contributed to success in violent intergroup conflict by promoting relatively sophisticated communication, formation of social alliances, and effective use of weapons. Those enjoying such success would presumably have left more descendants, who in turn were likely to possess these favored traits and capacities.

Freudian and Post-Freudian Psychoanalytic Theory

Sigmund Freud was the creator of psychoanalysis and in many ways the founder of modern psychiatry. He is particularly noteworthy for his emphasis on the role of the unconscious in human behavior. Freud himself was a pacifist, and he especially deplored what he saw as a vicious, lethal streak among human beings. In his later work, Freud attributed much of humanity's more "inhumane" behavior to the operation of *Thanatos*, or the death instinct, which he saw as opposed to *Eros*, the life instinct. In a famous letter to Albert Einstein, he noted, "We are led to conclude that this [death] instinct functions in every living being, striving to work its ruin and to reduce life to its primal state of inert matter."[7] When Thanatos is thwarted by Eros, its energy is displaced outward onto subjects other than oneself, resulting in aggression between individuals or among groups.

The notion of a death instinct remains associated with Freud's thought, and this idea was extended by one of his followers, Melanie Klein (the founder of object-relations psychoanalysis). But Freud also argued that, regardless of whether Thanatos exists within the human psyche or if we are "simply" aggressive by nature, civilization demands that people repress their primitive tendencies toward destructive and aggressive behavior if they are to live together with a minimum of violent conflict. Parents must provide discipline for their children, society must restrict its citizens, and ultimately, some form of supranational authority will be necessary to enforce a system of world government over individual states that would otherwise function anarchically, argued Freud. Hence, civilization demands the repression of both Eros and Thanatos, which in turn necessarily produces discontent (and neurosis) among its populace.

Another important Freudian concept especially relevant to war is that of *narcissistic injury*. Narcissism involves infatuation with one's self, and in moderation it is considered a normal stage in personality development. But when the individual associates himself or herself with a larger group, especially with the nation-state, slights or injuries to the group are easy to perceive as injuries to one's self. The resulting "narcissistic rage" may involve an unrelenting compulsion to undo the hurt; in the pursuit of this vengeful "justice," great violence may be self-righteously employed. Many of the most destructive wars in the 20th century were perpetrated by people seeking to retake territory that had been wrested from them by others (e.g., the French yearning to recapture the provinces of Alsace and Lorraine from Germany, which was a major reason for World War I, or the Vietcong and North Vietnamese, who sought during the Vietnam War to reunite their country). Other wars have been instigated by ethnic groups seeking to secede from a central governmental authority, only to precipitate intervention by armed forces from the nation-state from which they hoped to disconnect (as in Nigeria, Ethiopia, Indonesia, the former Yugoslavia, and Russia).

Like the Lorenzian and (to a lesser extent) the sociobiological and evolutionary psychological approaches, the orthodox Freudian perspective tends to be pessimistic about the prospects for ameliorating, much less eliminating, "this ineradicable defect in human nature." Thus, Freud maintained, for example, that we really shouldn't be so disillusioned about atrocities during wartime, because the notion that humankind was fundamentally civilized is itself illusory.

Furthermore, according to Melanie Klein and some of her followers, human aggression is ultimately rooted in the earliest "primitive" states of human existence, before there is an ego or language to modulate, rechannel, or defuse it. Human destructiveness manifests itself, among other things, in the "paranoid-schizoid" anxieties and defenses (such as splitting and projection) initially used by infants to ward off feelings of abandonment (by the mother or other caregivers) and fears of annihilation and disintegration. According to Kleinian theory, therefore, human aggression is implicit even in the womb; it emerges full-blown during the first years of life (when the infant quite literally bites the mother's hand and breast that feed it); and persists throughout the entire life span, either as unconscious sadomasochistic fantasies or overtly in self- and other-destructive behaviors. The goal of psychoanalytic therapy from a Kleinian perspective is accordingly to induce the "malignant" (destructive and disowned) parts of the self to become "reintegrated" within a "whole-object" psyche, not to seek in vain to eradicate aggression from either the individual or from the human species.

Some students of human behavior have concluded that much human misery, including even the penchant for war itself, derives in part from the consequences of being mistreated as children. It is further argued that many acts of violence toward children—whether overt, such as beating or sexual abuse, or more subtle, such as severe criticism and belittling by significant others in a child's early environment—have in turn been buttressed by the view that human beings are inherently sinful and depraved. From a more secular perspective, the neo-Kleinian psychoanalytic theorist and pediatrician D. W. Winnicott claimed that with "good enough mothering," the infant's proclivities toward aggression could be mollified; conversely, without a nurturing environment, babies and young children who are deprived of maternal love and positive reinforcement are at risk for developing pathological character structures and for engaging in self- and other-destructive behaviors.

Other prominent psychoanalysts have not been as pessimistic as most Kleinians and have in fact rejected the very notion of a death drive. Wilhelm Reich, for example, argued that the unprecedented violence and destructiveness unleashed on Europe during the first part of the 20th century were not simply the latest manifestation of the eternal battle between Eros and Thanatos, but could instead be better explained in terms of the historical development of character pathologies ("armor") and socially induced aggression under modern capitalism. And more contemporary schools of psychoanalytic theory and therapy—notably the ego, self, relational, and critical psychologists—have also stressed the roles of environment, culture, social interaction, and socialization in eliciting and reinforcing aggressive and destructive behaviors.

_____ "Innate Depravity" and "Human Nature"

Some thoughtful people have long maintained that human beings are innately depraved, nasty, and evil, basing this claim on a loosely argued blend of biology, moral outrage, and on occasion, theology. Looking over the blood-letting of the English civil war (1642–1649), Thomas Hobbes concluded that there was "a general inclination of all mankind, a perpetual and restless desire for power after power that ceaseth only in death."[8] To some extent, Hobbes's pessimism can be traced to a Biblical—especially to a conservative Christian—tradition that teaches that human nature is inherently flawed. Suffused with original sin, humans are deemed to be inherently incapable of becoming good. Consider these sentiments from the 16th-century theologian John Calvin, perhaps the most influential advocate of this perspective:

> Even infants themselves, as they bring their condemnation into the world with them, are rendered subject to punishment of their own sinfulness. . . . For though they have not yet produced the fruits of their iniquity, yet they have had the seed of it in them. Their whole nature is, as it were, a seed of sin and therefore cannot but be . . . abominable to God.[9]

In Calvinist theology, because of our allegedly innate human sinfulness, we were cast out of the Garden of Eden, doomed to death. We therefore deserve—indeed, we require—to be treated sternly and punished vigorously. In any event, according to this pessimistic Christian view, a true state of personal peace can be achieved only by grace, just as a state of political peace requires the Second Coming of Christ. And until then, war is inevitable.

This attitude is not limited to conservative Christians, however. Another approach, rarely articulated, emphasizes that human beings have not only a capacity for violence but also a deep-seated love of bloodletting, hatred, and destruction. In his letter to Albert Einstein, Freud observed that "man has within him a lust for hatred and destruction. . . . It is a comparatively easy task to call this into play and raise it to the level of a collective psychosis."[10] And in the 17th century, John Milton wrote that even if our species were rendered somehow impervious to injury from all outside forces, yet the perverseness of our folly is so bent, that we should never cease hammering out of our own hearts, as it were out of a flint, the seeds and sparkles of new misery to ourselves, till all were in a blaze again.[11]

From this perspective, especially endorsed by theologians such as Luther, St. Augustine, John Calvin, and Reinhold Niebuhr, as well as by religiously motivated political leaders such as Oliver Cromwell or satirists like Jonathan Swift, war is an evil unique to humanity. Niebuhr argued that it was the "sinful character of man" that necessitated "the balancing of power with power."[12] The philosophers Spinoza and Kant located the evils of human violence in the fact that our rational faculties are regularly overwhelmed by our irrational and untamed emotions.

This is only a very limited sampling of a widespread notion. Although it is quite difficult to prove, the idea of innate human weakness and depravity remains very popular, especially among the lay public. It has also been especially influential among those who are sympathetic to military force, if not to war itself. Thus, if human nature is inherently nasty and warlike, then we can never have any confidence in morality, law, or anything else to deliver us from war, since these are only frail, artificial institutions constructed by fundamentally flawed human beings. Because human nature presumably cannot be changed, the only recourse to safeguard personal or national security—regrettably—is to arms.

Criticisms of Human Nature Theories

The various human nature theories about the reasons for human violence all contain flaws. For example, human beings undoubtedly have the biological capacity to kill one another—proven by the fact that they have often done so. The danger is that such a broad generalization may be useless in analyzing the past or predicting the future. Other, more specific problems in these theories exist as well. For example, consider the following:

1.   Although war is a widespread human trait, it is not a universal one; certain cultures, such as the Tasaday of the Philippine Islands, the South African bushmen (or San), the Semai (in Southeast Asia), and the Inuit, apparently never engaged in war, although interpersonal violence was not unknown. Explanations based on human nature should apply to these peoples no less than to others. Although some societies are clearly more war prone than others, there is also no evidence whatever that such differences reflect inherent differences in human nature.

2.   Even among war-prone cultures, there have been many years of peace. If human nature caused World War II or the Vietnam War, then what about the peace that preceded and followed these wars?

If human nature causes war, then it must also cause peace—the neutrality of Sweden, the demilitarized U.S.-Canadian border, Gandhi's nonviolence. Any explanation that is so broad becomes useless. To paraphrase a military metaphor of Karl von Clausewitz, he who seeks to explain everything, explains nothing.

3. Even within war-prone cultures, there have been war resisters, peace advocates, and long-time nonviolent traditions such as the Mennonites and the Quakers; are they less "human," or less "natural," than their more violent fellow citizens?

4. The fact that animals behave in certain ways does not necessarily mean that human beings do so; we seem to be unique the capacity for complex, abstract, and symbolic thought, which give us the opportunity to reason, to analyze, and to rise above our unpleasant or dangerous inclinations.

5. If war is a result of a fixed human nature, then it is predestined and unavoidable, since we cannot—by definition—behave counter to our own nature. There is a special danger in the belief that war is inevitable, because it is likely to discourage people from seeking to end war and to promote peace. Moreover, it can also serve to *justify* war by making it appear somehow "good" because it is natural.

The above criticisms are all valid to a degree, especially when applied to naive or crude instinctivism. But they also oversimplify the more sophisticated human nature arguments. Thus, most biologically inclined theorists recognize that genetic factors do not irrevocably commit a person, or a society, to a given course of action. Rather, they create predispositions for behaving aggressively or violently when circumstances are appropriate; similarly, nothing in sociobiological or evolutionary psychological thought suggests that such predispositions could not be overridden by religious beliefs, historical circumstances, collective social action, and so on. There is nothing inconsistent with the proponents of such theories suggesting that human beings can say "No" to their genes, neurons, and/or hormones.

Human Nature and Genetic Determinism

There is a great difference between a possible genetic *influence* on war proneness and the doctrine of genetic *determinism*. The former implies the existence of tendencies, likely to be subtle and capable of being overridden, whereas the latter implies rigid, ironclad automatic responses. There may well be genetic and neurobiological influences that human beings, if they are to be peaceful, must overcome or sublimate; this is not to say that our genes, neurons, and/or hormones predetermine our behavior, condemning us to violence.

As to morality, advocates—and critics—of biologically based arguments should be wary of what the philosopher David Hume first identified—and later labeled by the 20th-century British philosopher G. E. Moore—as the *naturalistic fallacy*, the mistaken belief that "*is* implies *ought*." In other words, whatever insights biological and neurosciences might provide regarding how the natural world and the human brain work, these are distinct from ethical guidance as to what is good and what right conduct entails. Typhoid is natural; this does not mean that it is good. War may or may not be natural; whether it is good, however, is an entirely different question. In any event, if typhoid, or war, is to be prevented or cured, we must understand its causation, whether or not we are pleased by what we find.

Frustration-Aggression

Among explanations for war that do not depend on explicit assumptions about human nature, one of the most influential has been the frustration-aggression hypothesis, which was developed to explain individual aggressiveness as well. According to this theory, first proposed by psychiatrist John Dollard and his colleagues, aggressiveness is produced by frustration, which in turn is defined as "an interference with the occurrence of an instigated goal-response at its proper time in the behavior sequence."[13] Thus, if a hungry rat is presented with food, after which a glass wall is interposed between the animal and its desire, the rat is likely to become aggressive. A similar thing happens with frustrated human beings, people who have been seeking something unsuccessfully—food, political freedoms, access to a disputed territory, union with others who practice the same customs—or who have obtained partial success only to be prevented from achieving their ultimate goals.

In its initial formulation, frustration theory was presented rather dogmatically. "The occurrence of aggressive behavior always presupposes the existence of frustration, and contrariwise, the existence of frustration always leads to some form of aggression."[14] This rigidity led to problems comparable to those encountered with some human nature theories: The argument can become circular if all cases of aggression are defined as involving preexisting frustration, and vice versa, if any behavior that follows frustration is defined to be aggression.

Frustration theory has subsequently been modified to recognize that frustration creates a predisposition or readiness for aggression, by producing an intervening emotional state: anger. In addition, environmental stimuli—targets and/or cues—are necessary for aggression to be produced. Finally, an individual's learning experiences and society's expectations exert a powerful influence on the connection between frustration and aggression. Of course, other responses to frustration are also possible, namely, submission, resignation, alienation, withdrawal, avoidance, or even acceptance, but this does not in itself argue against the strength of the frustration-aggression link.

Frustration can also result in resentment, which (like the above responses) may or may not subsequently produce aggressive behavior. Frustration may be especially high when there is a discrepancy between expectations and realities: Bad social conditions, such as poverty or political repression, are made to seem even worse by high expectations that conflict with unpleasant realities. Accordingly, the "revolution of rising expectations," particularly in the less advanced economies, has been associated with frustration and violence.

Political and military authorities often respond to collective efforts to promote social change with increased repression, but the forceful repression of strongly felt needs (such as the yearning for Palestinian self-determination, and before that, of Zionists for a Jewish state) can in itself be highly frustrating and thereby ultimately increase hostility and aggression. In some cases, frustration finds its outlet in aggressive behavior against others who are not actually the perceived frustrating agent.

There is another possible twist to the connection between frustration and war, namely, boredom. It has been suggested that war is especially appealing to those whose lives are lacking in excitement and interest. "The absence of delight in daily living," wrote the historian John Nef, "has helped to leave many lives empty and sterile and so, fair game for any excitement, including the most terrific of worldly excitements, that of war."[15] Furthermore, once a society has elevated military values, has trained men and boys (and increasingly, women and girls) to be warriors, and has institutionalized and mythologized the war experience, people may be especially prone to be frustrated and bored with peace. Of course, warfare itself actually involves prolonged periods of boredom and monotony. The endless repetition, drill, and "hurry up and wait" behavior that characterize military routine are hardly antidotes for civilian ennui. Military boredom may lead, however, to frustration, which in turn leads to greater willingness to go to war, if only to "see action" and thereby finally to break the suspense.

Social Learning

Clearly, human beings are strongly influenced by their experiences—those that occur early in development and that also characterize later socialization —as well as society's norms and expectations. Most psychologists and sociologists maintain that human violence arises in response to experiences, rather than bubbling up out of our genetic constitution. "The important fact," wrote psychologist John Paul Scott, "is that the chain of causation in every case eventually traces back to the outside. There is no physiological evidence of any spontaneous stimulation for fighting arising within the body."[16] Scott has emphasized that individuals are particularly likely to fight if they have fought successfully in the past and that aggression often results from a breakdown in social structures. (It is also noteworthy, on the other hand, that some of the most aggressive societies have been highly structured: Nazi Germany and Fascist Italy, for example.)

Conditioning

One of the most important developments in 20th-century psychology revolved around the learning phenomenon known as *conditioning*, especially associated with the work of B. F. Skinner. The basic idea is that behavior will be influenced by its consequences for the individual: Certain behaviors tend to be *reinforcing*, that is, they make it more likely that the individual will repeat the previous behavior. Some authorities employ the phrase "instrumental aggression" to refer to aggressive behavior that is oriented primarily toward attaining some goal, such as winning a war or recovering territory, rather than causing injury as such.

Conditioning theory applied to human aggressiveness suggests that people will behave aggressively when such behavior leads to reinforcing (i.e., positive) results and, conversely, that the likelihood of aggression will be reduced if it leads to negative results. By extrapolation, members of whole societies can presumably be influenced similarly, making war more probable if their behavior has been positively reinforced (rewarded) or negatively reinforced (punished). For example, the international aggressiveness of Nazi Germany was positively reinforced during most of the 1930s by the appeasement policies of the West; by contrast, it can be argued that international adventuring on the part of the United States was negatively reinforced by its divisive and ultimately unsuccessful involvement in Southeast Asia (resulting in a subsequent reluctance to commit American ground troops to foreign combat, the so-called Vietnam syndrome).

Socialization to Aggressiveness

Some societies actively encourage aggressiveness from early childhood. For example, consider the Fulani people of northern Nigeria, among whom most males seek to embody the ideals of "aggressive dominance." As boys, young Fulani males are taught to beat their cattle to prevent them from wandering off and to fight back unhesitatingly whenever they have been attacked. If they refrain from retaliating, they are mocked as cowards. They show virtually no emotion when struck with sticks during increasingly serious fights, and by the time they are young men, the Fulani are proud of their battle scars. Not surprisingly, they are also prone to personal fighting as well as warfare.

Mark May, an influential social psychologist, summed up the dominant American view of the 1940s when he wrote that "men not only learn when it is best to fight or not to fight, whom to fight and whom to appease, how to fight and how not to; but they also learn whom, when, and how to hate." May went on to discuss the phenomenon of social learning for group aggressiveness:

> Learning to fight and to hate involves much more than learning to box, to duel, or to participate in other forms of group violence. Systematic education for aggressive warfare in ancient Sparta or in modern Germany includes, besides physical education in games and contests, universal compulsory military training; the inculcation of certain attitudes, prejudices, beliefs; and devotion to leaders and ideals. The whole purpose and direction of such education is toward group aggression.

Similar processes of socialization can also produce a group characterized by peace rather than by aggression. In such a group, according to May,

> there is the minimum amount of physical violence among the members. Antagonism, hostilities, and conflicts are held in check by customs, laws, and rules which are enforced in part by duly constituted author- ities and in part by inner compulsions of loyalties and the sense of social responsibility. Peace between groups as well as within a group is maintained by the joint action of external authority and social atti- tudes of tolerance and good will.[17]

Also important in this context is the phenomenon of "imitative learning," whereby individuals are prone to do something if they witness others doing the same thing. Thus, aggressiveness and hostility—or alternatively, an inclination to settle disputes peacefully—can become part of the ethos of a society.

Self-Fulfilling Behaviors

An important sociological concept is what Robert Merton has called the *self-fulfilling prophecy*, according to which a belief becomes true if enough people believe that it is true. In the realm of aggressive behavior, hostility often begets hostility on the part of others, which in turn not only reinforces the initial hostility but also intensifies it. People may create their own inter- personal environments simply by behaving with a certain expectation: If someone is suspicious, secretive, and blameful, he or she is likely to elicit comparable behavior. This pattern has the makings of a vicious circle, in which hostility becomes self-reinforcing in a kind of positive feedback. A similar pattern can apply to international relations as well. For example, if country A, convinced of the hostility of country B, increases its armaments, then B may well respond in kind. This in turn reinforces the "enemy image" already present, leading to further militarily oriented actions, each of which may truly be intended to be "defensive" but that, taken as a whole, diminish the security of all participants. Such a process characterizes much of the history of arms races.

Redirected Aggression

Other patterns in behavioral development also take place, often without the explicit intent of producing aggressiveness. In James Joyce's short story "Counterparts," a man who is browbeaten by his boss, and who then stops at a pub after work and is defeated at arm wrestling, finally goes home— and beats up his young son. This phenomenon is known as *displaced* or *redirected* aggression, whereby anger—often generated by other sources—is displaced or redirected to different targets. The Bible describes how the ancient Israelites would designate one animal as a *scapegoat*, which would be abused and driven from the herd, ostensibly taking with it the sins and anger of those who remained behind, uninjured, and purified.

Frequently, the victims of redirected aggression are smaller, weaker, or already the subjects of social abuse: a religious or racial minority, advocates of unpopular political doctrines, and so on. Blacks, communists in the United States, Arab immigrants in France, religious and ethnic minorities (especially those with dark skin, such as the Roma) in Russia and the countries spawned by the collapse of the former Soviet Union and Yugoslavia, all have borne the brunt of redirected aggression by people who have been themselves deprived or disadvantaged. Although local minorities provide convenient "targets of opportunity," foreign nationals are particularly targeted as objects of redirected group anger.

The Authoritarian Personality

Following World War II and the Holocaust in which six million of Europe's Jews (as well as millions of pacifists, gays, Roma, war resisters, mentally disabled people, political dissidents, and civilian noncombatants) were murdered, researchers led by the German philosopher Theodor Adorno and the American social psychologist Nevitt Sanford sought to identify those personal traits and experiences that predispose people toward anti-Semitism and related authoritarian and antidemocratic ideologies and practices. Their work resulted in the F-Scale (for Fascist), which gave a rough measure of an individual's tendency toward authoritarianism. The *authoritarian personality* was found to be positively correlated with a rigidly hierarchical family structure: the husband dominant over the wife, and parents (especially fathers) demanding unquestioned obedience and respect from their children. This moralistic and disciplinarian style of child rearing was often combined with a strongly nationalistic outlook, ready submission to powerful external authority, and fear of weakness and of moral "contamination" by "aliens and other outsiders."

The resulting *authoritarian personality structure* can engender an autocratic, xenophobic, and militaristic approach to social problems, both domestically and in foreign relations. Such people often (unconsciously) have a relatively poor self-image that makes them especially prone to following orders blindly, even if these orders involve inflicting injury on one's self or others and even if the behaviors involved go counter to fundamental precepts of traditional morality, such as "thou shalt not kill."

Closely connected with the notion of an authoritarian personality is the concept of *identification with the aggressor*, in which the victim tends to adopt the attributes of a powerful punishing agent (parent, government), in order to alleviate anxiety; in the process, the victim is transformed into an aggressor, either directly or indirectly by supporting aggression on the part of others. It may be significant that comparatively permissive societies seem to be less warlike than those with high levels of physical punishment of children and of sexual repression.

Alienation and Totalism

Psychoanalysts Erich Fromm and Erik Erikson have emphasized, more than their drive-oriented colleagues, the influences of culture, society, and the environment on people's propensity for engaging in violent and other antisocial conduct. They have also focused on the role of painful, or traumatic, experiences operating through nonrational psychic processes. Fromm has distinguished between *defensive aggression* and *malignant aggression*, with the latter involving a passionate drive to hurt others (sadism) or oneself (masochism). But unlike the human nature theorists, he attributes malignant aggression to social conditions rather than to innate human traits. In particular, Fromm blames *alienation*, an acute loneliness and disconnectedness from others, for the inclination by very alienated people to avenge their pain by acts of extreme destruction; they are also ripe candidates for inclusion in violent organizations, where they can lose themselves in a group that is united by their hatred of others. This might include the Ku Klux Klan and other neo-Nazis in the United States, skinheads in Great Britain, as well as other "terrorist" and hate groups worldwide. It must also be noted, however, that feelings of social and political alienation might also motivate psychologically healthy personalities to participate in social movements to *oppose* injustices and wars.

In a similar vein, Erikson has pointed out that, especially when it is changing rapidly, a society may generate ambiguities and unresolved stresses that combine with the individual's developmental problems to produce *totalism*, a susceptibility to all-or-nothing simplifications: us versus them, good versus evil, God versus the devil. Given the sacrifices that war demands—not only economic and political but also the willingness to sacrifice one's life and to go against the standard societal prohibition against taking another's life—it is not surprising that totalistic thinking and war should go hand in hand.

The Attractions of War

In *Notes From the Underground*, Dostoyevsky wrote, "In former days we saw justice in bloodshed and with our conscience at peace exterminated those we thought proper to kill. Now we do think bloodshed abominable and yet we engage in this abomination, and with more energy than ever."[18] This energy derives at least in part from the fact that some people at least find war a positive experience. Many combatants have extolled the sheer intensity of confronting the basic phenomena of life and death, and in the process, exploring the boundaries of one's capacities. For some soldiers, especially young men, there is something exhilarating about meeting death face to face, perhaps even heroically and for a noble cause, rather than to be overtaken alone in the night. Teilhard de Chardin (who served in World War I) wrote,

> The front cannot but attract us, because it is . . . the extreme boundary between what you are already aware of, and what is still in the process of formation. Not only do you see there things that you experience nowhere else, but you also see emerge from within yourself an underlying stream of clarity, energy, and freedom that is to be found hardly anywhere else in ordinary life. . . . This exaltation is accompanied by a certain pain. Nonetheless it is indeed an exaltation. And that is why one likes the front in spite of everything, and misses it.[19]

For others, there may be a compelling sexual component, as revealed in this passage from Norman Mailer:

> All the deep, dark urges of man, the sacrifices on the hilltops, the churning lusts of night and sleep, weren't all of them contained in the shattering, screaming burst of a shell? The phallus-like shell that rides through a shining vagina of steel. The curve of sexual excitement and discharge, which is, after all, the physical core of life.[20]

And most significant of all, perhaps, is the satisfaction of "belonging" and companionship, particularly a kind of male bonding, that most men do not experience during civilian life. Shakespeare's Henry V rhapsodizes about the pleasure the forthcoming battle holds for

> We few, we happy few, we band of brothers;
> For he to-day that sheds his blood with me
> Shall be my brother. (*Henry V*, IV, iii)

Or consider this commentary, from a combat veteran of World War II:

> We are liberated from our individual impotence and are drunk with
> the power that union with our fellows brings. In moments like these
> many have a vague awareness of how isolated and separate their lives
> have hitherto been. . . . With the boundaries of the self expanded, they
> sense a kinship never known before. Their "I" passes insensibly into a
> "we." . . . At its height, this sense of comradeship is an ecstasy.[21]

The American philosopher and psychologist William James (1842–1910)
believed that the raw emotional appeal of war constituted one of the greatest difficulties in overcoming it. In a renowned essay, James presented the
case for war's attractiveness:

> The war against war is going to be no holiday excursion or camping
> party. The military feelings are too deeply grounded to abdicate their
> place among our ideals until better substitutes are offered. . . . Modern
> war is so expensive that we felt trade to be a better avenue to plunder,
> but modern man inherits all the innate pugnacity and all the love of
> glory of his ancestors. Showing war's irrationality and horror is of no
> effect upon him. The horrors make the fascination. War is the *strong*
> life; it is life *in extremis*. . . . Inordinate ambitions are the soul of every
> patriotism, and the possibility of violent death the soul of all romance
> . . . If war had ever stopped, we should have to reinvent it . . . to
> redeem life from flat degeneration. . . . Its "horrors" are a cheap price
> to pay for rescue from the only alternative supposed, of a world of
> clerks and teachers, of . . . consumer's leagues and associated charities,
> of industrialism unlimited, and feminism unabashed. . . . Militarism is
> the great preserver of our ideals of hardihood, and human life with no
> use for hardihood would be contemptible. Without risks or prizes for
> the darer, history would be insipid indeed.

James then suggested that these attractions could be overcome only by sub-
stituting another crusade, which he called "the moral equivalent of war":

> A conscription of the whole youthful population to form for a certain
> number of years a part of the army enlisted against Nature . . . would
> preserve in the midst of a pacific civilization the manly virtues which
> the military party is so afraid of seeing disappear in peace. . . . So far,
> war has been the only force that can discipline a whole community,

and until an equivalent discipline is organized, I believe that war must have its way.[22]

None of these selections should be seen as reflecting enthusiasm for war, but rather a grudging recognition that *even* war has not only its horrors but also its attractions. A famous *bushido* tract from ancient Japan advises that "when all things in life are false, there is only one thing true, death."[23] The most war-prone ideologies generally claim that their long-term goal, however, is to eliminate war. But there is a notable modern exception: Fascism. Fascism has tended to glorify war, and (judging by its success in the 20th century), it struck a favorable chord in many people. "War alone," wrote Italian dictator Benito Mussolini,

> brings up to their highest tension all human energies and puts a stamp of nobility upon the people who have the courage to meet it. All other trials are substitutes, which never really put a man in front of himself in the alternative of life and death. A doctrine, therefore, which begins with a prejudice in favor of peace is foreign to Fascism.[24]

Of course, the fact that someone may be a fascist does not itself contribute a satisfactory explanation for his or her inclinations toward war. Rather, one must also consider those factors that presumably have led him or her to embrace such a war-prone ideology: frustration, authoritarian personality structure, inadequate nurturance during childhood, social and biological influences, and so on.

A final contributing reason for war, working at the individual level, may well be a kind of sanitized romanticizing of battle, found in many children's cartoons and toys, movies (such as the *Star Wars* films), music, art, and literature. For example, consider the following verse, by English poet A. E. Housman:

> I did not lose my heart in summer's eve,
> When roses to the moonrise burst apart:
> When plumes were under heel and lead was flying,
> In blood and smoke and flame I lost my heart.
> I lost it to a soldier and a foeman,
> A chap that did not kill me, but he tried;
> That took the sabre straight and took it striking
> And laughed and kissed his hand to me and died.[25]

To be sure, there also exists a rich catalog of antiwar songs, stories, movies, and poems, ranging from the delicate and plaintive (as in the song "Where Have All the Flowers Gone?") to the unrelentingly realistic and grotesque (as in *All Quiet on the Western Front, Johnny Got His Gun, Catch-22,* and

Saving Private Ryan). Opponents of war, however, are obliged to recognize those aspects of war that have long exercised a positive appeal for many humans.

Inhibitions Against War

The history of warfare shows that people are capable of the most heinous acts of brutality. From American history alone, consider the massacre of Sioux Indians at Wounded Knee in South Dakota in the late 19th century, or the massacre at My Lai in Vietnam about 100 years later: In both cases, hundreds of men, women, and children were slaughtered wantonly. Indeed, the preceding sections may leave the impression that war exerts a virtually irresistible attraction to human beings at the individual level, whether through our innate characteristics, our experiences, or via the lure of excitement, camaraderie, and ideology. But in fact, even beyond ethical and religious strictures, there are many inhibitions that serve to check the personal propensity for war.

One of these inhibiting factors is fear for one's own life. In Euripedes' *The Supplicants*, the Theban herald points out that "if death had been before their own eyes when they were giving their votes, Hellas [Greece] would never have rushed to her doom in mad desire for battle." There are, in fact, very few heroes during a war; most soldiers seek to do the minimum necessary to save themselves and their close colleagues.

As to alleged blood-lust and war fever, consider that during World War II, rarely did more than 25% of American soldiers fire their guns in battle; even during intense firefights, about 15% opened fire. And this applied to intensely trained combat infantrymen. A study sponsored by the U.S. Army concluded that "it is therefore reasonable to believe that the average and healthy individual—the man who can endure the mental and physical stresses of combat—still has such an inner and usually unrealized resistance towards killing a fellow man that he will not of his own volition take life if it is possible to turn away from that responsibility."[26] It can even be argued that, in many wars before 1950, fear of killing, rather than fear of being killed, is the largest cause of battle failure.

By the Korean and Vietnam Wars, however, the percentage of soldiers willing to fire their weapons appears to have gone up significantly, largely because of improved training and greater emphasis on establishing within-group solidarity among individual combat units. Army discipline has long been recognized as crucially important, largely because the side that broke and ran has historically been the one that was butchered. A major part of military training (especially in boot camp) seeks to countermand the basic moral teaching—not limited, incidentally, to Western tradition—"Thou shalt not kill." The goal of basic training, in the armed forces of most countries, has not so much been the teaching of new techniques and skills as the inculcation of new attitudes: unquestioning obedience to military superiors and an increased willingness to kill. Despite some resistance, most people can in fact learn these things, usually in just a few weeks. This should not be surprising, since a profound asymmetry of power exists between the recruit and the officers who train them: "Recruits usually have no more than twenty years' experience of the world, most of it as children, while the armies have had all of history to practice and perfect their techniques."[27]

Actual killing during combat is widely considered the role of enlisted men or, at most, junior officers. By 1914, for example, lieutenants and captains in the British Army led men into battle carrying only a swagger-stick or, at most, a pistol. "Officers do not kill," was the common understanding at that time, and there is reason to believe that, if they had the choice, most enlisted men would not have done so either. George Orwell, for example, who fought as an anti-Fascist volunteer on the Loyalist side during the Spanish Civil War, recounted that he was unable to shoot an enemy soldier whom he observed "half-dressed and . . . holding up his trousers with both hands . . . . I did not shoot partly because of that detail about his trousers. . . . A man who is holding up his trousers isn't a 'Fascist,' he is visibly a fellow-creature, similar to yourself, and you don't feel like shooting him."[28]

Some Issues in Nuclear Psychology

Because of its special features, nuclear war also merits special consideration at the level of individual psychology. Many aspects of nuclear psychology operate at the level of decision makers. Other factors, however, affect the psychological functioning of all human beings.

When it comes to nuclear war, feelings of attraction and revulsion are particularly intense. Some people evince a strange love for weapons of such all-encompassing power (hence, the title of the famous satirical movie *Dr. Strangelove, or How I Learned to Stop Worrying and Love the Bomb*). Others, by contrast, are especially repelled by the grisly prospect of ending life on so massive a scale. And yet, because a full-fledged nuclear conflict has not yet occurred, and because, in addition, the effects of nuclear explosions are so powerful as literally to stagger the human imagination, most people have difficulty focusing their minds and energies on such a topic, which is at once horrifying and yet strangely unreal.

When confronted with deeply unpleasant information, for example, people often respond with *denial,* a refusal to confront an unpleasant reality. This process is particularly well-known with respect to personal death: Virtually every cognitively unimpaired adult recognizes that eventually, he or she will die; however, most of us go about our lives as though our own death holds little reality. When confronted with the facts, we concur; if not, we often practice denial. Something similar can be identified with respect to the nuclear danger: Most of us go about our daily lives as though the prospect of instantaneous nuclear holocaust does not hang over us, simply because such an overwhelming threat is too painful and emotionally disruptive to admit into our moment-by-moment consciousness.

This behavior, although presumably adaptive for the individual, also has unintended and potentially dangerous consequences. By refusing to confront unpleasant realities, people who might otherwise become mobilized in opposition to nuclear weapons are likely to place their attention and energy elsewhere. Moreover, they abandon the field to those who have insulated themselves from the negative consequences of their activities, and who, by virtue of career advancement and/or ideology, have committed themselves to a more pronuclear, and possibly prowar, orientations.

Denial is encouraged by the fact that nuclear weapons tend to lack psychological reality: They are kept in secret, restricted installations, and in the United States, the Department of Defense refuses, as a matter of policy, either to "confirm or deny" their presence (even in other countries allied to the United States). This policy has ostensibly been adopted so as to keep information from would-be nuclear terrorists. Regardless, one important effect of official secrecy clearly is to keep the American public uninformed and, to some extent, to facilitate denial. Hence, for most people, nuclear weapons cannot be seen, touched, smelled, or heard, and so it requires a conscious effort to consider that they exist at all.

Closely related to denial is another personal, psychological phenomenon of the nuclear age, often called *psychic numbing*. This phrase was originally applied by psychiatrist Robert J. Lifton to the *hibakusha*, the victims of the atomic bombing of Hiroshima and Nagasaki. Psychic numbing refers to a loss of emotional sensitivity and awareness that appeared to result from the survivors' immersion in the mass death that characterized those events. It can be argued that to some extent, we are all victims of Hiroshima and Nagasaki, in that all of us suffer from some degree of psychic numbing, as the nuclear menace pervades our unconscious.

Another important psychological mechanism of the nuclear age has been called the "more is better syndrome." In some ways, it appears to be a vestige of prenuclear times, when security was obtained (at least in some cases) by accumulating more weapons than one's opponent. In a world bristling with nuclear overkill, it seems unlikely that "more" is even meaningful, let alone better, and yet the tendency persists for many people to think in this way.

____ A Final Note on Individual-Level Explanations of Wars

Approximately 1% to 2% of human deaths during the 20th century were inflicted by other human beings. In other words, 98% to 99% of recent human deaths were not caused directly by intentional, individually inflicted violence. Moreover, of those deaths that are caused by other people, the majority are due to collective violence rather than to individual aggression.

Many social scientists have insisted that war is a human invention, not a biological necessity. They cite the high level of social organization and structuring involved in any military enterprise and the fact that different societies make war, if they do so at all, in very different ways, depending on the social structures and technological options. Different societies also make war for different reasons, including pride, prestige, revenge, and the quest for resources. It can also be argued that decisions regarding war, especially in large, modern societies, are not made at the individual level, or at least not at the level of the average citizen. Certainly, such decisions do not involve the simple summation of all individual inclinations within the population, nor do they follow the results of plebiscites or referenda submitted to the citizenry to vote for or against a particular war. Rather, war is decided by political (and often military, economic, and strategic) elites, after which the populace generally goes along, sometimes eagerly, but usually only after considerable manipulation or even outright coercion. And sometimes, war isn't really deliberatively "decided" at all; it just seems to "happen," often by mistake or misjudgment.

In addition, although war typically *arouses* great passions, it is not always true that war is the *result* of such passions. In some cases, wars appear to have been chosen by intelligent, instrumentally rational individuals, after carefully calculating the costs and benefits of alternative courses of action. According to military historian Michael Howard:

> In general, men have fought during the past two hundred years neither because they are aggressive nor because they are acquisitive animals, but because they are reasoning ones: because they discern, or believe they can discern, dangers before they become immediate, the possibility of threats before they are made."[29]

Humans also fight when they can perceive—whether accurately or not— that they will gain substantially by doing so.

One influential view, then, is that, rather than being a result of some wild, instinctive human nature, war can be the consequence of our coolest, most cerebral faculties. Individuals may fight with passion when placed in warlike situations, but throughout history, authorities have often had to resort to force to induce their supposedly vicious, hot-headed, and war-loving citizens to fight at all. Traditionally, many soldiers have been forced into battle with guns at their backs, hating and fearing their officers and military discipline more than the "enemy." There have been many more draft dodgers and deserters than people protesting on the streets that they have not been provided with sufficient opportunity to go to war.

In any event, any serious effort to prevent war—and to establish a just and lasting peace—must take into account the inclinations and behavior of individual people, especially people with wealth and power. However, the "war against war" should not limit itself to the level of individual psychology, since, as we shall soon see, the behavior of organized groups may differ significantly from that predicted by a study of personal motivation and/or biology.

Notes

1. J. William Fulbright. Preface to Jerome D. Frank. 1967. *Sanity and Survival.* New York: Random House.

2. Hans Morgenthau. 1967. *Politics Among Nations.* New York: Knopf.

3. Konrad Lorenz. 1966. *On Aggression.* New York: Harcourt, Brace & World.

4. Robert Ardrey. 1966. *The Territorial Imperative.* New York: Atheneum.

5. Edward O. Wilson. 1971. In J. Eisenberg and W. Dillon, eds., *Man and Beast: Comparative Social Behavior.* Washington, DC: Smithsonian Institution Press.

6. Edward O. Wilson. 1975. *Sociobiology: The New Synthesis.* Cambridge, MA: Harvard University Press.

7. Sigmund Freud. 1964. Reprinted in J. Strachey, ed. and trans., *The Standard Edition of the Complete Psychological Works of Sigmund Freud.* London: Hogarth.

8. Thomas Hobbes. 1930. *Selections.* F. J. E. Woodbridge, ed. New York: Scribner.

9. John Calvin. 1956. *On God and Man.* F. W. Strothmann, ed. New York: Frederick Ungar.

10. Freud, *The Standard Edition.*

11. John Milton. 1953–1982. "The Doctrine and Discipline of Divorce." In *Complete Prose Works.* New Haven, CT: Yale University Press.

12. Reinhold Niebuhr. 1940. *Christianity and Power Politics.* New York: Scribner.

13. John Dollard et al. 1939. *Frustration and Aggression.* New Haven, CT: Yale University Press.

14. Ibid.

15. John Nef. 1950. *War and Human Progress.* Cambridge, MA: Harvard University Press.

16. John Paul Scott. 1975. *Aggression.* Chicago: University of Chicago Press.

17. Mark May. 1943. *A Social Psychology of War & Peace.* New Haven, CT: Yale University Press.

18. Fyodor Dostoyevsky. 1960. *Notes From the Underground.* New York: E. P. Dutton.

19. Pierre Teilhard de Chardin. 1965. *The Making of a Mind: Letters From a Soldier-Priest, 1914–1919.* New York: Harper & Row.

20. Norman Mailer. 1968. *The Armies of the Night*. New York: New American Library.

21. J. Glen Gray. 1967. *The Warriors: Reflections on Men in Battle*. New York: Harper & Row.

22. William James. 1911. "The Moral Equivalent of War." In *Memories and Studies*. New York: Longmans, Green.

23. Z. Tamotsu. 1937. *Cultural Nippon*. Iwado, ed. and trans. Tokyo: Nippon Cultural Foundation.

24. Benito Mussolini. Quoted in Seyom Brown. 1987. *The Causes and Prevention of War*. New York: St. Martin's.

25. From A. E. Housman. 1936. *More Poems*. New York: Knopf.

26. S. L. A. Marshall. 1947. *Men Against Fire*. New York: William Morrow.

27. Gwynn Dyer. 1987. *War*. New York: Crown.

28. George Orwell. 1968. *Homage to Catalonia*. New York: Harcourt Brace Jovanovich.

29. Michael Howard. 1984. *The Causes of War*. Cambridge, MA: Harvard University Press.

6 The Group Level

Man is a social animal who dislikes his fellow man.

—Eugène Delacroix

Regardless of how important individual reasons for wars may be, war remains fundamentally a group activity. A single person may be able to incite or catalyze international or domestic conflict by his or her personal aggressiveness, as did the assassin who killed Archduke Franz Ferdinand in 1914, thereby "causing" World War I, or Adolf Hitler, who "caused" World War II in Europe. Similarly, individuals can *go to* war, by enlisting or being conscripted. But an individual, by himself or herself, cannot *make* war, which is a group endeavor. As such, war has changed dramatically in the details of its conduct, though less in the motivations for it and the functions it serves.

Let us therefore take a closer look at the early history of warfare, and then briefly review its occurrence among premodern and nontechnological peoples, not necessarily because war was responsible for shaping our nature, but rather because it has characterized much of human history and prehistory.

War: Its Prehistory and Early History

War and Human Evolution

Very little is known about the earliest human warfare. It seems likely, however, that social grouping among primitive human beings was highly adaptive, that is, it probably contributed to their cultural and biological survival. By associating with other individuals living near them, our ancestors were able to share information and resources, to gain assistance in caring for their young, and to defend themselves against predators. Presumably, social groupings also enabled prehistoric (i.e., preliterate and therefore prior to historical documentation in written records), premodern (i.e., prior to the modern era, which in the West is generally acknowledged to date from about the 17th century), and contemporary nontechnological human beings (who live mainly in the "underdeveloped" "Third World") to bring down larger prey than would have been possible for a solitary individual hunter.

Some anthropologists have suggested that the early stages of human social evolution were promoted by selection for effective hunting, which favored the ability to fashion and use tools, to walk upright (thereby freeing the hands), and to communicate effectively with one's fellow hunters. This "hunting hypothesis" has been disputed, however, by others who emphasize the importance of gathering and digging roots. While the hunting hypothesis focuses on the dominant role of men, the foraging hypothesis places more emphasis on the role of women.

The role of war in early human evolution has also been disputed. One extreme view holds that war—even prehistoric or preindustrial war—is such a recent development that it exerted essentially no influence on the human species. The other view, and one that may be equally extreme, claims that warfare was an essential component of human evolution, perhaps the major selective force operating in our early history. From this perspective, groups that were more successful in hostilities with other groups were more likely to leave offspring who themselves possessed traits leading to such success.

The widespread dispersion of early human groups probably made contact —and thus, hostility—with other groups rare. Nonetheless, significant interactions likely still took place in regions of common interest: at waterholes, in areas of local food abundance, and so on. We may never know whether early war was important in shaping human evolution; even if it was, however, it seems unlikely that this would somehow doom the human species to unending war in the future. After all, war often entails such socially desirable elements as courage, initiative, coordination, self-restraint, and self-sacrifice. A winning group would presumably be one that cooperated well. Making airborne missiles, for example, whether spears or ICBMs, is not a frenzied act of passion, but rather a labor of considered intelligence. (Launching these missiles, especially in retaliation, however, may in part involve mental processes that are more primitive.)

No clear evidence of warfare—as opposed to fighting and skirmishing between mobile bands—can be found during Paleolithic (early Stone Age) or even Mesolithic times, from 10,000 to 8000 B.C.E. At this point, hunting and gathering societies were slowly replaced by economies based on the domestication of plants and animals. War is first discernible during the early Neolithic period, which began around 8000 B.C.E. The remains of the ancient city of Jericho (dating from 7500 B.C.E.) show clear signs of fortified towers and walls, suggesting military defenses, necessitated by the accumulation of wealth via trade, which in turn created targets for aggressive raiding or war.

Why Study Premodern and Nontechnological Warfare?

Anthropologists studying modern peoples have found examples of warfare that may in some ways predate the maintenance of fixed and fortified cities for the defending of accumulated wealth. Bear in mind that the actions of certain 20th-century nontechnological people, even if "primitive" by Western standards, are not really the same as those that occurred in earlier stages of human history. Nonetheless, by examining nontechnological "war" among contemporary people (e.g., in West Irian and Sierra Leone), we may learn something about our ancestors' behavior in pre-Neolithic days. And this in turn might yield some insight into underlying tendencies among human beings more generally, including modern people today.

A study of the diversity of human war making might lead to some useful generalizations beyond the following claims, most clearly articulated by the historian Arnold Toynbee: Extremes of climate (both very hot and very cold) are less conducive to the development of large-scale war making than are temperate climates; prairie and sea-coast dwellers tend to be more war prone than mountain or forest inhabitants; pastoralists (nomads) are similarly more war prone than are settled agriculturalists. We can also go beyond the simplistic (and misleading) generalizations that human beings have always fought wars, that they have hardly ever fought wars, that they always fight wars for practical reasons, or that they never do so.

_____ Functions of Nontechnological Wars

Most analysts of war, whether of technological or nontechnological conflict, agree that warfare is, in most cases, ethically a "bad thing." But there is legitimate disagreement, among sociologists studying Western war and among anthropologists studying its nontechnological counterparts, as to whether war is adaptive or maladaptive. (A phenomenon is considered adaptive or functional if it contributes positively to the success and survival of the individual, family, group, or society, that manifests it.) Thus, advocates of the latter, *dysfunctional* perspective emphasize the disruptive and retrogressive aspects of war: how it prevents growth, development, material, and social progress, as well as the obviously negative effects of increased suffering and death. Proponents of the former viewpoint claim that preindustrial and nontechnological war can be *eufunctional*—that is, it can serve a positive role by providing social solidarity within each competing unit, by yielding access to resources (notably food, territory, and/or mates), or by enhancing the prestige of the victors.

Walter Bagehot, a noted economist, expressed the eufunctional perspective when he wrote that "civilization begins because the beginning of civilization is a military advantage." Herbert Spencer, a distinguished 19th-century proto-sociologist, also emphasized the prosocial aspects of war: "From the very beginning, the conquest of one people over another has been, in the main, the conquest of the social man over the anti-social man." This is a challenging suggestion, especially for people who think of war as the extreme in antisocial behavior.

William McDougall, an influential American psychologist of the early 20th century, expressed a view that long prevailed among social scientists, and still has many adherents today:

> When in any region social organization had progressed so far that the mortal combat of individuals was replaced by the mortal combat of tribes, villages, or groups of any kind, success in combat and survival and propagation must have been favored by, and have depended upon, not only the vigor and ferocity of individual fighters, but also, to an even greater degree, the capacity of individuals for united action, good comradeship, personal trustworthiness, and the capacity of individuals to subordinate their impulsive tendencies and egoistic promptings to the ends of the group and to the commands of an accepted leader. Hence . . . such mortal conflict of groups . . . must have developed . . . just those social and moral qualities of individuals which are the essential conditions of all effective cooperation and of the higher forms of social organizations. For success in war implies definite organization, the recognition of a leader, and faithful observance of his commands, and the obedience given to the war chief implies a far higher level of morality than is implied by the mere observance of the primal law . . . those communities in which this higher morality was developed would triumph over and exterminate those which had not attained it in equal degree. And the more the pugnacious instinct impelled primitive societies to warfare, the more rapidly and effectively must the fundamental social attributes of men have been developed in the societies which survived the ordeal.[1]

This passage has been reproduced at length because it reflects an important bias among some students of peace and war, namely, that war contributes to humanity's "higher morality."

War is not a simple or unitary phenomenon among modern nation-states; neither is it readily explained among nontechnological peoples. The following functions of premodern war have been suggested:

1. Provide outlets for aggressiveness of young men, and thus reduce within-society tensions.

2. Provide opportunities for social advancement via enhancement of prestige.

3. Gain access to food resources, notably animal protein.

4. Obtain women from neighboring groups.

5. Obtain land from neighboring groups.

6. Correct imbalance in the sex ratio—in certain societies, female infanticide creates an excess of males, which can be corrected by mortality during war.

7. Achieve revenge, which often carries both symbolic and social payoffs.

8. Provide the opportunity for enlargement of tribal domain and (rarely) for certain individuals to establish large kingdoms or empires.

At its simplest level, nontechnological war appears to be largely concerned with interpersonal competition and struggles to obtain individual prestige, rather than with large-scale conflicts between social groups or even with the accumulation of land, women, or other resources. Thus, in premodern war, the involvement and motivation tend to be at the personal level, as compared with its modern counterpart, which is mainly directed toward conquest or the advancement of state interests. In modern technological warfare, personal involvement and motivation tend to be relatively less intense because the benefits to be derived are more diffuse, often ideological rather than practical and immediate. It should be noted, however, that anthropologists are divided over the degree to which ecological forces are responsible for human war, and if so, which forces might predominate. Despite their frequent disagreements, however, most anthropologists, like most sociologists, are united in rejecting the prospect that premodern war is a genetically driven need:

> The possibility of armed conflict has been embedded in the social and cultural experience of humankind at least since the palaeolithic era, when the spear and spear-thrower were developed, presumably for the purposes of hunting game. What does this mean for the future? It certainly does not mean that human societies are in some sense "programmed" for war, nor . . . that the history of human progress tells Hobbes' grim story after all. We do know that war is an aspect of many cultural ideologies, but we also know that ideologies—that is, people's statements about their beliefs—are flexible idioms that express selectively the cultural propositions that are capable of life in

human minds. This is cause for hope, since cultural analysis suggests that the causes of war lie not in the land, nor in some implacable demand for blood or honour, nor in human genes, but in imaginations that tolerate both the image and the reality of wholesale violence, at least for the moment.[2]

Characteristics of Premodern and Nontechnological Wars

The renowned anthropologist Bronislaw Malinowski identified six categories of armed aggressive behavior among nontechnological peoples:

1. "Fighting, private and angry," which serves as the prototype of criminal behavior

2. "Fighting, collective and organized," among groups within the same cultural unit

3. "Armed raids, as a type of man-hunting sport, for purposes of head-hunting, cannibalism, human sacrifices, and the collection of other trophies"

4. "Warfare as the political expression of early nationalism, that is, the tendency to make the tribe-nation and tribe-state coincide"

5. "Military expeditions of organized pillage, slave-raiding and collective robbery"

6. "Wars between two culturally differentiated groups as an instrument of national policy."[3]

Premodern war can be understood not only by examining the kinds of activities involved in Malinowski's list but also by considering its functions. "Among almost all American Indians," according to one authority, ". . . war existed to bring glory to the individual, and since war was relatively safe, everyone was happy even though few tactical, strategic and economic advantages for a whole people were obtained."[4]

Even the causing of death or injury was not always a goal for premodern warriors, and mortality appears generally to have been low; premodern and nontechnological "wars" often end after a single death or even a serious injury. The Dani people of New Guinea, for instance, traditionally do not use feathers on their war arrows, thereby reducing accuracy and keeping casualties down. And the Ibo of Nigeria used to count up their dead after a war, after which the side losing fewer warriors would compensate the "losers" with money, to avoid any grudges.

Among the American Plains Indians, the tribe was represented by a peace chief; the war chief, by contrast, served only during an actual campaign.

And even then, among many of the Plains tribes, a more glorious deed than killing one's enemies was to "count coup," or touch an adversary, either with one's hand or a special, ritualized stick, thereby humiliating the opponent and bringing great credit to the successful warrior. Self-renown, rather than death to one's enemies, was widely considered the highest goal. (The "war hero" is valued among technological peoples as well. The difference between premodern and modern peoples in this regard is that personal aggrandizement—for wealth and/or glory—is not supposed to be the most important reason for engaging in contemporary warfare; rather, the individual combatant is ostensibly acting as a defender of public security, national honor, and/or human rights.)

Trophy taking was, and still is, widespread in premodern war: heads among the New Guinea highlanders, scalps in the more aggressive Indian conflicts (especially with white invaders), foreskins among the ancient Israelites. Vestiges of this custom can be seen in modern times, in notches on guns in the Wild West, or "kills" painted on the fuselage of a fighter plane. However, the indiscriminate killing of old people, women, and children is rare in premodern cultures, even in the most heated of wars; the ancient Israelites and Mongols of the Middle Ages were exceptions. Even the notoriously "fierce" Yanomamo of the Amazon and warriors of the New Guinea highlands usually exempt women and children from hostilities, as well as anyone who has a personal relationship with a would-be attacker.

Premodern war has typically been bounded by numerous rules, which are specific to different tribes. For example, the Nuer of Sudan are forbidden to use spears against anyone living within a given proximity; beyond that distance, such lethal weapons are allowed. Among the Dani, truces automatically occur at nightfall, although the battle is considered unfinished until at least one person is killed on either side.

Among the most widespread customs associated with premodern warfare are those involving the extensive use of rituals to signal the initiation of warfare, as well as the change of one's status from civilian to warrior. Magic amulets are common, as well as special ways of shaving and adorning the body, typically with paints and/or feathers. Such techniques ostensibly help ward off evil and bad luck, but their more practical function appears to be the promotion of group solidarity. This includes modern-day uniforms and "totemic" symbols such as insignias, regimental banners, and national flags. Ritual abstinence, notably from food or sex, apparently helps relieve the guilt of killing while also signifying that one is clean, special, different, and thus permitted to do certain things that would be forbidden during peacetime. Repetitive dancing and singing, often with the use of drugs, have been characteristic of warfare among people in Asia, Africa, Polynesia, and certain American Indian tribes; this apparently reduces fear and helps cement commitment among members of a war party. Rehearsals of battle serve to diminish anxiety and also provide practice for warriors going into combat.

Typically, elaborate rituals are also performed after a battle, especially if the warrior has actually killed somebody. The great majority of societies consider that anyone who kills—even in war—is somehow "unclean" and must be ritually purified before being readmitted into civilian life: Fasting or abstinence are common, often with varying periods of isolation from the home group. In modern societies, returning soldiers are often accorded medals, parades, membership in special veterans' organizations, and their own cemeteries.

Patterns in Premodern and Nontechnological Wars _____

Although every episode of war—just like every human society—is to some extent unique, there are widespread patterns of warfare among nontechnological and premodern peoples, including the following:

1. *Social control.* In systems where formal machinery for resolving conflict is absent or weak, and no legal means exist for enforcing conformity, war serves as a method of social control. Thus, social unity within each band is enhanced.

2. *Limited destruction.* Resort to stylized symbols and agreements serve to limit the destructiveness of the conflict, maintaining a rough balance between the adversaries, who will, after all, continue to be neighbors. There is no direct parallel to the "total wars" of modern Western society.

3. *Internal logic.* Although the justification for the attack may seem irrational to the modern Westerner, it is consistent within a certain kind of cause-and-effect reference system, and it is not necessarily any less instrumentally rational than wars fought to determine the dynastic succession of an obscure line of royalty or trading rights that will influence only a tiny minority of the population on either side.

4. *Bargaining.* The process of bargaining is readily understandable cross-culturally, as well as the sly way the elders of an attacked tribe turned a potential disaster to their own benefit, which occurs, for example, among the Arunta in central Australia.

5. *Limited goals.* Premodern wars have usually been fought for limited goals, and in a limited way. Warfare among nontechnological peoples is typically of this sort—over revenge, women, animal protein, prestige, or occasionally, access to physical space for hunting, farming, or living. Only rarely does lethal group conflict erupt due to contesting ideologies. In fact, neighboring groups, usually the opponents in nontechnological wars, typically share the same culture, language, and worldview.

As an example of pretechnological warriors, consider the Yanomamo of the Brazilian and Venezuelan Amazon basin. They call themselves the "fierce people," and members of one village (perhaps 50–250 people) spend much time and energy making war on their neighbors. Most wars apparently take place over women, although Yanomamo men are highly pugnacious within their own villages as well; social interactions involve a large amount of bluff and bluster, and disputes (which break out frequently) are often settled by chest-pounding duels or club-fights in which the contestants take turns smashing each other over the head. The ultimate test of pugnacity and effectiveness, however, occurs during surprise raids on neighboring villages.

Blood revenge appears to be an important reason for war among the Yanomamo. Thus, of all males 25 years of age or older, 44% have participated in the killing of someone, and 30% of all adult male deaths are due to such violence. In the aftermath of a killing, the victimized group—and especially the relatives of the victim—feel obligated to retaliate against the killers, or at least against the village or relatives of the killers. This in turn promotes a never-ending cycle of retaliation; nearly 70% of all adults over 40 years of age have lost a close relative due to violence, and they generally feel obliged to retaliate in kind. Once caught in a cycle of quid pro quo of this sort, it is difficult to be extricated. Failure to respond, for example, invites additional attacks because the group is then seen as weak and vulnerable to further aggression. Moreover, participating in the system of blood feuds may provide reproductive benefits for those who survive: At least among the Yanomamo, men who have killed have more wives and more offspring than men who have not.

Alternatives to Nontechnological Warfare

There are a variety of seemingly peaceful societies, defined variously as (1) not having wars fought on their soil, (2) not fighting wars with other groups, or (3) not experiencing any civil wars or internal collective violence. (Interestingly, the frequency of external war has very little correlation with that of internal war.) Some examples of the most peaceable include the Semoi of Malaysia, the Siriono of Bolivia, the Mbuti pygmies of central Africa, the !Kung bushmen of the African Kalahari Desert, and the Copper Eskimos of northern Canada.

It is increasingly recognized that certain nontechnological people are notable not so much for their lack of aggression as for their effective and nonviolent way of coping with it. For example, the Eskimos of central Greenland slap each other's faces; in western and eastern Greenland, they engage in prolonged singing duels, with individuals competing to be more imaginative and to engage their audience more effectively. Many inhabitants of Alaska, Siberia, and Baffin Island have traditionally settled their disputes by wrestling. The Kwakiutl Indians of the northwest coast of North America have competed via potlatch feasts, in which chiefs sought to outdo each other by demonstrating how much wealth they could sacrifice. And the African Bushmen (!Kung) and pygmies use laughter and ridicule, rarely resorting to outright violence.

In other stateless human societies, war is either absent or quite rare. Among those factors that help prevent the outbreak of organized civil violence, the following appear to be especially important (although not all are present at the same time): (1) socialization toward the peaceful settling of conflicts and the disapproval of the use of violence or force, (2) the presence of a group or tribal decision-making system that is capable of applying effective sanctions against violent transgressors, (3) the opportunity for dissidents to emigrate to other groups, and (4) the existence of economic interdependence within the group.

As to the maintenance of peace between groups, several factors can be identified, although the enormous diversity of human cultures makes any generalizations hazardous. The perception of shared ancestry between different groups tends to inhibit violence between them, just as an emphasis on relatedness within a group (motherland, fatherland, "brothers and sisters," etc.) tends to foster greater internal group solidarity combined with an increased willingness to close ranks against other groups perceived as unrelated, foreign, and thus, enemies. Similarly, peaceful relations among groups are often enhanced by establishing kinship ties through marriage. For example, among the Mundurucu of Brazil, men reckon their kinship through the male descent line (*patrilineal*), but after marriage, husbands live in their wives' home community (*matrilocal*); as a result, attacks on different villages might require that men take up arms against their relatives. (The ancient Indian epic the *Bhagavad Gita* revolves around the internal conflict of a noble warrior, Arjuna, who is forced to make war on his relatives.)

According to the structuralist school of anthropology (whose most noted representative was the French anthropologist Claude Lévi-Strauss), a primary reason for the incest taboo is that by marrying outside the family, people establish cooperative relationships with other groups, thereby minimizing the likelihood of destructive warfare between these groups. The phenomenon of establishing politically useful alliances via marriages has a long history in the West as well, at least at the level of ruling houses among the European monarchies.

Underlying Group Processes

Human beings are highly social creatures. One of the most powerful human tendencies is to aggregate into groups, and somehow to distinguish the members of each group from other, comparable groups. This is typically achieved by shared language, customs, patterns of adornment, mythological and religious beliefs and practices, and so forth. Others who speak different languages (or even the same language, but with a different accent), who worship different gods, or who follow a different political or economic system are readily identified as different, and often perceived as threatening as well. Sigmund Freud once wrote of the "narcissism of minor differences," whereby many people tend to focus on, and exaggerate, relatively inconsequential cultural traits that distinguish themselves from their neighbors.

Benefits

Clearly, group life has important and empowering components, including the ability to pool resources, to cooperate, to achieve a division of labor, to learn and to teach, and simply to receive stimulation from the presence of one's fellows. As William James once wrote, "All the qualities of a man acquire dignity when he knows that the service of the collectivity that owns him need them. If proud of the collectivity, his own pride rises in proportion."[5] There is a powerful allure to being needed and appreciated, and a strong tendency to associate oneself with a larger whole, thereby enhancing one's self-esteem and self-worth.

Costs

But there are also disadvantages. Of these, one of the most significant is the loss of inhibitions than can result from immersion in a crowd, as a result of which a *mob psychology* can take over, through which individuals can engage in acts that would rarely if ever be done if they were acting alone. It can be debated whether war-making groups literally produce a new kind of entity, a social one having its own tendencies and characteristics, or whether groups simply give social sanction to individual tendencies, notably, aggressiveness, intolerance, and rage. Freud once commented that he could shame a single Nazi storm trooper, sent to search his apartment in Vienna, but when two were sent together, they became "good Nazis."

De-individuating

The process of *de-individuating* seems to involve three major components:

1. *The effect of validation by one's peers.* Members of homogeneous groups are more likely to respond to conflictual situations with hostility than are groups whose membership is more heterogeneous. Individual aggressiveness, when validated by the expressed aggressiveness of others, is

more likely to be released. The most strike-prone industries, to take another example, are those whose workers are isolated from the rest of the community and are drawn from ethnically similar backgrounds. One of the most important innovators in military science was the Dutch general Maurice of Nassau, Prince of Orange (1567–1625), who was the originator of close-order drill. According to a renowned historian, this innovation not only permitted closely coordinated maneuvers by large numbers of people, it also introduced an important psychological and sociological dimension, which largely explains why modern armed forces still use these techniques in basic training, more than 400 years later:

> When a group of men move their arm and leg muscles in unison for prolonged periods of time, a primitive and very powerful social bond wells up among them. This probably results from the fact that movement of the big muscles in unison rouses echoes of the most primitive level of sociality known to humankind. . . . Military drill, as developed by Maurice of Nassau and thousands of European drill-masters after him, tapped this primitive reservoir of sociality directly. Drill, dull and repetitious though it may seem, readily welded a miscellaneous collection of men, recruited often from the dregs of civil society, into a coherent community, obedient to orders even in extreme situations when life and limb were in obvious and immediate jeopardy.[6]

2. *Diminished individual profile.* Biologists have identified something known as the "selfish herd" phenomenon, whereby animals as diverse as fish or starlings appear to flock together because, by doing so, each individual increases the chances that its neighbor—rather than itself—will fall victim to an approaching predator. Animals in groups are also able to accomplish things, such as killing a prey animal or driving off a would-be predator, that could not be done by a solitary individual. Similarly, a human crowd seems to provide not only a feeling (as well as the reality) of strength in numbers but also a shield of protective anonymity. In addition, groups are usually associated with highly visible and persuasive leaders, who may provide impetus for group hostility by actively fomenting as well as directing violence that might not otherwise occur if individuals were left to their personal inclinations. And finally, the simple presence of leaders also tends to suggest to the group members that the leaders, rather than the followers, are likely to be at risk for retaliation, which in turn diminishes reluctance of the followers to participate.

3. *Contagious or imitative behavior.* A frustrated or angry person is much more likely to behave aggressively if he or she experiences others as doing so. This may involve not only "getting the idea" of violence but also gaining

a kind of social "permission" to behave in this way. Thus, it is well-known that violence (or, to put a more favorable cast upon it, resistance to oppression) tends to spread when others witness or hear about the events. A few examples of this include the French Revolution of 1789, the Luddite uprising in early 19th-century Britain, the U.S. ghetto uprisings of the late 1960s, and the Polish "Solidarity" strikes and Palestinian insurrections of the 1980s.

Dehumanization

Another prominent and troublesome characteristic of group functioning is the tendency to *dehumanize* members of other groups, that is, to give the impression—to compatriots, and at least on a subconscious level, to oneself —that the others are not really (or fully) human at all. Such dehumanizaton is especially easy to apply to those who are recognizably different because of language, appearance, cultural practices, religion, political ideology, and so on. Among various nontechnological peoples, even the word *human* is the same as the name for the tribe; members of different tribes are thus denied their humanity, as a result of which they can be killed with little or no remorse. Among modern technological peoples, language patterns during times of hostility reflect this tendency, especially with the use of animal terms to describe the opponent: vermin, insects, rats, pigs, dogs, and so forth. Even nonanimal slang terms have a similar effect: wogs, slants, kikes, niggers, krauts, honkies, reds, and so on.

The following news item appeared in the *San Francisco Bulletin* during the 1860s. It is a telling example of dehumanization in action:

> Some citizens of this city, while hunting in Marin County yesterday, came upon a large group of miserable Digger Indians. They managed to dispatch 30 of the creatures before the others ran away.[7]

This encounter—which apparently was a frightful massacre—is reported matter-of-factly, even proudly. It is noteworthy that the perpetrators were "citizens," not even duly constituted military authorities, and no question whatever was raised about the propriety of their acts, or the humanity of their victims. Furthermore, the language employed—"miserable" (implying lowly, not unhappy), "dispatch," and "creatures"—suggests that in killing them, the San Francisco citizens had performed a civic duty; certainly, they had not really slaughtered 30 innocent and defenseless people!

Group associations may also contribute to war by engaging people in a cumulative process by which the hostility of a few serves essentially to contaminate most, if not all, others. One writer poses the question as follows: "Imagine a group of tribes living within reach of one another. If all choose the way of peace, then all may live in peace. But what if all but one choose peace?"[8]

The problem could be that, like the proverbial rotten apple, a single highly aggressive tribe would either dominate its less aggressive neighbors, or it would catalyze a conversion to aggressiveness by any of the others. Such a transition could also occur, of course, as a result of a single aggressive individual, and indeed, perhaps that is part of the reason for aggressiveness on the part of social groups. It remains to be seen, however, whether the means of control would also be comparable.

A Final Note on Premodern and Nontechnological Warfare

We may never fully know the earliest history of human warfare, nor do we know whether premodern warfare among contemporary nontechnological, stateless societies casts much light on the evolution of human warfare generally. In addition to its intrinsic interest, however, premodern warfare undoubtedly illuminates at least some facets of modern, contemporary war that might otherwise be obscured by the complexity of modern social life and by our own involvement in current affairs. Moreover, certain fundamental underlying principles of individual motivation, group association, and intergroup aggression appear to be prefigured in an examination of nontechnological war.

Preindustrial, nontechnological war warrants attention, both for its own sake and for what light it may shed on wider (and possibly deeper) human patterns. The fact remains, nonetheless, that the fundamental issues of peace and war in the modern world are played out in a different arena, that of larger groups, often functioning at the level of nations.

Nations, States, Ethnic Groups, and Nationalism

Nations and States

In a sense, nations are ethnic groups writ large. Just as tribal or ethnic groups are composed of individuals sharing a strong sense of similarity and social identity, nations are similarly united, only the populations are much larger and, typically, more complex internally. *Ethnic* comes from the ancient Greek word *ethnos*, meaning a race, tribe, or group of people; the term *nation*, on the other hand, derives from the Latin *natio*, referring to birth (as in prenatal, or native). Although the word *nation* is often used loosely to indicate a state—that is, a political and geographic entity—in fact the term refers more precisely to a large group of people, ideally united by a common language, origin, history, religion, and culture. No formal process exists for identifying nations; rather, a nation exists when a group considers itself to be a nation and is recognized as such by already existing nations.

A *state*, by contrast, is a political unit, an area of land whose people are governed independent of other, comparable states. A nation-state exists if a nation and a state have the same geographic boundaries. For example, for a brief period after World War I, Lithuanians, Latvians, and Estonians each constituted separate nation-states, the Baltic states of Lithuania, Latvia, and Estonia. Then they were incorporated into a larger state, the former USSR, from which they gained eventually independence as the Soviet Union broke up. Russia today, like the former Soviet Union, on the other hand, is a large state, but not a single nation; rather, it is composed of many nationalities, including not only ethnic Russians but also Tatars, Mari, and many other ethnic groups.

Nationalism

The phenomenon of *nationalism* is one of the most powerful forces of modern times. It refers to the yearnings of a people to constitute themselves as part of a nation, typically to form a nation-state, and often to adjust geographic boundaries so as to increase the size of their domain, to incorporate others who share the same sense of national identity, and frequently to establish their nation as significant, if not preeminent. According to one definition, nationalism is "a people's sense of collective destiny through a common past and the vision of a common future."[9]

This hints at an important component of nationalism, namely, the emotional appeal of belonging, of shared deeds, and of extending the boundaries of one's self to comprise a larger and seemingly more glorious whole. In the words of 19th-century French philosopher and historian J. Ernest Renan, "What constitutes a nation is not speaking the same tongue or belonging to the same ethnic group, but having accomplished great things in common in the past and the wish to accomplish them in the future." In perhaps the most famous definition of this phenomenon, Renan also suggested that nationalism is

> a grand solidarity constituted by the sentiment of sacrifices which one has made and those that time is disposed to make again. It supposes a past, it renews itself especially in the present by a tangible deed: the approval, the desire, clearly expressed to continue the communal life. The existence of a nation is an everyday plebiscite.[10]

Increasingly, however, the sense of national identity has moved beyond the standard textbook definition, which emphasizes cultural unity. To a great extent, large nation-states are not so much natural social constructs as arbitrary groupings of people, cobbled together for political and economic purposes. The result has been a strong tendency to confer unity by establishing national symbols shared by many persons, regardless of their ethnic identity, thereby conferring unity. National flags, heroes, myths, and anthems —all have a remarkable hold over most people, and virtually all nations seek to inculcate recognition and respect for such symbols, typically requiring oaths, pledges, or other specific acts of allegiance.

During times of perceived stress—especially if the stress comes from an external threat—nationalist sentiments are likely to become particularly intense. Often the threat serves to enhance pronational emotions that may previously have been ebbing. The German invasion of the USSR, for example, enabled Stalin to build on a "war nationalism" that overcame much disaffection with his purges and heavy-handed dictatorship. (At the same time, some nationalists—notably in the Baltic states and Ukraine—attempted in the early phases of World War II to ally themselves with Nazi Germany, hoping to fulfill their own nationalist aspirations of separating from the Soviet Union.) The Japanese attack on China also evoked solidarity born of war nationalism, causing the government of Chiang Kai-shek and the revolutionary forces of Mao Tse-tung to make common cause, in the interest of Chinese national survival, against the invaders. Even long after national struggles have ceased, the existence of martyrs and of regular days for remembrance also serve to whip up nationalist sentiment and keep it fresh.

Nationalism can, in theory, be limited to love for one's nation; in practice, however, it is often combined with antagonism toward other nations. "By nationalism," wrote George Orwell,

> I mean first of all the habit of assuming that human beings can be classified like insects and that whole blocks of millions or tens of millions of people can be confidently labelled "good" or "bad." but secondly—and this is much more important—I mean the habit of identifying oneself with a single nation or other unit, placing it beyond good or evil and recognizing no other duty than that of advancing its own interests.[11]

This occurs, in part, because the nation provides a way of submerging the comparatively small, vulnerable individual self into a much larger, more powerful other. As theologian H. Richard Niebuhr describes the ardent nationalist,

> The national life is for him the reality whence his own life derives its worth. He relies on the nation as a source of his own value. He trusts it; first, perhaps, in the sense of looking constantly to it as the enduring reality out of which he has issued, into whose ongoing cultural life

his own actions and being will merge. His life has meaning because it is part of that context, like a word in a sentence. It has value because it fits into a valuable whole.[12]

Unfortunately, the tendency to identify one's group, tribe, or "own people" as a "valuable whole" carries along with it another tendency—nearly as strong—to devalue other, similar groups, or worse yet, to see them as threatening to oneself, one's group, and thus, one's fundamental values. Therefore, the "Others" become suitable targets for competition, conflict, and often violence.

The History of Nationalist Wars

Early-Modern European Nationalism

The sense of nationhood, as opposed to ethnic group or tribal affiliation, is relatively recent. During the Middle Ages, for example, individuals typically felt that they belonged to a city, or to a local reigning monarch. Thus, the loyalty of someone whom we now identify as "French" might have included local affiliation to family and village, and personal fealty to the duke of Lyons, the king of France, the Holy Roman Emperor, and the pope, but not to "France" as such.

European nation-states began to develop during the late Middle Ages. After the Treaty of Westphalia (1648), which ended the Thirty Years' War, and with improved travel and communication, peoples became increasingly aware of the existence of other peoples who were similar to themselves, as well as of others, generally farther away, who were quite different. Moreover, centralized authorities—abetted by gunpowder—were able to demolish the castles of local rulers and enforce a broader allegiance: to kings, whose domains also tended to include greater numbers of similar people. At the same time, loyalty to local rulers and religious leaders tended to diminish. Spain, Portugal, France, and England were nation-states by the 16th century; later, the phenomenon of nationalism, particularly in central Europe, received an enormous boost, largely in reaction to revolutionary and Napoleonic France.

In the course of its revolution in the late 18th century, France developed the first truly national anthem, "La Marseillaise," and substituted adherence to the nation for fealty to a monarch. In addition, Napoleonic conquests of other nations helped generate strong feelings of national pride on the part of those who had been invaded. Nationalistic sentiments were widespread by the early 19th century, largely coalescing around the doctrine of national self-determination, the belief that each national group had the right to form its own state. Under this impetus, Greece won its independence from Turkey in 1829, and Belgium was declared independent from the Netherlands in 1830. (The Dutch republic had achieved its own national self-determination several centuries earlier, from the Spanish empire, after a protracted and bloody conflict; the Dutch revolt was the first modern successful war of national liberation.)

Nationalism in the United States

Within the United States, the Revolutionary War was largely a war of independence rather than of nationalism. Nonetheless, nationalism later expressed itself through the doctrine of *manifest destiny*, which claimed that it was "manifestly" the "destiny" of the American people to expand across all of North America. Moreover, dreams of a major worldwide role for the United States led to other militaristic adventures, including the War of 1812. Senator Henry Clay of Kentucky, leader of an ultranationalist group known as the Warhawks, expressed both local pride and nationalist fervor when he proclaimed,

> It is said that no object is attainable by war with Great Britain. . . . I say that the conquest of Canada is in your power. I trust that I shall not be deemed presumptuous when I state that I verily believe that the militia of Kentucky are alone competent to place Montreal and all of Upper Canada at your feet.[13]

The resulting war was one of the smallest in U.S. history—1,877 Americans killed, 9,700 taken prisoner, and a cost of $200 million, including the burning of Washington, D.C., by the British. And no territory was gained. Nonetheless, U.S. nationalist sentiment contributed to such expansionist adventures as the Mexican-American War and the Spanish-American War, as well as to a growing series of armed interventions, notably in Latin America and the Far East.

European Nationalism in the 19th and 20th Centuries

By the late 19th century, European nationalism had become especially pronounced in Germany and Italy, each of which had been divided into numerous mini-states and principalities. Italian unification was finally achieved in 1870, after a militant struggle primarily against the Austrian empire (itself a state composed of many nations). Meanwhile, formal unification of such German mini-states as Saxony, Hanover, and Silesia was completed in 1871, with Prussia the undisputed leader of the new German nation-state. German unification was achieved by the Prussian leader Otto von Bismarck, who successfully engineered a series of wars, first against Denmark, then Austria, and culminating in the Franco-Prussian war.

Whereas Western European nationalism primarily involved the amalgamation of previously disunited regions and states, nationalism in Eastern Europe took a somewhat different form, ultimately resulting in the carving out of nation-states from the large, heterogeneous Ottoman (Turkish), Austro-Hungarian, and Russian empires. Nationalistic demands, especially on the part of the newly created Balkan states—and the tensions they provoked, especially within the Austro-Hungarian empire—played a major role in initiating World War I.

The Austrian leadership of that empire, for example, was desperately worried that it would not be able to hold together its rickety, heterogeneous assemblage of restive nations, consisting of Hungarians, Serbs, Croats, Montenegrins, Slovenes, and so on. Following the assassination in 1914 of the Austrian Archduke Franz Ferdinand by a Serbian extremist, the Austrians feared that Serbian nationalism was about to unleash nationalist demands that would ultimately result in the disintegration of the Austrian empire. And so it was decided to "punish" the Serbs. Russia stood by tiny Serbia, in a show of national solidarity (as it did during NATO's [North Atlantic Treaty Organization] bombing of Serbia in 1999; Serbs, like Russians, are ethnically Slavic). Germany, in turn, stood by Austria, which was its ally. France was already allied to Russia and was independently hungering to regain the provinces of Alsace and Lorraine, lost to Germany 40 years before, in the Franco-Prussian War. Furthermore, the war plans of Germany demanded an invasion of neutral Belgium, which in turn brought Great Britain into the war. National passions, fears, demands, and misunderstandings resulted in the first great 20th-century war.

Following World War I (or as it was called at the time, the Great War), numerous nations were not granted self-determination. The state of Yugoslavia, for example, was a patchwork quilt of seven "national republics"—consisting of Serbs, Croats, Bosnians, Macedonians, Slovenians, Montenegrins, and Albanians—all of whom consider themselves nations. These groups were held together, at least in part, by a powerful leader, Marshal Tito, a renowned anti-Nazi partisan during World War II. Following Tito's death, nationalist unrest commenced in Yugoslavia during 1988–1989, culminating in the relatively nonviolent secession of Slovenia and Macedonia, the moderately violent withdrawal of Croatia, and the extremely violent wars in Bosnia and Kosovo. As a general principle, the national aspirations of defeated people are often trampled on by the victors.

Nonetheless, nationalist sentiments can be extraordinarily resilient and persistent. For example, Poles retained their national identity for decades when "Poland" didn't exist (it was gobbled up in the late 18th century by Germany, Russia, and Austria). Citizens of Venice considered themselves Italians even while part of Austria, French-speaking residents of Quebec have resisted Anglicization of their culture by the rest of English-speaking Canada, most Basques consider themselves Basques rather than Spaniards, and so forth. (To be sure, there have been some examples of *assimilation*, in which isolated national groups lose their identity in favor of a larger group in which they are embedded. Most American Indians and Hawaiians, for example, despite awareness of their non-U.S. ethnic heritage, typically think of themselves as Americans.) Intrastate nationalist movements have generally resisted the efforts—even the violent efforts—of state governments to deprive them of their identity.

National Liberation and Revolutionary Nationalism

By the 19th century, the colonizing activities of the European powers had created a situation in which large segments of the globe were under military domination by people who had little similarity to, or cultural affinity for, the much larger number of "natives" being subjugated. Wars of national liberation were notably successful in Latin America during the 1800s, as the Spanish empire crumbled in the south, and the brief French ascendancy in Mexico was also ended. Revolutionary nationalism during the 19th century was less successful, however, in Africa and Asia: The Zulus were eventually crushed by the British in South Africa, for example, and despite bloody uprisings (of which the so-called Sepoy Mutiny, 1857–1859, is best known), Britain maintained control over India as well as Egypt and, indeed, over a large proportion of the inhabited planet. Although China was not directly occupied by imperialist powers, except for Hong Kong and Macao (both of which were returned to the motherland at the end of the 20th century), the weak and decentralized Chinese government was regularly humiliated and forced to submit to economic ravishment, including the forced "opening" of the country to opium trading. The resulting Opium Wars caused yet more resentment, adding to the growing urgency of Chinese nationalism, as did the Boxer Rebellion and the ill-fated Tai-ping Rebellion, from 1850–1864. (This latter struggle, little known in the West, resulted in an estimated 20 million fatalities.)

In the aftermath of the two world wars of the 20th century, revolutionary nationalism and counterrevolutionary and antimodern ethnocentrism have essentially triumphed throughout much of the "postmodern" world. In some cases this has occurred through protracted conventional war, in others by guerrilla operations, and in yet others by peaceful transitions, whereby the occupying colonial power granted independence, albeit grudgingly. Colonial holdings were not typically bounded in ways that were naturally (i.e., nationally) meaningful. As a result, many of the newly independent former colonies, especially those established since the end of World War II, have had to cope with substantial national and ethnic divisions of their own, many of which have led to war.

Types of Nationalist Wars

National Independence

National independence need not always be preceded by war. Burma, Malaysia, the Slovak Republic, Ukraine, the Baltic States, and Slovenia, for example, achieved statehood and self-determination with relatively little bloodshed. On the other hand, warfare is a frequent prelude to national independence, as witnessed by the birth of the United States. Indonesia fought for four years to gain independence from Holland (and East Timor fought Indonesia for its autonomy). Algeria became separate from France only after eight years of fighting, which cost 250,000 Algerian and French lives.

National Prestige

Many of the classic interstate wars of modern history have been stimulated by issues of national prestige. Enthusiasm within the United States for the Spanish-American War (1898) was generated by American desires to enter the arena of worldwide colonial acquisitions. The government of Spain, for its part, appears to have fought back largely because it would have been embarrassing to give up without doing so. Similarly, the aggressive appetite of both Germany and Japan in the 20th century was whetted by a pervasive sense that these great nations had not achieved world status commensurate with their economic or technological accomplishments, or their self-proclaimed racial superiority.

India has long taken the lead in condemning worldwide militarism in general, and the nuclear arms race in particular. But when Prime Minister Rajiv Gandhi announced in February 1988 that his country had successfully developed and tested a surface-to-surface liquid-fueled missile—entirely with Indian technology—he received a standing ovation in the Indian Parliament. And a decade later, India publicly exploded nuclear devices, supposedly in response to the nuclear threat posed to it by Pakistan. Of course, Pakistan claimed it had tested and developed its nuclear arsenal in response to the alleged threat to its national identity posed by a nuclear-armed India—and so it goes.

Pride and prestige, sometimes on a personal level as well, became a major factor in causing the United States to pursue its war in Vietnam. President Johnson persevered in that war in large part because of his private determination not to be "the first U.S. president to lose a war," and for President Nixon, the worst outcome for the United States in that conflict was "humiliation." "If, when the chips are down," he announced,

the world's most powerful nation, the United States of America, acts like a pitiful, helpless giant, the forces of totalitarianism and anarchy will threaten free nations and free institutions throughout the world. It is not our power but our will and character that is being tested.[14]

Frustration among American ruling elites was particularly acute during the period from late 1979 to early 1981, when revolutionary Iranians held the staff of the U.S. embassy captive. The resulting sense of national humiliation contributed greatly to the election of Ronald Reagan, and to the military buildup that followed. Similarly, the U.S. invasion of Grenada served partly to assuage the emotional pain of a devastating car bomb attack on the temporary U.S. Marine barracks in Beirut, Lebanon, just a few days before. U.S. bombers attacked Tripoli, Libya, in retaliation for acts of terrorism allegedly committed by Libyan nationals. And the United States sank Iranian naval vessels in the Persian Gulf. These actions provided an outlet for frustration and an opportunity to redeem a sense of diminished national pride. At the same time, what serves to redeem the pride of one nation typically diminishes that of another, leading in turn to a felt need for revenge, which creates yet more need to assuage the reinjured pride, and so on.

The United States is not necessarily any more vulnerable than other countries to perceived stains on its national honor, and it does not appear to be unusually likely to respond violently to affronts. On the other hand, being a superpower means that the United States possesses great military force (notably, nuclear weapons) that it is generally disinclined to use (although it is much less reticent about threatening and planning their use). And yet the impact of possessing these weapons depends largely on the perception that, if need be, they might be employed. Hence, a superpower attaches great importance to issues of national "credibility," seeing large consequences to what might otherwise be considered minor tests of will.

The maintenance of national prestige and the avoidance of humiliation loom large in the calculation of every state. For example, Arab pride has been sorely wounded by Israel's string of military victories; the October War of 1973, although technically yet another Arab defeat, came close enough to victory to demolish the myth of Israeli invincibility, and sufficiently restored Egyptian self-respect and prestige that President Anwar Sadat felt empowered to make his stunning trip to Jerusalem in 1977, to conclude the Camp David accords in 1978, and to sign an Egyptian-Israeli peace treaty (the first one between Israel and an Arab state) in 1979. Immediately after NATO's air war over Serbia and Kosovo—which Russia had opposed—Russian military units used a ruse to secure the airport in Pristina (Kosovo's capital), thereby attempting to assert Russian national pride in the face of NATO's overwhelming military might.

Secessionism

Sentiments of national unity are often associated with yearnings of a group of people to secede from a larger collectivity of which they do not feel a part. In 1967, for example, about 50,000 Ibos, who had migrated to northern Nigeria, were slaughtered by the more numerous Hausas, who resented Ibo economic success. Another one million Ibos were driven out of the north, after which the Ibo "nation" sought to secede and form its own nation-state of Biafra. The result was a civil war in which many hundreds of thousands died and many more suffered severe malnutrition and starvation. The war ended, unsuccessfully for the would-be secessionists, in 1970. Secessionism is a major factor in armed violence today, which has been particularly intense in the armed struggles by Kosovars and Chechens to secede from Yugoslavia and Russia, respectively.

Reintegrationism

People in a region occasionally seek to become associated with a homeland in which their nationality is represented. The Greco-Turkish hostilities over Cyprus were sparked in part by efforts on the part of Greek Cypriots to reintegrate their population into the Greek nation. Similar sentiments are shared by many Catholics in Northern Ireland, who would like their provinces to rejoin Eire (the Republic of Ireland) to the south.

Irredentism

After the political unification of Italy in the 19th century, the new government claimed that there remained other areas containing ethnic Italians that were "not yet redeemed" (*irredenta*) and that should eventually be incorporated within the Italian state. These regions were within the boundaries of other states, which, not surprisingly, were less than enthusiastic about acceding to the Italian demands. Irredentist claims have often led to war, as when French armies in the 15th century, led by Joan of Arc, sought to unite the French "nation"; or when the Spanish regions of Castille and Aragon fought the occupying Moors, also in the 15th century; or during the 20th century, when Hitler claimed Czechoslovakia and Poland in part because they contained German-speaking minorities. Irredentism continues in the modern world. Thus, at present, Japan claims the Kurile Islands, seized by the former Soviet Union at the end of World War II; Ghana claims all of Togo; and Morocco claims Mauritania.

International or Transnational Solidarity

The sense of "nationhood" often extends across political boundaries, resulting in strong feelings of empathy and connectedness with fellow nationals living in another state. When these people are considered to be abused, war can be evoked by a felt need to extend protection to fellow nationals living elsewhere. Thus, India felt justified in entering the 1971 Pakistani civil war because India's Bengali population found it intolerable to stand idly by during Pakistan's slaughter of its own Bengalis in what was, at the time, East Pakistan. Many Arab states send money in support of Palestinian nationalism, thereby expressing solidarity with fellow Arabs. The states of sub-Saharan Africa were especially opposed to South African apartheid because of the oppression of its black population. Turkey has come to the aid of the Turkish population on Cyprus, just as Greece has been seen as the protector of the Greek population there.

Of course, this is not the whole story, and the extending of international solidarity can also be a pretext for aggression. For a clear example, Hitler annexed Czechoslovakia and invaded Poland, using the alleged mistreatment of Czech and Polish "Germans" as an excuse. The U.S. invasion of Grenada in 1983 was officially justified at the time by the U.S. government's claim that American medical students on that island were in danger of being taken hostage, just as the U.S. invasion of Panama in 1989 was ostensibly undertaken to protect American lives in that country. In short, national solidarity has often been used to provide legal and political justifications that rationalize a conflict or intervention whose roots may well lie elsewhere.

In many cases, states stop short of war, but nonetheless provide "fraternal" aid to ethnic groups in other states. This is often done to promote their own interests, even if those interests are limited to satisfying otherwise restive, kindred national elements within their own borders. India, for example, with its large Bengali population, did not stand by while West Pakistanis slaughtered the Bengalis of East Pakistan. India was similarly drawn into the fighting in Sri Lanka (formerly Ceylon) because both India and Sri Lanka have a large Sinhalese population.

In some cases, a chain of "solidarity" can be forged, which more resembles a game of dominoes; the following pattern emerged in northern and eastern Africa during the 1970s:

> Libya supported Muslim Arab rebels against a Christian and animist Negro regime in Chad. The Chad government supported animist Negro rebels against the Muslim Arab regime in Sudan. The Sudanese regime supported Muslim rebels against the Christian regime in Ethiopia. And Ethiopia supported, along with Chad, the rebels in the Sudan.[15]

Russia is also an amalgamation of many ethnic groups (although much less so than the former Soviet Union, most of whose republics gained autonomy in 1991). Since there are also large ethnic Russian populations in many of the now-independent former states of the former USSR (in what Russia refers to as its "near abroad"), the danger exists that a nationalist government in Russia might attempt to intervene in, say, Estonia, Latvia, or Kazakhstan, ostensibly on behalf of Russians in those countries. This danger is augmented by the possibility that the Baltic states, and even Ukraine, might attempt to enter NATO. Moreover, Russian political and military leadership has been acutely concerned that Islamic fundamentalism might spread from the south to the heartland of Russia itself, which has provided a justification for wars in Afghanistan, Chechnya, and elsewhere. Russia's concern intensified, of course, after the attacks of September 11, 2001, on the World Trade Center and the Pentagon.

Nationalist Threats to States

One might ask why many governments so strenuously resist the various secessionist, irredentist, and reintegrationist national movements. Aren't the (West) Pakistanis better off not being artificially united to 100 million resentful Bengalis? What would be the harm to Spaniards if the troublesome Basques seceded and formed their own tiny nation-state? Part of the answer may itself reflect a kind of national pride, the hope for a larger and therefore greater state. In addition, the resisting peoples are typically those who profit economically and socially from the presence of the would-be seceders. British and American support for national self-determination for Kuwait (threatened by Iraq shortly after its independence in 1961 and invaded by Iraq in 1990) and Brunei (long coveted by Indonesia) derives largely from Western nations' and multinational corporations' needs for these (otherwise poor) countries' oil resources. Similarly, Belgium's support for attempts by residents of Katanga to secede from the Congo was keyed to the copper wealth of that province. Had Biafra been carved out of Nigeria, much of that state's industrial capacity and natural resources would have gone, along with the Ibo people. When Hitler seized the Sudetenland, he not only "liberated" three million Sudeten Germans, but also about three quarters of Czechoslovakia's industrial capacity.

When states are heterogeneous (composed of many ethnic groups and republics), political leaders often worry that demands for national self-determination may lead to additional popular demands and possibly to the breakup of the home country (as happened in the former Yugoslavia during the 1990s). Such fears drove the Austrian government's policies at the onset of World War I and the Russian government's actions in the late 1990s. Furthermore, it is not clear that further *Balkanization*—of Africa, India, or anywhere else—will necessarily further the cause of peace. Certainly, the Balkan peninsula, known as the "tinderbox of Europe," has not been a good advertisement for the benefits of nationalist sentiment, as was abundantly clear during the last decade of the 20th century.

Racial and Cultural Intolerance

Whenever individuals associate together, and especially if they do so on the basis of shared characteristics that exclude others and make for a distinction between "Us" and "Them," there are the dangers of racism, ethnocentrism, xenophobia, and other forms of intolerance. All of these can contribute to war and other violent acts against racial and ethnic minorities, as well as against "foreigners." Many of the world's hostilities involve different nationalities and ethnic groups in conflict. Of course, the mere fact of ethnic difference is not a sufficient cause for war; after all, many pluralistic societies live peacefully, both intranationally—the multiethnic population of Hawaii, for example, or multilingual Switzerland and Belgium—and internationally. In addition, distinct racial or cultural differences are not necessary for war, either: Paraguay and its racially and culturally similar neighbors fought some extraordinarily bloody wars in the 19th century, as did Austrians and Prussians, North and South Koreans, and North and South Vietnamese, not to mention the long and tragic history of civil wars within such ethnically homogeneous nations as Spain and China.

Ethnic Antagonisms and Ethnic Cleansing

A high proportion of armed conflicts, however, do involve members of different ethnic/religious/cultural/linguistic groups, such as Iraq (Arab) versus Iran (Persian), Jews versus Arabs in the Middle East, Irish Catholics versus Protestants in Northern Ireland, Tamil versus Sinhalese in Sri Lanka, Christians against Muslims in the former Yugoslavia and Russia, Tutsis versus Hutus in Rwanda and Burundi, and so on. The horrific culmination of these conflicts has been the forced "ethnic cleansing" committed by militarily superior groups of ethnic minorities, as in large areas of the former Yugoslavia and central Africa. The result has been the slaughter of hundreds of thousands, perhaps millions, of people and their dislocation from their ancestral homelands.

In a sense, there is nothing new about this. Hatreds based on ethnic and religious differences were at the root of many wars throughout history, including the Crusades of the Middle Ages (European Christians vs. Arab Muslims) and the Thirty Years' War (largely Catholics vs. Protestants), which devastated central Europe in the 17th century. To a degree, no clear separation can be drawn between national antagonisms based on religion and those based on differing race and ethnicity. Many of the recent African wars (Ibo/Hausa, Hutu/Tutsi) have been more ethnic than religious; the India-Pakistan wars, on the other hand, have been primarily religious, although the differences between Hindus and Muslims are so fundamental to Indian and Pakistani society that they include ethnic distinctions as well. The Iran-Iraq and Arab-Israeli conflicts involve both religious and ethnic differences, although the former have been more ethnic, and the latter, more religious.

Clearly, many other factors have been operating in each of these conflicts: border disputes, a history of antagonism based at least partly on generations of real or perceived oppression, economic rivalries, and the like. And typically, these various "causes" provide the immediate stimulus for each outbreak of violence. But it also seems clear that national and often racial sentiments linger in the background as a crucial underlying cause, and also as an explanation for the persistence and intensity of many conflicts. In addition, once war erupts—even if for other immediate reasons—the belligerents quickly seize on any discernible differences between themselves and their opponents, typically magnifying these differences, elevating their own traits, and devaluing those of the other side. Often it is sufficient just to point to the opponents as different—that is, as Hondurans rather than Salvadorans, or Koreans rather than Japanese—to evoke potent antagonisms. Dehumanizing language and racial/ethnic scapegoating are often introduced at this point as well.

A year after the beginning of World War I, Einstein lamented humanity's insistence on primitive hatred and its use of nationalism as the vehicle for that hatred:

> When posterity recounts the achievements of Europe, shall we let men say that three centuries of painstaking cultural effort carried us no further than from the fanaticism of religion to the insanity of nationalism? It would seem that men always seek some idiotic fiction in the name of which they can hate one another. Once it was religion; now it is the state.[16]

It is worth emphasizing that "state worship" and nationalism, of the sort that Einstein so decried, come together especially in fascism and in other ultranationalist ideologies of statism.

Nationalism and the Public Mood

Public opinion counts, especially when it comes to issues of peace or war. And this is even more true in a democracy. "Opinion," wrote Alexander Hamilton, "whether well or ill founded is the governing principle of human affairs." And Abraham Lincoln noted that "he who molds public sentiment goes deeper than he who enacts statutes or pronounces decisions."

Inflaming Public Sentiment

Wars can be provoked for many reasons, including so-called reasons of state (*raisons d'état*), which, at the outset, evoke very little nationalist passion on the part of the participants; rather, they proceed in large part from the machinations of leadership. To prosecute wars, however, especially in the modern era, it has proven necessary for governments, through the mass media, to inflame the public. Subsequently, states often find that it is easier to start a war than to control it or to stop it.

In 1853, for example, Britain and France entered a war between Russia and the Ottoman Empire, on the side of the Turks. They took this step after Russia annexed the principalities of Wallachia and Moldavia (now in Romania and Moldova) from the Ottoman Empire and then resoundingly defeated the Turks in a famous naval battle at Sinope. After the Crimean War began, Austrian diplomacy successfully maneuvered the Russian troops out of the two contested principalities, thereby removing the main political basis for the war. But its emotional basis remained unresolved: In the war fever occasioned by outrage over the "massacre at Sinope," as well as the excitement over launching an expeditionary force to punish the "evil" czar, the British and French governments soon found that they had a tiger by the tail.

The Western allies then decided to attack the Russian city of Sebastopol, on the Crimean peninsula, a seemingly vulnerable region that would provide the dramatic victory needed to satisfy the aroused British and French publics. Instead of the anticipated quick and easy victory, however, they got the heroic but stupid "charge of the light brigade," in which 500 out of 700 British cavalrymen were slaughtered (and subsequently immortalized in Tennyson's poem), as well as tens of thousands of additional deaths, mostly from disease. It had been thought that victory would be cheap and would take only a few weeks. Without the pressure of nationalist sentiment, there probably wouldn't have been any Crimean War at all, or at worst, a brief and relatively inconsequential conflict.

Manipulating Public Opinion

In modern times, most governments recognize that war requires the mobilization of national sentiment, and so if real affronts to national dignity, honor, or well-being are not available, pretexts are typically arranged. Even Hitler, who clearly sought to invade Poland in 1939, found it necessary to stage a phony "incident" to justify his actions and help arouse German national indignation: He staged an attack, allegedly by Polish forces (but actually by Germans wearing Polish uniforms), against a German radio station. The so-called Gulf of Tonkin Incident, in which U.S. destroyers were supposed to have been attacked by North Vietnamese forces, is now acknowledged to have been exaggerated and manipulated by the U.S. government, so as to induce congressional authorization and public support for the unrestricted involvement of U.S. combat units in Vietnam.

Effective orators and publicists have long been able to sway public mood, often generating enthusiasm for war. The ancient Greek historian Thucydides recounted that the Athenian general Alcibiades stirred up irresistible public enthusiasm for glory, booty, and adventure. "With this enthusiasm of the majority," noted Thucydides, "the few that liked it not feared to appear unpatriotic by holding up their hands against it, and so they kept quiet." The result was an expedition against Syracuse (in modern-day Sicily) that ultimately proved disastrous.

In the second century B.C.E., when Carthage had long ceased to be a threat to Rome, the elderly and eloquent Cato would repeat, after each of his speeches, *Carthago delenda est* (Carthage is to be destroyed). And in the ensuing Punic War, it was, by Rome. The U.S. entry into the Spanish-American War was promoted by lurid and often inaccurate accounts of alleged Spanish atrocities in Cuba: the so-called yellow journalism of the Hearst newspaper chain, which favored war. The U.S. battleship *Maine* was blown up while in Havana harbor, allegedly by Spanish agents; this acutely inflamed American passions, and "Remember the *Maine*" became a slogan of that war. Some historians now maintain that the *Maine* was actually sunk by a prowar group, to provide a pretext for the hostilities that followed.

Quenching Public Passions

There is a tradition of hoping and expecting that public opinion—acting through democratic government—might serve as a check on war. Once public opinion is mobilized in support of a war, however, an expeditious conclusion to that war is made virtually impossible. Even reasoned debate about ending the war becomes difficult, since in the passion aroused by the conflict, opponents of the national course of action, or those who urge a more conciliatory policy, are often branded by political and media pundits as unpatriotic or downright treasonous.

In addition, although a kind of exhaustion often sets in during a war, in most cases there is also a degree of enhanced determination as well as a feedback loop whereby sacrifice demands yet more sacrifice. During the Vietnam War, for example, its American advocates argued that the fighting should be continued and, in fact, intensified, to ensure an outcome favorable to the United States, to justify the expenditure of so many lives and so much revenue.

When wars were fought out of allegiance to the person of the local lord, king, emperor, pope, shogun, or maharaja, it was relatively easy to call a halt to the proceedings once the leaders in question decided to do so. But when wars are fought out of allegiance to national imagery, prestige, or ideology, against a rival seen to embody a detested alternative image—and when the efforts and emotions of an entire citizenry have been aroused—it becomes much more difficult to quench the flames, as is painstakingly evident in America's and its allies' responses to the attacks of September 11, 2001, on New York and Washington, D.C. To date, no modern nation's leadership, after declaring war, subsequently announced that it had changed its mind!

Most patriotic citizens criticize giving "aid and comfort to the enemy" but are conspicuously silent about those who, by their actions, create enemies. And although there are many terms, such as *treason, traitor, betrayal,* and so on, to describe undermining one's country by collaborating with an opponent, especially during war, there are no comparable phrases for those who err on the other side, that is, those who undermine their country by being excessively eager to fight or are unwilling to seek an equitable peace. During World War I, for example, the government of Britain resolutely refused even to consider examining on what terms—short of unconditional surrender—peace with the Central Powers might be negotiated, not even breaching the possibility that such peace might be achieved by Germany's agreement to withdraw from France and Belgium, as well as to return Alsace-Lorraine to France.

A further consequence of evoking public passions is that many present-day nationalist and ethnic wars remain unresolved, partly because relatively few recent wars have been successful in ending the underlying conflict that generated the war itself: Korea remains divided, heavily armed and hostile; India and Pakistan are in a state of ongoing antagonism (although Bangladesh is independent); the Middle East remains a tinderbox; and Cyprus, the Balkans, and much of central Asia and Africa are still divided among warring ethnic factions. Nationalist passions keep age-old rivalries simmering, interfering with the prospect of reconciling old disputes or healing ancient injuries. Moreover, modern nation-states have many more resources available than they had in the past. Superpower allies of the contestants also typically add to the persistence of some disputes by being reluctant to permit their clients to suffer an unconditional defeat: The former USSR kept resupplying the Arab states, the United States and China keep Pakistan armed against India, and so on. In some cases, however, closure on a nationalist war has been achieved, generally when the most intensely pronationalist side wins: This happened in Vietnam, as in most anticolonial wars of national liberation. In other cases, a decisive move by a national leader—as with former Egyptian president Sadat's overtures to Israel—can overcome the prowar drift of nationalist passion. (But it must regrettably be noted that several years after his courageous initiative, Sadat was assassinated by Islamic nationalists.)

Nationalism and Political Ideology

Even so potent a force as political ideology can appear pallid compared with the energies unleashed by nationalism, which is in a sense a primitive and widespread ideology of its own. The Soviets and the Chinese Communists were both officially Marxists, but for the most part, they have remained Russians and Chinese first, as witnessed by their armed border clashes and persistent antagonism in recent decades. Similarly, the Vietnamese and Chinese, despite a shared Marxist-Leninist ideology, fought a short but vicious war in 1979.

World War I

Perhaps the most dramatic case, however, of the triumph of nationalism over ideology occurred in the early days of World War I. (More accurately, nationalist and imperialist ideology clashed with internationalist and socialist ideology—and the former won.) In the years prior to World War I, the European Socialist and Social Democratic Parties were powerful, seemingly united, and for the most part committed to opposing the institution of war, which was seen by most socialists as part of capitalist exploitation of the proletariat. Through various resolutions associated with the Second International, as well as within each major European country, the large Socialist and Social Democratic Parties (most influentially, those of Germany and France) asserted that if war ever appeared imminent, their memberships would smother it by general strikes and, if necessary, insurrections. Solidarity among the working class would make war impossible: "They" might declare a war, but no one would come.

Before war was in fact declared, however, French socialists began worrying that German socialists would be unable to restrain German militarism, which would leave France fettered while Germany triumphed. German socialists, in turn, anguished that success on their part would leave Germany at the mercy of reactionary czarist Russia. In the end, an overwhelming majority within the Socialist Parties of each nation announced support for the coming war, because for *their* country, such a war would be defensive. The following declaration, by the Social Democratic Party of Germany in 1914, shows the tenor of thinking at the time:

> We are menaced by the terror of foreign invasion. The problem before us now is not the relative advisability of war or peace, but a consideration of just what steps must be taken for the protection of our country. . . . It devolves upon us, therefore, to avert this danger, to shelter the civilization and independence of our native land. Therefore, we must to-day justify what we have always said. In its hour of danger Germany may ever rely upon us. We take our stand upon the doctrine basic to the international labor movement, which at all times has recognized the right of every people to national independence and national defense, and at the same time we condemn all war for conquest.[17]

Ideology and Nationalism

On the other hand, sometimes ideology and nationalism go hand in hand, producing a combination that is especially potent. War-prone imperialist

France during the 18th and 19th centuries, for example, was committed to its *mission civilisatrice*, the notion that France had a special mission to civilize the non-French world. Similarly, German national militarism in the 20th century was buttressed by Nazi yearnings for a "thousand-year *Reich*" peopled by a triumphant "Aryan race." The former Soviet Union's support for Third World national revolutions derived in part from its devotion to Marxist-Leninist ideology, just as the American ideology of free-market capitalism and the vision of the United States as the "new Jerusalem," a shining "city on the hill," uniquely pleasing to God and man, undergirded U.S. territorial expansionism during the 19th century, and overcame its penchant for isolationism in substantial periods of the 20th century.

In most cases, peace movements fare poorly during wartime, overwhelmed by militant national enthusiasm. There are exceptions, however: Notably, a kind of "war weariness" can set in, especially when the war itself is controversial and/or appears to be stalemated. The Vietnam War was such an example, controversial from the start and terminated in large part because the enthusiasm of the American citizenry was insufficient, and turned increasingly to public outrage. World War I turned out to be much bloodier than expected, and after several years, seemed nowhere near resolution. Although citizen support remained generally high (except in Russia), mutinies became frequent: Fifty-four divisions (about one half the total) of the French Army mutinied in April 1917; 25,000 men were eventually court-martialed. Such behavior was contagious: The following month, 400,000 Italian troops deserted the field at Caporetto, and around the same time, German and Russian troops were fraternizing openly.

The Tension Between Peace and Freedom

Some of humanity's most stirring visions and most memorable sacrifices have been made ostensibly on behalf of freedom—typically efforts of national groups to achieve self-determination. Consider, for example, the blood-tingling sentiments of these lines from Robert Burns's poem (later set to music) "Scots Wha Hae," originally written in support of renewed Scottish national independence (Scotland was once an independent state, before being incorporated into Great Britain):

> By oppression's woes and pain! By your sons in servile chains!
> We will drain our dearest veins, but they shall be free!
> Lay the proud usurpers low! Tyrants fall in every foe!
> Liberty's in every blow! Let us do or die.

Many people think of nationalism and ethnocentrism as major reasons for wars, and they are at least partly correct. Certainly, nationalist sentiments, such as those expressed by Burns, are not likely to lead to the peaceful resolution of conflicts. It may be somewhat surprising, therefore, to learn that through much of the 19th and 20th centuries, nationalism was widely viewed as a potentially strong contributor to *peace*. After all, ethnically unified nations would seem least prone to civil war. However, the civil wars of Spain and China during the mid-20th century, and more recently, in the former Yugoslavia and in much of central Africa during the 1990s, give the lie to this somewhat wishful thinking.

On the other hand, by producing a crosscutting loyalty—one that transcends connections of economic class, local leadership, even religion—feelings of national identity and ethnic solidarity do appear to have sometimes contributed to peace and stability. Nationalism has helped end many instances of endemic subnational conflict. Following the establishment of nation-states in Western Europe, for example, the low-level feuding and banditry, as well as the religious and class violence that had long characterized that region, was virtually ended—at least until the resurgence of genocidal ethnic cleansing and xenophobia during the 1990s in the Balkans. The same can be said for much of prenational India, China, and Japan.

The Civil War, the bloodiest war in U.S. history, took place because feelings of regional identity (especially in the South) were stronger than national identity. Perhaps greater nationalism might have kept the peace, at least in this instance. The idea of nationalism as a route to peace is nonetheless ironic in that the first nation-state to have achieved what is generally regarded as the modern level of national self-consciousness—Napoleonic France—proceeded almost immediately to embark upon the most expansive, domestically motivated wars that Europe had experienced up to that time.

European Nationalism

Nationalist leaders, such as the apostle of Italian unification Giuseppi Mazzini (1805–1872), maintained that peace would ensue when every nationality constituted its own state. However, not surprisingly, advocates of national self-determination typically believed that peace itself was subordinate to freedom as an immediate goal. Mazzini himself, among the most literate and effective of the many young evangelists of nationalism in Europe during the 19th century, maintained that education and insurrection would liberate Italy:

> Education must ever be directed to teach by example, word and pen the necessity of insurrection. . . . Insurrection—by means of guerrilla bands—is the true method of warfare for all nations desirous of emancipating themselves from a foreign yoke. . . . It forms the military education of the people and consecrates every foot of the native soil by memory of some warlike deed.[18]

Twenty years later, Mazzini was still calling for "War, in the noble intention of restoring Truth and Justice, and of arresting Tyranny in her inhuman career, of rendering the Nations free and happy and causing God to smile upon them benignly."

Nationalist wars did in fact follow Mazzini's proclamation. In 1859, France defeated Austria and helped liberate Italy. Prussia and Austria "freed" Schleswig and Holstein from Denmark; then Prussia defeated Austria to help unite the German states, and followed this up by "liberating" Alsace and Lorraine from France in 1871. Throughout the 19th century, the various "captive nations" of Europe made numerous appeals to the European conscience: Montenegro, Romania, Serbia, Bulgaria, and Greece succeeded in gaining their independence from Turkey, although the Poles (under Russia) and Hungarians (under Austria) failed.

Much of European liberal thought of the 19th century reflected an important issue, which remains divisive among students of peace even today: What is the right course when two cherished goals—freedom and peace—conflict? Thus, in the late 19th century, there was widespread sympathy (and not just among ardent nationalists) for the struggles of Eastern Christians against Turkey, Poles against Russia, the Irish against England, Italians against imperial Austria, and before that, much of Europe against Napoleon. At the same time, it was widely recognized that the struggle for freedom may require breaches of the peace. There was real tension, therefore, in reconciling a cherishing of peace with a commitment to freedom. This conflict caused substantial difficulty, for example, for the British Peace Society, whose leader complained at one point that "this idea of nationality is a poor, low, selfish, unchristian idea, at variance with the very principles of advanced civilization."[19]

In 1867, the International League for Peace and Freedom was established in Paris. The guest of honor at its first meeting, the Italian patriot Garibaldi, called for replacing monarchy with democracy, separating church and state, and establishing, ultimately, a United States of Europe, if need be by war! There were also disillusionments. Widespread enthusiasm for the Balkan League (Greece, Bulgaria, and Montenegro, which is now a restive part of Yugoslavia), in its 1912 struggle with Turkey, was dampened when the victorious states refused to cooperate and began fighting among themselves, in part over conflicting claims to the newly established state of Albania. This in turn precipitated the Second Balkan War of 1913. More states means more boundaries, and hence more opportunities for antagonisms to proliferate. By the turn of the 20th century, therefore, the mainstream liberal European attitude toward nationalism had become ambivalent: support for oppressed minorities—captive nations within oppressive empires—tempered with anxiety about a world divided into numerous feisty, competing, and independent units. And by the beginning of the 21st century, despite widespread sympathy in the United States for the national aspirations of various ethnic groups (Chechens, Tatars, etc.) within Russia, the American government has maintained a policy in favor of maintaining Russia's geographic integrity. Similarly, U.S. foreign policy has consistently undercut the prospects of Kurdish nationalism, opting instead for the status quo.

The Post-World War II International Scene

In the sense of avoiding major armed conflict, Europe was largely peaceful from World War II until the Balkan wars in the former Yugoslavia and NATO's unprecedented military intervention in 1999. But Europe has also achieved a fair degree of national self-determination: Just about all French live in France, virtually all Germans in Germany (or Austria, or the German-speaking part of Switzerland), nearly all Poles in Poland, and so forth. There are, however, Austrians in northern Italy (the Tyrol), Hungarians in Romania, and until 1999, Albanians in Yugoslavia, as well as Gypsies (Roma) in much of Eastern Europe and many "guest workers" from northern Africa, southern Europe, and Turkey in northern and Western Europe. The presence of minority groups in many European countries has led to a backlash against foreigners, who are (usually incorrectly) perceived as taking jobs away from the ethnic majorities. Right-wing politicians have in some cases (notably Austria, France, Italy, and Switzerland) capitalized on widespread feelings of resentment and ethnic chauvinism. This has also led to substantial unease and occasional violence (especially in Germany).

In addition, there are simmering separatist movements among the Spanish Basques and Catalans, Catholics in Northern Ireland, and occasionally, Swiss in the Jura region, as well as tension between Flemings (speaking a Dutch/German dialect) and French-speaking Walloons in Belgium. These difficulties have been most acute in the former Yugoslavia, which literally came apart at the seams in the 1990s, and whose future is far from clear. The resurgence of jingoism, ethnocentrism, and xenophobia in many parts of western and central Europe shows few signs of abating during the first decade of the 21st century, and may well reverse the relatively halcyon conditions that prevailed in most of Europe during the second half of the 20th century.

Other regions of the planet did not experience the cold-war "peace" that prevailed in most of Europe between 1945 and 1990. Palestinians continue to strive for national self-determination, which may finally be in sight if Israel continues to make what it perceives to be concessions to the Palestinians and Arab nations surrounding it. India is a patchwork of dozens, perhaps hundreds, of potential nations speaking more than a thousand languages; China contains more than 50 million non-Chinese, of which the Tibetans are the most notably oppressed and resentful; and Russia, like its predecessor, the former USSR, is a vast heterogeneous assemblage of territories and regions dominated by different ethnic groups. Finally, the boundaries of many of the postcolonial African states are nothing less than a disaster, since they were drawn (by Europeans) with virtually no regard to the nationality of their people.

The Effects of Political Ideology

Finally, there is the prickly question of fundamental values: Peace, admittedly, is a great value, but is it infinitely valuable? Is peace so worthy an end that it should be maintained at all costs? And what of the connection between peace and freedom, or between peace and justice? What if justice—including national self-determination—cannot be obtained short of war? Since 1945, many Western advocates of peace have tended to see nationalism as an evil if practiced by the Western powers, not only because it has led in the past to imperialism, but also because it may contribute to a growing danger of nuclear war. At the same time, there is a tendency to look favorably on wars of national liberation, if directed by the oppressed against their oppressors; for example, the Algerian struggles against France during the 1950s and 1960s, the Mau-Mau movement for independence of Kenya from Britain during that same time, the Vietnamese conflict with the United States, and even the struggles by Chechens and Kosovars to detach themselves from Russia and Serbia, respectively.

At the same time, right-wing anticommunists, while deploring revolutionary nationalist violence (which they typically see as communist inspired and therefore especially "illegitimate"), have applauded various equally violent counterrevolutionary wars, such as that of the contras in Nicaragua, UNITA in Angola, and the mujahideen in Afghanistan. Seemingly, extreme right-wing and left-wing ideologues are willing to value freedom over peace, so long as freedom is defined as either (in the first case) freedom from Marxist governments, or (in the second) from colonial or right-wing military dictators.

During the second half of the 20th century, within the United States, there was a tendency among partisans of the political right (i.e., conservatives) to see antiestablishment revolutionary movements as necessarily aligned with worldwide communism. By contrast, centrists and leftists have been more likely to emphasize the nationalist, rather than the ideological, underpinnings of such activities. They point out, for example, that Marshal Tito, anti-Nazi partisan leader and later president of Yugoslavia, was a nationalist first, and a communist second (he withdrew Yugoslavia from the Warsaw Pact, for example). Similarly, Ho Chi Minh's commitment was to Vietnamese nationalism more than to communism of either the Chinese or Soviet variety. The effort to achieve freedom via national struggle has produced many wars of liberation and, more recently, of counterliberation. Moreover, enthusiastic adherence to the goals of the nation-state has also generated additional wars (of conquest), while setting the stage for a possible showdown between nuclear-armed nation-states.

The Question of "National Character"

There is no evidence for any genetically influenced behavioral differences among people of differing nationalities. Nonetheless, there remains a persistent belief that a nation can in some cases be characterized by certain summed personality traits. In fact, there have been numerous errors of political judgment resulting from a misreading of the "national character" of a prospective opponent. Hitler, for example—and Napoleon before him—felt that Britain was a "nation of shopkeepers," and therefore neither willing nor able to resist aggression. During the 18th century, Germans were widely considered to be either philosophical metaphysicians or incurable romantics, not cut out for heavy industry or any other practical undertakings; the Italians, by contrast, were seen as highly rational and scientifically inclined. Today, these stereotypes have been reversed.

Often such perceptions are self- (or rather, nation-) serving, as well as incorrect. During World War II, for example, part of the Allied justification for bombing German cities was that unlike the dauntless British moral fiber, the German will to persevere would "crack" under bombardment, leading perhaps to revolt and thereby shortening the war. Official government documents claim that

> the evidence at our disposal goes to show that the morale of the average German civilian will weaken quicker than that of a population such as our own as a consequence of direct attack. The Germans have been undernourished and subjected to a permanent strain equivalent to that of war conditions during almost the whole period of Hitler's regime, and for this reason also will be liable to crack before a nation of greater stamina.[20]

There is debate about whether strategic bombing actually shortened World War II by creating shortages of critical materials, notably ball bearings and petroleum, in the final months. However, it is widely acknowledged that, if anything, bombing *increased* the German will to resist. Certainly, the German national character did not crack. Later, the United States also underestimated the ability and willingness of the North Vietnamese to absorb bomb attacks and yet persevere in a war to which they, as a nation, were committed. Despite what are perceived to be eventual defeats, the Iraqis during the Persian Gulf War, Serbs during the war over Kosovo, and Chechens during the bombardments perpetrated by Russia all endured longer than most so-called U.S. political experts expected. This may in part be explained by a "rally 'round the flag" effect that strengthens ties of national and ethnic solidarity when under attack by a "foreign" power, even if the domestic regime is also perceived as corrupt and autocratic.

The persistence of the idea of national character is probably due to the fact that, while it is incorrect biologically, it has the appearance of psychological and sociological reality. Thus, a "national style," in speech, clothing, even responses to stress or to potential enemies, can sometimes be exhibited. These styles can and do change over time, but they nonetheless often have some limited consistency. For example, some Mediterranean peoples (Italians, Greeks) seem to be relatively more voluble and excitable than peoples from more northern climes (Scandinavians, Germans, British). Latin Americans and Arabs tend to maintain less interpersonal distance than do Americans or Europeans, which sometimes leads to misunderstandings at international gatherings. Japanese and Chinese seem (by mainstream American standards) unusually concerned with politeness and social formality. And Russians and Americans often misinterpret each other. For example, when Soviet Premier Khrushchev arrived in the United States for a summit conference with President Eisenhower, he unwittingly antagonized many Americans by clasping both hands above his head, in a gesture used to signal "victory" by U.S. prizefighters; in the former USSR, the same action was used to communicate friendship and solidarity.

Patterns of family life and personal development could also influence behavior patterns characteristic of the nation as a whole. According to the psychoanalyst Erik Erikson, the political appeal of Nazism to Germans in the 1930s was based at least partly on the authoritarian style of the typical German family, in which the father was often both tyrannical and remote:

> When the father comes home from work, even the walls seem to pull themselves together. The children hold their breath, for the father does not approve of "nonsense"—that is, neither of the mother's feminine moods nor of the children's playfulness. . . . Later, when the boy comes to observe the father in company, when he notices his father's submission to superiors, and when he observes his excessive sentimentality when he drinks and sings with his equals, the boy acquires . . . a deep doubt of the dignity of man—or at any rate, of the "old man."[21]

Such confusion makes social maturation difficult. Erikson claimed that if the Fuehrer had sought to appear as a straightforward father figure, he would have evoked ambivalence from the German citizenry. Instead, according to Erikson, Hitler appealed to the German national character as a glorified, indomitable older brother.

Whatever the role of national character, and of shared national or ethnic experiences in molding such apparent traits, the role of national self-image, or ethnic identity, is undeniable. Nations and ethnic groups invariably see themselves as well-meaning and motivated only by the purest of goals; their opponents, on the other hand, typically see themselves differently. For example, Americans generally saw their efforts on behalf of post-World War

II reconstruction (the Truman Doctrine and the Marshall Plan), which included assistance to defeated Germany and Japan, as generous and laudable. To the Soviets, this appeared entirely self-serving: a form of economic imperialism, a device to relieve American postwar overproduction, as well as a political weapon directed against the USSR.

More recently, many Americans see the post-Cold War status of their nation (having emerged—at least for a time—as the sole superpower) as a validation of its political and economic ideology of "democratic capitalism." At the same time, many other countries (especially France and Russia) increasingly regard this posture as U.S. arrogance and as a dangerously inflated self-righteousness combined with raw "hard" power.

_____ A Final Note on Nationalism and Ethnocentrism

Nationalism and ethnic solidarity can sometimes evoke compassion, love, and community pride and can even serve as a positive force for human cooperation and ecological awareness. Love of the land, the people, the culture, and the ecosystem can contribute to dignity, caring, altruism, and some of the finer emotions of which human beings are capable. At the same time, however, nationalism and ethnocentrism can become malevolent when they foster ethnic chauvinism, when they create violent divisions between people, and when they threaten to destroy the humanistic values they supposedly venerate. Nationalism and ethnocentrism pump people up, and they may often generate conditions that bring them down as well.

In his essay "Christianity and Patriotism," Leo Tolstoy pitied "the good-natured foolish people, who, showing their healthy white teeth as they smile, gape like children, naively delighted at the dressed-up admirals and presidents, at the flags waving above them, and at the fireworks, and the playing bands." Tolstoy warned that this euphoria is typically short-lived, and the flags and cheerful bands are quickly replaced by "only the desolate wet plain, cold, hunger, misery—in front of them the slaughterous enemy, behind them the relentless government, blood, wounds, agonies, rotting corpses and a senseless, useless death."[22]

One of the great challenges to students and practitioners of peace and conflict resolution is accordingly to channel the benevolent aspects of nationalism and ethnic solidarity while guarding against their horrors.

Notes _____

1. William McDougall. 1915. *An Introduction to Social Psychology*. London: Methuen.

2.   Carol J. Greenhouse. 1987. "Cultural Perspectives on War." In R. Vavrynen, ed., *The Quest for Peace*. Beverly Hills, CA: Sage.

3.   Bronislaw Malinowski. 1941. "An Anthropological Analysis of War." *American Journal of Sociology* 46: 521–550.

4.   H. H. Turner-High. 1949. *Primitive War*. Columbia: University of South Carolina Press.

5.   William James. 1911. "The Moral Equivalent of War." In *Memories and Studies*. New York: Longman, Green.

6.   William H. McNeill. 1983. *The Pursuit of Power*. Chicago: University of Chicago Press.

7.   Quoted in R. Heizer and A. Almquist. 1970. *The Other Californians*. Berkeley: University of California Press.

8.   Andrew Schmookler. 1984. *The Parable of the Tribes*. Berkeley: University of California Press.

9.   John Stoessinger. 1962. *The Might of Nations*. New York: Random House.

10.   J. Ernest Renan. 1882. *Qu'est-ce qu'une nation?* Paris: Calmann-Levy.

11.   George Orwell. 1953. *Such, Such Were the Joys*. New York: Harcourt, Brace.

12.   H. Richard Niebuhr. 1970. *Radical Monotheism and Western Culture*. New York: Harper & Row.

13.   Quoted in G. G. Van Deusen. 1937. *The Life of Henry Clay*. Boston: Little, Brown.

14.   Radio and TV address to the nation, April 10, 1970.

15.   David W. Ziegler. 1977. *War, Peace, and International Politics*. Boston: Little, Brown.

16.   Albert Einstein. 1979. *Einstein: A Centenary Volume*. Cambridge, MA: Harvard University Press.

17.   Quoted in Kenneth Waltz. 1959. *Man, the State, and War*. New York: Columbia University Press.

18.   Giuseppe Mazzini. 1891. *Life & Writings of Joseph Mazzini*. London: Elder & Co.

19.   Michael Howard. 1978. *War and the Liberal Conscience*. New Brunswick, NJ: Rutgers University Press.

20.   Quoted in C. Webster and N. Frankland. 1961. *The Strategic Air Offensive Against Germany*. London: HMSO.

21.   Erik Erikson. 1950. *Childhood and Society*. New York: Norton.

22.   Leo Tolstoy. 1987. *Writings on Civil Disobedience and Nonviolence*. Philadelphia: New Society Publishers.

7 The State Level

Nothing appears more surprising to those who consider human affairs with a philosophical eye, than the easiness with which the many are governed by the few.

—David Hume

We now come to the role of states in our analysis of the reasons for wars. As we have seen, popular usage often makes no distinction between the terms *nation* and *state*, although the former correctly refers to a collection of people, and the latter to an entity that functions in the world political arena. Inhabitants of the United States of America are especially likely to be careless in this usage, since unlike other nation-states, which typically refer to their subdivisions as provinces, regions, and the like, Americans tend to use the word *state* to mean the level of political division ranking just below the federal government.

Defining the State

More generally, however, a state can be defined as a sovereign political unit that may include many different communities and that operates via a centralized government, which has the authority and power to decree and enforce laws, collect taxes, and act as the legally recognized representative of its citizens in exchanges with other states, including the waging of war.

The relationship between nations and states is complex. Although there have long been efforts to make national and state borders coincide, thus creating nation-states, states also tend to suppress national movements within their borders. It has been estimated that there are about 200 states containing approximately 800 nationalist movements (more than 7,000 if ethnic identity alone is taken as the criterion for nationalism). At the same time, states promote their own, dominant form of nationalism. When nations are not organizing themselves into states, the leaders of states often seek to create nations by trying to unify the diverse peoples living within state borders.

The concept of statehood has often been imbued with an idealistic and almost metaphysical significance (so, for that matter, has the concept of nationhood). "What is the State essentially?" asked Randolph S. Bourne:

> The more closely we examine it, the more mystical and personal it becomes. On the Nation we can put our hand as a definite social group, with attitudes and qualities exact enough to mean something. On the Government we can put our hand as a certain organization of ruling functions, the machinery of law-making and law-enforcing. The Administration is a recognizable group of political functionaries, temporarily in charge of the government. But the State stands as an idea behind them all, eternal, sanctified, and from it Government and Administration conceive themselves to have the breath of life.[1]

This rather abstract description notwithstanding, the modern state performs numerous specific functions and has immense power, including the power to wage war. When discussion of the state is not enveloped in emotional rhetoric ("wrapping one's self in the flag"), states often justify their existence by appeals to political realism and to principles of efficiency and regularity. And yet scholars increasingly recognize that perhaps the most crucial characteristic of the state is its monopoly on the use of "legitimate" physical violence within its territory. That is, states reserve unto themselves the privilege of taking human life, without being answerable to any higher secular authority:

> The state claims the privilege of killing people for such crimes as treason, sedition, and murder and in such activities as wars, reprisals and pacifications. The state also tries to prevent any other person or organization from killing within its jurisdiction by enforcing municipal laws against homicides, insurrections, and invasions and from killing its nationals abroad by diplomatic protection and intervention. Since this monopoly in killing is conceived as a characteristic of the state in the abstract, the recognition by each state of other states implies recognition of the equal right of every state to exercise the monopoly within its jurisdiction. This jurisdiction, however, is not easy to define because of the migratory character of nationals and armies and the frequent instruction of armies to kill foreigners abroad and to protect nationals abroad from being killed.[2]

The two political ideologies that particularly value the state—elevating it above the individual—are the authoritarian left and the far right. Thus, in some Communist Party-governed countries, individuals may be held to be less important than the collectivity, typically represented by the state. Whereas Marxist theory calls for the eventual "withering away of the state," in practice, the governments of some Communist Party-ruled states are notably intrusive (as in China).

Speaking from the perspective of the far right, Benito Mussolini wrote,

> The fascist conception of life stresses the importance of the State and accepts the individual only in so far as his interests coincide with those of the State . . . the fascist conception of the State is all-embracing; outside of it no human or spiritual values can exist, much less have value.[3]

Increasingly, mainstream liberals and conservatives seem also to be placing greater emphasis on the state, liberals looking toward the promise of a benevolent "welfare state," and conservatives lauding the role of patriotism and the "national security state." Peace activists and progressive scholars, however, frequently criticize what they regard as excessive emphasis on states. They claim that an inordinately state-centered view of world politics makes the continuation of states a foregone conclusion, thereby shutting out the possibility of other kinds of political organization. But however the state is imagined, whether we like it or not, and whatever may be our goals for states in general and our own state in particular, states are the primary actors on the world's political stage (just as multinational corporations are the major actors on the world's economic stage), and so we had better understand what they are about.

State Sovereignty

An important concept related to the theory and practice of states is sovereignty, defined by French political economist Jean Bodin (in 1576) as "the state's supreme authority over citizens and subjects." In other words, under the doctrine of sovereignty, states are the final arbiter of earthly disputes and issues. There is no higher recourse. This is supposed to be true during peacetime, but is if anything exaggerated during war. Writing during the time of reigning monarchs, Bodin conceived of sovereignty especially in the sense of one's "sovereign lord," emphasizing the relationship of a subject to his or her ruler.

The Dutch jurist Hugo Grotius, writing a century later, made major contributions to the development of international law by considering the relationship of sovereign rulers to each other. He contended that in the light of state sovereignty, no ruler could be subject to legal control by another state. This principle still applies today, and it means that in theory the United States is legally on a par with, for example, Malta, an island state in the Mediterranean Sea, one tenth the size of Rhode Island and containing about one third as many people.

The Price of State Sovereignty

A crucial consequence of state sovereignty is international "anarchy." In a world composed of separate states, each of which is sovereign and thus, legally equal, there cannot be—by definition—any recourse to higher authority in the solving of disputes. Conflicting claims among cities can be adjudicated by the government of a province, or whatever may be designated the next higher administrative unit. Conflicts among provinces can be adjudicated by the federal government that in some sense sits "above" these provinces. But if different federal governments are truly sovereign unto themselves, there is no guarantee of orderly process—never mind harmony —when these entities quarrel. They may agree to submit their dispute to mediation, arbitration, or other forms of negotiation, or seek to employ diplomacy. But such efforts depend entirely on the voluntary goodwill of the states involved; that is, they involve temporary, and readily revoked, surrender of sovereignty. The Charter of the United Nations, for example, clearly says that it does not seek to restrict the sovereignty of the states making up this international organization.

When states disagree seriously, given that they are legally coequals, they are in theory "free" to engage in a violent test of strength, that is, war. (Or looking at it differently, one might say that sovereign states engage in war when they agree that war is the best way to resolve the issue between them.) In short, the doctrine of state sovereignty results in the lack of an overriding central authority with the legitimacy and power to carry out its decrees. Note that this does not necessarily imply disorder: In fact, much of the diplomatic exchange between states is highly structured. Rather, it follows from the absence of any overarching authority, superior to that of states themselves. Bodin as well as Hobbes recognized that interstate violence, or war, is the price paid for the system of state sovereignty, which, they claimed, maintains a degree of peace within states.

Others have placed much of the blame for war at the doorstep of the state system, although this has not necessarily led to rejection (even in theory) of the system of nation-states. More often, the mood is one of resignation:

> With many sovereign states, with no system of law enforceable among them, with each state judging its grievances and ambitions according to the dictates of its own reason or desire—conflict, sometimes leading to war, is bound to occur.[4]

Violations of State Sovereignty

The doctrine of state sovereignty is powerful. All states claim to support it, although in fact, efforts at spying and subversion (which are frequent and sometimes continual between certain states) are violations of that doctrine. Thus, when Marshall J. Pilsudski, Polish nationalist and dictator, advised the French government in 1933 to overthrow the German government while Hitler was still weak, it was judged that under the doctrine of state sovereignty, Germany had the "right" to choose its own government.

This "right" has only been selectively respected, however: In 1979, for example, when the government of Tanzania, with the aid of Ugandan exiles, invaded Uganda and ousted the Ugandan despot Idi Amin, other governments generally applauded or remained silent. In 1956, the former USSR trampled on Hungarian sovereignty, putting down efforts at liberalization; the same was done to Czechoslovakia in 1968, and Poland was implicitly threatened in 1981. (Later, under Gorbachev, the former Soviet Union peacefully allowed Poland, Hungary, and other members of the Warsaw Pact to go their own way, and several Eastern European nations are now members of the North Atlantic Treaty Organization [NATO], much to the consternation of many elements in Russia.) When a neo-Nazi political party became part of the governing coalition in Austria in 2000, many other governments expressed alarm, and the European Union (EU) nations sought to isolate Austria diplomatically. Others, including many people within Austria itself, expressed outrage at such actions and claimed these were efforts to interfere with that nation's sovereignty.

The former Soviet Union may also be said to have violated the sovereignty of Afghanistan following its 1979 military move into that country; supporters of this action, however, claim that the Soviets were merely responding to requests for assistance by the legitimate Afghan government. The U.S. government sought repeatedly to arrange for the assassination of Cuba's Fidel Castro in the 1960s, and it attempted to kill Libya's leader, Muámmar Gadhafi, by bombing his residence in 1986 (and killing members of his household). The CIA engineered the forcible overthrow of democratically elected governments in Guatemala and Iran in the 1950s, and in 1973 it provided assistance to the right-wing forces that overthrew the democratically elected Socialist government of Salvador Allende in Chile. These are only some of the more widely acknowledged examples.

When Britain, France, and Israel invaded Egypt in 1956, capturing the Suez Canal, international outrage (especially from the United States) forced them to withdraw, arguing the need to respect Egyptian sovereignty. Yet in 1984, the government of the United States secretly and illegally planted mines in certain Nicaraguan harbors, despite the fact that Nicaraguan sovereignty —at least in theory—is no less worthy of respect than Egyptian (or American) sovereignty. In 1988, the U.S. government arranged for the extradition of an accused drug smuggler from Honduras, in clear violation of the Honduran constitution and Honduran sovereignty. Outraged Hondurans rioted in response. And in 1989, when the United States invaded Panama in clear violation of Panamanian sovereignty, worldwide condemnation of the action was widespread but ineffectual. There are questions, as well, regarding the legitimacy of the attacks by the United States and its allies on Iraq (from the Persian Gulf War in 1990–1991 to the present), as well as on Afghanistan, Sudan, and Serbia. In short, while virtually all state governments pay lip service to the doctrine of state sovereignty, more powerful nations often invade and attack less powerful states as they see fit.

Limitations of State Sovereignty

States have traditionally been hesitant to allow the armed forces of another state to be stationed within their territory, or even to pass through it. During World War II, for example, Spain's fascist government of Francisco Franco, although sympathetic to Nazi Germany, would not permit German troops to cross its territory. However, sovereignty can be surprisingly flexible. The government of South Korea hosts thousands of U.S. troops and many U.S. nuclear weapons; South Korean military forces are essentially under U.S. command, largely a consequence of the Korean War. In a remarkable—if limited—surrender of sovereignty, the government of Sri Lanka invited Indian troops to enter that country, so as to police an attempted truce with Tamil separatists; this led to Indian troops engaging in hostilities with Sri Lankans on Sri Lankan soil. The violent conflict between Sinhalese and Tamils in Sri Lanka continues to the present and has, to some extent, spilled over into India (via assassinations and bombings).

In contrast, the states of Western Europe are also experiencing a kind of reduction in sovereignty, although this appears to be entirely voluntary. The European Parliament sets some economic and legal policy, in a sense over the heads of its constituent states, and the same can be said for the Western European economic union, the EU. For example, by eliminating tariffs toward other members and setting rules for the conduct of trade among their member states, the rules of the EU circumscribe the economic sovereignty of each participant, presumably for the good of all. In 1992, all trade barriers among the Common Market countries were lifted. By the end of the past century, a common currency—the euro—had come into existence, to replace the currencies of the member states in 2002. Some suggest that this may be preliminary to the eventual establishment of a "United States of Europe."

Other economic unions—such as OPEC, the Organization of Petroleum Exporting Countries—have not always succeeded in getting their member states to subordinate their desires to those of the group as a whole. When Saudi Arabia or Iran, for example, refuses to restrict or to raise its crude oil production, thereby foiling OPEC efforts to charge uniform oil prices, the members of OPEC defend their actions by relying on the principle of state sovereignty.

State sovereignty is to some extent enshrined in international law, part of which maintains that a procedure, if customary, has legal validity. States have consistently supported the concept of sovereignty, even if they violate it when it suits their purposes. But underlying the legalities, the fundamental legitimacy of sovereignty appears to rest on force: Just as states have a monopoly on sanctioned violence within their borders, there are no suprastate structures currently capable of overriding a state's claim of sovereignty. In *The City of God*, Augustine tells the story of a pirate who had been captured by Alexander the Great. Alexander asked him what was his justification for infesting the sea, "and the pirate answered, with uninhibited insolence, ' "The same as yours, in infesting the earth! But because I do it with a tiny craft, I'm called a pirate. Because you have a mighty navy, you're called an emperor.' "[5]

The State System

The Origins of States and the State System

Many theories have been proposed to explain the origin of the state. Aristotle maintained that it was "natural," and therefore needed no explanation. Rousseau viewed it as a historical curiosity. Some anthropologists have seen a relationship between the early production of agricultural surpluses (made possible by division of labor) and the presence of centralized organization to store, ship, and protect that surplus. Others have emphasized the early association of pretechnological civilization with arid environments (as in Babylonia and Egypt), as well as the possible advantage of economies of scale in providing for irrigation canals. On the other hand, in some cases (China, Mexico) states developed before irrigation. Orthodox Marxists maintain that states originated to police the dominance of one class over another. Many social scientists and historians, however, ascribe great importance to interactions among states, leaning toward what may be called the "conquest" theory to explain the origins of the state. Larger, well-integrated sociopolitical groups succeeded in conquering smaller, less integrated rivals, eventually leading to the modern state system, which is widely thought to have originated in Europe with the Peace of Westphalia (1648), which ended the Thirty Years' War.

But even before this, states constituted a powerful force over their subjects. For example, in Sweden, during the Thirty Years' War, most of the taxes raised were appropriated for the war effort. The state began rationing food to the civilian population, as well as establishing armaments monopolies, appropriating private lands, and selling war bonds. In the pursuit of armed might, the state began to penetrate nearly every aspect of civilian life. Several centuries earlier, distinctions had already been blurred between the sacred and the secular, between religion and civil society. Similarly, in the conduct of modern war, boundaries were gradually erased between state and society. Just as medieval knights were closely connected with the Catholic Church, 17th-century armies (especially the Protestant forces) made virtually everyone into functionaries of the state.

War and the State System

Whatever its origins, the organization of people into states constitutes a major fact of life in today's world, and the "state system" is crucial to issues of peace and war. Even though most people are organized in other ways as well—ethnically, vocationally, religiously, and so on—the state system has not only achieved a virtual monopoly over power (executions, wars) but also over political discourse and even the ability to imagine solutions to the problem of war. To a large extent, proposed courses of action within most peace movement traditions are "state centered," and within traditional governmental circles, policy options are focused almost entirely on the balance of power between major states.

Increasingly, as states came to be accepted almost without question as sovereign over individuals within their boundaries, they were left free to act with other states so as to maintain and enhance their power and international position. According to military historian Michael Howard, as often as not states fight "not over any specific issue such as might otherwise have been resolved by peaceful means, but in order to acquire, to enhance, or to preserve their capacity to function as independent actors in the international system at all." And French political theorist Raymond Aron argued that "the stakes of war are the existence, the creation or the elimination of states." In short, the wars between states, which characterize so much of the state system, are typically about states and the state system itself. On the other hand, since the end of World War II, the number of states in the world has tripled, largely because of decolonization, and yet the frequency of wars (as opposed to their intensity) has not increased correspondingly.

Certain states have been disproportionately involved in wars. These tend overwhelmingly to be the Great Powers, especially those of Europe. According to Quincy Wright, of the 2,600 most important battles involving European states between 1480 and 1940, France participated in 47%, Austria-Hungary in 34%, Great Britain and Russia in 22%, Turkey in 15%, and Spain in 12%. Of 25 interstate wars since 1914, the Great Powers were involved in 19. Today, the United States alone spends about 60% of all military budgets worldwide, and the Great Powers (United States, Russia, Great Britain, France, Germany, Italy, China, and Japan), nearly 90%. Several centuries ago, Spain, Turkey, Holland, and Sweden were involved in a high proportion of wars; with their decline as world powers, they have been substantially more peaceable as well.

These observations suggest that perhaps the problem of war is not so much a function of the *system* of states, but rather of *certain* states, and particularly, of the relative importance of these states. Furthermore, it can be argued that there is not, in fact, a "system" of states, but rather simply a number of separate entities, each pursuing its own interest (*Realpolitik*). And yet states often seem to act not only to preserve themselves but also to maintain the predominant international fabric of which they are part.

This leads to two rather different ways of thinking about the reasons for wars: (1) a kind of *systemic analysis*, in which the most significant factor is considered to be the preexisting organization—of states, of ideologies, or of individual or group inclinations—all of which inquire into the deep reasons for wars, versus (2) a *situational analysis*, which considers each crisis to be attributable largely to the situation presented by the crisis itself, a function of specific events, actors, and unique situations.

Finally, it should be emphasized that the system of states is not irretrievably wedded to war. After all, there have been numerous peaceful boundaries between states, such as the United States and Canada since 1812, the United States and Mexico since 1846, and Norway and Sweden since their peaceful separation in 1905. In addition, war between France and Germany, or Britain and France, is almost inconceivable today, although the animosity between both these states goes back literally hundreds of years.

Alliances Between States

States form alliances. They do so to increase their security, assuming that in unity there is strength. Surprisingly, perhaps, large states (such as the United States, Russia, Britain, and France) are more likely to enter into alliances than are small ones. Large states consider themselves to have large responsibilities and commitments, with their obligations often exceeding their resources; hence, they seek to ally with others. Alliances are also often formed among states that share common cultural or ideological features. They typically involve mutual pledges of assistance, often including the willingness to go to war in support of another alliance member.

Alliances as a Cause of War . . .

It has been claimed that alliances can help deter war by confronting a would-be aggressor with stronger opposition. But it can also be argued that, overall, alliances have served more as a cause of war. Even the signing of an alliance can be a serious provocation, leading to efforts to test, undermine, or break rival alliances. The evidence is equivocal, although certainly, alliances have a very strong influence on who goes to war and on which side, when and if war breaks out.

The events leading to World War I provide the most dramatic example of alliances among states contributing to war. Alliances among states can be double-edged swords: bringing about or preventing war, increasing or reducing tensions, tying states together in ways that may not be anticipated by the leaders and can only with difficulty be understood, later, by historians.

. . . . And the Absence of Alliances as a Cause of War

Ironically, just as World War I was caused in part by the state system of alliances, World War II was brought about in part by the absence of such alliances. Through much of the 1930s, Stalin sought to involve the Western powers in an alliance against Nazi Germany, but Britain and France, apparently disliking the Soviet Union even more than Hitler's Germany, resisted. Then, in 1938, French premier Edouard Daladier and British prime minister Neville Chamberlain agreed in Munich to allow Hitler to occupy the Sudetenland of Czechoslovakia. When Hitler also annexed Bohemia and Slovakia in the spring of 1939, Britain and France were finally ready to reinstitute the World War I Triple Entente against Germany. By this time, however, Stalin had given up on the West and had engineered his own pact with Hitler, calling for Germany and Russia to carve up Poland between them. When Germany invaded Poland in September 1939, France and Britain—having warned Hitler that they could not stand idly by—finally declared war on Germany. However, the ultimately successful alliance of Britain, France, the United States, and the Soviet Union did not come about until 1941, after Germany attacked its purported ally, the USSR. Japan, allied to Germany, then attacked the United States at Pearl Harbor, after which Germany declared war on the United States. Just as the rigidities of the pre-1914 alliances in Europe helped precipitate World War I, the failure of the anti-Nazi states to organize a united opposition seems to have encouraged German expansionism.

In more recent times, supporters claim that NATO (and presumably the former Warsaw Pact as well) kept the East-West peace between 1945 and the fall of the Soviet Union in 1991. An alternative view is that these alliances in fact heightened tensions that might otherwise have subsided. In any event, it is noteworthy that the end of the last Cold War has led to anxiety among many NATO officials that their alliance has become increasingly outdated, notwithstanding the leading role played by NATO in the militarily victorious campaign against Serbia in 1999.

Alliances and the State System

Winston Churchill, for all his opposition to Hitler, detested Stalin and the Soviet Union at least as much—until Hitler's attack on the USSR set the stage for Britain to ally itself with the Soviets against Nazi Germany. Again and again, alliances have been based primarily on matters of state convenience and power (Realpolitik considerations). Hence, they have shifted readily, depending on current perceptions of mutual advantage. As Great Britain's Lord Palmerston put it, "Great states have no permanent friends, only permanent interests."

Conventional political scientists have attempted to characterize the state system—both past and present—in terms of the pattern of major state actors and their alliances. Two primary dimensions are generally considered: polarity and connectedness. Thus, a bipolar system consists of primarily two states (such as the United States and the former USSR) with their associated allies as minor accompaniments. By contrast, a multipolar system might consist of many states (e.g., the United States, Russia, Japan, China, and the "superstate" of Europe). The dimension of connectedness refers to the closeness with which the various states are linked, and thus the probability that a perturbation in one will cause some change in another. If this probability is high, the states are said to be "tightly" connected; if low, they are "loosely" connected. Thus, the state system at any given time could conceivably be "tight and bipolar," "tight and multipolar," "loose and bipolar," or "loose and multipolar."

Much effort has been expended trying not only to assess the nature of the world state system but also to predict its future. Theories also abound as to which patterns are most war prone and which are most peace-stable. For example, perhaps bipolar systems are more stable because each side can attend more accurately to the behavior of the other. Or perhaps multipolar systems are more stable for the same reason that biologically diverse ecosystems are more stable than monocultures: There are more different players available to take up the slack and to prevent catastrophic breakdown. Many other interpretations are possible; the jury is still out on the war/peace significance of differing patterns of interstate alliances.

In any event, such issues are particularly the concern of political scientists and specialists in international relations, fields that are often closely allied with, and often apologists for, the state system. The field of peace and conflict studies, by contrast, tends to distance itself from analyses of this sort, considering instead that the state system is part of the problem, and thus not likely to be part of the solution.

Realpolitik and *Raison d'État*

When a state behaves in a particular way, supposedly doing so for its own good, the French say that it is demonstrating *raison d'état*, the state's own reasons for its actions. The phrase also implies the "right of a state" to act in its own best interests. Insofar as states are totally sovereign, raison d'état is sufficient justification unto itself, legally if not morally.

Closely related is the concept of Realpolitik, derived from the German, and referring to the conduct of international affairs under the assumption that a state's policy should be oriented toward and based on considerations of power, rather than on presumably "utopian" ethical ideals. Realpolitik is not necessarily any more "real" than other models of international relations, but its advocates fancy it to be.

In the early modern period, Niccolò Machiavelli was a major proponent of Realpolitik; during the 18th century, Prussia's Frederick the Great; and in the 19th century, Austria's Metternich, Britain's Palmerston, and Germany's Bismarck practiced the tradition with particular success. In the 20th century, former U.S. secretary of state Henry Kissinger (a historian of Metternich) was a well-known practitioner, as was the political scientist Hans Morgenthau. These influential figures, and many others, claimed that Realpolitik requires statesmen to base policy decisions primarily from considerations of power and state self-interest, in other words, raison d'état.

Realpolitik and Power

Hans Morgenthau was especially concerned with outlining the Realpolitik bases for state conduct in world affairs. He maintained that the primary national interest was the quest for national security and that this was to be achieved fundamentally through national power. The goal of international politics, in Morgenthau's view, was therefore the maximization of national power. According to Morgenthau, "Universal moral principles cannot be applied to the actions of states in their abstract, universal formulation, but they must be filtered through the concrete circumstances of time and place." Politics is reducible to one of three basic goals: "to keep power, to increase power, or to demonstrate power." Power is to the national leader what wealth is to the economist, or morality to the ethicist. States are assumed to be concerned—almost exclusively—with enhancing their power, and not hesitant about going to war to do so.

Note, however, that power is not strictly limited to military power. In 1941, the United States was far more powerful than Japan realized, not because of its military (which was relatively small at that time) but because of its population, its industrial potential, and its determination to prevail. Japan, similarly, is very powerful today, despite a relatively modest military force, because of the size of its economy and its ability to compete in international markets. (This in turn may be partly because Japan has invested in domestic productivity rather than weaponry.) There is also moral power, enjoyed by certain neutral states such as Sweden, Norway, and to some extent, India because of its history of Gandhian nonviolence. The power of a state can be defined as the ability of that state to influence the behavior of other states. As such, power ("soft power," in the words of political scientist Joseph Nye) can derive from unity, ideology, effective leadership, geographic position, cultural influence, health and educational level of its citizens, access to resources, no less than raw military force and the willingness to use it (or "hard power," in Nye's formulation).

Realpolitik and War

In the rough and tumble of Realpolitik, however, military power—however achieved, and whether direct or implied—is the "name of the game. Karl von Clausewitz, spokesperson for the military aspects of Realpolitik, made the renowned observation that war is "the continuation of politics by other means." He emphasized the subordination of military to political goals and wrote that although war is often brutal, it should not be senseless, but rather "an act of violence to compel the enemy to fulfill our will." According to Clausewitz, "Violence is therefore the means; imposing our will on the enemy, the end."

Part of the Realpolitik tradition in statecraft, accordingly, is the view that war is, ideally, not a consequence of error or irrational factors, but rather a result of a coolheaded decision that more can be gained by going to war than by remaining at peace. By extension, wars begin when two parties disagree as to their relative strength, and end when they are in agreement, that is, when the victor is revealed to be stronger than the vanquished. (Of course, given that most wars have a loser, it can be argued that 50% of the time, states are wrong, or their decision process was less than ideal.)

It would be simplistic, however, to assume that practitioners of Realpolitik are necessarily warmongers. Rather, they advocate a constant and, as they see it, hardheaded sense of the ways of international relations, limiting war only to those cases in which it will contribute to the "national interest." Hans Morgenthau, for example, strongly opposed the Vietnam War, but only because it was hurtful to the United States, not because it was wrong. Morgenthau wrote,

> The concept of the national interest presupposes neither a naturally harmonious, peaceful world nor the inevitability of war as a consequence of the pursuit by all nations of their national interests. Quite to the contrary; it assumes continuous conflict and threat of war to be minimized through the continuous adjustment of conflicting interest by diplomatic action.[6]

Realpolitik and Morality

When the Realpolitik of interstate behavior comes into conflict with more altruistic ethical principles, the latter almost always take a back seat. On the other hand, Realpolitik considerations have long been used to justify the actions of states in going to war, although often using terms of morality or idealism. Consider the following argument from 19th-century British prime minister William Gladstone: "However deplorable wars may be, they are among the necessities of our condition; and there are times when justice, when faith, when the failure of mankind, require a man not to shrink from the responsibility of undertaking them." He argued that Britain had a moral obligation to aid the Bulgarians, at the time oppressed by the Turks, whose rule, according to Gladstone, involved "the basest and blackest outrage upon record within the present century, if not within the memory of man."[7] Yet, just 20 years earlier, Britain had gone to war in support of that same Ottoman Empire, against Russia (the Crimean War). The issue at the time, far from the abuses and outrages of Turkish policy, was in fact Realpolitik, in this case the competition between Britain and Russia for influence in the Black Sea region.

Realpolitik seems to transcend traditional liberal, radical, and conservative political ideologies. Thus, the British liberal statesman James Bright resigned from the cabinet in 1882 to protest Britain's bombardment of Alexandria and occupation of Egypt: "Be the Government Liberal or Tory much the same thing happens: war, with all its horrors and miseries and crimes and cost."[8] (However Gladstone's attitude represented something of an ethical advance over previous principles of Realpolitik in that he emphasized the relation of war to the common interests of humankind, rather than simple considerations of state power.)

Ethical considerations loom large in more recent history as well. And yet, when ideals of nonviolence, fairness, and noninterference conflict with Realpolitik, the latter has generally triumphed. Immediately after World War II, for example, U.S. government officials harbored a number of former Nazi war criminals—especially those with expertise as rocket scientists or knowledge about left-wing movements in Europe—because it was believed these people could help the United States compete with and defeat the Soviet Union. The United States has repeatedly refrained from criticizing the ruthless tactics of China in forcing its rule upon Tibet, and in brutally suppressing the prodemocracy movement in 1989, because trade with China is deemed economically important to America, and because for a while China served as a convenient ally in America's competition with the former Soviet Union. Similarly, the United States was long willing to wink at Pakistan's violation of nuclear nonproliferation obligations because of that nation's role as a conduit for American military aid to the anti-Soviet mujahideen guerrillas in Afghanistan, and as a counterbalance to India, often seen by the United States in the past as tilting toward the former USSR.

On a wide scale, the United States has collaborated with right-wing dictators and despots, often ignoring their abominable human rights records, because their anticommunist stance was judged useful in America's competition with the former Soviet bloc. U.S. government policy seems to have resulted from a Realpolitik desire to oppose and undermine left-wing governments, as in Nicaragua (and in Cuba since 1961), or left-wing insurgencies against right-wing regimes friendly to the United States (as in El Salvador). During the Cold War, the USSR was often no less observant of Realpolitik, showing little hesitation about quashing prodemocracy movements in East Germany (1953), Hungary (1956), and Czechoslovakia (1968) —although it allowed these and its other Eastern European former allies to leave the Soviet orbit between 1989 and 1991 (when it collapsed).

Status Quo Versus Revisionist States

Considerations of Realpolitik also influence whether states are satisfied with current circumstances or advocate for change. The former are "status quo states," such as the United States; they generally seek to keep things as they are. Their wars are fought against those who try to change things, notably threatening aggressors such as Nazi Germany or, more recently, revolutionary nationalist movements. The doctrine of deterrence—which is not limited to the nuclear age, but which nonetheless looms especially large in the calculations of nuclear-armed superpowers, especially the United States—lends itself especially well to states whose primary desire is to prevent change. Thus, deterrence represents a way of preventing another state from aggressing; by its nature, its greatest success is when nothing happens.

On the other hand, "revisionist states" are those that typically believe their status is not commensurate with their power and aspirations: Japan in 1905 (on the eve of the Russo-Japanese War) and again in the 1930s and early 1940s, and Germany in the 1870s and again in the 1930s. It is debated whether the USSR in the late 20th century was a status quo or revisionist state. Under Gorbachev, it became increasingly revisionist at home and abroad, culminating in its release of control over the states of Eastern Europe. The United States seems to have become a seeker of the status quo both at home and abroad. It remains to be seen whether China—an emerging Great Power of the 21st century—will be predominantly revisionist or status quo.

Internal Cohesion

Considerations of Realpolitik and raison d'état may lead politicians to engage in foreign wars so as to consolidate their domestic situation. In addition, strong psychological and sociological pressures induce citizens to "rally 'round the flag," who may then ignore or postpone complaints with the current government so as to present a united front to the enemy. Jean Bodin, a major conceptualizer of state sovereignty, wrote that "the best way of preserving a state, and guaranteeing it against sedition, rebellion, and civil war, is to keep the subjects in amity with another, and to this end, to find an enemy against whom they can make common cause." Similarly, on the eve of the American Civil War, Secretary of State William Seward urged that President Lincoln consider declaring war on France and Spain, so as to unite Americans and preserve the union.

In George Orwell's *1984*, the world was divided into three megastates, which constantly made war against each other, not to win but rather to preserve their internal conditions:

> The war, therefore, if we judge it by the standards of previous wars, is merely an imposture. . . . But though it is unreal it is not meaningless. It eats up the surplus of consumable goods, and it helps to preserve the special mental atmosphere that a hierarchical society needs. . . . The war is waged by each ruling group against its own subjects, and the object of the war is not to make or prevent conquests of territory, but to keep the structure of society intact.[9]

Wars can serve states by providing an outlet for pent-up energy as well as surplus manpower. Discussing the Revolutionary Wars of France during the 1790s, the noted historian William H. McNeill suggested that they helped the newly established French government to go

> far towards relieving the social instability that had triggered revolution in the first place. Under the Directory, the mass of young men who had been unable to find satisfactory careers in civil occupations before the revolution were either successfully absorbed into the work force at home or living as soldiers at the expense of neighboring peoples, or else more or less gloriously dead.[10]

On the other hand, if wars have consistently been initiated so as to achieve internal cohesion, a correlation should exist between internal and external conflicts. Yet careful studies have not been able to demonstrate any significant statistical relationship between these variables. Moreover, wars initiated in the hope of achieving national unity and minimizing dissension don't always work out that way. If the war is prolonged and costly, citizen dissatisfaction can grow, despite the pressures for conformity that wars typically engender. Major reasons for resentment include the burden of added taxes to pay for the war, the mounting toll of casualties, unhappiness with the direction of the war, and especially, anger if the war is lost.

It is relatively rare that ethical considerations are particularly important in generating popular dissatisfaction with a regime's warlike behavior, although the Vietnam War was an exception. Practical concerns are generally paramount. Thus, enormous Russian casualties during World War I were important in precipitating the Bolshevik Revolution of 1917, and popular resentment at the conduct of the Falklands War led to the downfall of General Galtieri's Argentine government in 1982. On the other hand, the government of the Ayatollah Khomeini in Iran was if anything strengthened by its bloody war with Iraq in the 1980s, as was Saddam Hussein's regime in the 1990s, despite costly military defeats at the hands of the United States and its allies.

Finally, since warfare requires a degree of national unity and effective central coordination, states that are internally disunited may be especially cautious and hesitant to engage in a war they could end up losing. Following its defeat by Japan in 1905, for example, and having been shaken by an unsuccessful revolution, Russia was unwilling to risk war with Austria-Hungary when the latter annexed Bosnia and Herzegovina in 1908. By the late 1930s, the two most cohesive states of Europe were Germany and Italy; it seems doubtful that these states launched World War II so as to achieve further unity. By contrast, Britain and France appeared fractionated and distracted; hence, they seemed (to Hitler at least) unlikely to resist aggression. When Iraq launched its war with Iran, in 1980, the situation within Iran appeared chaotic, which seemed to make the Iranians *more* vulnerable to outside attack rather than especially war prone.

Arms Races

Short of war itself, an arms race is the most prominent and warlike form of competition between states. Arms races have been defined as "intense competitions between opposed powers or groups of powers, each trying to achieve an advantage in military power by increasing the quantity or improving the quality of its armaments or armed forces."[11]

Between 1945 and 1991, the nuclear arms race between the United States and the Soviet Union consumed considerable resources and attention. Despite the disintegration of the Soviet Union, the United States has continued to conduct an arms "race" against a range of hypothetical adversaries, including terrorists and rogue states. But arms races existed long before the invention of nuclear weapons. Moreover, arms races have long been a major arena for interstate competition, from the city-states of Greece to competing feudal overlords during the Middle Ages to modern times. As William James put it, "The intensely sharp competitive *preparation* for war by the nations *is the real war*, permanent, unceasing, and the battles are only a sort of public verification of the mastery gained during the 'peace' interval."[12]

Anxiety and the Fundamental Attribution Error

Reciprocal anxiety has often fueled arms races, with each side worried that the other was about to pull ahead or was already in the lead. Often, this involved incorrect estimates, which exaggerated the other side's forces. In 1914, for example, German intelligence estimated that the French Army had 121,000 more soldiers than the German army; at the same time, the French judged that the German Army exceeded the French by 134,000! During the period 1906–1914, when Great Britain and Germany were engaged in a vigorous naval arms race, each of the two states worried that the other was about to launch a preemptive attack. Such anxiety almost certainly played a part in the actual declaration of World War I. Edward Grey, British foreign secretary during the decade leading up to World War I, put it this way:

> Great armaments lead inevitably to war. The increase of armaments ... produces a consciousness of the strength of other nations and a sense of fear. Fear begets suspicion and distrust and evil imaginings, till each Government feels it would be criminal and a betrayal of its country not to take every precaution, while every Government regards the precautions of every other Government as evidence of hostile intent.[13]

Governments and citizens often tend to make what psychologists call the *attribution error*. This involves attributing one's opponent's behavior to ill-will and aggressive designs, while attributing one's own, comparable behavior to an understandable effort at self-protection.

Failure to Act

It can also be argued, however, that just as the pre-World War I arms races helped precipitate that conflict, the *failure* of the Western powers— notably Britain and France—to engage Germany in an arms race may have helped bring about World War II. Hitler appears to have been emboldened by what he saw as the rise of pacifism in Western Europe. When Germany first began violating the provisions of the Versailles Treaty (which called essentially for the demilitarization of Germany), England and France were considerably stronger than Germany, yet they did not respond. Thus, when Germany rebuilt its military and reoccupied the Rhineland, England and France failed to act or even to engage in significant arming of their own. The German General Staff is now known to have been quite apprehensive about these early aggressive moves by Adolf Hitler: Had the Western allies responded more forcefully, it is likely that Germany would have backed down, and Hitler's aggressive momentum might have been ended before it gathered steam.

Peaceful Resolution of Arms Races

In some cases, arms races have been resolved peacefully:

1. Great Britain versus France, navy, 1841–1865

2. Germany versus France, army, 1870s–1890s

3. Great Britain versus France and Russia, navy, 1884–1905

4. Chile versus Argentina, navy, 1890–1902

5. United States versus Great Britain, navy (cruisers), 1920–1930

6. United States versus the former Soviet Union, nuclear weapons, 1945–1991, and versus Russia, 1991–present.

In case 1, one side simply gave up; in case 2, the competition simply petered out, at least temporarily; case 3 was resolved by an alliance among the racers; case 4 ended with a resolution of the existing boundary dispute; case 5 (and case 4 as well) ended with an arms limitation treaty. The outcome of case 6 remains to be determined.

Factors Driving Arms Races

Many factors drive arms races: the financial profits to be made, desire for advancement on the part of individuals whose careers depend on success in administering or commanding major new weapons programs, political leaders pandering to bellicose domestic sentiment, and interservice rivalry within a state. One of the important factors leading to the U.S. entrance into World War I was Germany's decision to engage in unrestricted submarine warfare, which resulted in the sinking of the civilian ocean liner *Lusitania*. This escalation of the war by Germany was due at least in part to the fact that, while the German Army was fully engaged on both the western and eastern fronts, the German high seas fleet had been inactive, while Britain dominated the oceans, including the North Sea. A frustrated Admiral Tirpitz wrote,

> If we come to the end . . . without the fleet having bled and worked, we shall get nothing more for the fleet, and all the scanty money that there may be will be spent on the army. The great efforts of His Majesty the Emperor to make Germany a naval power will have been all in vain.[14]

It should also be pointed out that there is occasionally one other potential reason for these activities: genuine concern about the security needs of the state. Faced with an uncompromisingly hostile opponent, national leaders have often believed that military might was their only real protection. This leads to what has aptly been called the "security dilemma": When states perceive that they must increase their military power so as to achieve security, their rivals feel constrained to do the same. As a result, both sides enter into a dangerous competitive spiral by which all parties are made less secure. Each side seeks to resolve its insecurity by acquiring more weapons, which only leads to even more insecurity, which leads to even greater acquisitions of weapons, and so on.

British historian Herbert Butterfield suggested that perhaps "no state can ever achieve the security it desires without so tipping the balance that it becomes a menace to its neighbors." In the process, it becomes a menace to itself. But this has not prevented states from trying.

Arms Races and War

Do arms races lead to war? One influential point of view claims that they do. Another, equally influential view maintains just the opposite: By being militarily strong, a state prevents war. Arguing in favor of greater military expenditures, President Reagan, for example, claimed that the United States has never gotten into a war because it was too strong. (This ignores the Mexican-American and Spanish-American Wars, and perhaps the Vietnam War as well.) Proponents of military strength and arms races point to the "lessons of Munich," when World War II was made more likely by the failure of the West to answer Germany's strength with strength of its own: Opponents of arms races point to World War I, when arms races caused the European powers to blunder into an unwanted and unnecessary war.

It has proved virtually impossible to evaluate these propositions, although most attempts to examine the historical record have shown that arms races seem more likely to produce war than to prevent it. For example, one political scientist examined 99 serious international disputes between 1815 and 1965. Twenty-eight of these had been preceded by an arms race; 71 had not. Of the former, 23 (82%) resulted in a war, whereas of the 71 disputes not preceded by an arms race, only 3 (4%) resulted in war.[15] Although this study does not prove that arms races cause war, it does suggest that when a serious dispute occurs in conjunction with an ongoing arms race, war is far more likely than when the disputing nations have not also been competing militarily.

Nonetheless, many statesmen as well as citizens remain convinced that security often demands strength, and strength often cannot be obtained without an arms race. This theme is described in the famous Latin motto *si vis pacem, para bellum* (if you want peace, prepare for war). "A wiser rule," according to sociologist William Graham Sumner, "would be to make up your mind soberly what you want, peace or war, and then to get ready for what you want; for what we prepare for is what we shall get."

A Final Note on War and States _____

States seem more often to be the problem than the solution, when it comes to war, although most people would agree that if there is to be a solution, states will have to be a part of that as well. Increasingly, states appear to exist for their own sake, not for the benefit of their citizens. They enter into wars for raisons d'état, and terminate them for the same reasons. If defense is the primary reason for people to associate into those large political entities known as states, then what is to be done in the nuclear age, when that relationship has become potentially lethal, and one-sided as well? Nuclear weapons in particular may well exist almost entirely because of the purported Realpolitik benefits they confer on states that possess them; however, it is increasingly difficult to argue that they confer security on the individual. Indeed, citizens of nonnuclear states, such as New Zealand, Australia, Switzerland, Finland, and Sweden, are in many ways more secure, and prosperous, than citizens of the nuclear powers (except, of course, for the fallout, nuclear winter, and other devastating consequences they, and everyone else, would suffer in the event of a major nuclear conflict).

The novelist E. L. Doctorow wrote,

> The time may be approaching when we will have to choose between two coincident reality systems: the historical human reality of feeling, of thought, of multitudinous expression, of life and love and natural death; or the supra-human statist reality of rigid, ahistorical, censorious and contending political myth structures, which may in our name and from the most barbaric impulses disenfranchise 99 percent of the world's population from even tragic participation in their fate.[16]

With the world in ecological and social crisis, states have largely compounded these problems through increasing violence and militarism. If one is to oppose war, is it also necessary, then, to oppose the state? Can positive peace be achieved within the current system of states? And if so, what about the various positive roles of the state, such as maintaining order, social welfare systems, and common purpose? Many of the most important factors affecting people's lives occur on a global scale and are to a large extent beyond the ability of states to manage.

In the first part of the 21st century, some states may increasingly turn their attention toward some of the global problems facing all human beings, such as poverty, ecological destruction, and the urgent need for worldwide demilitarization, especially weapons of mass destruction. But except for nongovernmental organizations (NGOs) and international organizations such as the United Nations, it seems likely that Realpolitik and a narrowly defined sense of "the national interest" will continue to be the modus operandi for most states, particularly for great powers such as the United States. As a result, students of peace and conflict studies can anticipate efforts by many organizations to go beyond existing state boundaries and to seek alternative and/or additional ways of resolving these planetary issues.

Notes

1. Randolph S. Bourne. 1964. *War and the Intellectuals, Collected Essays 1915–1919*. New York: Harper & Row.

2. Quincy Wright. 1964. *A Study of War*. Chicago: University of Chicago Press.

3. Benito Mussolini. 1963. "The Doctrine of Fascism." In J. Somerville and R. Santoni, eds., *Social and Political Philosophy*. New York: Anchor.

4. Kenneth Waltz. 1959. *Man, the State, and War*. New York: Columbia University Press.

5. Augustine. 1950. *The City of God*. New York: Modern Library.

6. Quoted in J. E. Dougherty and R. L. Pfalzgraff. 1981. *Contending Theories of International Relations*. New York: Macmillan.

7. Quoted in J. Morley. 1903. *The Life of William Everett Gladstone*. New York: Macmillan.

8. Ibid.

9. George Orwell. 1984. *1984*. San Diego: Harcourt Brace Jovanovich.

10. William H. McNeill. 1982. *The Pursuit of Power*. Chicago: University of Chicago Press.

11. Hedley Bull. 1965. *The Control of the Arms Race*. New York: Praeger.

12. William James. 1967. *The Writings of William James*. New York: Random House.

13. Quoted in John G. Stoessinger. 1985. *Why Nations Go to War*. New York: St. Martin's.

14. Quoted in Stoessinger, *Why Nations Go to War*.

15. William D. Wallace. 1979. "Arms Races and Escalation." *Journal of Conflict Resolution* 23: 3–16.

16. E. L. Doctorow. "It's a Cold War Out There, Class of '83." *The Nation*, July 2, 1983.

8 The Decision-Making Level

The offhand decision of some commonplace mind high in office at a critical moment influences the course of events for a hundred years.

—Thomas Hardy

Large groups of people are usually led by much smaller groups, and in many cases, the ultimate decisions of war and peace are made by very few people, sometimes just one person. In our examination of the reasons for wars, it is therefore appropriate to consider decision making at the level of government and other influential leaders.

The Role of Leaders

There has long been debate over the role of crucial individuals in the making of history. So-called great man theories maintain that the personality of certain select, major figures has had a determining effect on world events. By contrast, theories of "impersonal forces" claim that most significant events would have happened no matter who was in charge, because they represent the culmination of large ebbs and flows of societies and historical trends, rather than resulting from the actions of a small, extremely influential minority.

In various writings, but most notably in *War and Peace*, Leo Tolstoy argued for the impersonal forces theory. He portrayed Napoleon as a bit ridiculous, imagining himself making important decisions such as whether or not to go to war, or how to conduct important battles; whereas, according to Tolstoy, major leaders are actually "history's slaves." In discussing the outbreak of war between France and Russia in 1812, the following questions are raised:

> What produced this extraordinary occurrence? What were its causes? The historians tell us with naive assurance that its causes were the wrongs inflicted on the Duke of Oldenburg, the non-observance of the Continental System, the ambition of Napoleon, the firmness of Alexander, the mistakes of the diplomats, and so forth and so on. . . . To us the wish or objection of this or that French corporal to serve a second term appears as much a cause as Napoleon's refusal to withdraw his troops beyond the Vistula and to restore the Duchy of Oldenburg; for had he not wished to serve, and had a second, a third and a thousandth corporal and private also refused, there would have been so many less men in Napoleon's arms and the war could not have occurred. . . . And there was no one cause for that occurrence, but it had to occur because it had to! Millions of men, renouncing their human feelings and reason, had to go from West to East to slay their fellows. . . . The actions of Napoleon and Alexander were as little voluntary as the action of any soldier who was drawn into the campaign by lot or by conscription. . . . To elicit the laws of history we must leave aside kings, ministers and generals, and select for study the homogeneous, infinitesimal elements which influence the masses.[1]

Tolstoy's view that the common people are as responsible as their leaders laid the foundation for his conviction that individuals have the opportunity —indeed, the responsibility—to take things into their own hands and refuse to fight.

With regard to its causes, probably no war has been analyzed in greater detail than World War I, because the interweaving factors that culminated in that war were unusually complex, and because so many relevant government documents are available to historians. No single villain (and certainly, no hero) emerges from all this scholarship, and some respected observers have even proposed that somehow, war was "in the air":

> What was in the air by 1914 was a spirit of violent repudiation of the age that can scarcely be accounted for in any objective historical or political terms, but only by a judgment on human character. The nineteenth century had abolished war; but the peace and stability of that world perished because men could hardly bear to live for a century with the kind of world they had made.[2]

This view does not ignore other concerns or causal factors, but it emphasizes the irrational and impersonal:

No single cause will explain the First World War. But the formal causes—the commercial and colonial rivalries, the cocked war establishments of Europe designed to mobilize, deploy, and conquer by the execution of a single and irreversible general-staff plan, the strident minorities and grandiose nationalisms, the disintegration of the Austro-Hungarian empire, the colonial rivalries, the rot of Turkey, the instability of the balance of power—all these pale before the fact that Europe in 1914 wanted war and got it.[3]

While this debate may be unresolvable, it is still necessary to attend to the specific issue of leaders and their decision making, if only because leaders do exist, they do make decisions, and moreover, there is good reason to think that these decisions are important—although perhaps not as important as most leaders themselves would like to think.

Strong Leaders

In the past, when rulers embodied the political and military power of their group, they clearly played a major role in deciding whether or not to go to war. In *The Education of a Christian Prince*, Erasmus urged,

Although a prince ought nowhere to be precipitate in his plans, there is no place for him to be more deliberate and circumspect than in the matter of going to war. Some evils come from one source and others from another, but from war comes the shipwreck of all that is good and from it the sea of all calamities pours out.[4]

The role of individual leaders may well have been unduly glamorized, and decision makers often receive credit—and blame—that they do not entirely deserve. And yet certain individuals, by the force of their personalities and the decisions they made, have had enduring effects on history. Sometimes, they represent the culmination of currents within their societies, and they may also catalyze other events. Nonetheless, people such as Alexander the Great, Genghis Khan, Charlemagne, Joan of Arc, Napoleon, Bismarck, Hitler, Stalin, de Gaulle, Mao Tse-tung, and Saddam Hussein have acted as lightning rods for popular discontent, and often, as precipitators of war. Less often have leaders of this ilk achieved renown as peacemakers.

On the other hand, when it becomes necessary for a state to accept defeat, a strong leader may be the only person capable of getting the populace to swallow the bitter pill. Marshal Pétain played this role in France in 1940, as did Carl Mannerheim in Finland in 1944, and Charles de Gaulle in France in 1961 by granting independence to Algeria. Perhaps the British people were better able to tolerate the post-World War II dissolution of their empire when it was conducted by Churchill, who was an avowed proimperialist,

just as the warming of Sino-American relations during the Nixon administration was facilitated by the fact that Richard Nixon's reputation as
a hard-line anticommunist insulated him against most accusations of
"appeasement."

Many leaders may be moved by the desire to go down in history as peacemakers. Thus, the dramatic warming of relations between the United States
and the former Soviet Union during the late 1980s and early 1990s must
be attributed, at least partly, to a partial shift in perceptions and goals
by President Reagan. This was even more the result of the commitment by
Mikhail Gorbachev to *glasnost* and *perestroika* ("opening" and "restructuring") inside the USSR. This produced a lessening of U.S.-Soviet tensions
and movement toward arms control, as well as a partial reduction of conventional forces in Europe and a decrease in the number of strategic nuclear
warheads. It almost certainly would not have taken place had any of
Gorbachev's more Stalinist rivals assumed power in the Kremlin. On the
other hand, Reagan's personal commitment to "Star Wars" (or SDI, the
Strategic Defense Initiative) hindered the prospects of even more dramatic
cuts in U.S. and Soviet nuclear weapons, just as U.S. insistence on "amend-
ing" the 1972 ABM (Anti-Ballistic Missile) Treaty, ostensibly to build a
National Missile Defense (NMD) system, threatens to have a similar effect
in the early 21st century.

Whereas the exaltation of national honor and state power has been cru-
cial throughout history, these general sentiments have been filtered through
charismatic personalities. Examples include Edward III and Henry V of
England in the 14th and 15th centuries; Philip II and Charles V of Spain
in the 16th; Charles XII of Sweden and Louis XIV of France in the 17th;
Russia's Peter the Great and Prussia's Frederick the Great in the 18th;
Napoleon Bonaparte in France, Abraham Lincoln in the United States, and
Bismarck in Germany in the 19th; and Mussolini of Italy and Hitler in
Germany during the 20th century.

The role of individual leaders is perhaps most clearly emphasized in the
events during the early days of World War II, when Britain stood virtually
alone against Nazi Germany. Churchill not only personified British defiance
and determination at that time, but he also helped generate it with such stirring rhetorical pronouncements as: "We shall fight on the beaches, we shall
fight on the landing grounds, we shall fight in the fields and in the streets, we
shall fight in the hills; we will never surrender." And when President Sadat
of Egypt went to Israel and negotiated a historic peace treaty with Israel's
Begin, through the mediating efforts of President Carter, it was a triumph of
the courage, vision, and hard work of a few individuals.

In many cases, of course, wars are imposed on their people by the decisions of their leadership. The various wars of succession during the 18th
century, for example, did not well up from public anger or concern; rather,
they were decreed by leaders for *raisons d'état*, and obediently entered into

by most of the populace. At other times, charismatic leaders from Alexander the Great to Hitler have succeeded in generating wartime enthusiasm (although admittedly, their messages could flourish only on fertile soil). In his war message to the American people in 1917, President Wilson expressed the oft-spoken distinction between people and their leadership, one that—true or not—has proven especially convenient during war:

> We have no quarrel with the German people. . . . It was not upon their impulse that their government acted. . . . It was a war determined as wars used to be determined upon in the old, unhappy days when people were nowhere consulted by their rulers and wars were provoked and waged in the interest of dynasties or of little groups of ambitious men who were accustomed to use their fellow men as pawns or tools.[5]

Weak Leaders and the Role of "Villains"

Of course, it is not necessarily true that only strong leaders initiate wars. The weak political personalities of Germany's Kaiser Wilhelm and Russia's Czar Nicholas rendered them unable to hold their general staffs in check; stronger leadership on their part might have prevented the First World War, just as stronger leadership in Britain and France during the 1930s might have averted the Second. (In the former case, such strength would have been needed to restrain those, within the country, who felt bound to follow predesigned mobilization plans, and who worried excessively about being preempted by the other side. In the latter case, strength was needed in restraining those outside the country—notably Hitler and Mussolini.)

The Cuban Missile Crisis—the closest humanity has apparently come to general nuclear war—was brought about in part because John F. Kennedy had felt browbeaten by Soviet Premier Khrushchev at their 1961 summit meeting in Vienna and had felt humiliated by the debacle of the failed American-supported invasion of Cuba at the Bay of Pigs. The following year, Kennedy was determined that he would not be pushed around again by the Soviet leader; fortunately for the world, Khrushchev was able (perhaps, due largely to insufficient military strength) to be willing to back down.

Lyndon Johnson also seemed to have been determined not to be defeated by the Asian Communists, Ho Chi Minh and the North Vietnamese. The war between Iran and Iraq during the 1980s depended in large part on personal animosity between the two leaders, Saddam Hussein of Iraq and the Ayatollah Khomeini of Iran. And the Persian Gulf War was fed by the hostility between Saddam Hussein and George Bush. The list goes on.

Sometimes, wars result from the overwhelming personal ambition of leaders, something that is not restricted to modern tyrants or would-be conquerors. Consider this boast from Xerxes, King of Persia in 480 B.C.E. (and recounted by Herodotus):

Once let us subdue this people [the Greeks] . . . and we shall extend the Persian territory beyond our borders; for I will pass through Europe from one end to the other, and make of all lands which it contains one country. . . . By this course then we shall bring all mankind under our yoke.[6]

Sometimes, the issue is face-saving, in which case leaders are especially likely to precipitate a crisis—or respond aggressively to one—if they are wary of opposition at home. Thus, President Truman, stung by criticism that he had "lost" China to communists, may have felt driven to intervene in response to the North Korean incursion at the start of the Korean War. Later, Truman hesitated to restrain General Douglas MacArthur from seeking to unify Korea by conquest of North Korea in 1950. John F. Kennedy seriously worried that he might be impeached if he did not respond forcefully to the discovery of Soviet missile sites under construction in Cuba. Also in 1962, India's Nehru had stirred up anti-Chinese feeling in India, and when the Chinese resisted Indian territorial encroachments, he had to choose between fighting and losing face, even though the Chinese had overwhelming logistic advantages and 10 times as many troops.

We know very little about what produces personalities that lead to national leadership, or what distinguishes a peacemaker from a warmonger. Alexander the Great grew up as one of many children in a royal, polygynous household. Contact with his father (Philip of Macedon) was rare, and young Alexander apparently had a very intense relationship with his mother, who was ambitious, energetic, demanding, punitive, and rather violent. Perhaps it is not surprising that Alexander's quest for approval included conquering much of the known world before he was 33. On the other hand, Prussia's Frederick—also known as the Great—had a submissive, ineffectual mother, but a demanding, callous, and rather brutal father (who forced him to witness the beheading of his boyhood friend). In his book *The Anatomy of Human Destructiveness,* psychoanalyst Erich Fromm argued that the early experiences of Hitler and Stalin produced a kind of malignant sadism (Stalin) and necrophilia (Hitler).

Genghis Khan, Attila the Hun, Timur, Hitler—these leaders often appear as villains, and rightly so, insofar as they figured prominently in precipitating wars that resulted in the deaths of millions. But what of Cecil Rhodes, an architect of British imperialism; Alfred Krupp, German weapons manufacturer extraordinaire; and J. Robert Oppenheimer and the other American physicists who created the first atomic bombs, or President Truman, who ordered their use, or the bomber crews who dropped them, or the patriotic citizens who paid their taxes in support of the war effort, and so on? The point is that it may be relatively easy to assign villainy to a select number of prominent individuals, but by most measures there is more than enough blame to go around.

Political revolutions are often precipitated by the popular perception that leadership is particularly corrupt or villainous. Although the new leadership may enjoy wider popular support (at least for a time), it may be as bad as, or worse than, what it replaces: Robespierre, for example, became more dreaded than Louis XIV, who was rather mild and fumbling by contrast. And Stalin was far worse than Czar Nicholas II. Moreover, heroes in one nation are often perceived as evildoers in another, and vice versa, as was the case during the Persian Gulf War, with Saddam Hussein and George Bush being demonized in each other's country.

It is often difficult to assign villainy in matters of politics, and especially in war and peace, because supporting reasons often exist for even the most violent and inhumane acts. Nonetheless, in certain cases, responsibility and blame seem sufficiently clear that widely accepted moral judgments have been made. After Pol Pot and his Khmer Rouge took power in 1975, at least a million people out of Cambodia's total population of seven million were killed, including virtually anyone perceived by the Khmer Rouge leadership to have Western connections, training, language, even eyeglasses. Idi Amin, formerly a Ugandan Army sergeant, took over the Ugandan government in 1971, initiating a reign of terror that is believed to have claimed more than 300,000 lives before Tanzanian troops, supported by Ugandan exiles, invaded Uganda in 1979 and drove Amin from power.

However, even (perceived) villainy—or at least, the extent of villainy—is open to dispute. The traditional, mainstream Anglo-American interpretation of the causes of World War II, for example, lays particular stress upon Hitler's aggressive designs plus, in a supporting role, British and French appeasement. But at least one revisionist historian, A. J. P. Taylor, has refused to heap all the blame on Hitler, viewing the Second World War instead as a continued pattern of German expansionism and militarism traceable at least to Bismarck. Also to blame in Taylor's view were the unsatisfactory (from the German perspective) Versailles Treaty that terminated the First World War and a large dose of faulty calculations both by Hitler and the Western leaders.

Regardless of the specific historical details, there may be some validity to placing substantial blame for many and perhaps most wars on a limited number of individuals. This view, however, must reconcile itself with the likelihood that even with a different cast of major characters, the outcome might have been fundamentally the same. Much of this blame should also go to what has been called the "military mind," which, according to the conservative political scientist Samuel Huntington,

emphasizes the permanence of irrationality, weakness and evil in human affairs. It stresses the supremacy of society over the individual and the importance of order, hierarchy and division of function. It accepts the nation state as the highest form of political organization

and recognizes the continuing likelihood of war among nation states
. . . . It exalts obedience as the highest virtue of military men. . . . It is,
in brief, realistic and conservative.[7]

As to the military's preoccupation with "security," to some extent it is
only doing its job—or at least, what society expects. "If you believe the
doctors," wrote England's Lord Salisbury, "nothing is wholesome; if you
believe the theologians, nothing is innocent; if you believe the soldiers, nothing is safe." There is, however, a crucial difference between the warnings of
doctors, theologians, and soldiers: We are not likely to make ourselves ill if
we obey our doctors, or to be damned if we obey our theologians. However,
the warnings of soldiers can lead to mistrust, arms races, and war. This is
illustrated, above all, in the tragic inflexibility shown by the belligerents in
World War I, which stands as an important cautionary tale for modern
times, when the mobilization time for nuclear-armed missiles is measured in
minutes.

Crisis Decision Making

Stimulated in particular by the close call of the Cuban Missile Crisis,
psychologically minded students of international relations have directed
considerable attention to the process whereby decisions are made, often
focusing on issues of perception and misperception, communication and
miscommunication, understandings and misunderstandings, and the effects
of crisis conditions and of small-group processes on decision making.

Small Groups

Major governmental decisions, especially regarding war or warlike actions,
are made by small ad hoc groups, that is, groups that may have been convened for that specific purpose. During the crisis at the beginning of the
Korean War, for example, 14 people participated in the emergency deliber-
ations of the U.S. government; during the Cuban Missile Crisis, the committee convened by President Kennedy had 16 members. The Politburo, the
core unit of decision making in the former Soviet Union, normally consisted
of 14 full members. In this context, it has been suggested that the United
Nations Educational, Scientific, and Cultural Organization (UNESCO)
charter should be rewritten to read, "Since wars begin in the minds of men
in the core decisional groups of the nation-states, it is in the minds of those
men that the defenses of peace must be constructed."[8]

It is often hoped a group will temper the enthusiasm and impetuosity of
a leader. However, studies suggest that the opposite is more likely to occur:
Group members tend to egg each other on, reinforcing tendencies present in

the most dominant individual(s). Social psychologists have found that risk taking tends to be more pronounced in groups than in individuals, because no one person must (or can) take responsibility for the outcome. Contrary to the widespread belief that "tough" leadership makes would-be aggressors back down, data indicate that the likelihood of war increases when leaders are willing to accept a high level of risk.

The greater the perceived outside threat, the greater the tendency to put up a united front, to suppress personal doubts and foster an illusion of unanimity. This tendency is enhanced by the fact that high-level leaders generally surround themselves with "yes men," people who agree with them and who rarely present contrary views. In short, leaders become victims of what social psychologist Irving Janis called "groupthink." This is

> a mode of thinking that people engage in when they are deeply involved in a cohesive in-group, when the members' strivings for unanimity override their motivation to realistically appraise alternative courses of action. Groupthink refers to a deterioration of mental efficiency, reality testing, and moral judgment that results from in-group pressures.[9]

Janis also emphasized that groupthink "is likely to result in irrational and dehumanizing actions directed against out-groups." The conclusion is that groups may be no more rational than individuals, and often less so. For example, following General MacArthur's success in repelling the North Koreans, the United States made the fateful decision to seek to unify all of Korea by force of arms. This eventually resulted in China crossing the Yalu River into Korean territory, and three years of stalemated war, with hundreds of thousands—perhaps more than a million—additional casualties. This decision was taken by a small group of American officials, strongly influenced by MacArthur's overconfidence. Discussion within the group shared and reinforced an illusion of invulnerability based in part on racial stereotyping of the enemy—the North Koreans—and the potential enemy, the Chinese. Experts with dissenting views were excluded from the decision-making process.

Excluding Bad News

This phenomenon is worth exploring in more detail: MacArthur's commitment to his goal of destroying the North Koreans made him insensitive to reports that would counsel caution to someone more open-minded. As a result, subordinates—eager to ingratiate themselves with their commander, or at least, to avoid antagonizing him—slanted intelligence reports to reinforce what they believed to be MacArthur's perception of the situation.

This is a widespread and dangerous phenomenon in crisis decision making: the fact that it may be based on incorrect information because the information sources have been hesitant to send bad news. For example, prior to World War I, Prince Lichnowsky, the German ambassador to Britain, reported (correctly) to the kaiser that Britain was prepared to declare war against Germany; he was alternately disregarded and derided as incompetent. By contrast, the German ambassador to Russia was praised for sending reassuring messages back to Berlin, stating that the czar was not likely to defend Serbia, even while that he was recording something very different in his personal notebooks. There are two useful lessons here: (1) When the bearer of bad tidings is likely to fare poorly, he or she may well doctor the message, and (2) people—including state leaders—often exhibit selective attention, so that if they are already committed to a course of action, they tend to disregard what they do not want to hear, focusing only on information that confirms their preexisting beliefs. Thus, Stalin actually ordered the execution of a Czech agent who warned in April 1941 (correctly, it turned out) that Nazi Germany was preparing an attack on the USSR. At the time, Stalin maintained that the spy must be a British provocateur, so convinced was he of British animosity toward the Soviet Union and of the reliability of his alliance with Hitler.

Decision-Making Pressures

Political crises may be defined as unanticipated threats to the values and institutions that leaders hold most important and that accordingly impel them to make prompt decisions. Decisions made during perceived crises are likely to be especially crucial for war and peace; unfortunately, it is precisely under such conditions—when stress is unusually high—that decision making is most likely to be flawed.

Crisis decision making is likely to have the following characteristics:

1. *Time pressure.* There is frequently a need (or a perceived need) for leaders to make decisions quickly.

2. *Heavy responsibility.* Most leaders are aware, some of them acutely aware, of the potential costs in human suffering if their decision results in war.

3. *Faulty and incomplete data.* Intelligence about the potential opponent (motivations, alternative options, strengths and weaknesses) is usually limited and inadequate. Under such conditions, there is a tendency for decision makers to rely on simplistic and often inaccurate stereotypes of the opponent.

4. *Information overload.* Many contemporary decision makers are inundated with large amounts of information, and although much of it may in fact be erroneous, decision makers typically do not know what information to ignore or believe.

5. *Limited options*. Decision makers often see themselves as having only a limited range of potential courses of action (in part, because the stress of the situation itself tends to limit creative problem solving); at the same time, the opponent is often perceived as enjoying a wide latitude of possible choices.

6. *Short-term over long-term*. Decision makers' attention tends to be focused on the immediate, short-term effects of a course of action, with relatively little patience for an assessment of the possible long-term implications of their decision. Their chief desire is then to act in such a way as to relieve the current, pressing crisis.

7. *Surprise*. Although the situation may not be entirely unexpected, an element of surprise is often involved, so that most crises appear to the decision makers to have to be resolved on the spot, without benefit of preanalyzed scenarios.

8. *Personal stresses*. Decisions of great import must often be made under conditions of sleep deprivation and sometimes under great anxiety, bordering on panic, for many decision makers.

All of the above factors combine to make it especially difficult for leaders—either singly or in small groups—to render intelligent and rational judgments. Writing of the Berlin Crisis of 1961, the Cuban Missile Crisis of 1962, and the U.S.-Soviet tensions raised during the Arab-Israeli Six-Day War (1967), former defense secretary Robert McNamara noted that

> on each of the occasions lack of information, misinformation, and misjudgments led to confrontation. And in each of them, as the crisis evolved, tensions heightened, emotions rose, and the danger of irrational decisions increased.[10]

Crisis Management

In view of the importance of such situations, a recent area of investigation, known as *crisis management*, has emerged. The goals of crisis management are not only (1) to prevent a crisis from escalating to war, but also (2) to keep the leaders in control of the situation and (3) to gain maximum advantage, whenever possible, from such crises when they occur. When crises involve the danger of war, especially nuclear war, decision makers on each side want to appear strong, fear to seem weak, and are eager to gain some advantage over the other that they would not like to see the other have over them. Crisis behavior then tends to become an exercise in "competitive risk taking."

The leaders on each side are inclined to engage in *one-upmanship*, hoping to induce the other side to back down, in a situation dangerously reminiscent of the game of chicken, whether nuclear weapons are involved or not. For example, a senior aide to President Kennedy recounted that during the Cuban Missile Crisis, former secretary of state Dean Acheson recommended bombing the Soviet missile sites, which had just been discovered in Cuba. When asked what, in his judgment, the Soviets would do in response, Acheson replied, "I think they'll knock out our missile bases in Turkey." "What do we do then?" "Under our NATO Treaty, we'd be obligated to knock out a base inside the Soviet Union." "What will they do then?" "Why, then we hope everyone will cool down and want to talk."[11]

Psychological Effects of Repetitive Crises

Even when an individual crisis is resolved peacefully (as in the case of the Cuban Missile Crisis), repetitive crises can produce an expectancy of war. For example, during the few years preceding the outbreak of World War I, Germany had been embroiled in numerous situations of near war—with Russia over Austria's annexation of Bosnia and Herzegovina, with Britain and France over Morocco—in addition to the navy race with Britain and an army race with France. Such situations can result in a feeling of fatalism as yet another crisis emerges, or an existing one is painfully prolonged and things appear to be leading slowly but irrevocably toward war. Finally, rationality and flexible decision making are often replaced by a sense on the part of leaders that they must accept the ensuing, and apparently inevitable, destruction to come.

Thus, on the eve of the First World War, the German kaiser exclaimed, in a fit of pique and resignation, "Even if we are bled to death, England will at least lose India." And when, after an ongoing series of economic and diplomatic confrontations with the United States, the Japanese government secretly decided on war with the United States, the Japanese war minister commented that "once in a while it is necessary for one to close one's eyes and jump from the stage of the Kiyomizu Temple" (a renowned suicide spot). Crises, in short, can be psychologically erosive, leaving war as apparently the simplest solution to unresolved political and diplomatic problems.

In some cases, though, a crisis, terminated short of war, has actually served to bring the two opposing sides closer together. In 1898, for example, a small contingent of French troops briefly occupied Fashoda, in Sudan, contesting the colonial claims of England. The ensuing "Fashoda crisis" generated enormous tension between France and England, nearly leading to war. It turned out, however, that this confrontation marked the high point of Anglo-French colonial rivalry, after which the two states became increasingly allied, leading to the entente of 1904 and to their subsequent friendship throughout the 20th century. Similarly, the Cuban Missile Crisis seems to have sobered the leadership of both the United States and the USSR, leading to a warming of relations the following year, including the signing of the

Atmospheric Test Ban Treaty, and eventually to a long period of détente, if not friendship.

Crisis in the Nuclear Age

Prior to World War I, mobilization of the Great Powers was extraordinarily fast, given the immense amounts of men and materiel involved, but it still required several days. In the nuclear age, mobilization requires mere minutes, and entire wars could be fought within hours. The quick-reaction regime of ballistic missiles has resulted in a chronic crisis mentality in leaders, advisers, and military chiefs. Thomas Schelling offers the following metaphor:

> If I go downstairs to investigate a noise at night, with a gun in my hand, and find myself face to face with a burglar who has a gun in his hand, there is danger of an outcome that neither of us desires. Even if he prefers just to leave quietly, and I wish him to, there is danger that he may *think* I want to shoot, and shoot first. Worse, there is danger that he may think that I think *he* wants to shoot. And so on.[12]

In the idealized case, crisis decision making is based on instrumental or strategic rationality. Decision making is seen as a variant of mathematical economics, a process of maximizing the difference between benefits and costs; this approach is especially popular among devotees of nuclear deterrence theory. Nuclear strategist Herman Kahn, for example, developed an elaborate classification of 44 different rungs of nuclear escalation, beginning with precise, low-intensity options such as "slow-motion counterproperty," through "augmented disarming attacks," and culminating in "spasm or insensate war."

The assumption that decision makers will remain rational during a full-fledged nuclear crisis, carefully picking and choosing among the various nuclear options while the bombs are going off all around, is one of the less credible aspects of modern nuclear strategy. In 1974, Secretary of Defense James Schlesinger testified to Congress about his judgment as to the feasibility of rationally conducting a "limited" nuclear war:

> If we were to maintain continued communications with the Soviet leaders during the war, and if we were to describe precisely and meticulously the limited nature of our actions, including the desire to avoid attacking their urban industrial bases . . . in spite of [the claims] that everything must go all out, when the existential circumstances arise, political leaders on both sides will be under powerful pressure to continue to be sensible. . . . Those are the circumstances in which I believe that leaders will be rational and prudent. I hope I am not being too optimistic.[13]

Evidence from history and psychology suggests that, almost certainly, he was.

The Effects of Crises on Rational Decision Making

What must be decided during a crisis? According to one political scientist, the tasks include (but are not limited to) the following:

(a) Identify major alternative courses of action; (b) estimate the probable costs and gains of alternative policy choices; (c) distinguish between the possible and the probable; (d) assess the situation from the perspective of other parties; (e) discriminate between relevant and irrelevant information; (f) tolerate ambiguity; (g) resist premature action; and (h) make adjustments to meet real changes in the situation (and, as a corollary, to distinguish real from apparent changes).[14]

There have been numerous cases of crisis decisions made hastily, emotionally, and erroneously. The psychological data are also clear that mild stress tends to facilitate human decision making but that intense stress is likely to be especially disruptive, resulting in actions that are increasingly self-defeating. During severe crises, therefore, good policy decisions become both more important and less likely. Information overload, for example, becomes a substantial problem:

As the volume of information directed at policymakers rises, the search for information within the communication system will tend to become less thorough, and selectivity in what is read, believed and retained takes on increasing importance. Unpleasant information and that which does not support preconceived beliefs is most likely to fall by the wayside.[15]

Laboratory studies have also shown that as perceived threat increases, messages sent and received tend to reveal assessments of the situation that are increasingly stereotyped and simplistic. There is a corresponding restriction in the range and originality of the options being considered. During real-life international crises, time pressures are often intensified by the use of deadlines and ultimatums. "Nothing clarifies the mind," according to Samuel Johnson, "like the prospect of being hanged in the morning." This may well be true, but it also seems likely that nothing fogs the mind like the prospect of immediately having to make a potentially catastrophic decision, in a stressful environment during a perceived crisis.

Experimental research has also shown that severe stress is particularly likely to impede precisely those decision processes needed during international crises: Verbal and logical performance deteriorates; problem solving becomes more rigid; tolerance for complexity and ambiguity diminishes (this is especially crucial because in the real world of international affairs, issues are rarely laid out in simple "either/or" terms); errors are more frequent; the focus of attention is reduced, both spatially and temporally; and decision makers become less able to discriminate the trivial from the crucial. In short, the decision maker finds himself or herself less able to see the problem clearly and to respond creatively.

Still, it remains uncertain whether simulation studies accurately reflect real experiences. But speaking from his own experience in the Kennedy administration, Theodore Sorensen noted that "I saw first-hand, during the long days and nights of the Cuban crisis, how brutally physical and mental fatigue can numb the good sense as well as the senses of normally articulate men."[16]

In general, we must conclude, with Robert Kennedy, that the effects of crises on human decision making are largely unpredictable: "That kind of pressure does strange things to a human being, even to brilliant, self-confident, experienced men. For some it brings out characteristics and strengths that perhaps they never knew they had, and for others the pressure is too overwhelming."[17]

Some Issues Regarding Perception and Cognition

It can be argued that most wars begin in error, since each side often feels at the outset that it will win—or else it wouldn't go to war in the first place. Insofar as this is true, then the process of war itself is a movement, from error, through agony, to a more accurate appraisal of the situation, since wars usually end when both sides agree as to which is the stronger. To be sure, some wars take place because one side is attacked, or perceives the other side as hostile and threatening, and it may fight back not because it expects to win but because it sees no viable alternative: For example, Poland, after Germany invaded in 1939; Finland, after the Soviet Union attacked in the same year; and Iraq during the Persian Gulf War. But in many other cases, human error—notably perceptual distortions—appears to have a role in causing war. Thus, Horatio, in Shakespeare's *Hamlet*, relates a tale

> Of carnal, bloody and unnatural acts,
> Of accidental judgments, casual slaughters,
> Of deaths put on by cunning and forced cause,
> And, in this upshot, purposes mistook
> Fall'n on th' inventors' heads.

Insofar as blunders and misperceptions have an important role in the real world as well, we have an obligation to be attuned to these sources of error.

"We can never walk surely," wrote the British statesman Edmund Burke, "but by being sensible of our blindnesses."

Even in the absence of a crisis, leaders and decision makers are often prevented from getting a clear, unbiased view of the situation. The result is a range of potential errors, resulting from misperceptions, misunderstandings, and/or miscalculations. Some of these, such as the tendency to disregard information that does not conform to one's preconceptions, have already been touched on. There are two major contending theories of perceptual distortion: cognitive theory, which is concerned with errors in the processing of information, and motivational theory, according to which the emotional needs of the decision makers are paramount. Here, we focus on the nature of misperceptions rather than on their causes.

Inaccurate Perception of Others

History is replete with examples of this phenomenon. Hitler, for example, disdained the British as "shopkeepers" and the Russians as "barbarians." Arabs who attacked the fledgling state of Israel with five armies in 1948 were highly (and inappropriately) confident of victory over a Jewish nation that had been seen, in modern history, as nonmilitarist. Conversely, the Israeli armed forces came to suffer from a misconception that Arabs were hopelessly incompetent in military matters; as a result, they nearly lost the 1973 Yom Kippur War.

Five different U.S. presidents apparently misread the determination of the North Vietnamese and their leader, Ho Chi Minh. They seemed convinced that the North Vietnamese's drive for unification would crumble if only more American military pressure were applied. Iraq, under Saddam Hussein, first apparently underestimated the resilience of the Ayatollah Khomeini and the Iranians, and later misperceived the determination of George Bush to undo Iraq's incursion into Kuwait. The list is very long; many decision makers have persistently underestimated their opponents. (Of course, it may be that we only become acutely aware of such errors because the results can be glaring. When, by contrast, decision makers correctly assess a would-be opponent, or overestimate its strength, the resulting inaction doesn't make headlines.)

Decision makers commonly misjudge the strength of allies as well. U.S. political leadership misjudged the status of the shah of Iran, until it was too late. According to one expert on the role of misperceptions in international affairs, American officials were so slow in recognizing the Iranian revolution because it went counter to many preexisting and reinforcing beliefs:

> Not only were the Shah and his regime perceived as strong, but also the specific image was supported by the general belief—based on good historical evidence—that leaders who control large and effective

internal security forces were not overthrown by popular protest. These preconceptions were reinforced by several others that were more peculiarly American: the menace to pro-Western governments comes from the left; modernization enjoys the support of the strongest political elements of society, and those who oppose it cannot be serious contenders for power; religious motives and religious movements are peripheral to politics.[18]

As a result, American decision makers not only misinterpreted events in Iran but also made inappropriate decisions based on those misperceptions. This difficulty was enhanced by the anguish associated with making difficult decisions: The harder it is to make a decision and to set a policy, the greater the resistance to reversing that decision once it has been made.

Many preconceptions are self-serving. Hawks, for example, tend to see an opponent as unrelentingly hostile and aggressive, so that even conciliatory moves are interpreted as clever maneuvers to make the other side let down its guard—thus further proving the correctness of the original impression. Doves tend to emphasize the role of perceptions, thereby sometimes excusing an unacceptably aggressive act as a consequence of misunderstanding or misperception. These have been called "motivated errors" and include, for example, the tendency among British leaders during the 1930s to underestimate German hostility and simultaneously to overestimate German strategic airpower vis-à-vis British cities. The former view was motivated by a determination to avoid a repeat of the senseless carnage that characterized World War I, while the latter view was also appealing to the appeasers because it made it all the more important that war with Germany be avoided. At the same time, the hawks also found it useful because it reinforced their assertion that Hitler was dangerous.

Misreading History

If one or a small number of articulated or unconsciously held values dominate policy formation, decision makers' perceptions are often modified to minimize psychological distress and to provide a congenial view of current events. There is also an understandable yearning by many leaders to avoid repeating past errors and instead to repeat past successes. Following the Franco-Prussian War, for example, two assumptions were widespread among many European politicians and generals: (1) The next war would be intense and brief, because (2) a long war would ruin a state's economy. The result was a desire to strike first and decisively; this contributed, in turn, to plans for total mobilization, with now-familiar consequences.

Past successes can also overshadow present realities. For example, NATO's (North Atlantic Treaty Organization) history of inaction during the Bosnian War in the early 1990s appears to have emboldened Serbian president

Milosevic to assume he would have a comparably free hand in subduing the rebels in Kosovo, but history did not repeat itself. Che Guevara's success during the Cuban revolution led him to believe that history would repeat itself in Bolivia; it also did not.

Decision makers have also erred by trying to avoid the mistakes of the past. Statesmen, like Britain's apparently well-intentioned Neville Chamberlain, appalled at the senseless and avoidable slaughter of World War I, were convinced that nonbelligerent, farsighted diplomacy would prevent similar disasters; hence, they were likely to favor appeasement. During the infamous Munich conference of 1938, Chamberlain acceded to Hitler's demand to annex the Sudetenland; a generation later, those remembering this great mistake and seeking to learn from it were likely to be very hard-nosed. Another case in point: After Egypt nationalized the Suez Canal in 1955, British Prime Minister Anthony Eden (one of Churchill's deputies during World War II) was convinced that the West was facing a "second Munich" or a "second Rhineland" unless it responded militarily. (In fact, 1930s-style appeasement probably might have prevented the First World War, and 1914-style intransigence might well have headed off the Second.)

Hitler also misread recent events. When Germany invaded Poland in 1939, Hitler did not expect that Britain and France would honor their commitments and declare war on Germany; after all, just six months earlier, they had refused to go to war over Czechoslovakia, which was militarily more valuable than Poland and also more defendable. The supposed "lessons of Munich," learned too late by the West, may have contributed to a hardening of Cold War alliances in the nuclear age, in the hope that if NATO made its commitments clear, similar outcomes can be avoided. Comparable perceptions by many American conservatives have also generated skepticism about arms control and disarmament.

Professional "security managers" generally give special attention to cases in which aggressive powers were not perceived as such until it was too late. As a result, they are inclined to overestimate the aggressiveness of a potential opponent. For example, when Argentine forces initially took over the Falkland Islands in 1982, Argentines looked as a historical analogy to the Indian takeover of Goa, a small colonial enclave on the Indian mainland whose loss was quickly accepted (without bloodshed) by the Portuguese government. To the British, however, the relevant metaphor was Hitler and the origins of the Second World War, and they responded not as Portugal did in 1961, but rather as they wished they had done in 1938.

States such as the United States, which have relatively limited historical experience in world affairs, may be unusually susceptible to drawing inferences from the small number of international events that have been significant for them. And the more recent the event, the more likely it is to be salient in memory, even if it may not be especially relevant: "If generals are prepared to fight the last war, diplomats may be prepared to avoid the last war."[19]

The Double Standard of Hostility

In 1970, during the Vietnam War, the United States bombed and invaded Cambodia, claiming that because Cambodia was providing haven and supply routes to the Vietcong and the North Vietnamese, it could legally be attacked, even though it was a sovereign, nonbelligerent state. In 1988, however, after Nicaraguan forces had pursued contra rebels to their staging and supply areas inside of neighboring Honduras, the Reagan administration decried what it called an "unjustified invasion" and dispatched 3,000 U.S. troops to Honduras.

In the late 1950s, the United States placed medium-range missiles, capable of reaching the Soviet Union, in Turkey and Great Britain; this was considered (by the United States) to be a defensive and justified action. But when, shortly afterward, the USSR sought to place medium-range missiles capable of reaching the United States in Cuba, this was deemed by the American government to be a dastardly, offensive, and unjustified act, and the Kennedy administration was willing to go to the brink of nuclear war to get them removed.

The principle sounds absurd, but is widely followed: When *we* (Russia, the United States, Iraq, whoever) do something, it is acceptable—often, laudable—but if *they* do the exact same thing, it is not. What is involved here, in part, is a profound absence of empathy, a failure to recognize that there is more than one way to look at a problem, and a refusal to consider that the motivations and actions of one side may be perceived quite differently by the other side. Herbert Butterfield attributed much of this widespread misperception to "Hobbesian fear":

> You yourself may vividly feel the terrible fear that you have of the other party, but you cannot enter into the other man's counter-fear, or even understand why he should be particularly nervous. For you know that you yourself mean him no harm, and that you want nothing from him save guarantees for your own safety; and it is never possible for you to realize or remember properly that since he cannot see the inside of your mind, he can never have the same assurance of your intentions that you have.[20]

During a 1989 speech at an East-West conference on reducing conventional forces in Europe, then secretary of state James Baker asserted, "Those in the West should be free of the fear that the massive forces under Soviet command might invade them. Those in the East should be free of the fear that armed Soviet intervention . . . would be used again to deny them choice."[21] Another, possibly more sensitive statesman might also have added something like the following: "Those in the East should be free of the fear that the forces of the West will invade them, as they have so often in the past," and perhaps even "Those in the West should be free of the fear that their own military forces might precipitate a war, which, although ostensibly fought on their behalf, would destroy them."

Among psychologists, three related theories have sought to explain this tendency to perceive the Other as hostile, while holding the Self blameless:

1. *Ego defense.* A theory of ego defense emphasizes that individuals would find it troublesome to admit that their activities threaten others; hence, they protect their self-images by maintaining their own innocence and benevolent intentions. When others then respond aggressively, this is regarded as "evidence" of their hostility, since it couldn't possibly have been evoked by us, "the good guys." President Eisenhower's secretary of state, John Foster Dulles, once noted that "Khrushchev does not need to be convinced of our good intentions. He knows we are not aggressors and do not threaten the security of the Soviet Union."

2. *Attribution.* Attribution theory suggests that individuals are intensely aware of the various external constraints on their behavior, including economic factors, the need to placate others, and so on. Any threat or actual harm to others is therefore unintended. By contrast, it is much more difficult to understand the complex forces acting to produce the behavior of others. Such behavior is therefore more likely to be seen as resulting from an oversimplified stereotype, rather than from the conflicted, multifactorial process known to operate within oneself and one's group.

3. *Projection.* Projection is the phenomenon in which people take certain unacceptable tendencies of their own, consciously or unconsciously expel and displace them onto another person, and then identify them in the Other instead of in themselves. Finding it painful to recognize nastiness, aggressiveness, and the like in oneself, it is more acceptable for many people to project such internal tendencies onto an opponent, and then criticize that opponent. "How wicked these people must have been," sobbed Hitler, as he observed the demolition of Warsaw, "to make me do this to them."

A perception of the Other as hostile has served as a self-fulfilling prophecy: Prior to World War I, for example, German leaders assumed (erroneously) that other statesmen were as willing to go to war in pursuit of their national interest as they themselves were. The result was a kind of hostile defensiveness, which heightened the anxiety of Germany's neighbors, in turn generating precisely the encirclement German leaders had so feared. (During the 1930s, interestingly, advocates of appeasement erred the opposite way: thinking Hitler wanted to *avoid* war as much as they did. Hence, they also may have made it more likely.)

Not surprisingly, wars fought because of the perception that an opponent is hostile, allied with an enemy, or bent on conquest tend to make that opponent hostile, allied with an enemy, and/or bent on conquest. Such wars vindicate the assumptions on which they were based. For example, the Vietnam War was presented by presidential administrations to the American public as a result of North Vietnam's (alleged) invasion of the South; this came to pass after U.S. bombing of the North triggered massive movement of North Vietnamese units into South Vietnam. Similarly, Soviet repression of reform efforts in Hungary and Czechoslovakia, out of the Kremlin's fear they were anti-Soviet, only increased anti-Soviet sentiment in Eastern Europe.

The double standard of hostility prescribes not only that one's own actions are blameless but also that one's opponents are relentlessly hostile. Prior to the First World War, Austria saw Serbia as populated by "devils," the Russian leadership was particularly distrustful of the Austrians, and while British diplomats were desperately trying to prevent war, the German kaiser wrote on a diplomatic note: "The net has been suddenly thrown over our head, and England sneeringly reaps the most brilliant success of her persistently prosecuted, purely anti-German world policy, against which we have proved ourselves helpless, while she twists the noose of our political fidelity to Austria, as we squirm isolated in the net."

Similarly, to many Israelis, their country seems small, isolated, and vulnerable. To many Arabs, and especially to Palestinians, Israel is a dagger wielded by Western imperialists, stabbing right into the midsection of the Arab world. The Sandinistas in Nicaragua saw the Reagan administration as an imminent threat to their survival; at the same time, Nicaragua was rhetorically branded by President Reagan as an imminent threat to the security of the United States, located merely "two days' drive from Harlingen, Texas."

Miscommunication

Some communication errors occur simply because people speak different languages and come from different cultures. For example, consider the "*mokusatsu* affair." In the early summer of 1945, the Allies, meeting in Potsdam, issued a surrender ultimatum to Japan. The official Japanese response was to "mokusatsu" the ultimatum, which was translated into English as "ignore." The Truman administration saw this as an outright rejection, whereas in fact, it should more accurately have been rendered as "withhold comment, pending deliberation." It is at least possible that, had there been better communication between Japanese and American decision makers, American atomic bombs might not have been dropped on Hiroshima and Nagasaki shortly thereafter.

In many other cases, and for diverse reasons, communication may result in what the French call *un dialogue des sourds*, "a dialogue of the deaf." Senders typically assume that if they spend much time and attention designing a message calibrated to convey a particular meaning, the receiver will necessarily understand it. Often, however, "messages" are not read as intended, whereupon warnings are not heeded, and the sender may even blame the receiver (unjustifiably) for intransigence or hostility. President McKinley, in 1898, sent what he thought was a blunt ultimatum concerning Cuba to Spain; the Spanish government erroneously interpreted the message as reassuring. The result, ultimately, was the Spanish-American War.

Numerous miscommunications seem to have taken place in the early stages of the Korean War. In 1950, Secretary of State Acheson testified to Congress that Korea was outside the United States' Pacific defense perimeter; the North Koreans, not understanding that these words were intended more for domestic consumption than as an international signal, felt emboldened to attack the South. Later, when U.S. forces were pushing far north of the 38th parallel (dividing North and South Korea), China sent numerous signals indicating that it would intervene if U.S. troops continued their military operations near the Chinese border. The United States, however, apparently did not pick up on these warnings. Furthermore, in seeking to reassure the Chinese that it did not wish to expand the Korean conflict, the United States referred frequently to a long-standing friendship between the American and Chinese people. At the same time, Chinese authorities had a very different perception of Sino-American relations, viewing the United States with deep distrust, as merely one of many imperialist exploiters of China during the 19th century, and more recently, as the inheritor of Japan's goal of an Asian empire. Similarly, Saddam Hussein may have felt emboldened to invade Kuwait in 1990 because he misinterpreted the statements of a high-ranking American diplomat then stationed in Baghdad, who indicated that her government does not take a stand on Iraqi territorial claims to Kuwait.

Overconfidence

Many people have a habit of hearing what they want to hear, and believing that something is true simply because they wish that it were so. Military leaders tend to be can-do people; it is their job to take an aggressive, problem-solving approach to their mission. Often there is no lack of intelligence (either data or IQ), but rather a reluctance to draw unpleasant conclusions.

For example, prior to the 1962 Sino-Indian War—a stinging defeat for India—Indian leaders may have assumed that the Chinese leadership was timid and that their military forces were superior to the Chinese, simply ignoring evidence to the contrary. The same kind of unwarranted self-confidence led the United States into the quicksand of Vietnam, with most American decision makers confident that there was "light at the end of the tunnel." In 1965, President Johnson was told by his joint chiefs of staff that "the communists" would be defeated in Vietnam within two years, if only sufficient additional military pressure would be applied. In 1971, the

Pakistani leadership—ignoring all evidence that India enjoyed clear superiority—nonetheless attacked its archrival seeking, unsuccessfully, to destroy the Indian Air Force on the ground, as Israel had succeeded against Egypt at the onset of the Six-Day War in 1967.

When the risks are high, one might expect that an uncompromising, self-critical honesty—if only for self-interested reasons—would develop. But the opposite occurs at least as frequently: Self-delusion is rampant in the events before a war and in its early stages. For example, Lord Asquith, British prime minister in the early days of World War I, claimed that the War Office "kept three sets of figures: one to mislead the public, another to mislead the Cabinet, and a third to mislead itself." On the eve of their attack on Pearl Harbor, Japanese leaders realized that it could only hope to prevail over the United States in a brief and limited war, so they convinced themselves that this is what would probably happen, especially if the United States were sufficiently shocked and crippled militarily at the outset.

Overconfidence has often cost states and leaders dearly. In the autumn of 1914, the kaiser promised Germany that its sons would be back "before the leaves had fallen from the trees." Hitler did not even have his quartermasters issue winter uniforms to his troops attacking the Soviet Union, so confident was he that the campaign would be over before winter (as it happened, many German soldiers died of exposure in Russia). In fact, most wars have been initiated on a note of confident optimism; in many cases, this optimism may itself have been a reason for the war. Only rarely have soldiers marched off to war in a mood of grim determination and resignation—those emotions usually come after hostilities have begun.

But it can also be argued that what is unintentional about most wars has not been the decision to fight, but the outcome. Wars have often turned out to be longer or costlier than expected at their outset. Above all, they typically result in the defeat of half the participants, virtually all of whom had initially expected to win.

Wishful Thinking

Wishful thinking is hardly a recent phenomenon. The defeat of its Armada, in 1588, marked the end of Spain as a global power. Before sailing, one Spanish commander "reasoned" as follows:

> It is well known that we fight in God's cause. So when we meet the English, God will surely arrange matters so that we can grapple and board them, either by sending some strange freak of weather, or more likely, just by depriving the English of their wits. If we come to close quarters, Spanish valor and Spanish steel—and the great mass of soldiers we shall have on board—will make our victory certain. But unless God helps us by making a miracle, the English, who have faster

guns and handier ships than ours, and many more long-range guns, and who know their advantage as well as we do, will never close with us at all, but stand aloof and blow us to pieces with their culverins, without our being able to do them any serious hurt. . . . So, we are sailing against England in the confident hope of a miracle.[22]

Of course, military adventures are often launched on something more than the "confident hope of a miracle." Nearly three quarters of all wars in the past 150 years have been won by the initiator, suggesting some tendency for accurate planning. However, there have been notable exceptions, including the American Civil War, World War I, World War II, the Korean War, the 1973 Arab-Israeli War, the Falklands War, the Iran-Iraq War, and the Persian Gulf War. The United States and the former Soviet Union became embroiled in their disastrous Vietnam and Afghanistan Wars, each confident of relatively easy victory against a small, impoverished, Third World state. Not surprisingly, brief interventions by powerful states into much weaker states (such as the United States in Panama in 1989) are more likely to be successful, at least in the short term. The long-term consequences of these invasions are more difficult to predict.

Negative, but Sometimes Accurate, Perceptions

The biases of certain leaders may well have contributed to dangerous and costly misperceptions. For example, the two most influential American secretaries of state in the period immediately following World War II, Dean Acheson (for President Truman) and John Foster Dulles (for President Eisenhower), were zealously, even rigidly, anticommunist, and profoundly distrustful of anything smacking of peaceful relations with the USSR. But one should beware of another potentially erroneous conclusion, namely, that international conflict arises solely from psychological errors and misperceptions. In some cases, negative perceptions are, regrettably, all too accurate. Conflict may arise not because the adversaries misunderstand each other, but rather because they understand each other all too well.

For example, in the 1930s, Neville Chamberlain seemed reasonable in his perception that peace in Europe could be ensured if only Hitler were granted what was widely acclaimed to be Germany's legitimate nationalistic ambitions; Winston Churchill, by contrast, was excoriated by critics who thought him irrational, hypermilitaristic, and bedeviled by all the bogeymen of misperception just discussed above. Of course, with the wisdom of hindsight we now know that Chamberlain was deceived and that Churchill saw the situation quite clearly. An accurate perception of Hitler as a dangerous warmonger might well have helped the Allies prevent World War II altogether, at least in Europe. In short, we must at least admit the possibility that sometimes states and their leaders are nefarious and war seeking. To see prospects for peace and harmony, to strive for mutual understanding and confidence building may not necessarily imply that one is naive or duped by the other side. But similarly, to be distrustful, to recognize danger, or enmity, is not necessarily to misperceive an adversary.

A Final Note on Decision Making

The making of war, and of peace, is the responsibility of human beings, typically of men (and increasingly women) who find themselves in positions of political and military leadership. To some degree, therefore, we are all at the mercy of those leaders whose decisions may be crucial for our survival. We thus have an interest in maximizing the quality of these decision makers and of the information available to them. Nonetheless, even with perfect perception of all current issues, decision makers are necessarily plunging into an uncertain darkness.

For example, some influential members of Spain's aristocratic military tradition believed, in 1898, that a war with the United States was necessary, in order to lose Cuba gracefully; they hadn't counted, however, on losing Puerto Rico and the Philippines, too, to America. "The future," wrote the eminent historian A. J. P. Taylor, "is a land of which there are no maps, and historians err when they describe even the most purposeful statesman as though he were marching down a broad highway with his objective already in sight."[23] It is of the greatest importance, then, especially in the nuclear age, that leaders be as free as possible from emotional and perceptual blinders in making the crucial decisions related to war and peace.

Notes

1. Leo Tolstoy. 1942. *War and Peace*. New York: Simon & Schuster.

2. E. Stillman and W. Pfaff. 1964. *The Politics of Hysteria*. New York: Harper & Row.

3. Ibid.

4. Desiderius Erasmus. 1936. *The Education of the Christian Prince*. New York: Columbia University Press.

5. Woodrow Wilson. 1965. *A Day of Dedication*. New York: Macmillan.

6. Herodotus. 1910. *History of Herodotus*. New York: E. P. Dutton.

7. Samuel P. Huntington. 1964. *The Soldier and the State*. New York: Vintage.

8. R. Falk and S. Kim. 1980. *The War System*. Boulder, CO: Westview.

9. Irving L. Janis. 1972. *Victims of Groupthink*. Boston: Houghton Mifflin.

10. Robert McNamara. 1986. *Blundering Into Disaster*. New York: Pantheon.

11. Quoted in Theodore Sorensen. 1965. *Kennedy*. New York: Harper & Row.

12.   Thomas C. Schelling. 1960. *The Strategy of Conflict*. Cambridge, MA: Harvard University Press.

13.   James Schlesinger. In John G. Stoessinger. 1985. *Why Nations Go to War*. New York: St. Martin's.

14.   Ole Holsti. 1971. "Crisis, Stress and Decision-Making." *International Social Science Journal* 23 (1).

15.   Ibid.

16.   Theodore Sorensen. 1964. *Decision-Making in the White House*. New York: Columbia University Press.

17.   Quoted in Holsti, "Crisis," op. cit.

18.   Robert Jervis. 1985. "Perceiving and Coping With Threat." In R. Jervis, N. Lebow, and J. G. Stein, eds., *Psychology and Deterrence*. Baltimore: Johns Hopkins University Press.

19.   Robert Jervis. 1968. "Hypotheses on Misperception." *World Politics* 20 (3).

20.   Herbert Butterfield. 1951. *History and Human Relations*. New York: Macmillan.

21.   Quoted in the *New York Times*, March 7, 1989.

22.   Quoted in B. and F. Brodie. 1962. *From Crossbow to H-Bomb*. New York: Dell.

23.   A. J. P. Taylor. 1955. *Bismarck, the Man and the Statesman*. New York: Knopf.

9

The Ideological, Social, and Economic Levels

Theories and schools, like microbes and corpuscles, devour one another and by their warfare assure continuity of life.

—Marcel Proust

Wars are caused not only by individuals, groups, states, and leaders but also—at a less tangible level—by underlying ideological, social, and economic factors. We look first at some of the more ideological and social reasons for wars, and then we turn our attention to cases in which economic issues figure more prominently. Then we briefly examine some of the social and economic effects of war and preparations for war. We conclude this chapter and the second part of the book with a summary of the reasons for wars.

Conflicting Ideologies

An ideology is an integrated but often unarticulated pattern of ideas upon which social and political actions are often explained, justified, and implemented. Ideologies are usually characterized by a certain number of rigidly held central propositions, a degree of comprehensiveness and systematization, and often, a feeling of urgency on the part of the ideologues about the need for and desirability of pursuing the favored approach. Ideologies are belief systems that pull together information, underlying assumptions, and global viewpoints that are generally not amenable to simple refutation. That is, differing ideologies weave together patterns of beliefs and basic premises that make up a self-contained thought system. Once accepted, such a belief system normally leads to only one admissible set of conclusions.

Ideologies can be organized around religious traditions, or around secular ways of life, such as capitalism, Marxism-Leninism, democracy, aristocracy, conservatism, liberalism, ethnocentrism, and nationalism. They are typically based on differing fundamental assumptions and cannot empirically be proved right or wrong. However, they can be powerful engines of human behavior, and when ideologies conflict, they can contribute to war.

Ideologies are not necessarily bad in themselves, however, nor is the word *ideology* necessarily pejorative. However, the term *ideologue* generally conveys negative connotations, indicating someone whose worldview and open-mindedness are distorted by adherence to a particular, and limiting, ideology.

Because they are deeply held, significant perceived ideological differences can contribute to wars of extraordinary brutality, with little or no quarter asked or given. The 18th-century wars of monarchical succession, for example, were fought among states that all accepted the same ideologies; hence, they were relatively brief and limited. By contrast, wars of religion, including the Crusades and Thirty Years' War, involved heartfelt ideologies and were exceptionally bloody. While the United States was fighting the Civil War (1861–1865), an immense tragedy based to some degree on differing ideologies, and in which perhaps 650,000 people died, the Taiping Rebellion, in which the Taipings sought unsuccessfully to overthrow the Manchu dynasty, was raging in China. This rebellion, driven by extreme zeal on the part of its Chinese Christian leader, resulted in nearly *20 million* fatalities, making it the most destructive civil war in history, and second only to World War II in total deaths.

Marxism, Capitalism, and Fascism

Among contemporary Western ideologies, Marxism in particular has addressed itself to the reasons for war and peace. According to orthodox Marxism (or Marxism-Leninism), capitalism results in two antagonistic classes, the proletariat (workers) and the bourgeois (owners), with the bourgeoisie (or the ruling class that owns the means of production) controlling the machinery of government. War is the external manifestation of this class struggle: War will therefore be abolished when communism has triumphed worldwide, following a possibly quite violent "transition" period from capitalism to socialism, a period known as "the dictatorship of the proletariat."

Mainstream Western capitalist ideology, by contrast, implies that the potential of individual "success" and social "security" is greatest in a situation of maximum economic freedom for markets and of freedom of thought and of speech for individuals. Wars are caused by many factors, but most notably by perceived threats to human freedom, such as those allegedly posed by "communist-inspired" revolutionary social and political movements.

Although fascist ideology has not been as clearly articulated as its Marxist-Leninist and capitalist counterparts, it can be viewed as a far-right-wing, nationalistic/militarist extension of capitalism, a worldview that places great reliance on social rigidity and respect for hierarchy. It glorifies patriotism, the state, and militarism, harking back to a "golden" and typically very romanticized past. Big business and conventional church-centered religion typically enjoy a prominent place in fascist states, so long as the former cooperates especially in the production of war material, and so long as the latter espouses doctrines that emphasize obedience to secular authorities (including the promise of heavenly reward for patriotic loyalty to the state), while demonizing any opponents of fascist rule. Racist appeals have also been important to most fascists, largely to buttress claims about the appropriateness of dominating other peoples and achieving the nation's legitimate "place in the sun."

Ideologies and Wars

Ideologies are a significant component of individual and collective worldviews, and as such, they can lead to perceptions that contribute to war making. For example, those American decision makers who saw the Sandinista government in Nicaragua as a manifestation of international communism were likely to consider it a threat to the peace and stability of the Western Hemisphere, whereas those who saw it as an example of revolutionary nationalism were more likely to recommend accommodation and coexistence, maybe even friendship. Similarly, rigid ideologues within the former Soviet Union were quick to brand reform efforts within such former Eastern European bloc nations as Poland, Hungary, and Czechoslovakia as part of the global capitalist and counterrevolutionary offensive against socialism. And these decision makers within the Kremlin, like their counterparts in Washington, at times also recommended and undertook military responses to these perceived threats.

World War II had clear ideological underpinnings: The Axis powers saw it as a crusade in defense of their nation-states and in opposition to communism, while the West saw it as the equally holy defense of democracy against Nazi Germany (whose National Socialist ideology can be seen as an extreme form of fascism) and fascist Italy and imperialist Japan. In the Atlantic charter of August 1941, Britain and the United States agreed to "respect the right of all peoples to choose the form of the government under which they will live." They also pledged "to see the sovereign rights and self-government restored to those who have been forcibly deprived of them," and promised to make "no territorial changes that do not accord with the freely-expressed wishes of the peoples concerned."

Although similar sentiments were expressed by political leaders before World War I, that conflict was not really an ideological war—until it began. World War I evolved into a kind of ideological conflict, especially on the part of the United States, not only "to make the world safe for democracy" but also as "the war to end all wars" (in the words of President Wilson). Before 1914, however, few people in the United States, Great Britain, or France had advocated war against Germany or Austria-Hungary simply because the Central Powers were autocratic and monarchic. Moreover, Russia under the czar (and then in World War II under Stalin) was extremely undemocratic. For the Germans, Austrians, and Turks, World War I became an ideological conflict in defense of monarchy and—more important—their national homelands.

The following is part of an address in 1917 by President Woodrow Wilson, in which he requested a congressional declaration of war:

> A steadfast concern for peace can never be maintained except by a partnership of democratic nations. We are glad . . . to fight thus for the ultimate peace of the world and for the liberation of its peoples, the German peoples included; for the rights of nations great and small and the privilege of men everywhere to choose their own way of life and of obedience. . . . America is privileged to spend her blood and her might for the principles that gave her birth and happiness and the peace which she has treasured . . . the world must be made safe for democracy.[1]

In the contemporary world, ideologies may make crosscutting demands. For example, although the state of Iran is Islamic, its populace is ethnically Persian and not Arab. During the Iran-Iraq War, therefore, many Arabs were forced to choose between their religious ideology (Islam) and their secular ideology (Arab nationalism). In most cases, they opted for the latter and supported Iraq over Iran.

Many wars, on the other hand, have been nonideological: (ostensibly) communist Vietnam against (officially) communist China in 1979, or right-wing capitalist Great Britain under Margaret Thatcher against right-wing Argentina under General Galtieri in 1982. And largely because of *Real-politik* considerations, states that one might expect to be ideological enemies have become allies instead: officially communist and atheist China and right-wing, Islamic Pakistan, for example.

Democracies and Wars

Human beings are organized into larger groups according to a variety of shared patterns: geographic proximity, religious affiliation, ethnic and national identity, political and economic systems. Often these patterns are crosscutting: Individuals of differing religions may find themselves within the same nation-state, people in different states may share the same ethnicity while in their own countries there may be many different ethnic groups, and so on. What role, then, do these differing patterns play in generating war? On the individual level, internal conditions strongly influence external behavior. But does this also apply at the level of states?

This question can be approached in many ways. At least partly because the Western states generally pride themselves in being democracies, and because it is widely believed that democratic governments are more peaceful than nondemocratic states, the focus here will be on the comparative war proneness of democratic and more authoritarian nations.

The results are a bit disconcerting: Statistically, at least until the second half of the 20th century, no significant difference had yet been demonstrated between the war proneness of democracies and despotisms, except for the virtual absence of wars *between* democratically elected governments. Authoritarian Sparta was no more aggressive or expansionist than democratic Athens; similarly, Franco's Spain, Somoza's Nicaragua, and Marcos's Philippines, although dictatorships, were not expansionist. By contrast, during the 19th century in particular, Britain and the United States engaged in expansionist wars. For the United States, these included successful wars against indigenous Native Americans, Mexico, and Spain, as well as the failed War of 1812 against Great Britain. And the British completed their acquisition of an immense global empire, it has been said, "in a fit of absent-mindedness."

The connection between democracy and war, although counterintuitive, should not be all that surprising. In feudal Europe and Japan, the aristocracy had a monopoly on war. As we have seen, this changed substantially with the spread of firearms, which made a commoner capable of stopping a charging horse and penetrating a nobleman's armor. Today, the military has become a relatively low-level and mercenary occupation in most democratic states. Moreover, the right to keep and bear arms (the Second Amendment to the U.S. Constitution) has been seen by many Americans as fundamental to democracy.

One's perception of the peaceableness of democracies may be strongly colored by the 20th century, in which most democracies became "status quo" powers, unlikely to engage in wars of aggression. However, the United States in particular took on the role of world policeman, thereby becoming embroiled, directly or indirectly, in armed conflicts on every continent but Australia and Antarctica. In addition, democracies have proven to be no less likely than more authoritarian states to fight when provoked—and they may be even more fierce in prosecuting such wars. "A democracy is peace-loving," claimed noted diplomat-historian George Kennan:

> It does not like to go to war. It is slow to rise to provocation. When it has once been provoked to the point where it must grasp the sword, it

does not easily forgive its adversary for having produced this situation. . . . Democracy fights in anger—it fights for the very reason that it was forced to go to war. It fights to punish the power that was rash enough and hostile enough to provoke it—to teach that power a lesson it will not forget, to prevent the thing from happening again. Such a war must be carried to the bitter end.[2]

Conservative politicians in particular (perhaps surprisingly) have distrusted democracy because of what they saw as its inclination *toward* war. Thus, England's 19th-century prime minister Disraeli maintained that if the British electorate were enlarged, "You will in due season have wars entered into from passion and not from reason." And young Winston Churchill pointed out (correctly) in 1901 that "democracy is more vindictive than Cabinets. The wars of peoples will be more terrible than the wars of kings."

Democracies in Peacetime

Peace is not a prerequisite for democracy, but it seems clear that democracies do better in times of peace than in times of war. In fact, whereas democracies do not necessarily lead to peace, the tendency may work in reverse: Peace predisposes governments toward democracy. Certainly, the converse holds: Wars often involve abridgment of rights of dissent and due process, even within democracies. They seem to require increased discipline, secrecy, unswerving and unquestioning devotion to the state, and obedience to its authority: All of these are easier to achieve with military governments. During World War II, for example, Churchill and his cabinet held almost dictatorial power in otherwise democratic Great Britain; indeed, that war produced a remarkable convergence in the political systems of all participants. There was also widespread suppression of dissent within the United States during World War I, the forced dislocation and involuntary internment of thousands of Japanese Americans in "relocation centers" (milder versions of concentration camps) during World War II, and attempts by some American political and police officials to suppress protest movements as demonstrations against the Vietnam War increased and its popularity sagged.

Some democracies nonetheless retain an abiding sense that the military is subordinate to the civilian sector. In the middle of the Korean War, for example, President Truman was able to fire General MacArthur, the most popular and successful military figure in the country, then at the peak of his powers. Comparable events would be almost unimaginable in countries lacking a similar tradition; for example, when Panamanian president Eric Delvalle dismissed the military chief, General Manuel Noriega early in 1988, the military backed Noriega, and Delvalle himself was forced from office. Similarly, in 1999 a conflict between Pakistani president Nawaz Sharif and General Purvez Musharraf led to a military coup that deposed the president.

Many military leaders are specialists in violence. It follows that they should be more willing, even eager, to enter wars, and moreover, they should be able to do so without the prolonged and divisive procedures found in most democracies. In the nuclear age, no formal declaration from the American Congress would be required for World War III to commence. But even without nuclear weapons, it can be argued that when it comes to the decision to go to war, democracies are not really democratic at all. The following selection—written by Randolph Bourne in the early days of World War I— conveys a sense of despair and disillusionment with governmental activities, even in a democracy:

The Government, with no mandate from the people, without consultation of the people, conducts all the negotiations . . . the menaces and explanations, which slowly bring it into collision with some other Government, and gently and irresistibly slides the country into war. For the benefit of proud and haughty citizens, it is fortified with a list of the intolerable insults which have been hurled towards us by the other nations; for the benefit of the liberal and beneficent, it has a convincing set of moral purposes which our going to war will achieve; for the ambitious and aggressive classes, it can gently whisper of a bigger role in the destiny of the world. The result is that, even in those countries where the business of declaring war is theoretically in the hands of representatives of the people, no legislature has ever been known to decline the request of an Executive, which has conducted all foreign affairs in utter privacy and irresponsibility, that it order the nation into battle. Good democrats are wont to feel the crucial difference between a State in which the popular Parliament or Congress declares war. But, put to the stern pragmatic test, the difference is not striking. In the freest of republics as well as in the most tyrannical of Empires, all foreign policy, the diplomatic negotiations which produce or forestall war, are equally the private property of the Executive part of the Government, and are equally exposed to no check whatever from popular bodies, or the people voting as a mass themselves.

The moment war is declared, however, the mass of the people, through some spiritual alchemy, become convinced that they have willed and executed the deed themselves. They then with the exception of a few malcontents, proceed to allow themselves to be regimented, coerced, deranged in all the environments of their lives, and turned into a solid manufactory of destruction toward whatever other people may have . . . come within the range of the Government's disapprobation. The citizen throws off his contempt and indifference to Government, identifies himself with its purposes, revives all his military memories and symbols, and the State once more walks . . . through the imaginations of men. Patriotism becomes the dominant feeling, and produces immediately that intense and hopeless confusion between the relations which the individual bears and should bear towards the society of which he is a part.[3]

Walter Lippmann, on the other hand, maintained that democracies are peaceful because of a certain public inertia:

> The rule to which there are few exceptions . . . is that at the critical junctures, when the stakes are high, the prevailing mass opinion will impose what amounts to a veto upon changing the course on which the government is at the time proceeding. Prepare for war in time of peace? No. It is bad to raise taxes, to unbalance the budget, to take men away from their schools or their jobs, to provoke the enemy.[4]

Democracy Relationship(s)

Thus, there appears to be a possibly paradoxical relationship between democracy and war: Once provoked, democratically elected governments fight fiercely, perhaps even more energetically than their less democratic counterparts, but most democracies tend to remain peaceful. The American experience during the latter part of the 20th century, however, suggests a troubling variation on this theme, namely, a penchant by the United States for brief, but militarily successful, wars of intervention in the affairs of less powerful nations. Both the 1983 invasion of Grenada and the 1989 invasion of Panama by the United States were illegal by most standards of international law, as was the American government's support for the contras in Nicaragua during the same period. Yet these warlike actions were quite successful domestically, boosting the popularity of Presidents Reagan and Bush. These belligerent activities were motivated, at least in part, by the perception (accurate, as it turned out) that the presidents in question would benefit politically. This raises the specter that presidents and other decision makers may seek to offset their domestic political difficulties by engaging in a quick war or "surgical strike" (as President Clinton did in Afghanistan and Sudan in the 1990s) that is relatively painless (at least for the American military, as were its campaigns against Iraq and Serbia) and popular. So long as public opinion responds favorably to such wars, especially around election time, democratically elected governments will be tempted to engage in them.

Capitalism and War

The relationship between capitalism and war seems similar to that between democracy and war. It was widely thought (except by Marxists, whose views are discussed later in this chapter) that capitalism would discourage war, since capitalism favors trade over the forcible seizure of land and political stability over instability, thus leaving the bourgeoisie and the multinational corporations they control free to maximize profits, with a minimal role for national governments. In the 19th century, influential sociologists such as Herbert Spencer and August Comte argued that of the two great styles of society—military and industrial—the latter would eventually win.

In fact, capitalist-industrial states have generally done well in war, and have been no less warlike than others, although often the pressure for war has usually come from other classes than the bourgeoisie. In the 19th century, for example, American agitation for the War of 1812 and the Civil War came primarily from the agrarian South and West rather than the mercantile East or North. In Britain, liberal merchants and industrialists were less supportive of imperialism than was the landed aristocracy. Japanese militarism was similarly spearheaded by the army and the peasantry rather than the capitalist classes, just as 20th-century German militarism came primarily from the aristocratic Prussian *Junkers* rather than from the business community.

Capitalists were not even united as to the merits of imperialism. Thus, the theory of "mercantilism" favored economic self-betterment via a favorable balance of trade (accumulating wealth by a nation's exporting more than it imports). In 1833, Thomas Macaulay expressed the perspective of English mercantilists as follows:

> It would be, on the most selfish view of the case, far better for us that the people of India were well-governed and independent of us, than ill-governed and subject to us; that they were ruled by their own kings, but wearing our broadcloth, and eating with our cutlery, than that they were performing their salaams to English collectors and English magistrates, but were too ignorant to value, or too poor to buy, English manufactures. To trade with civilised men is infinitely more profitable than to govern savages.[5]

Population Pressure and Other Social Stresses

Some scholars have argued that internal stresses make war more likely, even though there is at present little evidence to support this contention. The Vietnam War was clearly associated with an increase in domestic stress within the United States, but just as clearly, this increase was a result of that war rather than a reason for it. No correlations have yet been established between war proneness and population density, homicides, suicides, alcoholism, or urbanization. The role of population pressure, however, has repeatedly drawn attention.

The simplest claim is that expanding population drives a state to conquest, much as Hitler claimed that his conquests in Poland and the western

USSR were a result of the German need for *Lebensraum* (living space). Japan was, by many standards, overpopulated in the 1930s, when it was very aggressive. Today, however, it is even more crowded, and yet its aggressiveness is limited to foreign trade. Nor is this a recent phenomenon. Between the third and eight centuries A.D., for example, the population of Europe fell, yet this was a time of Roman imperial wars followed by smaller "barbarian" wars and the end of the *Pax* Romana. Later, the European population was reduced drastically during the Black Plague (14th century), and yet this period was characterized by the Hundred Years' War, and an uneasy transition from the religious wars of the Crusades to feudal wars among opposing princes. Moreover, rapid population growth during the first two centuries A.D. and during the 19th century was associated, not with increased war, but rather with the *Pax* Romana and *Pax* Britannica.

Any correlation between population and war proneness might, if anything, be counterintuitive. Smaller states, for example, have often worried that they were at risk of being attacked by larger, more populous ones (Belgium's fear of France, France's fear of Germany, Germany's fear of Russia, Vietnam's fear of China, Cambodia's fear of Vietnam, and Canada's fear of America—or at least of its mass culture—are notable cases). In fact, when they are not provoked, larger states seem if anything to be more inclined to (over)confidence and complacency. Nevertheless, high unemployment, homelessness, mass poverty, starvation, and general social dissatisfaction, whether in industrial regions or in rural societies in which population growth has exceeded available land, can lead to a dangerous kind of national restlessness.

Other, related patterns of war proneness and war avoidance have been suggested. For example, the historian Arnold Toynbee proposed that there are cycles of war weariness, in which the sad and bitter memories of a recent war restrain the populace until this short-term immunity from war wears off and wars become likely once again. The comparatively peaceful period in Europe following the Napoleonic Wars has been interpreted in this way. Toynbee recounts that during the 1920s, hiking with a knapsack was unpopular, presumably because it conjured up unpleasant military memories. It was, as he points out, an ominous sign when knapsacks came back into vogue in the 1930s.

On the other hand, the peace that typically follows a war may simply occur because there is nothing left to fight about, at least for a time. In some cases—when there was something to fight about—wars have followed hard upon one another, with no breathing space. For example, after fighting the Japanese invaders during the early 1940s, the Viet Minh continued battling the French forces that had reoccupied the Republic of Vietnam. Then, they fought the Americans. As soon as their devastating war with the Japanese was finished, the Chinese communists resumed, with scarcely a pause, their equally devastating civil war against Chiang Kai-shek's nationalist, right-wing and American-backed government. If wars necessarily lead to national exhaustion and therefore to peace (or at least to a cease-fire), one might expect that periods of peace would lead to a lower threshold for war, as the immunizing effects of painful memories wear off. But states such as Switzerland and Sweden, which have by now accumulated long histories of peace, do not seem any more war prone than others, such as Afghanistan, Israel, Iraq, and Ethiopia, that should rightly be tired of war.

Following the Vietnam War, by contrast, the United States went through a period when it was hesitant to engage in other military adventures; American conservatives in particular criticized this as the "Vietnam syndrome." It did not, however, appear to be a weariness with war in general so much as a determination to avoid "bad wars." And the Vietnam syndrome was short-lived, as evidenced by America's military involvements against Iraq, Serbia, and other perceived foes during the 1990s, as well as the current "war against terrorism." The former Soviet Union, following its extremely unpleasant military episode in Afghanistan, underwent a parallel "Afghanistan syndrome," which was also shed as Russia has battled "terrorists" in Chechnya from the mid-1990s to the present.

Poverty as a Cause of War

According to orthodox Marxist thinking, wars are caused by class struggles, including conflicts within societies as well as those between the upper classes of different societies for control over other countries. An official Soviet publication, *Marxism-Leninism on War and Army,* reads as follows:

> All wars in the past and present, those between exploiter states in pursuit of the selfish interests of the slave owners, feudal lords, and the bourgeoisie, as also the uprisings and wars of the working people against whom they rose . . . all these wars were caused by private ownership relations and the resultant social and class antagonisms in exploiter formations. . . . Wars are a means of rapid enrichment for the capitalists and, hence, a constant . . . companion of capitalism. The system of the exploitation of man by man and the system of the destruction of man by man are two sides of the capitalist order.[6]

And in the Communist Manifesto, we read that "in proportion as the antagonism between classes within the nation vanishes, the hostility of one nation to another will come to an end."

But one doesn't have to be a Marxist to see that poverty can breed dissatisfaction, which in turn can lead to war. During the Chinese Revolution, Josue de Castro, later president of the Executive Council of the Food and Agriculture Organization (FAO), wrote,

Some people think that Soviet infiltration and material aid are the principal explanation for the victories of the Communists over Chiang Kai-shek's troops . . . there is a more profound reason. The Communist revolution is winning in China today because, although Chiang Kai-shek has a powerful ally in the United States, the followers of Mao Tse-tung have a still stronger ally. That ally is hunger. . . . The fear of famine has been the great recruiting agent of Mao's armies. . . . The successes of Communism in China . . . are due to the fact that the Communists have promised freedom from the threat of starvation . . . . This Chinese hope is an exceedingly natural one, and . . . its frustration has been nothing less than inhuman.[7]

In 1962, President John F. Kennedy, referring specifically to Latin America, warned, "Those who possess wealth and power in poor nations must accept their own responsibilities. . . . Those who make peaceful revolution impossible will make violent revolution inevitable." Kennedy was echoing an influential view put forth by the English philosopher T. H. Green, in 1870:

The privileged class involuntarily . . . spreads the belief that the interest of the state lies in some extension without, not in an improvement within. A suffering class attracts sympathy from without and invites interference with the state that contains it. . . . The source of war between states lies in their incomplete fulfillment of their function; in . . . that there is some defect in the maintenance or reconciliation of rights among their subjects.[8]

Thus, socioeconomic deprivation was a major factor in generating popular support for Fidel Castro's successful revolt against Cuban dictator Fulgencio Batista in 1959, and for the overthrow of Nicaraguan dictator Anastacio Somoza in 1979. Right-wing violence has also been spawned by economic conditions, as witnessed by the (CIA-sponsored) overthrow of the democratically elected, Socialist president of Chile, Salvador Allende in 1973, as well as the coming to power of Adolf Hitler during the early 1930s, a time of severe economic stress in Germany. Efforts to destabilize a given regime by creating economic and social chaos testify to the widespread assumption that governmental stability can be diminished when domestic economic conditions are difficult.

Some of history's most notable revolutions (France in 1789, Russia in 1917, Italy's fascistic one in 1922, Iran's Islamic revolution in 1979, Haiti and the Philippines in 1986, and the "Velvet Revolution" in Czechoslovakia and elsewhere in Eastern Europe in 1989) have not involved lengthy civil wars, but rather an array of strikes and mass actions, in which the government lost the ability to control its own armed forces as a result of the disaffection of the people. More recently, military governments have feared their own people more than an external enemy; accordingly, police expenditures in less economically advanced countries have increased much more rapidly than have expenditures for external military forces. The large "defense" budgets of many Latin American and African countries, in particular, are directed almost entirely against their own populace rather than against some external and threatening enemy.

Poverty and Domestic Unrest

Poverty does not, however, inevitably breed war, or even revolution. The decade preceding the American Revolutionary War (1765–1775), for example, was not a time of poverty and deprivation, but rather of prosperity and expansion: Business was booming, and the number of ships in New York's harbor had nearly doubled in a decade. Even the French Revolution—long considered a classic case of hunger leading to violence—in fact took place at a time when conditions, although bad, were improving. According to Alexis de Tocqueville, "It is a singular fact that this steadily increasing prosperity, far from tranquilizing the population, everywhere promoted a spirit of unrest." Tocqueville also noted that "those parts of France in which the improvement in the standard of living was most pronounced were the chief centers of the revolutionary movement."[9]

Misery within a country, in short, does not necessarily lead to war. Germany was not belligerent during a period of runaway inflation in 1923, but rather in 1914, at a time of unparalleled prosperity. Hitler may indeed have been aided in his rise to power by the Depression of the early 1930s, but by the time of German expansionism (the late 1930s), prosperity was already returning.

"The revolution of rising expectations," rather than declining conditions may in fact be especially likely to lead to social violence. Some theorists have proposed that the crucial point at which a society becomes unusually violent depends less on so-called objective conditions than on a gap between prevailing conditions and a public *expectation*—that is, when the "want:get ratio" is high. Propaganda and agitation can, of course, intensify the effect of this gap.

In 14th-century England, a bloody revolt by Wat Tyler and his followers was stimulated by resentment at the high taxes imposed by the government, which sought to pay for the Hundred Years' War in France. Tax collecting at that time must have felt more like robbery than a legitimate civic function: The tax collector demanded money and yet the government offered essentially no services in return. Five centuries before Karl Marx, itinerant priest John Ball, one of the instigators of this revolt, spoke for an angry, resentful underclass:

My good friends, matters cannot go well in England until all things be held in common; when there shall be neither vassals nor lords; when the lords shall be no more masters than ourselves. . . . For what reason do they hold us in bondage? Are we not all descended from the same parents, Adam and Eve? And . . . what reason can they give, which they should be more masters than ourselves? They are clothed in velvet and rich stuffs, ornamented with ermine and other furs, and we are forced to wear poor clothing. They have wines, spices, and fine bread, while we have only rye and the refuse of the straw; and when we drink, it must be water. They have handsome seats and manors, while we must brave the wind and the rain in our labors in the fields; and it is by our labors that they have wherewithal to support their pomp.[10]

More recently, Franz Fanon, apostle of anticolonial revolutionary violence in post-World War II Africa, maintained that "violence is a cleansing force. It frees the native from his inferiority complex and from his despair and inaction; it makes him fearless and restores his self-respect."[11] And Che Guevara, comrade-in-arms of Cuba's Fidel Castro, asked,

Why does the guerrilla fighter fight? We must come to the inevitable conclusion that the guerrilla fighter is a social reformer, that he takes up arms responding to the angry protest of the people against their oppressors, and that he fights in order to change the social system that keeps all his unarmed brothers in ignominy and misery.[12]

Wars and Social Change

Civil wars generally occur when a disparity exists between the forces of socioeconomic change and the ability of existing political structures to accommodate these changes. Thus, the wars heralding the breakup of the Hapsburg and Ottoman Empires occurred when nationalist sentiments could not be satisfied within those existing systems. This is, however, a relatively new phenomenon: Prior to the late 18th century, wars had resulted largely from elite decision makers' ambitions for empire and conquest, from dynastic and Realpolitik squabbling, from messianic impulse, or for (perceived) self-defense. There had always been sporadic uprisings, such as that of the ill-fated Wat Tyler in England, or before that, the Spartacus revolt in ancient Rome. But with the U.S. War of Independence and, even more so, the wars of the French Revolution, organized violence between large armed groups came to be seen as a potential instrument for social change. Nearly 200 years ago, the newspaper *Patriote Français* exulted over the coming "expiatory war which is to renew the face of the world and plant the standard of liberty upon the palaces of kings, upon the seraglios of sultans, upon the chateaux of petty feudal tyrants and upon the temples of popes and muftis."

Although economic and social deprivations appear to have been important in unleashing rebellions such as that by Wat Tyler and civil wars such as the Chinese and Cuban Revolutions, they seem less likely to produce wars *between* states. In many cases, economic gain was a major motivating factor, especially the prospect of booty obtained by looting the defeated side. For example, the successes of the Macedonians under Alexander the Great, the Huns under Attila, the Mongols under Genghis Khan, and the remarkable advances of the armies of Islam during the seventh and eighth centuries A.D. all were due at least in part to the lure of direct economic gain. However, these armies were not so much driven by desperation about their personal well-being as by the hope of obtaining yet more booty.

Poverty may drive war in unexpected ways. In 1966, President Johnson sought to justify the presence of so many U.S. troops overseas (including, notably, those in Vietnam at the time). "There are three billion people in the world," he said while reviewing U.S. troops in Korea, "and we have only 200 million of them. We are outnumbered 15 to 1. If might did make right they would sweep over the United States and take what we have. We have what they want." Thus, when it comes to violence between states, poverty may be less influential in motivating the poor than in activating the wealthy to defend what they already have by taking measures ranging from "police actions" abroad to suppressing "civil disturbances" at home.

Economic conditions, however, can serve as an indirect cause of international war, as other states become nervous at the success of recently established revolutionary regimes. The French Revolution was stimulated in part by the outright physical hunger of a significant part of the French people. In turn, the new republican government was seen as a threat to the established monarchies of Europe, and efforts were therefore made to invade France and suppress that revolution. The resulting French Revolutionary Wars led to the ascension to power of Napoleon Bonaparte, and to the much larger Napoleonic Wars that were to engulf Europe.

Poverty as a Restraint on War

Overall, the correlations between poverty and war are unclear. Poor people are more likely to seek food and land than overseas conquests. In the contemporary world, impoverished peasants may occasionally pose a threat to their own governments, but not to their wealthy, well-armed neighbors. No one seriously believes that the poor *campesinos* of Mexico, for example, are going to invade the United States. It can be argued that, if anything, poverty has been more likely to restrain the military adventuring of states than to encourage it. Wars are expensive; it is costly to equip soldiers, navies, and air forces and to supply them in the field.

Truly desperate conditions, more often than not, reduce rather than enhance an army's motivation for fighting. For example, the terrible food, medicine, and supply situation (as well as despair over the high casualties and lack of battlefield success) led Russian forces to seek to end their war against Germany and Austria-Hungary from early 1917 onward. This was pursued with even greater determination following the Bolshevik Revolution later that year.

When England introduced the world's first nationwide income tax in the early 19th century, it was to pay the costs of the Napoleonic Wars. Only rarely has poverty pushed a country to war; more often, leaders have hesitated to make war unless their economies were strong enough to withstand the strain. By contrast, a degree of prosperity can make leadership pushy and dangerously self-confident. (It can also make them relatively peace loving—although highly militarized—like modern-day Switzerland and Sweden.)

Imperialism

Imperialism refers to the policy of extending one's rule over other, foreign peoples. It has an ancient history, beginning with the first efforts to conquer and subdue a foreign people. The Roman historian Tacitus commented, "Worldwide conquest and the destruction of all rival communities or potentates opened the way to the secure enjoyment of wealth and an overriding appetite for it."

Until the early 20th century, imperialism was widely accepted and even lauded—at least by the leadership of major imperialist states. At the same time, imperialism may have contributed directly to war and suffering, that is, by generating not only the direct violence of war but also the indirect, structural violence of colonial oppression. By the end of the 20th century, it seemed to many mainstream Western scholars that the world had passed into a postimperialist era. Therefore, suggestions that imperialism causes war may appear outdated. It should be emphasized, however, that imperialism still occupies an important place in Marxist and postcolonialist thinking on war, and moreover, the phenomenon itself can be very resilient, cropping up in many different forms. For example, "anti-imperialists" in both the less economically developed counties (especially in Latin America) and in advanced industrial nations (particularly in France, Italy, and Greece) decry what they perceive to be the economic and cultural imperialism of Western multinational corporations and American mass media.

A Brief History of Modern Imperialism

During its heyday from the 15th century through the end of World War I, imperialism had many backers, notably among conservatives such as Benjamin Disraeli, Lord Curzon, Rudyard Kipling, and Cecil Rhodes in England; Jules Ferry in France; and Theodore Roosevelt, William McKinley, and other "manifest doctrine" supporters in the United States. Imperialism was lauded as (ostensibly) helping to "modernize and Christianize" the savage, benighted peoples of the earth, whose improvement and care were "the white man's burden." Moreover, advocates were generally unapologetic about the value of imperial conquests in providing raw materials for domestic, Anglo-American industrial production and overseas markets for manufactured goods, as well as the prestige that befits a Great Power. "The issue is not a mean one," wrote Benjamin Disraeli, Conservative prime minister of Great Britain during the 1870s. "It is whether you will be content to be a comfortable England, molded upon Continental principles, and meeting in due course an inevitable fate, or whether you will be a great country, an imperial country."[13]

But imperialism has had numerous critics as well, especially from the political left. In 1902, in his influential book *Imperialism*, the liberal English economist John Hobson argued forcefully that imperialism was a social and economic wrong, indicating a defect in capitalism. In this view, imperialism results when nations enter the machine economy, with its advanced industrial methods, and manufacturers, merchants, and financiers find it more and more difficult to dispose profitably of their products. This in turn generates pressure for access to undeveloped overseas markets as well as to sources of raw materials.

Hobson's line of reasoning seemed especially cogent, coming as it did after such events as the Boxer Rebellion and Opium Wars in China, which in large part signified Chinese protests against Western economic domination of China and the insistence of the European imperialist powers (especially Great Britain) on opening China to the lucrative opium trade. The major intra-European conflict of the 18th century, the Seven Years' War (known in North America as the French and Indian War), was in some ways the first world war, brought about by worldwide colonial competition between England and France, a rivalry that was extended to India, the Caribbean, the west coast of Africa (over the lucrative slave trade), Canada and the upper Ohio valley, and the eastern Atlantic of colonial America. In addition, the Crimean and Boer Wars, as well as the Moroccan crises of 1905 and 1911, lent further weight to Hobson's critique of imperialism as a cause of war. "As soon as one of our industries fails to find a market for its products," we read in Anatole France's novel *Penguin Island*, "a war is necessary to open new outlets. . . . In Third Zealand we have killed two-thirds of the inhabitants in order to compel the remainder to buy our umbrellas and braces."

The Leninist Theory of Imperialism

The most detailed analysis of imperialism during the early 20th century was conducted by Lenin, in his book *Imperialism: The Highest Stage of Capitalism*. According to Lenin's view, which was strongly influenced by

Hobson, imperialism arises from the contradictions inherent in capitalism and is inevitable as capitalism proceeds:

> Capitalism has concentrated the earth's wealth in the hands of a few states and divided the world up to the last bit. . . . Any further enrichment could take place only . . . as the enrichment of one state at the expense of another. The issue could only be settled by force—and, accordingly, war between the world marauders became inevitable.[14]

Noting the participation of many Western European socialists in the First World War, Lenin also argued that war between capitalist states also served "to disunite the workers and fool them with nationalism, to annihilate their vanguards in order to weaken the revolutionary movement of the proletariat." In contrast to the liberal school of interpreting economic imperialism (Hobson), Lenin maintained that only revolution—not reform—could undo capitalism's tendency toward imperialism and thence to war. Lenin's became a major part of the orthodox Marxist interpretation of the reasons for war.

Undoubtedly, imperialism can lead to war between the imperial government and the local population: Examples include wars of occupation and conquest, such as the Maori wars in New Zealand, the Zulu wars in southeast Africa, and the Indian wars in the United States. These were followed in turn by wars of national liberation, for example, the Huk rebellion against the United States in the Philippines, the Mau-Mau rebellion in Kenya, the War of Algerian Independence, and so on. Intellectual disputes regarding modern imperialism centers on the questions of (1) whether capitalist states are necessarily driven to imperialism, and (2) whether imperialism has been a primary reason for war between imperial states.

In Lenin's view, the collapse of capitalism—predicted by Marx—was delayed because the capitalist states not only had bamboozled the proletariat into fighting the proletariat in other countries, but they had also used imperialism to acquire overseas outlets for their surplus goods and financial investments. Lenin applied his thesis to the reasons for World War I. By the early 20th century, almost the entire world had been carved into colonies or spheres of influence, with Britain's the largest. Germany, in contrast—although a rising power—had been effectively excluded. In the Leninist view, World War I was fought to determine whether Germany or Britain would be free to loot the world. In the words of one radical historian of that war,

> Each side was defending its imperialist interests by preventing the balance of power from being tipped in favor of its opponents. These imperialist interests were in the last analysis the private interests of finance and monopoly capital, which, through the influence of the plutocracy

on governments and public opinion, were identified in the minds of the rulers with "national honor and vital interests." There were, of course, other factors in the situation, and the psychological process by which promoting vested interests . . . is transmuted in men's minds into loyalty to religious, philanthropic, and patriotic ideals is complex and largely unconscious.[15]

Even when states are not directly competing for colonies, they are likely to conflict with other states, by intervening on behalf of their own nationals, or by competing with local forces or with the nationals of another would-be imperial country in some economically impoverished arena. Of the frequent U.S. interventions in Latin America, many occurred on behalf of private U.S. investments, notably those of the United Fruit Company. For example, in 1954 the CIA organized the overthrow of the democratically elected Arbenz government in Guatemala. Arbenz, a leftist, had sought to nationalize the United Fruit holdings in his country, distributing them to landless peasants and insisting that the company accept, as fair compensation, the value it had declared for tax purposes to the Guatemalan government that preceded him.

The U.S. obsession with Nicaragua in the 1980s, by contrast, seemed motivated largely by fear of a kind of ideological/social/economic domino effect: If a small poor state such as Nicaragua were to escape from the U.S. orbit, and to prosper as a consequence, perhaps this would encourage others to do likewise. This interpretation also explains the single-minded insistence by the Reagan administration on destroying the Nicaraguan economy, since by this strategy, even if the Sandinistas were not over-thrown, their revolution could be discredited if Nicaraguan society could be sufficiently damaged. If nothing else, the suffering of the Nicaraguan people could serve as an object lesson for what will befall any other client state that might seek to go against the United States. A similar interpretation might apply to the persistent hostility by the government of the United States toward Castro-led Cuba, although in this case, the political power of Cuban Americans, particularly in southern Florida, has also been key.

Reinterpretations and Rebuttals of the Leninist View of Imperialism

By the 1960s and 1970s, European imperial powers had dissolved their empires, and virtually all former colonies had gained political independence (even while their economic dependence on the West continued unabated). Accordingly, Leninist interpretations of Marxist theory were reconsidered. Contemporary neo-imperialism is now seen to operate more subtly, not through outright colonial control and only rarely via war. Rather, it typi-cally manipulates the economic, political, and sociocultural structures of less developed economies, maintaining them in a condition of dependency, by a process that Lord Lugard, British governor of Nigeria, called "indirect rule": control via indigenous ruling classes. For example, consider the role of the United States in Central America, France in western Africa, or Britain in its former colonies in eastern Africa and the Caribbean. Previous colonial masters no longer rule by naked military power. Rather, they exercise control over local economies—and often, sources of communication and information as well, such as the mass media and Internet access—typically relying on home-grown political flunkies recruited from the dominant socioeconomic classes. The emphasis here is not so much on war as on the structural violence found when one state dominates another.

Particularly influential in the development of what has become known as dependency theory are the Brazilian economist Andre Gunder-Frank, the American global systems theorist Immanuel Wallerstein, and the Norwegian peace researcher Johan Galtung. Galtung has developed a model in which both the neo-imperial state and the neocolony are divided into *center* (elites) and *periphery* (peasants and workers). According to this analysis, the neo-imperial system involves a connection whereby the center in the neo-imperial state is closely allied with the center in the neocolony, with antagonism between center and periphery in the neocolony, and a perceived disharmony of interest between peripheries in the neocolony and the neo-imperium. Instead of physical occupation, the imperial state provides limited economic aid, relatively abundant military aid, and intellectual under-pinning and legitimacy to a colonial center that actively oppresses its own people, for the benefit of the two centers, both colonial and imperial.

According to the neoliberal economist Walter Rostow (who, along with his brother E. V. Rostow, supported and helped design the Vietnam War), the acquisition of colonies—especially during the 19th century—was not warranted by European capital markets nor by military or strategic consid-erations, but rather by competition for prestige:

> The competition for colonies was conducted for reasons that were unilaterally rational on neither economic nor military grounds; the competition occurred essentially because competitive nationalism was the rule of the world arena and colonies were an accepted symbol of status and power within the arena.[16]

The question still remains: Regardless of the underlying reasons for im-perial competition, to what extent did this competition lead to war among the competitors? The issue is not resolved. In World War I, for example, the prime movers—Austria, Serbia, and Russia—were involved in a relatively straightforward struggle over prestige, territory, power, national self-determination (Serbia), and survival as an imperial state (Austria), not primarily in a competition for overseas possessions or raw materials. More-over, the common interest in shared trade between, say, Britain and Germany may well have been greater than the rivalries over international markets and imperial ambition. In addition, overseas businesses may often be considered as much the pawns of governments as their manipulators.

Prior to the Russo-Japanese War, Russian private investors put money into timber near the Yalu River, in a region under dispute with Japan. Apparently, they were put up to it by the government, which sought to use these investments as an excuse to further its own expansionist goals. Economics, in short, may be manipulated by politics, no less than the other way around.

The following arguments have also been raised against the Leninist view that capitalism leads to imperialism, which leads to war:

1. Economic interests do not always strictly determine foreign policy. In some cases, foreign policy even goes against economic interests.

2. Foreign investments do not always yield a higher rate of return on investments. In fact, there is growing evidence that 19th-century imperialism nearly always injured the imperial power more than it helped it.

3. Although the total investment of major capitalist countries in less developed economies is (and has been) large in absolute numbers, it has always been a very small proportion of the domestic economic investment: typically less than 10%. It is very difficult, therefore, to argue that capitalism relies greatly on foreign investments in order to survive.

4. Foreign capital has increasingly been invested in other developed countries rather than being sunk, "imperialistically," into less developed countries. Japanese finance capital and Arab oil money, for example, have been invested heavily in the United States, Great Britain, and Western Europe.

It is also difficult to argue, for example, that participation of the United States in the Vietnam War was primarily economically motivated. Thus, Vietnam's teak, tungsten, and modest off-shore oil deposits paled by contrast with the cost of that war for the United States: 50,000 U.S. lives, $150 billion. In addition, the stock market fell whenever it appeared that the Vietnam War would be prolonged, further suggesting that it was not good for American business.

The Military-Industrial Complex

The link between economics and war is often a real one, particularly as this connection operates in contemporary capitalist societies through money making, the global reach of multinational corporations and the Internet, and the "military-industrial complex." Although this phrase has become especially popular among its left-wing critics, it was first introduced by the relatively conservative American president Dwight Eisenhower, in his 1961 Farewell Address:

> We have been compelled to create a permanent armaments industry of vast proportions. . . . This conjunction of an immense military establishment and a large arms industry is new in the American experience. The total influence—economic, political, even spiritual—is felt in every city, every statehouse, every office of the federal government. . . . In the councils of government, we must guard against the acquisition of unwarranted influence, whether sought or unsought, by the military-industrial complex. The potential for the disastrous rise of misplaced power exists and will persist.[17]

This alliance of military and industry has been joined by scientists, research universities, mainstream labor unions, and government. And it is more firmly entrenched than ever.

Forerunners of the Military-Industrial Complex

The American military-industrial-science-labor-government complex since the Second World War is not totally new in human experience. Those with a financial and social interest in war making have long had a disproportionate influence on the policies of governments. In the days of warrior-kings, they *were* the government. During ancient times, soldiers were rewarded with a proportion of the spoils of a sacked city. Mercenary armies, by definition, fought for pay and/or a share of the booty. Much of the martial enthusiasm that marked the Muslim conquests of much of Europe and the Mediterranean world during the Middle Ages, for example, has been attributed to fact that Islamic warriors were fighting not only for their faith but also for their personal enrichment. In the late 16th century, Spanish soldiers—fighting the Dutch effort at independence—sacked Antwerp (then the richest city in northern Europe), when Philip II of Spain went bankrupt and could not make good on their back pay.

"The orientation toward war," wrote the economist Joseph Schumpeter, "is mainly fostered by the domestic interests of ruling classes, but also by the influence of all those who stand to gain individually from a war policy, whether economically or socially."[18] From early in the industrial age, the great armaments manufacturers—Krupp in Germany, Vickers and Armstrong in England, Remington and Colt in the United States, and more recently, Dassault in France—all profited when their country went to war. They even profited when other countries went to war, by selling arms to the belligerents —often to both sides.

During the 1930s, a U.S. Senate committee, chaired by Senator Gerald Nye, investigated the charge that U.S. arms manufacturers were responsible for American entry into the First World War. Although the Nye Committee was unable to prove these allegations, the "merchants of death" theory gained credibility. On the other hand, popular pressure in opposition to military spending has also influenced government decisions: Britain and France, for example, found it very difficult to maintain large military forces during the early 1930s because of popular antimilitary sentiment, and the United States and Russia have succeeded in restricting at least certain aspects of their nuclear competition.

The Contemporary Military-Industrial Complex

And this pattern continues today: Arms sales have been the number one export for Brazil, France, and Israel. With the exception of Japan, arms make up a major proportion of the exports of every industrialized state, with the United States, Russia, and France leading all the others in absolute terms (and with the United States by far the largest arms peddler to the world).

Huge amounts of money are made on armaments, both through domestic weapons programs and in sales to other nations. Within the United States, during the latter part of the 20th century, about 10% of all business derived from military-related production, more yet for large corporations such as Lockheed, General Dynamics, Boeing, and Northrop, which in some cases derive up to 50% of their profits from military-related production. In certain regions of the United States, such as California and parts of the Southeast, military spending has accounted for upward of one third of all jobs.

In addition, influential politicians have often succeeded in bringing extraordinary amounts of military business to their local districts. The Charleston, South Carolina, district of former representative Mendel Rivers, a longtime chairman of the House Armed Services Committee, contained an Air Force base, a Marine air station, an Army depot, several naval hospitals, a naval weapons station and supply center, a Polaris submarine base, as well as AVCO, Lockheed, Sikorsky, and GE plants. The military payroll alone in this one congressional district exceeded $2 billion. Not surprisingly, Mr. Rivers—who was responsible for overseeing military expenditures—was inclined to see "the Soviet threat" almost everywhere and to support a high level of military preparedness. Moreover, he was regularly reelected to Congress by his appreciative constituents.

There has been a Soviet, and now Russian, counterpart to the Western military-industrial complex. Nikita Khrushchev called them the "metal eaters," the alliance of industrial bureaucrats and military leaders in the former USSR. In a society that long valued heavy industry and national defense over civilian goods, military production received highest priority in the former Soviet Union until Gorbachev came to power in 1985 and initiated *glasnost* and *perestroika* (which were to some extent reversed by Yeltsin after 1991). The future of such reforms under Putin and succeeding Russian presidents remains uncertain.

In many industrial states, career advancement within the military is most readily achieved when associated with some major military building program. In the United States, a kind of "revolving door" operates, whereby senior government officials are recruited by military contractors after their retirement. While in government service, many of these people (often from industry or the military in the first place) are typically reluctant to alienate the military contractors who are potential employers after their retirement. Nonetheless, whereas preparations for war may be profitable, the fighting of wars—especially nuclear wars—is likely to be a losing proposition.

A key issue, therefore, is not so much war-profiteering as war-preparation-profiteering. In limited cases, wars can help stimulate an economy; the Great Depression of the 1930s ended with the onset of World War II. However, peace researcher Lewis Richardson concluded that fewer than one third of wars from 1820 to 1949 were generated by economic causes, and these were limited to small wars rather than large ones. Economics clearly influences military spending levels as well as specific procurement decisions (the purchase of one weapons system over another). The profit motive may contribute indirectly to war by supporting arms races and by creating important constituencies with an interest in the maintenance of international tension, which in turn makes it difficult to achieve disarmament or even arms control. But it appears that the military-industrial complex does not directly cause war.

The Economic Effects of Wars

When it comes to the effects of war on a country's economy, not surprisingly, the location of the war is crucial: A war on one's own territory can be devastating; on someone else's, it is much less painful and can even help an economy. The Napoleonic Wars, for instance, put a special premium on iron, which in turn hurried along Britain's entry into the Industrial Revolution:

> Indigent and underemployed men do not buy cannon and other expensive industrial products. But by putting indigent thousands into the army and navy and then supplying them with the tools of their new trade, effective demand was displaced from articles of personal consumption towards items useful to big organizations—armies and navies in the first place, buy factories, railroads, and other such enterprises in times to come. Moreover, the men who built the new

coke-fired blast furnaces in previously desolate regions of Wales and Scotland would probably not have undertaken such risky and expensive investments without an assured market for cannon. At any rate, their initial markets were largely military.[19]

There is another view, however, namely, that war has done little to stimulate industrial progress, whereas industrial progress has done much to stimulate war and to make it more horrendous when it occurred. Wars rely heavily on peacetime scientific and economic achievements, such as: advances in metallurgy, transportation, chemistry, medicine, communication, transportation, mathematics, even food processing and preparation. War is very often a parasite on civilian economies, taking much and contributing little. During the 1980s, declines in American economic productivity and trade deficits were due largely to the Reagan administration's investment of substantial national resources—both human and material—in the military economy. By contrast during the "economic boom" (for the affluent) in America during the 1990s, defense spending and investment were held relatively constant.

As to the vaunted spin-offs from military technology, if governments and corporations had really wanted no-stick frying pans, or computer miniaturization, they would have been able to create these things much more rapidly, and cheaply, by investing directly in such technology. Moreover, military research and development is typically insensitive to cost, while very demanding as to performance. As a result, advanced weaponry tends to be very expensive, but not useful in the civilian marketplace. Consumers, for example, don't need toasters that will operate at 80° below zero, or mega-computers that can perform "Star Wars" calculations in nanoseconds; rather, they need reliable, inexpensive items that benefit their lives.

In most economically less developed nations, wars have contributed nothing positive to the local economy, whereas the physical, economic, and social effects of wars have been horribly destructive. Wars lay waste to nations not only by the direct detonation of weapons but also by the disruption of economies. It has been estimated, for example, that in 1988, after nine years of war, food production in Afghanistan was only about one quarter its prewar levels. And in that same year, Angola spent 60% of its income on military forces, defending itself against guerrillas supported by South Africa, Saudi Arabia, and the United States. This destitute state, which invested only $49 per capita in educating its children, also spent $133 per capita on its military.

Furthermore, emergency and relief efforts—difficult enough to mount successfully in peacetime—can be lethally disrupted. During 1984 and 2000, Ethiopia suffered serious famines in which hundreds of thousands starved and millions were malnourished. In 1988, Ethiopia received $534 million from abroad for famine and development aid; at the same time the government was spending $447 million on military forces to fight its civil wars in Eritrea and Tigre, as well as the Ogaden. Also, relief convoys, conducted by the Red Cross, were unable to make deliveries of needed food to people in the rebellious areas of Eritrea and Tigre. The Ethiopian government claimed that such convoys would not be safe, while critics accused it of withholding food as a weapon against the rebels and of spending three fourths of the national budget on arms and internal security when poverty and hunger remain Ethiopia's most pressing needs.

The Effects of Military Spending

Some people argue that military spending is economically beneficial, providing jobs, permitting federal governments to target areas needing financial investment, and generating demand that can stimulate a lagging economy. On the other hand, most experts agree that in the long run, military spending is economically damaging. (Of course, the primary justification for military spending is not economic but rather that it supposedly enhances national security; economic arguments are generally seen to be secondary to that more fundamental justification.)

Economic criticisms of military spending as detrimental to a society focus on five areas:

1. *Employment.* Although military spending creates jobs, it almost invariably results in fewer jobs than would be generated by the same funds spent for civilian purposes. This is especially true for high-tech military procurement, notably for aerospace and nuclear weapons. Such expenditures are capital-intensive—that is, they cost a lot of money, but hire relatively few people—as opposed to such labor-intensive expenditures as education, health care, and construction.

2. *Inflation.* Military spending is perhaps the most inflationary way for a government to spend money. By using up major resources without producing consumable goods, military spending reduces supply while also increasing demand for raw materials, thereby contributing to inflation in two ways. Moreover, costs tend to rise yet further when the supply of money and credit increases without corresponding increases in productivity. The result is the classic inflationary process: too much money chasing too few goods.

3. *Deficits.* Governments can only obtain military forces by paying for them. The immense federal deficits of the Reagan administration, for example, occurred largely because the U.S. government chose to lower taxes while dramatically increasing military expenditures.

4. *Productivity.* Industrial productivity is strongly influenced by the availability of scientists and engineers to provide innovative tech-

nologies, and the ability of federal governments to invest in civilian research and development as well as the renovation of aging industrial plants. Military economies tend to dominate scientific and R&D (research and development) activities, thereby robbing the civilian economy. As a result, there is a strong inverse correlation between military spending as a function of gross national product (GNP) and growth in economic productivity: States such as Denmark, Canada, and Japan—which invest in their domestic rather than their military economies—during the 1980s grew more rapidly than nations such as the United States or Great Britain, whose priorities were reversed.

5. *Unmet social needs.* Resources spent on the military are not available to be spent in other ways. A "substitution effect" tends to operate, whereby expenditures for submarines, missiles, and machine guns, for example, are deleted from money available for hospitals, day care centers, and schools. One half of 1% of one year's world military spending would purchase enough farm equipment, according to the Brandt Commission on North/South Issues, to permit the world's low-income countries to reach food sufficiency within a decade. The world's annual military budget in 1987 equaled the total income of the population of the 44 poorest nations on earth: 2.6 billion people. Global military expenditures that year reached an all-time high of $1.8 million per minute, at a time when people were dying from hunger-related, preventable diseases at a rate comparable to one Hiroshima bomb every two days. Also in 1987, a UN conference on the relationship between military spending and economic development was attended by 128 countries; the United States boycotted this meeting, claiming that disarmament and development are separate issues.

Military spending is also a serious problem in nations such as the United States, Israel, and Russia. During most of the 1990s, Russia acknowledged the need to reduce military spending so as to address its inadequate domestic productivity; more recently, however, Russian politicians have reexpressed their desire for Russia to resume Great Power status, which is usually acquired through military posturing. The problem is even more acute in many developing countries. In the 1970s, for example, military spending in Africa increased by 6.6% per year, while economic growth was only 0.4%. Taken as a proportion of GNP, military expenditures of the world's richer states have actually declined since 1960, whereas those of the poorer states have increased; countries that cannot meet the basic social needs of their people have been spending a larger share of their meager incomes on weapons and soldiers than the richer states spend of their much more abundant income.

"Every gun that is made," said President Eisenhower, "every warship launched, every rocket fired signifies, in the final sense, a theft from those who hunger and are not fed, those who are cold and are not clothed. The world in arms is not spending money alone. It is spending the sweat of its laborers, the genius of its scientists, the hopes of its children."[20]

A Final Note on the Reasons for Wars

Wars—and the preparations for wars—take place within contexts that transcend individuals and their group affiliations. These contexts include such diffuse but extremely important factors as ideologies, economic forces, and sociocultural conditions. There are no simple cause-and-effect relationships in this realm. Rather, war, like other forms of violent human conflicts and human behavior more generally, is an *overdetermined* phenomenon: Multiple factors, some short term and relatively easy to discern (such as an assassination) and others that are long term and harder to pinpoint (such as cultural antagonisms), predispose decision makers to take the fateful steps leading to wars.

A somewhat oversimplified but not simplistic mnemonic device for remembering some of the multiple factors leading to wars is represented by the acronym EGGIEs: ego, greed, groups, ideologies, and extenuating circumstances (of which the two most significant historical variables have been leadership and technology).

From this perspective, wars are fought because powerful and influential individuals, usually in search of personal aggrandizement or revenge ("ego"), and often motivated to increase their wealth and/or power ("greed"), persuade, manipulate, and/or command their compatriots ("groups") to pursue their personal and national agendas ("ideologies") by force of arms—despite the opposition of other individuals in different groups and/or nations, who would oppose them, by violent means if necessary. Leadership, both good and bad, and technology (including the never-ending search for "the winning weapon") can sometimes make the difference between winning and losing any particular war. And even deeper underlying factors, such as possible hormonal imbalances and/or brain and genetic abnormalities, may also predispose certain individuals to commit excessively aggressive and violent actions (thus possibly adding another "G"—"gonads"—to the acronym).

Although wars are extremely complex phenomena and often elicit the entire range of human motivations and conduct, they are, like all human artifacts, modifiable and preventable. In the remainder of this book, we consider a number of ways to reduce the incidence and virulence of wars (building negative peace) and to lay the groundwork for a world "beyond war" (building positive peace).

Notes

1. Woodrow Wilson. 1965. *A Day of Dedication*. New York: Macmillan.

2. George F. Kennan. 1951. *American Diplomacy, 1900–1950*. Boston: Little, Brown.

3. Randolph S. Bourne. 1964. "The State." In *War and the Intellectuals, Collected Essays 1915–1919*. New York: Harper & Row.

4. Walter Lippmann. 1955. *The Public Philosophy*. Boston: Little, Brown.

5. Quoted in Mary Kaldor. 1987. "The World Economy and Militarization." In S. Mendlovitz and R. B. J. Walker, eds., *Towards a Just World Order*. London: Butterworths.

6. *Marxism-Leninism on War and Army (A Soviet View)*. 1974. Soviet Military Thought, No. 2. Washington, DC: United States Air Force.

7. Josue de Castro. 1952. *The Geography of Hunger*. Boston: Little, Brown.

8. Quoted in Michael Howard. 1978. *War and the Liberal Conscience*. New Brunswick, NJ: Rutgers University Press.

9. Alexis de Tocqueville. 1955. *The Old Regime and the French Revolution*. New York: Doubleday.

10. Quoted in Arthur Bryant. 1966. *The Fire & the Rose*. New York: Doubleday.

11. Franz Fanon. 1963. *The Wretched of the Earth*. New York: Grove.

12. Che Guevara. 1968. *Guerrilla Warfare*. New York: Monthly Review Press.

13. Benjamin Disraeli. Quoted in Michael Howard. 1978. *War and the Liberal Conscience*. New Brunswick, NJ: Rutgers University Press.

14. V. I. Lenin. 1939. *Imperialism: The Highest Stage of Capitalism*. New York: International Publishers.

15. K. Zilliacus. 1946. *Mirror of the Past*. New York: Current Books.

16. Walter Rostow. 1960. *The Stages of Economic Growth*. Cambridge, UK: Cambridge University Press.

17. Dwight D. Eisenhower. 1961. *Peace With Justice: Selected Addresses*. New York: Columbia University Press.

18. Joseph Schumpeter. 1955. *Imperialism and Social Classes*. New York: Meridian.

19. William H. McNeill. 1982. *The Pursuit of Power*. Chicago: University of Chicago Press.

20. Eisenhower, op. cit.

A Beijing citizen pauses in front of tanks, June 5, 1989.
(Photo © Bettmann/CORBIS)

PART III

Building Negative Peace

Every noble work is at first impossible.

—Thomas Carlyle

Throughout history, people have recognized the absurdity and horror of war, even as they have engaged in it. There has been no shortage of proposed solutions to the problems posed by war. The simplest solution, perhaps, can be derived from the failed "war on drugs": Just say no. But as in that other "war," this turns out to be no solution at all. Although seemingly straightforward moral judgments and outright condemnation are undeniably appealing, most nations have been no more able to go "cold turkey" on war than individuals have on drugs. Mark Twain once noted that it was easy to stop smoking—he had done it many times. Similarly, it has been easy to prevent war; many different solutions have been proposed, and some of them have even been implemented (to varying degrees).

Perhaps these solutions are not sufficiently innovative, forward-thinking, or creative. And others may not be practical or even feasible. Perhaps the problem is that no one solution has been pushed hard and far enough. Or perhaps war is still with us because these various solutions have not been attempted in the right combination, or with the right adjustment or nuance. Perhaps they actually are working, only slowly, so that peace—like President Herbert Hoover's claim about prosperity during the Great Depression—is just around the corner. On the other hand, perhaps they have not and will not, so that something else is needed. If so, let us hope that by reviewing humanity's efforts to prevent war, we can at least save peacemakers of the future from repeating the errors of the past. And maybe, we can inspire greater efforts, and achieve greater success, in the days to come.

Some historians have pointed out that the political and social reality of recent centuries have not coincided exactly with their calendar definitions. Thus, the 19th century can be seen to have begun, effectively, with the French Revolution (1789) and ended with World War I (1914), while the 20th century began, in a sense, in 1914 and ended with the collapse of the Soviet Union in 1991. If so, then we are already well into the 21st century; and yet, in terms of dramatic changes in war and peace, we have disappointingly little to show for it, astoundingly little, compared to the opportunity we have been granted to remake the world.

"War is waged," wrote St. Augustine, "so that peace may prevail. . . . But it is a greater glory to slay war with a word than people with a sword, and to gain peace by means of peace and not by means of war."[1] In the following seven chapters, we examine efforts to gain peace by means of peace. It is no easy quest. As General Omar Bradley put it:

> The problem of peaceful accommodation in the world is infinitely more difficult than the conquest of space, infinitely more complex than a trip to the moon. . . . If I am sometimes discouraged, it is not by the magnitude of the problem, but by our colossal indifference to it. I am unable to understand why . . . we do not make greater more diligent and more imaginative use of reason and human intelligence in seeking . . . accord and compromise.[2]

What, then, does human reason and intelligence have to offer by way of preventing war and creating peace?

"There is no way to peace," wrote the great pacifist A. J. Muste, "peace is the way." But if we are to follow it, the way to peace must at least be discerned, even if dimly. And like the blind men and the reasons of war, the causes of peace are also multifaceted. Most likely, just as no one body part defines an elephant, there is no one way to peace but rather many ways—some of which might lead down blind alleys, some to dangerous cliffs, and others to yet more paths, each with additional branching points and an unending series of twists and turns. In Part III, we walk a short way down some of the most prominent of these paths.

Notes

1.   St. Augustine. 1950. *The City of God.* New York: Modern Library.

2.   Quoted in Alan Geyer. 1982. *The Idea of Disarmament.* Glencoe, IL: Brethren.

10 Diplomacy, Negotiations, and Conflict Resolution

We have met the enemy and he is us.

—Pogo

*Disagreements must be settled, not by force, not by deceit or
trickery, but rather in the only manner which is worthy of
the dignity of man, i.e., by a mutual assessment of the reasons
on both sides of the dispute, by a mature and objective
investigation of the situation, and by an equitable
reconciliation of differences of opinion.*

—Pope John XXIII, *Pacem in Terris*

One way of achieving peace is for the contending sides in a dispute to reach a mutually acceptable agreement among themselves. When such agreements or understandings are obtained among states, through the efforts of trained governmental representatives, often employing stylized communication, we say that diplomacy has taken place; the people who practice this art are known as diplomats. (There is also a more cynical view of diplomats, who have been defined as "men [and increasingly, women] sent abroad to lie for their country.")

Peace researcher and political scientist Anatol Rapaport has usefully distinguished among fights, games, and debates. In a fight, the intent is to defeat the opponent, sometimes even to destroy him or her. Rules may exist, as in a prizefight, but they may also be ignored—as in a street fight, or a particularly vicious war—and the means are nonetheless violent. In a game, by contrast, each side tries to outwit the opponent, playing strictly within certain rules. And in a debate, the goal is to persuade the opponent of the justice or correctness of one's cause. The process of conflict resolution, ideally, is closest to a debate, just as wars are fights, although as we have seen, with some aspects of a game as well. However, as we shall now see, even diplomacy and negotiations involve elaborate rules, and not uncommonly, the threat of fighting as well.

Although ways of fighting have changed through history, the basic techniques of negotiations scarcely have. In essence, negotiators have two things that they can offer: threats and promises. These can be backed up by varying degrees of goodwill or ill will, and a continuum from blind trust to iron-clad verification. Negotiations, however, can succeed only if there is a set of outcomes that each party prefers to reaching no agreement. Admittedly, the participants to a dispute (especially if they are governments) occasionally engage in negotiations just to appear virtuous. But there is good reason to think that in most cases at least, a negotiated settlement is preferred over either a failure to agree, or the use of violence to force an outcome. The trick is to find a peaceful settlement that will be acceptable to both sides.

In the course of seeking to achieve agreements and resolve disputes short of violence, the contending parties typically try to obtain the most favorable outcome possible for their side. The process of give-and-take and the strategies for succeeding—in reaching an agreement, and also getting the best outcome—involve skill at negotiating. This applies both to the governments in question and also, frequently, to third parties who are called in to help the disputants reach an agreement. Techniques for successful negotiations therefore can contribute greatly to the peaceful resolution of conflicts. Finally, in our search for various routes toward peace, we must ultimately consider the phenomenon of conflict resolution more generally, not only in the international sphere but also with respect to domestic antagonisms, and even interpersonal as well as intrapsychic efforts at resolving conflict.

It is important to realize how often we negotiate solutions to conflict, typically on the interpersonal level. Disagreements between siblings over who gets to sit in a given chair, within families over what television program to watch, or between coworkers over whether or not to have an office party—such disputes are typically resolved, and nearly always short of violence. This fact highlights the many routes available for dealing with conflict; it is something we do every day. And yet one of the most pervasive myths of our current culture of militarism is that war and preparation for war are "natural," unavoidable phenomena, whereas peace and preparations for peace are hopelessly unrealistic. We are surrounded with subliminal messages to the effect that peacemaking is an impossible dream, whereas war making—or at best deterrence or a kind of armed standoff—is the only realistic option. Hence, it is important to affirm and make visible the peacemaking that happens all around us, most of the time. Often peacemaking receives society's attention only when it takes place at the highest government level.

Summitry

In ancient times, leaders were themselves renowned warriors, and not uncommonly, they would meet person to person, to settle their disputes via individual combat. At other times, at least according to folklore, champions would be selected, one from each side, to fight it out: The classic example was David versus Goliath. In historic times, leaders are more likely to be political figures, and their meetings are intended to help establish or cement relationships or to engage in personal resolution of disputes between their countries (while also playing to their domestic constituencies).

When the leaders of two major groups meet, this is referred to as a summit meeting. There have been many; for example, President Richard Nixon's meeting with Chinese leader Mao Tse-tung in 1972 was especially dramatic, as was Egyptian president Sadat's journey to Jerusalem and his meeting with Israeli prime minister Begin. In both these cases, the states involved had previously been bitter enemies, so antagonistic, in fact, that they were not even communicating with each other. Hence, the mere fact that political leaders were meeting and talking amicably sent a powerful signal about the possibilities of peaceful coexistence.

During the Cold War, the term *summit* was largely reserved for meetings between leaders of the two superpowers, at that time the United States and the USSR. Here too, it was widely thought that if only the leaders could meet and talk over their disagreements, as intelligent and concerned human beings, then peace would reign. Unfortunately, there is no reason to expect this. In some cases, summit meetings were merely cosmetic, perhaps improving the international atmosphere but offering few if any specific changes, and thereby often disappointing those who had hoped for more. A 1955 summit meeting between Nikita Khrushchev and Dwight Eisenhower fell into this category, along with the 1985 meeting between Mikhail Gorbachev and Ronald Reagan in Geneva. At other times, minor progress was achieved, largely by signing agreements that the diplomats had laboriously worked out in advance: a 1972 summit between Richard Nixon and Leonid Brezhnev, for example, at which the SALT I (Strategic Arms Limitation Talks) agreement was signed, or a 1987 meeting in Washington, D.C., between Gorbachev and Reagan at which the INF (Intermediate Range Nuclear Forces) agreement was signed.

It should be pointed out, however, that summit meetings occasionally made things worse, resulting either in feelings of ill will or dangerous misjudgments by one or both parties. An example of the former is the 1986 summit meeting between Gorbachev and Reagan in Reykjavik, Iceland, which terminated in animosity and subsequent claims by each side that the other misunderstood and/or misrepresented what had transpired. Similarly, a summit meeting between John F. Kennedy and Khrushchev in Vienna during 1961 appears to have been a personal embarrassment for JFK (who was younger and less experienced than his Soviet counterpart), and it may have led to Khrushchev's inaccurate estimation that the U.S. president could be pushed around, which in turn set the stage for the Cuban Missile Crisis. It may also have contributed to Kennedy's determination that he would be especially tough in the future.

With the end of the Cold War, meetings between world leaders have rarely carried the same emotional freight as in the recent past and have generally received less public attention. Also contributing to their lowered visibility is the fact that such meetings have become somewhat more frequent, at least on a multilateral basis, with regular convocations of the world's major industrial states (the so-called Group of Seven, plus Russia), as well as frequent trade and other ministerial meetings.

Summit meetings notwithstanding, it is not necessarily true that closer relations and greater communication among world leaders will make war less likely. Kaiser Wilhelm of Germany and Czar Nicholas of Russia, for example, were first cousins, and on the very eve of World War I, they sent each other a flurry of telegrams signed "Willy" and "Nicky"! Summit meetings and personal relationships, in short, can be helpful, but they can also cause problems, depending on the issues and the personal dynamic between the leaders, or provide only an illusion of warmth and mutual understanding.

A Brief History of Diplomacy

In the past, diplomats were drawn from the same social and economic class (upper), and in most cases they spoke the same language, literally: French. Although there is a long history of monarchs sending ambassadors to the courts of other rulers, it is generally agreed that the current system of diplomatic protocol was established by Cardinal Richelieu, the chief minister— some would say, chief manipulator—of the early-17th-century French king, Louis XIII.

Although there has always been a peculiar stiffness to official diplomatic discourse and protocol, such formalities have evolved over many years so as to enhance precision of communication, and whenever possible, reduce the chances that personalities will interfere with formal and serious communication between governments. Historically, ambassadors were the personal representatives of one sovereign to the court of another, and this polite fiction is still maintained, even in the case of democracies: Upon their arrival, ambassadors typically present their credentials to the head of state of the host country. In modern times, electronic communication has largely bypassed the individual diplomat when it comes to the establishment of important international agreements, but the role of person-to-person contact, even at the highest levels, remains important.

Ironically, states communicate with each other least frequently and least clearly during war—precisely when such communication is likely to be the most needed. At such times, and occasionally when interactions become severely strained during peacetime, diplomatic relations are broken off, and each state recalls its ambassador. Otherwise, officials are available to correct possible misunderstandings, clarify positions, and when all else fails, simply to buy time, occasionally in the hope that tense situations will eventually blow over. As we shall see, diplomacy has failed in many cases; however, there have also been successes.

Some Diplomatic Successes in Averting War

In 1987, Indian military exercises near the Pakistan border alarmed the Pakistanis, whose forces were mobilized in response. Soon, more than 300,000 armed men were facing each other across a border that has known substantial violence in the past. Tensions gradually eased, however, via urgent diplomatic exchanges between the two sides; among other things, both agreed (verbally) to refrain from attacks against the other's nuclear facilities. Also in 1987, Greece and Turkey exchanged threats over Turkish plans to prospect for oil near several islands in the eastern Aegean that were under Greek ownership but very close to the Turkish mainland. Like India and Pakistan, these two states also have a long history of antagonism and warfare (Greece was long dominated by Turkey, as part of the Ottoman Empire, and the two states have also engaged in threats as well as fighting over the fate of Greek and Turkish ethnic nationals on the island of Cyprus). Once again, tensions were gradually cooled, at least in part because both sides feared to antagonize their North Atlantic Treaty Organization (NATO) ally, the United States, with the possible cut-off in military aid that might ensue.

In many cases, multilateral diplomacy has negotiated an end to fighting; for example, termination of the wars in Bosnia and Kosovo, and an apparent peace agreement in Northern Ireland. It may be overly optimistic, however, to consider these to be diplomatic successes, since they may also be examples of diplomatic failures that resulted in war, followed eventually by diplomacy-assisted termination once one or both sides tired of the war's costs. (But even in this minimal sense, diplomacy can be profoundly useful, as a means whereby warring sides communicate their desire for peace.)

Some Diplomatic Failures

Sometimes diplomats make things worse. They are human beings, after all, and as such, fallible. Moreover, although it is hoped that direct, personal interactions can reduce the likelihood that nations will resort to force in order to settle their differences, such interactions also provide the opportunity for interpersonal hostility. Perceived slights among rulers and diplomats have, on occasion, endangered the peace. Late in the 17th century, France and

Spain nearly came to blows when a coach carrying the Spanish ambassador to England cut in front of the French ambassador, on a London street. In 1819, the Dey of Algiers, angered about the failure of the French government to make good on a debt, struck the French consul three times with a flyswatter. This insult precipitated a naval blockade by the French and ultimately served as an excuse for what became the long-time occupation of Algeria.

Even at its best, diplomacy breeds a certain deviousness and social artifice that most people find laughable, if not downright unpleasant. During the protracted negotiations leading to the Treaty of Paris after Napoleon's defeat, the famed Austrian diplomat Metternich was told that the Russian ambassador had died. Story has it that he responded, "Ah, is that true? I wonder what he meant by that."

Efforts at diplomatic clarification sometimes backfire, making things worse: For example, in late July 1914, Sir Edward Grey, the British foreign secretary, warned Kaiser Wilhelm that if a general war occurred, Britain would enter it on the side of France and Russia. Rather than deter Germany (as Grey had intended), this was seen as a threat, which made Wilhelm more belligerent, convinced of a plot against him by the Triple Entente. Similarly, at almost precisely the same time, the German chancellor, Bethmann-Hollweg, sent the following diplomatic message to Sazonov, the Russian foreign minister: "Kindly call M. Sazonov's serious attention to the fact that further continuation of Russian mobilization measures would force us to mobilize and in that case European war could scarcely be prevented." This only made Sazonov and the Russian government more intransigent, convinced that Germany was aiming at sovereignty in the Balkans, including control of the Dardanelles.

Sometimes statements by diplomats, intended for domestic consumption, have had serious international repercussions. In 1950, for example, Secretary of State Dean Acheson gave a speech in which he outlined the U.S. "defense perimeter" in the Pacific; this appeared to exclude Korea, which gave the North Korean government the false impression that the United States would not forcibly resist an invasion of South Korea. Shortly before invading Kuwait, Iraqi leader Saddam Hussein met with U.S. ambassador to Iraq, April Glaspie. Ms. Glaspie responded to a query by stating that the United States "takes no position" on Iraqi territorial claims to Kuwait. This was taken by the Iraqis, incorrectly, to mean that the United States would not become involved in the event of an Iraqi invasion.

The prospect of a negotiated settlement is nearly always a desirable one, especially if the alternative is war. However, sometimes war can be made more intense by the fact that diplomats are striving to bring the fighting to a close, as each side seeks to make gains on the battlefield that might influence the ultimate peace settlement. Middle East diplomats noticed that the proposals put forward by Count Bernadotte, the first UN negotiator sent to settle the 1948 war, closely reflected the immediate battlefield situation; as a result, both sides paid less attention to him and put more effort into achieving military gains so as to influence the negotiations in their favor. Similar intensification of war-fighting took place about the time that serious peace negotiations were under way at Panmunjon, in Korea, in 1953. During the end stages of the Bosnian War in the early 1990s, all sides tended to initiate offensives, hoping to improve their bargaining position in the eventual postwar settlement. For this reason, it is generally recommended that the first step in negotiating peace is an immediate cease-fire.

On occasion, diplomacy has even been consciously employed by leaders eager to initiate war. The most famous example of this was the Ems telegram, which was craftily abbreviated by Bismarck to make it appear to the French that Kaiser Wilhelm had snubbed the French ambassador. In Bismarck's own words, he "waved a red flag in front of the Gallic bull." The bull charged, as Bismarck had calculated, and ran into a Prussian steel wall in the ensuing Franco-Prussian War. In this case, Bismarck could have simply declared war on France, but he wanted to goad the French into appearing to be the aggressor to ensure the cooperation of the independent south German states of Bavaria, Wurtemberg, Baden, and Hesse and also to prevent other states (notably Russia and Austria-Hungary) from aiding France. In this case, then, diplomacy was used to create war, and to isolate one side.

Classically, European diplomacy served to make peace in ways that tended to avoid excessive humiliation of the loser, so as not to foment grievances that would lead promptly to additional war. Some territory would be transferred, fortresses would be surrendered and frontiers adjusted, indemnities might be required and reparations exacted. For example, following the Peace of Utrecht, in 1714, France and its neighbors ceased fighting any major battles over the succession to the Spanish and English thrones. The peace in Europe was basically kept for the next few decades by this diplomatic style of mutual concessions and avoidance of humiliation, combined with respect for each other's vital interests.

But more recently, especially with national wars replacing sovereign's wars, concessions have often been cause for lasting resentment, which have in turn sowed the seeds for subsequent wars. Thus, France's loss of Alsace and Lorraine during the Franco-Prussian War—and its national fervor for reclaiming these lost regions—did much to bring about World War I. The German anger and humiliation associated with the Treaty of Versailles (which ended that war) led in part to World War II. By contrast, the diplomatic settlements at the end of World War II, although imperfect, have had greater staying power.

Diplomacy of this sort, however, is not so much an alternative to war, or a means of avoiding it, as an adjunct to national hostilities. "Diplomacy is a disguised war, in which States seek to gain by barter and intrigue, by the cleverness of wits, the objectives which they would have to gain more clumsily by means of war," wrote Randolph Bourne.

Diplomacy is used while the States are recuperating from conflicts in which they have exhausted themselves. It is the wheedling and the bargaining of the worn-out bullies as they rise from the ground and slowly restore their strength to begin fighting again. . . . Since [diplomacy] is a mere temporary substitute, a mere appearance of war's energy under another form, [its] effect is almost exactly proportioned to the armed force behind it. When it fails, the recourse is immediate to the military technique whose thinly veiled arm it has been.[1]

Accordingly, let us turn to the relationship between diplomacy and military force.

Diplomacy and Military Force

According to one influential viewpoint, diplomacy is only as effective as the military power available to each side, the threats that underwrite courteous diplomatic interchanges. "Diplomacy without armaments," according to Frederick the Great, "is like music without instruments."

There have been many examples of diplomatic intimidation, some successful, some not. During the late 1930s, Hitler successfully bluffed and bullied the Western democracies into successive territorial concessions—occupation of the Ruhr Valley, union with Austria, annexation of Czechoslovakia—largely because Germany had become militarily powerful, and Britain and France, remembering the pointless devastation of World War I, were eager to avert a repetition of that carnage. Shortly after taking office in 1992, President Clinton sent diplomatic representatives to the Haitian colonels who had kept democratically elected Jean-Bertrand Aristide from assuming power in that country. At the same time, a military invasion force was readied, and only when reports reached Port-au-Prince that U.S. aircraft were en route did the junta agree to step down—peacefully. As another example, after years in which NATO dithered and thousands of Bosnians died, the Serbs of Yugoslavia and Bosnia finally agreed to a serious settlement of the Bosnian War only after NATO actually initiated bombing of Serb positions. (This is not a precedent that gladdens the hearts of peace advocates, but its reality must be acknowledged.)

On the other hand, military threats have backfired. During the early 1980s, the USSR sought to deter Western Europe from deploying Euromissiles, by threatening, in the event of war in Europe, nuclear retaliation against any state that accepted them. By making itself appear more belligerent, the Soviet Union reinforced the arguments of those who proclaimed the need for the Euromissiles in the first place. The Euromissiles were deployed anyway, only to be subsequently removed via bilateral U.S.-Soviet negotiations.

Otto von Bismarck, the 19th-century chancellor of Prussia and architect of German unification, was hardly a pacifist. Yet, while he freely employed military force, he also understood its limitations. During the Austro-Prussian War, for example, the Austrians were badly defeated at the battle of Koniggratz, far more soundly than anyone had expected. At this point, political pressure quickly developed within Prussia for a wider victory over Austria, including the dismemberment of the Austrian empire itself. But Bismarck insisted on limiting Prussian demands to the provinces of Schleswig and Holstein, thereby preventing war with France and possibly Russia and Britain. As the archdiplomat Metternich once put it, "Diplomacy is the art of avoiding the appearance of victory."

In contrast to Bismarck's sensitivity to the dangers of pushing one's victories too far, during the Korean War General Douglas MacArthur and President Harry Truman were insensitive to the costs of similarly pressing the North Koreans and Chinese. After a surprise landing of U.S. forces at Inchon had resulted in dramatic gains in the autumn of 1950, UN (mostly U.S.) troops advanced deeply into North Korea. This led in turn to large-scale Chinese involvement and massive bloodshed on both sides, ending three years later in a stalemate, which could have been achieved with much less suffering had the Western leaders shown greater far-sightedness. The lesson of Koniggratz—that military restraint can often lead to greater diplomatic and long-term success—had not been learned.

Another kind of bargaining, on the other hand, has occasionally been useful in diminishing levels of violence. Often termed "tacit bargaining," this involves reaching agreements without actually spelling out the terms of the understanding. Because threats are strongly implied in such tacit bargains, they have most commonly taken place in close association with conditions of war or other violence. For example, during the Korean War, a tacit bargain existed on both sides: The Chinese would refrain from attacking U.S. aircraft carriers, supply lines, and bases in Japan, while similarly, there would be no bombing of North Korean supply lines in China. In the Middle East today, there is another tacit bargain: Israel will not flaunt its secret stockpile of nuclear weapons and the Arab states will not call attention to them. To some extent, this understanding serves the interests of both sides: The Israelis would rather not acknowledge their nuclear capability, and the Arab states would rather not have to respond publicly to its existence. Neither the Korean War nor the Middle East nuclear examples are particularly satisfying to students of peace, since they both involve at best a kind of stand-off (the Middle East), and at worst, the legitimation of violence (Korea). Skilled diplomats and negotiators generally hope for better.

Rules and Goals of Diplomacy _____

In *Poetry and Truth*, the great German writer Goethe acknowledged, "If I had to choose between justice and disorder, on the one hand, and injustice and order, on the other, I would always choose the latter." Many others—notably Metternich in the 19th century, and one of the 20th-century's best-known students of Metternich, Henry Kissinger—followed suit, and made stability a goal in itself. Diplomacy, in such hands, should not necessarily be seen as always desirable, since regrettable goals, not just stability but also repression and other forms of injustice, can be achieved through diplomacy. Diplomacy and techniques of negotiation in general are of interest in peace studies insofar as they represent nonviolent ways of resolving conflict short of overt violence. It is a different question whether the end result of diplomacy, or other forms of conflict resolution, results in a better world.

Hans Morgenthau,[2] perhaps the 20th century's most influential advocate of Realpolitik in international relations, proposed numerous rules for diplomacy, which, he hoped, would help states resolve conflicts short of war while also pursuing their own self-interest in international affairs. In summary, Morgenthau's rules included the following:

Do not be a crusader. Avoid "nationalistic universalism," the insistence that the goals of one's own nation are appropriate as universal goals for all nations. As the 19th-century French foreign minister Talleyrand put it, *pas trop de zèle* (not too much zeal). Such excessive zeal was shown in the enthusiasm of U.S. National Security Council aides to assist the contra rebels in Nicaragua, even at the cost of illegal activities and, ultimately, great harm to U.S. influence and prestige.

Employ a narrow definition of vital national interests, namely, the survival and maintenance of socioeconomic well-being. Morgenthau emphasized that in the nuclear age, states cannot afford war—or the risk of war—for anything short of their most supreme security interests. This implies, among other things, a substantial winding down of international treaty commitments. (Under such restrictions, for example, humanitarian interventions such as the UN's ill-fated efforts in Somalia would be prohibited.)

Be willing to compromise on all national interests that are not truly vital.

Try to see the other side's point of view, recognizing that the other side will also have vital national interests, and should not be pushed into compromising them.

Distinguish between what is real and what is illusory; do not allow considerations of honor, credibility, or prestige to override issues of real national security.

Never paint yourself into a corner; always retain avenues of retreat (or advance).

Do not allow an ally (especially a vulnerable one) to make decisions for you; as a corollary, do not allow yourself to be drawn into someone else's fight.

Always keep military factors subordinate to political ones. Remember that military planners know "nothing of that patient, intricate, and subtle maneuvering of diplomacy, whose main purpose is to avoid the absolutes of victory and defeat and meet the other side in negotiated compromise."

"Neither surrender to popular passions nor disregard them."

Following Napoleon's defeat in 1815, Western Europe entered into a period of relative stability, based in large part on the system established by the victors at the Congress of Vienna. Some of this "success" was because all the major players accepted the agreed system as legitimate, and everyone felt about equally rewarded and equally slighted by the outcome. As Henry Kissinger put it,

> Since absolute security for one power means absolute insecurity for all the others, it is obtainable only through conquest, never as part of a legitimate settlement. An international settlement which is accepted and not imposed will therefore always appear *somewhat* unjust to any one of its components. Paradoxically, the generality of this dissatisfaction is a condition of stability, because were any one power *totally* satisfied, all others would have to be *totally* dissatisfied and a revolutionary situation would ensue. The foundation of a stable order is a *relative* security—and therefore the *relative* insecurity—of its members.[3]

In contrast to Morgenthau's conception of value-free diplomacy is the notion that issues of right and wrong lie at the heart of international disputes. Unfortunately, states generally find it easier to look dispassionately at conflicts in which they are not themselves embroiled; once physically and emotionally involved, the process of moralizing often becomes intense, leaving only victory as a tolerable outcome. U.S. president Woodrow Wilson had urged the participants of World War I to seek a "peace without victory" and "a peace between equals," until the United States entered that war. Then, even the American Peace Society declared that "this is not a war of territory, of trade routes or of commercial concerns, but of eternal principles. There can be no end of war until after the collapse of the existing German government."

Historically, many of the crucial aspects of diplomacy have been carried out largely in secret. Secrecy was subsequently blamed, by many, for the errors and miscalculations that led to World War I, and President Wilson accordingly called for "open covenants openly arrived at." On the other hand, although secret diplomacy sounds inherently unpalatable, especially to a democratic society, it remains true that when conducted in public, diplomatic negotiating isn't conducive to compromise. Each side fears appearing soft, or a dupe, and is inclined to play to domestic public opinion, making arguments and advancing proposals that may be politically popular, even if it knows that other solutions may be fairer, and even more desirable. So there is much to be said for diplomacy that is carried out not so much "in secret" as under a mutual understanding that not every offer and counteroffer will be leaked to the waiting world. It may not be coincidental that some of the noteworthy diplomatic successes of recent years, such as the Mid-East Oslo Accords, the Dayton Accords that ended the Bosnian War, and the termination of fighting in Kosovo, all followed secret negotiations.

Track II Diplomacy

Since the late 1970s, there has been growing interest in so-called Track II diplomacy, also sometimes called unofficial or "encounter group" diplomacy. Track II diplomacy is unofficial in that it need not involve formal negotiations between representatives of different states; rather, it revolves around relatively informal interactions among representatives of opposing groups. It contributes largely to laying the social and political groundwork needed in order for government leaders to act. It also can be seen as representing a way of solving problems independent of the nation-states themselves.

In Track II diplomacy, people are brought together, typically in the presence of an experienced third party or facilitator, for the purpose of achieving mutual understanding, exploring their commonalities as well as differences, and establishing interpersonal relationships despite the political disagreements between their "home" groups. This has been attempted, often with remarkable success, in groups of Catholics and Protestants from Northern Ireland, Greek and Turkish Cypriots, Israelis and Palestinians, and Tutsis and Hutus in eastern Africa. Typically, the individuals in question are relatively influential in their communities: doctors, lawyers, professors, journalists, midrange politicians, and military officials. Success is never guaranteed, and there is typically substantial distrust and, often, numerous minor incidents, especially at the outset. Over time, however, most of these "encounter groups" have produced very positive results.

The most dramatic example of Track II techniques employed successfully at the highest levels of government occurred during the Camp David meetings in 1977. Hosted by then U.S. president Jimmy Carter, who served as the facilitator, Israel's prime minister Menachim Begin and Egypt's president Anwar Sadat spent 13 days at the rustic presidential retreat in Maryland. The meetings took place without the formalities, protocols, and rigid negotiations characteristic of traditional summit meetings or bargaining sessions.

Rather, there was no formal agenda, no intrusive press, and—perhaps as a result—some highly emotional interchanges. Although the Camp David meetings did not solve all Middle East problems, or even all areas of Egyptian-Israeli dispute, they did turn out to be highly productive.

Interestingly, just as the meetings were about to end, apparently in failure because of the Israeli prime minister's refusal to sign any accord, a breakthrough occurred: At Begin's request, President Carter was autographing photographs of the three Camp David participants, to be given to the Israeli leader's grandchildren. President Carter personalized his autograph, dedicating each photo to each of Prime Minister Begin's grandchildren, by name. Then, as President Carter recalled,

> I handed him the photographs. He took them and thanked me. Then he happened to look down and saw that his granddaughter's name was on the top one. He spoke it aloud and then looked at each photograph individually, repeating the name of the grandchild I had written on it. His lips trembled and tears welled up in his eyes. He told me a little about each child and especially about one who seemed to be his favorite. We were both emotional as we talked quietly for a few moments about grandchildren and about war.[4]

Shortly afterward, Begin indicated his willingness to sign the accords, and the Camp David "process" ended on a strong—even euphoric—note of accommodation, agreement, and mutual respect. Regrettably, a similar Track II approach was not attempted for the Egyptian and Israeli advisers and midlevel leaders at Camp David; their involvement in and commitment to the Camp David process would presumably have been greater had they been included as well. Nonetheless, the result has been a historic peace— although a "cold peace"—between Israel and Egypt, followed in the late 1990s by a similar peace treaty between Israel and Jordan.

The Camp David experience indicates something of the possibilities when individuals come together on a personal level, with time, goodwill, a skillful facilitator, and, perhaps, some luck as well. Employing this same model, President Clinton helped facilitate similar preliminary negotiations between Israel and Syria early in 2000.

Third-Party Involvement

Consider a married couple who have been squabbling, for example, over how to divide household chores. Left to themselves, they may be unable to reach agreement, in part because each individual sees only his or her viewpoint. Moreover, each may hesitate to give in, even partially, for fear that any concession might be seen as an admission that he or she has a weaker case. Similar deadlocks are seen in other situations of conflict, such as disputes between labor and management. In such cases, disagreements between contending parties—whether individuals, organizations, or states—are sometimes more readily resolved if a third party is brought into the process. For domestic disputes, marital counselors may be helpful; for labor disputes, trained mediators or arbitrators, often provided by the government. A similar process can apply to international disputes.

An outside expert may be called in to help clarify the issues, resolve misunderstanding, and suggest areas of compromise and common ground. A third party—unbiased and trusted by both sides—can sometimes help reach agreements for which everyone may be grateful but that (for a variety of reasons) neither party could suggest, or even accept if it had been proposed by the other. Imagine, for example, that two adjacent states are disputing the location of the border in a strip of land 100 km wide, between them. If A proposes placing the border right down the middle, giving 50 km to each side, then B might use this "opening" to bargain further, "splitting the difference" between them, and proposing a border so that B gets 75 km and A, 25 km. In such a case, the side that first proposes a compromise finds itself at a disadvantage. One obvious solution, therefore, is for a third state, C, to propose independently that A and B agree to 50 km for each. (Unfortunately, international disputes are rarely this simple, given historical backgrounds, social factors, political passions, military alliances, and economic considerations, as well as geographic factors such as marshes, rivers, or mountains, etc.). It is also important to bear in mind that disputes always occur on at least two levels: the specific issue under dispute and also the underlying question of who wins, who is more powerful, and what this portends for subsequent interactions.

The Functions of Go-Betweens

There are several specific ways in which third parties can be helpful to disputants. First, they can serve as go-betweens, providing what is known as their "good offices." This may simply involve making a meeting place available, on neutral ground. The Scandinavian states, as well as Austria and Switzerland, have often made themselves available as sites for international dispute settlement; when in doubt, international diplomats typically meet in Geneva.

Since most Arab governments—except for Egypt and Jordan—do not officially recognize the state of Israel, it is especially important for third parties to provide a means of communication between them. Of course, when the third party is a high-ranking representative of a major power, he or she presumably does not merely act as a messenger, but also can engage in various forms of arm-twisting, for example, threatening to cut off economic or military aid unless some proposed compromises are accepted. This further suggests why some forms of diplomacy are best conducted in secret: It may be politically unacceptable, for example, for a state to appear to knuckle under to such pressure, although it may be better for everyone concerned if it does so. At the same time, powerful countries are able to "sweeten the deal," as with the United States providing billions of dollars in aid to both Israel and Egypt in the aftermath of the Camp David agreements. The promise of similar assistance also underlines the prospects of further Arab-Israeli peace deals (as does the fact that with the dissolution of the Soviet Union, states such as Syria lost their prospect of assistance from their major backer).

During 1967, Greece and Turkey—both U.S. allies and NATO members—were threatening to go to war over Cyprus. The U.S. emissary, Cyrus Vance, eventually succeeded in persuading both sides to step down their military preparations and to accept an expanded role for the UN peacekeeping force already on that island. Alexei Kosygin, Soviet premier at the time, was similarly successful in inducing India and Pakistan to terminate their second Kashmir War (1966), in part by secret arm-twisting. In the early 1990s, the Norwegian foreign minister was especially influential in facilitating the Oslo Accords between Israel and the Palestinians, and in 1999, the president of Finland served as go-between when NATO forces and Yugoslavian president Slobodan Milosevic ended the war in Kosovo.

Third parties, if they have the respect of the contenders, can also serve a valuable role as "fact finders," ascertaining, for example, whether a disputed border was crossed, how many political prisoners are held in specified jails, how large the military forces involved are, or what the economic situation is in a particular region. International organizations, notably the United Nations, have been especially helpful in this respect, establishing various commissions of inquiry: to evaluate conflicting claims. In certain cases, basic facts are in dispute; in others, the disagreement is not over numbers or other data, but rather over values—not over what is true, but what is right.

Mediation and Arbitration

Aside from providing a place to meet, facilitating communication, and occasionally, twisting a few arms, third parties can basically fulfill two diplomatic functions: mediation and arbitration. Mediators make suggestions that might be agreeable to both sides. Like marriage counselors, mediators try to resolve disputes, but adherence to their suggestions is entirely voluntary. By contrast, in the case of arbitration, both sides agree in advance to accept the judgment of the arbitrator. Mediation therefore involves less of a threat to sovereignty; it is accordingly less radical and more often acceptable to contending states. A third procedure, adjudication, involves making decisions with reference to international law. We therefore consider it in a subsequent chapter.

There is nothing new in the practices of mediation and arbitration. They were especially frequent and successful in Europe during the late Middle Ages, from about the 13th to the 15th centuries. The success of third-party involvement at this time was apparently due to several factors. Family ties among diverse political leaders were frequent (not uncommonly, heads of state were cousins or even closer). The economic costs of war were widely recognized to be exceptionally high and local treasuries often teetered on the edge of bankruptcy. Finally, a powerful third party was available to aid in the settling of disputes, namely, the Catholic Church and its emissaries.

A particular advantage to mediation and arbitration is that a third party can sometimes succeed in fashioning a solution that both contending parties find acceptable, but neither would be willing to propose for fear of being seen as too conciliatory, and thus, weak. Opposing governments often face a dilemma: Even when a compromise is feasible, both sides want to project an image of power. Accordingly, the mediator or arbitrator can suggest something that, privately, both sides want but that neither is willing to propose. During the Geneva Conference of 1955—which ended the French occupation of Indochina—Britain, China, and the Soviet Union mediated between France and the Viet Minh. In this case, as with many others, it can certainly be argued that mediation did not resolve the dispute; it only postponed it. Five years after Soviet premier Kosygin's successful mediation between India and Pakistan, war broke out between these two countries (although this time, the issue was Bangladesh). But even apparent failures may sometimes be helpful; as Winston Churchill once noted, "Jaw, jaw, jaw is better than war, war, war." Sometimes, moreover, there can be a real advantage in postponing war, if, over time, passions cool and peaceful solutions eventually become possible. And sometimes, of course, mediation is altogether successful. President Theodore Roosevelt, for example, won a Nobel Peace Prize for his successful mediation between Russia and Japan, which ended the Russo-Japanese War.

When both sides agree to abide by the judgment of a third party, we say that the dispute has been submitted to arbitration. One of the most important historical cases is the so-called *Alabama* claim, known for a Confederate warship that had been purchased (illegally) in Britain, a neutral country, during the U.S. Civil War. The U.S. government subsequently demanded reparations for the damage done to U.S. shipping by the *Alabama* and other similar ships, and in 1872, both sides consented to arbitration. An independent panel eventually awarded the United States more than $15 million in damages, which Britain paid, thereby lowering tensions between the two countries. In fact, the now-close relationship between Britain and the United States can be counted as beginning with this successful arbitration.

_____ Negotiating Techniques for Resolving Conflict

Numerous techniques are available to arbitrators. One promising example is the "last best offer." Imagine two sides disagreeing over the amount of money to be paid for ownership of a disputed island. Rather than making offers and counteroffers, each side is told to give the arbitrator its last best offer, from which the arbitrator will choose the one that seems the most fair. The arbitrator cannot decide to split the difference, since this would only encourage each side to be intransigent. In the last best offer technique, by contrast, each side is nudged to be as conciliatory as possible, in hopes that its offer will be the one accepted.

Resolution Versus Dominance

In 1964, conservative American policy analyst Fred Charles Iklé wrote an influential book titled _How Nations Negotiate_. It was focused on how one nation (the United States) can best the other side, and concluded as follows:

> A good negotiator should be . . . patient in working for seemingly lost causes, because by doing so he may slowly change the opponent's views and objectives. . . . Above all, he must maintain the will to win.[5]

This view would probably still be endorsed by the majority of diplomats and negotiators today. However, if negotiations are to help resolve conflict, rather than become arenas for yet more conflict, another perspective is needed. In short, this perspective views negotiations as a means whereby contending parties seek to resolve their differences, not to prevail over each other. It suggests that to be fruitful, negotiations must be seen as non-zero-sum solutions, interactions in which my gain is not necessarily balanced by your loss, or vice versa. It aims to achieve win-win solutions in which all sides are better off than they were before.

Compromise

The most obvious, and in some cases the most common, negotiating technique is to compromise, that is, to reach an agreement that is in some sense intermediate between the demands of both sides. There are, however, several disadvantages to this method. For one, a compromise may leave both sides dissatisfied. In some cases, this may actually be desirable, so that a "fair" decision may be defined—only somewhat tongue in cheek—as one that leaves everyone equally unhappy. But one side's claim may in fact be just and the other's unjust; in such a case, a compromise simply rewards the unjust side while penalizing the just one. Compromise assumes that both contenders are equally worthy, so that "splitting the difference" between them will produce a fair settlement. But what if state *A* arbitrarily insists on imposing a 50% tariff upon all imports from state *B*, but refuses to allow *B* to tax its imports? Clearly a "compromise" that allows a 25% unilateral tariff would not be fair and is unlikely to be acceptable—at least, not to state *B*.

In certain cases, however, one side can "win" without the other "losing." For example, Franco-German relations were bedeviled through the first half of the 20th century by a dispute over ownership of the Saar region, a rich industrial sector of the Rhineland. Following World War I, occupation and mining rights to the Saar were ceded to France; French control was reasserted after World War II. But the region's population was (and still is) overwhelmingly German, and the governments in Paris and Bonn eventually cooperated to resolve this issue: After a plebiscite in 1955, France permitted the Saar to rejoin West Germany. This negotiated agreement, in which France ostensibly "lost," served everyone well, since it proved to be a cornerstone for subsequent Franco-German cooperation and friendship.

Positional Versus Integrative Bargaining

Compromises are often the outcome of what has been called "positional bargaining," in which each side stakes out a position, and then holds to it. Positional bargaining clearly does not encourage flexibility and reasonable stances or attitudes; rather, intransigence is rewarded, and willingness to compromise (or even to suggest compromise) is penalized. Thus, in positional bargaining the participants are rewarded for staking out a "hard" position and sticking to it, and penalized, in turn, for being "soft." As a result, "good" bargainers are those who remain relatively intransigent—that is, who make it difficult or unlikely that an agreement will be reached. Fortunately, there is a third way, known as "integrative bargaining" or "principled negotiating."

Integrative or principled bargaining tries, among other things, to separate the actual dispute from the underlying interests of each side. The goal is to focus on the latter and avoid getting bogged down in the former. As negotiators Roger Fisher and William Ury recount,[6] consider the story of two sisters who quarreled over an orange; they decided, finally, to compromise, each getting one half. One sister then proceeded to squeeze her half for juice while the other used the peel from her portion to flavor a cake. By compromising—an old and honorable solution—they overlooked the integrative solution of giving one all the peel, and the other all the juice.

Or imagine once again that two states disagree over a boundary. The real dispute may not be over territory as such, but rather one state's desire for access to certain transportation routes, along with worry by the other that granting such access would diminish its military security. In such a case, integrative bargaining would seek to identify the underlying issues and solve them directly, perhaps reaching an understanding in which the needs of both sides are integrated into one solution: for example, access to the desired transportation routes, for an agreed annual fee, along with a bilateral treaty specifying strict limitations on the nature of the vehicles or number of personnel permitted to travel along them. (An agreement of this general sort permits Palestinians living in the West Bank and the Gaza Strip to go back and forth, with Israel in between.)

Numerous tactics may be employed by negotiators seeking to bridge differences between contending sides. They include focusing on the shared interests of both sides, rather than on the demands as such, diminishing the role of personalities (i.e., separating the people from the problem) and "fractionating" the conflict (i.e., separating a dispute into resolvable and tractable components), then working on the former. Such tactics also contribute to a process of confidence building, which increases the probability that more difficult issues will be solved in the future. In fact, researchers in this area have become increasingly interested in enumerating possible confidence-building measures (CBMs) as better than ICBMs at keeping the peace. The idea is that having made some degree of progress, disputants will likely try all the harder for additional success and be less inclined to resort to violence.

Certain disputes—such as the story of the oranges—have a high "integrative potential" in that they inherently lend themselves to agreements that leave all parties entirely satisfied. Other cases are more difficult, as when, for example, buyer and seller disagree over the price of a house. Even here, however, there is room for integrative agreements: modifications in the interest rate, the date of occupancy, the amount of principal to be paid off by certain dates, and so on. In such cases, it may be possible to integrate the interests of both sides, essentially by reaching agreement on other dimensions aside from those initially in dispute (in this case, the purchase price).

Methods of Integrative Bargaining

Let us now examine five different methods[7] by which integrative agreements might be reached, taking as an example a hypothetical dispute between a husband and wife over where to spend their two-week vacation: The wife wants to go to the seashore, the husband to the mountains. One solution is to compromise, and spend one week at each; they would like, however, to find some more satisfactory settlement.

Expanding the pie. Sometimes solutions can be achieved by increasing the amount of a resource in short supply. Perhaps the couple could arrange to take four weeks of vacation, thereby spending two weeks at each location. This is not as utopian as it may seem, since expanding the pie need not necessarily involve getting something for nothing. Thus, if they value their vacation enough, it might be possible, for example, to work overtime during the rest of the year so as to pay for it. For such solutions to work, however, each party must not find the other's preferred outcome to be aversive; that is, it could work if neither has an intrinsic objection to the other's preference, but simply a stronger desire for his or her own choice. In our example, the husband must be able to tolerate going to the seashore, and the wife to the mountains. Solutions of this sort are largely based on efforts to help each side get what it wants and to do so by increasing the amount of a limited resource (time, money, land, people, security, hard currency, etc.).

Nonspecific compensation.   In this case, one party "gives in" but is repaid in some other way. The husband, for example, may agree to go to the seashore, but only if he is relieved of housecleaning chores for the next four months. By extension, a country may permit a neighbor to flood its markets with exported goods if the exporting country agrees to provide a certain number of jobs for citizens of the importing country. Solutions of this sort require information about what is particularly valued by both parties, and what one party may be able (and willing) to provide to another in return for getting its way. An important factor is whether some form of compensation exists that may be of low cost to the donor and high value to the recipient: Perhaps the wife doesn't particularly mind doing the husband's share of the housecleaning, at least for a few months, and perhaps the exporting country actually needs the labor skills of the importer.

Logrolling.   If both parties differ on issues within the main ones under dispute, and if they differ in their priorities regarding these issues, then the possibility exists for creative "logrolling," which is, in a sense, a variant of nonspecific compensation. For example, perhaps the husband-wife disagreement over vacations also involves differences of opinion about the preferred accommodations. Let us say that the wife favors simple, rustic beach cottages, whereas the husband is looking forward to an elegant mountain resort. Perhaps, then, the husband will be quite happy going to the seashore, so long as the wife agrees that they stay in a fancy seaside resort (or alternatively, maybe a rustic cabin—desired by the wife—in the mountains—preferred by the husband). For solutions based on logrolling to be developed, it helps to identify potential concessions, and especially to ask, "Are some of my low-priority issues of high priority to the other party?" or vice versa.

Cost-cutting.   Solutions based on cost-cutting are those in which one party essentially succeeds in "winning," but the costs to the other party are reduced or eliminated. Thus, cost-cutting solutions are more one-sided than those discussed above, but they are nonetheless feasible and potentially stable, if the side that "gives in" truly does not suffer any disadvantage from the agreement. In the case of the husband-wife vacation dispute, perhaps the husband had resisted going to the seashore because he feared being lonely and isolated while his wife was windsurfing; in this case, a cost-cutting solution—and one that could be entirely satisfactory to the husband—might be for the couple to agree to go to the seashore, but to do so along with some of their friends, who could provide company for the husband.

Cost-cutting differs from nonspecific compensation in that it involves a kind of "specific compensation," a particular kind of recompense directed toward one of the parties, but not really compensation for a painful outcome so much as a way of making the settlement agreeable for the "loser." For cost-cutting to be successful, there must be clarity as to the reasons either side opposes the desires of the other, and an openness (especially on the part of the side giving in) to considering ways in which it might be possible to give in without really losing.

Bridging. Bridging occurs when the two parties agree to a solution in which neither side wins or loses, but rather both agree to a different option from the ones each originally favored. This solution must address the primary interests that actually underlie the specific issues in dispute. Thus, if the husband wanted to go to the mountains to hike and the wife wanted to go to the seashore for the sun, perhaps it would be possible to find a beach resort near hiking trails (or a vacation site where the mountains are dry and sunny). Successful bridging requires that the parties refocus their negotiations from an insistence on their *positions* to an examination of their underlying *interests*. Why are they pushing for their particular position? Is there some alternative outcome that would meet their actual needs? Is it really the mountains, or the seashore, that they want, or do these simply provide a means of achieving some other goal, such as sunshine, exercise, comfort, adventure, simplicity, and so forth?

Additional Negotiating Techniques

Apparently trivial details can become surprisingly influential in the negotiating process. In some cases, for example, attention to the physical arrangement of participants may be important: Thus, it can even be helpful to seat the contenders on the same side of a table—opposite the negotiator, whose job is to articulate the disagreement—thereby literally facing the problem together, rather then contentiously facing each other. This sometimes encourages both sides to cooperate rather than compete, to concentrate on solving the problem rather than defeating each other. In other cases, a wise conflict resolver will simply ignore uncooperative statements, rather than allowing them to derail an agreement; during the Cuban Missile Crisis, the U.S. government received two communications from Nikita Khrushchev, Soviet premier at the time, one conciliatory and the other contentious. At Robert Kennedy's suggestion, the United States simply ignored the latter and responded to the former.

Clarity is generally a virtue; in some cases, negotiated agreements come unraveled or become a source of irritation when they are interpreted differently by the different parties. For example, Britain and the United States felt that at the Yalta conference toward the end of World War II, the Soviet Union had agreed to allow pluralistic democracy in postwar Poland. Soviet diplomats (and some U.S. participants as well), on the other hand, argued differently. It is also possible, however, that if the expectations and intentions of each side had been spelled out in detail, an even greater falling out would have occurred. Part of the negotiator's art may therefore include recourse to equivocal and imprecise language. Nobel Prize-winning Canadian diplomat Lester Pearson put it this way:

> I know that there have been occasions, and I have been concerned with one or two, when, as the lesser of two evils, words were used . . . that could be interpreted somewhat freely and therefore could be used not so much to record agreement as to conceal a disagreement which it was desired to play down and which, it was hoped, would disappear in time.[8]

To avoid misunderstandings, a negotiator might request that each side state, as clearly as it can, the arguments of the other side. This can help build empathy, a deeper awareness and appreciation of the other's perspective, and of the constraints felt by the other. (Remember that in serious disputes, each side is often intensely aware of the limitations on its own behavior, while considering that the opponent has great latitude; failure to reach agreement is then likely attributed—by each side—to the other's intransigence.)

Adequate empathy can lead to another helpful exercise, the "yesable proposition." In this case, each party to a dispute is asked to consider formulating a proposition that the other side is likely to accept. This is a subtle but important shift: In most cases, each side makes demands—indeed, the nature of the negotiating process encourages them to do so—that are likely to be outrageous and unacceptable. In the search for yesable propositions, both sides are more likely to uncover shared interests, based on which a mutually acceptable outcome might become clear.

In the course of seeking an agreement, it can be helpful to make proposals through an intermediary—often a low-ranking one—so that they can be disowned if the other rejects it out of hand. This avoids the embarrassment that could result from acrimony and ridicule; by having the capability of denying that any such opening was ever made, either side may be more willing to make an initial attempt. For example, during the Cuban Missile Crisis, Premier Khrushchev chose a low-ranking Soviet embassy official to convey his proposal: removal of Soviet missiles from Cuba in return for a U.S. pledge not to invade that island. In addition, this message was sent to a news broadcaster rather than directly to U.S. officials.

Additional suggestions include the following: Avoid ultimatums, do not impugn the motives of the other side, try to keep from playing to the crowds, be flexible but not spineless, avoid *ad hominem* (personal) attacks, avoid nonnegotiable ploys, and do not be so desperate for agreement that you sacrifice future peace for short-term palliatives.

What counts, in the long run, is reaching agreements without either side giving in or resorting to violence. Sometimes it may be possible, even desirable, to paper over disagreements so as to buy time for new events to unfold or for old disputes to grow stale. And of course, there is no guarantee that all disputes can be resolved by negotiations. A positive outcome, for example, requires a degree of goodwill and a genuine desire to reach an agreement. It also requires willingness to "bargain in good faith." There have been cases in which good faith was not shown. For example, the Soviet government in 1939 was openly negotiating with Britain and France for a mutual defense pact against Nazi Germany while at the same time secretly organizing the now-infamous nonaggression pact that briefly allied Stalin with Hitler and paved the way for Germany's invasion of Poland. Similarly, Japanese diplomats were negotiating with their U.S. counterparts on December 7, 1941, when Japanese forces attacked Pearl Harbor. And when, in 1955, Soviet negotiators accepted U.S. disarmament proposals, complete with international verification procedures, the U.S. delegation promptly withdrew them —having never expected that they might be accepted!

More recently, Serbia's Slobodan Milosevic repeatedly claimed that his country was not providing military assistance to Bosnian Serbs and that Serbia forces were not participating in "ethnic cleansing" first in Bosnia then later in Kosovo. And Iraq's president Saddam Hussein has persistently violated numerous agreements previously made, especially regarding inspection of possible weapons facilities.

Nonetheless, there is good reason to believe that such cases are exceptions. The desire for nonviolent resolution of conflicts is, if anything, stronger and more widespread today than at any time in the past. In addition, other factors—domestic opinion, international law, international organizations, the shared costs of violence—combine to make nonviolent conflict resolution an attractive alternative to the use of force, so long as the participants (including the mediator if there is one) is both skillful and persistent.

A Final Note on Conflict Resolution

Ultimately, belief in the feasibility of nonviolent conflict resolution— whether by diplomacy or negotiation, between two parties or with the assistance of a mediator or arbitrator—is just that, an exercise of faith: faith in the underlying goodwill of most people and in their fundamental rationality. Such faith may or may not be warranted. Certainly, the human species has long displayed a penchant for irrational acts, personal as well as collective. But skeptics might consider that the alternative—war—is usually no more rational. Moreover, if it seems unrealistic to rely on the rationality of one's opponents, bear in mind that the fundamental peacekeeping strategy of the nuclear age—deterrence—relies precisely on just this kind of instrumental rationality and mutual dependence. How much better, therefore, it is to employ such negotiating tactics for the pursuit of conflict resolution rather than to resort to conflict prolongation or, worse yet, violence as final arbiter of disputes.

Notes

1. Randolph S. Bourne. 1964. *War and the Intellectuals, Collected Essays 1915–1919*. New York: Harper & Row.

2. Hans Morgenthau. 1978. *Politics Among Nations*. New York: Knopf.

3. Henry Kissinger. 1957. *A World Restored*. Boston: Houghton Mifflin.

4. Jimmy Carter. 1982. *Keeping Faith*. New York: Bantam.

5. Fred Charles Ikle. 1964. *How Nations Negotiate*. New York: Harper & Row

6. R. Fisher and W. Ury. 1981. *Getting to Yes*. Boston: Houghton Mifflin.

7. Derived from Dean G. Pruitt. 1983. "Achieving Integrative Agreements in Negotiation." In M. H. Bazerman and R. Lewiski, eds., *Negotiating in Organizations*. Beverly Hills, CA: Sage.

8. Lester B. Pearson. 1949. *Diplomacy in the Nuclear Age*. Cambridge, MA: Harvard University Press.

11 Peace Through Strength?

*Have you walked up and down upon the earth lately? I have;
and I have examined Man's wonderful inventions. And I tell
you that in the arts of life man invents nothing but in the arts
of death he outdoes Nature herself, and produces by chemistry
and machinery all the slaughtered, of plague, pestilence, and
famine . . . when he goes out to slay, he carries a marvel of
mechanism that lets loose at the touch of his finger all the
hidden molecular energies, and leaves the javelin, the arrow, the
blowpipe of his fathers far behind. In the arts of peace Man is a
bungler . . . his heart is in his weapons. . . . Man measures his
strength by his destructiveness.*

—the Devil, in George Bernard Shaw's *Man and Superman*

When asked about the most important way of maintaining peace, most people—including government leaders—point to military strength. The slogan of the Strategic Air Command (SAC) unblushingly proclaims, "Peace is our profession." (Below this sign at SAC headquarters, someone once scrawled, "Mass murder is our specialty.") Not surprisingly, however, advocates of peace studies generally look askance at the traditional reliance on military force to maintain peace, viewing armed force as part of the problem, not the solution.

Like it or not, and agree with it or not, "peace through strength" was probably the most politically potent and influential concept of war prevention throughout the 20th century. It is also probably the most perilous, and is a viewpoint against which peace studies must struggle. Whether or not it "worked" in maintaining peace in the past, and whether it will work in the 21st century, "peace through strength" undoubtedly succeeds in two senses at least: It directs the expenditure of vast quantities of national wealth, and virtually all major governments adhere to its precepts. The major challenge of peace studies is to break away from the existing war system—which includes reliance on peace through strength—and to establish a viable ecology of peace whose strength does not derive from violence or the threat of violence. Hence, some professional students of peace may even object to including a chapter called "Peace Through Strength" in a text such as this. But any modification of current policies would be enriched by understanding the background to our current system and the assumptions under which, in large part, it currently operates. If students of peace are not to be dismissed as incurably romantic or hopelessly uninformed, it behooves them to understand the arguments, if only to refute them.

The motto "Peace through strength" is a modern version of the Latin *vis pacem, para bellum* (if you want peace, prepare for war). It has been taken as axiomatic by entire generations of conservative politicians and military leaders. In all fairness to them, we should at least consider that this perspective may be more than a rationalization for the maintenance of large and threatening armed forces, sought for other reasons that are rarely acknowledged (economic gain, career benefits, distracting the populace, and/or the satisfaction of personal psychological needs to feel potent and powerful, to have clearly defined enemies, etc.). There have been, and still are, people who sincerely believe that the only way to achieve peace is by the ability and willingness to employ military force. In this chapter, we briefly examine their arguments.

Balance of Power

Generally, a geopolitical "balance of power" is obtained when the primary contending states are roughly equal in their military strength. Thus, balance of power is intimately associated with the assumption of "peace through strength," as seen in this observation by Henry Kissinger:

> Throughout history the political influence of nations has been roughly correlative to their military power. While states might differ in the moral worth and prestige of their institutions, diplomatic skill could augment but never substitute for military strength. In the final reckoning weakness has invariably tempted aggression and impotence brings abdication of policy in its train. . . . The balance of power has in fact been the precondition for peace.[1]

How Balance of Power Works

In its traditional usage, balance of power involves a tacit agreement among governments that power will be distributed among the various states so as to prevent any one from becoming so strong as to threaten the others. Thus, it relies fundamentally on deterrence, the expectation that a would-be aggressor would refrain from attacking opponents who are more powerful than itself, or who are capable of inflicting unacceptable damage if they were attacked. Hence, adherence to balance of power implies a continuing arms race, or possibly, mutual agreements to keep the system stable by keeping the mutual threat symmetrical. To some extent, the Cold War involved maintaining a balance of power (more accurately, perhaps, a balance of terror) between the nuclear forces of the United States and the Soviet Union. Before that, and especially during the 18th and 19th centuries, balance of power referred less to arms races than to a constantly shifting system of alliances whereby states arranged themselves to keep any one from being too powerful. When they occurred, wars were generally fought for limited objectives rather than universal, crusading goals. Balance of power also represented an extreme of *Realpolitik*, in that states were expected to shift alliances readily, looking out only for their own benefit.

Just as we can never conclude with certainty that nuclear deterrence prevented a specific war, we also cannot know with confidence when (or if) balance of power considerations inhibited states from going to war. But it seems clear, for example, that at the conclusion of the Gulf War in 1991, the United States was loathe to push for the overthrow of Saddam Hussein's government in Iraq, in part out of concern that a stable even if dictatorial and aggressive Iraq served as a useful counterbalance to the power of Syria and of Iran, neither of which were Western allies.

On the other hand, there have been many cases in which a state's willingness to disrupt the balance has precipitated war with others, who sought to preserve it; for example, Germany's invasion of neutral Belgium in the early days of World War I led Britain to enter that war. Speaking in Parliament at that time, British foreign secretary Edward Grey argued that "I do not believe, whether a great Power stands outside this war or not, it is going to be in a position at the end of it to exert its superior strength . . . to prevent the whole of the West of Europe opposite to us . . . falling under the domination of a single Power."

Great Britain as "Balancer"

During the 1930s, Winston Churchill sought to rally Britain against the growing might of Nazi Germany. He pointed out that for centuries English foreign policy had been to ally itself with the weaker powers in Europe, in opposition to the stronger, to prevent the emergence of any threat to British security:

For four hundred years the foreign policy of England has been to oppose the strongest, most aggressive, most dominating Power on the

Continent. . . . We always took the harder course, joined with the less strong Powers, made a combination among them, and thus defeated and frustrated the Continental military tyrant whoever he was, whatever nation he led.[2]

Thus, when Spain was strong and threatening, England fought Spain (defeating the Armada in 1588). Then, when France under Louis XIV appeared capable of dominating Europe, England joined military alliances against it, repeating the process against Napoleon. For much of its history prior to the 20th century, England saw itself as the "balancer" in world affairs, and some historians claim that the *Pax* Britannica was due to Britain's success in preventing any one state from becoming dangerously powerful. In part because of its relative invulnerability as an island nation with the world's most powerful navy, Britain felt safe enough to refrain from keeping a large army, which in turn made it less menacing to others. And because of its prior unsuccessful earlier efforts to conquer France, Britain after 1815 had no serious continental ambitions. Moreover, British success in enriching itself via its overseas colonies left it free to pursue a relatively peaceful policy in Europe, which in turn may have given balance of power a relatively good name—probably better than it deserved.

In a passage described by historian Arnold Toynbee as "excruciatingly complacent," historian Edward Gibbon wrote,

The balance of power will continue to fluctuate, and the prosperity of our own or the neighboring kingdoms may be alternately exalted and depressed; but these partial events cannot essentially injure our general state of happiness, the system of arts, and laws, and manners. . . . In peace, the progress of knowledge and industry is accelerated by the emulation of so many active rivals: in war, the European forces are exercised by temperate and indecisive contests.[3]

Shifting Alliances

The primary anxiety of the United States, USSR, and most Arab states during the Iran-Iraq War of the 1980s was not the bloodshed and destruction of the war itself, but rather that the winner would emerge as the predominant power in the Persian Gulf region. Hence, assistance tended to flow to whichever side was losing.

Following World War II, the United States and the Soviet Union emerged as the two dominant states of the world, initiating a "bipolar" balance of nuclear power, with each state seeking to buttress its position by the establishment of competing alliances and courting the favor of neutral countries. With the end of the Cold War, that situation has changed dramatically, with the United States emerging as the undisputed single great power, especially in military terms (the "indispensable nation," according to Secretary of State Madeleine Albright). It remains to be seen whether other countries will come to fear and/or resent such an imbalance, and whether such feelings will precipitate new alliances seeking to reestablish a new balance.

Since 1991, the emergence of China and Japan (along with the "Asian tigers" of South Korea, Thailand, Malaysia, Singapore, and Taiwan) as well an increasingly united Western Europe has created a kind of "multipolar" balance, especially in the economic sphere. Some authorities claim that multipolar systems are more stable and less warlike than bipolar systems because they involve (1) more crosscutting loyalties, (2) less anxious attention directed to any one state by another, and (3) the fact that increased armaments by one state (an incipient arms race) has less impact on the security of any other state. On the other hand, equally competent authorities point out that satisfactory balances may be more difficult to achieve with the many different actors of a multipolar system and also that the greater diversity of interests and demands provides more opportunities for conflict.

Problems With Balance of Power

Advocates of balance of power often assume and sometimes assert that such a balance deters war. It remains uncertain, however, whether wars are more or less likely during conditions of balance. Thus, the Peloponnesian War presumably would not have occurred if Athens and Sparta had not been so close in strength as to constitute a threat to each other. This may also have been the case for the Punic Wars between Rome and Carthage. During the *Pax* Romana, Rome was supreme in the Mediterranean world; there was no balance of power, yet there was comparative peace. Similarly, there has never been a war between the Soviet Union and Bulgaria, or between the United States and Canada or Mexico (at least, recently!), in part because of the *imbalance* of power in these cases.

Promoting War

Wars often occur when rival states disagree about their relative strength; they end when both sides agree. The war itself terminates disagreement: The stronger is acknowledged by having won, and the weaker, by having lost. Looking at the distribution of power at the conclusion of wars, we can conclude that indecisive wars, which resulted in a relative balance of forces, were more likely to result in another war shortly thereafter, whereas decisive victories led more frequently to periods of peace.

During the heyday of balance of power, a coalition of European states regularly took the field against whatever ruler seemed about to establish hegemony: against the Hapsburgs in the late 16th and again in the early

17th centuries, against the French in the late 17th and again in the early 19th centuries (first Louis XIV and then Napoleon), and against Germany and its allies in World Wars I and II. Perhaps balance of power "worked," in that it prevented domination by a single state, and likely tyranny as well. But it has not prevented war. In fact, it may well have promoted it. After all, the underlying goal of balance of power is not to deter war, but rather to preserve the balance and, thus, national sovereignty and the system of states of which the balance is comprised. Sometimes, it operates via war. Accordingly, standard progressive doctrine has long maintained that wars are caused by arms races, military-industrial complexes, misunderstandings and misperceptions, secret diplomacy, *and* balance of power.

Slight Imbalances and Their Effects

Evidence also suggests that wars tend to break out when there is a slight imbalance, especially if one side has grown rapidly but has not yet reached the power of its opponent. In this situation, the status quo power (the one seeking to maintain things as they are) feels threatened that the balance is about to tip against it, sometimes calculating that war now is preferable to waiting for the upstart to gain yet more strength. States actively committed to a balance of power, in short, have an incentive to attack their neighbors whenever they perceive an adverse shift in that balance. Whether that attack is justified as preventive (to forestall gradual change and eventual war) or preemptive (jumping the gun to short-circuit an attack that is considered imminent), states find themselves impelled to jump through a "window of opportunity" and begin a war, lest it become a "window of vulnerability" through which they are attacked. This occurred to Germany, for example, in 1914. In July of that year, General von Moltke, the German chief of staff, wrote, "Basically, Russia is not at the moment ready for war. Nor do France or England want war now. In a few years, on all reasonable assumptions, Russia will be ready. By then it will overwhelm us with the number of its troops."[4]

Balance of power theories contain an important and often unstated assumption: Given the opportunity, a stronger state will attack a weaker one. This, presumably, is why severe imbalances in strength must be prevented. Whereas there have been numerous cases of such aggression taking place (e.g., China attacking Vietnam in 1979, the USSR attacking Finland in 1939, Italy attacking Ethiopia—then known as Abyssinia—in 1934), it also remains true that the world abounds in unbalanced power relationships, many of them even involving neighboring countries, which have not resulted in war. We rarely see a headline such as "Brazil did not invade Uruguay today." The fact that power imbalances do not necessarily produce war has not, however, diminished the cogency of the concept for those who believe strongly in it.

Additional Problems

Reliance on balance of power to prevent war presents other difficulties as well, several of which have been touched on in previous discussions:

1. *Increased involvement in wars.* When and if war breaks out in a balance of power system, a larger number of states will likely be involved, since various governments will have been allying themselves with one side or the other. World Wars I and II, for example, became worldwide conflicts because so many different countries were involved.

2. *Instability.* The relative balance is never static, which leads to constant anxieties and adjustments, some of which may generate instability. (Balance of power thus resembles deterrence, not only in some of its underlying assumptions, such as imminent hostility, but also in the liability that it requires constant and possibly dangerous readjustments.)

3. *The balance backfire.* Efforts to upset the balance, on the part of an ambitious ruler or state, may readily succeed and lead to war. For example, the Soviet Union was widely perceived to be upsetting the nuclear balance when it attempted to place nuclear missiles in Cuba in 1962; from the Soviet perspective, the United States had already upset that balance several years earlier by placing missiles in Turkey and England. In any case, the Soviet response, and the subsequent U.S. reaction, precipitated the Cuban Missile Crisis, which led to humanity's closest ever brush with all-out nuclear war. This suggests that whereas there may be a strong temptation to produce an *imbalance* in one's favor, such actions may backfire, generating a crisis and possibly leading to war.

4. *Military alliances.* George Washington reflected a fundamental distrust, when in his Farewell Address, he urged the United States to avoid "entangling alliances." Of course, it should also be pointed out that alliances—crucially important to any balance of power system—do not always promote war, either. It has been argued that the North Atlantic Treaty Organization (NATO), balanced by the Warsaw Pact, promoted peace and stability in Europe for 45 years after World War II. Immediately prior to World War I, Kaiser Wilhelm sought to restrain his Austrian ally from attacking Serbia; had he succeeded, textbooks such as this might now be extolling the benefits of balanced alliances in preventing war! The fact remains, however, that military alliances have often led to war, with the major participants sometimes drawn in through the actions of their proxies and out of fear that inaction would mean a loss of national honor (today referred to as "credibility").

Collective Security

Advantages

Closely related to balance of power, but nonetheless distinct from it, is the concept of collective security. In systems of collective security, states promise to refrain from using force against other members of the "collective," except that they agree to band together against any member who attacks any other within the group. Collective security differs from balance of power in that it relies on the participation of each state, as an individual, nonaligned entity, as opposed to a balance of unstable, constantly shifting alliances. Note that NATO and the former Warsaw Pact would not count as examples of collective security, since they were predicated on mutual defense against a potential aggressor from *outside* each alliance, whereas collective security pacts are specifically directed at defense against any aggression from *within* the pact. Early in its history, some statesmen hoped that NATO might exemplify collective security, and include the Soviet Union, for example, among its members. However, the system of post-World War II alliances degenerated from collective security to "selective security," a series of bilateral and regional arrangements that—notably in the case of NATO and the Warsaw Pact—set themselves up as competing, opposed alliances. It is debatable whether these alliances prevented war or maintained nearly two generations of hostility.

Among the advantages of collective security is that, by agreement, any aggression would be forcefully opposed. By contrast, in balance of power systems, a would-be aggressor might attempt something, calculating that so long as the other participants considered that the balance (from their perspective) was not adversely affected, a relatively small power grab might be successful.

Disadvantages

There have been problems with collective security. Such agreements, for example, are only as good as the will of the participants to abide by them. Given the extreme destructiveness of war, states may be understandably reluctant to meet their treaty obligations. This is especially true unless their populace strongly supports the military action that is called for. And finally, given the social and especially the economic interdependence of modern states, even responses short of war—for example, boycotts, trade embargoes —may cause real hardship, thereby making political leaders hesitant to take such steps.

Also, collective security arrangements, when they involve small states with large and powerful friends, can give rise to highly destructive and interminable wars. Left to themselves, for example, the war between North and South Korea would almost certainly have ended quickly, one way or another. But as it happened, the United States and China became deeply involved, and the conflict was therefore greatly prolonged and intensified. A similar process occurred in the struggle between North and South Vietnam, between the contra rebels and the government of Nicaragua, between Angola's elected government and insurgent UNITA forces. The Middle East was kept simmering, if not boiling, in part by assistance provided by the United States and the Soviet Union, primarily to the Israelis and the Arabs, respectively. (It is not coincidental that most Arab states have been more willing to consider reconciliation with Israel since their superpower backer, the former USSR, has disappeared.) By contrast, wars between India and China, and Britain and Argentina, have been comparatively decisive, in part because they were fought without significant military involvement by allies on either side.

In addition, "allies" sometimes attack each other. The USSR, for example, invaded fellow Warsaw Pact members Hungary (1956) and Czechoslovakia (1968) and threatened a similar move against Poland when the Solidarity movement initially attempted to lead that country to ideological and socioeconomic independence. Likewise, the United States has invaded various states of the Western Hemisphere on numerous occasion, most notably the Dominican Republic (1965), Grenada (1983), and Panama (1989).

National Security Via Military Force

Given the uncertainties of maintaining peace through balance of power or collective security, it is not surprising that many government leaders opt for going it alone—not necessarily avoiding alliances, but rather placing their primary emphasis on being sufficiently strong to deter war by the military power of the state, standing by itself. Just as balance of power and collective security systems depend ultimately on a contest of strength, the doctrine of peace through strength is similarly committed to military force.

Richard Perle, a very hawkish assistant secretary of defense during the Reagan administration, once said, "Those who believe that the way to maintain peace is by being weak are over and over again shown by history to be wrong." Here, the political right wing is in agreement with some more violence-prone elements of the far left. Mao Tse-tung wrote that "we do not desire war, but war can only be abolished through war—in order to get rid of the gun, we must first grasp it in hand." In fact, the lessons of history are more equivocal. Diplomatic historian George Kennan suggests that "modern history offers no example of the cultivation by rival powers of armed force on a huge scale that did not in the end lead to an outbreak of hostilities," adding that "there is no reason to believe that we are greater, or wiser, than our ancestors." Moreover, there is every reason to believe that in the nuclear age, the consequences of worldwide hostilities could be far more severe than they have ever been in the past.

As we have seen, strong states are far more likely than weak ones to be involved in wars, especially if the weak ones maintain a position of neutrality, and even more so if their "weakness" is really a refusal to provoke or threaten others. Thus, Switzerland and Sweden have been war-free for centuries, and although they are far weaker than the larger, more belligerent countries nearby, they are militarily rather strong. In other cases, small, weak countries have indeed been conquered or absorbed by their more powerful neighbors: Latvia, Lithuania, and Estonia were annexed by the Soviet Union just prior to World War II; Hawaii was incorporated within the United States; Tibet was similarly overrun by China; and the Portuguese enclave of Goa was swallowed up by India.

Military Strength and Failure

There is a primitive logic to the notion that one is better off being strong than weak. And yet overwhelming military strength has often resulted in failure. The United States, for example, was victorious in essentially every major military engagement of the Vietnam War. The world's strongest military power dropped 8 million tons of bombs (making more than 20 million craters) and nearly 400,000 tons of napalm, killing approximately 2.2 million Vietnamese, Cambodians, and Laotians, maiming and wounding about 3.2 million more, and leaving more than 14 million homeless—but was defeated. Israel is more than a match for all its Arab neighbors combined and is infinitely more powerful—militarily—than the largely unarmed Palestinians inhabiting the West Bank and Gaza—and yet Israeli security (and even control of its occupied territories) is by no means ensured. Similarly, the Soviet Union was enormously more powerful than the Afghan rebels who eventually compelled it to retreat, just as its successor state, Russia, was unable to subdue tiny, rebellious Chechnya during a ruinous war from 1994 to 1996 and was still attempting to do so in the early 21st century. As with the United States in Vietnam, the Soviets were almost always victorious on the battlefield, although defeated in their ambitions.

Pyrrhus was a king in ancient Greece. During the third century B.C.E., he lost nearly all his men in the battle of Asculum, in which the Romans were defeated; upon being congratulated for his victory, he replied, "One more such victory and we are utterly undone." Hence, the phrase, a "Pyrrhic victory." This paradox—that military force, even military victory, does not necessarily lead ultimately to success or even security—is especially true with respect to nuclear weapons, as a result of which nuclear countries find themselves holding a tiger by the tail. Part of the irony lies in the fact that by committing a state's existence to military success, leaders paradoxically place its security in the hands of one's opponents.

Security Through Superiority?

Government leaders typically argue that their prime responsibility is the maintenance of "national security," a phrase that is readily invoked but only rarely scrutinized. It is easy to equate strength with safety, weakness with danger. Fearing to be seen as too weak, too accommodating, too easily pushed around, government leaders are prone to use threats of military force in efforts to coerce an opponent, or to inhibit further adventuring. Sometimes this works; at other times, the bluff is called. After the Iraqi invasion of Kuwait, President Bush demanded a withdrawal and then—to the surprise of many, and admittedly, for a variety of reasons—the United States did in fact force such a withdrawal. A similar combined U.S. and NATO demand preceded military action against the Serbs in Kosovo. At other times, preemptive saber-rattling may discourage unwanted actions by other parties; China, for example, has made it clear that it would respond militarily to any unilateral assertion of independence on the part of Taiwan, which the Chinese maintain is an integral part of "one China." (The United States has similarly threatened to respond with military force if China seeks to reunite itself with Taiwan by force.)

During times of international tension, participants are likely to be especially aware that the other is aggressive, dangerous, and likely to probe for weakness, being deterred only by strength. In the early days of the Korean War, and again during the Cuban Missile Crisis, White House aides argued that the Soviets were following the Leninist maxim "If you strike steel, pull back, if you strike mush, keep going." So, better to meet the enemy with steel than with mush. And of course, so long as both sides do this, they can justify their policies by pointing to the other side's policies, and the other side's steel as well. By a kind of self-fulfilling logic, both sides would be correct.

However, the inherent logic of forever seeking superiority crumbles when one considers its role in generating the security dilemma. Nonetheless, thinking of this sort has long dominated the national security managers of many states. Through much of the 19th century, for example, Britain proclaimed the "two-power standard," by which the Royal Navy ought always to be at least equal, and preferably superior, to the combined navies of the next two most powerful states. This was considered necessary to guarantee British national security. The British sought absolute security, despite the fact that, as Henry Kissinger has put it, "the desire of one power for absolute security means absolute insecurity for all the others."

Hence, it is not surprising that the British and German naval establishments competed vigorously during the first decade or so of the 20th century, or that the tension generated by this competition contributed to the outbreak of World War I. This Anglo-German arms race also exemplifies another difficulty in trying to achieve peace through strength: the fact that new manifestations of "strength" can undermine a state's preexisting security. For example, the Royal Navy was quite far ahead of its German counterpart when the British Admiralty introduced a new class of extra-large, heavily armed and armored battleships, known as dreadnoughts, after the name of the first such ship. At a stroke, this unilateral act—which was the logical culmination of seeking to maintain peace through strength—made much of the Royal Navy obsolete and forced Britain to engage in a more intense competition with Germany, and from a position of reduced advantage, since the Germans began constructing their own dreadnoughts.

Something similar happened repeatedly in the nuclear arms race, in which the United States, the consistent leader and innovator, introduced new delivery systems or warheads, only to find the Soviet Union following suit, after which both sides were less secure than they were before the escalation.

Military Interpretations of National Security

Typically, national security is seen as deriving from military strength. Accordingly, it is very scarce and a zero-sum game, in that the more one side gets of it, the less there is for the other. Such a mind-set suggests three rejoinders:

1. *Military strength is often a two-edged sword, evoking less security rather than more.*   This security dilemma arises because states, trying to enhance their security via military forces and alliances, succeed only in making other states less secure, which in turn respond militarily themselves, as a result of which everyone is less secure and worse off. The United States may well offer the most dramatic example: Highly prosperous, surrounded by two great oceans and happy Canada to the north and hapless Mexico to the south, not since the War of 1812 has the United States had to worry seriously about invasion by a foreign power. And yet nuclear weapons in particular (as well as risks of terrorism, whether nuclear, chemical, biological, or conventional) have given Americans substantial reasons to worry about "national security," and personal security as well.

2. *The tendency is to think of security as an exclusive, competitive accomplishment: Security for me can be purchased only at the cost of insecurity for you.*   In fact, however, national security can be a positive-sum game, in which both sides can win. Indeed, in a world of growing interdependence, as well as the shared danger posed by weapons of mass destruction, true and enduring national security can only be achieved *mutually*.

3. *In their quest for national security, government leaders may—intentionally or not—actually create "enemies" so as to justify their continuing position of power and authority with their own society.*   In addition to producing a situation of reduced security, which presumably is unintentional,

leaders who create enemies can also facilitate the social and economic exploitation of their own populace and a degree of enhanced solidarity of a population under attack, a process likely to be wholly intended, although rarely identified as such.

It is an ancient pattern. For example, during the latter stages of the Roman republic, the populace was wantonly exploited and pillaged, by its own leadership, in the name of "security." Enemies were created to justify ruinously high taxes, the appropriation of private holdings, and the abridgement of personal liberties. In his essay "The Sociology of Imperialism," economist and historian Joseph Schumpeter unsparingly criticized "that policy which pretends to aspire to peace but unerringly generates war, the policy of continual preparation for war, the policy of meddlesome interventionism." He went on to describe these excesses on the part of Rome's rulers, which should serve as a warning to the excessively enemy prone even in the 21st century:

> There was no corner of the known world where some interest was not alleged to be in danger or under actual attack. If the interests were not Roman, they were those of Rome's allies; and if Rome had no allies, then allies would be invented. When it was utterly impossible to contrive such an interest—why, then it was the national honor that had been insulted. . . . The whole world was pervaded by a host of enemies, and it was manifestly Rome's duty to guard against their indubitably aggressive designs.[5]

"Meddlesome interventionism" is not limited to the ancient past; it is with us today, as many inhabitants of developing countries can attest. Moreover, residents of many countries continue to be kept anxious, impoverished, and imperiled by those who see enemies everywhere. The United States is not immune, as General Douglas MacArthur pointed out (himself no shrinking violet when it came to military response to perceived enemies). "Our government has kept us in a perpetual state of fear," he wrote in his memoirs, "kept us in a continual stampede of patriotic fervor—with the cry of a grave national emergency. Always there has been some terrible evil at home or some monstrous foreign power that was going to gobble us up."[6] With the end of the Cold War and the dissolution of the Soviet Union, contemporary purveyors of ever new "enemies" have been challenged to fill the gap, employing, by turns, the following: Cuba, Libya, Iraq, North Korea, international terrorism, and a generalized "unpredictability." Some have even indicated nostalgia for the Cold War!

Other National Security Considerations

Although there is often a legitimate military dimension to national security, it must be emphasized that national security cannot be measured by military parameters alone. It is also a function of economic strength, political cohesiveness, social equity, cultural outreach, and environmental soundness. National security is diminished if the populace is inadequately housed or fed, or when medical care is insufficient. For a state to neglect its own people in pursuit of "national security" is very much like a person destroying his or her house to obtain materials with which to build a fence around the devastated shell.

In this respect, historian Paul Kennedy has developed the influential thesis that great powers tend to rise and then fall in a predictable cycle, as their world ambitions make excessive demands on their domestic productivity:

> A nation projects military power according to its economic resources but eventually the high cost of maintaining political supremacy weakens the economic base. Great powers in decline respond by spending more on defense and weaken themselves further by directing essential revenues away from productive investment.[7]

This argument points in turn to the rise and fall of Hapsburg Spain and the British Empire, and it was influential in the toppling of the Soviet Union, whose economy was unable to sustain a continuing 14% expenditure on the military sector. It also suggests that we look critically at whether the United States might experience a similar decline, especially as it stubbornly refuses to reduce its absolute level of military spending despite the absence of an identifiable enemy. In contrast to the United States, whose military expenditures comprise about 6% of its gross national product (GNP), military spending in Japan is only about 1% of its GNP, which freed money to help finance its remarkable post-World War II economic boom. It is notable that about 10% of Japanese government investment in research and development goes into military products, whereas the analogous figure for the United States is a whopping 70%. The Japanese were pioneers in developing and marketing VCRs, automobiles, cameras, and so forth, which they sell to the world economy, and despite some economic difficulties in the 1990s, they continue to enjoy an enormous financial surplus. By contrast, by becoming the world's leading producer of high-tech military gadgetry, the United States has specialized in items that are typically purchased by U.S. taxpayers, contributing to inflation, a large trade deficit, and national debt.

"The problem in defense," said President Eisenhower in 1953, "is how far you can go without destroying from within what you are trying to defend from without."

Bargaining Chips

"We arm to parley," said Winston Churchill, and indeed, political leaders have long maintained that one of the benefits of armaments is that they provide leverage in disarmament or arms control negotiations with the other side. Generally, whenever two sides agree to divest themselves of weaponry (something that happens very rarely) or to refrain mutually from acquiring certain military forces—by either qualitative or quantitative restrictions—both sides are expected to forgo something comparable. If one side is militarily weak and the other strong, then what incentive is there for the latter to build down? One answer, then, is for both sides to make themselves comparably strong at the outset of any serious disarmament discussions.

There is some support for this idea, especially in the nuclear age, when serious, joint efforts at nuclear arms control gathered momentum only in the late 1960s, when the Soviet Union essentially achieved military parity with the United States. At the same time, it has often happened that weapons originally justified as bargaining chips were never cashed in. Rather, they tended to develop a powerful constituency—civilian contractors who build them, military commanders who deploy and command them, politicians in whose district they are constructed and/or sited—and so they have often insidiously become part of the arsenal, whether needed or not.

On the other hand, most American conservatives recoil at any diminution in U.S. military expenditures, pointing to the alleged impact of the Reagan-era military buildup in "defeating" the Soviet Union. They suggest that continued overwhelming U.S. strength will provide immediate security and also discourage other would-be rivals from increasing their military power to the point of eventually threatening the status of the United States as the world's only superpower. Nonetheless, military pressure most commonly undercuts the conciliators on the opposing side and leads to a corresponding military buildup in return. If the military had been in charge of negotiating the Montreal Protocols, for example, which established standards for ozone protection, we might all be stockpiling chlorofluorocarbons as bargaining chips.

Appeasement, Provocation, and Deterrence

Just as doves point to the dangers of overarming and of provocation—referring especially the lessons of World War I—hawks point to the dangers of underarming and of appeasement, especially the lessons of Munich and World War II. The Soviet experience during World War II, in which they suffered a massive surprise attack by German forces in June 1941, had a counterpart in the traumatic U.S. experience, in the surprise attack by Japan at Pearl Harbor in December of that same year.

World Wars I and II

The security dilemma is not unique to modern times or the nuclear age. In the decade before World War I, for example, German and British naval leaders each worried that the other might be planning a preemptive attack on the other's fleet. And as we have seen, one of the driving forces behind the actual declarations of war by Germany and Russia in 1914 was anxiety over the consequences of allowing the opponent to mobilize first. A would-be defender, seeking to achieve peace via strength, must walk a narrow line between, on the one hand, provoking the war it wants to prevent (the experience of both sides in World War I) and, on the other, failing to prevent war by being perceived as too weak or lacking in resolve (the "Munich syndrome" in 1938, or Bosnia vis-à-vis Serbia in the early 1990s).

In 1914, British foreign secretary Sir Edward Grey announced that "Britain probably would be unable to stand aside" if war came to Europe; a clearer statement of intent to stand by France if war came to Europe might have made Germany more hesitant. Similarly, France had a treaty with Czechoslovakia in 1938, committing the French nation to Czechoslovakia's defense. But France had vacillated when Germany remilitarized the Rhineland (in defiance of the Versailles Treaty, which had ended World War I), and annexed Austria, so Hitler was convinced that France would find some way to weasel out of its obligation to Prague. He was right. He thought the same thing about his attack on Poland, but that time he was wrong.

The Nuclear Age

Supporters of "peace through strength" like to point to the fact that no U.S.-Soviet war took place in the nuclear age, even during periods of intense rivalry and antagonism. But it is not possible to assess this claim. Perhaps peace prevailed between the two superpowers simply because they had no quarrel that justified fighting a terribly destructive war, even a conventional one. It is not at all clear, for example, that the Soviet leadership was ever itching to invade Western Europe, restrained only by the other side's nuclear arsenal. Such post facto arguments—especially negative ones, purporting to show why something has *not* happened—are in fact impossible to prove. (If a dog barks in the night, we might be able to say with confidence that it did so "because" someone walked by. If it does not bark, however, we may never know "why.")

In addition, it should be pointed out that in the context of world events, the 45 years from World War II to the end of the Cold War was not really all that long. More than 20 years separated World Wars I and II; before that, there were more than 40 years of peace between the end of the Franco-Prussian War and World War I, and 55 years had elapsed since the previous major war, which ended with Napoleon's defeat at Waterloo in 1815. The point is that periods of peace are not unheard of, even in war-torn Europe. Furthermore, when peace ended and the next war began, it was fought with the weapons available at that time, which for the next major war might well include nuclear weapons.

In short, it may be inaccurate—even premature—to congratulate ourselves, or our nuclear weapons, for keeping the peace. The story is told about the man who sprayed perfume on his lawn every morning. When his perplexed neighbor asked about this strange behavior, the man replied, "I do it to keep the elephants away." The neighbor protested, "But there aren't any elephants within ten thousand miles of here." Whereupon the man announced, triumphantly, "You see, it works!"

There is also a logical fallacy at work here: If nuclear weapons had failed to keep the peace, and we had a nuclear war, then there would be no one around to argue about their effectiveness as peacekeepers! Moreover, while it is possible that the post-1945 U.S.-Soviet peace was achieved "through strength," it is also possible that it has occurred *in spite of* the provocations of deterrence rather than because of them. Thus, the presence of nuclear weapons on hair-trigger alert capable of reaching each other's homeland has certainly made both sides nervous and edgy. Although in 1962, during the Cuban Missile Crisis, the two sides refrained from active hostilities, largely because of the unacceptable costs of nuclear war, the crisis itself was brought about because of the provocative nature of the weapons.

There have also been many cases in which the possession of strong military forces—including nuclear weapons—has not deterred war. The Chinese, Cuban, Iranian, and Nicaraguan revolutions all took place despite the fact that the United States was allied with the governments previously in power and possessed nuclear weapons. Similarly, the United States lost the Vietnam War, just as the USSR lost in Afghanistan, despite the fact that both countries were not only nuclear armed but much stronger than their opponents. Nuclear weapons also did not aid Russia in its unsuccessful war against Chechen rebels in 1994–1996 and again from 1999 to 2000, nor have they helped insulate the United States from terrorist threats, which are more likely to be made via nuclear weapons than deterred by them. It was a nuclear-armed United States that "lost" China and a nuclear-armed Soviet Union that "lost" China once again, in the early 1960s. (It may seem odd, incidentally, that such a huge nation can have been so frequently misplaced!)

One of the most unstable world regions has long been southern Asia. (Unlike the United States and the Soviet Union during the Cold War, India and Pakistan share a common border and have fought four wars; by contrast, the United States and the USSR were global and ideological competitors but without a history of direct bloodshed or conflict over specific real estate.) Since 1998, India and Pakistan have also been nuclear armed. Although it is possible that the mutual possession of nuclear weaponry will induce both countries to be more cautious than they might otherwise be, most observers do not derive comfort from the fact that nuclear deterrence is potentially operating in this case.

Arms races in general can be criticized as a kind of action-reaction sequence, in which an action by one side led to a reaction by the other, which generates, in turn, yet another action. Closely related are "worst-case analyses," in which the military establishment of each side—seeking to be prudent—assumes the worst of the other's capabilities and intentions. The result is a process of "threat inflation," in which each side takes an alarmist view of the threat that the other poses and, as a result, overreacts, thereby further escalating the competition and nervousness on both sides. "The worst aspect of this development," wrote Albert Einstein, "lies in its apparently inexorable character. Each step appears as the inevitable consequence of the one that went before, and at the end, looming ever nearer, lies universal annihilation."[8]

The Use and Abuse of Threats

The most extreme example of attempted peace through strength and threats has involved nuclear weapons. Arguments in their favor rely, as we have seen, on the concept of deterrence and the presumption that in the absence of immense destructive power, the United States would be susceptible to attack, blackmail, and/or domination. Supposedly, we are made safe by nuclear weapons. It may not be the best of all imaginable worlds, we are told, but perhaps it is the best of all realistically possible worlds, in that it keeps our enemies at bay. As we read in Shakespeare's *Henry IV*, part 1, "Out of this nettle, danger, we pluck this flower, safety." And as Winston Churchill proposed, referring specifically to nuclear deterrence, "Safety will be the steady child of terror, and survival, the twin brother of annihilation."

Fear, Stubbornness, and Opportunity

When we seek to maintain peace through strength, we basically rely on the effectiveness of threats. In *The Strategy of Conflict*, a now-classic analysis of threats in international affairs, Thomas Schelling distinguished between "compellent" and "deterrent" threats: the former are more aggressive, forcing the opponent to *do* something, surrender something of value, and so forth. The latter are intended to *prevent* the opponent from acting in a way that the threatener finds undesirable: deterring aggression, dissuading the opponent from subverting another state, and so on. Schelling also pointed out that force can be used for its punishment or shock effect, aside from its military usefulness: Sherman's march through Georgia, General Sheridan's genocidal tactics against the Comanches, German use of V-1 and V-2 weapons against Britain in World War II, or the atomic bombing of Hiroshima and Nagasaki. States also tend to employ force when they see a need to shore up their credibility.

Deterrence theory and the assumptions of "peace through strength" can have a pernicious effect. Nuclear deterrence in particular depends on a mutually threatening posture, as each side seeks to impress the other with its toughness and willingness to use force if provoked. Thus, conflicts that may in themselves be of no intrinsic consequence for either side and that may even occur far from the borders of either country become imbued with a peculiar significance: that of indicating the credibility, reliability, toughness, and hence, the security of one side (or both). It then becomes vital to intervene in virtually any struggle, just to prove that "we" will not be pushovers and to ensure that our "national will" is not about to be tested again in the future, or doubted. For example, concern about avoiding the image of the United States as a "pitiful, helpless giant" served as a major motivator for U.S. perseverance in the Vietnam War.

It is possible that deterrence—especially nuclear deterrence—made the superpowers cautious in their provocations of the other. However, deterrence also encourages a kind of "competitive risk taking," in which the bolder, tougher, more violence-prone player appears likely to win. But when two sides collide, each determined to be the tougher, peace through strength can succumb to war through stubbornness, as with World War I.

Moreover, a cogent argument can be made that when they are assessing whether or not to go to war, political leaders do not necessarily follow the expectations of deterrence theory, which assumes that states regularly assess their potential prospects vis-à-vis one another and are likely to leap through any "windows of vulnerability" that might reveal themselves. Thus, advocates of peace through strength assume that military weakness relative to another state invites attack, whereas strength deters it. But in fact, wars have been precipitated much more often by *fear* (of the other side being stronger, or—even more often—that it will shortly become stronger) rather than by overconfidence. Thus, at the eve of World War I, Germany and Austria feared being encircled and outmaneuvered by the Triple Entente, just as the Israeli attack on Egypt and Syria in 1967 was brought about by fear that its Arab neighbors were getting too strong. Similarly, the USSR did not invade Afghanistan because it felt especially strong but because it felt *weak* and threatened by the prospect of a hostile Islamic state on its southern border.

There is abundant evidence that states are more likely to be influenced by their own internal political needs than by their objective military strength vis-à-vis an opponent. Thus, Argentina clearly was militarily inferior to Britain when it attacked the Falkland Islands in 1982, just as India clearly was militarily inferior to China when it provoked the brief and (for India) disastrous Sino-Indian War over the disputed Himalayan region of Ladakh in 1962. (It is also noteworthy that in both these cases, the unsuccessful attacker was not deterred by the fact that the "victim" possessed nuclear weapons.) Similarly, the deteriorating political fortunes of India's ruling Hindu fundamentalist party were revived after India's nuclear testing in 1998, and its successful repulsion of Pakistan in Kashmir in 1999, just as the election of Russia's Vladimir Putin in 2000 was ensured by his vigorous promotion of the comparatively popular Second Chechen War in 1999–2000.

Finally, we note that reliance on threat as an arbiter of victory may also lead to a false estimate of the other's threshold, which can be dangerous in the extreme if both sides engage in a game of nuclear "chicken," each determined that the other must be the one to swerve.

The Prisoner's Dilemma

Advocates of peace through strength often maintain that states have no choice: They must maintain and even increase their armaments—as well as a credible threat to use them if called on to do so—because if they relied less on military force, they would be at the mercy of another state that continued to arm heavily. Hence, each state may find itself forced into a warlike posture that neither wants, but both are unable to escape. This situation has long been recognized, and modeled mathematically, as the so-called Prisoner's Dilemma. Analyses based on the Prisoner's Dilemma have a prominent place in mathematical game theory, strategic analysis, social psychology, and even evolutionary biology, which attempt to model various competitive interactions. Understanding this system is therefore important, not only for the light it might shed on threats, competition, and the problems of cooperation but also for what it reveals about the mind-set of people whose opinions are influential in shaping major military and political decisions.

The Prisoner's Dilemma is also a model for the evolution of cooperation versus competition. In its very simplified imaginary world, individuals (or states) have two options, call them "cooperate" (or disarm) and "defect" (or arm). If both cooperate, then both receive the payoff R, the reward for cooperation; if both defect, then both receive the payoff P, the punishment of mutual defection; if one defects and the other cooperates, than the defector receives T, the payoff for uncontested competitiveness, and the one who cooperates (disarms, etc.) while the other takes advantage of the situation receives S, the sucker's payoff.

Basically, a Prisoner's Dilemma occurs when the payoffs are in the following relationship: $T > R > P > S$. In this case, the "players" are tempted to get T, fearful of getting stuck with S, and so they wind up getting P (a punishing arms race) when the best mutual payoff would have been R, the reward for cooperation or mutual restraint.

The Prisoner's Dilemma is a useful way of modeling the dilemma of thinking that one must be "nasty" for fear that anyone who is "nice" is at the mercy of others who persevere in being nasty. On the other hand, it may well be unduly pessimistic, in that it assumes only two choices, whereas in reality, individuals or states have a variety of options. They can try a mix of tactics: disarm in one respect, build up in another, delay a modernization program, and so on. The simplified model also requires that there is only one payoff and that everything depends on that. In reality, states interact many times in succession, and they can vary their behavior depending on what happened the previous occasion. And if both sides have an interest in generating a sequence of cooperative interactions, then, as political scientist Robert Axelrod has demonstrated in his highly acclaimed book *The Evolution of Cooperation*, cooperative outcomes can yield the highest payoff.

In short, the Prisoner's Dilemma can be useful in clarifying our thinking, and indeed, variants of it are used extensively by analysts in the promilitary strategic community. But it should be remembered that such an approach carries many hidden assumptions and that individuals—and states—must avoid becoming Prisoners of their own narrow-minded Dilemmas.

Nonprovocative Defense

Finally, having considered the major traditional doctrines related to peace through strength, and found them wanting, let us turn to another concept, one more likely to commend itself to military-minded seekers after peace. It is variously known as *defensive defense, nonoffensive defense, alternative defense, transarmament,* or *nonprovocative defense*. This approach seeks to make war less likely through a substantial restructuring of strategic planning and the actual disposition of forces. Thus, although most countries describe their military as "defense" forces, they almost always have a large offensive component, which leads in turn to the widespread "security dilemma." By contrast, under a regime of nonprovocative defense, states would emphasize weapons that are unambiguously defensive and would reconfigure their forces so as not to threaten other states. The goal would be to establish a regime in which defense dominated offense, in which states felt secure in their ability to repel an aggressor, but felt insecure in their ability to successfully attack another.

How It Might Work

Specifically, tanks would be prohibited, whereas antitank defenses permitted; bombers would be prohibited, but antiaircraft batteries and short-range fighter-interceptors permitted; heavily armored mechanized forces would be prohibited, but lightly armed, mobile infantry units permitted; supplies would be prepositioned, and defensive networks constructed throughout the countryside. Such arrangements are not suitable for attack, but can help comprise a formidable defense. U.S. military thinking has not been especially receptive to nonprovocative defense, although European planners have shown substantial interest.

One difficulty with implementing nonprovocative defense is the potential difficulty of distinguishing unambiguously between defensive and offensive forces. Fighter aircraft, for example, can be used to supplement offensive operations, as well as to defend against invaders. Armored personnel carriers can be either aggressive or defensive, as can destroyers and even submarines. Even fixed defensive fortifications can serve the offense: The Siegfried Line, built by Germany along its border with France, made it less likely that France would assist its Polish ally while the Nazis made war in the east. Of more current relevance, a "ballistic missile defense" system (previously known as "Star Wars"), although touted as defensive by its advocates, alarms others who see it as possibly offensive, encouraging its possessor to initiate an attack with confidence (whether or not well-founded) that it will be immune to retaliation.

In other cases, the distinction is more clear-cut: minefields and immobile tank-traps are unambiguously defensive, while nuclear weapons are offensive (even if they ostensibly provide deterrence).

Nonprovocative defense would require a substantial change in doctrine, abandoning existing plans for "forward-based defense," "deep strikes," and the like, tactics that call for "defending" a country by carrying the fight deep into opposing territory. Instead, countries would concentrate on a "defense in depth," emphasizing small mobile units trained to mount defensive operations, if necessary deep within their own borders. Certain states—notably the United States—specialize in "projecting power" far from their shores. These forces—aircraft carriers, long-range fighter-bombers, mobile artillery, amphibious assault units—are not used for defending one's own borders; rather, their purpose is overwhelmingly to intervene (or threaten to intervene) in other countries, generally far from home. Nonprovocative defense would require that states forgo such activities.

A world in which interstate war is significantly less likely must be considered a potential advance. In this regard, the prospects for nonprovocative defense, although cloudy, are not altogether bleak. The idea of confining each state's "defense forces" to real defense, thereby making was less likely, reducing tensions, and saving money to boot, has an undeniable practical appeal. (It must be emphasized that nonprovocative defense would not offer any less defense than current military postures; in fact, by being less threatening to would-be opponents, it should reduce the probability of armed hostilities, thereby providing much *more* defense.) In addition, unlike most arms control or disarmament proposals, the transition to nonprovocative defense does not require complex bilateral or multilateral negotiated agreements; any state that wishes to can make the shift unilaterally.

Several have already done so. A number of countries, notably the European states that practice "armed neutrality," are living, practical examples of successful nonprovocative defense. For example, Switzerland requires that all men between 20 and 50 years of age participate in a civilian militia.

The Swiss Army emphasizes antiaircraft systems, tank-traps, and other anti-tank defenses, as well as a high degree of mobility, keyed to the mountainous Swiss homeland. Supplies have been cached throughout the country; thousands of strategic demolition points have been identified and prewired, so as to slow any invader; and the Swiss Air Force features short-range fighter-interceptors, deliberately excluding long-range heavy bombers. The net result is a robust military capability, but one that is distinctly nonprovocative and also oriented toward deterrence by dissuasion rather than by threat.

Sweden is yet another example of a modern state that has achieved a kind of peace through strength, by emphasizing truly defensive and nonprovocative strategies. Sweden has also sought to enhance its own security by promoting disarmament—especially nuclear disarmament—as a major issue on the world agenda. Thus, Swedish politicians have long been prominent in disarmament efforts, and the Swedish government funds what is probably the preeminent peace institute, the Stockholm International Peace Research Institute (SIPRI).

A Final Note on Peace Through Strength

In today's world, the pursuit of security clearly must be deepened (beyond military strength) and widened (beyond national security). Specifically, security must be recognized as encompassing economic, political, social, and environmental considerations. National security can no longer be achieved by any country acting alone; that is, real security must be mutual, or better yet, global. With the Cold War fading into memory, the inability of most people—notably, of the United States, richest and most powerful country on earth—to articulate a nonmilitary, nonconfrontational vision of peace and global security must count as one of the great failures of the late 20th century, and one of the profound opportunities of the 21st. Moreover, it is noteworthy that the United States, despite being unchallenged as the supreme military power in the world, was profoundly vulnerable to a massive terrorist attack on September 11, 2001. If nothing else, this highlights the limitation of defining "security" in strictly military terms.

During the period of U.S.-Soviet confrontation, it was widely estimated that about 85% of U.S. military expenditures was directed toward meeting that perceived challenge. Now, with the Soviet Union having disintegrated, the U.S. military budget has declined by less than 10%. With the USSR and international communism no longer a perceived threat to U.S. security and hegemony, U.S. military doctrine calls instead for the ability to fight and prevail in two simultaneous wars! Such is the power of "peace through strength" —at least as an assumption that drives policy.

Following the terrorist attacks on the United States on September 11, 2001, and the military response in Afghanistan, it seems likely that U.S.

military doctrine will be changed, placing greater emphasis on rapidly deployable "special operations forces." Not surprisingly, the apparently successful prosecution of a war generally leads to short-term enthusiasm for "peace through strength" policies. It remains to be seen, however, whether such policies lead to genuine and lasting security.

Thus, perhaps the last word should belong to Calvin Trillin, who penned this bit of cynical doggerel with an eye to Russia's brutal effort to impose its will by force on the breakaway republic of Chechnya. His lines may well apply to all such efforts at achieving peaceful ends by strictly military means:

It seems so familiar to me: They know one more tank, one more gun'll
    Allow best and brightest to see the light at the end of the tunnel.[9]

Let us therefore turn to the question of disarmament and arms control.

Notes

1.   Henry Kissinger. 1979. *White House Years*. Boston: Little, Brown.

2.   Winston Churchill. 1948. *The Gathering Storm*. Boston: Houghton Mifflin.

3.   Edward Gibbon. [1782] 1932. *The Decline and Fall of the Roman Empire*. New York: Modern Library.

4.   Quoted in Richard Ned Lebow. 1981. *Between Peace and War*. Baltimore: Johns Hopkins University Press.

5.   Joseph Schumpeter. 1988. "The Sociology of Imperialism." In *Two Essays by Joseph Schumpeter*. New York: Meridian.

6.   Douglas MacArthur. 1965. *A Soldier Speaks*. New York: Praeger.

7.   Paul M. Kennedy. 1987. *The Rise and Fall of the Great Powers*. New York: Harper & Row.

8.   Albert Einstein. 1960. *Einstein On Peace*. New York: Simon & Schuster.

9.   Calvin Trillin, in *The Nation*, February 17, 2000.

12 Disarmament and Arms Control

You cannot simultaneously prevent and prepare for war.

—Albert Einstein

No one—not even the most ardent advocate of disarmament—claims that doing away with weapons will solve the problem of war. So long as the underlying causes of personal, group, and state instability remain, and so long as human beings possess the capacity and inclination to resort to violence under certain circumstances, war will continue to haunt us. Nonetheless, advocates of peace often favor getting rid of weapons or at least exercising strict control over the ones remaining. In this chapter, we examine some aspects of disarmament and its close cousin, arms control.

Different Visions of Disarmament

Arms Control and Gun Control

There have been many different visions of disarmament. Perhaps the simplest is general and complete disarmament, or GCD (general = all countries; complete = all weapons). Not surprisingly, there are problems here, one of which is how to define a weapon. Dynamite, for example, can make an effective weapon, but it is also used for legitimate commercial purposes such as mining or demolition.

And what about firearms? Many citizens of the United States, for example, maintain that "the right of the people to keep and bear arms shall not be infringed," as stated in Article 2 of the U.S. Bill of Rights. Others point to this article's precise wording, which begins "A well-regulated militia being necessary to the security of a free State," inferring that this constitutional guarantee applies only to governmental entities, not to individuals.

In many ways, the heated debate over gun control in the United States mirrors issues of arms control and disarmament more generally: Opponents point to a perceived inalienable constitutional right (to keep guns) and to the supposedly comparable inalienable necessity of state sovereignty (to maintain national weaponry). Similarly, opponents of gun control point to the fact that crime rates are high in the United States and that "if guns are outlawed, only outlaws will have guns," just as opponents of arms control and disarmament point to the anarchy prevailing in international affairs and to the danger that a disarmed country will be at the mercy of aggressive states. At the same time, advocates of gun control emphasize that the easy availability of firearms contributes mightily to the high rate of violence, just as advocates of arms control and disarmament note the widespread "security dilemma," whereby the pursuit of military power tends to make everyone less secure. Opponents of gun control argue that "an armed society is a polite society," whereas advocates point to the rate at which members of armed societies tend to kill one another. Even as gun control opponents are fond of suggesting that "guns don't kill people; people do," arms control opponents emphasize that the problem is not military hardware, but the aggressive designs of certain malevolent leaders, while to proponents of gun control as well as arms control and disarmament, it is simply absurd to think that more weapons—whether personal firearms or national military forces—ultimately makes for safer individuals or a safer world.

It is noteworthy that once a society is heavily armed, control and elimination of personal weapons might make disarmed individuals especially vulnerable to those who cheat and retain their weapons; a similar concern is expressed with regard to the disarmament of states. In both cases, the possession of weaponry is like riding a tiger: a situation not only dangerous in itself, but requiring great care in extricating one's self. Note, also, that just as most contemporary proposals for gun control in the United States involve elimination of firearms that are especially lethal (e.g., automatic weapons) or likely to fall into the wrong hands (e.g., "Saturday night specials"), and generally call for careful monitoring rather than total elimination, a parallel can once again be drawn with proposals for arms control.

Maintenance of National Security Capabilities

A less ambitious goal than GCD was proposed by President Woodrow Wilson in his Fourteen Points, which he recommended as international goals at the end of World War I. Wilson called for national disarmament "to the lowest point consistent with domestic safety." This suggests that states would be allowed to retain police forces, but nothing capable of threatening other states. A police force adequate for China, however, might be quite threatening to Korea or Vietnam. And a Russian police force could threaten Bulgaria. At the Versailles Conference, Wilson's proposal was watered down to "the reduction of national armaments to the lowest point consistent with *national* safety" [italics added], terminology that leaves much open to interpretation. A state like Poland, for example, located on the wide plains of Europe and surrounded by large and potentially threatening neighbors, might seem to require a larger military force than does Switzerland, which has many natural mountain barriers. And the United States, with friendly neighbors north and south, and oceans east and west, would appear to need relatively little in the way of military force, unless (as was the case for most of the 20th century) it considers that its national "safety" requires a military presence—via bases, advisers, and/or the capacity for intervention—in countries overseas.

Disarmament is not uniquely applied to sovereign governments. Among the most contentious issues arising between governments and insurgent movements are typically those involving potential disarmament of the latter. Not surprisingly, governments often refuse to negotiate with armed opponents; it is equally easy to see why revolutionary groups typically resist being disarmed! This can readily lead to a kind of "chicken and egg problem," in which each side refuses to budge until the other does so. For decades, for example, the Israeli government refused to negotiate with the PLO, considering them armed terrorists, just as "decommissioning" (disarming) of the Irish Republican Army has long been a precondition set by the British government in Northern Ireland before any peace plan could be implemented.

Selective Disarmament

Another possibility is to disarm selectively, focusing on offensive weapons. This was the goal of the Geneva Disarmament Conference of 1932; it failed because of inability to reach general agreement on exactly which weapons are defensive and which are offensive (states typically define their own armaments as the former and those of their opponents as being the latter). When the United States ended its occupation of South Korea in 1949, it removed airplanes and tanks, seeking in this way to ensure that South Korea would not be emboldened to attack the North. One result was that the North, instead, attacked the South, which found it very difficult to mount an effective defense after being deprived of these "offensive" weapons.

Probably the most popular version of selective or qualitative disarmament is the enthusiasm that countries have for disarmament of the other, but not for itself. This was especially notable during the U.S.-Soviet arms race, when many observers concluded that the two superpowers essentially colluded in creating a "duopoly," whereby the two superpowers excluded others from being major players on the world stage. There is a fable that describes a disarmament conference held among the animals. The eagle, eyeing the bull, recommends that all horns be cut off. The bull, looking at the tiger, suggests that sharp teeth and claws should be pulled. The tiger, sizing up the elephant, urges that tusks be filed down. The elephant, looking at the eagle, insists that all would well if only wings and beaks were clipped. Then the bear, speaking in tones of sweetness and reason, spoke up, "Come now, my friends, let us abandon these halfway measures and agree to abolish all weapons, and simply resolve any disagreements with a great, friendly hug."

Weapons of Mass Destruction

Even without full-fledged adoption of nonprovocative defense, the possibility exists for mutually agreed restrictions on obviously offensive weapons, such as bombers, motorized artillery, and the like. Perhaps the greatest prospect—as well as the greatest need—for selective disarmament concerns atomic, biological, and chemical weapons ("weapons of mass destruction" or so-called abc weapons), because of the unique threats they pose. In addition, nuclear weapons—especially when combined with fast and highly accurate delivery systems—are unusual in potentially generating their own instability, because they might arouse fear of a preemptive strike. This makes selective disarmament agreements especially important and of incalculable value.

Military Budgets

Reductions and restrictions in military budgets have often been discussed. Not surprisingly, there are problems as well. For example, if all states are restricted to a maximum total expenditure, then the same national defense would be purchased for Luxembourg, which has a small border and few enemies, as for Russia, which has an immense border and much greater legitimate need for defense. But if larger states are permitted larger military budgets (such as an agreed percentage of area, population, or of their gross national product [GNP]), then they might pose a threat to smaller states. In addition, difficulties arise in determining the actual military expenditures of many states that do not publish reliable figures. Even the budget for the U.S. Department of Defense is misleading: It does not include the costs of nuclear bombs and warheads, for example, which are included in the Department of Energy budget.

Proportional Limitations

Agreement was reached in the past over the relative proportions of certain naval vessels to be permitted the major powers, with set ratios allotted for each state. Similarly, various numerical restrictions have been established in

the past for certain kinds of strategic nuclear weapons. However, considerations of prestige have typically made it difficult for states to accept smaller
forces than their rivals. And a further problem remains: How shall these
proportions be allocated? If by population, then, again, larger states will
receive larger forces, thereby constituting a greater threat to their neighbors.
During the Geneva Conferences in the 1920s and 1930s, for example, France
requested force allotments that would make up for the fact that its traditional rival, Germany, had a larger population and industrial capacity. Not
surprisingly, Germany disagreed. And there is also the difficult question of
alliances. During the Euromissile negotiations in the early 1980s, the Soviet
Union emphasized that since the nuclear forces of Britain and France (not
to mention China) were directed against the USSR, it should be permitted
to maintain forces that equaled those of all the North Atlantic Treaty
Organization (NATO) countries combined, and not just those of the United
States.

Weapons-Free Zones

The idea of weapons-free zones is to agree on the elimination of weapons
within a designated geographic area. For example, under the Treaty of
Tlatelolco (named for a suburb of Mexico City), most of the states of the
Western Hemisphere agreed not to develop or deploy nuclear weapons.
Similar suggestions, especially for nuclear-free zones, have been made for
Africa, the Middle East, Australasia, the Balkans, and Scandinavia. Agreement to forgo all weapons within a designated zone, or even just those of a
certain type, can help diminish anxiety that a local rival is seeking to gain
superiority. Consequently, such agreements could diminish pressure to push
ahead with armaments that—when matched by the opponent—would ultimately diminish the security of all concerned. Thus, they offer the prospect
of emerging from the Prisoner's Dilemma (see Chapter 11).

For example, the Rush-Bagot Treaty of 1817, which arranged for the
demilitarization of the U.S.-Canada border, helped set the stage for persistently good relations between these two North American neighbors. This
was no merely cosmetic treaty. It called, among other things, for a 3,000-
mile unfortified border and for the actual dismantling of a number of naval
vessels, which had been built on the Great Lakes and were too large to be
sailed out. It is also worth noting that this agreement was reached only two
years after the United States and Britain—then governing Canada—had
fought a war, including several naval battles on the Great Lakes. Looking at
U.S.-Canadian relations today, we blithely take peace for granted, but at the
time of the Rush-Bagot Treaty, things were very different. Even the treaty
itself did not immediately lead to peace; rather, distrust and several near
wars characterized the ensuing several decades. Undeniably, however, in
this case, a serious disarmament agreement hastened a genuine peace. If

threatening naval vessels had been allowed to continue patrolling the Great Lakes, and if military fortifications had been constructed along the U.S.-Canada border, relations between the two countries would probably have gone quite differently.

Another type of disarmament agreement, similar to the establishment of a weapons-free zone, occurs when all parties agree to the neutralization of a particular country. Following World War II, for example, the victorious allies occupied Austria. By the Austrian State Treaty of 1955, all sides agreed to end that military occupation, signing an accord whereby the state of Austria was essentially demilitarized and pledged to Cold War neutrality.

A Brief History of Disarmament

Self-Serving Plans

Governments have on occasion tried to reduce armaments, and sometimes they have even succeeded. But the history of such efforts is largely one of failure. In 1766, Austria proposed a bilateral arms reduction to Prussia's Frederick; he refused. In 1787, France and Britain agreed to a short-lived freeze in naval construction, and the Russian czar unsuccessfully proposed general arms reductions in 1816. Financial considerations have been important in prompting disarmament efforts. After the Napoleonic Wars, for example, Czar Alexander led an (unsuccessful) effort to save governmental funds via multilateral disarmament. Later, Czar Nicholas II convened the first Hague Peace Conference in 1899, once again in an effort to stave off an arms race that threatened to lead to bankruptcy. But political motivations —especially the desire to appear peace loving—have also been important. After taking office in 1981, for example, President Reagan showed himself to be not only uninterested in disarmament but downright antagonistic to it, especially during his first term in office. Later, the U.S. government begrudgingly entered into arms negotiations with the Soviet Union, almost certainly as a response to mounting political pressure, both within the United States and in Europe.

Other practical concerns have motivated disarmament efforts as well. For example, when Nicholas II suggested a freeze on all military budgets in 1899, Russia already had the largest army in Europe; a freeze would have perpetuated that asymmetry. Churchill proposed a naval-building "holiday" to the Germans during 1912–1914, when Britain was ahead, especially in battleships. Immediately following World War II, the United States proposed the Baruch Plan, which would have required that all states surrender the possibility of producing their own nuclear weapons, *after which* the United States would place its nuclear facilities under international supervision. This would have left the United States the only state with the knowledge and ability to produce nuclear weapons in the future. The Soviets countered with a plan whereby the United States would dispose of its nuclear facilities first, after which other states would join in. (It was argued in the West that the USSR, as a vast and secretive society, would have had a greater opportunity to cheat if it sought to do so.) In short, disarmament negotiations and conferences have often served as a forum for advancing the interests of each state and prosecuting interstate rivalry, rather than as a means of diminishing those rivalries.

Between World Wars I and II, Britain and the United States, the great naval powers, sought to abolish submarines (which were threats to the preeminence of their surface fleets) but to keep battleships and cruisers. France, a traditional land power, fought restrictions on tanks and heavy artillery. During nuclear arms negotiations in the 1980s, the Soviet Union tried to restrict cruise missiles, forward basing of nuclear forces, and most new technological developments in the arms race: all areas in which the United States was ahead. The United States, in turn, urged reductions in large throw-weight intercontinental ballistic missiles (ICBMs) (where the Soviets were ahead), while zealously protecting bombers and submarine-based missiles (where the United States has long been particularly strong).

Germany disarmed briefly after World Wars I and II; ditto for Japan after World War II. But in these cases, the victors simply imposed disarmament on the losers; there is no evidence that the people of Germany and Japan suddenly came to appreciate the merits of disarmament. Shortly afterward, the United States encouraged its new ally, West Germany, to re-arm during the 1950s and eventually to join NATO, much to the dismay of the USSR. And throughout the 1980s, U.S. government officials urged Japanese leaders to devote a larger share of their national budget to their military forces. (By tradition, since World War II this had always been less than 1% of its GNP, and by its postwar constitution, Japan is pledged never to maintain offensive military forces.)

Unsuccessful Attempts

Some attempts at renouncing war, by treaty, have been notably unsuccessful. By the early 1920s, the Treaty of Versailles appeared to be unraveling with Germany refusing to pay its obligatory World War I reparations and France responding by sending troops to occupy Germany's Ruhr Valley. The German foreign minister then organized a peace conference involving the major European powers, hoping to head off the establishment of a new anti-German alliance. At a major meeting in Locarno, Switzerland, numerous agreements were reached, including demilitarization of the Rhineland and a mutual defense treaty linking France to both Poland and Czechoslovakia. Enthusiasm ran high for the outlawing of war altogether, and shortly thereafter, French foreign minister Aristide Briand proposed to U.S. secretary of state Frank Kellogg that, on the tenth anniversary of the U.S. entry into World War I, France and the United States sign an agreement outlawing war between the two states.

The U.S. government responded with unexpected enthusiasm, urging that the proposed instrument be expanded to a worldwide renunciation of "war as an instrument of national policy," in addition to further agreement that "the settlement or solution of all international disputes or conflicts . . . shall never be sought except by peaceful means."

Unfortunately, the Kellogg-Briand Pact was utterly unenforceable, and—along with the "Spirit of Locarno"—may have ultimately done more harm than good, since it gave a false sense of security to states that were already peace loving, and a smokescreen behind which aggressive states were able to pursue their ambitions. The Kellogg-Briand Pact has become a prototype of meaningless and often misleading "statements of principle." On the other hand, such agreements may be important in affirming a widespread yearning for dramatic reductions in armaments; violations of the Kellogg-Briand Pact were also used against former Nazi officials in the Nuremberg Trials, after World War II (see Chapter 14).

Modest Successes

There have been, in addition, some modest examples of successful non-nuclear disarmament. The Washington Naval Conference resulted in a 1922 treaty that caused the United States, Britain, and Japan to scrap 40% of their capital ships (battleships and aircraft carriers). Remaining capital ships for the United States, Britain, Japan, France and Italy were fixed in a ratio of 5 : 5 : 3 : 1.67 : 1.67. By this agreement, Britain—weakened by World War I—finally agreed to abrogate its policy of naval superiority, although the United States actually made the largest material concessions. A decade later, in the London Naval Treaty of 1930, these limits, including restrictions on total tonnage, were extended to cruisers. At this second conference, the major powers were unable to reach agreement on limiting destroyers and submarines, however, and France and Italy did not sign at all. The Italians had demanded naval parity with the French, who found this unacceptable. Japanese militarists also chafed under their restrictions, and Japan renounced both treaties in 1934 when a new, more nationalist government came into power.

Despite their ultimate failure, these agreements probably helped diminish tensions during the years immediately following World War I, as well as postponing the economic stress of a costly naval arms race during that period. But they may also have contributed to the rise of Japanese extremism, as well as impeding attempts by Britain and America to keep up with the naval threat that Japan eventually posed. The actual disarmament achieved by the Washington Naval Treaty was due in large part to the audacious proposals put forth by U.S. secretary of state Charles Evans Hughes; it must be accounted a success (although admittedly a short-lived one), in terms of the weapons eliminated, but clearly not an unambiguous triumph for the disarmament process. If nothing else, however, it demonstrated at least the possibility of some kind of disarmament—in some cases.

This checkered history has led to a rather jaded view of disarmament proposals, one that is—unfortunately—justified in some cases. Disarmament policies have often served simply to demonstrate to public opinion that efforts are being made in a noble direction and that any failures are due to the stubbornness of other countries.

To be sure, there have been many well-meaning attempts at establishing GCD. All of them, however, have been failures, usually resulting—at best—in certain minor restrictions, such as the elimination of expanding (dumdum) bullets or prohibitions against the use of poison gas. When Albert Einstein was asked his opinion of the Geneva disarmament conference of 1926, he responded:

> What would you think about a meeting of a town council which is concerned because an increasing number of people are knifed to death each night in drunken brawls, and which proceeds to discuss just how long and how sharp shall be the knife that the inhabitants of the city may be permitted to carry?[1]

At another such conference, this one held in 1931, great excitement ensued when several Afghans were found to be in attendance. The conference organizers were delighted that the idea of disarmament had spread so far and was being so widely accepted. But when asked why they were attending, the Afghans replied that "if these nations really are going to disarm themselves, perhaps we can pick up some weapons cheaply."

Arms Control

In the aftermath of World War II—widely seen not only as a "good war" but also as one that had been hastened by the West's reluctance to arm adequately in the 1930s—public enthusiasm for disarmament waned significantly. The two emerging superpowers each proposed plans for disarmament, but these were almost certainly a mixture of propaganda ploys and efforts to achieve a unilateral advantage over the other. By the late 1950s, governments began to turn their attention from disarmament to a more modest and attainable goal, especially as regards nuclear weapons, namely, arms control.

There were many reasons for this shift. Following Stalin's death, the Cold War thawed somewhat. Improvements in technology permitted verification with higher confidence, especially by satellite surveillance. The ongoing arms race had heightened citizen anxiety and pushed the West in particular to recognize the growing dangers posed by radioactive fallout from above-ground nuclear testing. And finally, with their acquisition of ICBMs and a growing nuclear arsenal, the Soviet Union achieved essential strategic parity with the United States, thereby permitting both superpowers to negotiate seriously, from a position of more or less equivalent strength. (It has been said that there are two rules for negotiators: Don't negotiate when you are behind, and don't negotiate when you are ahead. Hence, the best opportunity for progress often comes when two sides are functionally equal.)

To dovish critics, arms control is a mere smokescreen, a thinly veiled excuse for continuing to accumulate additional weapons, all the while quieting the public with claims that "progress" is being made. Moreover, arms controllers are concerned with managing and stabilizing the arms race; disarmers, by contrast, do not seek to stabilize the arms race, but rather to *destabilize* it, and end it altogether. To hawkish critics, it should be added, arms control is only somewhat more acceptable than unilateral disarmament (which is utterly anathema); it is considered a snare and a delusion whereby a nation allows itself to be outmaneuvered at the bargaining table by its adversary. If one is opposed to any agreement on arms limitation, or at least to any agreement that applies equally to all sides, then it is no surprise that any such agreement is perceived as damaging to national security. This opposition is typically based on the presumption that the other side is untrustworthy and will cheat, and also on a determination to settle only for victory—or, in the case of an arms race, remaining continually ahead. To some extent, a free-for-all arms race, unfettered by international agreements, also smacks of the economic free market, so beloved by political conservatives.

These, then, are some of the hidden, nefarious goals of arms control: gain a unilateral advantage either by ending competition when you are ahead or by steering competition into an area of one's advantage, establish a monopoly that effectively subjugates other states, create the false impression of progress, thereby quieting domestic dissatisfaction. The official, legitimate goals of arms control are as follows:

1. *Reduce the likelihood that war will break out, by removing some of the more threatening situations or weapons.*   For example, World War I might have been averted if some agreement could have been reached that dampened competition for early mobilization on both sides. The de-alerting of nuclear missiles should diminish fears of a surprise attack, thereby also reducing the danger of war being provoked by error or false alarm.

2. *Prevent competition that could be not only financially ruinous but also destabilizing.*   The Washington and London Naval Treaties were in fact arms control or partial disarmament agreements, which temporarily precluded

some aspects of naval competition among the Great Powers. The ABM Treaty of 1972, by which the United States and the Soviet Union agreed not to develop or deploy significant antimissile weapons, was especially attractive because it headed off a strategically futile and economically intolerable spiral of competition between the offensive and defensive weapons of each side. (In 2002, the United States unilaterally with drew from this treaty, with consequences yet to be seen.)

3. *Create an environment of increasing trust and confidence.* By reaching agreements—even over trivial issues—contending parties can progressively gain greater confidence in each other, as they become increasingly familiar with their counterparts, comfortable with their motivations, and thus, more willing to engage in serious agreements in the future. Of course, this also presupposes that the participants are well-meaning and that the agreements in question will be adhered to. Otherwise, such agreements can backfire.

The vast majority of arms control agreements have in fact been lived up to, and this has on balance created a climate of trust that is favorable to yet more progress. Furthermore, agreements themselves sometimes establish mechanisms for airing and resolving grievances: The SALT I Interim Agreement between the United States and the USSR, for example, created the Standing Consultative Commission (SCC), which was able to resolve numerous Soviet and U.S. accusations of noncompliance.

4. *In the event that war breaks out, arms control can still have been helpful if, because of preexisting arms control agreements, the war is less destructive than it otherwise would have been.* The banning of dumdum bullets has helped, in a small way, to make war more "humane." The major powers also appear to have destroyed biological warfare agents, following an international agreement in 1972, and chemical weapons stocks as called for in an international agreement in the late 1990s. (One hypothetical danger here is that in making war less destructive, it might also be rendered more tolerable and therefore a more acceptable instrument of national policy; after all, nuclear deterrence rests on the proposition that by making the costs of war *in*tolerable, it will be prevented.)

Nuclear Weapons Treaties

Many arms control treaties have been signed since 1945, most of them related in one way or another to nuclear weapons. Although the list is long, however, it is not impressive, because countries were generally willing to restrict only those activities that they were not interested in pursuing anyhow. For decades, arguably, the real arms race was not between the United States and the USSR, but rather between the builders of nuclear arms and those who would restrict these weapons. If so, there is no question who won, most of the time, as evidenced by the tens of thousands of weapons and delivery systems that were constructed. But there have been some successes for the controllers, and we turn now to them. We shall not attempt a complete overview of arms control treaties and accomplishments, just a brief summary of some salient points, by grouping these treaties into logical categories.

Geographic Treaties

The Antarctic Treaty (1959) essentially demilitarized the Antarctic Continent. The Outer Space Treaty (1967) banned "weapons of mass destruction" from orbit and from celestial bodies. The Sea-Bed Treaty (1971) prohibited the implanting of such weapons on the ocean floor. These treaties have been successful and uncontroversial; critics contend, however, that they restricted armaments of a kind and in a place where states had not been contemplating military activity in any event—kind of like banning weapons from Saturn.

Test Ban Treaties

The Partial Test Ban Treaty, or PTBT (1963), capped many years of public protest against rising levels of worldwide fallout from atmospheric nuclear tests. In this treaty, signatories agreed to refrain from atmospheric, outer space, or undersea testing of nuclear weapons. However, testing was not stopped altogether; the perfection of existing warheads and the development of new ones continued to go forward, with testing moved to underground sites. The governments of China and France, moreover, refused to sign the PTBT, and persisted in testing above ground (China) and beneath the ocean (France), until the 1990s, and India and Pakistan detonated relatively low-level nuclear explosions in 1998.

The Threshold Test Ban Treaty, restricting testing to 150 kilotons (more than 10 times the Hiroshima explosion) was signed in 1974 but went unratified by the U.S. Senate. The same was true of the so-called Peaceful Nuclear Explosions Treaty, signed in 1976, and which applied these limits to "peaceful" as well as warlike explosions. Critics long argued that these limits were so high as to be meaningless, and thus that the two treaties are shams; in addition, they point out that no nuclear tests are peaceful. At the time of the PTBT, the real goal of most antitesting advocates was—and continues to be—a Comprehensive Test Ban Treaty (CTBT), which would constrain all nuclear testing, underground as well as above ground. It has been the announced goal of all U.S. administrations since that of Dwight Eisenhower. That goal remains elusive, despite the fact that all major countries participate in a moratorium in such testing, and a CTBT was signed in 1996, and ratified by the Russian Duma (legislature) in 2000. However, in a stunning defeat for nuclear arms control, in 1999 the Republican-dominated U.S. Senate defeated attempts to ratify this treaty, claiming that (1) such a ban could not be satisfactorily verified and (2) even if it could, continued testing is necessary to ensure the reliability of the existing nuclear arsenal. This rejection did much to deprive the United States of any pretense of leadership in promoting nuclear disarmament or even arms control. It also raised the dangerous proposition that other countries, notably Pakistan and India, will continue to develop their own nuclear arsenals.

Mutual Understandings and Improvements in Communication

The "hot line" agreement (1963) established an emergency communications link between Washington and the Kremlin. This was subsequently updated and modernized, with the addition of satellite links and "crisis control centers" in each capital. In the Nuclear Accidents Agreement (1971), the two superpowers agreed to notify each other in the event of accidental or unauthorized nuclear detonations, and the High Seas Agreement (1972) sought to establish rules of conduct to minimize the chances of oceanic collision and misunderstandings during naval maneuvers. In 1975, nearly all European states agreed to the Final Act of the Conference on Security and Cooperation in Europe (CSCE, better known as the Helsinki Accords), which essentially ratified the post-World War II map of Europe, and also arranged for advance notification of large military exercises.

Nonnuclear Weapons

The Biological Weapons Convention (1972) committed the signatory states to refrain from developing, producing, or stockpiling biological weapons (primarily viruses and bacteria). Chemical weapons, however, were not included. The Environmental Modification Convention (1977) prohibited the alteration of the environment, including climate, of an adversary, and the Chemical Weapons Agreement of the 1990s has led to reductions in major powers' chemical arsenals.

Strategic Nuclear Weapons

The first set of Strategic Arms Limitation Talks, or SALT I, resulted in an Interim Agreement (1972) that established numerical limits for each side's guided missile submarines, submarine launched missiles, and ICBMs. It granted the Soviets higher numbers in these categories, to compensate for the U.S. lead in "MIRVed" warheads (equipped with multiple, independently targeted reentry vehicles), submarine systems, strategic bombers, and the fact that U.S. "forward-based systems" in Europe (such as F-111 bombers) could reach the USSR but had no Soviet counterparts. Later, the Vladivostok Accords (1974) set equal numerical limits for strategic launch vehicles, for MIRVing, and for antimissile systems.

SALT II, negotiated through the 1970s, called for greater detail in numerical limits: restrictions on the number of MIRVed ICBMs, as well as on the various permissible combinations of bombers with and without cruise missiles, MIRVed SLBMs (submarine-launched ballistic missiles) and other fine points. It fell victim to domestic U.S. politics, having been strongly opposed by influential right-wing groups; accordingly, it languished in the U.S. Senate.

Under the Reagan administration, the United States unilaterally breached certain terms of SALT II, and then belatedly began negotiations on a replacement, known as START (Strategic Arms Reduction Talks). Critics maintained that these talks were begun with no serious expectation of success, but only to quiet the U.S. peace movement. The START I Treaty was eventually signed and ratified by the U.S. Senate, as well as the Russian Duma. It called, among other things, for a complex mix of reductions in missile launchers, cutting U.S. and Russian warheads to about 6,500 on each side.

In 2000, the Russian Duma ratified the START II agreement, by which the two sides agreed to a maximum of 3,500 warheads each, by 2007. This treaty also bans multiple-warhead missiles, long considered dangerously destabilizing. Russia—eager to reduce the cost of maintaining such expensive arsenals—has urged that START III, the next step, ought to decrease the number of strategic warheads to 1,500, although the United States has resisted such reductions. At the same time, the ABM Treaty has emerged as a stumbling block, with the United States arguing for its amendment and Russia desiring to maintain its current provisions. The possibility nonetheless exists that the United States will agree to substantial reductions in warhead numbers (desired by Russia), in return for Russian acquiescence to U.S.-inspired loosening of the ABM Treaty.

The ABM Treaty and Star Wars

The Anti-Ballistic Missile (ABM) Treaty, signed in 1972, was part of SALT I. It was a watershed in strategic doctrine in that both sides essentially pledged themselves to mutually ensured destruction: an agreement that nuclear deterrence between the United States and the USSR would be based on the mutual vulnerability of each state. Although both sides have continued to abide by this treaty, it is under attack, especially by U.S. plans to develop, test, and deploy a form of Ballistic Missile Defense (BMD), or "Star Wars" (initially designated by the Reagan administration as the Strategic Defense Initiative, or SDI).

Initially proposed as a "defensive" shield against Soviet nuclear missiles, a BMD system has been touted post-Cold War as offering possible protection against a terrorist attack, or one launched by a fledgling nuclear state, such as North Korea. Critics question whether it could work, given that offensive countermeasures appear to have the advantage, especially since only a small number of warheads would have to penetrate such a BMD. In addition, a system of this sort runs the risk of making other nuclear powers nervous, since it could conceivably be paired with a U.S. first strike, as follows: Suppose that a surprise U.S. attack eliminated a large proportion of another country's missiles. A BMD system, incapable of defending against a first strike, could in theory nonetheless be effective against the "ragged retaliation" that would take place if the victim sought to strike back with its limited forces that would be remaining. The result of such a "defensive" system— even one of limited effectiveness—could therefore be to encourage its possessor to strike first, confident that the victim could not retaliate. Hence, a system described as defensive could also appear offensive, and therefore very provocative, to a potential opponent, such as China, for instance, which fields between one and two dozen ICBMs and might well feel a need to increase its arsenal in response.

Euromissiles

The so-called Euromissiles provide a notable example of limited but genuine nuclear disarmament. They were a very contentious issue during the period 1979–1989, beginning with the Soviet deployment of medium-range, SS-20 missiles in Europe, which NATO insisted on matching with Pershing II and ground-launched cruise missiles of its own. The ensuing situation was potentially dangerous, since the Euromissiles on both sides were not only highly accurate but had very short flight times, which threatened to precipitate a "hair-trigger" pattern of mutual anxiety. Fortunately, the Euromissile crisis was resolved when both sides accepted the "zero option," whereby the INF (Intermediate Range Nuclear Forces) Treaty eliminated this entire class of nuclear weapons.

Future Prospects

Most of the above events occurred within the context of the Cold War, a period of antagonism, distrust, and overt geopolitical, military, and ideological competition between the United States and the former Soviet Union. With this time past, there would seem to be immense opportunity to capitalize on history and achieve genuine abolition of nuclear weapons. Admittedly, the "genie cannot be put back in the bottle"—that is, the knowledge of how to make nuclear weapons cannot be undone—but the weapons themselves can be deconstructed. Numerous specific suggestions have been made for *vertical disarmament*, dramatic reductions in nuclear stockpiles worldwide, as well as for *horizontal disarmament*, the physical separation of warhead and missile components so that no country could quickly make use of whatever weaponry they may retain. With long-range (satellite) as well as on-site verification, there is no question that such developments are technically feasible; lacking is political will.

Ironically, at a time when it is most attainable, the future of nuclear disarmament is very much at risk. On the positive side, the total number of deployed warheads in the combined Russian and American nuclear arsenals has declined significantly from a peak of around 65,000 in 1985 to about 18,000 in 2000 (with another 16,000 in storage). Yet after signing the START II Treaty in January 1993, formal negotiations on START III had not even begun by the early 21st century. In addition, the collapse of the Soviet Union generated major concerns about the control of nuclear weapons and materials in Russia and in other parts of the former Soviet Union (the problem of "loose nukes"). Most ominously, perhaps, political and military developments in the two countries regularly threaten to halt, if not reverse, progress made in nuclear disarmament.

A major contributor has been pursuit by the United States of a series of policies that threaten to undermine American-Russian relations. These include the expansion of the NATO alliance, including former Soviet allies (such as Poland, Hungary, and the Czech Republic), which move NATO's borders closer to Russia and look offensive (at least to wary Russian nationalists), movement toward deployment of theater and national missile defenses (along with substantial support among congressional conservatives for scrapping the ABM Treaty), insistence on preserving the capability to rapidly expand the U.S. strategic nuclear arsenal, aggressively sponsoring research on new nuclear weapons designs, along with the U.S. Senate's refusal to ratify the CTBT. During the 1990s, moreover, the U.S. government was notably lacking in creativity or even, perhaps, interest in pursuing nuclear disarmament, a hesitation that has long bedeviled all governments: fears of being considered "soft on defense." To make matters worse, the United States continues its military spending at close to Cold War levels.

For Russia, collapse of its conventional military power has led the armed forces to rely more on nuclear weapons in defense planning (seeking to obtain "more bang for the buck" or, we might say, "more rubble for the ruble"). This has led to Russia renouncing the previous Soviet policy of no-first-use of nuclear weapons. Since the USSR's collapse, the Russian parliament has been dominated by political forces that are highly skeptical of American intentions and of further disarmament initiatives. It has been preoccupied with economic stagnation, political infighting and corruption, and military challenges by would-be secessionist provinces, such as Chechnya. Uncooperative American military policies, meanwhile, have provided Russian hard-liners with further justification for resisting nuclear disarmament, and even arms control.

Nonetheless, numerous opportunities exist to take advantage of the (possibly fleeting) window of opportunity opened by the collapse of Soviet communism. These include a "consolidate-monitor-dismantle" initiative that would encompass the thousands of tactical nuclear warheads (not covered by the strategic arms control reduction process) and place them under secure control, in preparation for dismantlement. U.S. and Russian forces could take thousands of strategic nuclear warheads off hair-trigger alert, which would reduce the risks of accidental nuclear war. A START III Treaty could be promptly negotiated and rapidly brought into force, establishing levels of around 1,000–1,500 strategic nuclear warheads (still many more than are needed for any reasonable degree of deterrence). Retraining and alternative employment opportunities can be made available for nuclear weapons designers, to ensure that their expertise is not diverted to nuclear "wannabe" nations. Overall, the United States should recognize that nuclear security can be most effectively achieved by bilateral and multilateral initiatives designed to reduce and dismantle threatening weapons, rather than insisting on "going it alone."

Putting this more strongly: The end of the Cold War and the collapse of the Soviet Union has given humanity the opportunity to free the world of nuclear weapons and other weapons of mass destruction, if not literally and for all time, then at least practically, as realistic threats to national and species survival.

Some Conventional Arms

Exporting Weapons

The United States is without question the major purveyor of arms to other countries of the world, supplying, for example, approximately 58% of the world's weaponry from 1992 to 1996. A proposed modification would involve adoption of a legislatively mandated code of conduct governing U.S. arms transfers, requiring that arms would be made available only to regimes that are democratic, that respect human rights, that are not engaged in aggressive military policies, and that make their military plans and activities "transparent," that is, available for public scrutiny. This goal is not unreasonable or beyond reach; it would limit the likelihood of possible tragedies such as the use of U.S.-supplied weapons in the slaughter of East Timorese by the Indonesian government, as well as other situations, such as in Iraq and Somalia, in which U.S. military assistance "boomeranged" and provided technology and training that were used against U.S. and UN peacekeepers.

U.S. secretary of state Madeleine Albright, in a September 1998 speech at the United Nations, admitted that arms exporting states "bear some responsibility" for trade that "fuels conflict, fortifies extremism and destabilizes entire regions." President Clinton made history in 1999 when he apologized for the U.S. role in training and arming Guatemalan troops who committed acts of genocide against the indigenous population. It is controversial and unresolved whether, or to what extent, U.S. or UN forces should become involved in cases of within-country genocide or "ethnic cleansing." At the same time, it should be an easier decision for countries such as the United States to limit their own culpability by refusing to provide weapons and training to regimes likely to engage in such outrages.

Prohibition of Land Mines

There are more than 100 million antipersonnel land mines lurking underground in over 40 countries, notably in Cambodia, Angola, Mozambique, Bosnia, and Afghanistan. Hundreds of thousands of persons—most of them civilians, especially farmers working their fields or children at play—are maimed or killed by these devices every year. International outrage, not surprisingly, has been growing. In 1997, the International Campaign to Ban Landmines and its coordinator, Jody Williams, were awarded the Nobel Peace Prize for their efforts toward the elimination of this scourge. More than 100 countries gathered in Ottawa, Canada, to sign a comprehensive land mine treaty that would prohibit the "use, stockpile, production, and transfer of anti-personnel landmines." This treaty entered into force in 1999, by which point it had been signed by 135 countries, and ratified by 71. Although the United States has promised increased funding for humanitarian demining, it has refused to sign the Ottawa Treaty, maintaining that military necessity requires the United States to retain the option of using land mines on the border separating North and South Korea.

U.S. policies concerning land mines include an export moratorium, planned destruction of its 3 million "dumb" antipersonnel mines, renunciation of using such mines except in Korea, and the claim that no more antipersonnel mines will be used even in Korea after 2006—with this loophole: Exempted from the above prohibition is the use of "mixed mine systems" containing *both* antitank and antipersonnel mines. According to U.S. policy, these systems can and will be used indefinitely.

Pitfalls of Arms Control Agreements _____

It sometimes seems as though the threat of weaponry can be ended via treaties and appropriate negotiated agreements. But even if we leave aside the problem of underlying hostilities, there are numerous pitfalls lurking along the road of negotiated arms control.

Numerical Obsessions

Arms reduction treaties usually involve things that can be counted, which in turn gives inordinate importance to quantitative as opposed to qualitative factors. For example, given the current levels of destruction available to nuclear powers, the actual count of warheads or missiles can be misleading and distracting, especially since asymmetries in force structures make it possible for partisans on either side to point selectively to certain measures, thereby making it seem that their side in unacceptably behind. By focusing on the need for nuclear parity, excessive "bean counting" tends to discourage interest in "sufficiency," in which states would assess what they need for their legitimate defense needs, rather than seeking to match their opponent in every category.

Slowness

Arms control negotiations are almost always slow. It took three years for the United States and the USSR to agree on SALT I, seven years for SALT II, and another seven years for the INF Treaty. Moreover, for reasons of pride and ideology, new presidents tend to discard what their predecessors have accomplished, insisting on starting afresh. It is also inherently more difficult to reach the political consensus needed to ban or even restrict a weapon than to meet the engineering requirements of designing and constructing it; as a result, by the time negotiators wind up banning a weapon, it may be virtually obsolete, while new weapons are being planned and produced. (On the other hand, it is worth pointing out that when political will is present, agreements can be made quickly; the PTBT, for example, was negotiated in a matter of weeks.)

"Leveling Up"

It is easy to decide to build more weapons; such decisions are *unilateral*. It is much harder, by contrast, to decide on a *bilateral* or *multilateral* halt, or even a ceiling, because such decisions must be made in concert with others. There is also a reluctance to destroy expensive weapons that have already been deployed. So rather than accept a limit below one's current level, negotiators are inclined to accept—as a limit for all—the level of the side that is currently higher. Often treaty limits are even set above those of either side, whereupon they become production goals, stimulating an arms race rather than damping it.

The "Balloon Principle"

When some weapon is constrained, states tend to put effort into another system, one that is unconstrained and that then expands, like a balloon that is squeezed in one place and pops out somewhere else. For example, after the PTBT was ratified, the rate of nuclear testing (underground) actually *increased*. After SALT I, which did not restrict the number of warheads per missile, there was a great increase in the strategic arsenals of each side, as both sides proceeded with MIRVing.

Bargaining Chips

It is widely held that bargaining should proceed from a "position of strength," that is, lots of weapons. At a time, for example, when even its advocates agreed that the MX missile was not supportable on its merits, it was promoted as a way of buttressing the ongoing strategic arms negotiations. We have seen that weapons, originally justified as bargaining chips, tend to be retained when the negotiations fail. It has also been suggested that governments sometimes begin negotiations so as to build support for the procurement of weapons, ostensibly as bargaining chips.

National governments also sometimes find themselves having to bargain with their own military-industrial leadership. For example, the vast increase in underground testing that followed the PTBT took place because President Kennedy had to agree to it in order to garner support within the Joint Chiefs of Staff for the PTBT. Similarly, President Nixon purchased military support for SALT I by supporting a vigorous MIRVing program, and President Carter had to support the Trident and MX programs in return for SALT II, which has not been ratified.

Linkage

Arms control skeptics often claim that agreements should be held hostage —"linked"—to other aspects of the other side's behavior. This suggests that such treaties are favors extended to the other side, whereas in fact if they are of any value, it is as positive-sum game developments that are beneficial to both.

Moreover, as President Kennedy pointed out,

A sea wall is not needed when the seas are calm. Sound disarmament agreements, deeply rooted in mankind's mutual interest in survival, must serve as a bulwark against the tidal waves of war and its destructiveness. Let no one, then, say that we cannot arrive at such agreements in troubled times, for it is then that their need is greatest.[2]

Legitimating an Arms Race

Only rarely (e.g., the INF Treaty, the ABM Treaty) have treaties actually stopped serious weapons competition. More often, they have gone along with continuing trends and have in effect ratified arms races themselves, providing government leaders with a touchstone by which they can assure their citizenry that even escalations in weaponry are consistent with treaty obligations. The presence of arms control agreements sometimes allows leaders to claim that they are pursuing an end to a given arms race, while actually managing and channeling it.

False Confidence

In the 21st century, nuclear weapons have become so unpopular in many places that their very legitimacy has once again been seriously questioned. In the past, however, popular revulsion at such weapons came largely from signs that governments were not sincere about trying to restrain or abolish them. By providing occasional arms control "successes," all the while ensuring that weapons regimes remain fundamentally undiminished, governments may succeed in quieting public opposition while essentially maintaining a dangerous status quo. With the ratification of the PTBT in 1963, for example, the upsurge in antinuclear sentiment largely subsided, although the arms race continued, and in fact increased, with nuclear testing having gone out of sight and, for most people, out of mind. Hawks, by contrast, tend to worry that arms control agreements produce a false sense of confidence in the other direction.

The Paradox of Small Arsenals

By the peculiar logic of deterrence, there can be a kind of safety inherent in relatively large nuclear arsenals. This is because when a country has many potential weapons available for retaliation, an opponent would likely be especially reluctant to initiate a first strike, knowing that some of the victim's weapons would likely survive and be available for devastating retaliation. At the same time, countries with a large arsenal are likely to be aware of such reluctance by would-be attackers, and therefore less nervous and hence less likely to misinterpret false alarms or crisis conditions as indicating an imminent attack against themselves. This might otherwise engender a "preemptive" response to an attack that has not begun!

By the same logic, it has been argued that reductions in nuclear arsenals below a certain (unspecified) level could actually diminish stability, since a country with, for example, just a handful of nuclear weapons might be a tempting target by an opponent, especially during a tense political or military confrontation. At the same time, possessors of such a potentially vulnerable arsenal, knowing its vulnerability, might be inclined to "use them or lose them." Accordingly, some strategic analysts claim that the nuclear standoff between India and Pakistan—each side having small numbers of nuclear weapons—may be less stable and more dangerous than the Cold War balance of terror between the United States and the USSR.

Benefits of Arms Control Agreements

We live in a real world, not an ideal one. Just as this incontrovertible fact is regularly used to justify the presence of armed forces, it also explains efforts to control them. There are enormous risks in permitting uncontrolled arms races; hence, it seems essential that non-zero-sum game solutions to humanity's shared dilemma be identified and acted on, since nothing less than survival is at stake.

In this regard, it appears that arms control and continued efforts at disarmament have a crucial role to play. Good agreements can inhibit wasteful competition (e.g., the ABM Treaty), reduce worldwide pollution (the PTBT), diminish the chances of accidental war (the hot line), and even eliminate dangerous weapons (the INF Treaty). In his Farewell Address, President Eisenhower emphasized that

> the conference table, though scarred by many past frustrations, cannot be abandoned for the certain agony of the battlefield. Disarmament, with mutual honor and confidence, is a continuing imperative. Together we must learn how to compose differences not with arms but with intellect and decent purpose.[3]

Verification

Successful arms control (and disarmament as well) must rely on something more than trust. Specifically, compliance must be verifiable. During the Cold War, the Soviet Union, with its traditionally closed and secretive society, was consistently averse to on-site verification, which it long considered unacceptably intrusive and a license for spying. So, just as the Soviets once cynically pressed for widespread (and unverifiable) disarmament schemes, the United States—no less cynically—would insist on ironclad verification procedures that they knew would be vetoed by the Soviets. These issues are no longer likely to block agreements, and in fact, Russia has in many ways been more open to U.S. arms inspectors than have some U.S. military contractors, which periodically object to what they fear might be industrial espionage. At the same time, verification has on occasion been hotly contested, notably in the aftermath of the Gulf War, with Iraq's resentment of UN arms inspectors and its periodic refusal to permit on-site monitoring of Iraqi weapons facilities. On several occasions, indeed, this issue has precipitated bombing of Iraq and has also delayed the lifting of UN economic sanctions.

Verification is not simply an excuse for avoiding arms control or disarmament, however; it is also important in its own right. No one can seriously expect that either side will tolerate substantial cuts in its own arsenal unless it can be confident that the other side is abiding by its share of such agreements. It is reasonable to assume that certain reductions—even if made unilaterally—will not diminish a state's security. So long as hundreds of warheads remain in a country's arsenals, it would not matter if the other side squirrels away a few hundred more than are called for in any build-down agreement. Even in this case, however, verification may well be helpful, and perhaps necessary, if the reductions are to be acceptable to the hard-liners on each side.

Techniques and Prospects

A useful distinction can be made between "absolute" or legalistic verification, by which *any* violation will be detected with absolute certainty, and "functional" or realistic verification, according to which some violations may be missed, but any that could be of strategic significance will be detected. With the advent of spy satellites and other detection techniques, functional verification can generally be ensured; insistence on absolute verification, by contrast, is tantamount to insistence on no agreement at all.

A variety of verification procedures are available. Most treaties provide for verification by "national technical means," which refers to a variety of long-range reconnaissance procedures that do not directly intrude on the side being monitored. Of these, satellite observation is the most powerful and important; increased sensitivity and sophistication of satellite monitoring have led some enthusiasts to claim that U.S. spy satellites such as the "Big Bird" can read the license plates in downtown Baghdad. Although this may be an exaggeration, technical advances currently permit ground resolution of as little as 12 inches. Infrared imaging can even penetrate cloud cover and detect changes in work patterns inside factories.

Governments have additional sources of information. Radar, for example, provides for accurate detection, tracking, and monitoring of missile tests, thereby assessing compliance with treaty restrictions. Seismic instrumentation has become so sensitive that nuclear explosions as small as 1 kiloton reportedly can be distinguished from natural events such as earthquakes; this appears to hold even for so-called decoupled explosions, detonated in sites designed to absorb the blast effects. An array of tamper-proof black boxes, installed within national territory, can provide a very high level of reassurance that no one is conducting nuclear tests. National technical means of verification also include the capability of electronic signal interception, whereby countries listen to the communications of the other. Taken together, these various capabilities are important not only in the information they provide but also in their potentially deterrent effect. Thus, no country can be confident that its activities will not be detected by others, after which they would be free to renounce its adherence to any violated agreement.

There have been failures in verification, however. For example, it is said that at the end of the Gulf War, when Iraqi weapons installations were forcibly inspected, UN teams were surprised at Iraq's progress in constructing nuclear warheads. But as a general rule, verification of military *capabilities* has been remarkably reliable; breakdowns, when they have occurred, have more commonly been in a "softer" area, notably political *intentions*. The West was caught off guard, for example, by the rapidity of the Soviet Union's disintegration, by the rampage of Hutus against Tutsis in Rwanda, and by Serbian ferocity toward Kosovar Albanians.

We may also assume that the current technical verification regime—impressive as it may be—represents only a small fraction of the information potentially available to interested parties. Thus, in a substantially disarmed world, it is likely that a large fraction of military budgets, now devoted to the procuring of weapons and the maintenance of large armed forces, would instead be devoted to improved verification capabilities. Detection would replace destruction as the primary goal of the "national security" apparatus of all major powers. With such motivation, verification procedures will, if anything, become more precise and reliable. It must be emphasized, however, that ultimately, adherence to arms control or disarmament treaties must be in the real, long-term interests of the countries involved. Insofar as that is true, and recognized as such, the temptation to cheat will be greatly diminished.

Economic Conversion

The economy of the United States is heavily militarized, as was that of the Soviet Union; indeed, the ruinous economic pressure of keeping up in the arms race appears to have contributed substantially to the Soviet Union's disintegration. The economies of other states, such as Israel, Iraq, and North and South Korea, are even more heavily oriented toward military expenditures and production, as measured by the proportion of GNP devoted to military purposes. Converting such economies from military to civilian functions poses special challenges as well as opportunities. It had been expected in most liberal political circles that the end of the Cold War would generate a substantial "peace dividend," as military spending was redirected toward the civilian economy, with resulting benefits in terms of meeting unmet social needs (domestically and around the world), paying off the national debt, and/or significant tax cuts. By and large, this has not happened. It seems clear that economic conversion—from a military to a civilian economy—deserves a place in the U.S. national agenda, both to generate political pressure for the process itself and to ensure that it is carried out intelligently.

Challenges

Large military expenditures tend to create their own constituency, which in turn makes disarmament—and even arms control—politically difficult. When big corporations and their many employees make large amounts of money based on current market demands, the result is powerful pressure to continue business as usual, even if the military/strategic justification for just "business" has evaporated! Moreover, whole regions now rely on military spending, and many U.S. politicians attribute their election and reelection to success in bringing some of the Pentagon "bacon" home to their constituents. Disarmament—even if it is partial—can thus appear to threaten the livelihoods of many people. Not only do economic factors make disarmament politically unattractive to many government leaders (in other countries as well as the United States), but the reality is that large-scale demilitarization of an economy would in fact require a major overhaul, in some cases generating real hardships, at least until funds and priorities are rearranged. Thus, the closing of only a relatively small number of military bases in the United States during the 1990s generated heated political opposition.

Opportunities

On the other hand, military spending is, on balance, more hurtful than helpful to a national economy. In the long run—and aside from its major benefit in diminishing the likelihood of war—restructuring from a military to a civilian economy offers the promise of (1) reducing inflationary pressures, (2) increasing employment, (3) lowering the deficit, (4) improving productivity, and (5) freeing up resources—human as well as financial—for needed social programs. While pessimists may choose to bemoan the problems posed by economic conversion, it is equally valid—if anything, more so—to consider economic conversion as a wonderful opportunity yielding a potential "disarmament dividend"—which provides yet another reason for moving toward a demilitarization of security.

Economic conversion has been achieved in the past. Following World War II, the U.S. military budget plummeted from nearly $76 billion in 1945 to less than $19 billion in 1947. As part of this postwar demobilization, the armed forces went from 11 million troops in 1945 to 2 million two years later, yet unemployment never exceeded 4% during this period.

Skeptics point out, however, that successful post-World War II conversion in the United States was based in part on conditions that would not be repeated in the event of comparable conversion today. For example, many women who had been recruited into the workforce in the early 1940s returned home to raise families, thus making room in the workforce for demobilized servicemen. In addition, a large pent-up consumer demand accumulated during the war years, when new automobiles, for example, were not produced, since factories had retooled to make jeeps, tanks, and military trucks. On the other hand, the U.S. economy is far larger today than it was in 1945, and the number of people to be "demobilized" is far smaller. If substantial government expenditures are ever redirected away from the military, these funds will not simply evaporate; rather, they will be available for use in other areas (except for the proportion left unspent, to diminish the federal deficit). And such expenditures actually produce more jobs, per dollar spent, than does military spending, since the latter is "capital intensive," using large amounts of money to employ relatively few people. Moreover, national and global needs are immense and include funding for education, health, renewable energy, pollution abatement, housing, environmental protection, and public transportation; rebuilding roads, bridges, and other structures; retooling the industrial base for the production of affordable consumer goods; reconstructing our blighted cities; reforestation and other types of land reclamation; providing drug treatment and rehabilitation; establishing more humane penal institutions, and so on. Literally billions of dollars and millions of workers would be released as resources were redirected from destructive to constructive purposes. It would seem to indicate a stunted imagination to consider this a calamity to be avoided rather than an opportunity to be embraced.

Conversion Planning

Estimates show that most people employed in today's military-industrial complex could be retrained for productive work in the domestic economy within about six months. Mid- and upper-level managers and engineers would require somewhat more extensive retraining, since they have generally specialized in making narrowly focused, cost-insensitive products, rigidly defined within certain bureaucratic guidelines. In short, they are accustomed to pleasing the Pentagon, not the public. But there is no reason to think that this cannot be changed. The United States already maintains an Office of Economic Adjustment, concerned with helping local communities mitigate the effects of plant and base closings. Such work could readily be expended on a national scale. Some industries and labor unions have (in most cases begrudgingly) begun making contingency plans for converting their activities to domestic and civilian purposes, although peace groups have thus far done the bulk of the work. Careful conversion planning could yield several payoffs: (1) In the event of a transition from a military to a genuinely nonmilitary economy, dislocation would be greatly reduced, and (2) the existence of realistic, mutually beneficial plans would make the disarmament process itself more feasible politically (on the other hand, this helps explain the reluctance of government, industry, and some communities to engage in such planning!).

Economic conversion is especially important as a practical nuts-and-bolts consequence of disarmament, as well as a necessary prerequisite for real movement in that direction. It is discouraging, however, that despite the immense opportunities afforded by the end of the Cold War, the U.S. government remains generally resistant to the concept of economic conversion and averse to planning for it. It seems likely that a substantial change of "mind-set" will be needed.

Graduated and Reciprocated Initiatives in Tension Reduction

In his book *An Alternative to War or Surrender*, psychologist Charles Osgood proposed a practical strategy whereby states might achieve substantial progress in reducing tensions as well as the level of armaments. He called it GRIT, for "graduated and reciprocated initiatives in tension reduction." The idea is quite simple: Just as individuals, or states, increase tension by a series of unilateral escalations, it is also possible to proceed down the tension ladder by a series of unilateral initiatives in the opposite direction. Arguments between two people, for example, often escalate through a series of annoyances, insults, and affronts to each other, with increasing distrust and animosity. However, people also often "make up," and this generally requires a reaching out from one to the other; that is, it begins with some sort of unilateral initiative.

Comparable initiatives can be applied to international affairs, quite possibly with comparable results. These initiatives are not intended as appeasement. Rather, Osgood points out that when individuals, or states, make conciliatory gestures, substantial pressure builds up in favor of matching gestures from the other side. It is possible—even likely—that the initial phases of GRIT will encounter skepticism. Over time, however, assuming that the initiatives are maintained and (better yet) intensified, powerful psychological and social pressure build up to reciprocate, which in turn contributes to a process of mutual tension reduction that can be as real as the process of tension escalation that preceded it. Osgood recommends that a national policy of GRIT follow certain basic rules:

1. Each step should be small, so that the initiator does not at any time run risks with its military security.

2. Each initiative should be taken in the interest of reducing armaments and reducing tension; initiatives should not be accompanied by threats or efforts at coercion, which tend to harden the opposition.

3. Each initiative should be publicly announced and carried out with maximum publicity.

4. Each action should be real and meaningful, not something that would be done in any case, like retiring an obsolete weapons system or withdrawing from territory already known to be indefensible.

5. The GRIT initiatives should be continued, and if necessary repeated several times, in the hope of generating a like response. If it fails, a GRIT strategy could always be abandoned, with little loss and no diminution to national security. ·

The United States and the USSR apparently used a GRIT-like strategy of progressive mutual disengagement to defuse a highly tense situation during the Berlin crisis, when U.S. and Soviet tanks were literally facing each other. President John F. Kennedy apparently was aware of GRIT in the summer of 1963, when he initiated a series of outreaches to the USSR, beginning with the announcement that the United States would stop atmospheric testing, and not resume unless the Soviets did so first. Premier Khrushchev responded positively and announced a decrease in production rates for strategic bombers. Numerous tit-for-tat benefits followed, including the hot line agreement, a large wheat sale, the PTBT, and overall, a dramatic lowering of East-West tensions. (The Soviets liked the interaction so much that they coined their own phrase to describe it, "the policy of mutual example.")

There are many possibilities for GRIT-ty initiatives in today's world. If there is any benefit to being overarmed, perhaps it is that it provides an opportunity for all parties to initiate substantial reductions—in both armaments and tension—without diminishing security. GRIT could also be usefully applied to the many conflicts between adjacent rivals, such as India and Pakistan, Israel and its Arab neighbors, and so forth. In such cases, it appears that the limiting factor is less likely to be national security as such than local public opinion. This makes peace-related education and outreach all the more important.

A Final Note on Disarmament and Arms Control _____

In 1981, when he received the Albert Einstein Peace Prize, diplomat/historian George F. Kennan assessed the nuclear arms race as follows:

> We have gone on piling weapon upon weapon, missile upon missile, new levels of destructiveness upon old ones. We have done this helplessly, almost involuntarily: like the victims of some sort of hypnotism, like men in a dream, like lemmings heading for the sea, like the children of Hamlin marching blindly along behind their Pied Piper. And

the result is that today we have achieved . . . in the creation of these devices and their means of delivery, levels of redundancy of such grotesque dimensions as to defy rational understanding.[4]

Kennan concluded as follows:

We are confronted here, my friends, with two courses. At the end of the one lies hope—faint hope, if you will, uncertain hope, hope surrounded with dangers, if you insist. At the end of the other lies, so far as I am able to see, no hope at all. Can there be—in the light of our duty not just to ourselves (for we are all going to die sooner or later) but of our duty to our own kind, our duty to the continuity of the generations, our duty to the great experiment of civilized life on this rare and rich and marvelous planet—can there be, in the light of these claims on our loyalty, any question as to which course we should adopt?

Disarmament is a long-standing, traditional value, to which—like Mom and apple pie—many people pay lip service, yet efforts at disarmament typically bog down when it comes to the specifics of implementation. The devil, it is often said, is in the details. Nonetheless, it should be remembered that human beings have used weapons and war in efforts to resolve their differences for thousands of years; it is not reasonable to expect that such ancient habits will be overturned in a matter of years, or even decades. And whereas the goal of absolute disarmament may seem unlikely, short-term disappointment in this respect should not blind us to the benefits to be obtained from various accomplishments along the way. Most of all, we must recognize that disarmament is a *process*, not an *event*. It is more a verb than a noun, more a way of progressing than a finished and concluding masterpiece to be unveiled to the admiring world with a grand *"voila!"* Like perfect grace, disarmament may never be altogether achieved, but that doesn't mean that it is not a valid goal, or even a route toward possible salvation.

Notes

1. Albert Einstein. 1960. *Einstein On Peace*. New York: Meridian.

2. Quoted in Alan Geyer. 1982. *The Idea of Disarmament*. Glencoe, IL: Brethren.

3. Dwight D. Eisenhower. 1961. *Peace With Justice: Selected Addresses*. New York: Columbia University Press.

4. George F. Kennan. 1981. *The Nuclear Delusion*. New York: Pantheon.

13 International Organizations

Nothing will ever be attempted if all possible objections must be first overcome.

—Samuel Johnson

Conflict situations can be resolved in two basic ways, contrasting options that peace researcher Kenneth Boulding called "associative" and "disassociative." The latter involves reliance on military strength and political separation, based on the notion that "good fences make good neighbors." Associative solutions, on the other hand, are efforts to tear down walls, to join together. As we have seen, prominent among the causes of war —as well as a major obstacle to disarmament and even arms control—is the existence of feisty, sovereign states that are by definition disassociative relative to each other. In this chapter, we examine deeply associative solutions that go beyond the current state-centered world system and look toward larger patterns of integration: international law, world government, and ethical and religious norms. In the current chapter, we consider middle-road associative possibilities, ways of ameliorating—although not eliminating— the often-troublesome role of states. We start with the League of Nations, since its failures have much to teach us.

The League of Nations

Most European citizens and leaders alike were shocked and sobered by World War I. One result was the creation of the League of Nations, a notable, although unsuccessful, effort to transcend some of the problems of state sovereignty and to produce a war-free world. World War I was the greatest and most disastrous war in the Western world up to that time, and the old balance of power system was widely blamed for that conflict; hence, balance of power as a way of maintaining the peace was temporarily discredited in its aftermath. President Woodrow Wilson argued cogently that wars would continue so long as states had to be responsible for their own defense. To prevent states from forming competing groups, each arming and plotting against the other, Wilson urged the establishment of a League of Nations, which all states would join, and which would function by "collective security."

Structure and Function

Under the terms of the league, formally inaugurated in 1920, states retained their sovereignty in domestic affairs and in virtually all foreign dealings as well. However, as part of its covenant (constitution), members pledged to refrain from the use of force against any other state and to submit any disputes to arbitration or an investigation by the league's council. This body was similar to the Security Council of the current United Nations, having the Great Powers as permanent members and a varying number of rotating members; it was to be the league's primary peacekeeping agency. In Article 16 of the League Covenant, signatories pledged that

> should any Member of the League resort to war . . . it shall ipso facto
> [by this fact] be deemed to have committed an act of war against all
> other Members of the League, which hereby undertake immediately to
> subject it to the severance of all trade or financial relations, . . . and the
> prevention of all financial, commercial or personal intercourse between
> the nationals of the Covenant-breaking State and the nationals of any
> other State, whether a Member of the League or not.

In addition, the league's council was authorized to recommend to member states that specific military forces should be raised and employed against the violator. The hope was that by virtue of their membership in the league, all states would obtain an equal measure of security, which in turn would remove any temptation for alliances. Any aggressor would also be deterred by the prospect of having to face the collective might of all other league members. The consequence of aggression having been made clear, it was further expected that secret diplomacy would be unnecessary, to be replaced by "open covenants openly arrived at."

Although President Wilson was the intellectual father of the League of Nations, the United States never joined, because the U.S. Senate refused to ratify league membership. In reaction to the carnage of World War I, isolationist sentiment in the United States prevailed over internationalism. Germany did not join until 1926, and it withdrew in 1933, when the league refused to lift the arms restrictions imposed earlier on Germany by the Treaty of Versailles. The Soviet Union did not join until 1934, by which time the league's authority had already been severely undermined by its inability to act decisively following Japan's conquest of Manchuria.

Early Challenges

During its first decade, the League of Nations functioned reasonably well, largely because there were no world-shaking crises. It successfully ended fighting, for example, between Bulgaria and Greece in 1925, and between Lithuania and Poland in 1927. In 1932, Bolivia and Paraguay went to war over a disputed border region known as the Gran Chaco; an arms embargo against both states, organized by the league, contributed—although not decisively—to resolution of that conflict. Later, however, when disputes arose involving powerful states, the league proved ineffective.

Throughout the 1920s, Manchuria had been nominally under Chinese political control, but in fact it was economically exploited by Japan, which also controlled Korea. In response to growing militant nationalist sentiment, Japan invaded Manchuria in 1931, using a small railroad explosion (most likely initiated by the Japanese themselves) as pretext. The League of Nations protested, asking Japan to withdraw, but the Japanese ignored the league's objections and proceeded to set up the puppet state of "Manchukuo." The league also set up the Commission of Inquiry, which took nearly one and one-half years to issue a final report (in 1933) that found Japan clearly guilty of unprovoked and unjustified aggression. However, the collective security provisions of the league's covenant were not invoked, because of the legal nicety that Japan had not formally declared war! The only result, therefore, was moral condemnation and league refusal to recognize the legitimacy of the conquest; for example, currency and postage stamps from Manchukuo would not be accepted by other states. Japan thereupon withdrew from the League of Nations.

The Abyssinian Crisis

The crisis that led most directly to the collapse of league authority and ultimately, the organization itself, was the Italian invasion of Abyssinia, now Ethiopia. Italy, which already occupied Eritrea (subsequently incorporated into Ethiopia, and more recently an independent state since the early 1990s), had long coveted nearby Ethiopia. Under the fascist dictator Benito Mussolini, Italy nurtured dreams of reestablishing the glory that had been Rome, beginning with colonial conquests in Africa. In 1934, when Italian forces in Eritrea were obviously preparing to invade, Ethiopian king Haile Selassie appealed to the League of Nations for assistance. But no action was taken, since no aggression had yet taken place.

When the Italian invasion actually occurred a year later, the League of Nations immediately condemned Italy as an aggressor and voted to apply a full range of economic sanctions, except for oil importation, which alone would have crippled the Italian war effort. Moreover, the Suez Canal was not closed to Italian shipping, and no military action was taken—or even seriously considered—against Italy. Because neither Japan, Germany, nor the United States belonged to the league, economic sanctions were unavailing; furthermore, by trading with Italy, these states—the United States in particular—could easily have defeated any oil embargo, while also enriching themselves in the process. The overwhelming "community of power" that Wilson had envisioned to oppose any aggressor simply did not materialize. Italy completed its conquest of Ethiopia, and Selassie's 1936 appearance before the League of Nations, as an exile, served to emphasize the failure of that organization.

Postmortem on the League of Nations

It is important to understand why the League of Nations failed, not simply for the sake of history, but because these factors shed light on the difficulties of keeping peace via international cooperation. No single reason can be identified for the league's failure; rather, a series of factors combined to doom it.

Nonsupport From Major States

The league depended on the support of the major states. Whereas it acted effectively in the case of minor conflicts, it was unable to enforce its will against stronger powers. There was no clear-cut international peacekeeping force, and no reliable mechanism for recruiting it if need be. The Soviet Union, through its Pacific forces, might have become involved in the Manchuria invasion, but it was convulsed at the time with Stalin's purges. The United States was not a league member, and never joined. Britain had sufficient naval forces to "project power" into either Manchuria or Ethiopia, but was more concerned with protecting itself from a growing German threat.

U.S. Refusal to Join

The United States never joined the League of Nations. Not only did this deprive the league of U.S. input, such as the possibility of U.S. support for military intervention against an aggressor, it also meant that the United States could serve as "strikebreaker," foiling any attempts at economic sanctions against such an aggressor, even if the league mustered the will to attempt such a response. Eventually, Germany and Japan also left the league, making the prospects of economic sanctions even less credible.

Lack of Interest in Remote Conflicts

For collective security to be successful, all significant participants must agree that "peace is indivisible," that is, that a threat to the peace of any nation—no matter how small or seemingly insignificant—is a threat to themselves. But when conflicts are seen as remote and not significantly affecting the security interests of other states, governments have tradition- ally been hesitant to commit themselves to economic costs—and even more so, to military adventures—that might preserve the peace or restore the status quo ante (the preexisting situation) in some far-off land such as Manchuria or Ethiopia.

Former British prime minister Neville Chamberlain was roundly criti- cized (especially with the advantage of 20/20 hindsight) for having urged Great Britain not to assist Czechoslovakia in its 1938 crisis with Germany over the Sudetenland, maintaining that it was a "quarrel in a faraway coun- try between people of whom we know nothing." And yet, if indifference is dangerous, interventionism is not much beloved either. What in fact are the legitimate boundaries of governmental concern? Or—more narrowly—of national security? The USSR evidently figured in 1956 that its "peace" required a notably unpeaceful intervention in Hungary; ditto for 1968 in Czechoslovakia. In 1962, the United States stayed out of hostilities between India and China, but almost went to nuclear war over Soviet missiles in Cuba and intervened actively (if covertly) in Nicaragua and El Salvador. Where, today, is the real U.S. frontier? Does it extend to the former Yugoslavia, Korea, Indonesia, Congo, Taiwan?

Selfish Collusion

Closely related to the problem of indifference and interventionism is that of selfish collusion. Once states begin acting in what they consider to be their own selfish national interest, systems of collective security begin breaking down. This was most dramatically shown in the case of Italy's invasion of Ethiopia. At that time, Britain and France hoped to obtain an alliance with Mussolini, or at the least, to keep Italy from joining forces with Germany. Several years after the league's inaction in Ethiopia, it was revealed that Britain and especially France had actually conducted secret negotiations with the Italian government, in which they sought to win over Mussolini by promising Italy a free hand in gobbling up Ethiopia. The result? The Italian people became united behind his successful expansionist policies, Mussolini was emboldened to attempt further aggression, and the League of Nations became an international laughing stock, woefully unable to contain the aggression that was eventually unleashed against Britain and France themselves. And Mussolini allied himself with Hitler after all.

Confusion Over the Nature of Aggression

There have long been problems in defining *aggression*. Clearly, the ritual declaration of war is insufficient, as shown by the absurdity of claiming that Japan did not violate the league's covenant in 1931 since it did not technically declare war. One definition frequently employed is "violation of territorial integrity and political independence," but even this leads to difficult and confusing cases. For example, consider the Six-Day War in 1967, when Israel attacked its Arab neighbors. This appears to have been clear-cut Israeli aggression, involving as it did a violation of the territorial integrity of the Egypt's Sinai peninsula, Syria's Golan Heights, and Jordan's proprietorship of Jerusalem. Clearly, Israel "started it." But just prior to the Israeli attack, Egypt's president Nasser had closed an international waterway, the Straits of Tiran, to Israeli shipping, thereby blockading Israel's use of its important port of Aqaba. And such a blockade has itself traditionally been considered an act of war. (For their part, the Egyptians claimed that the straits are in Egyptian territorial waters.) As to the Golan Heights, Israel claimed that this region had been used by Syria to violate Israel's territorial integrity, and Israel also claimed ancient, biblical rights to Jerusalem. Nasser, in turn, had claimed previously that the very existence of the state of Israel is an act of aggression against the Arab peoples.

Some other examples follow. Was it aggression when the United States sent troops into South Vietnam, given that this was at the request of the internationally recognized government there? And what about the Soviet troops sent to Afghanistan, in response to a similar request by the recognized Afghan government? What about the U.S.-sponsored mining of Managua harbor in 1984, which was clearly against the wishes of the legally constituted and recognized Nicaraguan government at the time? Or what about sending military advisers and munitions to revolutionary movements in a foreign country (Angola, Nicaragua, Afghanistan, Cambodia, etc.)?

It is also clear that Serbia did not commit international aggression in Kosovo in 1999, since the latter had long been part of the former. Can a country commit aggression against its own people? What of the Iraqi government's use of poison gas against Kurds (legally, Iraqi citizens), or similar outrages by Turks against Kurds, or Indonesian soldiers against independence-minded East Timorese?

A Brief History of the United Nations

As World War II drew to a close, the victorious allies—once again traumatized by war and disillusioned at the failure of the state system to prevent it—decided once more to establish an international body that would work toward the abolition of war. They also hoped that this new organization, known as the United Nations, would avoid some of the pitfalls that had doomed the League of Nations. The idea developed in part from the Atlantic Charter, signed in 1941 by Winston Churchill and Franklin Roosevelt, by which the two leaders committed themselves to a postwar world with economic cooperation and eventual disarmament. The formal idea of an international organization for preserving world peace was approved by Roosevelt, Churchill, and Stalin during a conference in Tehran in 1943. Specific plans for such an organization were drawn up at the Dumbarton Oaks Conference, outside Washington, in late 1944.

It was agreed that all governments would be welcome, with membership in a large General Assembly, but that primary enforcement power would lie in a Security Council, with the United States, the Soviet Union, Britain, France, and China being permanent members. Finally, in the spring of 1945, delegates from 50 countries met in San Francisco at the United Nations Conference on International Organization, which established a charter for the United Nations. The preamble to that charter reads as follows:

> *We the peoples of the United Nations* determined to save succeeding generations from the scourge of war, which twice in our lifetime has brought untold sorrow to mankind, and to reaffirm faith in fundamental human rights, in the dignity and worth of the human person, in the equal rights of men and women and of nations large and small, and to establish conditions under which justice and respect for the obligations arising from treaties and other sources of international law can be maintained, and to promote social progress and better standards of life in larger freedom, *and for these ends* to practice tolerance and live together in peace with one another as good neighbors, and to unite our strength to maintain international peace and security, and to ensure, by the acceptance of principles and the institution of methods, that armed force shall not be used, save in the common interest, and to employ international machinery for the promotion of the economic and social advancement of all peoples, *have resolved to combine our efforts to accomplish these aims.*

The United Nations first formally convened in 1946, in London; it moved to its present location, by the East River in New York City, in 1952.

The Basic Structure of the United Nations

There are several major differences between the United Nations and its predecessor, the League of Nations. For one, whereas the United States remained aloof from the league, it became a charter member, and in many ways, the most important single actor, in the UN. For another, the United

Nations, unlike the League of Nations, was constituted to have many other important functions beyond those dealing strictly with the avoidance or termination of wars. A branch of the UN, the Economic and Social Council, was established, with many specialized agencies concerned with various economic, educational, health, scientific, and social issues—such as the Food and Agriculture Organization (FAO), the World Health Organization (WHO), the World Bank and International Monetary Fund, UNICEF and UNESCO (to which the United States no longer belongs), as well as lesser-known organizations, such as the International Civil Aviation Organization, the International Telecommunication Union, and the World Meteorological Organization. The major organs of the United Nations and their prime missions are as follows:

- Security Council: Issues of war and peace
- General Assembly: The main parliamentary, budget, and decision-making organ
- Economic and Social Council: Quality of life worldwide
- International Court of Justice (also known as the World Court), located at The Hague, Netherlands: Adjudication of international legal disputes
- Secretariat: Essentially the executive organ of the UN, led by one individual, designated the secretary-general.

The United Nations and the State System

To understand the United Nations and assess its actual and potential contributions to peace, it is important to realize what it is *not*. Thus, it is not a world government, or even an effort at establishing one. It does not offer an alternative to state sovereignty; in fact, the UN was established with a number of guidelines to ensure that, if anything, state sovereignty supersedes it. Accordingly, although the UN often proclaims high-minded goals and resolutions, the decisions and actions taken by the UN are not above the national interests of the states that comprise it. It is not a substitute or cure-all for the current state system; rather, it is in large part a *reflection* of that system; a mirror not a panacea. It is not a solution to problems of personal aggressiveness, poor decision making, nationalism, oppression, or ethnic strife. It did very little to ameliorate or end the Cold War. It is limited to the actions of states, and it can solve only problems that those states want to solve, in ways that are approved by the existing states. Whatever one's disappointments in how it has functioned, it cannot fairly be said that the UN has failed its member states; rather, if there has been failure, it is the states—especially the permanent members of the Security Council—that have failed the UN.

Shortly after the United Nations was founded, it became apparent that the United States and the Soviet Union were not going to cooperate very

much, if at all. In fact, the Cold War quickly began in earnest. In the early
years after the founding of the United Nations, the United States had a number of allies in the General Assembly and was thus able to use the United
Nations to prosecute its side of the Cold War. The USSR, in turn, was isolated and forced to use its veto in the Security Council on numerous occasions. However, UN membership expanded rapidly, due largely to an influx
of newly independent former colonies. In 1946, there were only 55 members
of the UN; by 1960, there were 99, and by 1982, 157. By the late 1950s, the
United States could no longer count on an automatic two thirds majority in
the General Assembly, as most of the new states considered themselves nonaligned, and in 1966, the United States was forced to cast its first veto in the
Security Council. For decades, during which the United States refused to
recognize the Maoist government of mainland China, that country had been
excluded from the United Nations. By 1971, however, a watershed was
reached when—over U.S. objections—mainland China was seated in place
of Taiwan (whose presence as a Security Council member had been something of a farce since 1949). UN security operations had earlier ceased to be
a means whereby the U.S. prosecuted the Cold War, and the UN entered
more clearly into a phase of limited peacekeeping and peacemaking.

Attitudes Toward the United Nations

Many conservatives in the United States have long been uncomfortable
with the United Nations, seeing it as—at minimum—an infringement on
national sovereignty. "Get the U.S. out of the UN," read bumper stickers
and the occasional roadside sign, "and get the UN out of the U.S." As economically developing countries have become a numerical majority in the
UN, right-wing opposition to it has intensified. Annoyance with the organization has been especially fueled by the fact that every state has only one
vote in the General Assembly, no matter how small it may be or how despot-
ically governed. Moreover, the UN General Assembly has voted for numerous resolutions that many Americans have found disagreeable, such as one
stating that Zionism (support for the establishment of Israel) is a "form of
racism," as well as the seating of China. Moreover, the UN tends to embrace
concerns that U.S. conservatives generally oppose, namely, disarmament,
economic and social equality, environmental protection, and women's
rights. And finally, conservatism and nationalism tend to be tightly linked,
and many conservatives oppose any organization, such as the UN, that they
see as threatening the absolute national sovereignty of their country. As a
result, the United States has lagged seriously behind in paying its dues, being
more than $1 billion in arrears throughout the 1990s, and periodically at
risk of losing its vote in the General Assembly as a result.

From a peace studies perspective, the major failing of the United Nations
has been its inability to achieve global disarmament, to prevent wars, and to

end those wars that it could not prevent. On the other hand, the UN offers a vision of superordinate goals: the coming together of sovereign states because of a commitment—albeit sometimes a modest one—to planetary concerns. It may also help legitimize the idea of world government. In the meanwhile, the UN does good work in bettering the social, economic, educational, medical, scientific, environmental, and cultural condition of humanity. This is desirable in itself, and it also helps create conditions more conducive to "positive peace." In addition, the UN has had some (admittedly limited) success in acting directly to make peace and to keep it. Let us turn now to an overview of the UN record in this respect.

Peacemaking Efforts of the United Nations

Hopes for what the United Nations might accomplish have gone through several stages. In the immediate aftermath of World War II, it was hoped that the grand alliance that defeated Germany and Japan would hold together and that the major powers, acting in concert, would fashion a truly functional system of collective security. The Security Council was empowered to identify an aggressor and then to request various member states to provide military force as necessary to enforce the peace. To keep disagreements from escalating and possibly even causing war between them, the permanent members of the Security Council were each given veto power over any such decision: This meant, in effect, that the UN would be paralyzed if any one of its major members opposed a given action. Although this feature has often prevented UN involvement in many cases where it might have been helpful, the Security Council veto has also acted as a "circuit breaker," preventing the system from overloading and possibly blowing itself apart when it faced situations that were especially contentious. As a result, the UN became virtually powerless for resolving disputes in which any of the permanent members feel that they have a high stake. But on the other hand, it has been able to function much longer than its predecessor, the League of Nations, and—especially in issues involving the lesser states—more effectively as well. The UN has been involved in a wide array of armed disputes, and its roles have varied from brokering peace, to active peace*making* (which has sometimes been distressingly close to war fighting) to peacekeeping.

Brokering Peace

Shortly after its founding, a UN-sponsored commission arranged a cease-fire between Indonesian independence fighters and their Dutch colonial occupiers, bringing the combatants together for a peace conference that ultimately approved independence for Indonesia in 1949. Later, in the 1960s, the United Nations arranged for Indonesian sovereignty over West New Guinea

(West Irian). In 1999, the UN supervised elections by which the people of East Timor indicated their overwhelming support for independence from Indonesia (in 1973, Indonesia had replaced Portugal as colonial overlord in East Timor, and subsequent Indonesia repression cost the East Timorese perhaps 200,000 lives). By mid-1999, an armed contingent led by Australia had secured an apparent peace. Although the UN did not prevent war in colonial or postcolonial Indonesia, it did serve as a useful intermediary, and to some extent, a face-saving way for decolonization (probably inevitable in any event) to proceed.

Similarly, the United Nations arranged for several cease-fires during wars between India and Pakistan over Kashmir, in the late 1940s and mid-1960s; the issue itself has never been resolved, and additional India-Pakistan warfare broke out along the "line of control" in Kashmir in 1999, despite UN protestations. The UN has also been involved as an armed intermediary, supervising cease-fires on Cyprus, Angola, Namibia, and Mozambique, among other trouble spots, and monitoring democratic elections in numerous countries, including El Salvador and Cambodia. Although the UN was not formally a belligerent in Bosnia, in Kosovo, or during the Gulf War (military operations in these cases were carried out by the North Atlantic Treaty Organization [NATO], under leadership of the United States), it was called in afterward, to help monitor cease-fires and achieve a degree of subsequent "nation building."

Korea

When World War II ended, Soviet troops occupied Korea north of the 38th parallel, with U.S. troops controlling the South. A UN commission sought unsuccessfully to unite the country. In June 1950, North Korean forces invaded the South, believing they had been provoked, and initially achieved dramatic success, leading to U.S. intervention. Meanwhile, the Security Council identified the North as the aggressor and voted for UN members to send troops to assist the South, designating the U.S. military leadership as commanding UN forces in Korea. This vote occurred because the Soviet delegation was boycotting Security Council meetings to protest the UN refusal to seat a delegation from mainland China, which had recently replaced the Nationalist Chinese government after a long and bloody civil war. Hence, the Soviets were unable to veto Security Council proceedings.

Although 16 UN members sent troops and 41 sent supplies during the ensuing Korean War, the United States contributed over 95% of both supplies and troops, as well as virtually all the commanders and major decisions. In fact, the so-called police action in Korea by UN forces was essentially a ratification by the United Nations of a military policy that the United States had already initiated unilaterally. When the Chinese then entered the Korean conflict in October 1950, the Security Council met to discuss further action, but by that time, the Soviet delegate had returned and vetoed any proposed military response. The United States reacted by taking up the matter in the General Assembly, which passed the "Uniting for Peace" Resolution, stating that when the Security Council was unable to act in repelling armed aggression, the General Assembly had the right to call on member states to do so. The USSR denounced this move as a subversion of the Security Council's powers, but the UN, by this strategy, continued its active involvement in the Korean War until China and the United Nations (really, the United States) signed a cease-fire agreement in 1953. No peace treaty has yet been signed.

In the case of Korea, the United Nations was in a sense functioning close to what the original designers of the world organization had in mind, except for the fact that it was largely acting on behalf of one superpower (the United States) and against the interests of another (the USSR). This occurred in part because of the Soviet tactical error in boycotting Security Council proceedings, and because many governments feared that failure to act on North Korea's invasion of the South would doom the UN to irrelevance, like the League of Nations before it.

The Congo

After 55 years of Belgian rule, the Congo (subsequently Zaire, and then the Democratic Republic of the Congo) became independent in 1960. However, Belgium had done virtually nothing to establish a well-trained and well-educated indigenous civil service. With Belgian withdrawal, chaos ensued. Belgian troops then returned, ostensibly to keep order, but in the opinion of many, to reclaim their colonial hold on the country. Meanwhile, stability in the Congo—and in much of the rest of central Africa—was further threatened by the attempted secession of mineral-rich Katanga Province, which also received assistance from European mercenaries. At the request of the Congolese leadership (who themselves were bitterly divided on most issues), the Security Council sent UN forces to the Congo.

At its peak, the Congo operation was a substantial military commitment, totaling 20,000 men and also fighter aircraft. The Soviet Union soon considered that the United Nations was aiding right-wing forces and vetoed subsequent UN actions in the Congo, whereupon operations were—as in the case of Korea—authorized by the General Assembly. The Katanga rebellion was eventually ended, and a right-wing military government under Mobutu Sese Seko was established, whereupon the UN forces finally withdrew in 1964.

After decades of corrupt dictatorship, Mobutu was finally ousted in 1998, although the situation in Congo remains violent and unsettled, with numerous adjacent states fighting ongoing patterns of civil and cross-border wars that verge on being "Africa's first continental war," in which the United Nations may well become involved once again.

The Arab-Israeli Wars

Over Arab opposition, the General Assembly approved a British plan in 1947, dividing Palestine into a Jewish state and an Arab state, with Jerusalem to be governed under UN auspices. When Israel was declared an independent state in 1948, it was invaded by armies from Egypt, Syria, Lebanon, Iraq, and Transjordan (now Jordan). The General Assembly and Security Council tried vainly to stop the fighting; a Swedish diplomat, sent to the Middle East as a potential mediator, was assassinated by Jewish extremists. Eventually, U.S. diplomat and UN mediator Ralph Bunche established an armistice in 1949, for which he received a Nobel Peace Prize. Bunche met with representatives of the Arabs and Israelis on the island of Rhodes (because the Arabs did not extend diplomatic recognition to Israel, Bunche had to shuttle messages between different floors of a hotel in order to achieve written agreement). However, the issue had been resolved not so much by UN diplomacy as by force of arms, that is, the effective defeat of the Arab armies in the field. Indeed, the underlying issues were not resolved.

By the end of the fighting, Israel had expanded its borders over those earlier approved by the United Nations, and hundreds of thousands of Arab refugees (known as Palestinians) fled to neighboring Arab states, where they remain today, stateless, largely unassimilated, and demanding a homeland. In 1956, Egypt had blockaded Israeli shipping in the Gulf of Aqaba and nationalized the Suez Canal, whereupon Britain and France, in coordination with Israel, invaded Egypt and captured the Sinai peninsula as well as the Suez Canal. Not surprisingly, Britain and France vetoed action by the Security Council; the General Assembly then called for a cease-fire, which was finally achieved several months later. In this case, UN pressure was relatively unimportant, however; Britain and France were largely pushed to withdraw by the vigorous opposition of their close ally, the United States. But the General Assembly did arrange for UN troops to guard the border between Egypt and Israel, which agreed to pull back to the 1949 cease-fire line.

This UN presence, the United Nations Emergency Force (UNEF), represented a very important and innovative step, first proposed by Canada's Lester Pearson (for which he won a Nobel Peace Prize) and administered by Secretary-General Dag Hammarskjöld: a new system that came to be known as "peacekeeping." The idea was not to favor either side but to enforce the peace by interposing a lightly armed UN presence between the belligerents. By what Hammarskjöld called "preventive diplomacy," UN peacekeepers could help to patrol and maintain otherwise shaky cease-fires; at minimum, this would prevent further bloodshed. At maximum, it could gain time and help create conditions under which creative diplomacy might help resolve the conflict. In Hammarskjöld's conception—which has been retained ever since—the UN would seek to isolate local conflicts from big-power involvement, in part by recruiting peacekeepers largely from smaller states.

Limitations on the UN Use of Force

The UN's ability to serve as an active peacemaker and peacekeeper has been severely limited. For one thing, member states have never been able to agree on maintaining an independent UN force with sufficient military strength and political independence to deter would-be adversaries.

In the case of many large-scale conflicts, the United Nations was uninvolved, or impotent, reduced to making futile pleas for peace, or—worse yet—failing even to make any statement at all. For example, the UN briefly discussed but stayed out of the Vietnamese invasion of Cambodia in 1978, which overthrew the murderous, pro-Chinese government of Pol Pot, as well as the subsequent Chinese "punishment" of Vietnam in 1979. Indeed, the UN has been especially hamstrung when it comes to conflicts involving the permanent members of the Security Council. The UN played no part, for example, in ending the struggle between Algeria and France—in which 10% of Algerians perished before ultimately winning their independence—because France, as a permanent Security Council member, wielded a veto. In response to the Iranian hostage crisis in 1979–1980, the Security Council toothlessly requested that Iran release the U.S. hostages, but the USSR vetoed a recommendation for economic sanctions. The UN also did essentially nothing to end the Vietnam War, the Soviet involvement in the civil war in Afghanistan, U.S. military subversion of Nicaragua, or Soviet incursions into Hungary and Czechoslovakia, Chinese oppression in Tibet, and Russian military excesses in Chechnya.

The United Nations was also unable to intervene and prevent ethnic warfare in Bosnia and Kosovo, because Russia—ethnically and historically allied to Serbia—threatened to veto any such actions. (Eventually, military intervention was achieved by NATO, with the UN subsequently enrolled to assist peacekeeping after the heavy fighting was over.)

The United Nations eventually intervened in a chaotic situation in Somalia, ending disastrous famines, but after U.S. forces suffered a small but humiliating military defeat, UN activities were withdrawn. Similarly, the UN—to its shame—did nothing to prevent genocide by the Khmer Rouge in Cambodia during the 1970s, or by Rwandan Hutus against Tutsis in 1994.

The Promise of Peacekeeping

On the other hand, the fact that the United Nations hasn't prevented or stopped all wars does not mean that it has not been effective and useful in

certain cases. Although the UN has not been a panacea, it has achieved remarkable successes; as of the year 2000, it has negotiated 172 peaceful settlements, helping bring about an end to the Iran-Iraq War, the civil wars in El
Salvador and Namibia, and withdrawal of Soviet troops from Afghanistan.
The UN has also supervised elections in Angola and East Timor; even though
these events were followed by sporadic continuation of a civil war in the former
case, and Indonesian-inspired murder and brutality in the latter, the prospect
of free and fair elections must be seen as a hopeful harbinger for the future.

Peacekeeping troops—lightly armed, blue-helmeted "soldiers without
enemies"—currently serve as valuable buffers between contending forces in
many hot spots worldwide. They have also been important in monitoring
compliance with cease-fires, supervision of disengagement lines, the maintenance of a "no man's land" between belligerents, and so forth. When
neutral forces are interposed between opponents, suspicious events are less
likely to be misinterpreted as a provocation, and intentional provocations
themselves are less likely.

UN operations in the Golan Heights, for example, have been notably successful. This elevated region along the Israeli-Syrian border has great strategic value, since it constitutes a high spot from which one can look down on
either Damascus or Jerusalem. Under UN supervision, the Golan Heights
was effectively demilitarized, setting the stage for peaceful negotiations for
its eventual return from Israel to Syria.

Largely because of financial limitations, UN peacekeeping forces were,
ironically, scaled back around the turn of the 21st century, just at the time
when they seem especially important. In 1988, UN peacekeeping forces were
awarded a well-deserved Nobel Peace Prize for their crucial and courageous
efforts, and in 2001, another Peace Prize went to the UN as a whole and to
Secretary-General Kofi Anan.

The United Nations has met with some success in preventing the escalation of hostilities, and sometimes, in helping to terminate them. This is quite
different, however, from preventing war. It must be admitted that in many
cases the UN has only been "effective" after the guns have spoken, and/or
depleted treasuries and popular impatience have forced governments to seek
some kind of settlement as a result. A peacekeeping regime, on the other
hand, helps produce an atmosphere of calm, in which a just and peaceful
solution can be negotiated. But even successful peacekeeping can have draw-
backs as well. Although it may save lives at the time, it may also help perpetuate a crisis, by reducing the urgency of reaching a political solution. By
taking the edge off a conflict, in a sense it prolongs that situation, making
it more tolerable and even part of the way of life in the affected region.
Another downside to peacekeeping is that occasionally, UN forces have
been inserted when there is no peace to keep. In addition, these forces may
be inadequately trained or equipped or provided with guidelines for military
engagement that render them ineffective. For example, outgunned UN

forces were unable to prevent the slaughter of perhaps thousands of Bosnian Muslims in Srebernica, and several hundred UN peacekeepers were taken hostage by Sierra Leone rebels in 2000.

UN Peacekeeping and the United States

International peacekeeping is not merely an altruistic endeavor (although it is also that). Thus, peacekeeping directly serves the security, political, and commercial interests of the United States. When she was U.S. ambassador to the United Nations, Madeleine Albright stated that "whether measured in arms proliferation, refugees on our shores, the destabilization of allies, or loss of exports, jobs, or investments, the cost of runaway regional conflicts sooner or later comes home to America.... Without the U.N., both the costs and the conflict would be far greater." At the dawn of the 21st century, however, the fate of peace operations hangs in the balance, in part due to crippling funding shortfalls. Although the UN is often a first line of crisis response overseas, the United States (and to a much lesser extent, a few other nations) consistently falls behind in paying dues and peacekeeping assessments. These overdue bills limit the United Nations' ability to respond rapidly to crises and implement needed reforms. Ironically, given its reliance on the UN as a potential means of preserving peace and preventing genocide, the U.S. Senate has balked at paying its UN bill of more than $1 billion, which represents *one third of 1%* of planned U.S. annual military budgets, which are in the range of $300 billion dollars, extending into the indefinite future! If the United States is to avoid the costs and dangers of a unilateral role as world policeman, it would seem that, if anything, greater—and certainly not less—reliance on the UN is in order.

Other Functions of the United Nations

Third-Party Mediation

UN mediators have occasionally served as valuable third parties, helping belligerents to reach acceptable and face-saving agreements. Former secretary-general Javier Perez de Cuellar and other UN diplomats were instrumental in helping reach an agreement whereby Soviet troops began leaving Afghanistan in 1988; the secretary-general and his deputies have also served as intermediaries, helping achieve a long-awaited cease-fire in the Iran-Iraq War that same year. And in 1988, Dean Rusk—secretary of state during the Cuban Missile Crisis 26 years before—revealed that President Kennedy had prepared a memo to be proposed by then secretary-general U Thant, in the event that the United States and the Soviet Union appeared irreconcilably headed toward war. The memo suggested a "compromise" that the U.S. government had already decided would be acceptable—but only if it came from a disinterested third party, not the Soviet Union. The compromise—that the United States would remove its land-based missiles from Britain and Turkey in return for the Soviets dismantling their Cuban missiles—proved unnecessary, since Premier Khrushchev subsequently agreed to Kennedy's terms. It does, however, show the value of a respected and disinterested third party. (Even if the UN had prevented only one nuclear war—and done nothing else—this would have been more than enough to justify its existence!)

A Forum for Debate

On occasion, the United Nations is derided as a mere debating society. But in fact, even debating societies can be very useful, providing opportunity for government representatives to meet each other and exchange views, often without the glare of publicity. (In the words of one observer, the UN "has become indispensable before it has become effective.") There have also been cases—and doubtless will be others in the future—in which outraged domestic public opinion has pressed a government to respond to some international event, while at the same time peace has been best served by inactivity by the governments themselves. "Blowing off steam" is generally less harmful than blowing up people. In such cases, the UN provides an opportunity for states to meet their adversarial obligations symbolically rather than through bloodshed.

For example, U.S. authorities judged (no doubt correctly) that it would be unwise to intervene militarily when the Soviet Union invaded Hungary in 1956, so its delegates roundly condemned the Soviets in the United Nations, thereby giving American public opinion the impression that something was being done on behalf of the Hungarians. The Soviets had comparable opportunities when the United States unilaterally dispatched troops to Lebanon in 1958, and to the Dominican Republic in 1965. Similarly, Arab delegates get to castigate Israel regularly, attacking them verbally while their armies generally refrain from doing so militarily.

Prevent Major Power Conflicts

It is widely acknowledged that the United Nations has moved away from its original concept of providing collective security. Peacekeeping, on the other hand, has emerged as a successful innovation, not only in itself but also as a means of defusing the likelihood that the major powers might intervene. Originally, it had been hoped that concerted military action by the major powers would keep the peace; now, we find the UN operating under an opposite assumption, that peace will be enhanced specifically by excluding the major powers from crises, and recruiting peacekeepers from smaller, neutral states. Former secretary-general Dag Hammarskjöld admitted in 1961 that the UN could not serve to overcome superpower rivalry, such as disputes over Berlin, or regarding nuclear weapons. But it could work, he maintained, to localize disputes in which the superpowers did not have an overriding interest. By bringing in the small powers, the United Nations' preventive diplomacy keeps the superpowers out, thereby averting a major confrontation, while also working to defuse local crises. In Hammarskjöld's words, the job of the UN was "not to bring mankind to Heaven, but rather, to save it from Hell."

Constraints on the Use of Force

In theory, the United Nations has the authority, through its charter, to raise military forces and interject them into a conflict, without the permission of the conflicting parties. Article 42 of the UN Charter authorizes the Security Council to call for military operations against aggressors, and Article 43 calls on member states to provide such forces as requested. Moreover, Article 39 of the UN Charter says that the Security Council shall

> determine the existence of any threat to the peace, breach of the peace, or act of aggression and shall make recommendations, or decide what measure shall be taken . . . to maintain international peace and security. . . . Such action may include demonstrations, blockade, and other operations by air, sea, or land forces of Members of the United Nations.

Note that a buildup of forces, an oppressive social system, or even the ascension to power of a militaristic government could legitimately be defined as a "threat to the peace." In theory, therefore, the UN has substantial discretionary powers for the use of force. In practice, however, it has been very cautious.

Not only has it generally kept out of superpower affairs, the United Nations has studiously avoided involvement in most civil wars as well. It is worth noting that if the UN were to take its original mandate literally, and squash any threat to peace, then in the process it might well be squelching any hopes for national liberation on the part of Eritreans, Kurds, Basques, Afghans, Salvadorans, Kosovars, and so on. For better or worse, the UN operates under numerous constraints.

This seeming weakness of the United Nations is more a reflection of the weakness of the world system as a whole: the fact that the world has been divided into contending and sovereign states, each of which nearly always evaluates a policy through the lens of national rather than international benefit.

Sensitivity to State Sovereignty

The United Nations attempts to be sensitive to issues of national sovereignty, trying not to force choices between allegiance to the state, on the one hand, and to the world body, on the other. For example, since the Korean War and the controversial Congo intervention, prospective host countries have had the option of forbidding any UN peacekeeping presence; the UN can send observers into a country only if it is specifically invited to do so And the UN generally withdraws its forces whenever the host country so requests (as happened in Egypt in 1967). "The umbrella was removed," complained Israeli diplomat Abba Eban, "at the precise moment when it began to rain." As a result of such sensitivity to matters of state sovereignty, the UN has been less forceful than it might otherwise be, but it has also been able to exist in a changing world of jealous and strong-minded states. This kind of flexibility and adaptability has served it well, and kept it around for those cases in which it has been able to make its mark.

At the same time, UN policies have also shown flexibility in this regard. Thus, at the conclusion of the Gulf War, Iraq—as the defeated party—was forced to undergo detailed on-site weapons inspection by UN investigators. Although this resulted in the detection and destruction of many munitions, it also became a sore spot in UN-Iraqi relations, as the Iraqi government regularly interfered with these inspections, and UN (largely U.S.) forces frequently responded by bombing suspected sites. Rarely has the conflict between claims of state sovereignty and the demands of the larger international community been more clear.

The framers of the UN Charter had hoped that the major powers would stand united against aggression and that upon them would fall the responsibility for maintaining peace and order. The United Nations was thus ill-equipped to deal with the major East-West schism that developed. The competing superpowers, not surprisingly, elected to handle their own controversies by themselves (e.g., the Berlin and Cuban Missile Crises, or the various strategic arms negotiations, in which the UN had essentially no part). Similarly, the major powers continue to vigorously rebuff what they see as UN interference in their own foreign policy goals: The United States did not consult with the UN before sending troops to the Dominican Republic in 1965, or to Grenada in 1983. And when tensions arose between the Soviet Union and its Eastern European allies, no UN force interposed itself along the Soviet-Polish or Soviet-Romanian borders. At the same time, the UN has increasingly become a forum for addressing the tension between the industrialized, mainly wealthy North, and the largely impoverished, dissatisfied South. To some extent, the various economic and social agencies of the UN also help redress this imbalance.

Functionalism

When we consider the possible role of the United Nations in promoting peace, we are most likely to think about disarmament conferences and such relatively direct measures as peacekeeping or mediating. But according to advocates of another approach—"functionalism"—the long-term prospects of peace are enhanced even more by other, humanitarian activities that cut across state and national borders.

Doing Good

Functionalism can best be understood by reference to the so-called functional agencies, such as the WHO, the FAO, and the International Postal Union (IPU), which are typically given short shrift in discussions of the United Nations. The aims of these organizations do not include the establishment or maintenance of peace as such, but rather such goals as eradicating malaria, providing protein to growing children, or seeing to the fair exchange of international mail. Here is a small sample of some of the humanitarian efforts and successes of the UN (such accomplishments, in themselves, are a useful corrective for much anti-UN cynicism).

- A 13-year effort by the WHO eradicated smallpox worldwide in 1980. The WHO also helped wipe out polio from the Western Hemisphere. In 1974, only 5% of children in developing countries had been immunized against these "preventable plagues": polio, tetanus, measles, whooping cough, diphtheria, and tuberculosis. By 1995, as a result of the efforts of UNICEF and the WHO, the immunization rate was close to 80%, saving the lives of more than three million children each year.
- The United Nations has also provided famine relief to millions of people. The International Fund for Agricultural Development, for example, provides economic credit for poor and marginalized groups, benefiting more than 230 million people in nearly 100 developing countries, while building the potential for long-term hunger relief. In 1996 alone, 27 million refugees—mostly women and children—received food, shelter, medical aid, education, and repatriation assistance from the UN High Commission for Refugees.
- Through sponsorship of several international treaties, the United Nations has been a leader in efforts to protect the ozone layer and curb global warming.
- UN forestry action plans help limit deforestation and promote sustainable forestry practices for 90 countries.
- The United Nations has been active in providing safe drinking water for 1.3 billion people in rural areas, and it maintains ongoing efforts to help prevent overfishing and clean up pollution.

- UN programs have helped raise the literacy rate of women in developing countries from 36% in 1970 to 56% in 1990, and 68% in 2000.

De-emphasizing the Role of States

In the eyes of its proponents, functionalism is way of de-emphasizing the role of states, and even to some extent undermining their authority. Functionalism pins its hopes on a three-pronged strategy:

1. By reducing human misery, as by eradicating diseases, developing new strains of food crops, disseminating technological know-how, promoting literacy, and so forth, it is hoped that war will be made less likely.

2. By showing that institutions other than the state can attend to human needs—sometimes much better than the states do—it is hoped that state sovereignty will gradually be undermined. (This is a goal of many "functionalists," and not one that is explicitly endorsed by the UN itself.)

3. By providing opportunities for interactions across political borders, it is hoped that mutual understanding, tolerance, and respect will be enhanced.

It is difficult to evaluate the success, or the future prospects, of functionalism. Although conventional wisdom has it that misery leads to war, no clear evidence supports this claim, at least with regard to international war. And prosperity often seems to have made violence more likely, not less, in that strong and wealthy states, flushed with self-confidence, may be more inclined to engage in military adventures, while weaker ones—being less able—tend to be more cautious. On the other hand, making a better life for people might well decrease the chances of rebellions and civil wars, which have comprised the bulk of recent wars. And certainly, the humanitarian goals of functionalism are worthwhile in themselves, regardless of whether they result in fewer wars.

When it comes to undermining the authority of states, functionalism may be on stronger footing. Thus, some social scientists (stemming from the political philosophy of Hobbes, Locke, and Rousseau), emphasize the so-called social contract, whereby loyalty of citizen to the state is supposed to result from a kind of exchange: The state provides certain benefits to the populace, and in return, the people support the state by, for example, going to war when told to do so. But if inoculations are provided by doctors from the WHO, or new tractors by technicians from the FAO, or literacy programs by teachers from UNESCO, it is at least possible that in subtle ways the state's claim to the loyalty and gratitude of its citizens will be eroded. Within a domestic society, individuals have many crosscutting loyalties:

They may be members of the PTA, a trade union, a garden club, and also a particular church. This prevents any one cleavage from becoming dominant, and it leads to a general sense of social solidarity. Perhaps something of this sort can be achieved internationally. With this in mind, the hope of functionalists is also that by experiencing the benefits of cooperation across traditional national and state boundaries, people could be weaned away from narrow, nationalistic concerns and gradually imbued with an ethos that is more cooperative as well as transnational.

Enthusiasts of this approach should be cautioned, however, that states have historically insisted—in most cases, successfully—that loyalty to their political entity supersedes other affiliations: social, political, intellectual, emotional, economic. They have obtained the cooperation and often the lives of their subjects while often providing very little in return. States jealously guard their sovereignty, and seem unlikely to permit functionalist activities that risk subverting the loyalty of their citizens. One difficulty impeding the worldwide campaign against AIDS, for example, has been the refusal so far of many African states even to admit that they have a problem, for fear that it will result in a loss of international prestige and tourist dollars.

Nonetheless, by accepting the authority of certain functional agencies, states are in fact accepting certain limitations on their sovereignty, which is probably a healthy step. For example, the use of airspace and sea lanes is now increasingly governed by decisions made by the International Civil Aeronautics Organization and the International Maritime Consultative Organization, respectively. In these considerations, might no longer makes right, nor can a given state follow its own rules and procedures, without regard to others. To cite another example, in international telecommunications, the best frequencies are not simply preempted by the most powerful broadcasters; rather, it is universally recognized that to be legitimate, broadcasting frequencies must be allocated by the International Telecommunication Union.

Finally, it seems clear that communication and interaction of the sort provided by UN agencies would be beneficial. The 19th-century British statesman Richard Cobden advocated "as little intercourse as possible between Governments, as much connection as possible between the nations [i.e., peoples] of the world." And in his now-famous correspondence with Albert Einstein, Sigmund Freud opined that "anything that creates emotional ties between human beings must inevitably counteract war. . . . Everything that leads to important shared action creates such common feelings." Again, however, we caution that most wars have occurred between neighbors, who often know each other quite well. It is interesting, for example, that one of the factors aggravating relations between the United States and Canada, which are otherwise very close, is Canadian irritation at U.S. domination of the communications industry—radio, television, books, and magazines— which tends to make the smaller state a cultural colony of the larger. Closer contact can breed greater resentment.

With the end of the Cold War, the United States, Russia, and the other successor states to the USSR have embarked on numerous cooperative efforts, notably in space and in the destruction of some nuclear missiles. In these cases, it appears that cooperation has been primarily a result of improving relations rather than a cause. Nonetheless, the possibility always exists that positive experiences among individuals and governments will lead to a snowballing, positive feedback effect, which in turn can lead to improved relations at the official level. In this regard, there have doubtless been gains from sister city relationships, or even international pen pals, all of which serve to break down the political, geographical, and ideological barriers between states. Turkey and Greece, for example, have a long history of hostility. In 1999, both countries experienced disastrous earthquakes in rapid succession, and in each case, aid was provided to the victims. The resulting "earthquake diplomacy" appears to have thawed relations between these old rivals.

It has even been suggested that a more dramatic shared threat—such as an invasion or asteroid from outer space—might be needed to get many other feuding countries to put their antagonism and mistrust aside. In the meanwhile, others have proposed combined efforts to send a manned mission to Mars, to eradicate illiteracy and diseases such as malaria or tuberculosis, and so forth. While it is important not to be so idealistic as to lose touch with real limitations, it may be equally important to recognize that certain advances hold the prospect of benefiting humanity in more ways than the obvious.

Regional Organizations

Although the United Nations has so far largely failed as an organ of collective security, it has been more successful on a smaller, regional level with the establishment of many different organizations. In examining this approach, also known as "regionalism," we do not include the establishment of competing military alliances, such as NATO, the Warsaw Pact, the Southeast Asia Treaty Organization (SEATO), and the Central Treaty Organization (CENTO). These military groupings were directed *outward* against potential aggressors and were not designed as collective security organizations, intended to protect all members against an aggressor from *within* the region. Regional organizations include the Organization of African Unity (OAU), the Organization of American States (OAS), the Association of Southeast Asian Nations (ASEAN), and the Arab League. In some cases, these organizations have helped maintain the peace. Although not strictly collective security systems, they at least provide for third-party pressure to be brought to bear against member states that might otherwise go to war.

In 1960, the OAS was able to resolve accusations by Venezuela that the Dominican Republic was employing political subversion against it. When the "Soccer War" broke out between El Salvador and Honduras in 1969, the OAS was able to arrange a cease-fire and to provide independent observers to supervise its details. Early in 1979, the OAS severely criticized and isolated the government of Nicaraguan dictator Anastacio Somoza; this may have contributed to his ouster less than a year later. Then, after an obviously fraudulent election in Panama in 1989, the OAS roundly condemned Panamanian military leader Manuel Noriega, thereby officially serving notice that U.S. displeasure with Noriega was shared by virtually all governments of the Western Hemisphere; this provided additional pressure toward his removal. However, the OAS vigorously disapproved of the U.S. invasion of Panama in 1989; like other regional organizations, it favors multilateral rather than unilateral acts.

The OAU, for its part, has helped facilitate the settlement of border disputes between Morocco and Algeria, and among Kenya, Somalia, and Ethiopia, as well as having a major role in coordinating African opposition to South African apartheid. A military force from various western African states, notably Nigeria, helped stabilize the chaotic post-civil war situation in Liberia. In other cases, regional alliances have sought UN assistance: The United Nations was called in, for example, after the British Commonwealth of Nations couldn't solve the India-Pakistan disputes over Kashmir and Bangladesh. It should be noted, by the way, that the UN Charter explicitly endorses regional peacekeeping organizations.

In other cases, the United Nations has notably taken a back seat to regional organizations, as evidenced by the role of NATO military forces in enforcing peace in Bosnia, and—most dramatically—in Kosovo. In this case, the UN was initially unable to act because of Russian and Chinese opposition, based in part on ethnic solidarity in the case of Russia, as well as concern by both countries that a precedent of UN intervention within a country's territorial borders might eventually have implications for their treatment of some of their own rebellious provinces, notably Chechnya and Tibet. And so, the military action in Kosovo was carried out by NATO, in an extension of its traditional role, and representing a kind of collective security action, even though the former Yugoslavia is outside the territory of any NATO member.

On balance, however, regionalism has not been especially successful, generally for the same reasons that the United Nations has been limited in its peacemaking: State sovereignty restricts its effectiveness. In addition, regional organizations have in the past become vehicles for superpower domination. OAS members, for example, were largely coerced by the United States into supporting sanctions against Cuba and approving the U.S. invasion of Grenada. During the 1982 Falklands/Malvinas War, the OAS largely stood by Argentina, out of regional and anticolonial loyalty, yet it was fractionated because the English-speaking Caribbean states sympathized with Britain.

IGOs, NGOs, TNOs, and MNCs

States can also cooperate by forming intergovernmental organizations (IGOs), such as the Organization of Petroleum Exporting Countries (OPEC). If, as Mao said, power once grew out of the barrel of a gun, it can also grow out of a barrel of oil: The oil revenues of the Middle East OPEC members in 1970 totaled $4 billion; just four years later, following price increases by the oil cartel, the figure was $60 billion. International cartels can be effective in raising certain prices; although this helps states exporting these commodities, it often hurts other states, which have to pay more for the products in question. Moreover, increases in international prices do not always help the poor, even in exporting countries; for example, unroasted coffee rose from $.60/lb in the mid-1970s to more than $3.00 per lb in the late 1970s. As a result, the price to growers rose from 9¢ per lb to 14¢ lb, which did not even keep up with inflation. And the pay raise to laborers was even less. The OPEC oil embargo of 1973 was particularly painful to oil-poor developing countries, whose economic growth was strangled by having to pay increased prices for petroleum. There is, accordingly, no clear evidence that monopoly cartels by producers, exporters, importers, and so forth will further world peace, except perhaps indirectly by weakening the traditional, state-centered world system. They seem as likely to foster war, by generating intolerance, resentment, and further inequities of wealth.

Another notable IGO is the European Coal and Steel Community (ECSC), established in 1950 to integrate the industrial economies of West Germany, France, Italy, and the Benelux countries (Belgium, the Netherlands, and Luxembourg). By 1958, the ECSC had become a larger, more integrated entity, the European Economic Community, also known as the Common Market. It consists of 12 members, with a total population and gross national product (GNP) exceeding that of the United States. Most trading and transportation barriers throughout Western Europe have been eliminated, and 11 states are members of the European Monetary Union, increasingly employing a common currency, the euro. This process of transnational integration could ultimately lead to eventual political union, a kind of United States of Europe.

Finally, connections across international borders do not require the direct action of governments. There are many different kinds of nongovernmental organizations, or NGOs,[1] including many of the world's religions (e.g., the Roman Catholic Church, Society of Friends) and other groups whose affiliations cut across political boundaries, such as the Rotary Clubs International, the International Physicians for the Prevention of Nuclear War (winner of the 1986 Nobel Peace Prize), CARE, the International Olympic Committee, Amnesty International, and a wide array of scientific, educational, business, and other professional organizations. The number of NGOs has been increasing rapidly, from 176 in 1909 to more than 38,000 in 1999. Some of these groups seek as part of their agenda to break down the traditional barriers between states; most commonly, however, the various NGOs simply go about their affairs, which, as it happens, are best served by cutting across state boundaries. They are subtly, benevolently, subversive of state authority. Whereas international organizations embody the principle of national sovereignty; transnational organizations (TNOs) try to ignore it.

One of the most important transnational phenomena of the late 20th century is the emergence of powerful multinational corporations (MNCs). Such companies as General Motors, Microsoft, Exxon, General Electric, Shell Oil, CIBA/GEIGY, and McDonalds typically have commercial operations spread through a wide diversity of states. Great controversy surrounds the role of these MNCs. On the one hand, given the size of these businesses— many of which have annual earnings larger than the GNP of a midsized country—they should be powerful actors on behalf of transnational integration. And since profitable operations generally require a smooth international environment, it would seem that the influential multinationals seemingly would act to reduce the probability of war, pouring their financial resources like oil on troubled waters. Furthermore, it can be argued that by entrapping different countries in a web of economic interdependence, MNCs make war less likely, exemplifying a kind of benign functionalism— although one that is oriented toward profits instead of good deeds.

On the other hand, war has in the past been precipitated by economic entanglements; for example, during the 1930s, Japan was dependent on the United States for oil and iron ore, and this dependence led to competition, resentment, and fear that the United States intended to strangle further Japanese expansion, which was true, and which in turn contributed to the Japanese decision to attack Pearl Harbor in 1941. As to the multinationals themselves, their pursuit of profits rather than peace can sometimes involve the fomenting of disorder, via revolution or coup (e.g., Kennecott Copper and ITT in Chile, in 1973) or counterrevolution (e.g., the influence of United Fruit in inducing the United States, through the CIA, to overthrow the democratically elected Arbenz government in Guatemala in 1954).

In 1935, the U.S. Marine Corps commandant, General Smedley Butler (winner, incidentally, of three Congressional Medals of Honor), offered this remarkable first-person testimony to the role of MNCs in generating military intervention:

> I spent 33 years in the Marines, most of my time being a high-class muscle man for big business, for Wall Street and the bankers. In short, I was a racketeer for capitalism. I helped purify Nicaragua for the

international banking house of Brown Brothers in 1910–1912. I helped make Mexico and especially Tampico safe for American oil interests in 1914. I brought light to the Dominican Republic for American sugar interests in 1916. I helped make Haiti and Cuba a decent place for the National City [Bank] boys to collect revenue in. I helped in the rape of half a dozen Central American republics for the benefit of Wall Street. In China in 1927 I helped to see to it that Standard Oil went its way unmolested.

I had a swell racket. I was rewarded with honors, medals, promotions. I might have given Al Capone a few hints. The best he could do was to operate a racket in three city districts. The Marines operated on three continents.[2]

Charles Wilson, U.S. defense secretary during the Eisenhower administration, once announced that "what is good for General Motors is good for the country." In many cases, government officials have apparently acted on this presumption, engaging military forces worldwide in support of various MNCs, especially in the developing world. There is nothing unique about this: The British East India Corporation, for example, was one of the guiding forces behind English colonial expansion during the 18th and 19th centuries, just as the Hudson's Bay Company and the large railroads (such as Union Pacific) helped motivate the decidedly unpeaceful expansion of Canada and the United States throughout North America.

Furthermore, although the multinationals do provide (usually low-paying) jobs in their host country, they also extract resources, paying the lowest possible prices for raw materials as well as labor. In the process, they contribute to the long-term environmental degradation of host (i.e., exploited) countries while also keeping these countries economically and often politically dependent on the MNC. The resulting *dependencia* relationship (from the Spanish word for dependency) can be seen as a kind of neocolonialism that brings economic and social enslavement, and neither prosperity nor peace.

In this regard, the WTO, founded in the mid-1990s to replace the international economic structure known as GATT—the General Agreement on Tariffs and Trade—also deserves mention. It exemplifies the complexities of multinational economic integration, widely known as globalization. Essentially, globalization refers to the fact that worldwide communication and transportation has created what is increasingly a single, global economy. The WTO is especially devoted to establishing "free trade," by eliminating tariffs and opposing—by economic sanctions if need be—national policies that it perceives as being in restraint of unfettered international trade. As a result of such globalization, MNCs have been increasingly free to move factories to countries offering the lowest wage scales, and minimal protection for human rights as well as the environment. On the positive side, such activities offer jobs to impoverished people in developing countries who might not otherwise be employed. On the negative side, union rights and worker safety laws are frequently nonexistent in such cases, and the WTO has been roundly criticized as being a tool of the MNCs, simply fostering a "race to the bottom," when it comes to human rights as well as environmental protection. A major challenge for the WTO, and for the MNCs whose interests this organization seems to represent, is to expand their concerns to include sustainable economic development for all people, and not just for a privileged few.

A Final Note on International Organizations

Although their record has not been perfect, there is much to applaud in the activities of international organizations. Some of these—notably the United Nations—promote human and planetary betterment in numerous ways, including but not limited to the keeping of *negative peace*, that is, the prevention or termination of war. They also represent a partial step in the progression from individualism through nationalism to globalism, a transition that may well be essential if we are ever to give peace a realistic chance. As such, international organizations can be seen as possible halfway houses toward the establishment and solidification of international law, and perhaps even world government.

Notes

1. Peace researcher Johan Galtung has pointed out that the term *nongovernmental organizations* is regrettable, since by defining such organizations with respect to governments, it gives too much importance to the latter; analogously, consider replacing "governmental organizations" with "nonpeople organizations." In place of NGOs, therefore, Galtung suggests using "interpeople organizations" or some equivalent phrase.

2. Smedley Butler, untitled article in *Common Sense*, November 1935.

14 International Law

The international community should support a system of laws to regularize international relations and maintain the peace in the same manner that law governs national order.

—Pope John Paul II

Schemes for ending war—for creating negative peace, and ultimately, positive peace as well—often founder on the problem of states. By zealously (and jealously) guarding their sovereignty, states undermine or, at best, diminish the authority and effectiveness of international organizations such as the United Nations. Even when these organizations claim to be consistent with state sovereignty, in fact there is an unavoidable tension between a state-centered world system and one organized around different fundamental values. By providing political units around which dangerous and misleading notions such as "peace through strength" can congeal, nationalism and state-centeredness give legitimacy to the use of violence in settling disputes. By emphasizing the similarities and often suggesting some kind of superiority on the part of each group of people, and cutting them off from others, the current political divisions of our planet make disarmament seem terribly difficult, perhaps impossible. By rewarding those who behave violently—so long as such violence, or the threat of violence, is successful—our current world system works strongly against peaceful ethical or religious resolutions of conflict. And by fractionating the people of the world, political organization based on nation-states makes it very difficult to deal effectively with problems that cross traditional borders and that require global solutions. In a sense, we already have a kind of "peace system," whereby deterrence ostensibly prevents war between the major powers, while lesser conflicts go on, often civil and ethnic wars of great brutality. According to "realists," this may be the best that could be expected. Others, especially those committed in peace studies, are looking for something better.

In short, many people are becoming increasingly aware that our current state-centric system is part of the problem and that for the solution, we must go beyond the nation-state. In this chapter, we consider some of the directions that such a quest might take. All governments operate by laws, the rules of behavior that specify what is permissible and—more commonly— what is not. Even in our current system of separate states, a legal framework undergirds the relationship of states to one another. It is known as international law, and we review it in this chapter. Then, in the next chapter, we address the question of world government, a dream (for some, a nightmare) that constitutes a frontal assault on state sovereignty itself.

The Sources of International Law

We are all familiar with domestic law, with its prohibitions against violent crimes such as murder, robbery, or assault, as well as the way it regulates the nonviolent conduct of daily living, from the flow of traffic to the work of businesses, and the standards of acceptable conduct in private and public life. Less familiar, by contrast, is international law, the acknowledged principles that guide the interactions between states and that set limits on what is and what is not permissible. People live within societies, not between them, so we have done more to encourage *intra*national law than *inter*national law. And yet international law does exist; in fact, the current body of international law is very large. Just as most daily life among individuals within a society is peaceful, most interactions among states on the world scene is also peaceful, in accord with expectations, and thus, in a sense, "legal."

Unlike domestic law, which in the United States is codified in constitutions, amendments, and the specific laws passed by federal, state, and municipal law-making bodies, the body of international law is relatively chaotic, spread over history, and generated in many different ways. There are four major sources of international law: (1) classical writings that have become widely accepted, (2) custom, (3) treaties, and (4) the rulings of international courts.

Classical Writings

In the 16th century, the Spanish legal scholar Francisco de Victoria developed the thesis that war must be morally justifiable and could not simply be fought over differences of religion or for the glory of a ruler. He also maintained that soldiers were not obliged to fight in unjust wars, even if so commanded by their king. But the best-known and most influential example of classical international law was the work of the Dutch legal scholar Hugo Grotius. In his treatise *On the Law of War and Peace* (1625), Grotius maintained that there was a fundamental, "natural law," which transcended that of nations, and which emanated from the fact that people were ultimately members of the same community. Grotius argued strongly for the sovereignty of individual states, within their own realms. From this, he concluded that states must avoid interference in the internal affairs of other states. Grotius pointed to the agreements that states have made among themselves, and which have proved to be durable: peace treaties, decisions as to the allocation of fishing and navigation rights, commonly accepted boundaries, and so on. The Grotian tradition thus derives the legitimacy of international law from the legitimacy of states themselves. But it goes further in seeking to derive principles whereby the behavior of one state toward another can be regulated, arguing that "natural right" must govern the interactions among states and that this supersedes the authority of the states themselves. As Grotius saw it (and subsequent international law has affirmed), international "society" exists, which requires certain norms of conduct among states, including rules governing what is acceptable during war itself. For Grotius, war is not a breakdown in the law of nations but rather a special condition to which law still applies.

One of the earliest and most effective examples of international law in action was the battle against international piracy, during the 16th through 18th centuries. It was widely agreed at the time—even by England and France, for example, which were bitter enemies and which often outfitted or tacitly supported pirates against each other—that all states had jurisdiction over acts of piracy on the high seas, and essentially this unanimity of states permitted concerted and successful action. It is noteworthy, however, that pirates were apprehended by the military forces of individual, sovereign states, and tried by domestic courts, rather than by some international legal body.

The term *international law* first appeared in 1783, with the publication of Jeremy Bentham's *Principles of International Law*. Accordingly, it is worth emphasizing that whatever its shortcomings, nearly all progress in international law has taken place in just a few hundred years; in fact, things have really gathered steam in the past 50 years. Humanity might therefore be on the threshold of dramatic new developments.

Custom

Custom is one of the most important and least appreciated sources of international law. For example, consider the "rules of diplomatic protocol," whereby diplomats from one country are considered immune to arrest or detention in another. This is clearly in the interest of all countries, since if the representatives of opposing states could legally be harassed, communication between them could quickly cease, to the disadvantage of all sides. Diplomats are occasionally expelled from a host country, usually for "activities incompatible with their diplomatic status" (i.e., for spying), in which case some of the other side's diplomats are typically expelled in retaliation. But normally—that is, customarily, and thus by international law—diplomats are allowed substantial leeway, including guarantees that they will be able to communicate freely with their home government. (The strength of this presumption is shown by the outrage when it is violated, as when U.S. diplomats were held hostage in Iran during 1979–1980.)

Another example of international law derived from custom—or perhaps we should say "in the process of being derived" because it is currently in flux —is associated with the concept "common heritage of mankind" (CHOM). This developing notion has figured in the Law of the Sea and Antarctic Treaties, as well as the Montreal Protocols directed at reducing the production of chemicals implicated in destroying the earth's ozone layer. According to CHOM, the fact that certain entities—the ocean bed, Antarctica, the ozone layer—transcend state sovereignty means that individuals or states may not simply exploit or despoil them as they wish. Rather, as part of the common heritage of humankind, these things (and presumably, others as well) are entitled to protection under international law. At present, CHOM is of uncertain but growing status as an established principle of international law. It also exemplifies the important principle that international law, no less than domestic law, must be flexible and responsive to change and growth in accepted standards. Note that insofar as it has been successful, CHOM has thus far applied only to areas that are not within the accepted jurisdiction of existing states; the approach has not yet been effective, for example, in preserving tropical rain forests, whose ownership is zealously insisted upon by each state in question.

Treaties

International treaties are analogous to contracts among individuals. And of course, there have been many treaties, covering not only the termination of wars but also agreements about boundaries, fishing and navigation rights, and mutually agreed on restrictions as to permissible actions during war. Treaties are not always honored, but in the vast majority of cases, they have been. Backing away from treaty obligations results in substantial loss of face, and once branded a treaty breaker, a state may not be able to establish useful, reliable relationships with other states. Through treaties as well as customary practice, international law provides "rules of the road" by which international interaction, beneficial to each side, can be conducted. As a result, states have an interest in abiding by them.

Courts

Finally, international law—just like domestic law—requires courts to hear disputed cases and render decisions. The first example of an international court was the Central American Court of Justice, established by treaty in 1908 by five Central American republics. During its 10-year life span, this pioneering court heard 10 cases; in one, it resolved a dispute in which Honduras, El Salvador, and Guatemala teetered on the edge of war. The European Community has established the Court of Justice, which hears disputes arising from treaties establishing the Common Market; in addition, the European Court of Human Rights, at Strasbourg, hears human rights cases involving citizens of any of its 21 member states.

Best known and most important, however, is the International Court of Justice (formerly the Permanent Court of International Justice, during its tenure under the League of Nations), located in The Hague, Netherlands, and administered by the United Nations. Also known as the World Court, this institution consists of a rotating membership of world jurists. It issues decisions about international law that are generally considered authoritative, although typically unenforceable.

An International War Crimes Tribunal was convened during the 1990s and has held trials against individuals accused of participating in genocide in Bosnia and Rwanda. This tribunal has also indicted more than a dozen Serbian leaders for war crimes in Kosovo. It has barely begun to move against Cambodian Khmer Rouge officials, however. The governing statute of a new International Criminal Court was agreed on in 1998, despite U.S. objections and refusal to sign. (Essentially, the United States has objected to the possibility that its nationals might ever be brought before such a court, but seems quite willing to support the indictment, trial, and imprisonment of citizens of other countries.)

The verdict on international courts is mixed. On the one hand, states are gradually becoming more accustomed to letting go of enough sovereignty to settle disputes in court instead of in combat. But on the other, adherence to the dictates of the World Court is entirely consensual—it is up to the consent of those involved—whereas adherence to domestic law is obligatory. Imagine a community in which accused lawbreakers could be brought to trial only if they agreed that the laws applied to them, and further, imagine that they could decide whether or not to abide by the ruling of the courts!

Enforcement of International Law

The major problem with international law, therefore, aside from its diffuseness, is enforcement. Because enforcement provisions are generally lacking, some people contend that in fact international "law" is not, strictly speaking, law at all, but rather a set of acknowledged customs, or norms of behavior. The importance of norms alone should not be underestimated; in fact, most human behavior occurs with regard to widely shared norms, not law itself. Nonetheless, domestic law is the last resort (short of violence, which domestic law typically prohibits), and law is effective at least in part because if worst comes to worst, and a lawbreaker is apprehended and found guilty of violating the law, he or she can be held accountable, suffering fines, prison terms, and so on. In the case of domestic law, individuals acknowledge (whether overtly or not) that they are subordinate to the state and its machinery of enforcement, for example, the police, court bailiffs, the national guard. When it comes to relations among states, by contrast, the "individuals" insist on their sovereignty; they most emphatically do not recognize that there is an authority that supersedes themselves. If individual people behaved this way, it is unlikely that domestic law would effectively regulate their behavior. The major problem with international law, therefore, is that individual states insist on a kind of latitude that they would never allow their own citizens.

Let us briefly consider the role of sanctions (punishments for noncompliance) in law more generally. There are three primary incentives for obeying any law, domestic or international: self-interest, duty, and coercion. For example, most individuals stop at red lights not because they fear getting a traffic ticket, but rather because they know that otherwise, they are more likely to have an accident. Rules may therefore be followed out of purely utilitarian concerns, in this case, interest in their own personal safety. Laws provide a way of regulating human conduct, ideally for the benefit of all: You can proceed with reasonable safety through an intersection when your light is green, because you know that opposing traffic has a red light, and you have some confidence that other drivers will respect this law, just as you do.

In addition, individuals may follow the law because they feel themselves duty-bound to contribute toward an orderly society that functions with respect for authority. As members of society, who benefit from it, individuals assume a responsibility toward it. That is, some people are influenced by normative considerations, or a kind of Kantian categorical imperative to do what is right and good for its own sake. And finally, some people are induced to be law-abiding by fear that "violators may be prosecuted" and forced to succumb to the state's authority if they are found guilty. Although the role of such coercive factors cannot be denied, coercion is not the only reason why most people obey the law. And similarly, the absence of such coercion does not invalidate international law, or render it toothless.

States have numerous incentives, both positive and negative, for abiding by their legal obligations to other states. If a state defects from its legal obligations, adversaries may well retaliate, one's friends and allies are liable to disapprove, and world opinion is likely to be strongly negative, leading to ostracism and possible economic, political, and cultural sanctions. More-over, governments themselves have a strong stake in their own legitimacy, and—even in totalitarian states—adherence to law is fundamental to such legitimacy. Furthermore, a strong case can be made that enforcement per se is less important in inducing compliance with any law—domestic or inter-national—than is the aura that surrounds all law. Thus, in a law-abiding society, police forces do not make law respectable; rather, it is underlying respect for the law that enables police forces to function effectively. Accord-ing to this view, what is primarily lacking in international law is not really a mechanism for enforcement but rather a deeply felt sense that such law carries its own moral imperative.

Conflict With State Sovereignty

It simply isn't true that all is anarchy in the international arena, any more than all is peaceful in the domestic sphere: More than one quarter of all wars, for example, are civil wars. States generally obey the law—out of a combined sense of duty and self-interest—even though coercive sanctions, as understood in domestic law, are absent. States engage in nonviolent commerce—exchange of tourists, diplomats, ideas, trade—according to certain regulations, and usually with goodwill and amity. Moreover, states usually do not enter into treaties unless they intend to abide by them, and they only acquiesce with customary norms of behavior when they anticipate that over the long run, they will benefit by doing so. But at the same time, they typically cling to various aspects of sovereignty. Most treaties—notably those involving nuclear weapons—include a provision permitting signatories to withdraw within a set period of time, typically three or six months, if their "supreme national interests" are jeopardized. And who makes this decision? The state itself.

States can be defined as those political entities that claim a monopoly of legitimate violence within their borders. When they engage in what they claim is lawful violence outside their borders, states typically maintain that (1) they are acting in self-defense (the USSR in World War II, Israel in the Six-Day War), (2) they are fulfilling treaty obligations (France and Britain in World War II), (3) they are intervening on the side of legitimate authority (the United States in Vietnam, the USSR in Afghanistan), (4) the situation is anarchic and lacks a legitimate authority (the United Nations in the Congo or Somalia), (5) the conflict is within the realm of international legal obliga-tions (the United Nations in Korea), or (6) the conflict presents an overrid-ing moral imperative, such as the prevention of genocide (the North Atlantic Treaty Organization [NATO] in Kosovo). In short, state sovereignty con-tinues to reign—at least when it comes to the interveners. And usually, a semblance of international law is invoked as well. States have been especially hesitant, moreover, to circumscribe their day-to-day authority. It is significant that whereas the Hague Conferences, for example, produced a few halting restrictions on the waging of war, they were unable to establish any significant binding rules for peace.

States are also selective even when it comes to accepting the jurisdiction of the International Court of Justice, a process known as *adjudication*. Adjudication is very similar to arbitration in that the decision of the third party is binding. The only difference is that in adjudication, the decision is based on international law and rendered by a world court, rather than made by an arbitrator. The Soviet Union historically refused to submit disputes to this body, and the United States has been no better, despite the fact that in 1946, it formally agreed to refer all of its international disputes to the International Court of Justice. At that time, the U.S. Senate attached an amendment, known as the Connally Reservation, stipulating that the World Court will not have authority over any disputes that "are essentially within the domestic jurisdiction of the United States of America as determined by the United States of America." With this loophole, the United States is free to "determine" that any dispute is essentially within its domestic jurisdiction, thereby avoiding international adjudication whenever it wishes.

This stance is not unusual. France, for example, refused to acknowledge jurisdiction of the World Court when it tested nuclear weapons on French possessions in the Pacific, despite complaints of international illegality from New Zealand, Australia, and other Pacific states. Similarly, when the World Court ruled against the United States and in favor of Nicaragua in a case deriving from U.S. mining of Nicaraguan harbors during 1983 and 1984, the United States simply shrugged aside this verdict, claiming that in this instance it did not recognize the authority of the court.

Law, Power, and Social Change

Law is an important part of human life; some would even say that it is crucial to civilization. Despite concerns about enforcement—and anxiety when, as in the case of international law, enforcement powers are lacking—law is in many ways the antithesis of rule by brute force. Might does not make right; law does (or better yet, it should reflect what is right.) As a result, most good, decent people are presumed to be law-abiding, and in fact, rule by law is almost inevitably seen as preferable to rule by force. We should also be aware, however, that law can be an instrument of oppression. Laws are made by those in power, and as such, they serve to perpetuate that power and to prevent social and political change. Thus, laws—international as well as domestic—serve best in a conservative, relatively unchanging environment. Developing and revolutionary states often point out that international laws were established by Western powers in support of their domination.

The clearest example might well be the Treaty of Tordesillas (1494), following Columbus' "discovery" of the New World, whereby the pope "legally" divided that world into Spanish and Portuguese domains—without any regard for the people already living there.

Similarly, Western international law relies heavily on the basic principle that *pacta sunt servanda* (treaties should be honored). But consider cases in which a puppet ruler, imposed by a foreign colonial power, signs a treaty granting economic privileges to that power; if an indigenous, representative government eventually replaces the colonial authorities, should the new government be obliged to fulfill those obligations? For example, rights to the Suez Canal were originally "negotiated" with a British-installed government in Egypt; similarly, the U.S. naval base at Guantánamo, in Cuba, derives from an agreement reached by the U.S.-backed Batista dictatorship that was overthrown in the Cuban revolution. Nonetheless, the power of previous treaties (plus, in the case of Guantánamo, the power of the United States) has generally been such that even treaties negotiated by a previous regime are typically continued in force. When the Soviet Union dissolved, its major successor state—Russia—not only acceded to the previous USSR's seat in the United Nations, but Russia also undertook to meet the USSR's treaty obligations, including those pertaining to nuclear weapons.

Not surprisingly, however, economically developing and, to a lesser extent, revolutionary nationalist states are often inclined to repudiate *pacta sunt servanda* and to rely instead on an opposing doctrine, which is also recognized under law: *rebus sic stantibus* (circumstances have changed). The principle states that international laws must be living documents, subject to modification and, if necessary, annulment whenever conditions become substantially different from those obtaining when an agreement or treaty was reached. In addition, agreements made under duress—like contracts signed with a gun to one's head—are not generally considered valid.

International law must be flexible, if only because of the march of technology. For several centuries, for example, ever since a Dutch ruling in 1737, *territorial waters* have been considered to extend three miles from shore; this distance was based on the effective range of shore-based cannons at the time. Now, new guidelines are being sought, with controversy fueled by disagreement among states, especially between the exploiters and the exploited. The former, particularly the developed industrialized states with relatively little shoreline (such as Britain and Japan), argue for narrow territorial waters, while those with extensive coastal waters (such as Brazil or Thailand), and which seek to protect their fishing industry from foreign fleets, argue for a 200-mile limit.

These issues were partly resolved by the Law of the Sea Treaty, completed after decades of wrangling. This treaty also arranged for mechanisms of dispute resolution, waste disposal, and navigation procedures, but under the Reagan administration, the United States refused to sign, maintaining that the treaty's call for an intergovernmental body to supervise mining on the deep-sea bed constituted "international socialism." This highlights once again the susceptibility of international law to asserted claims of state sovereignty, as well as the growing pressure of North-South cleavages. The United States eventually signed this treaty.

_____ Hidden Strengths of International Law

Governmental Respect for Law

Most governments do not routinely flout the law, not even their own domestic statutes, over which they have complete control. In most democratic countries, governments accede to legal decisions, even those that go against them. Citizens of the United States, for example, often take for granted the fact that in many cases, they can, if they wish, bring legal action against their own government. And if the courts—which are themselves organs of the government—rule against the government, citizens can receive compensation or other redress for their grievances, even though governments, not the courts, have the strong-arm potential of enforcing their will. This emphasizes the primacy of law over force. For example, following a labor strike during the Korean War—an action that supposedly threatened U.S. war production at a critical time—President Truman sought to nationalize the U.S. steel industry. The Supreme Court, however, overruled this action and the government obeyed the law, albeit reluctantly. Because democratic governments have a long-range interest in settling disputes amicably, an interest that supersedes its short-term interest in winning a given dispute, they tend to accept legal rulings, even those that they dislike.

In international affairs, such acceptance is less likely, unless the opponents are so mutually balanced that the costs of losing a case are less than the costs of further wrangling, and possible war. For example, in 1960 Nicaragua complied with an order from the International Court of Justice to cede certain territory to neighboring Honduras, as agreed in an arbitration conducted in 1906 by the king of Spain, Alfonso XIII. The consequences of possible war, as well as the loss of prestige that would have come from defying the World Court, combined to pressure Nicaragua into abiding with this decision, while also providing an excuse for doing so. Thus, although some Nicaraguan nationalists opposed giving up the land, the government was able to carry out the unpopular decision by reference to Nicaragua's obligation under international law and by placing the responsibility on a prestigious third party.

Tacit Acceptance and Expectation

International law often appears weaker than it really is. This is because violations, when they occur, are often sensational and dramatic, whereas compliance is taken for granted. When domestic law is broken by individuals, only rarely are we moved by this to question the appropriateness of the law itself, and never to doubt the existence of such law. But a different standard is often applied to international law: When states violate international law, they may or may not be condemned by public opinion, but almost invariably, the law *itself* is called into question and the purported weakness of international law is once again lamented. Just as we are not told about the vast majority of people who obey domestic law every day, we do not see headlines proclaiming, "Paraguay today complied with its treaty obligations regarding its border with Bolivia, and therefore no invasion took place."

Virtually the entire civilized world was shocked, by contrast, when Chancellor Theobald von Bethmann-Hollweg justified the German invasion of Belgium in the early days of World War I by describing the international guarantee of Belgian neutrality as a "mere scrap of paper." On the one hand, this announcement—and even more so, the brutal invasion itself—showed the truth of the chancellor's assertion: Belgian neutrality was in fact "only" an international agreement, lacking any guarantee and incapable, by itself, of keeping out the invading German divisions. But on the other hand, the level of international outrage showed that international law, even when it lacks a means of enforcement, is nonetheless real in its effects on public perception. In addition, we should note that the immediate reason for Britain entering the war against Germany was in fact the German violation of Belgian neutrality; so in a sense, international treaty law was ultimately enforced in this case. Had Germany respected the law, it might have won the war.

The Law of War

War—the violent, large-scale attempted resolution of conflict—can be seen as the antithesis of law, whose goal after all is the ordering of relations without recourse to violence. Cicero first wrote that *inter arma silent legis* (in war the law is silent). This is taken to mean that the justifiability of any given war is outside the purview of international law, since states are sovereign authorities unto themselves, and thus free to make war or not, as they choose. Under this view, since there is no higher authority than a state, no one can claim that a state is making war unlawfully.

"For as long as men and women have talked about war," writes ethicist Michael Walzer,

> they have talked about it in terms of right and wrong. And for almost as long, some among them have derided such talk, called it a charade, insisted that war lies beyond (or beneath) moral judgment. War is a world apart, where life itself is at stake, where human nature is reduced to its elemental forms, where self-interest and necessity prevail. Here

men and women do what they must to save themselves and their communities, and morality and law have no place.[1]

Nonetheless, a body of law is widely thought to apply to states under conditions of war. Legal scholar Quincy Wright has even defined war itself as "the legal condition which equally permits two or more hostile groups to carry on a conflict by armed force." Therefore—at least according to some experts—war is a highly formalized interval when violence may *legitimately* be practiced between two opposing groups. Enough agreement exists within the community of nations that belligerents and neutrals alike recognize the existence of certain accepted standards: "Although war manifests the weakness of the community of nations," Wright has pointed out, "it also manifests the existence of that community."

On occasion, members of that community coalesce around acts that are sufficiently outrageous, as with the banning of chemical and biological warfare and the use of dumdum bullets. For example, the international conscience has been deeply offended by the use of children—some as young as eight—in military engagements. In Geneva in 2000, the UN Convention on the Rights of the Child was revised, raising the minimum age for participation in armed conflicts from 15 to 18 and defining recruitment of soldiers under the age of 15 as a war crime. (The United States eventually signed, after having long objected to such a provision, insisting on its "right" to recruit 17-year-old volunteers, and even to send them into combat. At the same time, rebel groups rather than national armies are especially likely to employ grossly underage child soldiers, and such groups generally show relatively little inclination to abide by the international laws of war.)

The Nuremberg Principles

States that are party to international treaties may find themselves subject, even against their will, to the legal restraints of these treaties. The losers in World War II, for example, were tried—and many were convicted—for having waged aggressive war in defiance of their obligations under the Kellogg-Briand Treaty. These trials, conducted in the German city of Nuremberg, were unique in developing the legal doctrine that individuals are personally liable to criminal prosecution for crimes against international law. This includes illegal resort to war as well as violations of accepted restraints as to appropriate conduct during war, notably the treatment of prisoners and the waging of genocide.

Telford Taylor, the chief Allied prosecutor at Nuremberg, wrote that

war consists largely of acts that would be criminal if performed in time of peace—killing, wounding, kidnapping, destroying or carrying off other people's property. Such conduct is not regarded as criminal if it takes place in the course of war, because the state of war lays a blanket of immunity over the warriors. . . . But the area of immunity is not unlimited and its boundaries are marked by the laws of war.[2]

Some critics objected to these proceedings, claiming that the Nuremberg Trials were simply examples of "victors' justice" and not real international law. Nevertheless, the so-called Nuremberg Principles have served as a benchmark in efforts to introduce humane and reasoned limits to acceptable wartime behavior. Thus, the international military tribunal that convened in Nuremberg specified a series of international crimes. Article 6 of the Nuremberg Charter identified the following:

1. Crimes against the peace, namely, planning, preparation, initiation or waging of a war of aggression, or a war in violation of international treaties, agreements or assurances, or participation in a common plan or conspiracy for the accomplishment of any of the foregoing.

2. Crimes against humanity, namely, murder, extermination, enslavement, deportation, and other inhumane acts committed against any civilian population, before or during the war, or persecutions on political, racial, or religious grounds . . . whether or not in violation of the domestic law of the country where perpetrated.

3. War crimes, namely, violations of the laws or customs of war. Such violations shall include, but not be limited to, murder, ill-treatment or deportation to slave labor or for any other purpose of civilian population of or in occupied territory, murder or ill-treatment of prisoners of war or persons on the seas, killing of hostages, plunder of public or private property, wanton destruction of cities, towns, or villages, or devastation not justified by military necessity.

Article 7 specified that "the official position of defendants, whether as Heads of State or responsible officials of Government departments, shall not be considered as freeing them from their responsibility or mitigating their punishment." And according the Article 8, "The fact that the defendant acted pursuant to orders of his Government or of a superior shall not free him from responsibility."

Whereas the German defendants at Nuremberg were tried for crimes they committed that were subsequently ruled to have been against international law, a series of lesser-known trials was conducted in Tokyo, of Japanese officials accused in large part of crimes of *omission*—that is, illegal failure to act. For example, Koko Hirota, Japanese foreign minister from 1932 to 1937, failed to insist on an end to Japanese atrocities against civilian Chinese during the "rape of Nanking," and General Tomoyuki Yamashita, commander of Japanese troops in the Philippines, was found guilty of failing to restrain the troops under his command when they committed atrocities against Filipinos as well as U.S. prisoners of war. Several decades later, when U.S. Army lieutenant William Calley was tried and found guilty for his role in the cold-blooded slaughter of hundreds of old people, women, and children—known as the My Lai massacre—during the Vietnam War, it appears to have been the first time a state had accused one of its own soldiers of war crimes. Calley's higher-ranking commanding officers were not tried, however, despite the fact that parallels can be drawn between the actions of General William Westmoreland (U.S. military commander in Vietnam) and General Yamashita, and between Secretary of State Dean Rusk, Secretary of Defense Robert McNamara, and indeed, former presidents Johnson and Nixon, and Minister Hirota. So again, whereas international laws exist, and have been enforced, such enforcement has been highly selective.

The treaties that were violated by the Nuremberg defendants, originating from the Geneva and Hague Conventions, specified limitations on such things as naval or aerial bombardment. But they also made allowances for "military necessity," which can be stretched to permit nearly any act in wartime, however outrageous. Similarly, even the toothless Kellogg-Briand Pact was interpreted by many as permitting "wars of self-defense," as does the current UN Charter: Article 51 grants states the "inherent right of individual or collective self defense." Self-defense would clearly justify Poland's short-lived response in seeking to resist the German invasion in 1939, but what about France's response: namely, declaring war on Germany? (France was bound by treaty to help defend Poland.) And what about the Israeli invasion of Egypt in 1967, in which Israel clearly struck first, but in which it was argued that Egyptian behavior constituted a real provocation as well as an imminent threat that justified a "preemptive" attack by Israel? Similarly, the "Brezhnev Doctrine," by which the USSR justified its invasion of Czechoslovakia in 1968, was described as simply self-defense by socialist people against Western-inspired counterrevolutionaries. And the "Reagan Doctrine," under which the United States assisted right-wing revolutionaries seeking to overthrow leftist governments in Angola or Afghanistan, was also described by its supporters as aid to people seeking to defend themselves. Apologists for wars of self-defense and self-determination have thus far always been able to find loopholes in international treaties large enough to drive an army through. And when it comes to governments using force against their own citizens—such as Serbia in Kosovo or Iraq toward its Kurdish population in the north as well as the so-called swamp Arabs in the south—the obligations and restraints of international law are murkier yet.

In short, when states consider that their security interests require it, violations of international law have occurred, and they can be expected to continue. Many scholars argue, incidentally, that the very possession of nuclear weapons runs counter to international law, because it involves preparations for genocide; it seems likely, however, that if these and other undiscriminating weapons of mass destruction are to be abolished, it will be for reasons other than their "illegality."

A Final Note on International Law

International law has many imperfections. It appears to have exerted some useful restraints in some cases while being woefully inadequate in others. The major powers give it less credence than do the militarily weaker states, in part because the former have recourse to their military strength, whereas the latter are generally more invested in the rule of law, which offers them the possibility of a "level playing field" in contests with larger, stronger opponents. Some authorities recommend only a modest role for international law in the future, avoiding what Stanley Hoffmann called "the Charybdis of subservience to state ambitions and the Scylla of excessive pretensions of restraint" and recognizing that "it is in the interest of international law itself to put states' consciences neither to sleep nor to torture."[3] Another view is that international law is a beginning, something on which to build a world without boundaries, or at least, one in which the sanctity of state sovereignty is greatly curtailed in the interest of human survival as well as quality of life.

Notes

1. Michael Walzer. 1977. *Just and Unjust Wars.* New York: Basic Books.
2. Telford Taylor. 1970. *Nuremberg and Vietnam.* Chicago: Quadrangle.
3. Stanley Hoffmann. 1971. "International Law and the Control of Force." In K. Deutsch and S. Hoffmann, eds., *The Relevance of International Law.* New York: Anchor.

15 World Government

I have long believed the only way peace can be achieved is through World Government.

—Jawaharlal Nehru

As we enter the 21st century, it is clear that most of the problems afflicting our planet and our species transcend the boundaries of the nation-state. For example, following a catastrophic accident at the Soviet nuclear plant in Chernobyl in 1986, radioactive contaminants were deposited throughout much of the world. Wind patterns and fallout do not respect national boundaries—similarly, for the greenhouse effect: global warming due to increasing atmospheric levels of carbon dioxide and other chemicals. A comparable case can be made for most of the world's other ills, including poverty, overpopulation, racism, resource shortages, hunger, and injustice. The notable exception, war, is itself largely a *product* of the nation-state.

The Need for World Government

Ever since the Tower of Babel, people have been plagued by their own political disunity. A potential solution, proposed in one form or another for literally thousands of years, has been to erase the existing political boundaries and to replace them with government structures at the largest, most inclusive level, namely, world government. This suggestion has been raised most urgently with regard to war and its prevention, since when it comes to war, nation-states have been only reluctantly and haltingly part of the solution; in the eyes of many, they are part of the problem. And for some, they are

387

virtually the whole problem. War making has fractured the human community along ideological, social, and geopolitical lines. The prevention of war, accordingly, may well require that this community be reforged on a global scale.

The shortcomings of the world political system have been readily apparent through the greater part of modern history. But these weaknesses are even more obvious in the nuclear age, in which nationalist passions and the jockeyings of states literally threaten an end to the entire human experience. Many informed people have long looked for alternatives to the nation-state system; not surprisingly, in an age of diminishing resources, shrinking distances, and ever more devastating weaponry, advocates of world government speak with a particular urgency.

In the medieval world, the typical European owed allegiance to his or her feudal lord, who in turn may have been subject to the secular authority of the Holy Roman Emperor and the religious power of the pope. At least in theory, the world was integrated in a roughly pyramidal power structure. Then came the great so-called wars of religion, culminating with the Thirty Years' War and the signing, in 1648, of the Treaty of Westphalia, which inaugurated the state system that was eventually extended into the modern pattern of nation-states. For citizens in pre-Westphalian, medieval times, concerns were overwhelmingly bounded by day-to-day events taking place in local surroundings: the happenings in local fields, woods, nearby towns and the closest castle with its protector (or oppressor) nobility. The Westphalian world expanded the allegiance of state and national subjects to include lands and people more distant than one's immediate surroundings. In addition, technological advances, especially in transportation and communication, made it unavoidable that individuals became involved with other places and other people beyond their closest neighbors.

Continuing this line of thinking, it can be argued that we now live in a post-Westphalian world, one in which the state or nation-state system is as obsolete as its feudal antecedents. Our mounting problems, notably pollution, poverty, resource depletion, and the destructive effects of war, should supersede the old, traditional political boundaries. They have made it imperative that we think as planetary citizens. The world, in short, has become functionally integrated, even while it remains politically fragmented.

The appeal of world government is basically that superior authorities ought to be able to force quarreling subordinates to refrain from violence; to respect larger, common interests; and to solve their disputes in some other way. When two individuals disagree about something, they are expected to settle the dispute in a law-abiding manner; they are not permitted to go "outside the law" and start shooting each other. Settling disputes by a duel, popular in previous centuries, is analogous to nation-states "settling" today's disputes by war. The former has been universally outlawed; the latter has not—or rather, not yet. Similarly, individual households are not "sovereign."

They do not have the right to dump toxic chemicals into "their" stream, thereby poisoning their neighbors' water supplies; why, then, should "sovereign" states be permitted to do this?

International organizations such as the United Nations, as we have seen, offer frameworks for transcending political boundaries, but they operate within the present system of sovereign states, which are free to disagree, overrule, or simply ignore these organizations if they choose. Similar limitations apply to international law, although here, once again, some of the fundamental ingredients for transcending state sovereignty are present. What is missing is the ability of a larger authority to impose restraint on the states themselves. Whatever their underlying causes, wars take place because there is no higher authority to prevent them. In modern times, the parts (states) claim to be greater than the whole (humanity, and the planet Earth). With a world government, this would likely change: States would be prohibited from imposing themselves on their neighbors, whether economically, ecologically, or militarily, just as domestic governments now prevent individuals from overstepping their bounds or settling their disagreements by duels, and just as federal governments keep the peace among their provinces or smaller, constituent republics.

_____ A Brief History of Plans for World Government

Many proposals have been advanced for world government of one sort or another. Most of the early suggestions advocated the dominance of one ruler or superstate. For example, Dante, in _De Monarchia_ (1310), suggested a universal empire with a single ruler, who would guarantee peace. Early in the 17th century, the duke of Sully, Maximilien de Bethune, proposed a "grand design" for European peace, involving a council consisting of representatives from all European states. The French monk Emeric Cruce developed a proposal in 1623 calling for a world structure, including not only Europe but also India, China, the kingdoms of Africa, and representatives of the pope and the Jews.

The 17th and 18th Centuries

By the 17th and 18th centuries, there had been a flourishing of proposals designed to establish some form of worldwide political restraints on war making. William Penn, in 1693, wrote _Essay Toward the Present and Future Peace of Europe_, which included a general parliament with military force to compel observance of its decrees. In 1713, the Abbe de Saint-Pierre, in his _Project for Perpetual Peace_, called for a "Senate of Europe" consisting of 24 representatives, including one from each European state, a plan that received much attention, and criticism as well. Voltaire, for example, noted that the states in question would overwhelmingly be monarchies and maintained that for peace to be preserved, democracy was necessary—and at that time, democracy was unthinkable as a practical matter, just like world government itself.

Notable among such proposals, in addition to the efforts of Penn (*Essay Toward the Present and Future Peace of Europe*, 1693), Saint-Pierre (*Project for Perpetual Peace*, 1713), and Jeremy Bentham (*Plan for a Universal and Perpetual Peace*, 1789), was one advanced by the French philosopher and novelist Jean-Jacques Rousseau (1712–1778). In his *Discourse on the Origin of Inequality*, Rousseau concluded that ownership of private property was the underlying cause of war; he therefore proposed that to achieve world peace, it would be necessary to abolish private property worldwide. His work, in turn, leads to an interesting—if currently unanswerable—question: If war is a result of a specific form of social organization, is this reason to condemn the society, or to justify certain wars? Thus, many theorists have argued that the defense of property is a legitimate reason for war.

Probably the most notable design for a potentially workable form of world government was put forth by the great German philosopher Immanuel Kant. In his small but wide-ranging book *Perpetual Peace* (1795), Kant made the first major effort to focus specifically on the dangers of arms races and armaments, rather than just proposing yet another kind of world parliament. He also argued strongly for "republican" governments, that is, democracies, as being most likely to keep the peace. In addition, Kant maintained that in spite of the evil of which human beings are capable, the continuing cultural progress of humanity will enable them to use reason and logic to act increasingly on behalf of moral perfection. Consistent with the philosophy of the Enlightenment, Kant maintained that ethical and intellectual truth exists independent of time, place, and matter and that this truth is binding on all people because our rational capacities transcend day-to-day circumstances and permit us to grasp certain fixed principles.

Kant's views should be contrasted with those of Thomas Hobbes, who, 150 years earlier, had emphasized that perceptions are individual and personal, rather than universal, and that because of this, individual perspectives are bound to diverge, so that agreement among different and contending agents requires enforcement by fear and physical power. Whereas Hobbes's emphasis on conflicting interests served to justify the existence of a powerful political state, Kant was concerned with preventing the excesses of state power, especially when states interact violently with one another. Kant proposed a worldwide organization that would be bound by international law and composed of a federation of free states. His work represented a growing tendency toward what may be called "optimistic internationalism" among peace theorists and devotees of world government. (It may also have been discouraging to many that shortly after Kant's book appeared, the Napoleonic Wars convulsed Europe.)

Whereas Hobbes had argued that war is our "natural" situation, the French political philosopher Montesquieu, in his *Spirit of Laws* (1748), maintained that the blame lay not in human nature, but squarely on the system of political states:

> As soon as man enters a state of society he loses the sense of his own weakness; equality ceases, and then commences the state of war. Each particular society begins to feel its strength, whence arises a state of war between different nations.[1]

Montesquieu was joined in this belief by Rousseau, who argued that war could be prevented only by severing the bonds by which the state held people together: "It is only after he is a citizen," noted Rousseau, "that he becomes a soldier." Rousseau also maintained that "conquering princes make war at least as much on their subjects as on their enemies" and that "all the business of kings . . . is concerned with two objects alone; to extend their rule abroad or make it more absolute at home." Hence, the enemy was not only the political state but most especially the institution of monarchism.

Kant also identified the state as the prime war-causing culprit, but rather than focus on the problem posed by the state's very existence, Kant located the blame in what he called the "lawlessness" of how states interact with one another. For Kant, some form of "external coercion" is therefore necessary to establish peace between states.

The Early 20th Century

The 19th century was not notable for serious proposals concerning world government, at least in part because the post-Napoleonic Concert of Europe did a reasonably good job at keeping the fragile peace. After World War I, however, and the subsequent failure of the League of Nations, there was a flurry of renewed interest in world union, led by groups such as the United World Federalists. In fact, some tension has arisen between supporters of the United Nations and world federalists, who believe that international organizations of this sort tend to enhance state authority rather than transcend it. Some argue that so long as international organizations are structured around the preservation of state sovereignty, they are not so much stepping-stones to world government as threats and impediments to its implementation.

The Clark/Sohn Plan

The most elaborate and detailed scheme for world government was developed in 1966 by the legal scholars Grenville Clark and Louis Sohn.[2] It basically called for transforming the United Nations into a world peacekeeping unit, whereby states would retain their sovereignty *except* in matters of disarmament (which would be mandatory) and war (which would be prohibited). Clark and Sohn proposed to increase the power of the General Assembly and to change its voting procedures, making decision making largely proportional to population. Under the Clark/Sohn plan, the four largest countries (China, India, the USSR, and the United States) would have 30 votes each, the next eight largest would have 15 votes each, and so on. An Executive Council would be authorized to intervene militarily world-wide, so as to prevent war. Unlike the present Security Council, however, there would be no veto, although a clear majority (12 of 17 members) would have to approve any armed action, and this vote would have to include a majority of the largest states. An Inspection Commission would ensure that disarmament is total; after a two-year census of each country's military forces, it would supervise 10% annual reductions, across the board. A World Peace Force, under UN auspices, would consist of from 200,000 to 600,000 professional volunteers, initially using supplies and weapons obtained as the member states disarmed themselves. Nuclear weapons would not normally be supplied to this force, but they could be obtained if needed—from a Nuclear Energy Authority—to deter the use or threatened use of nuclear weapons by any state that kept a small cache.

The Clark/Sohn plan, although wonderfully detailed and specific, does not offer any suggestions as to the means of achieving this goal, of getting from "here" to "there." It does illustrate, however, that there is no shortage of precise ideas about possible future world governments. Another sugges-tion, for example, has called for vesting war/peace decisions within the General Assembly, but modifying the requirements for passing a major vote by specifying that such a vote must include two thirds of the states of the world, as well as two thirds of the population of the world and two thirds of the contributors to the UN budget. Such a "binding triad" would thus include most of the countries, most of the people, and most of the world's economic/military/political strength. It would accordingly be more legitimate, in a sense, than the current situation, in which resolutions can be passed by states that represent only a small fraction of world population or actual power, or blocked in the Security Council by another minority, one that pos-sesses power but may lack population as well as moral legitimacy. Clearly, the current global geopolitical situation does not encourage respect for the institution, at least among those influential states that might be outvoted. Whatever the strengths or weaknesses of the binding triad proposal or of the Clark/Sohn plan, or others, the point is that world government has not been stymied by a shortage of good ideas, but rather by a lack of political will.

Pros and Cons of World Government _____

Despite the attractiveness of the idea of world government, the fact is that people—once organized into relatively large units—have generally shown far more eagerness for splitting off than for joining together. There have been virtually no examples of the successful merging of states. The union of North and South Vietnam might be one such case, although it was only achieved via appalling violence—and despite substantial resistance from many of the South Vietnamese themselves; moreover, Vietnam had previously been a single country, so that the outcome was not so much the merging of different states as the reunification of a state that had been artificially separated. The same can be said of the reunification of Germany in 1989 after its post-World War II separation into West and East.

At one time, Egypt and Syria attempted a peaceful merger, establishing the United Arab Republic (UAR), but that union was quickly disbanded. When consolidation does occur, a smaller unit is typically swallowed up by a larger, often against its will: Tibet was incorporated into China, Goa into India, the Baltic states into the USSR after World War I. A major reason, indeed, for the breakup of the USSR was the fact that it was an artificial entity, composed of numerous republics, each of which maintained a national, ethnic identity that resisted decades of domination and efforts to subordinate its local loyalty to a larger Soviet whole. Furthermore, much of the tension in the world today is generated specifically by regions desiring not to submerge their identity but rather to *separate* themselves from control by a larger whole: Catholics in Northern Ireland, Quebecois in French Canada, Basques in Spain, Tamils in Sri Lanka, East Timorese in Indonesia, and so on.

The Maintenance of Peace

The argument for peacefulness under world government is derived largely from analogy: Since domestic governments enforce peace (e.g., between New York and Pennsylvania in the United States), or attempt to do so (Armenia and Azerbaijan in the former USSR), a world government would presumably do the same, treating nation-states much as municipal governments now treat their citizens, or as federal governments now treat their subordinate provinces or constituent republics. But analogies do not always hold. Moreover, federal governments do not always create or maintain peace: Civil wars are distressingly common, and often highly destructive. Europe during the 19th century, for example, was composed of feisty, sovereign states, while the United States was a single, ostensibly united country. And yet the war casualties suffered by the "United" States during its civil war (about 600,000) were almost precisely equal in number to the casualties suffered by Europe during the entire century between 1815 and 1913.

Perhaps if they were not held forcibly within a larger state, independent republics would be freer to work out their ethnic conflicts in peace. Or alternatively, maybe they would go to war: Ethnic antagonisms within the former Yugoslavia, for example, were kept from erupting into violence because of the inhibiting and unifying influence of the central government in

Belgrade, under a widely respected leader, Marshal Tito. With that central force removed, the constituent republics (notably Serbia, Croatia, and Bosnia) were vulnerable to violent appeals to previously submerged nationalistic passions.

The Danger of Oppression

To some people, the prospect of a world government is truly frightening. These include many—notably in the United States—associated with various self-styled "militia" and "patriot" movements, who seriously entertain the delusion that an oppressive world government, most likely under the auspices of the United Nations, is ready to swoop down in fleets of black helicopters and deprive them of their civil liberties (notably, their guns). Such right-wing delusions aside, a serious argument can be made that as a cure, world government might be worse than the disease.

If large political units tend to be unresponsive to the needs of their citizens, and are sometimes downright oppressive, imagine the danger inherent in government by a worldwide "superstate," with the power to enforce its decrees on everyone. (The Clark/Sohn plan carefully ensured that the armed forces of several countries, combined, would exceed those of the world force, thereby hedging against centralized despotism.) But why, critics ask, should we expect better government from a world authority than we now get from national governments? And, it is worth noting, only about half of states today experience functioning representative democracies. So what, if anything, guarantees that a world government would not be a worldwide tyranny? Most of us want to have our cake and eat it too: peace *and* freedom, international order *and* national sovereignty. But perhaps these goals are conflicting. If so, and if we have to choose, which is preferable? Or perhaps we can hope for a compromise, maybe along the lines of the Clark/Sohn plan, something that offers restrictions on the state's ability to make war, but without impinging on other aspects of domestic life.

This may be easier said than done, however. For one thing, powerful states are usually not interested in world government; actually, they are not just uninterested but often vigorously opposed, since world government would require that they give up some of the influence and power that they exercise today. It might also make them subject to certain basic principles of equality and fairness, from which they are at present largely exempt. In some cases—notably that of the United States—state sovereignty combined with military/economic/scientific/political might has been a means of achieving and maintaining inequitable access to the world's riches. What if, having surrendered its military autonomy, the United States is faced with a demand from the economically less developed states that it cease consuming scarce resources and polluting the planet out of proportion to its population, or that it redistribute its wealth? Would world government mean that we would have to share? If so, many U.S. citizens might prefer autonomy and gluttony, even at the risk of occasional war. (Especially insofar as military-technological advantages—evidenced in the Gulf War and the war in Kosovo—continue to make such wars relatively casualty-free, at least for the United States.)

Critics of world government also point to what they see as an inconsistency. World government is supposed to be necessary because the ferocious Hobbesian world of independent nation-states is simply too violent and irresponsible to continue unchecked. But then, advocates of dramatic change turn right around and assert that such fierce competitors and vicious inclinations can be rendered peaceful by a kind of world government modeled after the ideals of John Locke and other 19th-century Euro-American liberals: a limited, mild, and democratic authority that is based largely on mutual consent. Such a "Lockean" government might indeed be more palatable than its "Hobbesian" alternative, but if the problem is so grave, it might simply be inadequate. In short, a Hobbesian world may require a Hobbesian government. The problem is that a Hobbesian government is likely to be very unpleasant. And it would be even more unpleasant—and more difficult to reform—if its resources and authority were global rather than merely national.

On the other hand, there is no reason why a functioning world government could not allow current national governments to continue exercising autonomy and sovereignty in their internal affairs. Maybe the issue is posed incorrectly: Rather than worrying about what national governments would have to surrender, perhaps we should focus on what they would be gaining. World government could then be viewed not so much as requiring us to give up something that we now have (state sovereignty and the ability to threaten and wage offensive war) but rather offering us the opportunity to gain something that we now lack and desperately need (extending the peaceful rule of law to international affairs, and with it, a massive increase in genuine national security).

As to criticism that world government would deprive states of one of the most important perquisites of state sovereignty—deciding whether or not to go to war—it is sobering to realize that such independence as the nation-states now cherish is in part illusory. The Soviet Union, for example, had no choice about entering World War II; when it was attacked by Germany in June 1941, it was forced to respond. Similarly, the United States was propelled into World War II not so much by a declaration of war by the U.S. House of Representatives as by decisions made by the Imperial War Council in Tokyo.

Limitations in Power

It is often said that the current international system of state sovereignty is essentially one of anarchy and that the fruit of such anarchy is war. The antidote for anarchy is authority, but any authority with worldwide reach and substantial coercive powers might be excessively strong and, thus, repressive. On the other hand, there might be an opposite danger, namely, the risk that a global authority could be weak and thus too hesitant to maintain adequate order. When the state loses respect and power—which could happen to a "world-state" as well—the doors are open to chaos, violence, social disruption, and, then, to fascist appeals for exaggerated structure and "traditional values." For example, in 1919, Italian poet-agitator Gabriele D'Annunzio and his followers moved to occupy the city of Rijeka in Yugoslavia, holding it for 16 chaotic months, while indecisive government authorities in both Yugoslavia and Italy tried unsuccessfully to establish public order. The breakup of the Soviet Union permitted old ethnic animosities to erupt in violence, and the economic and social disruption within Russia itself has provided fertile ground for the growth of aggressively nationalist and even fascist political movements.

Advocates of world government emphasize that any viable world authority would have clear enforcement powers but that these powers would also be carefully circumscribed and limited. As with the U.S. federal government, rights not specifically granted to a world authority would be reserved for its constituent states. After all, in our private lives, we cherish certain personal rights while also accepting restrictions on them: One person's freedom to swing his or her arm ends, for example, where someone else's nose begins. Under world government, nation-states would have to accept just two restrictions circumscribing their freedom (1) to maintain armed forces and (2) to behave aggressively against other states.

Similarly, there need be no anxiety that world government would necessarily mean the homogenization of national identities. Within the United States, Florida is still recognizably distinct from Alaska, and Maine from Arizona, just as national cultures within Russia range from urban Muscovites to tundra-dwelling indigenous people of Siberia, from industrialism to semi-nomadic Islamic pastoralism. As Israeli prime minister Golda Meir once pointed out: "Internationalism doesn't mean the end of individual nations. Orchestras don't mean the end of violins."

The Dream of World Government: A Waste of Time? ____

There is one other potential problem of world government, however, one rarely confronted by peace advocates: namely, that by focusing on it, devotees may lose touch with the world and its serious problems as they now exist. Or they may simply be ignored by the self-styled "realists" who run today's states, and by extension, the world. Lost in dreams of utopia, hungering after what may turn out to be nothing more than "globaloney," students of world government run the risk of being marginalized, considered irrelevant to "serious" discourse on issues of war and peace. If advocates of peace studies withdraw into musings over ideal but impractical solutions to real problems, they essentially give over the reins of power to those willing to deal instead with current reality. And time itself is critical, since world government will certainly not happen tomorrow, while wars are happening today. Even Freud, who supported the idea of world government, also warned about unrealistic dreams that "conjure up an ugly picture of mills which grind so slowly that, before the flour is ready, men are dead of hunger."

But no serious student of peace or devotee of world government recommends putting all of one's eggs in the one distant basket of global political union. It is not necessary to choose between nuclear arms reductions and world government, between peace in the Balkans and global disarmament, or between ecological harmony and transnational thinking and acting. In addition, even while we need to engage ourselves in immediate, practical, pressing issues, isn't there also a need to focus on ultimate goals, even if they seem—at the moment—to exceed our grasp? Can serious students of world peace ignore the need for global structural change, or the importance of planning not just for tomorrow but also for the more distant future? As General Omar Bradley once pointed out, "It is time we steered by the stars and not by the lights of each passing ship." Isn't this a "realistic" agenda as well?

Accordingly, we might ask the self-styled realists—the practical, hard-headed men (and they largely are *men*) if it is truly realistic to believe that the state system, with its divisions and contradictions, its history of repetitive warfare and state-centered selfishness, can be relied on to keep the peace and create a decent and humane planet into the indefinite future. Clearly, world government is unlikely to be perfect, but in view of the imperfections of the current state system, it seems unlikely to be worse, or more dangerous, than our current plight. The dangers of a world with some form of centralized, war-suppressing government pale in contrast to the dangers of a world without it.

According to historian Arnold Toynbee, "War has proved to have been the proximate [immediate] cause of the breakdown of every civilization which is known for certain to have broken down." And William McNeill, another noted historian, concluded a masterly survey of the role of armed forces and technology in human society by recommending that all but a token number of nuclear warheads ultimately be dismantled, with a monopoly of atomic weaponry to reside in a "global sovereign power."

> Nothing less radical than this seems in the least likely to suffice. Even in such a world, the clash of arms would not cease as long as human beings hate, love, and fear one another and form into groups whose cohesion and survival is expressed in and supported by mutual rivalry.

But an empire of the earth could be expected to limit violence by preventing other groups from arming themselves so elaborately as to endanger the sovereign's easy superiority. . . . When and whether a transition will be made from a system of states to an empire of the earth is the gravest question humanity confronts.[3]

Prospects for World Government

Despite its flaws, dangers, or difficulties, world government may well be essential. However, just because something is desirable—even necessary— does not mean that it will come to pass. A drowning person may *need* a life preserver, just as we may need world government, but necessity does not create miracles. People sometimes drown. Thus, it is not sufficient simply to state that world government is a prerequisite for survival, especially in the nuclear age. Maybe we will not survive.

Commitment to States

The pressures against world government are strong. People retain a deep loyalty to their nation-states, and also a powerful distrust of large central- ized systems. In addition, like so many proposals for dramatic reform (e.g., disarmament), the "devil is in the details." How do we get from here to there? In 1712, the French Abbe de Saint-Pierre proposed his pan-European Union, complete with a Senate of Peace, which would have authority over military forces sufficient to compel any recalcitrant ruler to submit to the will of the larger unit. Interestingly, the French foreign minister at the time, Andre Fleury, did not question the desirability of such a system, but he pointed out to Saint-Pierre: "You have forgotten an essential article, that of dispatching missionaries to touch the hearts of princes and to persuade them to enter into your views." Jean-Jacques Rousseau also applauded the scheme, but called it an "absurd dream," since sovereigns would never agree that their shared interest in peace supersedes their personal interest in power.

For government leaders to agree to a world government would be equivalent to slaveholders banding together to outlaw slavery. But slavery has in fact been outlawed worldwide, sometimes (notably, in the United States) only after much bloodshed. It might also be worthwhile to examine in greater detail how certain nation-states (e.g., Sweden, Holland, Portugal, Spain) have made a seemingly healthy transition from world power to rela- tive insignificance. This might serve not only to prepare the United States for the possibility of future decline in a world of continuing nation-states but also perhaps to suggest how the state system itself might be afforded lesser prominence and perhaps eventually eased out of existence.

At present, no powerful country seems any more prone to relinquish sovereignty and embrace world government; in most respects, such states remain fiercely independent. Tradition in the capitalist West tends to be deeply suspicious of large and powerful governments and is particularly jealous about guarding political freedom. And whereas Marxist theory calls for the eventual "withering away" of the state, the former Soviet Union and its allies were rarely any more receptive to world government. When the state is taken to embody the needs and aspirations of its citizens, there is little reason to surrender the state's power. Even "peace groups" were described as unnecessary in most Soviet bloc states, since the state itself was purported to be everybody's collective "peace group." (*It* was not the problem; *other* states were the problem!) Traditionally, the political right wing has engaged in relatively more militaristic flag-waving patriotism, while accusing the left of being part of, or duped by, various "international conspiracies," generally communist inspired. However, the heyday of socialist internationalism, as we have seen, was in the late 19th and early 20th centuries; in recent decades, many leftists have shown as much adherence to their own nation-state as have partisans of the political right. And in much of the developing world, militant nationalism is even more pronounced than in the industrialized North.

Beyond the issue of whether government leaders are capable of divesting themselves of the power that comes with state sovereignty is the question of whether most human beings have sufficient flexibility and generosity of spirit to embrace world citizenship over comparatively narrow, national concerns.

Examples of a Wider Identity

Although we do not know whether people are capable of considering themselves part of a united planet, the prospects may not be all that bleak. The United States of America, for example, is a very diverse country, made up of Caucasians, African Americans, Native Americans, Asian Americans, Catholics, Protestants, Jews—and yet, despite some prejudice, the country as a whole enjoys a reasonable degree of coherence. Although cynics may say that U.S. citizens are united by a shared fear of "the other"—Chinese, North Korean, or Cuban communists, Islamic terrorists, international Mafia-style gangsters—the United States also derives unity from a shared cultural and social identity, a shared history, and shared ideals. Certainly, the human species is capable of establishing even wider affiliations than between Maine and Hawaii, if such feelings of connection are encouraged from birth and reiterated by teaching, symbols, slogans, and a range of appeals, to emotion as well as reason. Such active propagandizing in favor of world citizenship may well be necessary, but it would hardly be unique: We are all subjected to vast amounts of pro-national and pro-state propaganda. A psychology of world citizenship might indeed be attainable, and without anything qualitatively different from what now passes for laudable patriotic teachings.

Take another example: People calling themselves "Germans" and "French" have long been at each other's throats, via their respective governments, the nation-states we identify as Germany and France. And yet quite near these perennially warring states, several million very "French" people live—and have lived for centuries—peacefully with about three times as many equally "German" people. The difference is that in the former case, a sovereign state of Germany has confronted an equally sovereign France, whereas in the latter, "French" and "German" have submerged war-making authority in the sovereignty of a third shared entity, known as Switzerland (which also contains a third large subpopulation, one that is Italian speaking). Similarly, English and Irish, Italian and Austrian, Vietnamese and Chinese, Arab and Jew, all have waged brutal wars across the globe—but when they become citizens of the United States of America, they submit themselves to a common identity and live together peaceably, at least for the most part. Clearly, it can be done.

The Case of the United States of America

Consider once again the present United States of America: When California, for example, has a dispute with Arizona regarding water rights, the two governments do not call up their militias and fight it out. The "law of force" is subordinated to the "force of law," and both sides submit arguments, if need be, to the U.S. Supreme Court. Then, they abide by the ruling. The states of the United States do not walk about like gunslingers from the Wild West, revolvers on their hips, ready to settle disputes by the fastest draw. Rather, just as individuals submit themselves to the rule of municipal law, the states submit themselves to the authority of the federal government—at least in certain carefully circumscribed areas, including the resolution of disputes among them.

Following the Revolutionary War, the United States under the Articles of Confederation was a loose amalgamation of states, headed toward disaster because of its virtual anarchy: Maryland and Delaware fought an undeclared "oyster war" over fishing rights to the Potomac River; nine states had navies of their own; state militias were separate and distinct armies; seven of the states even printed their own currency; New York placed a tariff on wood from Connecticut and on butter from New Jersey, Boston was boycotting grain from Rhode Island, various states imposed taxes on shipping from other states, and so on. Things were a mess, just as they are in the world today.

With the writing of the U.S. Constitution, however, a strong federal system was created, out of whole cloth. Advocates of world government point to this transition that gave birth to the United States of America as "the great rehearsal" for world federalism, a transition that the world system can also make if and when the need is widely recognized. Skeptics argue that the early American states were already homogeneous in culture and tradition, in language and ethnic background, unlike the world states of today. But in fact, there was substantial diversity in the 1780s: Catholics were denied the vote in Rhode Island, and the Catholic priesthood was itself illegal in Massachusetts, whereas Pennsylvania and Delaware were proud of their religious diversity. As just noted, no common system of taxation, currency, or trade existed, and interstate travel was often blocked by local restrictions. Moreover, the southern states practiced slavery, cherishing it as an essential part of their way of life, while majority opinion in the northern states was opposed to slaveholding.

Just as some people today fear a potential world superstate, the delegates to the Constitutional Convention also feared to establish a potential despotic dictatorship. Yet the framers of the Constitution recognized as well that the 13 states were threatened with war and unacceptable chaos, and so they successfully designed a workable federal union, one that preserved the rights of states in regulating their internal affairs while establishing a strong federal system capable of providing unity and ensuring the peace. They did this by establishing a careful, democratic system of checks and balances. At present, the states of Europe, with all their similarities and all the obvious benefits of federation, have moved haltingly but with increasing confidence toward a limited and fragile form of union.

Eleven different European states recognize the euro as a common currency; furthermore, within many countries of Europe, passports and visas are now entirely unnecessary, and passage through international borders— previously heavily controlled and guarded—is now usually very fast and no more consequential than going from Texas to Oklahoma, and this despite a history of major wars and a present reality of numerous distinct and cherished linguistic and cultural traditions.

The reality of what the United States accomplished—in the face of grave doubts—suggests the magnitude of what can be achieved. The problem in 1787 was for people to learn to think nationally about the United States, rather than locally. Now, the problem is for people to learn to think internationally, about the planet, rather than nationally.

Must world government wait, then, until humanity has achieved a higher level of spiritual development? It is true that the "founding fathers" are currently revered in the United States, but they were human beings, just like us. It is also true that the U.S. Constitution was not perfect (although it was certainly better than what preceded it). Moreover, no one in the late 18th century claimed that a strong federal government could not be enacted until all the inhabitants of North America had first become saints.

Toward World Government? _____

Several transgovernmental movements have sought to go beyond the current state system by establishing links that intentionally defy present political boundaries; for example, during the Cold War, the European Nuclear Disarmament movement consciously strove to move "beyond the blocs" separating East and West in Europe. A number of international tribunals have worked toward delegitimizing certain warlike actions of states, trying to apply principles of international law, even though such proceedings have lacked enforcement capability. For example, the Russell Tribunal in the 1960s excoriated the U.S. role in Vietnam; in 1982, another tribunal of international legal experts heard testimony and condemned the existing nuclear weapons regime at a meeting held, fittingly, in Nuremberg. The MacBride Commission in Britain investigated Israel's 1982 invasion of Lebanon and pronounced it a violation of international law. Such tribunals and peace movements generally are unpopular with the governments of nation-states because they seek to restrict war-making capacity, and also because they represent a budding transnational sensitivity, which might one day undermine state authority more generally.

If these activities truly threaten the current system of state sovereignty, it is an example of the important sociological principle that "if people define situations as real, they are real in their consequences." If we define ourselves as bound irreparably to the current state system, then we are so bound, by a kind of self-fulfilling prophecy. But the more we look beyond the states— and the more we find when we do so—then the more we may find ourselves liberated. Indeed, one of the things that keeps us prisoners of the state system is our inability to envision alternatives to it. Not many people, as recently as 1990, would have predicted a 21st-century world in which South Africa has become a democratic, multiracial state or in which the Soviet Union has dissolved and with it, the Cold War. Two futures are easy to imagine: This world ending with the "bang" of nuclear war or with the "whimper" of continued degradation (ecological, social) plus ongoing conventional wars. Both of these are plausible but undesirable extrapolations of the status quo. World government—in whatever specific form—offers a potential third way.

Recent decades have also seen a proliferation of planetary conferences, reflecting and dramatizing the fact that as advances in communication and transportation make the world smaller, the costs and responsibilities of technology—no less than its benefits—require attention on a global scale. Thus, there has been a World Population Conference in Bucharest, a Wood Food Conference in Rome, a World Women's Conference in Beijing, and numerous gatherings to discuss problems of pollution, the world status of indigenous people, the fight against racism and against AIDS, the linkages between disarmament and development, the problems of global warming, ozone depletion, destruction of the world's rain forests and the need to protect biodiversity, and so on. With or without world government, it is clear that worldwide problems cannot be solved by governments remaining stiffly within their traditional state boundaries.

Not surprisingly, the new social movements tend to be either local, community based, or region centered (and thus, below the level of the state) or transnational and global (above the level of the state). Moreover, states themselves have already begun to surrender some aspects of sovereignty, as we have seen in the case of certain international organizations as well as the general acknowledgment of—if not universal obedience to—international law. Perhaps this is a foot in the door. Or perhaps it simply reflects a cynical strategy by the states themselves: Give up a few insignificant crumbs while at the same time remaining as unwilling as ever to permit any meaningful challenge to their authority. But more subtly, many nation-states have already surrendered some aspects of their autonomy: The United States government, for example, is not politically "free" to declare war on Canada. A kind of de facto (in fact) restriction of state sovereignty has thus already come into effect, even though it is not yet de jure (in law). And even now, with no true apparatus of world government in place, the nuclear weapons of France, Britain, and the United States, at least do not directly threaten one another. Conventional war is even unthinkable between certain long-time rivals such as Britain and France, Holland and Britain, Finland or Turkey and Russia, France and Germany, or Japan and the United States.

Kenneth Boulding refers to the appearance of "zones of peace," which

> probably began in Scandinavia after the Napoleonic Wars between Sweden and Denmark, spread to North America about 1870, to Western Europe, Japan, Australia, and New Zealand after the Second World War. Now we have a great triangle of stable peace, stretching roughly from Australia to Japan, across North America, to Finland, with about eighteen counties which have no plans whatever to go to war with each other. This has happened without much planning or even understanding.[4]

Interest in world government tends to increase after major world wars: notably, World Wars I and II in the 20th century. Just as community pressure for a traffic light on a dangerous corner often does not peak until a child is killed at the intersection, perhaps another major war, or a close call, will be necessary for people to rise up and demand a dramatic reworking—if not a surrender—of state sovereignty. In the meanwhile, it should be emphasized that "futurism" need not be limited to technological panaceas and derring-do, a world of organ transplants, cyborgs, and Star Wars. It can also include moving beyond the state.

It is also important not to discount the role of vision and visionaries. Before we can ever establish a better world, we must first imagine it. This is not to deny the importance of dealing with the world as it is. It simply emphasizes that to "accept" current realities is not necessarily to accept them as god-given, engraved in stone, immune to challenge and to change. The world system of states, no matter how firmly entrenched, is nothing more than a human creation, and a relatively recent one at that. There is no reason to think that it is so perfect or so powerful as to be a permanent part of the human condition. "The dogmas of the quiet past," wrote Abraham Lincoln, "are inadequate to the stormy present. We must think anew and act anew." Only if we think, plan, dream, and act for a future world that is better than today's or yesterday's can we have any hope of attaining such a future.

A Final Note on World Government

Let us conclude with one of the premier theorists and advocates of a new future world order, Richard Falk:

> More and more various civil societies are experiencing disillusionment with facets of the old ways, but have yet to comprehend the feasibility of full-fledged alternatives. Our task is to join in the work of converting this societal disillusionment into creative social action to overcome the menace and begin to fulfill the promise contained in our situation. Never has the dual reality of danger and opportunity been more deeply grounded in the historical situation than it is at present.[5]

In Part IV, we examine some of the options currently under consideration for establishing positive peace in a world grown not only increasingly endangered but also increasingly interdependent. But first, we complement this chapter's discussion of worldwide political transcendence by exploring one more avenue for the building of negative peace, namely, ethical and religious traditions, by which many people have already superseded traditional state boundaries.

Notes

1. Charles L. des Montesquieu. 1949. *The Spirit of Laws*. New York: Hafner.
2. Grenville Clark and Louis Sohn. 1960. *World Peace Through World Law*. Cambridge, MA: Harvard University Press.
3. William H. McNeill. 1982. *The Pursuit of Power*. Chicago: University of Chicago Press.
4. Kenneth Boulding. 1965. *Stable Peace*. Austin: University of Texas Press.
5. Richard A. Falk. 1987. "The State System and Contemporary Social Movements." In S. H. Mendlovitz and R. B. J. Walker, eds., *Towards a Just World Peace*. London: Butterworths.

16 Ethical and Religious Perspectives

The God of peace is never glorified by human violence.

—Thomas Merton

War almost always involves killing, one of the most drastic actions a person can take. Killing another human being, except by accident, in self-defense, or out of insanity, is condemned in modern societies—unless done during war, in which case it is not only permitted but applauded. In fact, in war, particularly good killers are often accorded high honors. Not surprisingly, therefore, war has received substantial attention from ethicists and theologians. However, the relationship between moral teaching and war has long been ambiguous; advocates of peace have often derived inspiration and strength from such teachings, while at the same time, the war prone have also turned to religious and moral authorities (sometimes the same ones!) to support their arguments as well.

It may be that a concerted nationwide and planetary opposition to war will ultimately derive considerable impetus from ethical and religious sources; nonetheless, it remains true that some versions (or perversions) of ethics and religion have also fueled much warfare in the past, and may continue to do so in the future. Although we turn to religious and ethical traditions with hope, in fact the world's organized moral systems historically have been more likely to support militarism than to oppose it. Sometimes, as we shall see, religious authorities have been among the primary cheerleaders for war making. At other times, their stance has been passive acquiescence. In czarist Russia, for example, Russian Orthodox priests traditionally said a funeral mass for peasants when they were inducted into the army. Commonly, religious and ethical values were limited to self-protective and self-serving doctrines, such as immunity for the clergy and mixtures of reassurance and solace for the soldiery and endangered civilians. The following inscription (loosely translated) is commonly seen even today on houses in the various small villages of Bavaria: "Saint Florian, protect our town, pass by my house, burn others down"!

On the other hand, religious and ethical concerns must be central to the establishment of peace. Moral decisions cannot be avoided: There was, after all, virtually nothing scientifically or technically wrong with Auschwitz, Dachau, or the bombings of Dresden and Hiroshima. (The latter, especially, was a major scientific and technical achievement.) Criticism, or condemnation, must come—if at all—in moral terms. In the modern world, religion in particular has been transformative: Islam in post-shah Iran, Catholicism in Poland, Episcopal bishop Desmond Tutu and others who fought apartheid in South Africa, not to mention the role of Protestant Christianity in fueling the civil rights movement in the American South during the 1960s, as well as the impact of numerous churches in opposing the war in Vietnam, and nuclear weapons during the 1980s.

Warfare is typically overlain with numerous rules and elaborate structures of right and wrong. But fundamentally, it is an inversion of one of the most basic strictures of social life: Thou shalt not kill. Hence, it carries an inherent moral dilemma. (This, incidentally, may also be why war is so often the midwife of social change. Having broken out of the prescriptions of what is permissible and what is not, situations of war occasionally open up possibilities for rearranging the social order.) Any serious turnabout in fundamental attitudes regarding the acceptability of war will almost certainly involve ethical and religious formulations; conversely, no such turnabout will be possible if it is not somehow anchored in ethical and religious precepts. This, plus the support now provided by ethics and religion to peace workers and war boosters alike, makes it all the more important that students of peace pay close attention to these issues.

War and General Ethics

Mainstream Western ethical and religious thought typically condones war in particular cases; occasionally, as in fascist doctrine, war is even embraced with great enthusiasm. But when considering war in general, human ethical judgment by and large is critical. Approval—when it comes (and sooner or later, it usually does)—is largely restricted to specific wars, in which people are confronted with particular conflicts and identifiable enemies who typically are also perceived as threats. One might argue that the specifics are what count: Just as there is no such thing as "war" taken in the abstract, but rather specific wars, it avails nothing if ethicists condemn war in general but lend their approval to each particular war as it comes along. But this conclusion misses a potentially important characteristic of most ethical thought:

a predisposition *against* violence and killing. This fundamental and often unspoken precept may contribute importantly to the eventual delegitimation of war that is a goal of peace studies.

Presumption Against War

Like the presumption of innocence in legal proceedings, a widespread moral orientation presumes that the way of peace is better than the way of war. For war to be justified, therefore, in a world that prides itself on possessing moral values, the burden of proof must lie on those who would make war.

According to Immanuel Kant, war involves an inevitable moral descent. It deprives the enemy of the respect that is fundamentally due to all persons by virtue of their humanity. Kant emphasized that we should treat people as rational people intrinsically deserving respect (i.e., as *ends*), whereas war often requires the combatants to see each other as mere *means*, as objects, numbers, or targets. Frequently, commanders even treat their own soldiers as cannon fodder. This underlying depersonalization runs counter to deepseated moral precepts, hence the widespread need, even on the part of aggressors, to justify their actions in moral terms.

In addition, today most reasonable citizens recognize that might does not make right. When trial by combat became legal in Burgundy in A.D. 501, the clergy at the time objected, whereupon King Gundobald replied: "Is it not true that the event of national wars and private combats is directed by the judgment of God, and that his providence awards the victory to the juster cause?" Times have changed, and dramatically so; thus, no modern state currently condones the settling of private disputes by violent combat between the contending individuals. When state or national disputes are settled by war, however, it is analogous to settling personal disputes by individual combat, with the outcome presumably a function of strength, not of merit. Hence, such procedures are difficult to justify.

One of the most dramatic and famous exceptions to the Western moral injunction against the politics of "might makes right" occurred in the ancient Athenian campaign against the island of Melos. The Melians had favored Sparta during the Peloponnesian War, but sought to maintain neutrality since they were geographically close to Athens, which was far stronger than tiny Melos. After a lengthy siege, the Athenians delivered an ultimatum to the inhabitants of Melos: Surrender and be enslaved, or be destroyed. When the Melians protested the unfairness of this choice, arguing that they had not given Athens any cause for such violence, the Athenian spokesman answered in a speech that is renowned for its brutal honesty: "Right only comes into question when there is a balance of power, while it is Might that determines what the strong extort and the weak concede." The strong do what they will; the weak endure what they must. Ultimately, all Melian males were killed, and the women and children taken as slaves.

The Athenian disregard for conventional civil morality is shocking, and the fact that it is so upsetting is itself testimony to the virtually universal presumption that, in essentially all war, blame is heaped on the opponent. It is almost unheard-of for a belligerent to announce: "We have decided to make war on our neighbor, not because of any misdeeds on their part, or for any righteous cause, but because we desire to plunder their resources—including their women—settle on their territory, enhance our prestige, enrich our arms manufacturers, provide amusement and occupation for our dissatisfied young men, and/or deflect domestic criticism." Rather, even when the aggressive design is transparent, the other side is almost always blamed; such convenient fictions provide a shred of moral legitimacy to which the populace may cling and behind which the leadership may hide.

Blaming the Other Side

Wars are often preceded by efforts to emphasize the perfidy of the other side, or if necessary, to create "incidents" that make the war more acceptable. Many historians suspect, for example, that the sinking of the U.S. battleship *Maine* was either an accident or a deliberate provocation, initiated by persons hoping to goad the United States into declaring war on Spain in 1898. Similarly, Hitler repeatedly claimed that ethnic Germans within Czechoslovakia and Poland were being criminally maltreated, and prior to the invasion of 1939, German forces even staged a phony "attack," ostensibly by Polish troops against a German radio station near the border. The Gulf of Tonkin incident (1964) was essentially manufactured by President Lyndon Johnson as a successful ploy to paint North Vietnam as an aggressor against the United States and to get Congress to approve direct U.S. military intervention in the conflict in Southeast Asia. The second Russian war in Chechnya (1999–2000) was justified domestically as a response to the bombing of several apartment houses in Moscow—terrorist acts that were never proven to have been undertaken by Chechens and that some critics even suggest were initiated by the Russian government as an excuse for mobilizing public opinion in favor of crushing a troublesome, independence-minded republic.

Government leaders are only rarely as direct as the Athenians confronting Melos. In addition to setting up justifications, often phony ones, statesmen almost invariably describe their wars as being moral, often moral crusades. Thus, for many in the United States, the Vietnam War was a crusade to defend the democrats of Saigon against the butchers from Hanoi, just as the murderous contras in Nicaragua were likened by President Reagan to the American founding fathers. For Hitler, expansion of the Third Reich was required to save the world from Jews and communists. For the Soviet Union, interventionism was justified to protect the human rights of Afghans (especially the women, oppressed by Muslim fundamentalism), and to liberate

Hungary from the horrors of counterrevolution. For China, occupation of Tibet was explained as necessary to banish Tibetan feudalism. For India, their long-sought goal of dismembering Pakistan was clothed in the high moral purpose of aiding the persecuted Bengalis in East Pakistan. The U.S. insistence on driving Iraq out of Kuwait during the Gulf War was presented as a high-minded pursuit of international justice, whereas in all likelihood, it was primarily driven by worry about securing Kuwaiti oil, as well as domestic political needs. The North Atlantic Treaty Organization (NATO) war in Kosovo may well have been driven by NATO's desire to prove its relevance in a post-Cold War world, but it was publicly justified as purely moral in purpose: to prevent genocide by Serbia against native Kosovars. And so it has gone.

On the other hand, we should not be unduly cynical about the flexibility of ethical outrage. It is all too easy to criticize the ease with which moral indignation is aroused in support of organized killing. After all, politics is a difficult and messy occupation, and nowhere is it more difficult or messier than when it comes to decisions about war. In the view of some authorities, such as Reinhold Niebuhr, the necessity for tough, practical choice and action in a world of moral ambiguity transforms politics into nothing less than tragedy: "Politics will, to the end of history, be an area where conscience and power meet, where the ethical and coercive factors of human life will interpenetrate and work out their tentative and uneasy compromises."[1]

An alternative view, however, is that especially when it comes to issues of war and peace, death and life, there is no room for compromises or moral equivocation. Under such circumstances, it is not enough to choose the lesser of two evils. One must choose what is right.

Utilitarian Versus Absolutist Ethics

This raises an important distinction, between *utilitarian* and *absolutist* ethics. The former (also sometimes called "consequentialist") places particular value on the balance of benefits and costs associated with any act. For example, many sensitive and thoughtful people maintain that violence—even war—can be justifiable if it occurs in pursuit of some lofty goal, such as human freedom. More than 2,500 years ago, when the invading Persians called for their opponents to surrender, the greatly outnumbered Greeks responded as follows: "A slave's life thou understandest, but, never having tasted liberty, thou canst not tell whether it be sweet or no. Ah! Hadst thou known what freedom is, thou wouldst have bidden us fight for it."

Ethicist Michael Walzer argued that only aggression can justify war. He defined aggression as the "use of force of imminent threat of force by one state against the political sovereignty or territorial integrity of another," further arguing that "once the aggressor state has been militarily repulsed, it can also be punished," the goal of such punishment being to deter others, to exact legitimate retribution, and to restrain or reform the aggressor, as is done with respect to criminals in civil life.

Critics claim that ethics of this sort can have tragic effects, especially if mass violence is rationalized by verbal niceties that conveniently redefine "aggression," or the legitimate limits to "punishment." Once the door is opened to official sanction for violence, they argue, consequentialist or utilitarian ethics can rapidly become apologies for mass murder; the deliberate killing of civilians, for example, can be deemed permissible if enough can be gained by it. The alternative, absolutist (or "deontological") ethics, would include such stances as absolute pacifism. In this view, no killing is permissible, no matter what good is achieved, or what evil is averted thereby. (To be consistent, absolute support for destroying one's opponent should also logically be included here, but absolute ethics of this sort are rarely encountered in modern times.)

Our primary interest is to assess the contributions of religious and ethical precepts to the establishment of peace. Nonetheless, an accurate portrayal requires that we first examine the ambiguity of their roles, starting with some of the ways in which religion has disturbed the peace, rather than promoted it.

Religious Support for War

We have already seen that religious intolerance has led to many wars throughout history; in addition, religions have contributed to warfare directly, by their own internal demands and expectations.

Judaism

Jewish doctrine is inconsistent with respect to war. Whereas European Jews have traditionally been strongly peace oriented, the ancient Israelites were notable warriors, and indeed, the Old Testament is replete with bloody accounts of the so-called commanded wars, in which God urged his people to destroy others: "When the Lord your God has given them over to you, and you defeat them, then you must utterly destroy them; you shall make no covenant with them, and show no mercy to them" (Deuteronomy 7:2). For several thousand years, however, after the domination of Judaism by the Romans, Jewish tradition emphasized pacifism, only to experience a renewed warlike ethos in association with the founding of the state of Israel and in the aftermath of the Holocaust of the late 1930s and early 1940s, when approximately six million European Jews were slaughtered. Today, the Israeli army (technically known as the Israeli Defense Forces) is widely considered the most effective fighting force, person for person, in the world.

Islam, Hinduism, and Buddhism

Other religious traditions—less important in the United States but influential worldwide—have also displayed a positive attitude toward war. Best known among these is the jihad or holy war among Muslims, in which fallen warriors are considered to be guaranteed entry into heaven. Many Islamic scholars maintain that jihad applies most clearly to internal struggle, a personal "war" against one's own disobedient and thus ungodly inclinations. However, there also exists a parallel tradition that emphasizes the "glory" of dying in defense of Islam. Hinduism contributed to Gandhian nonviolence, but it has also had a rigorous military tradition. The great Hindu texts emphasize the duty of devout Hindus to fight even for a cause with which they may disagree: Bhisma, a hero in the *Mahabharata*, fought on behalf of the reigning government, even though he recognized the other side as more just. And in the *Bhagavad Gita*, the hero Arjuna is enjoined to kill even his friends and relatives, if his duty so demands. Moreover, battle is seen as a kind of divine, selfless action (*karma yoga*), and Arjuna, the man and warrior, is advised by Krishna, the warrior-god, to cease all personal striving: "Be thou merely the means of my work."

Peace has long been a central doctrine for Buddhism, like Christianity, but it has traditionally been more inward- than outward-looking. Specific war resistance as a self-conscious Buddhist goal has historically been rare. Notable exceptions were the United Buddhist Church in Vietnam and elsewhere in Indochina, especially after the early 1960s, when some Buddhists committed self-immolation (suicide by burning themselves) as a means of personal protest against the killing during the Vietnam War, and more recently, in Burma (Myanmar), protesting a dictatorial military junta. Subsequently, an intentional Buddhist peace tradition has emerged, emphasizing "engagement" in the world no less than pure contemplation, especially under the influence of the Vietnamese Zen teacher Thich Nhat Hanh.

Christianity

Christianity, too, has a complex relationship to war. Although as we shall see, many of its founding principles emphasize pacifism, turning the other cheek, and loving one's neighbor, Christianity (along with Islam, Hinduism, and Shinto, the predominant religious tradition of Japan) constitutes one of the great warrior religions of history. There is a fundamental Christian ambiguity toward war, reflected in the attitude toward the cross. On the one hand, it is supposed to be the ultimate symbol of God's peace and love, divine grace with which to replace violence and sin. But on the other, the cross has long been seen as a new and more effective sword with which to smite the forces of evil. Thus, Saint Paul warned that "if thou dost what is evil, fear, for not without reason does it [government] carry the sword. For

it is God's minister, an avenger to execute wrath on him who does evil"
(Romans 13:4).

Christianity was the eventual heir to the dying Roman Empire, and as
such, many of its early wars were unsuccessful, although fought with increasing fervor. The "holy war" tradition in Christianity is a direct descendant of
the commanded wars of the Old Testament and was especially potent during the Middle Ages, most dramatically during the Crusades. Saint Bernard
of Clairvaux, in the 12th century, delivered the following sermon in support
of Christian efforts to drive Muslims from Palestine:

> A new sort of army has appeared. . . . It fights a double war; first, the
> war of the flesh and blood against enemies; second, the war of the
> spirit against Satan and vice. . . . The soldier of Christ kills with safety;
> he dies with more safety still. He serves Christ when he kills. He serves
> himself when he is killed.[2]

In 1215, the Catholic Church took the important step of forbidding participation of priests or bishops in trials by combat. God, it was decided, was
not concerned with such demeaning matters; nonetheless, the tendency to
see wars as divine judgment and retribution continued, in part as a carryover
from the time when various Old Testament prophets warned that the
sinning city of Babylon would be punished by God, via war. From the 16th
to the 18th centuries, Christians continued a similar perspective; war was
widely seen as "God's beadle," chastising the ungodly, the sinners, those
who were insufficiently devout and righteous.

War has also been seen by many Christians as curiously attractive
precisely because it satisfies a guilt-ridden need for punishment, something
that has also long been prominent in Christian tradition. For example, the
General Court of Massachusetts declared in 1675 that war with the Indians
was brought about because the Puritans had ignored previous warnings
from God and that therefore "God hath heightened our calamity, and given
commission to the barbarous heathen to rise up against us, and to become
a smart rod and severe scourge to us." And so, although war was widely
perceived as undesirable and punishing, it was nonetheless considered to
have been ordained by God. Thus, under certain circumstances (i.e., when
the clergy approved), war was a legitimate endeavor for Christians. Not
only did war represent God's vengeance on the wicked, it could also serve as
a hair shirt, a kind of penance for the war maker, a chastisement for people
who had been backsliding, who needed its miseries to remind them of their
wickedness and smallness, and of God's almighty power.

At other times, religious zealotry served to legitimize the conquest of
nonbelievers. "Conversion by the sword" was a notable stimulus for the
expansion to Islam from A.D. 700 to 1450, but was also prominent among
Christian war makers.

Even as recently as 1914, the Bishop of London urged his countrymen to

kill Germans—kill them, not for the sake of killing, but to save the world, to kill the good as well as the bad, to kill the young men as well as the old . . . As I have said a thousand times, I look upon it as a war for purity, I look upon everyone who dies in it as a martyr.[3]

And of course, German priests and ministers were simultaneously reassuring their countrymen, *Gott mit uns* (God is with us). Warfare is bad enough; when religious zealousness adds absolute certainty of one's righteousness, then it becomes even worse. "Men never do evil so completely and cheerfully," noted Pascal, "as when they do it from religious conviction."

Religious Support for the Status Quo

Religious leaders and traditions have not only been accused of serving as cheerleaders for war but have also been condemned for hindering human freedom by serving as a bulwark in favor of the status quo. Christian doctrine in particular has been criticized for legitimating the oppression of women, blacks, sexual minorities, and the impoverished. The faithful often have been called upon to support law and order (favored code words for government-sponsored repression), as a way of keeping human "sinfulness" under control. In short, religion has often served to keep people submissive, weak, and accepting of their oppression. Not surprisingly, therefore, revolutionary socialist doctrine has generally been antagonistic to organized religion. Consider the following by Karl Marx:

The social principles of Christianity justified the slavery of antiquity, glorified the serfdom of the Middle Ages, and equally know, when necessary, how to defend the oppression of the proletariat. . . . The social principles of Christianity preach the necessity of a ruling and an oppressed class, and all they have for the latter is the pious wish the former will be charitable. . . . So much for the social principles of Christianity.[4]

During World War II, Joseph Goebbels—the Minister of Propaganda in Nazi Germany—suggested to German religious leaders, "You are at liberty to seek your salvation as you understand it, provided you do nothing to change the social order." Similarly, the Russian Orthodox Church was permitted to operate more or less freely in the former Soviet Union, so long as it did not challenge the political dominance of the Communist Party.

But in fact, Christian doctrine is not inevitably wedded to entrenched power, supportive of government-sponsored war making, and consistently opposed to social betterment. God, in short, is not necessarily a conservative, right-wing militarist. "Liberation theology," which originated in Latin America, proclaims a vigorously *social* gospel, emphasizing the social sensitivities of Christ, and the need for the modern-day Catholic Church to align itself on the side of the poor, the despised, and the disenfranchised. The General Conference of Latin American bishops, in Puebla, Mexico, in 1979, issued the following statement:

> From the heart of Latin America, a cry rises to the heavens ever louder and more imperative. It is the cry of a people who suffer and who demand justice, freedom, and respect for the fundamental rights of man. . . . We identify, as the most devastating and humiliating scourge, the situation of inhuman poverty in which millions of Latin Americans live.[5]

Christian "Realism"

To some extent, each Christian denomination has its own tradition with respect to war; often, in fact, the same church has differing, conflicting approaches. Thus, there are pacifist Baptists and highly militarist Baptists, nonviolent Lutherans and Lutheran paratroopers. Undoubtedly, the most carefully enunciated and influential Christian doctrine with respect to war has been a middle-of-the-road approach known as Just War doctrine.

Certainly, there is nothing new in seeking to provide ethical underpinnings for the initiation and conduct of war. The ancient Romans and Greeks developed carefully reasoned rationales for their wars, and 2,000 years earlier, the Code of Hammurabi, the earliest written set of legal regulations, begins with the statement that the Babylonian leader seeks to "establish justice in the earth, to destroy the base and the wicked, and to hold back the strong from oppressing the feeble . . . and to illuminate the land."

The Late Roman Empire

Substantial evidence suggests that the early Christian Church was pacifist; indeed, pacifism seems to have distinguished early Christianity from both the warlike Roman Empire and the equally violence-prone Old Testament Jewish tradition (the latter included the Zealots, who were Jewish terrorists and assassins seeking to coerce Roman withdrawal from ancient Palestine). Many early Christian martyrs died for refusing service in the Roman legions. By the fourth century A.D., the secular fortunes of Christianity improved, and with the conversion of the Roman emperor Constantine, Christianity became the official religion of the Roman state. Almost overnight, Christianity went from a minority and prophetic movement to the prime defender of Roman government and society. Its transformation was such that soon *only* Christians were permitted to serve in the Roman army. (It was in the context of taking up secular—especially war-related—burdens that the Catholic Church became the *Roman* Catholic Church.) When the Roman Empire was threatened by "godless barbarians" such as the Goths, Vandals, and Huns, Christianity quickly developed a more practical and accepting view of organized violence, a middle ground between the bloodthirsty commanded wars of the Old Testament and the uncompromising pacifism of the early Gospels. The result was a series of careful rules by which a Christian could engage in a "just war."

The Augustinian View

Major contributions to Just War doctrine can be found in the writings of medieval secularists such as DeVittoria, Suarez, and Grotius, as well as in the work of Saint Thomas Aquinas. The main contributor to Christian Just War theory, however, was Saint Augustine, Bishop of Hippo in the fourth century A.D. Augustine was primarily concerned with justifying Christian participation in the defense of Rome. In *The City of God*, Augustine wrote that "it is the wrong-doing of the opposing party which compels the wise man to wage just wars" and that "war with the hope of peace everlasting" to follow was preferable to "captivity without any thought of deliverance."

To Augustine, and the large tradition of "Christian realism" that followed him, peace was "tranquility in order." Augustine thus prefigured the tension between the devotees of order (often represented in modern times by the political right wing) and justice (typically represented by the political left). In the Augustinian view, peace often requires violence against evildoers, and the soldier who goes to war in defense of right—and order—does not violate the commandment against killing. "They who have waged war in obedience to the divine command, or in conformity with His laws" wrote St. Augustine, in *The City of God*, "have represented in their persons the public justice or the wisdom of government, and in this capacity have put to death wicked men; such persons have by no means violated the commandment: Thou shalt not kill."

War, in Augustine's view, must be based ultimately on "Christian charity," that is, the defense of a neighbor who has been unjustly attacked. Nonetheless, a Christian was expected to go to war, if at all, with a heavy heart, and only after carefully examining his conscience, because the presumption was at all times supposed to be in favor of peace. Thus, Augustine emphasized that when the Christian goes to war, he must do so with anguish and deep regret. Whereas the City of God is founded on an act of loving grace, the City of Man, in Augustine's view, is founded on war: "Whatever part of the city of the world raises the standard of war, it seeks to be lord of the world: in fact, it is enthralled in its own wickedness." Since the evil exists, the Christian is supposedly obliged to struggle against it. Much debate has arisen, however, over whether this is really a necessity, a permission, or an excuse. In certain hotly contested cases, wars themselves seem to be the greater immorality. Opposition to the Vietnam War in the United States, for example, was fueled by a passionate sense that this war was unjust in its origins, and also unjustly fought. The "Call to Resist Illegitimate Authority," issued in 1969 during the height of antiwar sentiment, asserted that "every free man has a legal right and a moral duty to exert every effort to end this war." This raises the painful but unavoidable question of personal responsibility, which is especially acute when society is perceived to be prosecuting an immoral war.

Just War Doctrine

There are two major components to Just War doctrine. The first refers to the justification of fighting a particular war—known by its Latin phrase, *jus ad bellum*, or the justice of a war. It spells out the requirements that must be met in order for a Christian to identify a particular war as acceptable. The second major component of Just War doctrine is *jus in bello*, or justice *in* a war. Whereas *jus ad bellum* concerns whether or not a war ought to be fought, the rules for electing war versus peace, *jus in bello* deals with the manner in which such a war may be engaged, the rules for conducting any given war. Thus, a just war (one that meets *ad bellum* criteria) may be fought unjustly (if it fails to accord with *in bello* restraints), and similarly, an unjust war can be prosecuted justly.

Jus ad Bellum

The generally acknowledged criteria for *jus ad bellum* are as follows:

1. *Last resort:* War must not be entered into with undue haste or unseemly enthusiasm, but rather only if all other means of resolution have been explored and found inadequate.

2. *Legitimate authority:* The decision to go to war cannot be made by disgruntled individuals or self-appointed groups; it must come from duly constituted state authority.

3. *Right intention and just cause:* War is unacceptable if it is motivated by aggression or even revenge; it must be consistent with Christian charity and/or self-defense. (Interestingly, Augustine specifically excluded self-defense, arguing that it was acceptable only to wage war in defense of *others*.)

4. *Chance of success:* Futile resistance cannot be justified; only when there is reasonable chance of a beneficent outcome may the Christian consider that a war is justifiable.

5. *Goal of peace:* Looking ahead to the conclusion of the war, it must be possible to envision a peace that is preferable to the situation that would prevail if the war was not fought.

Conditions 3–5 are sometimes summarized as the "principle of proportionality," which states that for a war to be just, its overall moral benefits must exceed its costs. Thus, the principle of proportionality recognizes that war is inherently evil, and therefore it can be justified only if it leads to an even greater overall good. In practice, once a state's leadership decides on war, the overwhelming majority of its religious figures almost always pronounce it to be just, whereupon the average citizen or soldier goes along. But at the same time, the requirements for *jus ad bellum* arguments provide—at least in theory—a yardstick whereby "good" Christians can personally evaluate the legitimacy of a state's call to arms.

Jus in Bello

Once a war is under way, it can, in Just War doctrine, be fought justly or unjustly. The generally acknowledged *in bello* restraints can be summarized in two principles, double effect and discrimination. The principle of double effect is a specific application of the *ad bellum* doctrine of proportionality, described above. Just as wars can be seen to have good and bad overall effects, the principle of double effect states that specific *in bello* actions— those taken during a war—typically have two effects: a "good" effect in bringing the war to a successful conclusion, and a "bad" one in causing pain, death, and destruction to combatants and often noncombatants as well. According to the principle of double effect, therefore, such actions as bombings and invasions can be countenanced only if the good effect outweighs the bad. Military means and the cost of war must be proportional to a moral end and its presumed benefits.

The second component of *in bello* restraints, the principle of discrimination, is synonymous with "noncombatant immunity." It states that civilians must not be the direct, intentional object of military attack. This principle recognizes that civilians will often be killed during hostilities, but the direct targeting of noncombatants is prohibited. In practice, however, the principle of discrimination further acknowledges that noncombatants will often be targeted "indirectly," and such activities, so long as they are ostensibly inadvertent, are generally condoned. For example, when strategic bombardment seeks either to destroy war-production facilities or to diminish the other side's morale, as in the firebombing of German and Japanese cities during World War II, the practical effect has typically been the massacre of tens of thousands of noncombatants.

Various attempts have been made to establish *in bello* restraints on the conduct of war. The medieval "Truce of God" defined certain days as unacceptable for fighting, and the "Peace of God" prohibited direct attack against certain persons: travelers, merchants, clergy, and farmers. The "code of chivalry" established rules concerning who may fight with whom, and regarding the treatment of prisoners (i.e., if they were members of the nobility). The Second Lateran Council, in 1215, even banned the use of certain weapons, notably the crossbow. Significantly, however, these prohibitions applied only to use against *Christians*; the crossbow could still be employed against Muslims, during the Crusades. But even this prohibition eventually faltered, and in fact, there have been very few examples of weapons that have been effectively banned because their use was judged immoral.

Chemical weapons appear to be an exception. Although used widely during World War I, they were also universally condemned and hardly employed at all during World War II. On the other hand, this restraint may have been more a function of deterrence than of moral considerations, since each side knew that the other was capable of retaliating with comparable weapons. Moreover, chemical weapons have been used during the 1980s, notably by the Iraqis against the Iranians, and also against Kurdish rebels in northern Iraq. Biological weapons are universally condemned and have been essentially banned, although stockpiles are still maintained in certain cases, supposedly so as to facilitate the design of countermeasures.

Violations of Noncombatant Immunity

Perhaps the most notable feature of *in bello* restraint, however, and its most tragic failures, involve violations of noncombatant immunity, a trend that has been increasing since 1914. For example, although military casualties were roughly comparable during World Wars I and II, civilian casualties were substantially higher in the latter. This seems due to two factors: (1) the greater involvement of entire populations in a nationwide war effort, thereby blurring the distinction between military and civilian, and (2) the invention of increasingly more destructive and less discriminating weapons, most of which also operate at great distance. Nuclear weapons represent a culmination of this trend.

Strategic bombing of cities became increasingly frequent during World War II. There had been great public outcry at the fascist bombing of Guernica during the Spanish Civil War, the Japanese bombing of Chinese cities such as Nanking, and the German bombing of Rotterdam and Warsaw. By the time of the London blitz and the subsequent Allied bombings of civilian populations in Germany and Japan, however, countercity targeting was virtually taken for granted. Night bombing was safer than daytime raids for the attacking side, but was substantially less accurate than bombing by day; hence, it was virtually impossible to conduct precision attacks on specific, military targets or even on war industries, as was seen to some degree in NATO's bombing raids on Belgrade in 1999. Rather, whole cities became targets. Tens of thousands of civilians died in the nighttime firebombing of Dresden, Hamburg, Tokyo, and Osaka. Munitions were specifically designed to increase the probability of creating firestorms, and bombing patterns were employed to create a ring of fire, trapping civilians within.

Lewis Mumford denounced the Allied saturation bombing of German civilian targets in World War II as "unconditional moral surrender to Hitler," and David Lilienthal, later the first chairman of the Atomic Energy Commission, warned, "The fences are gone. And it was we, the civilized, who have pushed standardless conduct to its ultimate." Others, of course, argued that strategic bombing in general, and the atomic bombing of Hiroshima and Nagasaki in particular, was morally justified under the doctrine of double effect, claiming that the good effect (the supposed hastening of the end of the war) overrode the bad (the killing of hundreds of thousands of civilians). But in fact, moral standards were not abandoned altogether. It is interesting to note that a plaque in Westminster Abbey commemorates the Royal Air Force (RAF) pilots of Fighter Command who died defending Britain against German bombers, whereas there is no comparable recognition of the (equally brave) fliers of Bomber Command who died while raining destruction on German cities.

It is noteworthy that ethical considerations such as noncombatant immunity have been influential even in the propaganda associated with war. Typically, each side will accuse the other of causing civilian casualties. President Truman even described the first atomic target, Hiroshima, as "an important military base," whereas it definitely was not. (By late summer of 1945, U.S. bombers had been striking targets throughout Japan at will; all targets of military significance had already been attacked, most of them many times.) Rather, Hiroshima was chosen specifically because its military irrelevance had caused it to escape prior attacks, and as an intact city, it was capable of providing a clear demonstration of atomic destruction.

Another ethical justification for overriding the principle of noncombatant immunity is that such immunity is a dangerous and misleading nicety that makes war seem civilized, and therefore, acceptable. Why, one might ask, is it considered an atrocity to throw a human being into a fire, but a legitimate military activity to throw fire on a human being? The firebombing of Dresden took place during the last days of the Second World War, when its outcome was already known, and when the city itself was swollen with thousands of refugees and in the middle of a children's carnival. Commenting on the presumed immorality of the Dresden firebombing, a British RAF official maintained that it is not so much this or the other means of making war that is immoral or inhuman. What is immoral is war itself. Once the full-scale war has broken out it can never be humanized or civilized, and if one side attempted to do so it would most likely be defeated. So long as we resort to war to settle differences between nations, so long will we have to endure the horrors, barbarities, and excesses war brings with it. That, to me, is the lesson of Dresden.[6]

In the early 19th century, the Prussian military theorist Karl von Clausewitz had also argued against the concept of restraints in war:

He who uses force unsparingly, without reference against the bloodshed involved, must obtain a superiority if his adversary uses less vigour in its application. . . . To introduce into a philosophy of war a principle of moderation would be an absurdity. War is an act of violence pushed to its utmost bounds.[7]

And yet, the horrors of unrestricted warfare are so great that it is only natural to be grateful for whatever *in bello* restraints the human mind can conceive and agree to—however imperfect, or how frequently violated in practice. During the U.S.-led bombing of Kosovo and, later, Afghanistan, notable effects were made to minimize civilian casualties, the exact number of whom may never be known.

Religious Pacifism

Neither holy wars nor Just War doctrine constitutes a unique contribution of Christianity to religious ethics and warfare. Holy wars trace their ancestry to the warlike traditions of the Old Testament, and Just War doctrine is essentially a reworking of Greco-Roman ethics. It is in the doctrine of *pacifism* that Christianity makes its most notably distinct contribution to Western religious ethics and warfare. In many ways, Christianity marked the advent of organized pacifism in the West, at least in the sense of doctrinal refusal to participate in military service.

The Second Commandment calls us to love our neighbor as ourselves, but the New Testament, especially the Gospel according to Saint John, goes farther, enjoining followers to love their *enemy*, and actively to return good for evil. Among modern Christian churches, the historic "peace churches," including the Society of Friends (Quakers), Mennonites, and the Church of the Brethren, are notable for their literal adherence to pacifist doctrines as enunciated, for example, in Christ's Sermon on the Mount:

You have heard that they were told, "An eye for an eye and a tooth for a tooth." But I tell you not to resist injury, but if anyone strikes you on your right cheek, turn the other to him too. . . . You have heard that they were told, "You must love your neighbor and hate your enemy." But I tell you, love your enemies and pray for your persecutors. (Matthew 5:38–46)

Pacifist traditions have also persisted as minority views within mainstream churches, including Catholicism, via such organizations as Pax Christi. The Fellowship of Reconciliation (FOR) is an ecumenical effort to unite and coordinate religious pacifists of all faiths. In addition to opposing military policies, pacifists refuse personal participation in wars, most directly by resisting conscription. They often practice tax resistance as well, which frequently takes the form of refusing to pay the proportion of national taxes that goes toward the military. Some governments, including that of the United States, have reluctantly accepted the legitimacy of conscientious objectors, so long as some form of alternative service is available; on the other hand, war resisters have traditionally been persecuted, sometimes killed, and even today are often imprisoned for their views.

Many pacifists agree with G. K. Chesterton's sardonic observation that "the Christian ideal has not been tried and found wanting. It has been found difficult and left untried." Mennonite theologian John Howard Yoder was one who tried:

Christians whose loyalty to the Prince of Peace puts them out of step with today's nationalistic world . . . are not unrealistic dreamers who think that by their objections all wars will end. The unrealistic dreamers are rather the soldiers who think that they can put an end to wars by preparing for just one more. . . . Christians love their enemies not because they think the enemies are wonderful people, nor because they believe that love is sure to conquer those enemies. . . . The Christian loves his or her enemies because God does, and God commands His followers to do so; that is the only reason, and that is enough.[8]

Religious pacifists such as Yoder emphasize that people were created in God's image and that Christ died for all humanity. Hence, they maintain that the Christian has no choice: He or she must follow Christ's injunctions and model, refusing to do violence against others, especially if this might entail taking another's life—regardless of what the secular authorities might demand. Noted pacifist A. J. Muste made numerous impassioned calls for noncompliance with the military draft, which he termed an act of "holy disobedience." It is interesting to note that in Western religious traditions, disobedience is widely considered to be the primary human sin (witness Satan's disobedience to God, or Adam and Eve's alleged transgressions in the Garden of Eden). And yet a case can be made that throughout human history, far more harm has been done by obedience to authority than by disobedience.

Nuclear Ethics

Although considerable debate surrounds religious and ethical approaches to war, when it comes to *nuclear* war, the issues are somewhat more clear-cut. And despite the end of the Cold War, it must be emphasized that there continue to be thousands of nuclear weapons maintained in different countries and that their use—by "terrorists," "rogue states," newly proliferated nuclear powers, or even the declared nuclear weapons states—cannot be precluded so long as they exist. Most authorities agree that a nuclear war could never meet Just War criteria. Noncombatant immunity could not be maintained, although some hawkish ethicists argue that civilians might legitimately be killed in such a war so long as they are not targeted directly, as such. In 1966, the Second Vatican Council concluded that "any act of war aimed indiscriminately at the destruction of entire cities or of extensive areas along with their populations is a crime against God and man itself. It merits unequivocal and unhesitating condemnation." In their pastoral letter in 1983, the American Catholic bishops added that "this condemnation, in our judgment, applies even to the retaliatory use of weapons striking enemy cities after our own have already been struck."

It is difficult to imagine what kind of "good effect" could balance the "bad effect" of killing millions of people, possibly hundreds of millions, and maybe even threatening the continuation of life on earth. Moreover, nuclear war would seem to fail each of the various *ad bellum* considerations listed previously. Accordingly, the U.S. Catholic bishops concluded that "our No to nuclear war must, in the end, be definitive and decisive."

Ethics and Nuclear Deterrence

Although there is general (but by no means universal) agreement among civilians that nuclear war must necessarily be profoundly immoral, much debate surrounds the question of whether nuclear *deterrence* is equally unacceptable. The question is, can a country legitimately threaten something that would be immoral if carried out? Protestant ethicist Paul Ramsey used this metaphor to describe the dilemma:

> Suppose that one Labor Day weekend no one was killed or maimed on the highways, and that the reason for the remarkable restraint placed on the recklessness of automobile drivers was that suddenly every one of them discovered that he was driving with a baby tied to his front bumper! That would be no way to regulate traffic even if it succeeds in regulating it perfectly, since such a system makes innocent human lives the direct object of attack and uses them as a mere means for restraining the drivers of automobiles.[9]

Ramsey's point is that moral error lies first in the intention to do wrong, and only later in the act itself. This is why intended wrong (such as homicide) is considered more serious than accidental wrong (such as manslaughter), and doing the right thing for the wrong reason is nonetheless considered an ethical transgression. To rework Ramsey's metaphor, imagine that society decreed that in the event of murder, punishment would befall not only the murderer but also all his friends and relatives. This would clearly be an unethical system, *even if it worked.*

Nonetheless, Ramsey ends up defending the legitimacy of nuclear deterrence, so long as it is limited to counterforce targeting. He admits that an adversary might be restrained by fears of collateral effects—the practical awareness that nuclear retaliation, even if ostensibly aimed at military targets only, would cause enormous destruction to the country and civilian populace at large. But so long as this is a by-product of the intended, discriminate targeting, apologists for nuclear deterrence deem it acceptable.

Other thinkers justify nuclear deterrence with the argument that sometimes it is necessary to commit an evil (threatening nuclear war) in order to prevent an allegedly greater one (war itself, and/or—at least during the Cold War—communist domination of the United States). On the other hand, the paradox remains that only by making credible threats can nuclear deterrence possibly work, and only by meaning these threats—that is, deploying weapons and using strategies that are intended to be used—can they be effective. So the effectiveness of deterrence varies directly with the likelihood that if one's bluff is called, nuclear war will follow.

The American Catholic bishops, in their 1983 pastoral letter, *The Challenge of Peace*, were unequivocal in rejecting *any* use of nuclear weapons:

> We do not perceive any situation in which the deliberate initiation of nuclear warfare, on however restricted a scale, can be morally justified. Non-nuclear attacks by another state must be resisted by other than nuclear means. Therefore, a serious moral obligation exists to develop non-nuclear defensive strategies as rapidly as possible.

In spite of this sentiment, the bishops wound up with a strictly conditional *acceptance* of nuclear deterrence, echoing the judgment of Pope John Paul II, who said in a speech at Hiroshima that "in current conditions, deterrence based on balance, certainly not as an end in itself but as a step on the way toward a progressive disarmament, may still be judged morally acceptable." As time goes on, however, ethicists may well ask whether deterrence has truly been used as a step toward disarmament or as an end in itself, and also a means of justifying yet more weaponry (e.g., "modernization" having been justified as a means of "enhancing deterrence.") Thus, the United Methodist Council of Bishops went farther than their Catholic counterparts, and refused to condone nuclear deterrence:

The moral case for nuclear deterrence, even as an interim ethic, has been undermined by unrelenting arms escalation. Deterrence no longer serves, if it ever did, as a strategy that facilitates disarmament. . . . Deterrence must no longer receive the churches' blessing, even as a temporary warrant for the maintenance of nuclear weapons.[10]

Supporters of deterrence have argued that nuclear weapons are moral and acceptable because they preserve the essential values of Western, Christian civilization. By attributing the collapse of communism to the West's perseverance in maintaining and adding to its nuclear arsenals, nuclear supporters justify the continued maintenance of such arsenals, as a deterrent to other states and ideologies as well as a hedge in case Soviet-style communism should reappear. Moreover, nuclear supporters do not discount the possibility that limited nuclear wars could be fought, and even won, which, if true, would diminish the ethical onus of fighting such wars and of preparing for them.

On the other hand, opponents maintain that nuclear weapons are themselves profoundly immoral and that willingness to employ these weapons is simply unacceptable. In the words of diplomat/historian George Kennan,

The readiness to use nuclear weapons against other human beings—against people whom we do not know, whom we have never seen, and whose guilt or innocence it is not for us to establish—and in doing so to place in jeopardy the natural structure upon which all civilization rests, as though the safety and the perceived interests of our own generation were more important than everything that has ever taken place or could take place in civilization; this is nothing less than a presumption, a blasphemy, an indignity—an indignity of monstrous dimensions—offered to God![11]

A Final Note on Ethics and Religion

It remains uncertain whether ethical and religious precepts and courageous leaders might ultimately lead the way toward the abolition of war and the establishment of peace. Absolute prohibitions—against killing, for example —have rarely been followed with absolute fidelity. And given that human beings have so often used moral or religious certainty as a justification for repression, intolerance, and cruelty, there is some reason to be distrustful of any form of moral absolutism. On the other hand, it may be that at this stage of human history, when the very survival of humanity hangs in the balance, revulsion against organized violence is an absolute necessity as well as a realistic hope. The remarkable changes in the human situation—notably the collapse of the Soviet Union and the end of the Cold War, as well as the end of apartheid in South Africa—offer exciting possibilities for redirecting human endeavor toward life instead of the mechanisms of oppression and death.

Having now completed our review of negative peace—that is, prospects and proposals for preventing war—let us bear in mind that in the long run, such prevention will be a shallow victory if it does not include the establishment of positive peace as well. Hence, in Part IV, we turn from war to peace, just as we hope that someday, the world will.

Notes

1. Reinhold Neibuhr. 1932. *Moral Men and Immoral Society*. New York: Scribner.

2. Saint Bernard of Clairvaux. 1980. *Sermons*. Geneva, Switzerland: Slatkine Reprints.

3. Quoted in Roland Bainton. 1960. *Christian Attitudes Toward War and Peace*. Nashville, TN: Abingdon.

4. Karl Marx. 1964. *On Religion*. New York: Schocken.

5. Quoted in Penny Lernoux. 1982. *Cry of the People*. New York: Penguin.

6. Quoted in D. Irving. 1963. *The Destruction of Dresden*. New York: Holt, Rinehart & Winston.

7. Karl von Clausewitz. 1976. *On War*. Princeton, NJ: Princeton University Press.

8. John Howard Yoder. 1982. "Living the Disarmed Life: Christ's Strategy for Peace." In J. Wallis, ed., *Waging Peace*. New York: Harper & Row.

9. Paul Ramsey. 1968. *The Just War*. New York: Scribner.

10. United Methodist Council of Bishops. 1986. *In Defense of Creation: The Nuclear Crisis and a Just Peace*. Nashville, TN: Graded Press.

11. George F. Kennan. 1982. "A Christian's View of the Arms Race." *Theology Today* 39:2.

On November 12, 2001, the Security Council of the United Nations adopts resolution 1377, calling on all states to become parties to the international conventions and protocols relating to terrorism. (UN/DPI Photo by Eskinder Debebe)

PART IV

Building Positive Peace

We travel together, passengers on a little
spaceship, dependent on its vulnerable reserves
of air and soil; all committed for our safety
to its security and peace; preserved from
annihilation only by the care, the work and the
love we give our fragile craft, and, I may say,
each other.

—Adlai E. Stevenson

Preventing war is a necessary condition for the establishment of real peace, but it is not sufficient. A world without war is certainly to be desired, but even this would not really produce a world at peace. In short, it is not enough to be against something, namely, war. We need, as well, to be in favor of something, and that something must be positive and affirmative, namely, peace. Of necessity, therefore, the positive peace toward which peace studies strives must be part of a broader, deeper effort to rethink the relationship of human beings to each other and to their planet. As difficult as it will be to obtain negative peace—the prevention of war—it may be even more of a challenge to achieve positive peace, since a world without violence would be a significant challenge to our basic way of living, not just our ways of occasionally dying, and killing.

The field of peace studies is unusual not only in its cross-disciplinary approach to the understanding and prevention of war but also in its efforts to envision and help establish a desirable and attainable peace. But if war seems difficult to define—as evidenced by disagreement about the role of formal declarations, number of casualties, nature of the combatants, level of violence, and so on—peace can be even more elusive. Nonetheless, it is possible to sketch the outlines of a just and sustainable peace, recognizing that in a world that is not only beset with violence but that also relies on violence and on the structures of violence, efforts toward such a peace may be not only visionary but also radical, even revolutionary.

As this world enters the 21st century, it is becoming increasingly clear that ideologically based political and military competition is outdated, dangerous, and also irrelevant to humanity's fundamental needs. Ardent militarists seem more and more to be ideological dinosaurs, formidable but dated, moving clumsily and even stupidly across a rapidly changing landscape. It is necessary that we end militarized competition, but we must not stop there. As we probe the issue of positive peace, it will become apparent that ideological and military disputes of the sort that so preoccupied the post-World War II world should give way to planetary issues (many of which reveal tensions along a North-South axis): concerning human rights, poverty, and the environment, and on the fundamental principles of nonviolence in politics and in personal life.

As we have seen, much importance has been attributed to the so-called Just War doctrine. The conditions for a "just peace" are no less strenuous or important. For many in the West (at least, those who are relatively affluent and well educated), hope for a peaceful world is equated with continuing the status quo, with some improvements around the margins, such as guaranteed health care, children in a good college, and an ever-increasing stock portfolio, whereas for many in the lesser developed countries, it is reflected in basic aspirations for human rights, national autonomy, and economic well-being. For a growing number of people around the globe, just peace also entails achieving a viable relationship with the natural environment.

Whereas the absence of war is relatively easy to define—but still susceptible to dispute—reasonable people are even more likely to disagree about what constitutes a desirable condition of positive peace. It brings up what we might call the "car-canine problem": Imagine a dog that has spent years barking and running after cars. Then one day it catches one. What does it do with it? What would devotees of peace do with the world if they had the chance?

17   Human Rights

Injustice anywhere is an affront to justice everywhere.

—Martin Luther King, Jr.

Like Mark Twain's celebrated remark about the weather, we can say that many people talk about human rights, but relatively few do anything about it. And yet this issue is very serious. A great many human beings are denied some of the most basic human rights: Nearly one half the world's people are denied democratic freedoms and participation; about one third face severe restrictions on their right to own property; over one half of Asia and black Africa do not have access to safe water; jails are filled with political prisoners, many of them held without trial and victimized by torture; child labor is widespread; women are often deprived of the economic, social, and political rights that men take for granted; many workers are not only non-unionized but prohibited even from forming unions; the right of conscientious objection to military service is not recognized in most countries; censorship is widespread; and billions of people are illiterate, chronically sick, without adequate shelter, and just plain hungry. Human rights, it seems, are more honored in the breach than the reality. Nonetheless, concern with such rights has, if anything, been growing in recent years. Real progress is being made, and more yet can be anticipated.

A Brief History of Human Rights

It is tempting to claim that human rights are as old as the human species, but the truth seems to be quite different. Even if human rights themselves are

God-given, inalienable, and fundamental, the conception of human rights as such—and respect for them—is relatively new. Individuals may possess rights and privileges, but these have traditionally been considered the province of society, to be bestowed or revoked by the larger unit (band, tribe, village, city, state) at will. In virtually all societies, for virtually all of human history, ultimate values have been derived from the social order, not the individual. Hence, an individual human being could not claim entitlement to very much, if anything, simply because he or she existed as a human being.

Some elements of traditional cultures support the concept of human rights as wide-ranging and universally derived. Confucius, for example, argued that "within the four seas all men are brothers," and Buddhists believe in "compassion for every living creature." But in fact, the idea of human rights as currently understood is largely a Western tradition, deriving especially from the work of John Locke and John Stuart Mill. Locke maintained that the fundamental human right was the right to property, the primary one being the right to the secure ownership of one's own body; civil and political rights flowed, in his view, from this. And Mill strove for a set of rights not covered by the state. Thus, there is some truth to the criticism that Westerners advocating human rights may occasionally be guilty of moral arrogance, seeking to export their own rather culture-bound ideas, especially their emphasis on civil/political freedom.

It should also be emphasized that Western political thought is not limited to individualism and human rights; rather, it coexists with respect for—and occasionally, virtual worship of—the state. According to influential theorists such as Hegel and Herder, rights are enlarged and created for individuals only through the actions of the state. And for orthodox Marxists, value derives only from the social order: There is no meaning, in doctrinaire Marxist analysis, to individual rights prior to those granted by society. Although communist societies are supposedly designed to maximize the benefits of every person, the "rights" of each individual may come to naught if they run counter to the greater good of society as a whole. Individuals can expect to receive benefits from a community only insofar as they participate in it and further its goals. And as we shall see, even today—with communism largely a memory and ever-increasing agreement on the meaning and desirability of human rights—there continues to be substantial disagreement as to priorities.

Human Rights in Modern Times

Internationally, there was little concern with human rights until after World War II. Despite the Enlightenment, despite modern capitalism's emphasis on individual property rights, and despite Western democracy's emphasis on individual political rights, as a practical matter state sovereignty has long taken precedence over human rights. When the world-wide modern state system was established in the mid-17th century, governments agreed—ostensibly in the interest of world peace—not to concern themselves very much with how other governments treated their own citizens. Within its own boundaries, each state was supreme and could do virtually as it wished.

Gradually, however, human rights law developed, initially out of concern with protecting persons during armed conflict. The Geneva Convention of 1864, for example, sought to establish standards for treatment of wounded soldiers and of prisoners. (It is ironic that war—one of the most inhumane of human situations—should have led to the first organized recognition of shared humanitarian values.) The International Committee of the Red Cross is a nongovernmental organization (NGO) long concerned with international human rights; it was organized by a group of Swiss citizens who had attended the 1864 Geneva Conference. The Red Cross remains active today, seeking especially to ensure fair treatment of people during armed conflict; it has also participated in several modifications and revisions of the Geneva Convention, most recently in 1977.

Following World War I, there was widespread recognition that one cause of that conflict had been the denial of national rights, within large empires such as Austria-Hungary's. Hence, human rights received explicit attention from the League of Nations, which emphasized that the rights of minorities must be respected by larger federal governments. Labor rights—the right to organize, the right to decent working conditions and wages, restrictions on child labor—were the focus of the International Labor Organization, which later persisted within the United Nations, and also won a Nobel Peace Prize. Opposition to slavery catalyzed numerous early human rights organizations, such as the Anti-Slavery League. (Many people do not realize that in many countries slavery was only abolished during the 1950s; some claim that it is still being practiced today, notably in Mauritania, Pakistan, and Sudan.)

Organized, worldwide concern for human rights did not really coalesce until after World War II, perhaps in part as a reaction to the devastating denials of rights that occurred in association with that conflict. In the aftermath of the Nazi Holocaust, the world's conscience was finally activated —partly out of regret for those who had suffered, and partly too out of enlightened self-interest. Martin Niemöller put it memorably:

First they came for the Jews and I did not speak out—because I was not a Jew. Then they came for the communists and I did not speak out —because I was not a communist. Then they came for the trade unionists and I did not speak out—because I was not a trade unionist. Then they came for me—and there was no one left to speak out for me.[1]

(In fact, Pastor Niemöller himself became a victim of the Nazis.)

Since 1945, many people have begun to speak out for themselves and for human rights of every sort. Before we review some of the legal protections, conventions, and treaties that have resulted, let us consider what is meant by human rights, and how they have come to be asserted.

The Political Philosophy of Human Rights

Human rights implies a new way of viewing the relationship of governments and their citizens, whereby governance is intended to enhance the dignity of human beings, not exploit them. It is useful to consider three major political philosophies of human rights, each divisible into two branches.

Liberalism

In traditional liberal thought, human rights exist not only because of their contribution to human dignity but also because human beings, themselves, naturally possess such rights. "The object of any obligation in the realm of human affairs," according to philosopher Simone Weil,

> is always the human being as such. There exists an obligation towards every human being for the sole reason that he or she is a human being, without any other condition requiring to be fulfilled, and even without any recognition of such obligation on the part of the individual concerned.[2]

In Jefferson's phrase, people have certain "inalienable rights," which may not be denied. The liberal view of human rights thus corresponds to the "natural law" perspective. Social democracies, such as Sweden, are also constructed along liberal lines, but with a stronger dose of economic egalitarianism. Thus, while the classical liberalism of the United States stresses equal civil and political rights, with freedom of socioeconomic competition, egalitarian liberalism such as Sweden's (and to a lesser extent, those of Canada, Australia, and Germany) places greater emphasis on a right to a minimum degree of socioeconomic standards as well.

Conservatism

Traditional Anglo-American conservatism is rarely articulated today with respect to human rights, because conservatism is in large part a philosophy of unequal rights and privileges and, as such, difficult to defend in an avowedly egalitarian age. But the unspoken tenets of conservatism are nonetheless influential in practice. Classical Western conservatism can be said to have originated with Plato, who argued in *The Republic* that all people are not equal and that the best form of government is therefore not democracy but rule by philosopher-kings. More than two millennia later, this belief in unequal rights underpins many right-wing governments, from the "classical conservatism" of the military juntas that ruled Brazil and Greece to the various U.S.-sponsored Central American governments through most of the late 20th century (Guatemala, Honduras, Panama) to the neofascist dictatorships as occurred in Chile, Paraguay, Indonesia, and the Philippines, in which rights were reserved only for the most powerful.

Collectivism

Finally, there is a third branch of human rights philosophy, which for want of a better term, might be called "collectivist." As with liberalism and conservatism, it can be subdivided into two branches, Marxist and nationalist. For Karl Marx, individuals were not fully independent actors; rather, they were controlled by economic forces engaged in a relentless class struggle. In the Marxist view, the liberal emphasis on individual rights is therefore misplaced, a bourgeois luxury, ideological form without social substance. Instead, rights are conferred by society, and they should belong exclusively to the proletariat or working class. Such an approach leads automatically to an embrace of socioeconomic rights and economic equity, with a downplaying of civil/political rights. Thus, in Marxist societies, freedom of speech and opinion have been permitted insofar as they do not conflict with the stated goals of group advancement and welfare. The state, and not the working class, typically became paramount.

The second version of collectivist human rights has a leftist flavor but is not, strictly speaking, Marxist. It originates instead in the experience of national liberation movements, and it places special emphasis on the right to national self-determination and economic development, from which all other rights are then derived. Believers in the human right of national self-determination downplay the individual as well as the social class, although they remain committed to equal rights. Emphasis instead is on the rights of a national grouping. This approach lay behind the "Universal Declaration of the Rights of Peoples," which grew out of an influential 1976 meeting of highly regarded, nongovernmental spokespeople from the developing world. Its concern with "people's rights" clearly distinguishes this approach from the Western focus on "individual rights."

Choosing the Appropriate Philosophy

Not surprisingly, there is substantial debate over which human rights model is most appropriate for any given country. The two major contending Western systems of the past—capitalism based on classical liberal principles and Marxism based on a particular collectivist philosophy—historically have brought into being deep structures of oppression. Thus, although Marxism explicitly claimed that the state will eventually disappear, the fact remains that Marxist state structures showed no tendency to do so; in fact, they became notably oppressive in their own right, until, as in the case of the Soviet Union, they simply crumbled (which is very different from Marx's original conception, under which the ideal workers' state would wither away only after all its goals had been achieved). Even more than liberal capitalist states, Marxist governments have tended to be super-states, abusing power via ossified bureaucratic structures that were generally insensitive to personal civil and political liberties. It should also be pointed out, however, that liberal capitalist democracies were persistently antagonistic toward the revolutionary Marxist states; this in turn lent some credibility to the latter's claim that their state power had to be maintained as a guard against counter-revolution.

By contrast, the supposedly "minimal states" envisioned by some Western liberal philosophers, and established especially in northern Europe and North America, have been primarily concerned with balancing the various political powers of government, and between governments and the people. Social and economic "rights" are generally treated as secondary, as capitalist/democratic societies rely on market mechanisms and an ethos of individual competition. Only begrudgingly have the capitalist/democratic states recognized a social responsibility toward their populace.

On balance, capitalist democracies give insufficient attention to socio-economic rights, while state socialist governments take inadequate account of civil/political ones. It seems clear that economic development is generally more rapid under capitalism, and indeed, the economic stagnation of most communist countries appears to have contributed mightily to their dramatic political decline. At the same time, relatively little benefit from economic development actually reaches the poorest citizens of most capitalist states. The rapid transition to a primitive kind of capitalism on the part of Russia and its former satellite states has been accompanied, in most cases, by immense wealth on the part of a small minority of successful entrepreneurs (and more than a few outright crooks and beneficiaries of rampant crony-ism, as state assets were sold off at ridiculously low prices). At the same time, living conditions for the majority have if anything worsened. In such cases, political freedoms have expanded dramatically across the board. Whereas economic *opportunities*—at least in theory—have improved immensely for everyone, in practice, most people formerly living under Soviet-style communism and now experiencing Western style "freedom" have undergone a deterioration in the status of their socioeconomic rights.

What Are Human Rights?

After doing much to spark the American Revolution, Thomas Paine went to France at the time of the French Revolution. There, he is said to have had the following conversation with Benjamin Franklin, U.S. ambassador to France. "Wherever liberty is," said Franklin, "there is my country." To which Paine replied, "Wherever liberty is *not*, there is mine." Despite their seeming disagreement, Paine and Franklin were united in espousing the same basic view of human rights, the one that is most readily identified by most people in the United States even today: individual liberty.

Individual Liberty Versus Socioeconomic Rights

Even individual liberty is not unidimensional. It involves many things, notably bodily freedom from torture, unjust imprisonment, and execution, as well as intellectual freedom to speak, write, and worship and various political freedoms, including the right to peaceful assembly, to freedom of association, and to vote by secret ballot. Numerous other human rights have also been identified and proposed, including notably what have been called "socioeconomic rights," such as the right to work, decent housing, education, medical care, and adequate food. To some extent, the United States and most other economically advanced capitalist states associate human rights with the first category, whereas communist (Marxist-Leninist) states and impoverished, Third World, undeveloped, "underdeveloped," or "developing" states have long given greater weight to the second. Those who are wealthy and privileged characteristically favor maximum individual freedom (especially, freedom of economic competition) and a minimal role for government, which at least in the United States often leads in turn to opposition to the "welfare state." Those lacking in wealth and power are typically more in need of laws and specified rights, to be ensured by society. Hence, there is a tendency among some Western governments to describe socioeconomic rights as not really "human rights" at all, but rather, goals or aspirations for society.

A global consensus has been developing that incorporates not only the traditional American concern with political liberty but also an additional concern with socioeconomic rights, as well as other values that are difficult to pigeonhole. In some especially dramatic cases, alternative visions of human rights are different indeed: the "right to life" (of a fetus) versus a woman's "right to choose" (whether to have an abortion). Many other rights are also asserted, which are not quite as controversial—states' rights, consumer rights—but to claim that something is a "human right" is to claim something particularly fundamental and weighty. It should not be done lightly.

Cyrus Vance, secretary of state during the Carter administration, gave the following categorization of human rights from the dominant U.S. perspective:

> First, there is the right to be free from governmental violation of the integrity of the person. Such violations include torture; cruel, inhuman, or degrading treatment or punishment; and arbitrary arrest or imprisonment. And they include denial of fair public trial and invasion of the home. Second, there is the right to the fulfillment of such vital needs as food, shelter, health care, and education. . . . Third, there is the right to enjoy civil and political liberties: freedom of thought, of religion, of assembly; freedom of speech; freedom of movement both within and outside one's own country; freedom to take part in government.[3]

This listing, although useful, omits certain other categories of rights that many people consider important, such as the right to security from mass destruction and to a safe natural environment. One simple categorization parallels the famous French motto "liberty, equality, fraternity": (1) political and intellectual rights, (2) economic and social rights, and (3) the right to peace and to a safe natural environment. Of these, the first ("liberty") is the most widely accepted in the West; the second ("equality") remains controversial, especially in the United States; and the third ("fraternity") is the most unsettled—and for some, unsettling—of all.

Large numbers of people, especially in developing countries, attribute great importance to socioeconomic rights. In the words of Léopold Senghor, former president of Senegal, "Human rights begin with breakfast." Without such an awareness, it is all too easy for relatively well-off Westerners to sneer at the poor "rights" records of other countries, oblivious to their own shortcomings in the eyes of others. In addition, if Westerners would recognize the validity of socioeconomic rights, then governments such as Libya under Gadhafi or Cuba under Castro—which to many in the West are failures because of their lack of representative government, widespread censorship, and other civil-political inadequacies—can at the same time be acknowledged as effective, even admirable, in other domains, such as public health or literacy. This is not to claim that success in some dimensions of human rights cancels outrages in another; rather, it helps permit a more balanced perception of systems that might otherwise seem unidimensionally evil, and whose high level of local, domestic acceptance would otherwise be difficult for Americans to understand.

Indigenous People and Others

There are about 250 million indigenous people worldwide, representing national majorities in, for example, Guatemala and Bolivia, and small minorities in Brazil, Australia, Russia, and the United States. Regardless of their numbers, indigenous people are generally in dire straits, sometimes—as in Guatemala and Brazil—having suffered genocide even in recent times. For example, a UN investigation concluded in 1999 that three former Guatemalan presidents had been involved in genocide, state terrorism, and torture as part of a brutal counterinsurgency campaign conducted by the Guatemalan military during the 1970s and 1980s; this resulted in the deaths of more than 200,000 people, most of them Mayan Indians.

In other cases, indigenous people are severely maltreated, and/or they enjoy dramatically fewer opportunities and privileges than their nonnative counterparts:

- Australian aborigines are on a per capita basis the most imprisoned people on earth, with a incarceration rate 16 times that of the Caucasian population.
- Even aside from being the targets of government-inspired atrocities, the life expectancy of Mayan Indians in Guatemala is 11 years shorter than that of the nonindigenous population.
- The average per capita income of Native Americans is half that of the rest of the U.S. population.
- Large dams have devastated the homelands of indigenous peoples in Canada, Brazil, Norway, the Philippines, and India, depriving them of an arguably crucial human right: to live in their ancestral homelands.

And this is but a partial list.

Other groups can also be identified as having particular human rights claims and vulnerabilities: mentally ill persons, children, homeless persons, racial and sexual minorities, handicapped persons, convicts, unskilled workers, migrant laborers, refugees, political dissidents, the elderly, and so on. Ideally, human rights such as civil freedoms, economic opportunity, protection from mass destruction, and the right to a safe and clean environment will be equally shared by all people. In practice, these rights must often be defended most vigilantly for those groups that have thus far been the most victimized.

Women's Rights

Women comprise more than 50% of the world's population, and yet they are an oppressed group. For centuries, women have suffered from patriarchal social structures that devalue their personhood and deny many of their basic human rights. This includes a diverse array of abuses, such as footbinding in precommunist China; the forced seclusion and isolation of women in certain contemporary Hindu and Muslim societies; sexual mutilation, as currently practiced on millions of young women in numerous African societies; polygamy; restricted or nonexistent choice as to marriage; and—even in ostensibly liberated societies such as that of the United States and Great Britain—greatly restricted economic and professional opportunities along with underrepresentation in political life. In can be argued that whatever the sources of well-being in the world, women as a group consistently enjoy less of them; this includes intangibles such as opportunity as well as physical assets such as property.

Some History

In the West, concern with women's rights dates from the Enlightenment. These rights were set out clearly, for example, in Mary Wollstonecraft's *A Vindication of the Rights of Women*, published in England in 1792. This brief and powerful book emphasized the importance of providing education for women equaling that available to men. (Even in the 21st century, however, illiteracy rates remain consistently higher for women than for men, especially in developing countries.) Social philosopher John Stuart Mill was also especially eloquent about the necessity that women receive opportunities for economic and social advancement that are comparable to those available to men. During the late 19th and early 20th centuries, crusaders for women's rights were especially concerned about obtaining *suffrage*, the right to vote and to hold political office.

By the mid-20th century, something of a shift occurred, with growing consciousness in Western liberal circles of the degree to which women were also oppressed in the domestic sphere. Especially influential were these milestone books: *The Second Sex*, by Simone de Beauvoir, which raised feminist consciousness by pointing out the extent to which men were traditionally considered the "subjects" of modern life whereas women were merely "others" and secondary "objects"; *The Feminine Mystique*, by Betty Friedan, which identified the deadening domesticity to which women were typically relegated; and *The Female Eunuch*, by Germaine Greer, which castigated the sexual passivity to which many women were traditionally forced. Added to this were innovations in birth control technology (especially the development of contraceptive pills), as well as the U.S. civil rights movement, which raised public awareness about the need to reevaluate and reconfigure the role of women in the home, workplace, and the public sphere.

In the West

Although women's suffrage is essentially universal in the West, women's participation in the political process or in the business and professional world is nonetheless often constricted by the traditional idea that "a woman's place is in the home" (which is not that far removed from the Nazi motto for women: *Kinder, Kirche, Kuche*—children, church, and cooking). Advocates for women's rights point out that women are typically paid 80% of what men receive for comparable work, demanding instead, "equal pay for equal work." The numbers of women in executive-level positions in the U.S. corporate world remains very low. The effort to expand women's social and political options involves a continuing effort to challenge social stereotypes of women as dependent, weak, passive, and hyperemotional relative to men. Although some countries (Great Britain, Norway, Israel, India, Sri Lanka, Pakistan) have had woman prime ministers, no woman has been elected president of the United States, and indeed, the U.S. Congress has not even passed an equal rights amendment. Women's reproductive rights remain precarious, as evidenced by ongoing efforts on the part of social conservatives to restrict access to abortions, and to roll back *affirmative action* programs that benefit women as well as minorities.

So on the one hand, there are struggles to protect those modest advances that have been achieved. In addition, a continuing debate within the feminist and women's rights movement revolves around the degree of change to be sought: whether radical restructuring of society (ranging from private domestic relationships to the sinews of our public life), or whether change should be incremental, within the basic social structures that currently exist. Such debate is not necessarily a weakness of the women's rights movement; rather, it reflects the vigor and heterogeneity of its devotees, paralleling ongoing discussion within other peace movements.

In Developing Countries

In most economically developing countries, the goals of the women's movement tend to be more basic: increased literacy, health care, and an end to polygamy and *brideprice* (whereby men literally purchase a wife). In many traditional societies, especially in Africa, millions of women are subjected to genital mutilation, which is often justified as a legitimate cultural practice but that causes immense suffering, as well as diminished sexual pleasure, not to mention high mortality rates. Many Muslim countries insist on highly restrictive dress codes for women, legally sanctioned violent— often lethal—responses to sexual infidelity, and frequently, the denial of educational, social, and economic opportunities. Women are prohibited from driving a car in Saudi Arabia, for example, and the fundamentalist Taliban government of Afghanistan denied basic education to women and prohibited women from working outside their houses; indeed, women were not even permitted to go outside at all unless accompanied by a male relative. As egregious as these conditions were, it is noteworthy that the U.S. military pressure that eventually brought down the Taliban was not motivated by outrage at the terrible state of women's rights in Afghanistan, but rather in response to attacks on the World Trade Center and the Pentagon.

In many countries, women cannot own property and may not obtain a divorce without their husband's consent. Many feminists point out that although Western society may well be unacceptably repressive, the sad fact is that most developing countries are even worse, with women widely subjected to lower legal status, institutionalized economic deprivation, cultural subordination, economic deprivation, and outright political repression.

Feminism and Peace

Women's rights have also become increasingly tied to an integrated pro-peace agenda. This reflects, among other things, the fact that whereas men are the primary wagers of war, women have long been among those most likely to suffer (because of their vulnerability as part of the civilian population). Feminists also point out the likely connection between patriarchy (male dominance) and war making, as reflected in what appears to be a greater male propensity for violence, in hierarchical structuring of systems of power, and in the exalting of threats and physical force over consensus building. Feminist scholar and peace educator Betty Reardon also emphasizes that "traditional gender roles have assigned the main functions and maintenance of *quotidian* ["daily, and domestic"] security to women while excluding them from participation in the exercise of power over national and global security" and that "this arrangement has made women more vulnerable to the violent consequences of militarized security," an arrangement that is especially unfair given that "the substance of daily life, the domestic and social chores upon which everyday human life depends, the functions that make all other human activities possible are women's work. Public decisions of life and death are not." In Reardon's view—and that of a growing number of feminist peace workers—this must change: "The feminist challenge is becoming a challenge to the war system itself."[4]

Reflecting this sense of both increased vulnerability and yet, paradoxically, the prospect of enhanced political power, there have been several major intergovernmental conferences concerned with women's rights: in Mexico City, Copenhagen, Nairobi, and Beijing. These meetings, held in conjunction with the United Nations, have produced numerous documents detailing various women's rights—including, but not limited to, the right to physical security—and have also brought together diverse groups, especially through the actions of numerous NGOs.

Ever since *Lysistrata*, the classic Greek play by Aristophanes, women have taken part in efforts to end war and violence (although, to be sure, some have also participated in such activities, or even instigated, and—rarely—led them). Many women have also engaged in direct action in support of an avowedly feminist peace agenda. "Women in Black," composed of Israeli and Palestinian women, have been urging an end to Israeli military occupation of the West Bank and Gaza, as well as to terrorism; they have also appeared at other sites of violent conflict such as the former Yugoslavia. The Argentinean "Madres de la Plaza de Mayo," beginning in the 1970s, protested the "disappearances" (in most cases, the kidnapping, torture, and murder) of their children, raising national and international consciousness about crimes against humanity on the part of their government, and shaming political leaders into action. Similar courageous and effective actions have been taken by the Chilean "Association of the Relatives of the Detained and Disappeared." The "Soldiers' Mothers' Movement" in Russia has actively interfered with the drafting and brutalization of Russian conscripts—especially in the USSR's war in Afghanistan and Russia's war in Chechnya—in the process becoming an important political force. It is noteworthy that these and other groups have carried their message via direct actions and nonviolent public protest, rather than mere lamentation.

Some Areas of Controversy

In many cases, the distinctions between civil-political and socioeconomic rights may be arbitrary. The right to free speech, to vote, or to be free of torture are clearly different from the right to eat or to work. But what about the right to form a trade union—is that civil-political or socioeconomic? And what about the right to an education? As we shall see, human rights and "development" policy frequently intersect in the realm of "basic human needs." The list is very long, and yet, this does not mean that the issue of rights is meaningless or unimportant. Nor does it mean that real and meaningful progress cannot be made.

It seems unavoidable that sometimes various rights will conflict. In a famous opinion, U.S. Supreme Court Justice Oliver Wendell Holmes concluded that the right to free speech did not extend to yelling "Fire" in a crowded theater. The "right" to a drug-free environment may conflict with the "right" to privacy, just as the "right" of people in developing countries to healthy babies has already been found to conflict with the "right" of the Nestlé company to market infant formula. In Islamic states, women's "rights" are often subordinated to the "rights" of people to practice the religion of their choice. A woman's "right" to control her own body, including an abortion if she desires, runs contrary to a fetus's "right" to life; the "right" of religious freedom can conflict with a child's "right" to necessary medical care, as when fundamentalist parents refuse life-saving treatment for their child; the public's "right" to safe air travel appears to have triumphed over individual "rights" not to be searched without a warrant; and the list goes on.

However they are sliced, many human rights are essentially claims against the authority of governments. As such, they are freedoms *from*: guarantees that governments will refrain from behaving badly toward their own people. These can be distinguished from freedoms *to*: the asserted obligations of society to help its members to achieve a better life. It is a distinction that somewhat parallels the one between negative and positive peace: between those rights asserted *against* governments (no war, no intrusions into personal freedom) and those expected *of* them (establish positive peace, provide for basic human needs). In most cases, the first category (negative rights) seem easier for governments to achieve; certain states may simply lack the financial resources to make substantial improvements in socioeconomic conditions, but they all can stop torturing, murdering, and oppressing their people in other ways.

Although human rights constitute a diverse and sometimes confusing array of causes, from peace, women's rights, environmental protection, and penal reform to national independence, they share a common humanizing focus, placing individuals at the center of public policy. "The goal of human rights advocacy," writes one authority, "is to insist that the power, security, and economic well-being of states and their ruling elites be accompanied by concern for the average citizen and/or the least well-off in political and economic terms."[5]

The Legal Status of Human Rights

Explicit statements of human rights are most clearly associated with various international agreements, nearly all of which have been developed since the Second World War, and which derive their legal status from international law.

UN-Related Agreements

Although the UN Charter serves as a kind of international constitution, it lacks a Bill of Rights, specifying which human rights are to be protected. The UN-sponsored Universal Declaration of Human Rights (UDHR) was passed unanimously in 1948, enumerating these rights. The United States was a major contributor to the UDHR; much of its impetus came from Eleanor Roosevelt, widow of U.S. president Franklin D. Roosevelt.

The UDHR consists of 30 articles, of which the first 21 are primarily civil/political, prohibiting torture and arbitrary arrest, guaranteeing freedom of assembly, religion, speech, emigration, and even the right to vote by secret ballot. The remaining articles are concerned with socioeconomic and cultural rights, including the right to work, to an "adequate" standard of living, to education, to some form of social security, and even specifying the right to vacations with pay.

The UDHR is not technically binding in the sense of an international treaty; it is a recommendation only, with no provisions for enforcement. Nonetheless, it has had substantial impact on thinking worldwide, is widely respected, and has legitimated concern with human rights; it has even been incorporated into many national constitutions. To some degree, the UDHR has become part of customary international law, and accordingly, many judicial scholars argue that it has the literal force of law, although it is often violated. (It should be noted that customary law is more universal and more durable than treaty law.)

Numerous worldwide legal instruments have built on the UN Charter and the UDHR, including an array of covenants, conventions, treaties, and declarations, of diverse legal meaning, but all helping to further define the concept of human rights. Of these, the most important are the Convention on the Prevention and Punishment of the Crime of Genocide (1948, only belatedly ratified by the United States) and the International Convention on the Elimination of All Forms of Racial Discrimination (1965—the United States has not ratified). There have also been two UN human rights covenants, signed in 1966, which entered into force in 1977, when they were ratified by a sufficient number of national governments, but again, not by the United States. These are the International Covenant on Civil and Political Rights and the International Covenant on Economic, Social, and Cultural Rights. There have also been two 1977 Geneva Protocols on Armed Conflict, both of them controversial and not universally in force, in addition to various instruments concerned with specified rights, such as those of refugees and children, as well as denunciations of apartheid and numerous declarations that were less formal in character.

Some scholars and political decision makers dispute precisely what obligations member states undertake when, in the UN Charter, they agree to "promote universal respect for and observance" of human rights. Nonetheless, an underlying consensus has emerged that governments have no business engaging in a "consistent pattern of gross violations of human rights." Thus, whereas isolated incidents are unlikely to generate worldwide outrage, "gross violations," if they recur, merit condemnation and, ultimately, such actions as censure, economic boycott, and possibly even military intervention. Abuses of this sort could include widespread torture, mass arrests and imprisonment without trial, genocide, vicious policies of racial segregation and debasement, and forced relocation of entire populations.

Human Rights and the Nation-State

Some halting progress has been made as *national* courts have begun ruling to enforce *international* norms with respect to human rights. For example, in a celebrated legal case, *Filartiga v. Pena*, a U.S. court ruled in 1980 that politically inspired torture and murder were so clearly prohibited by international agreements on human rights that the United States had jurisdiction to prosecute a Paraguayan national for events occurring within Paraguay. In 1998, the British government arrested former Chilean dictator Augusto Pinochet and nearly put him on trial for thousands of cases of torture and the "disappearance" of political prisoners while he had been dictator of Chile (Pinochet narrowly avoided legal action because he was judged too old and feeble to stand trial, and he was deported to Chile). Nonetheless, this case constitutes an important precedent, one that might well be expanded to allow prosecution of the many ex-heads of state—typically living in comfortable exile—who ordered or condoned murder and torture while in office. The ultimate significance of such prosecutions would likely go beyond the satisfaction of justice, notably by putting current despots on notice that they may well have to answer for crimes committed on "their watch."

As controversial as the Pinochet case has been, there is nothing new about governments criticizing human rights abuses in other states, although it is novel for them to place national leaders under arrest for human rights violations committed while they were heads of state. Governments have long found it useful to complain loudly about the actions of other governments—especially those to which they are not allied—while turning a blind eye to their own misbehavior. The real crunch between states and human rights concerns the degree to which a state is willing to forgo part of its own sovereignty and permit its own human rights practices to be the subject of international scrutiny, judgment, and influence—if not control.

Resistance to Western Intervention

Although many Western citizens often assume that people from other cultures would necessarily applaud their actions on behalf of worldwide human rights, sometimes the response is less than enthusiastic. Partly, this is because of the moral arrogance with which the primarily Western concept of human rights is exported to other societies. Partly, it is because people from developing countries remain very aware of Western imperialism and the fact that in the past, the West's legitimate promotion of human rights has been used as a moral pretext in connection with colonial conquest: for example, bringing an end to "barbarous" practices such as the Indian custom of *suttee* (burning a widow on her deceased husband's funeral pyre), foot-binding, or female infanticide. In addition, many developing countries are intensely committed to socioeconomic rights, and they believe—rightly or wrongly—that progress in this respect may require a strong governmental authority, exerting some restrictions on civil and political rights.

Following World War II, more than 80 former Western colonies won their political freedom, liberating more than one billion people in the world's most massive transfer of political power. But national independence does not necessarily guarantee the rights of individuals. In some cases, quite the opposite takes place, especially when the newly established government is shaky; threats to the security of the nation serve as a handy excuse for denying individual rights, and in fact, many newly independent countries are politically insecure, for a variety of reasons. There is accordingly a strong tendency for such states to be run by dictatorial, often military, governments, and for such governments to be especially repressive of human rights.

The Primacy of State Sovereignty

The greatest underlying conflict between human rights and the nation-state is one that is characteristic of virtually all governments. It derives from the very nature of state sovereignty and the point that a call for human rights is generally a claim on behalf of individuals *against* the state. Whether demanding that states refrain from mistreating their people (negative rights) or that they commit themselves more aggressively to their betterment (positive rights), claimants for human rights typically push governments in directions they would not otherwise choose. International standards of human rights may represent assaults on state power and sovereignty by restricting what a state can do (and sometimes, telling it what to do), even within its own borders. This could include disapproval by the international human rights community of a country's internal policies, notwithstanding that such policies may be fully "legal" according to its own domestic laws. For example, South African apartheid laws were not internationally acknowledged as legitimate, despite the fact that they were duly passed by that country's legislative parliament. The North Atlantic Treaty Organization's (NATO) brief but violent air war in Kosovo was largely a response to the widespread perception that the Serbian government was abusing the human rights of Kosovars, and international intervention occurred despite the fact that Kosovo at the time was unquestionably part of Yugoslavia. (The Kosovo intervention was at least partly a Western effort to compensate for the fact that other countries did nothing to prevent genocidal slaughter in Rwanda five years earlier.)

Paradoxically, a concern for human rights may actually enhance state sovereignty. States that by and large adhere to international standards of human rights (the Western democracies generally) normally experience a higher level of legitimacy and security than those that routinely trample on them. No serious observer of the United States, Western Europe, Australia, or Japan seriously worries that any of these governments will be overthrown by coup or revolution—unlike the fate of others that abused human rights, such as Duvalier in Haiti, Somoza in Nicaragua, or Ceausescu in Romania.

The Role of Politics

Governments are often asked to report on the status of human rights within their own borders. It can be argued, however, that leaving states to report on their own human rights situation is like having the fox report on the status of the chickens. The assessment by outside experts, including dissidents, is generally much more critical as well as believable than judgments made by nationals about their own government's behavior.

The United Nations has also played politics with human rights. Thus, the UN Human Rights Commission has generally been willing to criticize pariah states such as Israel and (during its apartheid regime) South Africa, but not the major powers. On the other hand, organizations such as the Red Cross, the International Labor Organization, UNESCO, UNICEF, the Food and Agriculture Organization (FAO), the World Health Organization (WHO), and the High Commission on Refugees have done much to improve human rights within offending states. Private NGOs, notably Amnesty International (which won a Nobel Peace Prize in 1977), have sometimes been effective in improving conditions for specific political prisoners, and on many occasions, even winning their release. But such groups have typically focused on individual cases, avoiding the more troublesome, general issue of state sovereignty versus human rights.

The view of classical Western liberalism has long been that the individual—linked to freedom and equality—is the ultimate end of government policy and that the individual must never be a mere means to state security. In 1978, U.S. president Jimmy Carter proclaimed that "there is one belief above all others that has made us what we are. This is the belief that the rights of the individual inherently stand higher than the claims or demands of the State."[6] Nonetheless, states traditionally value themselves more than their component citizens; beyond this, it has been common practice that states trample wantonly on human rights, especially the human rights of citizens of other states. This occurs either directly, by military intervention and economic pressure, or indirectly, by the support of military superpowers for repressive regimes among economically developing countries.

The Problem of Enforcement

Faced with the awesome, sovereign power of states, it can seem that the international human rights regime is woefully inadequate, based as it is on mere legalisms or exhortations, devoid of enforcement mechanisms. But legal systems always have difficulty controlling powerful actors: labor unions in France, for example, or large corporations in the United States. And ultimately, most of them rely on voluntary compliance. Some states have in fact complied voluntarily with international human rights norms, largely to achieve international legitimacy as well as to avoid ostracism.

Frustration with the rights-denying policies of states occasionally spills over into efforts to transcend the authority of states. Although lacking in legal authority, individuals of high moral and international standing have on occasion gathered together to fill what they see as a vacuum in the protection of human rights. So-called people's tribunals have periodically convened to draw attention to various human rights abuses. Most notable of these was the Russell Tribunal, which roundly criticized U.S. policy during the Vietnam War. The League for the Rights of Peoples, established in Rome in 1976, has held numerous sessions, condemning political repression under Marcos in the Philippines and offering a retrospective on Turkish genocide against Armenians during 1915–1916 and on Brazil's behavior toward its indigenous Amazonian population. It has also criticized Indonesia's strong-arm tactics in East Timor, U.S. intervention in Central America, and Soviet intervention in Afghanistan, as well as questioning the legitimacy of nuclear weapons. Such actions are of uncertain effectiveness, but they do attract a degree of public attention while also serving to undercut the presumption that only state-centered approaches are relevant in dealing with violations of human rights.

New Approaches to Human Rights

An emphasis on human rights is a fundamentally new way of thinking about human dignity and world politics, reflecting as it does the determination that states must meet certain standards, both in their own domestic affairs and in their international relations. Even now, after several decades of vigorous pro-human rights advocacy, states typically act with primary regard to their power and perceived national interests rather than according to the ideals of human rights. There is, as a result, the constant danger that concern for human rights will be sacrificed on the altar of state sovereignty, expediency, and *Realpolitik*.

Human rights advocacy differ greatly from Realpolitik in that it involves a different perspective from which to view the human condition and the goals of society and politics: People are seen as citizens of a larger community rather than merely individual sovereign actors, and as ends rather than means. As opposed to the relatively narrow focus of states, concern with superordinate human rights requires that political barriers be transcended, in the search for human dignity on the widest possible scale. With this in mind, let us now turn briefly to the special case of human rights policy in the United States.

Human Rights Policy and the United States

The U.S. government thinks of itself as being especially supportive of human rights. After all, the Declaration of Independence states,

> We hold these truths to be self-evident, that all men are created equal,
> that they are endowed by their Creator with certain inalienable Rights,
> that among these are Life, Liberty and the pursuit of Happiness—That
> to secure these rights, Governments are instituted among Men, deriv-
> ing their just powers from the consent of the governed.

The right to "Life" includes the right to self-defense, and protection against
unwarranted attack and unjust government; the right to "Liberty" includes
freedom of speech, of public association, of religion, and to establish a government of one's own choosing; the right to "pursuit of Happiness" includes
the right to own property and to enjoy the fruits of one's labor. The U.S.
Constitution was later amended to include a much-cherished Bill of Rights,
which specifically guarantees freedom of religion, speech, the press, and
peaceable assembly and the right to petition the government for redress of
grievances, the right to keep and bear arms, freedom from unwarranted
search and seizure and from self-incrimination, the right to a fair and speedy
trial, and protection against excessive bail.

On the other hand, the new United States was not exactly a paragon of
human rights: Slavery was practiced in the South, and women were denied
the vote. Even today, racial discrimination is widespread, and the United
States still has not passed an equal rights amendment, explicitly guaranteeing equal rights and legal protection to women, including such basic concepts as equal pay for equal work. Moreover, many other nations frequently
see the United States as a repressive opponent of human rights, rather than
as U.S. citizens typically consider their country to be: a white knight on
horseback, defending individual freedoms. In the past, this critical attitude
was promoted by U.S. military intervention in Vietnam and Central
America, long-standing association with an array of oppressive right-wing
dictatorships, economic exploitation of many developing countries, cod-
dling of apartheid in South Africa, tacit support for Israeli oppression of
Palestinians in the occupied territories, and vigorous initiation and further-
ance of the nuclear arms race. In addition, the United States has pursued a
rather intolerant, single-minded sponsorship of free enterprise capitalism as
the sole acceptable solution to the world's ills while urging civil and political liberties, at the same time opposing most efforts at promulgating socioeconomic rights.

Messianic Zeal

One of the more pernicious doctrines under which human rights have
been and continue to be violated is the notion that one's ideas are so
good, so pure, and so correct that anything is justified in pursuit of them.
Totalitarian states, fascist and communist alike, have justified violent
repression of their own population in the name of a "greater good," either

the glory of the fatherland (fascist) or the dictatorship of the proletariat (communist). And the United States has not been immune to a dose of messianic ideology, beginning early in its history, when the fledgling country viewed itself as a "shining city on a hill," and a self-proclaimed "light unto the nations."

U.S. National Security Council directive no. 68, issued in 1950 at the dawn of the Cold War, noted that "the integrity of our system will not be jeopardized by any measures, covert or overt, violent or nonviolent, which serve the purposes of frustrating the Kremlin design." This directive has never been rescinded; in effect, it gives the U.S. government license to intervene—both domestically and overseas—in ways destructive of human rights (psychological, political, and economic, to say nothing of arranging for assassinations and various forms of social destabilization) so long as such activities are aimed at "frustrating" the goals of its opponents—in the past, the Soviet Union, and more recently, "international terrorism" and various "rogue nations." The result included a range of interventions abroad, as well as the toppling of governments, attempts (on several occasions) to assassinate Fidel Castro, and apparent collaboration in the murder of Vietnam's Diem, the Congo's Lumumba, and Chile's Allende, as well as bombing a presumed chemical warfare factory in Sudan, subsequently shown to be a pharmaceutical plant.

To some degree, concern with human rights has long motivated U.S. foreign policy, and at least some of this concern seems to have been honest. On the other hand, outrage at the mistreatment of people by occupying governments has also served to help justify wars of colonial expansion on our part: The Mexican-American and Spanish-American wars are notable examples from 19th-century history, just as the U.S. intervention in Vietnam was propagandized, in part, by alleged abuses on the part of the Vietcong and North Vietnamese. The U.S. military's response to Iraq's invasion of Kuwait was publicly justified, in part, by continued U.S. government reference to purported human rights outrages committed by the occupying Iraqis, such as Kuwaiti infants being allegedly tossed from incubators. (These reports were subsequently revealed to be fabrications.)

As noted, U.S. concern with human rights sometimes has had a messianic quality, as revealed by then president Jimmy Carter's observation: "Because we are free, we can never be indifferent to the fate of freedom elsewhere." And the U.S. entry into both World Wars I and II was facilitated by the argument that both wars were in defense of liberty and democracy. Nonetheless, U.S. foreign policy has not always been directly influenced by concern about human rights in other countries. More important has usually been concern for U.S. power and U.S. profit. When democratically elected leftist governments threatened to practice something less than their predecessors' anticommunist zeal, and/or when such governments threatened to restrict the profits of U.S. companies abroad, the United States often intervened to replace them with other regimes, more friendly to U.S. corporate interests, as happened in Guatemala, Iran, and Chile. Typically, the human rights records of these new governments were far worse than their predecessors'.

Traditional National Self-Interest

Despite its avowed commitment to human rights as part of American democratic ideology, the truth is that U.S. human rights policy was influenced largely by traditional self-serving Great Power concerns. Shortly before the outbreak of World War II, for example, the U.S. government refused to permit the immigration of tens of thousands of German Jews attempting to flee growing Nazi persecution. Motivated in part by anti-Semitism, as well as by concern to avoid the economic and social stresses such immigration might produce, the United States chose to adhere strictly to its narrowly written laws governing immigration and naturalization, rather than to a broader conception of human rights. The Truman administration gave some initial support for human rights, through the UN Charter and the UDHR, but as the Cold War heated up, things changed.

During the second half of the 20th century, U.S. human rights policy was subsumed into a foreign policy based largely on anticommunism and containing the Soviet Union. This in turn produced alliances with a large number of repressive governments, which were said by the U.S. government to constitute part of the "free world," regardless of the degree of their own human rights violations, so long as they professed anticommunism. Despite a respite during the presidency of Jimmy Carter, when human rights briefly became a touchstone of foreign policy, the U.S. government generally downgraded human rights, a tendency that reached its maximum during the Reagan administration, when socioeconomic rights were essentially ignored, as were human rights violation by right-wing, anticommunist military dictatorships. The human rights policy of the United States became characterized by selective outrage.

Nonetheless, with the end of the Cold War, there is some evidence that U.S. human rights policy has become depoliticized and less directly tied to its confrontation with opposing ideologies. But moral considerations are still not paramount. Thus, NATO's war in Kosovo was motivated not only by concern for the rights of Kosovars but also by a yearning to demonstrate that organization's relevance given that its opponent—the Warsaw Pact—no longer existed. And economic as well as domestic political considerations continue to loom large. For example, in dealing with Cuba and China, the United States has remained far more antagonistic toward the former than toward the latter, although both violate civil/political rights, with China's offenses being if anything more egregious than Cuba's. American considerations of Realpolitik appear to be paramount: Unlike Cuba, China is a major trading partner with the United States, while anti-Castro Cuban exiles represent a potent force within U.S. politics.

Clearly, there are two horns to the dilemma of human rights and U.S. foreign policy: on the one hand, a real sympathy for human rights (especially the civil/political kind), and on the other, a felt need to respond to concerns of national security, geopolitical maneuvering, state power, and profit.

Human Rights and Peace

Human rights and peace are inextricably connected, in several ways. First, the denial of human rights is itself a denial of real peace. A world in which there is no armed conflict but in which fundamental human rights are thwarted could not in any meaningful sense be considered peaceful. Speaking at the United Nations, Pope John Paul II explicitly linked human rights and war:

> The Universal Declaration of Human Rights has struck a real blow against the many deep roots of war since the spirit of war in its basic primordial meaning springs up . . . where the inalienable rights of men are violated. This is a new and deeply relevant vision of the cause of peace. One that goes deeper and is more radical.[7]

The pope's perspective applies to socioeconomic rights no less than civil/political ones. As Scandinavian peace researcher Asbjørn Eide has noted, "Whether a child dies in infancy due to poverty and consequent malnutrition and lack of hygiene, or if it grows up and at a later stage is executed as a political opponent, the society in which this happens must be considered hostile to human rights."[8] And, we might add, to peace as well.

Second, there appears to be a connection between the way a state treats its own population and its inclinations toward other states. As Franklin Roosevelt put it, "We in this nation still believe that it [self-determination] should be predicated on certain freedoms which we think are essential everywhere. We know that we ourselves will never be wholly safe at home unless other governments recognize such freedoms." And in fact, democratic states have never made war against other democracies. (On the other hand, not all dictatorships are aggressive: Fascist Spain stayed neutral during World War II, and neither neofascist Paraguay nor neo-Stalinist Albania were international aggressors.)

To some extent, the foreign policies of states reflect their domestic inclinations. During the heyday of the Soviet Union, it was apparent that a state that often denies political freedoms to its own people is unlikely to be especially respectful of such freedoms in other countries. And similarly, the relative disinterest of the United States in promoting economic justice at home has long paralleled its opposition to any serious efforts at reconstructing the international economic system.

The denial of human rights can also provoke breaches of the peace, if other states become involved. Humanitarian intervention of this sort may be legal; certainly, there is ample precedent in the classical writings of international law. In Vattel's *The Law of Nations*, the author claimed that "nations have obligations to produce welfare and happiness in other states. In the event of civil war, for example, states must aid the party which seems to have justice on its side or protect an unfortunate people from an unjust tyrant."[9] Great Britain, France, and Russia intervened in 1827 when Turkey had been using especially inhumane means to put down Greek aspirations for independence, and the world cheered. U.S. intervention in the Cuban civil war of 1898 was intended, according to the congressional resolution at the time, to put an end to "the abhorrent conditions which have existed for more than three years in the island of Cuba, have shocked the moral sense of the people of the United States, and have been a disgrace to Christian civilization."

On the other hand, claims of humanitarian intervention have often been used as an excuse for aggression (of which the Spanish-American War may well be an example). Violations of Nicaraguan human rights, for example, were cited by the United States as justification for its efforts to overthrow the Sandinista government, although no comparable justifications were ever used by the United States to overthrow rightist regimes, including the earlier Somoza dictatorship, which had been far more abusive of human rights.

Finally, one of the widely recognized human rights—specified in the first article of both 1966 Human Rights Conventions—is that of national self-determination. Abuses of this right often lead directly to war, especially civil war, making this issue especially difficult. The pursuit of human rights may in fact lead more to violence than to peace, since human rights often are won by struggle and confrontation. Furthermore, it is not obvious whether all claims for national self-determination are worthy of success: Should there be independent states of Kurdistan, Baluchistan, Chechnya, Kosovo? And what about the national aspirations of (at least some) Basques, Welsh, Scots, Quebecois, native Hawaiians, and Puerto Ricans? The UN Security Council has determined that at least in certain cases, such as anticolonial struggles, a continuing denial of human rights constitutes a threat to international peace. (This was applied to Zimbabwe, Namibia, and South Africa.)

In summary, the connection between human rights and peace is complex and multifaceted. It is useful to claim that human rights contribute to peace, but in fact, it may be that the most fundamental connection is that such claims permit adherence to human rights, as a desirable end in itself, regardless of whether, in the short term at least, this actually promotes peace as narrowly defined.

The Future of Human Rights

What of the future? Several things can be said with confidence. The first is that the question of human rights will continue to demand attention on the international agenda. Concern for human rights is so widespread, resonating so deeply as a fundamental aspiration of most human beings, that most governments will be forced to pay attention—even though in many cases (perhaps most) they would rather not. Some progress has in fact been made, and not only with the disintegration of most Marxist states and the initiation of democracy in Russia and most of the former Soviet bloc. The following, for example, have implemented substantial civil/political rights despite having also had a history of despotic rule: Chile, Brazil, Argentina, Malaysia, South Korea, the Philippines, Haiti, and Indonesia. And other countries, despite considerable poverty, have made strides in securing broader socioeconomic rights for their people: These include Sri Lanka, Taiwan, Nigeria, and Kenya.

Competing Conceptions of Human Rights

A second conclusion is that the question of human rights will continue to be controversial, with different conceptions competing with each other, while the very notion of human rights competes with the basic inclinations of states to engage in amoral, Realpolitik maneuverings. The dilemma may be profound. Consider these Realpolitik questions, for example, from the perspective of a government leader. What should a state do, for example, when confronted with this choice: It desires a particular strategic relationship with another state, but that other state engages in human rights abuses. Which should be sacrificed, national strategy or a commitment to human rights? Reinhold Niebuhr argued that "group relations can never be as ethical as those which characterize individual relations." Similar thinking inspired some Marxist-Leninist leaders to rationalize the power politics by which their states generally function, as well as their failure to "wither away," as Marx had originally promised. Several centuries ago, Niccolò Machiavelli, in *The Prince*, wrote that "a man who wishes to make a profession of goodness in everything must necessarily come to grief among so many who are not good." This may have been largely an excuse, justifying a ruler's amorality, but it also expressed a genuine dilemma.

Perhaps, on the other hand, the "natural law" school is correct and support of human rights is simply the right thing to do, period, regardless of its practical consequences. Consider this observation from German philosopher Karl Jaspers, who addressed himself to the question of "metaphysical guilt," following the Holocaust. Jaspers wrote,

There exists a solidarity among men as human beings that makes each co-responsible for every wrong and every injustice in the world, especially for crimes committed in his presence or with his knowledge. If I fail to do whatever I can to prevent them, I too am guilty.[10]

There is yet another possibility, a way station between the amorality of Realpolitik and the absolutism of inflexible ethical norms for their own sake. Some argue that power (or at least, security) can readily be reconciled with human rights. After all, the United States has found that brutal, oppressive regimes—Somoza's in Nicaragua, the shah's in Iran, Marcos's in the Philippines—do not always make reliable allies. And Mikhail Gorbachev's policies of *glasnost* and *perestroika* in the USSR between 1985 and 1991 reflected at least in part the fact that in the long run, national security may be enhanced, not diminished, by allowing human rights to flourish, even at the cost of traditional measures of national power.

Former secretary of state Cyrus Vance once offered the following similar observation:

We pursue our human rights objectives, not only because they are right, but because we have a stake in the stability that comes when people can express their hopes and find their futures freely. Our ideals and our interests coincide.[11]

Promoting Human Rights

It is difficult to imagine exactly what a U.S. foreign policy would be if it were organized primarily around the promotion of human rights worldwide. However, the following specific actions, which have already been taken at different times in support of human rights, suggest the benefits to be gained from a continuation, to say nothing of an expansion, of such policies:

Subtle diplomacy. Quiet, persistent pressure raised with offending governments has the advantage that the government in question need not worry about losing face if and when abuses are corrected. Admittedly, however, there is a disadvantage, beyond the possibility of being simply ignored, namely, that a government may claim to be employing subtle diplomacy while it is actually doing nothing.

Public statements. This involves drawing world attention to specific abuses and to governments that violate human rights. It may include publicly dissociating one's own government from the unacceptable behavior of another. Human rights compliance can be promoted by publicizing violations through the publication of reports conducted by respected, impartial investigative commissions; especially in a world climate committed to human rights, most governments seek to avoid the embarrassment that comes with being branded a violator of these rights.

Symbolic acts. Sending support to dissidents, either by words, by contact with opposition figures, or by otherwise indicating disapproval of abuses, is a way of emphasizing to both the offending government and its people that human rights violations are noticed and rejected.

Cultural penalties. By isolating offenders at international cultural events, including athletic exhibitions and other exchanges, such governments are made to feel like pariahs. Although it is easy to scoff at such minimal "penalties," pride and the universal desire to be accepted add weight to such actions.

Economic penalties. Applying trade embargoes, renouncing investment in the offending country, refusing development loans and other forms of foreign aid: These actions can hurt the economy of offending countries, thereby putting pressure (often on the more wealthy and influential citizens) to modify policies and/or oust the government. Both cultural and economic penalties were applied, with some success, to the apartheid regime of South Africa.

Immigration. Human rights activists, dissidents, and those being deprived of their human rights can be permitted to enter the United States. In the past, the "right" of immigration was applied selectively, facilitating immigration by people fleeing leftist countries whose human rights policies the United States wished to criticize while making it very difficult for refugees from rightist countries that are allied to the United States, and whose human rights policies it was inclined to ignore or whitewash.

Legal approaches. International law can be applied more vigorously, by identifying, indicting, and when possible, arresting and trying violators of human rights overseas, just as people involved in the international drug trade have occasionally been indicted and, when possible, extradited for trial. A large opportunity exists for the apprehension of national leaders who presided over abuses in their own countries; if successful, such actions could also serve as a substantial deterrent to future outrages.

Multilateral approaches. The United States can commit itself to the various human rights organizations now active worldwide, especially the UN Commission on Human Rights. There are many other possibilities, such as the regular publication of a UN-sponsored catalog of human rights abuses, to be subject to international scrutiny. Regimes with disproportionately large military spending tend generally to be the worst human rights abusers (and it can also be argued that such spending drains funds that might otherwise be available to help secure socioeconomic rights). Thus, the ratio of military to domestic national spending could be publicized for each state, and governments be expected to explain and justify their priorities.

Destabilization and belligerency. In the past, the United States actively sought to destabilize the governments of certain countries—for example, Nicaragua—allegedly because of their human rights abuses. This remains an option, although of questionable legality or morality, unless the abuses are sufficiently flagrant, and unless the policy is applied even-handedly to all regimes, regardless of ideology. The human rights abuses of Nazi Germany and imperial Japan may have facilitated the U.S. decision to make war on them, although these abuses actually became more serious after war was declared. The Tanzanian invasion of Uganda, which ultimately toppled the government of Idi Amin, won widespread support because Amin's human rights record was particularly atrocious.

A Final Note on Human Rights

For most of the world's people, security—national no less than individual —has been undermined, not by excessive attention to human rights but by insufficient concern on the part of their governments. In the short run, attention to human rights can be destabilizing, as the final Soviet leadership discovered. In the short run, repression can clamp a lid on a boiling pot of unmet human rights, but in the long run, political stability—either within a state or between states—can be constructed only by turning down the heat. Thus, it can be argued that, ultimately, human rights are not only compatible with genuine security (of individuals and governments) but are necessary for it.

We conclude this chapter with an account by Jerome Shestack, a long-time human rights activist. Shestack recognizes the extraordinarily difficult and seemingly hopeless task of securing human rights worldwide, in the face of human cruelty, frailty, misunderstandings, and the power of states. He conjures up the Greek myth of Sisyphus, who was condemned to spend eternity pushing a boulder up a hill, only to have it roll back again just as he reaches the top. Sisyphus' task is absurd, and yet—echoing the existential philosopher Albert Camus—Shestack points out that

> Sisyphus may turn out to be a more enduring hero than Hercules. For if, as Camus taught, life itself is absurd, Sisyphus represents the only triumph possible over that absurdity. In his constancy to reach that summit, even with failure preordained, Sisyphus demonstrated that the human spirit is indomitable and that dedication to a higher goal is in itself man's reason for living. . . . The realities of the world may foredoom a great part of the struggle and make most of the effort seem

abysmal. Yet, the very struggle itself takes on symbolic meaning, enhancing human dignity. And when all is said and done, there is no other humane course to pursue.[12]

Notes

1. Quoted in J. Bentley. 1984. *Martin Niemöller*. New York: Free Press.
2. Simone Weil. 1952. *The Need for Roots*. New York: Putnam.
3. Cyrus Vance, Law Day address at the University of Georgia, 1977.
4. Betty Reardon. 1985. *Sexism and the War System*. Syracuse, NY: Syracuse University Press.
5. David Forsythe. 1989. *Human Rights and World Politics*. Lincoln: University of Nebraska Press.
6. State Department news release, January 4, 1978.
7. Address to the UN General Assembly, October 3, 1979.
8. Asbjørn Eide. 1977. *Human Rights in the World Society*. Oslo: Norwegian Peace Research Institute.
9. Emmerich de Vattel. 1883. *The Law of Nations*. Philadelphia: T. and J. W. Johnson.
10. Quoted in Louis Rene Beres. 1984. *Reason and Realpolitik*. Lexington, MA: Lexington Books.
11. Testimony to the Senate Committee on Foreign Relations, 1980.
12. Jerome J. Shestack. 1978. "Sisyphus Endures: The International Human Rights NGOs." *New York Law School Law Review* 24: 89–124.

18 Ecological Well-Being

When we see land as a community to which we belong, we may begin to use it with love and respect.

—Aldo Leopold

The word ecology derives from the Greek *oikos*, meaning house. It refers to the interrelations between living things and their environments, which includes other living things (plants, animals, microorganisms), as well as inanimate factors such as climate, rocks, water, and air. Despite widespread dreams of space travel and the colonization of other planets, the fact remains that for the foreseeable future at least, human beings have only one home. Good planets are hard to find. The planet Earth is also home to millions of other species, virtually all of them intimately connected to each other and ultimately, to us.

Enhanced Environmental Awareness

Environmental awareness has emerged fitfully over many centuries. Within the United States, it did not begin to achieve widespread public attention until the last third of the 20th century, with increased public dismay about air and water pollution, the effects of persistent pesticides such as DDT (cogently described in Rachel Carson's influential book, *Silent Spring*), and human overpopulation (forcefully argued in Paul Ehrlich's *The Population Bomb*). Following Earth Day in April 1970, it appeared that the U.S. environmental movement had come of age.

Additional milestones in ecological consciousness-raising were the powerful writings of Aldo Leopold, stressing the need for an "ecological conscience," and the study *Limits to Growth*, which argued that economic and population growth, widely taken for granted as desirable and inevitable, are in fact undesirable and unsustainable. For a time, this perspective was seen by many social activists as a distraction from legitimate socioeconomic needs, and even, in some cases, as a plot to ensure continued underdevelopment of impoverished countries. Now, many people working closely with social movements in developing countries are increasingly convinced that environmental/ecological/resource issues are at the heart of their struggle. In addition, concern for indigenous people—their culture, livelihood, and integrity—requires recognition of their place in the complex web of natural ecosystems. The web of life has been fraying; peace requires that it be rewoven, or at least, allowed to regenerate on its own.

From 1980 to the Present

By the 1980s, substantial progress in raising ecological awareness had been made in the United States—both in legislation and in public attitudes—but the environment itself continued to deteriorate, at least in part because of the policies of the Reagan administration, which prized short-term economic growth over consideration for the environment. As part of their strong commitment to free enterprise, most political conservatives have remained opposed to active government intervention on behalf of environmental protection, preferring to leave the free market as free as possible, regardless of the environmental impact.

Nonetheless, environmental concern has become more widespread in other countries as well. The Green Parties of Europe periodically make strong showings in national elections, and also in elections to the European Parliament. By the end of the past century, the environment had been very much on the front pages: Serious heat waves and drought, alternating with occasional severe flooding, gave cogency to concern about greenhouse warming. Fires ravaged the American west, including Yellowstone National Park, as well as huge tracts in Mexico, Brazil, and Indonesia. The earth's protective ozone layer has been shown to be thinning, perhaps dangerously. Nuclear accidents at Three Mile Island in the United States (1979) and Chernobyl in the USSR (1986), combined with the revelation that U.S. nuclear weapons plants had secretly and recklessly fouled thousands of acres with radioactive waste, tarnished the image of nuclear power as a "pollution free" energy panacea. Waste disposal became a worldwide problem, along with toxic contamination and floods exacerbated by forest destruction. Famines scourged Africa, soils became increasingly degraded, and the human population surged to more than six billion. The world's rain forests have diminished rapidly, and the world's wildlife has become impoverished, with many "charismatic" species (giant pandas, tigers, rhinos, even elephants) as well as a host of lesser known ones pushed to the edge of extinction. To some degree, politicians who have made careers fighting one human enemy or another have begun to consider the need for all people to cooperate in protecting the environment of the only planet we have.

The Environment and National Security

In the final analysis, a world at peace must be one in which all living things experience themselves as being "at home." This does not require a state of perfect, unchanging harmony; indeed, our planet has never known an extended period of utter balance, static immobility, or unchanging equilibrium. A world in equilibrium, however, must be distinguished from one in stagnation. Life itself involves change: consumption, synthesis, metabolism, locomotion, reproduction, competition, evolution. But life has also depended on a kind of fundamental, underlying stability, at least in the longer run—that is, measured in hundreds, thousands, even millions of years. In recent years, some of the crucial relationships between the world's species and between those species and their environments have become increasingly tenuous, and this in turn has begun to threaten the quality of life, both human and nonhuman, on our planet. It also threatens to undermine the integrity of our fundamental life-support systems: the air we breathe, the water we drink, the food we eat, and the diverse fabric of living things that provides emotional and spiritual sustenance as well.

One of the most important—and overdue—shifts in human thinking noticeable in the early 1990s was the growing realization that national security must be defined in broader terms than the strictly military. As our planet becomes increasingly interconnected politically, economically, and socially, and also increasingly endangered, the health, well-being, and security of every individual become inseparable from the health, well-being, and security of the earth itself. In his famous "strategy of peace" speech, delivered at American University in 1962, President Kennedy noted,

> We are devoting massive sums of money to weapons, that could be better devoted to combating ignorance, poverty and disease. . . . We all inhabit this same small planet. We all breathe the same air. We all cherish our children's future. And we are all mortal.

Our connectedness—to each other and to other forms of life—is rapidly emerging as something beyond mere rhetoric or metaphor. Observing the growing numbers of species pushed to extinction, growing numbers of people feel a sense of foreboding for the human future. In the looming threats to clean air, clean water, the integrity of the earth's atmosphere, and in an era of diminishing resources, people are recognizing threats to their own well-being that are as real as any military threat emanating from an armed opponent. Ecological thinkers maintain, as well, that human beings have an obligation to be something other than a generalized predatory and destructive species. Rather, they must exercise wise stewardship over the planet's wild things and wild places, not just for our own benefit but as a moral and ethical imperative. Other environmentalists see the connection between despoiled, depleted, and polluted lands and human misery. It is becoming increasingly clear that we cannot fully make "peace" until we make peace with our planetary environment. Moreover, in responding—albeit belatedly—to the various looming environmental threats, we will not be running the risk of anything like the "security dilemma," in which military "preparedness" actually threatens to bring about the danger it is intended to surmount. Environmental sensitivity and protection seem likely to be largely win-win propositions, although as we shall see, there are also economic, social, and political conflicts to be faced. Nonetheless, environmental concerns, once considered an indulgence of the rich, are increasingly recognized as fundamental to a decent life for everybody.

In the absence of dramatic environmental disasters, public attention rarely focuses on the continuing plight of a silently deteriorating planet. Many of the most serious and adverse environmental effects (climate change, resource depletion, overpopulation) will not become grossly apparent until some time later in the 21st century, but paradoxically, if we wait until then, we may well have foreclosed the opportunity to intervene effectively. As with the prevention of war, the prevention of ecological disaster requires that we intervene *before* catastrophe actually takes place, whereupon effective responses are virtually impossible.

The Tragedy of the Commons

A model—first described in a scientific article by ecologist Garrett Hardin[1]—helps us understand one of the major factors underlying environmental problems. The model considers the sort of situation that long obtained in Britain, in which some grassland was privately owned, and another part, the "commons," was shared property of the community at large. Various citizens owned sheep, which they could graze on their own private lands or on the public commons. It was well-known that overgrazing was harmful to the productivity of the grassland, and so, shepherds generally avoided overgrazing their own property. But they treated the commons differently: The shepherds recognized that a healthy commons was of benefit to everyone, but each also reasoned that if he refrained from grazing his sheep on the commons, then others would doubtless take advantage of this restraint, and fatten their sheep on the public lands. As a result, tendencies to be prudent and ecologically minded were suppressed because individual sheep owners reasoned that if they did not take advantage of the commons, then surely someone else would—so, if the commons was going to be degraded anyhow, they may as well be the ones who do it! The result was deterioration of the commons, until it was no longer fit to support sheep, or shepherds.

The tragedy of the commons, then, is that individuals—each seeking to gain personal benefit—find themselves engaging in behavior that is to the disadvantage of everyone. It can also be generalized to other difficulties, whenever short-term selfish benefit conflicts with long-term public good. For example, there may be short-term self-centered benefit to a factory owner in using the atmosphere as a public sewer; after all, even if his effluents pollute the air, it is a cost that is borne more or less equally by everyone who breathes, whereas the factory owner personally is saved the expense of having to install pollution control devices. Similarly with overuse of scarce resources: It may be inconvenient to recycle and in fact, easier for individuals simply to throw their garbage away, or to use more than their share of scarce commodities. After all, they may derive some personal gain or enhanced convenience by doing so, while the cost—in overcrowded dumpsites or worldwide resource shortages—is by contrast a diffuse and general one, borne by all. Besides, if they don't abuse the environment, then surely someone else will (which is just what the sheep owners told themselves about the commons).

The tragedy of the commons has global dimensions: Scandinavian forests and lakes suffer from acid rain because of the effluents of English smokestacks, while Britain gets the economic benefit. Japan and Norway periodically defy international outcry while hunting the world's great whales to the verge of extinction. Brazil seeks to benefit economically from the Amazon rain forest, even though such "benefit" requires that it be destroyed, to the ultimate detriment of everyone.

Some Major Environmental Problems

Pollution

Modern life produces large amounts of by-products, many of which are quite toxic. These include pesticides, herbicides, nitrates, phosphates, heavy metals, petroleum products, and numerous other poisons, including contamination from military uses and abuses of the air, water, and soil. For many years, the atmosphere, fresh waters, and the oceans have been considered publicly owned and thus suitable as public sewers for all manner of unwanted substances. Automobiles spew out vast quantities of additional air pollutants, as do power generators and the widespread, large-scale burning of forests and grasslands, especially in the developing world. The American Lung Association estimates that air pollution alone is responsible for $40 billion in annual damage, counting medical expenses as well as damage to crops and buildings. And this is just in the United States, where air quality standards are among the highest in the world.

Even though industrialization generates much air and water pollution, the wealthier countries ironically tend to have cleaner air and water, on average, than the poorer ones. Since pollution control devices may be costly, they are often unattainable for countries that are already poor. Environmental protection has thus become a luxury that most developing countries cannot afford—although in the long run, they cannot afford *not* to protect their environments. At present, however, multinational corporations have been preferentially establishing factories in countries where poverty and politically pliant leadership have resulted in minimal standards of environmental protection. The air in Mexico City, Manila, or Bombay, for example, is among the worst on earth. Major rivers in such regions are often little more than open sewers.

The problem is not altogether intractable, however. Industrial pollution can be diminished greatly, not only by end-of-the-pipe treatment of effluents but also by reducing the waste stream itself. A modest federal tax on carbon and other emissions can go far toward stimulating conservation and pollution reductions, although domestic industries—and many developing countries—object vigorously, complaining that such a tax would inhibit their ability to compete internationally. Therefore, innovations of this sort would probably be most acceptable if adopted by many states simultaneously. Attempts to respond in this manner have been bedeviled by demands by developing countries that they be given special dispensation when it comes to curtailing toxic emissions—since, after all, the developed countries attained their status largely without worrying about such constraints—while developed countries tend to insist that all states, rich and poor alike, should be treated equally in this regard.

The nations of the world do not have to wallow in their own toxic waste, polluting the air and water, and poisoning those—especially the poor—who cannot afford to live in safer, cleaner environments. Moreover, in a resource-limited world, it should also be recognized that pollution equals wastage: Mercury belongs in thermometers, not in fish; sulfur belongs in matches and pharmaceutical drugs, not as sulfuric acid in dead lakes, and so on. Environmental protection can thus be good economics as well as good aesthetics, considering beneficial consequences in terms of diminished cost for health care and enhanced opportunities for fisheries, forestry, hunting, "ecotourism," and so forth. Thus, a thorough cleanup of air and water has practical benefits as well as ethical advantages.

There are signs of international cooperation in cleaning up the planet, along with growing public awareness of the problem. International protocols have been signed restricting emissions of nitrogen, sulfur, and chlorofluorocarbons (CFCs, which eat away the ozone layer) and reducing the production of greenhouse gases, notably carbon dioxide. Although progress has been spotty toward establishing a widely recognized Law of the Sea, hope exists for such an agreement, which would not only regulate the exploitation of the ocean's' resources but also limit the amount of oceanic pollution to be allowed. A comparable Law of the Atmosphere may also be anticipated.

The growth of nuclear energy constitutes one of the most pernicious environmental problems, especially for economically less developed nations (including Russia, India, Ukraine, and China, which have come to rely on it for a significant percentage of their energy needs). Despite claims of the nuclear power industry, military contractors, and the government, nuclear power is not "clean." Neither is nuclear military production. In the United States alone, more than 100 commercial reactors plus a handful of weapons reactors (as well as several hundred naval power plants) produce an average of 30 metric tons of nuclear waste per reactor per year.

The Greenhouse Effect

Since the middle of the 20th century, scientists have warned that human technology and economic "progress" has been disrupting the worldwide carbon cycle, one of many fundamental processes on which life on earth depends. Then came the 1980s and 1990s, in which the 14 warmest years of the past century all occurred during the same two-decade period. It suddenly became increasingly apparent—even to indifferent citizens, antagonistic industrialists, resistant planners, and obtuse politicians—that the "greenhouse effect" had already begun to arrive.

The greenhouse effect begins when energy from the sun warms the earth. This energy is most familiar to people as visible light. However, the earth then radiates heat back, largely in the form of infrared radiation. This is readily absorbed by the atmosphere, much of it by "greenhouse gases," notably carbon dioxide. If it were not for this atmospheric absorption of heat reradiated by the earth, our planet would become lifelessly cold. But as the quantity of these gases has been increasing, the atmosphere has apparently become a heat sink, absorbing so much warmth that the earth's climate has begun to change. (It is called the "greenhouse effect" because a similar principle keeps greenhouses substantially warmer than their surroundings, relying in this case on the structural characteristics of glass rather than the chemical properties of carbon dioxide: Light passes easily through the glass of a greenhouse, but the reradiated infrared energy is trapped inside. A similar process occurs when an automobile is left in the sun.)

Throughout geological time, carbon levels in the atmosphere do not seem to have fluctuated dramatically. Under natural conditions, carbon is released into the atmosphere as a result of the respiration of animals and the burning or decomposition of organic materials. Similarly, carbon is removed from the atmosphere and "fixed" in the bodies of plants via photosynthesis. With the coming of the industrial revolution, this cycle has been unbalanced, with much more carbon newly released to the atmosphere than is being fixed in plants. The combustion of fossil fuels (coal and oil) has been especially responsible, but the burning of forests and grasslands has also added substantially to the atmosphere's carbon load. About two thirds of the planet's excess carbon comes from fossil fuels (emitted especially by automobiles and trucks, power generation, and heavy industry) with about one thirds coming from burning and rotting vegetation (especially savanna fires in Africa and burning of the Amazon rain forest as well as other tropical forests, notably in the Democratic Republic of the Congo and Indonesia). In addition, the steady destruction of the world's forests (for fuelwood and to clear land for cultivation and/or grazing) not only adds carbon dioxide directly but also destroys the major means by which carbon is naturally removed from the atmosphere.

Increasing carbon dioxide levels might result in an increase in world temperatures by 3° to 9° F by the year 2050. This change may sound small, but for comparison, consider that when average temperatures were only about 9° colder than they are today, the world experienced an Ice Age. The worldwide temperature increase due to the greenhouse effect would represent a rate of climate change 100 times faster than at any time in recorded history, with results likely to be catastrophic. Agriculture would be profoundly disrupted. Large numbers of species would almost certainly die; accompanying droughts (because of higher evaporation rates) would add to the calamity. As the oceans expand because of the higher temperatures, and some melting occurs in the polar ice caps, sea level would rise, causing potentially devastating floods to low-lying terrain. (Many of the world's great cities are coastal and at sea level, including Los Angeles, San Francisco, New York, Rio de Janeiro, Manila, and nearly the entire population of Bangladesh.)

Carbon dioxide is not the only greenhouse gas. Others are nitrogen oxides, methane (produced in landfills, termite mounds, the digestive processes of cattle), and CFCs (also implicated in the destruction of the ozone layer). Per molecule, in fact, these chemicals are far more heat-absorbing than CO_2 (carbon dioxide); however, they are much less abundant.

There seems no way to reverse the greenhouse effect in the short run. However, it can be ameliorated, essentially buying time for future generations. One practical series of solutions is the adoption of a triad: renewable energy sources (wind, solar, etc.), strict conservation, and reforestation. There are many possibilities for action; for example, a tax on carbon emissions could exert economic pressure for the development and use of noncarbon energy sources. We don't know for certain about the exact dimensions of the greenhouse threat, but such uncertainty has never stopped human beings when it came to other threats, notably that posed by international aggression: for example, the Allied mobilization against Germany and Japan in the 1940s, as well as during the Cold War that followed. The threat posed by the greenhouse effect may be every much as great, or greater. Thus far, however, human response has been much more restrained.

The major culprits—that is, the major carbon emitters—are the United States, China, and Russia. However, any state, once it becomes heavily industrialized or highly dependent on coal (such as China), will contribute more than its share to the earth's carbon load. After much controversy, more than 150 countries—including the United States—signed the Kyoto Protocols in 1997, which committed them to cut their carbon dioxide emissions by 2010; few concrete steps have been initiated, however, to carry out this agreement, and the Bush administration refused to comply, calling instead for more research. If greenhouse warming is to be slowed, policymakers must agree to restrictions that are both far-seeing and enforceable.

Ozone Depletion

Chemically, ozone is O_3, a molecular form of oxygen. When near the ground, ozone contributes to air pollution, especially photochemical smog. But in the upper atmosphere, it behaves more benevolently, absorbing dangerous ultraviolet radiation and preventing it from reaching the ground. (Excessive ultraviolet exposure can cause sunburn, skin cancer, and blindness.) Atmospheric scientists have noted that the ozone layer, especially above the Antarctic, has been thinning dangerously. Major culprits are CFCs, chemicals that have been widely used in industry, as aerosol propellants and refrigerants and in the manufacture of polystyrene foam.

As with the greenhouse effect, ozone depletion is difficult to track down as to precise cause, and even its effects are diffuse. Unlike wars, epidemics, or famines, atmospheric deterioration generally does not photograph well or lend itself to dramatic 30-second "sound bites." But for all its subtlety, it is no less real. This is once again a kind of tragedy of the commons, in that individuals, or individual industries, have little motivation to behave responsibly toward the atmosphere unless others are persuaded or coerced into behaving similarly. The same applies to countries: Unless all states can be persuaded to act together, there is little motivation for any one to act separately. Thus, there is likely to be an immediate economic cost, for example, in taxing carbon emissions or forbidding the use of CFCs.

This makes it especially heartening that in the case of ozone depletion, at least, some cooperation has been achieved. In an important success for the United Nations Environment Programme, most of the world's heavily industrialized countries have agreed to the Montreal Protocols, pledging themselves to a dramatic cut in CFC production. Although it affects only one of the many environmental problems that require attention—and in the opinion of many experts, even in this case, it is too little and possibly even too late—it represents an important political and psychological victory for environmental consciousness and basic planetary hygiene.

Depletion of Tropical Rain Forests and of Biodiversity

The world's tropical rain forests are the greatest repositories of biological diversity—sheer numbers of species—on earth. They are also among the most endangered. They cover only about 7% of the earth's surface, but they are home to a staggering 50% to 80% of all plant and animal species. Of the estimated 5 to 30 million species on earth, only about 1.7 million have even been identified. It is difficult to assess the value of such species, that is, their value to *Homo sapiens*. Seen as entities in themselves, with their own intrinsic worth, each is irreplaceable and priceless. In addition, rare species often prove of direct human benefit, for example, providing raw materials for treatment of cancer and other diseases.

It is also noteworthy that more than a third of all plant and animal species (excluding fish and invertebrates) live exclusively on a mere 1.4% of its land surface. These "hot spot" regions are concentrated in the tropics: notably Madagascar, Brazil, Borneo, Sumatra, a few other Southeast Asian islands, the tropical Andes, and the Caribbean. On the one hand, this concentration underscores the risk of extinction; on the other, it suggests that by focusing on protection of a relatively small total area, substantial insurance for the world's biodiversity can yet be obtained.

Nonetheless, widespread land hunger combined with government eagerness for "development" has resulted in the destruction of vast amounts of tropical rain forests, notably in South America, Africa, and Indonesia. Regions that are especially threatened include the island of Madagascar (home to many unique, "endemic," species) where more than 90% of the original vegetation is gone, the eastern slope of the Andes, the monsoon forests of the low Himalayas, the Atlantic coastal forest of Brazil, and Malaysia. Less than one twentieth of the world's tropical forests are under any protection whatever, and those that are, often are protected on paper only: They remain subject to extensive poaching, lumbering, grazing, and so on, largely because of human poverty and local dense population.

Economic factors typically loom large in this ongoing tragedy. Tropical rain forests occur in economically developing countries, which are often desperately poor and thus eager to attempt anything that promises economic improvement, even if the "gains" are only short-lived. Moreover, these countries tend to be suffering from painfully high national debt, so that funds are desperately needed to make the interest payments. Some Central American countries, for example, clear their remaining rain forests to raise beef so as to earn money from U.S. fast-food restaurants, and many Southeast Asian states export teak and mahogany, similarly destroying their own countryside, in return for short-term gains (which tend to benefit only a small proportion of the local population).

Meanwhile, 11 million hectares of tropical forests—about the area of Virginia—are cleared annually. More than 8 million hectares of Brazilian rain forest are burned annually, to clear land for cattle ranching. In his book *Earth in the Balance*, Al Gore asked, "If, as in a science fiction movie, we had a giant invader from space clomping across the rain forests of the world with football field-size feet—going boom, boom, boom every second—would we react?"[2] His point is that this is happening right now.

As worldwide awareness of the plight of the rain forests has increased, so has international pressure on those states that are currently devastating theirs. But this too raises difficulties. For example, having largely massacred the indigenous inhabitants of North America, and greatly abused their own environment (also making themselves rich in the process), Americans are on poor moral ground lecturing Brazilians to refrain from doing to the Amazonian "frontier" what they have done to their own. The environmental and social challenge in developing countries is to emulate the prosperity of the industrial states without repeating their mistakes. Conservation efforts must also contend with a fierce nationalism, often evoked when the wealthy North lectures the impoverished South about what the latter should do with their own lands.

Few issues, short of war itself, give greater clarity to the absurdity of state sovereignty in an interdependent world than does environmental conservation. Brazil, for example has its ancient battle cry, *A Amazonia e nossa* (the Amazon is ours). And after years of selfish, destructive ecological and political imperialism in Africa, for example, Europe has little moral basis for urging the Indonesian government to spare its watersheds. Imagine the response if the British government had sought to prevent the United States from slaughtering its own indigenous bison herds during the 19th century.

It will not be easy to persuade inhabitants and governments in poor countries—or the rest of us, for that matter—that the Amazon, the upper Congo watershed, the New Guinea lowlands, and indeed, all of the planet, belongs to all of us. But there is also some cause for hope. Worldwide awareness of the plight of the rain forests has increased greatly. Funds have been established to help preserve these irreplaceable regions. The field of restoration ecology has also gathered momentum, investigating ways to restore previously devastated lands. Local governments have begun to realize that their own economic, social, cultural, and even political health requires that they preserve a healthy environment. And some organizations have begun experimenting with "debt for nature swaps," in which the external debt of certain developing countries is purchased at a substantial discount (say, 50 cents on the dollar) and then used, in turn, to purchase nature reserves. In this way, countries like Ecuador and Bolivia have been able to retire some of their debt while also preserving some of their natural environment—to everyone's benefit.

The field of ecotourism has also been blossoming, giving countries that are wildlife-rich but cash-poor a financial incentive to preserve their living resources. Rwanda, for example, has been able to reap substantial income by providing opportunities for wealthy nature-loving tourists to observe free-living gorillas. (The alternative is to clear the forests, and destroy the gorillas, for short-lived subsistence farming, which is also less remunerative.) More than 10% of Costa Rica's land is now protected, much of it in national parks, and if the worldwide environmental movement continues to show the political vitality it has demonstrated, other countries can be expected to follow suit.

Renewable Resources

A fundamental principle of environmental stewardship is that we must respect the natural cycles on which all life depends. There is simply no viable alternative to some form of global balance: between carbon emissions and carbon fixation, between soil erosion and soil formation, between tree cutting and burning and tree planting and growth, between births and deaths. In the long run, we simply cannot take more away from the land than we —or nature—put back. Moreover, we must plan for the long run. A commitment to positive peace recognizes that it is ethically unacceptable, and ultimately impractical as well, to purchase short-term gratification and growth while robbing future generations. Whereas it is relatively easy for most people to see the foolishness of "mining our capital" when it comes to nonrenewable resources, it is less obvious—but no less important—to behave responsibly with regard to renewable resources as well.

Forests and soils are especially poignant and worrisome cases of renewable resources that are being dangerously disrupted. Over geological time, for example, soils were formed more rapidly than they eroded, which bequeathed all of us a life-sustaining layer of topsoil averaging about 6"–10" deep worldwide. But deforestation, erosion, overgrazing, and the like have dangerously degraded this natural legacy. It may be difficult to believe today, but in ancient times, northern Africa was the granary of Rome. Now, much of northern Africa is desert, and *desertification* is advancing south across Africa at a frightening pace. The process of "desertification" must be distinguished from drought. Desertification—a major threat to soil—is not a natural process, but rather the consequence of human mistreatment, whereby the rich organic material is washed or blown away, leaving relatively coarse rocky materials, which cannot sustain plant life and also are unable to retain moisture. This contributes to erosion and further degradation. The resulting sand dunes or gullies are nonproductive and very difficult to reclaim, even for wildlife habitat.

According to an assessment by the United Nations Environment Programme, 4.5 billion hectares—35% of the earth's land surface—are threatened by desertification. Of this vast region, three quarters have already been at least somewhat degraded. In the United States today, farmers lose six tons of topsoil for every one ton of produce grown. Atmospheric sensing stations in Hawaii can detect when spring plowing begins in China because of the increased particulate matter as airborne soil lost to the land! Worldwide, approximately 25 billion tons of topsoil are lost to erosion every year; this is nearly equivalent to the amount covering the wheatlands of Australia.

As the population increases—especially in the poorest countries—marginal land is brought under cultivation, leading to further erosion by wind and water, desertification, and additional loss of long-term productivity. Up to the middle of the 20th century, worldwide crop production increased at least in part because additional lands were brought under cultivation. Then, further increases in agricultural yields were achieved during the 1950s and 1960s through the "green revolution," which involved improved genetic varieties, fertilizer use, and the cultivation of new land. But the limits of such advances are rapidly being reached: Per capita productivity in Africa, for example, has actually begun *declining*, and there are no major new regions—anywhere—that can be brought under cultivation, at least not for long. In addition, overuse of existing croplands can exact a heavy price. In addition to erosion, for example, millions of acres of cropland are being destroyed by *salinization*: When underground soil drainage is insufficient, irrigation water—loaded with fertilizer and other salts—puddles up and evaporates, leaving an implacable manmade saline desert, which already covers vast areas of previously productive land and is expanding rapidly.

The World Bank has introduced a new concept, "food insecurity," which refers to those people who lack enough food for normal health and physical activity. Central African states are especially food insecure, notably Ethiopia, Congo, Uganda, Chad, Somalia, and Mozambique. Moreover, developed states may not be immune. Thus, by the end of the 20th century, the U.S. grain harvest fell below consumption for the first time in recent history.

The destruction of productive soil is very difficult to reverse, but not impossible. Overgrazed and overcultivated land must be allowed to lie fallow, sometimes for many years. Land that is especially vulnerable must be taken out of active production. The United States had led the way in this regard; the Food Surplus Act is intended to shift millions of acres of highly erodable land into meadows or forests. (This does not actually represent a sacrifice, since such land is not highly productive, and moreover, it cannot produce worthwhile yields for very long before being seriously degraded.)

The basic principle of sustainability applies to forest growth and regeneration as well. In short, if we destroy more than is created, we are cutting into the productive substance of the planet. And such imbalance cannot continue for long. If we cut and burn more than grows in that same period of time, then forests (or other resources) are diminished, weakened, and ultimately,

destroyed. In most developing countries, forest cover is declining dangerously, through logging, land clearing, and firewood gathering. In a mere
eight years. for example, India lost 16% of its forest cover; as a result, fuelwood prices in India's 41 largest cities increased by nearly one half, exacting a painful toll on that nation's poor. It doesn't take a higher degree in
mathematics or forestry to see that such trends cannot continue for very
long and that such degradations must inevitably have devastating effects on
wildlife, soil formation and maintenance, water quality, atmospheric equilibrium, and—not least—human well-being. In central Europe and North
America, acid rain generated by industrial air pollution, especially coal-fired
power-generating plants, has already damaged up to 25% of the forests, and
rendered thousands of lakes uninhabitable to fish and other aquatic life.
Forest destruction, in turn, leads to soil erosion, degradation of water quality, and increased runoff; for example, years of forest destruction in the
Himalayan foothills above Bangladesh has contributed to devastating
floods, which take an enormous toll in lives and property.

Such tragedies exemplify several important environmental themes:

1. *Political boundaries are virtually irrelevant to the world's ecology.*
   Forest cutting in northeastern India, Nepal, and Bhutan results in
   widespread destruction downstream, in Bangladesh.

2. *Environmental issues are not only the legitimate worry of the
   affluent.* Poor people—and often poor countries—are typically
   located where the environment has been most severely abused and
   are liable to suffer most seriously from environmental disasters.

3. *Environmental abuse can generate short-term profits, but invariably at the cost of long-term declines, both environmental and economic.* Natural systems underpin all national economies; as the
   former deteriorate, so will the latter. As a result, sensible policies
   must reflect environmental wisdom no less than economic, social,
   and political realities.

4. *Natural processes must be respected.* Human beings can intervene
   in those processes—we can unbalance them, and sometimes even
   restore them—but we cannot transcend them.

It is possible, fortunately, to turn the tide on forest loss. Tree planting on
a massive scale will help overcome greenhouse warming, reverse erosion,
and improve water and air quality, while also providing fuel and wildlife
habitat. South Korea has begun to do just this, China is on the verge, and
India at least has developed a forward-looking plan to reclaim its forests.
Trees do grow back, and reforestation is generally feasible, so long as the
money is available and people understand the need.

One of the most important renewable resources involves the production
of food itself. Nontechnological farmers obtain small yields, and they are

often thought to be inefficient compared with modern, high-tech agriculture. But in fact, much of the productivity of agro-industry is achieved by using vast amounts of energy. On average, every 1 calorie expended by non-technological farmers (as human and animal labor) yields 5 to 50 calories of food energy. By contrast, the intensive, mechanized farming practiced in the United States expends 5 to 10 calories of energy (mostly as petroleum, some as fertilizer and pesticide), to produce just 1 calorie of food. We grow a lot of food, but we do so by expending even more energy, which not only contributes to greenhouse warming but also depletes our most important non-renewable resource, fossil fuels.

Activism

In the United States

Environmental activism takes many forms. Within the United States, it is largely expressed through legislation and direct citizen participation. Legislative environmentalism involves the passing of laws designed to protect environmental values, to preserve wild and open space, to restrict pollution typically by establishing air or water standards to which states and local municipalities are required to comply, to prohibit the sale of materials derived from endangered species, and so forth. A landmark piece of legislation required that before the government expended federal funds on any project likely to produce adverse environmental impacts, an Environmental Impact Statement must first be prepared and evaluated; this statement must employ scientific studies to evaluate the extent of the impact and whether adverse effects can be diminished, and to provide objective information as to whether the project should be permitted to go forward.

Often legislative remedies are incomplete, in part because governments are frequently hesitant to enforce regulations that they see as harmful to business interests. In such cases, citizens may have access to legal procedures, obtaining court injunctions to prevent illegal actions, and in some cases, to force governments to enforce their own laws. The field of environmental law has grown rapidly, and groups such as the Environmental Defense Fund bring polluters and land despoilers to court; there has also been some progress in identifying environmental values (the right to clean air, water, an environment with wildlife) as having legal standing similar to personal property rights or the right to privacy.

Finally, there is the question of direct action, analogous in many ways to nonviolent antiwar resistance. Groups such as Greenpeace have blockaded whaling ships and sewage outfalls, and by a variety of dramatic and often courageous acts, including boycotts and sit-ins, called public attention to other environmental abuses, such as the clubbing of baby seals or improper disposal of nuclear waste. Such actions often include civil disobedience and can be controversial. The radical environmental organization Earth First! sometimes resorts to ecological sabotage ("ecotage"), as by vandalizing land-clearing equipment, or "spiking" trees (hammering large nails into them, thereby making it dangerous to log them). Governments have occasionally responded with violence and outright terrorism, as when French intelligence agents blew up the Greenpeace vessel *Rainbow Warrior*, which had been protesting French nuclear weapons testing in the South Pacific.

Not surprisingly, there has been some tension between large, relatively wealthy and well-connected environmental organizations that are often headquartered in Washington, D.C., and seek to exert influence at the national level, and local, grassroots activists, who are often on the "front lines." Nonetheless, the environmental movement in the United States has been gaining strength, although there seems little immediate prospect for electoral success of a United States Green Party modeled from the European experience.

In Other Countries

Grassroots environmentalism has, if anything, been developing more strongly in other countries. One of the most remarkable is the Chipko, or "Hug-the-Tree" movement of India. Beginning in the 1970s, Chipko developed in remote villages in the southern foothills of the Himalayas. It arose spontaneously, based on a cultural heritage that held a deep respect for the region's lofty mountains, magnificent forests, and clear streams. A series of disastrous floods clearly resulted from extensive deforestation; local activists responded by literally hugging the great trees, and in time-honored Gandhian fashion, lying down in front of logging operations. The Chipko strategy has since been used to save other natural areas in India, and it has also spread to other countries, where environmental concern is often most strongly developed among the poor, who rely most deeply on the land.

Another epic struggle has pitted indigenous Amazonian tribes, rubber-tappers (who earn their living extracting latex sap from free-growing rubber trees), anthropologists, and environmentalists against land development interests, especially in Brazil. In this case, ecological exploitation has been intimately connected with violence, notably genocidal extermination of whole villages and indigenous tribes, by private "armies" hired by landowners and abetted by the military.

Small-scale, grassroots organizing is occurring worldwide on behalf of the environment and its people. There are tens of thousands of community development groups in India alone, and their focus, increasingly, is on ecologically sensitive, sustainable development. Similarly, more than 100,000 "Christian base communities" have sprung up in Brazil, while in Africa and Asia in particular, women have been especially prominent in struggling for local reforestation, soil preservation, and the like. It cannot honestly be said that the tide has turned. Every year, in fact, the planet seems on balance to be losing rather than gaining. Beyond this, there has been a worldwide trend for environmental activists—often allied with human rights workers on behalf of indigenous peoples—to be persecuted by governmental authorities that stand to make large amounts of money by following destructive land-use and resource-extraction policies. But at least the battle has been joined.

A Sustainable Future

A sustainable society is one that is fundamentally in equilibrium with its environment, which meets its needs without diminishing the prospects of future generations. The alternative—nonsustainable exploitation—can produce short-term benefits but long-term disaster. Ecosystems (and presumably, entire planets) can be destroyed by thoughtlessness and failure to take the long view.

There is little question that human societies must ultimately meet the fundamental criterion of sustainability. It has been suggested that some of the world's great civilizations—Sumerian, Mayan, Roman—may have declined in part because they were destabilized internally by depletion of their underlying resource base. Today, very few knowledgeable people question the ultimate desirability, even the necessity, of a sustainable world economy. There is considerable debate, however, over the best route to sustainability, and even about when the limits to growth must be faced. Some people retain faith that technology will somehow save us, as it often has in the past. Others maintain that the earth is blessed with abundant resources—natural as well as human—sufficient to see us through any crisis that will arise, at least for the foreseeable future.

Faith in Technology

The argument goes that as resources are used up, the ensuing shortages will serve as incentive to (1) find new reserves; (2) reduce the rate of consumption, for example, by increasing efficiency; and (3) substitute abundant resources for those in short supply, such as making telephone lines out of fiber-optic tubes instead of copper. Necessity (or more precisely, higher prices) will be the mother of invention as a resource-poor world finds new solutions to old problems. In the recent past, fossil fuels largely replaced wood and animal power in providing energy for heavy industry, and aluminum has to some degree supplemented iron as a construction material. Who is to say that humanity will not continue to be equally inventive? New resources, new forms of energy, and new ways of replenishing the earth may be just over the horizon.

The difficulty with such thinking is that innovations cannot be counted on, whereas the depletion of known resources is absolutely certain. (There was immense excitement in the late 1980s about the possibility that "cold fusion" would provide cheap, abundant, clean energy; that hope now appears illusory, and we must conclude that there probably is no free lunch in our environmental future.) Moreover, even when they do prove successful, "solutions" often carry a new array of problems along with them: Fossil fuels pollute the atmosphere, high-technology mining operations are often energy-intensive themselves, and so on. A starry-eyed confidence that technology or inventiveness will always save us—like Flash Gordon or the Lone Ranger riding heroically to achieve a last-minute rescue—may well become a tragic disappointment.

Thresholds

Many environmental experts fear, in addition, that we cannot continue on our present course much longer without causing irreversible damage. There could well be key thresholds in the planetary environment that, once crossed, may permanently impair the earth's ability to meet our needs in the future. If the atmospheric load of greenhouse gases becomes too high, the ozone layer too sparse, soils too eroded, air and water pollution too severe (or some combination of these and other factors), if forest clearing and desertification go too far, then at some point, the planet may simply become incapable of nurturing life, regardless of our attempts to remedy things. Thus, it could be that the current generation has the enormous responsibility of determining the habitability of our planet, and not just for ourselves but for myriad other species as well. In this regard, time is not on our side: Soil, once eroded away, can take centuries to be replenished; certain forms of contamination (plastics, nuclear waste, long-lived pesticides) will probably be around longer than human history has thus far endured; the atmosphere, once warmed, may be impossible to cool; and species, once extinct, cannot be recreated.

There are solutions, however, some of them short-term stopgaps, others more promising for the long haul. Certain countries—notably the wealthy ones—have even stabilized their population, which, by definition, is a major step toward sustainability. Others—such as China—are working hard to do so. Energy efficiency can be increased dramatically, and alternative, renewable sources can be expanded. Reforestation, soil conservation, wildlife preservation, and strict antipollution controls are all eminently feasible. In most cases, the sticking point is political will.

Human Perception

Many dramatic human achievements require that a perceptual threshold be crossed. Before this happens, relatively few people have any deep dissat-

isfactions with the status quo; the result is business as usual. Then, charismatic leaders, catastrophic events, and/or successful education campaigns
may combine to force a dramatic perceptual shift, after which the world
appears transformed, after which sometimes it becomes transformed in reality as well. These events often have a distinct ethical/religious component,
but simple self-interest may also be effective: Consider the abolishment of
slavery and of hereditary monarchies, and—increasingly—worldwide revulsion against nuclear weapons. It may be that with the various combined
threats to the worldwide environment, and the intense publicity they have
generated in recent years, ecological wholeness is about to receive the attention and action that it warrants.

Interconnections

A world at peace is one in which environmental, human rights, and
economic issues all cohere to foster maximum growth and well-being.
Ecological harmony cannot realistically be separated from questions of
human rights or economic justice. The right to a safe environment, to clear
air, and to pure water is no less a human right than the right to freedom of
expression or dissent, equal employment opportunity, or participation in
the political process. Environmental degradation is also intimately connected to poverty: Wealthy states are often able to export their most odious
environmental abuses (sometimes literally, as in the case of toxic materials),
and impoverished states are often forced, by their poverty, to accept the
situation. The plowing of steep, erosion-prone slopes (which permanently
destroys soil) and large-scale intrusions onto wildlife habitats (which contributes to extinction) are in large part a response to land hunger in rural
countries, where a small minority of wealthy people own the great majority
of the arable land, thereby pushing people to environmentally abusive
behavior, simply to survive. In addition, within any given state, wealthy
people are able to purchase environmental amenities, while the poor find
themselves living in polluted, degraded surroundings.

Ecological well-being cannot be achieved piecemeal. The rain forests will
continue to be abused so long as there are too many people in too little
space; indeed, overpopulation has an impact on every environmental issue.
Poverty often leads to land degradation, as hungry, desperate people are
likely to clear and cultivate regions that should be left untouched. The burning of fossil fuels produces air pollution as well as greenhouse gases; greenhouse warming will greatly increase food insecurity by reducing agricultural
productivity; accordingly, solution of these and other problems must be intimately tied to providing adequate, safe energy.

Environmental problems are integrated in another sense as well. Many
of the most severe ecological threats are worldwide in scope, including
the greenhouse effect, air and water pollution that affects many states, or
the threat to the planet's ozone layer. Others, although occurring within

national boundaries, affect the world economy and/or the worldwide quality of life, such as the loss of species diversity, soil destruction, unsustainable demands on the world's renewable resources, and the heedless depletion of nonrenewables. Deforestation in Nepal causes flooding in Bangladesh; water overuse by the United States deprives Mexico of the Colorado River; pollution of the Rhine by Swiss and German chemical industries makes its water toxic for the Dutch who live downstream; whaling by the Japanese destroys these magnificent animals for everyone; and so on.

Finally, the various environmental and social issues are themselves interlocking: Population stabilization, as we shall see, will likely occur only when poverty is reduced; developing countries will be able to devote themselves to the preservation of their unique wild resources only if and when their debt burden is relieved; energy use will be sustainable only if it does not burden the air and water with additional pollutants. It seems undeniable that world cooperation on the environment is every bit as necessary as on economic matters, or on issues of military security and disarmament.

Tension Between Economics and the Environment

In the long run, there is only compatibility between economics and ecology, because what destroys the environment also destroys economies. But economic planners typically look only to the immediate future, and in the short run, jobs, profits, and development often conflict with environmental preservation. Air and water pollution control costs money, and installing such controls may make an industry uneconomic, hence leading to plant closings and loss of jobs. A sound environment may demand that wetlands be preserved (to absorb variations in the water table, as breeding grounds for fish and other aquatic organisms, etc.), but such preservation may come at the cost of restrictions on development (fewer new shopping centers, housing sites, and industrial parks).

Ultimately, economic development and environmental protection are not antagonistic; they are intimately connected. Vast numbers of people rely directly on the natural surpluses produced by a healthy environment: harvesting fish from wild populations in oceans, rivers, and lakes, obtaining game from the land, and fuel from the forests. A Mauritanian cattle herder does not need advanced training in ecology to know that "the land is tired," nor does a Philippine fisherman require a degree in marine biology to recognize that fish don't thrive where the ocean is polluted. Guatemalan peasants know all too well the consequences of plowing land that is too steep, and it is not only wealthy, amateur bird-watchers who mourn the loss of brilliant animals such as the quetzal, which has a prime place in Central American cultural identity.

But it is not only distant "primitives" who are immersed in the environment: We all depend on stable hydrological cycles for water, on atmospheric processes for air, on a stable world climate, and on the productivity of the world's organic soils. Environmental degradation, in the long run, translates directly not only into a less interesting and less beautiful planet—one deprived of wildlife, for example, or scenic values—but it also means thirst, hunger, poverty, sickness, and misery.

Nonetheless, battle lines still continue to be drawn in many cases between those who see themselves as defending the environment and those who champion jobs and economic development. In the Pacific Northwest of the United States, for example, a major controversy has erupted between conservationists and the timber industry. A rare bird, the northern spotted owl, nests only in relatively large, undisturbed tracts of old-growth forest. But the timber in these forests is also coveted by loggers. It remains to be seen whether a lasting accommodation can be reached in this and other acute conflicts between economics and ecology. It should be emphasized, however, that in the long run, a successful timber industry requires a continuing supply of trees, just as the spotted owl does. Accordingly, it seems not only possible that a win-win solution can be achieved, but also necessary, because neither the economy nor the environment can be victorious if the other is defeated.

Political Ideologies

Critics of environmental policies in the West sometimes assume that capitalism is largely to blame; after all, a system that exalts profits above everything seems unlikely to prize environmental values. And without doubt, the industrialism of capitalist states is intimately connected to their many environmental abuses. But socialist states have been no more sensitive to environmental issues, and in some cases, less so. In the former Soviet bloc, for example, the single-minded pursuit of production goals often took the place of profits, with the environment being seriously abused. The difference between traditional economics (whether market oriented or centrally planned) and sustainable economics is that the former is concerned with how to produce what for whom, whereas the latter expands the definition of "for whom" to include future generations.

Within the former Soviet Union, the once-majestic Aral Sea dropped 40 feet because of destructive, short-sighted dam and irrigation projects. The Neva River, near St. Petersburg's Hermitage Museum, is befouled with oil. Swimming is regularly curtailed at Black Sea resorts, due to typhoid and dysentery contamination. Environmental restrictions on the development of Siberia are almost nonexistent, and ignored when present. Forest destruction in the former East Germany, Czechoslovakia, and Poland were among the most severe on earth, and many regions of Poland in particular became drastically polluted through chemical and other toxic wastes.

Rigid adherence to production goals—regardless of environmental consequences—combined with state ownership made the tragedy of the commons even more widespread than in market-oriented societies. Private greed was largely replaced by public greed. The difference between capitalism and communism, it has been said, is that in the former, man exploits man, whereas in the latter, it was the other way around! In both cases, it has been the environment—and ultimately, everyone—that loses.

Making Peace

A world of increasingly scarce and endangered resources might be one in which people are motivated to cooperate, for everyone's benefit. But it might also be one in which conflict and violence are exaggerated, as wealthy states seek to achieve continuing access to raw materials and to hold onto their advantages while poor ones attempt to translate their existing resources into power, or simply to retain them in the face of growing demands. It would be especially tragic if a world made tense by ecological scarcity slides into war, which, in addition to its human toll, destroys yet more of the nonhuman environment.

But we are not doomed to repeat the mistakes of the past. The future can be reclaimed. Doing so, however, requires not only forbearance with respect to war but an active commitment to peace. This in turn must involve not only measures directed to preventing war but also those needed to build peace, including public as well as private commitment to invest heavily in environmental protection and restoration. But such investments require time, effort, and money. The following goals are minimal, but also achievable: reforesting the earth and stopping current deforestation; slowing and eventually stabilizing population growth; increasing energy efficiency; developing renewable energy sources; retiring Third World debt; protecting topsoil from erosion, desertification, and salinization; preserving representative, adequate-sized samples of the planet's pristine ecosystems and its wildlife; and protecting the air, water, and land from harmful, persistent pollution. Such accomplishments will not come cheaply. Some estimates suggest that they would require annual expenditures, over the next few decades, in the range of $200 billion per year. (The General Accounting Office estimates that it will cost about $150 billion just to clean up the mess already existing at U.S. nuclear production facilities.) And with so many pressing demands on government budgets, it is not clear where such resources would come from.

However, it is difficult to argue that the goal—a habitable, sustainable planet—isn't worth such a cost. Moreover, even a price tag of $200 billion annually is only about one fifth of the world's annual military expenditures, which currently exceed $1 trillion per year. It may well be that we cannot make peace with the planet until nations make peace with each other. If national security is eventually redefined in broader terms than mere military security, such a transformation may well be possible. After all, the

Netherlands currently spends about 6% of its gross national product (GNP) defending itself against the ocean, a far greater expenditure for its national security than it spends on its NATO obligations.

On the other hand, it is not necessary that we wait for the dawning of universal brotherhood for us to make a major contribution toward correcting the sad state of the world's environment. There are certain key states, which, by acting decisively, could greatly mitigate our current environmental difficulties. For example, the United States, China, and the states comprising the former Soviet Union produce fully 50% of the world's CO_2 emissions; Brazil, Indonesia, and Congo hold 48% of all virgin tropical rain forest; China and India together account for 35% of the world's annual population increase; and the northern tier of industrial states is responsible for virtually all of the world's acid rain production.

The result is a two-pronged lesson. First, to make peace with the earth, we must also make peace with each other. But second, just as some people claim that "peace begins with me," impressive strides toward environmental peace can begin with the actions of individual countries as well, not only to showcase what can be done but also to get results. Otherwise, it is possible that before the physical and biological limitations of the earth take a more direct toll, a period of Hobbesian strife will ensue; chaos and war—with all its profoundly anti-ecological effects—may add to the devastation. It remains to be seen whether environmental threats, even when shared, result in a tendency to unite as inhabitants of a shared planet, or more narrowly, as members of separate and embattled nation-states.

Environmental Ethics

This chapter—like the rest of this book—has been motivated by a need to identify real-world problems and suggest real-world solutions. Thus, it is driven more by considerations of practicality than by ethics. However, just as there is an underlying ethic to peace studies itself (the desirability of peace, negative as well as positive, and the iniquity of violence), we can also identify deep-seated ethical aspects to environmental sensitivity. In the Indian cultural heritage, for example, human activity is guided by three values of life: *artha* (which is essentially resources), *kama* (the needs and desires of human beings), and *dharma* (right conduct, or what people *ought* to do as opposed to what they *want* to do). *Dharma* also involves the proper utilization of resources, restricting their use to the satisfaction of one's primary needs, and not appropriating the resources of others. To do otherwise is to steal from others and from the world. In this worldview, *Dharma* consists of mediating skillfully and thoughtfully between desires and resources; there is therefore a close interlinking between justice and ecological and social harmony. Activities that are wasteful or destructive of natural resources must therefore be rejected, on ethical grounds as well as for practical reasons.

As historian Lynn White pointed out in an influential essay,[3] Judeo-Christian tradition is quite different. It emphasizes a separation between human beings, on the one hand, and the biological world of beasts and fields, on the other. Human beings are seen as having been created in the image of God, as against the gross and nonspiritual material world. Christians and Jews have been told to "go forth and multiply" and to "subdue the earth." Having emphasized such a distinction between people and the natural world, Judeo-Christian teaching established a context for destruction and exploitation, providing the intellectual and emotional underpinning to what has since become our ecological crisis. Nonetheless, White concludes his essay by describing an alternative tradition in Western theology, the gentle, nature-centered, and compassionate acceptance of Saint Francis of Assisi; he proposes Francis as the patron saint of ecologists.

Other thinkers have also proposed the establishment of ethics on a less human-centered and more tolerant and diversity-oriented basis. There may be deep benefits to adopting a more humble and accommodating view of the world and our place in it. If human beings saw themselves as part of the life process rather than its most celebrated rulers, the result may well be a kinder, more tolerant, and gentler way of living, not only with our planet but also with each other. Moreover, a growing trend in Judeo-Christian theology has been emphasizing the human responsibility to act as reliable stewards on behalf of God's creation.

It seems likely that the great environmental struggles, on which the future viability of the world's ecology will depend, will be played out during the early part of the 21st century. If we are to rise to this challenge, we will have to see ourselves as part of planetary processes, not set apart from the earth. We must follow the rate of soil erosion as closely as the rate of inflation; we must expend at least as much concern about keeping up with air and water quality standards as about keeping up with the stock market. We must begin to reconsider basic questions about common benefit versus individual rights: Individuals may be able to afford two automobiles, for example, or a large family, but can the planet?

Environmental ethics, as proposed by Henry David Thoreau and then John Muir, and more recently by Aldo Leopold and others, seeks to respect the living (and nonliving) world as having value in itself, not simply because of its possible utility or threat to human beings. It emphasizes that peace may ultimately require a much broader view of the human community, in which people are not only responsible for their own actions, the actions of other people, and their effects on other people, but also their effects on all other life forms. The West has long had a code of interpersonal ethics, the Ten Commandments. As of the 18th and 19th centuries, it developed codes of societal ethics: capitalism, democracy, liberalism, conservatism, socialism. To complete this triumvirate, perhaps what is needed from the 21st century is a code of environmental ethics.

A Final Note on Ecological Well-Being

Perhaps the fundamental lesson to be derived from a search for ecological wholeness and well-being is the idea of underlying unity. All things, quite literally, are linked to all others, such that any striving for peace must take account of this connectedness: of living things to the soil and to the atmosphere as well as to all other living things, of people to their natural environment as well as to their man- and woman-made social systems and to each other, of the past to the future of this planet, and of risks to opportunities for every one and every thing.

"What is man without the beasts?" a Native American, Chief Seattle, is said to have asked in 1854.

If all the beasts are gone, man would die from a great loneliness of spirit. For whatever happens to the beasts, soon happens to man. All things are connected. . . . Whatever befalls the earth befalls the sons of the earth.[4]

Notes

1.   Garrett Hardin. 1961. "The Tragedy of the Commons." *Science* 162: 1243–1248.

2.   Al Gore. 1992. *Earth in the Balance: Ecology and the Human Spirit*. Boston: Houghton Mifflin.

3.   Lynn White. 1967. "The Historical Roots of Our Ecologic Crisis." *Science* 155: 1203–1207.

4.   Chief Seattle. 1984. *Chief Seattle's Speeches*. Seattle, WA: Friends of the Earth.

19 Economic Well-Being

If a free society cannot help the many who are poor, it cannot help the few who are rich.

—John F. Kennedy

Peace implies a state of individual and collective tranquility, calm, and satisfaction. But it is very difficult to be tranquil or calm or satisfied when denied such basic needs as food, clothing, shelter, education, and medical care. It is even difficult to establish ethical guidelines—let alone to abide by them—when fundamental necessities are not available. Bertolt Brecht puts it well in his play *The Threepenny Opera*:

> First feed the face, and then tell right from wrong.
> Even noblemen may act like sinners,
> Unless they've had their customary dinners.

Moreover, even when their bellies are at least minimally full, many people rarely feel peaceful when they perceive that their economic conditions are far inferior to those of others. Not surprisingly, therefore, there is little peace in a world characterized by painful differences between the rich and poor, between the haves and the have-nots. Poverty, as we have seen, may not lead directly to war, but it certainly is not conducive to peace. Revolutions in particular have been stimulated and maintained by grinding economic privation. And it seems likely that one of the most important, but rarely acknowledged, reasons why the rich states maintain large military forces is that they are concerned with preventing any fundamental reorganization in the worldwide distribution of power and wealth. Saint Francis, commenting on the "plight" of the wealthy, noted that "he who has property also needs weapons and warriors to defend it."

But most of all, inequality in resources and opportunities is a direct burden on the poor themselves (poor people as well as poor countries). When poverty is persistent, degrading, miserable, life-shortening, life-threatening, and life-denying, it is an affront to human dignity. The search for peace must accordingly include a search for human economic and social betterment. (At the same time, it must be recognized that not all economically "poor" people feel miserable and abused, especially in Buddhist countries, for example, where material condition is considered less important than spiritual well-being.)

Most of the world's people are so preoccupied with their own immediate problems (of which poverty looms especially large) that wider preoccupations such as nuclear weapons, even peace and war, or the condition of the natural environment seem almost irrelevant. Political imagination is typically constrained by such immediate issues: in Latin America, debt, democratization, and poverty; in Africa, famines, displaced persons, debt, racial and religious violence; and so forth. The concrete day-to-day struggles of average people to lead tolerable lives occupies most of the energies of the overwhelming majority of humanity. Most Americans, by contrast, know what it is to be hungry on occasion, but have had blessedly little experience with *hunger*.

Efforts to eliminate poverty, or—not necessarily the same thing—to maximize wealth, have stimulated some of the major socioeconomic schemes of modern times, notably capitalism and communism. Accordingly, we shall not attempt here to reinvent the wheel by drafting blueprints for a preferred world economy. We instead try to sketch out some of the primary issues, identify some of the major controversies, and point toward possible courses of action.

Like war, poverty is not an abstraction, although we often speak of it in general terms. Just as there are specific wars, there are specific, flesh-and-blood people, and particular regions of especially bleak poverty, even in so-called wealthy countries. As with war, there are also questions of definition and identification: What is poverty? How do regions and countries differ? Is it getting better or worse? Yet just as political theory helps us identify and understand the reasons for and prevention of war generally, it can do the same for poverty, even though, as in efforts to understand war, theory yields many different explanations, some of them conflicting in their interpretations and their recommendations.

The Problem of Poverty

In its simplest terms, poverty exists when people do not have sufficient access to the "good life," however this may culturally be defined. Of course, one person's good life is another's luxury. For a middle-class American, the good life may require two cars, a color TV, at least one satisfying vacation annually, and the ability to send one's children to the college of their choice. For a resident of Manila's Tondo slum, it may be regular meals, a sewer system, one day off per month, and the ability to keep one's children from dying of diarrhea. The official "poverty level" in the United States would be considered a luxury level in much of the developing world. (At the same time, consider the following figures for the technologically advanced countries: 80% of global suicides, 74% of heart attacks, 75% of "television zombies," 56% of impotence and frigidity, 98% of illicit drug consumption—out of only 10% of the world's population.)

The most dramatic examples of clear-cut poverty on a global scale concern underindustrialized states of the South. Variously labeled "Third World," "underdeveloped," "developing," "have-nots," "lesser developed countries" (LDCs), and so on, it remains clear that these states are significantly poorer than their Northern, industrial cousins. It is also clear that these states have generally (although not universally) been subject to colonization and exploitation by the wealthier states, at least in the past.

Physical and Psychological Effects of Poverty

One of the most important, if least recognized, aspects of poverty is its psychological effects, the bitter pill of perceived injustice and inequality that must be swallowed by those who observe the affluence of others while still mired in their own poverty. Even if one's purchasing power is adequate for survival, it can be painful to witness a dramatically higher level of consumption on the part of others—and with increased communication and transportation, even the most isolated people, living traditional and impoverished lives, are exposed to examples of affluence. The results are deep mental suffering: envy, shame, and either despair or anger. (Moreover, as we shall see, along with "development" in the previously impoverished countries, there seems to be an inevitable widening of the gap between rich and poor, as has been the case—although to a lesser extent—for the United States as well.)

Beyond the phenomenon of envy, there is the painful physical fact of deep, absolute poverty. Hunger is the most obvious manifestation, with disease being inevitably associated as well. Other deficits usually accompany poverty: Poor housing and inadequate sanitation contribute to disease, as does inadequate nutrition. Health care is minimal or nonexistent. Educational opportunities are very limited, because areas of extreme poverty frequently have few and typically inadequate schools, and also because the very poor often need their children to work, so they are denied whatever limited educational opportunities may be available. The result is a deepening of the cycle of poverty, making it even more difficult for such people, or their descendants, to escape. Not surprisingly, life spans are significantly shorter among the very poor.

National and Global Inequalities

Poverty may be measured in absolute terms (sheer deprivation of food, poorer health, shortened life expectancy, etc.) or in comparative measures (inequality in the distribution of wealth, such that a small proportion of the population monopolizes more than its fair share of wealth, leaving the majority with less income and fewer assets per capita). In addition, trends in poverty are also important: The per capita income in Bolivia, Ecuador, Venezuela, and Peru was lower in 1999 than in 1989; in Nigeria, workers in the year 2000 earned 40% less than they did in 1990.

But relative inequality in wealth is perhaps even more appalling, even in the wealthy United States, where the top 20% of the population receives more than 50% of the annual gross national product (GNP), while the lowest 40% gets less than 15%. Interestingly, even under communism, Soviet-bloc states were not substantially more egalitarian: In Bulgaria, for example, the top 20% earned 33%, and the bottom 40% earned 27%. (States of the former Soviet bloc were actually more equitable than appears from these statistics, however, since health care, education, housing, and some degree of employment were more or less guaranteed.) Within most newly democratizing, fledgling capitalist countries, disparities in wealth have become extraordinarily wide: In Russia, for example, the newly ascendant top 1% of the population controls more than 20% of that country's wealth, while those at the bottom—notably elderly people on pensions and children—have seen their standard of living plummet as the communist-era socio-economic safety net has been frayed almost to the point of nonexistence.

The developing world is one of widespread and appalling contrasts, gleaming high-tech development alongside chronic and unremitting poverty. Moreover, the absolute gap between global rich and poor is widening. In many cases, the degree of deprivation is hidden by governmental manipulation of statistics. In Chile, for example, instead of assessing malnutrition by considering a child's weight in relation to his or her age, it is estimated by weight in relation to height; thus, a child whose growth is stunted is declared to be adequately nourished! Examples abound of governmental callousness toward the poor—even in the United States—in large part because the poor tend to have a very small say in governmental decision making, which generally takes place on behalf of the wealthy and powerful. During the Reagan administration, for example, an effort was made to cut school lunch programs for the poor by declaring ketchup a vegetable.

Although poverty is a worldwide phenomenon, it is not homogeneously distributed. There are poor people living in rich countries (e.g., parts of Appalachia in the United States) and wealthy people in the poorest countries:

multimillionaire plantation owners in Bangladesh or the Philippines. Poverty, however, is generally easy to identify, wherever it is found: high levels of unemployment, poor nutrition, inadequate health care and education, little or no savings, high levels of indebtedness, low levels of investment, inadequate housing, and often, ecologically depleted environments.

It should also be emphasized that although urban slums are devastating in their impoverishment, and typically receive the bulk of public attention, in fact the *favelas* of São Paulo, the barrios of Mexico City, and the slums of Cairo or Kinshasa are a relatively recent and minor phenomenon; despite their terrible squalor, the urban poor are generally *better off* than their rural cousins. This is part of the reason why Third World cities are doubling in size every 10–15 years, as impoverished, landless peasants flock to the cities, creating situations that become ever more desperate and unmanageable. Even now, however, more than 70% of the world's poor still live in rural villages, in India, Africa, Indonesia, and so on. Among the rural poor, illiteracy and the great epidemic diseases—malaria, cholera, tuberculosis— are at an all-time low, but the good things in life (and some of the necessities, such as an adequate diet) are no more available than they were before. Historically, rural interests have been overrepresented in Western democratic republics, notably England and the United States. By contrast, rural people—especially the very poor—are characteristically underrepresented in political and economic decision making on the part of less developed countries. The rural poor in particular tend to be ignored not only because their poverty makes them less consequential in the "corridors of power" in faraway cities but also because the rural poor are especially likely to be seen as irrelevant and also an embarrassment to those elite decision makers who look to the wealthy North for material goods, for images of their country's future, and for—not least—their own advancement.

Although the United States is, by many measures, the wealthiest country in the world, it does not rank very high regarding socioeconomic equity: fifth in worldwide literacy rate, seventh in public school expenditures per capita, eighth in public health expenditures per capita, 14th in life expectancy, 16th in percentage of women enrolled in universities, 18th in infant mortality rate (lower than Cuba, incidentally), and 20th in teachers per school-age population. There are more homeless people on the streets of the United States than in China, and an estimated 20 million Americans are functionally illiterate. In the richest country in human history, one child in five lives in poverty.

Causes of Poverty

"The rich are different from you and I," F. Scott Fitzgerald is said to have commented to Ernest Hemingway, whereupon Hemingway responded, "Yes, they have more money."

It is not terribly useful to conclude that poverty is caused by an absence of money. But what, then, are the underlying causes? There have been many explanations, some of which may even be correct. In certain cases, the natural resources of a country are so poor that wealth is virtually impossible to create. The African state of Chad, for example, is so arid as to be agriculturally unproductive; it also lacks significant mineral resources. By contrast, wealthy countries such as the United States tend to be resource-rich. But this argument is not altogether satisfying: Japan, for example, has relatively few natural resources, yet despite recent setbacks it has become an economic giant. The same is true in Hong Kong, South Korea, Singapore, and Taiwan, as well as in certain wealthy but resource-poor European states such as Belgium and the Netherlands. In a sense, some states can be considered especially resource-rich (Venezuela, Saudi Arabia, Kuwait), while others are capital-rich (Singapore, Luxembourg, Hong Kong, Taiwan, Japan). Some—notably the United States—are rich in both resources and capital, whereas others—Chad, Bangladesh—appear to be poor in both. Clearly, however, resources alone do not explain everything.

Government Policies

Government policies can also contribute substantially to poverty. Many analysts have attempted to explain the "economic miracle" of Japan (even though the Japanese economy suffered during the 1990s, it has remained one of the strongest on earth). There seems little doubt that social organization—in Japan's case, most notably a powerful work ethic—helped boost economic productivity. Alternatively, where poverty is widespread and has existed for thousands of years with little sign of improvement, a kind of fatalistic lethargy often sets in. Government policies can have substantial impact in such cases, either encouraging grassroots self-help or deepening the plight of a country's majority. The Congo (formerly Zaire), for example, is "rich," as measured by natural resources. Yet 80% of Congolese are desperately poor, and real wages are only about one tenth what they were at independence in 1960. At least some of the responsibility must be borne by long-time dictator Mobutu, who stole more than $5 billion directly from the national treasury. National wealth was similarly plundered by the likes of Marcos in the Philippines and Suharto in Indonesia. Fiscal mismanagement and irresponsibility—often bolstered by a rigid adherence to discredited ideology—have also resulted in economic degradation. An example is Romania, a country abundantly endowed with natural resources (notably oil) but that was reduced to painful poverty by destructive Stalinist-style policies.

Political leaders frequently take power by promising to represent the oppressed and underprivileged. Once in office, however, rulers often find it advantageous to cater to the powerful (i.e., in most cases, the wealthy). Carlos Menem, for example, was elected president of Argentina in 1989 by espousing a "Peronist" economic policy, which historically has allied itself with organized labor and Argentina's impoverished peasantry. Once in office, however, and pressured by rampant inflation as well as a massive international debt, Menem promptly began cutting back on Argentina's welfare state. A similar transition occurred during Corazon Aquino's "reform" government in the Philippines, which back-pedaled on promised land reform. There are many reasons for such policy shifts, including keeping the military happy (thereby allowing the government to remain in power), satisfying the demands of foreign bankers (notably the World Bank and the International Monetary Fund, which typically insist on domestic fiscal "austerity" in return for loans or debt relief), as well as the occasional lure of personal payoffs. It should also be reiterated that short of revolution or the overt threat of revolution, the very poor generally have a disproportionately small voice in government decision making.

Political Ideology

Social and political factors also can contribute to income disparities. According to Marxists, capitalism itself is largely to blame: Capitalist societies are stratified by economic class, with the owners of corporations exploiting the workers, thereby keeping them poor. According to mainstream capitalist economic theory, wealth is most likely to be generated by an unfettered free market; poverty is due to lack of effort, will, or ability, to bad luck, or to the allegedly negative influence of government interference. According to the classical economist Adam Smith, private enterprise, if left to its own devices, will act as though guided by an "unseen hand," to produce the maximum economic good for the maximum number of people. Implicit in capitalist economic theory is the idea that some people will inevitably do less well than others. This difference is presumably due at least in part to unavoidable differences between them; it is not the job of society to establish socioeconomic equality. Moreover, if government intervenes to redistribute wealth, this will not only diminish the efficiency with which new wealth is produced, it also constitutes a major blow to individual liberty.

Even most capitalist societies, however, do not subscribe to purely laissez-faire theories, in which governments are expected to take a purely hands-off attitude. Various "safety net programs" have been established in the United States, for example, including Head Start, Aid to Families with Dependent Children, and so on. Most other Western democracies are substantially more involved in the economy, especially at the federal level, seeking to maintain and improve the economic lot of their poorest citizens. In the past, conservative ideologies attributed poverty to alleged natural inferiority; more recently, the scapegoating tends to be more subtle, pointing to cultural circumstances and thereby relieving society of its social responsibility.

Poverty and War

Finally, there is a complex causal relationship between poverty and war. Preparing for war occasionally yields economic benefits: Many advances in the aircraft industry, radar, computers, and so on were stimulated by military research and development. But on balance, it is clear that domestic social progress, if it was the goal, would be produced far more effectively by targeting financial resources explicitly at domestic needs. Moreover, considering the immense destructiveness of war itself, there can be no question that on balance, war is impoverishing. It is essentially a parasite, feeding off the economic and social strength of societies, and like most parasites, it weakens its host.

As we noted previously, military industries provide employment, but they actually create fewer jobs than if comparable sums were expended in the civilian sector. Similarly, military expenditures are by their nature inflationary, and they do not contribute to equitable distributions of wealth, since they are strongly biased toward high-tech materials and highly trained white-collar employees. And perhaps most important, military spending uses funds that therefore become unavailable for environmental protection, medical or educational programs, construction of low-income housing, or rebuilding the national infrastructure.

Socioeconomic Development: Prospects and Problems

"Development" has long been seen as the key to the Third World's economic future. As President John Kennedy put it, "A rising tide lifts all boats." The idea is to improve the economic situation in the world generally, as a result of which, some economic benefits would be enjoyed by everyone, including the poorest countries and the poorest segments of society. In the jargon of the 1980s, a dynamic world economy would generate benefits that would "trickle down" to all inhabitants. On the other hand, it must be pointed out that when one is chained to the bottom, a rising tide can be rather frightening. Moreover, famed U.S. labor leader George Meany once noted that during his decades as a licensed plumber, he had seen lots of things trickle down—but that money wasn't one of them!

Growth and Modernization

During its heyday in the 1960s and 1970s, the idea of development theory was that economic progress would spread from the industrialized states to the Third World and that foreign aid, as well as enhanced trade and credit provided by the North, would help speed the process. Instead of dividing up the global pie differently, the wealthy states would simply help to bake a larger pie.

Development theory still persists in various forms. It also gave rise to numerous government programs, including the Alliance for Progress (within the Western Hemisphere) and the Peace Corps. Development theory is closely allied to classical free enterprise economic models, which espouse the basic theme of "grow now, redistribute later." Developing countries, according to this view, should strive to attract more, not less, foreign capital and to emphasize efficiency and growth as their goals. There have been some dramatic success stories in economic development, notably the so-called Asian Tigers: Hong Kong, Singapore, South Korea, and Taiwan. Moreover, those economies that were least integrated into the world free market system, such as North Korea and Myanmar (Burma), have been among the least dynamic.

Disappointments

Development theory still persists in various forms. But the great majority of poor countries have not had positive experiences with growth and development in recent decades, which has led to growing dissatisfaction and increasingly militant demands on the part of the world's poor.

One of the major disappointments of development has been a phenomenon sometimes referred to as *marginalization*, whereby increases in the size of the middle and upper classes are actually accompanied by deeper poverty on the part of the very poor. There may always be relative poverty—some people at the poor end of the income spectrum—just as there will always be those who are comparatively wealthy. The tragedy of marginalization is that it involves an increase in absolute amounts of poverty. In short, the benefits of economic growth in the poorest countries have not reached the lowest levels of society, and the poorest of the poor are pushed more and more to the margins of subsistence. This condition, whereby development causes increased disparity in income, is associated with low per capita school enrollment and high birthrates. Regardless of its causes and correlates, however, the distressing fact remains that in many if not most cases, development has been a cruel joke, as the already low-income poor have faced the prospect and reality of *declining* incomes.

Globalization

Dramatic advances in communication and transportation, plus the remarkable growth of computer technology generally, have provided impetus for the *denationalization* of economies and the advent of *globalization*. In a globalized economy, a product may be designed in Italy, fabricated in

Malaysia using raw materials from Brazil, then sold in Australia—to the economic benefit of a corporation based in Chicago! Not surprisingly, globalization is a two-edged sword. On the positive side, it offers the prospect of some employment for impoverished people in nonindustrial countries, and thus, a possible "hand up" in their lives. It connects such people for a while to the world economy, and it may involve them and their government leaders in a web of interconnections that promises to break down parochialism and reduce the likelihood of armed conflicts. But there are also negative aspects to globalization.

For example, in the absence of carefully enforced international standards, multinational corporations are sorely tempted to scour the globe for the lowest-paid workforce, for the least available worker safety and health benefits, and for minimal if not nonexistent environmental protections. The ensuing "race to the bottom" benefits such corporations and—in the short run—consumers, since consumer products can therefore be produced cheaply. At the same time, higher-paid, better-protected workers (such as many in the United States), suffer in return, as their jobs disappear, while low-paid workers in poor countries are denied basic and essential protections. In addition, excessive focus on the elimination of trade barriers at all costs has resulted in a lowering of environmental standards (since they, like labor standards, have often been judged to be "unfair restraints on trade").

From the end of World War II until the early 1990s, the primary vehicle for globalization was GATT, the General Agreement on Tariffs and Trade. Currently, such issues are taken up by the World Trade Organization, or WTO, which has concerned itself almost exclusively with lowering trade barriers between countries. Globalization has the potential to help alleviate world poverty while protecting worker rights and the environment; thus far, however, it has not lived up to those hopes and instead has tended to enhance corporate profits over human and environmental values.

Some countries have begun to move away from a simple progrowth and development model. Sri Lanka, for example, succeeded in significantly reducing abject poverty by devoting half of its national budget to free rice, education, and health services and to subsidized food and transportation. As a result, life expectancy has risen dramatically, approaching that of more "developed" countries. (Tragically, ethnic conflict between Tamil and Sinhalese has interfered with, and to some degree overshadowed, the recent remarkable social accomplishments in Sri Lanka.)

For most of the world's impoverished countries, development poses a difficult dilemma: On the one hand, an economic system emphasizing free markets, open trade, and foreign investment offers the prospect of efficient, rapid growth and potentially massive production. But on the other hand, such a system also tends to enhance the schism between rich and poor.

At the same time, another perspective—quite different from development theory—has been gaining credibility. According to this influential critique, often known as *dependencia* theory, the Western model of "development" has actually been harmful to most of the world's people.

Dependencia Theory

This perspective on international poverty originally derived from the economic situation in Latin America, a region that has long been economically and politically subservient to the United States. Under the influence of radical economic theorists such as Andre Gunder Frank, the term, based on the Spanish word for *dependency*, has also been applied to other regions, wherever indigenous peoples and resources are believed by many social critics to be exploited by the wealthier, industrialized states of the North.

The basic idea of dependencia is that poverty in what Johan Galtung called the "periphery" (the less-industrialized South) occurs in large part because of affluence by the "center" (the industrialized North). Poor countries are thus not so much underdeveloped as overexploited, such that their poverty is not somehow due to neglect by the wealthy North, but by too much attention. Countries such as the Democratic Republic of the Congo, Indonesia, Brazil, India, and Malaysia are rich; only their people are poor! According to dependencia theory, not only did the North exploit the South overtly during the days of colonialism, but such exploitation has continued, covertly, even after outright imperial control was terminated. Even now, the wealthy, powerful North takes advantage of the South by manipulating markets, credit, and trade balances. In the past, repressive control was exerted directly, by armed forces of occupation; such control is currently indirect, through surrogate local rulers (the so-called *comprador* class), who are clients of the wealthy states and who profit personally by impoverishing their own people while being essentially in league with the Northern powers. As a result, the great majority of Third World people are victimized by their own governments as well as by the industrialized states. Unlike the relationship between, say, the United States and France, in which benefits often flow in both directions, exchanges between either of these wealthy Northern powers and Mauritania, for example, are likely to be exploitative and distinctly one-sided.

The Debt Problem

In addition to poverty itself, most of the world's nonindustrialized countries have another problem, one that saps revenues, limits domestic spending options, and sits like an ogre inhibiting progress along the path of economic betterment: debt. Forced to pay billions of dollars annually, out of a national economy that is barely keeping its head above water, these countries have virtually no hope of achieving prosperity for most of their citizens, as they are literally unable to invest in their own economies.

The debt crisis was precipitated in large part by a widespread recession among the wealthy states. The stage was set during the 1970s, as costs sky-rocketed for petroleum, weapons, and food—all of which were purchased by developing countries, in part using funds that Northern banks eagerly made available. By the 1980s, interest rates rose dramatically while commodity prices plummeted, whereupon debtor states found themselves increasingly hard-pressed to meet the interest payments on their loans. Ever since, the poor countries have been finding themselves falling ever farther behind in their capacity to pay; their plight has been like that of the coal workers in the song "Sixteen Tons": "You load sixteen tons and what do you get? Another day older and deeper in debt."

Under certain circumstances, the International Monetary Fund permits rescheduling of this crushing debt burden, but only if the debtor country agrees to "austerity programs," which typically require drastic cutbacks in government subsidies of food, transportation, health care, and education, as well as anti-inflation policies that substantially increase unemployment and underemployment. A related strategy has been to provide new loans to enable debtors to pay the interest on old loans—a "solution" that is unlikely to inspire much long-term confidence.

The human cost of international debt has been staggering. A UNICEF report estimated that approximately 500,000 children die annually because of economic decline or stagnation in the world's poorest states, conditions that generate government cutbacks in basic health services, primary education, and food and fuel subsidies. This occurs when family incomes for a billion people have been *declining*, especially in Africa, South America, and southern Asia.

Under the circumstances, some of the most impoverished and indebted states have begun to threaten default on their loans. One alternative—debt rescheduling and outright debt forgiveness—has been proposed and encouraged by several religious institutions (notably the Roman Catholic Church), but shows no signs of being acted on.

Ethics and Equity

Amid these conflicting ideologies and attempts, a fundamental question remains: Why should the wealthy states agree to forgiving the debt burden of poor countries, or indeed, to any policies designed to reduce the inequality in world wealth? Do the wealthy countries have any obligation toward the poor ones? Some theorists claim that no such obligation exists. An extension of laissez-faire capitalism and the ideology of "rugged individualism" is that poverty is the unavoidable consequence of differences (among countries no less than among individuals) and that inequality should not only be tolerated but even celebrated, since it indicates that "merit" is being rewarded. By this argument, it is in fact immoral to redistribute wealth, since such redistribution necessarily involves taking away resources that rightfully belong to someone while conferring it on others who presumably are not worthy; otherwise, they wouldn't be in such need.

But in fact there are many reasons for opposing inequalities in global wealth. One is the notion of *distributive justice*, that is, a virtually universal sense that gross inequity is of itself unfair, even when it might not be the result of unjust practices. Certainly, there is something ethically repugnant about the spectacle of dire, unremitting, life-threatening poverty coexisting with extreme luxury. For some, it is a moral imperative based essentially on charity: When suffering exists, people have a duty to attempt to alleviate it.

America ethicist and political philosopher John Rawls has developed a theory of rights that emphasizes liberty and equity. According to this influential view, "Social and economic inequalities are to be arranged so that they are . . . to the greatest benefit of the least advantaged." In his book *A Theory of Justice*, Rawls proposed that we evaluate any social institution from "behind the veil of ignorance," that is, considering every system as though we have no foreknowledge as to our own specific place within that system: Not knowing whether we would be privileged or not, how would we feel about being part of a given social form? (Our view of the Hindu caste system would probably be affected if we had a high probability of being an "untouchable," for example.)

Moreover, it is not unreasonable to suggest that the poverty of the many is somehow connected to the extreme wealth of the privileged few. Wealth amidst poverty is often the result of extortion, theft, unmerited good luck, and so on. But beyond the issue of fairness and merit, there looms the question of distributive justice. Should society intervene to ensure equitable distribution of wealth? Or should certain minimum levels of economic welfare be established? If so, then how? And what should they include—housing, education, medical care, guaranteed employment? If so, how can we make room for individual initiative and ensure that people will contribute their "fair share"?

A classic Marxist maxim is "from each according to his ability, to each according to his need." But in practice, it has proven difficult to assess and reward need, and even more difficult to induce people to contribute according to their ability, unless they perceive that a direct personal benefit will flow from their labors. This is one reason for the relatively low productivity of most communist economies. Beyond this, is it necessarily true that everyone should be treated equally? With respect to legal entitlements or political rights, most people would agree that the answer is yes. But in other respects, it is clearly, no: Criminals, for instance, are treated differently from law-abiding citizens. What about reward for special effort or skill? Is inequality of compensation in itself unjust? And what about unequal wages between farmer and factory worker, computer entrepreneur and common laborer, villager and city dweller, Eskimo and Polynesian? Is economic inequality any more acceptable between different countries than within a single country?

Hunger

Approximately 15% to 20% of the human population suffers from under-nutrition, primarily insufficient protein and/or calories. About 70% of the world's hunger is found in nine countries: India, Bangladesh, Pakistan, Indonesia, the Philippines, Congo, Cambodia, Brazil, and Ethiopia.

The Extent of the Problem

The average inhabitant of southern Asia consumes fewer than 2,000 cal-ories per day, as compared with more than 3,000 for the average American. The average Asian consumes about 400 pounds of grain per year, almost all of it directly as grain. The average American, by contrast, consumes an extraordinary 2,000 pounds of grain/year, but of this, only about 150 pounds are eaten directly as grain (the most energy-efficient way); about 100 pounds are consumed as alcohol, and most of the remainder is eaten much less efficiently, as meat. (When calories are transferred from grain to live-stock and the meat eaten by human beings, between three fourth and nine tenth of those calories are lost.) Approximately one billion people are chron-ically undernourished, while food imports have increased, reinforcing Third World dependence as well as vulnerability to droughts, hurricanes, floods, earthquakes, and the like.

The simple capacity to raise food is certainly relevant, and in this respect it is especially troubling that per capita food production in many impover-ished states, notably in central Africa, actually went *down* during the 1980s and 1990s. Poor countries produce less food, at least in part because being poor, they cannot afford modern agricultural technology: Rice yields in India and Nigeria, for example, are only one third those of Japan, and Brazil's corn yields are only one third that of the United States. Approximately one tenth of the world's land surface is now under cultivation, but little increase can be anticipated, since most of the remaining land is desert, mountainous, arctic, or otherwise uncultivatable. Nonetheless, despite serious problems of desertification, erosion, and pollution, worldwide agriculture raises 2.5 times the grain needed for human consumption. Inequities in such consump-tion, however, are dramatic.

A Matter of Distribution

To a very large extent, the problem of world hunger is not really so much a production problem as it is a *distribution* problem. In Mexico, for example, where as many as 80% of the country's rural children are undernourished, livestock consume more grain than the entire rural population, and the meat is then exported to the United States. Throughout much of Africa, land that once grew sorghum and corn—for local consumption—is now owned by multinational agribusiness conglomerates and is used for the production of cotton and coffee for export. Local people are thereby denied native grains while also finding themselves unable to pay for imported wheat and rice. People may have desperate needs, but in classical economic terms, this doesn't constitute "demand" unless they can pay for what they want. Moreover, the rich have greater influence on the politics of decision making. As a result, when poor countries are capable of production, there is a tendency to make luxury goods (for export) rather than necessities for domestic consumption.

Fewer than 3% of the world's landowners—many of them absentee and/or large agribusiness firms—own nearly 75% of all cultivatable land. In some areas, this inequity is even greater: 1% of the population of northeast Brazil, for example, owns 45% of the land, much of it used to grow sugar, which generates money for the owners but provides virtually no food for the vast majority of the population. Peasant farmers, desperate to raise their own food, find themselves forced to cultivate erosion-prone hillsides and infertile terrain, which in turn are quickly overcultivated and depleted, leading to ecological ruin and yet more poverty and famine.

In 1974, Frances Moore Lappé wrote *Diet for a Small Planet*, in which she argued the need for people to eat lower on the food chain (less meat, more grain, etc.). In 1986, in her book *World Hunger*, Lappé saw the problem differently: World grain production alone, she estimated, is enough to provide 3,600 calories per capita per day—enough to make everyone overweight! The World Bank estimated that world grain production alone could provide 3,000 calories along with 65 grams of protein per person per day, more than the highest estimates of minimum nutritional requirements. If only 2% of the world's grain output were redirected toward those who need it, hunger would essentially be eliminated from the world.

But the greed of agribusiness shippers and brokers, plus control of land by a small elite, leaves hundreds of millions of people hungry every day. Subsistence farmers typically rely on their own seed—derived from this season's crops—to provide for the next season's planting; agribusiness companies, oblivious to this human necessity, developed "sterile" plant strains, which would require that new seeds be purchased every year. Although public outrage resulted in recall of these "innovations," they indicate the pervasive and continuing conflict between corporate profit and human need. The politics of scarcity, which dominate the lives of most Third World people, have scarcely been examined in the overfed First World.

Population

As we have seen, positive peace involves a web of interconnected relationships. This is especially true of the population problem. Population—the sheer press of human numbers—makes itself felt in every aspect of the human condition, but environmental and economic issues are especially prominent. On the one hand, the negative impact that human beings exert on their environment is largely a function of technology: Compare the damage done to a tropical rain forest, for example, by 10,000 indigenous hunters, gatherers, and horticulturists, who have lived in relative balance with the forest for thousands of years, with the damage wrought by 10,000 people armed with bulldozers, dynamite, asphalt, and guns, who threaten to destroy whole ecosystems in a matter of years. And yet the sheer numbers of people also contribute substantially to environmental problems. Even among nonindustrialized countries using minimal technology, expanding population threatens to destroy major wildlife forms because of habitat destruction (e.g., the fencing and plowing of land otherwise needed for jaguar habitat in Belize) and hunting (e.g., poaching of elephants and rhinos in Tanzania). Too many people results in too much consumption, which in turn pollutes the air and water, creates unmanageable quantities of solid waste, and threatens to exceed the productive capacity of any given region—and ultimately, the entire planet—to provide nourishment, decent living conditions, and an acceptable environment. Many of our environmental problems doubtless can be ameliorated in the short term by social, political, and technological innovations, but even with the best of policies, there must ultimately be a stabilization of the human population, or else no solutions will ever hold for the long haul.

This is especially true of attempts at economic self-betterment. All too often, countries seem poised to make real gains in their living standards only to have the progress nullified by an exploding population. No country can "pull itself up by its bootstraps" if the weight of the human population is so great as to tear those straps.

Some Trends in Population Growth

The human species is several million years old. World population, however, did not reach the one billion mark until about the year A.D. 1600. This increase was due largely to the Agricultural Revolution, begun around 8000 B.C.E., with the domestication of plants and animals. It in turn resulted in better diets, more reliable food supplies, and the opportunity for division of labor. After that long journey to the first billion, it took only 300 years to add the next billion. This happened around 1900, stimulated in large part by the Industrial Revolution (which made energy available via mechanization and the use of fossil fuels) as well as advances in public hygiene, vaccination, and control of certain major epidemics. The third billion arrived in just one sixth that time, in 1950, and the fourth, by 1975. Human population reached five billion in the 1980s and six billion at the onset of the 21st century. And it is still climbing. In short, not only has the world population been growing, but for a time, the rate of that increase itself increased, because, as the English economist Malthus pointed out, human population increases geometrically (or exponentially).

Considering worldwide population as a whole, the actual rate of increase has slowed in recent years, although because the overall population has continued to grow, actual numbers added per year has actually *increased*. In some cases—notably, the developed economies of the West—population levels are stabilizing, and thus, cause for hope rather than alarm. It is anticipated, for example, that the U.S. population will even decline slightly by the mid-21st century, after the momentum of the "baby boomers" carries the population to about 300 million. Similarly, the population of most northern European states is expected to decline by as much as 10% by the year 2025. (Some effects of declining birthrate in these countries are already apparent, including the accommodation of increasing numbers of "guest workers" from Turkey, Iran, northern Africa, and Asia, along with attendant ethnic and racial tension, and a rise in right-wing, neofascist ideology on the part of some indigenous Europeans.)

On balance, however, total world population seems destined to increase dramatically, doubling in another 40 years. About 30% of the world's people live in developed countries, although the percentage of world population increase attributable to these countries is less than 10%. The world adds the equivalent of a new Mexico—an additional 100 million people—every year, with more than 90% of this growth occurring among the poorest countries. This gives some credence to the old adage that the rich get richer and the poor get children. To maintain a constant population size, women must bear on average, two children in their lifetime. The U.S. average is 1.8, but in rapidly expanding populations such as Nigeria and Kenya, the numbers reach a whopping 6.6 and 8.0, respectively. The cause of this increase, quite simply, is an excess of births over deaths, which, as we shall see, leads to a deepening of the planetary ecological crisis plus enhancing the poverty within which such population growth takes place.

This tidal wave of population growth has had results that are little short of cataclysmic, making a mockery of efforts at economic and environmental self-improvement. Take the situation in just one country: Nigeria, the most populous in Africa. Since 1950, Nigeria has grown from 43 million to 125 million persons, and by 2025, that number is expected to swell to more than 300 million. Some people contend that concern about overpopulation—especially when the worried parties are Caucasian—is actually a concealed form of racism; this accusation is at least plausible, since rapid population increases are largely occurring in Africa, Latin America, and parts of Asia. But it should be emphasized that the costs of overpopulation are borne overwhelmingly by the poor and marginalized people who are themselves overcrowded. Countries in which resources are already stretched to the limit are required, by virtue of their expanding human populations, to increase demands on water, soil, wildlife habitat, education, and health and other human service budgets that are already dangerously depleted. Struggling, debt-ridden governments have in many cases already reached or surpassed their abilities to provide even basic services to their people. In 1969, for example, Mexico City had a population of 9 million people; in 1999, there were more than 20 million people in this huge, almost ungovernable city.

The point is that continued high population growth in the poorer countries will not only prevent a closing of the economic gap between rich and poor, it will actually *widen* that gap. The rates of *income* growth in rich and poor countries are roughly comparable; accordingly, it is the different rate of *population* growth that keeps the latter from catching up. This problem is particularly acute in the Indian subcontinent, Africa, and Latin America.

The Demographic-Economic-Environmental Trap

There is a real danger that some states may never emerge from what might be termed the "demographic-economic-environmental trap." In such cases, rapid population growth contributes to increased demands on natural and socioeconomic systems, which are then overtaxed and begin to collapse. People commonly respond with higher birthrates, which in turn produce yet more ecological and socioeconomic pressure, which ultimately impoverishes the land and the people, leading to catastrophic mortality, notably from starvation and epidemics, and possibly direct violence as well.

Population levels, ecological factors, and economic conditions are all intimately related. Thus, every environment can be said to have a *carrying capacity*, the number of people who can be supported by the soil, forests, grassland, croplands, water, and other resource supplies of that region. If demand exceeds carrying capacity, the effect is like "mining capital" rather than "living off one's interest": It cannot be sustained for long. For example, in many areas of the world, wood is used for fuel. More people result in more demand for wood, which leads to cutting, perhaps in excess of the amount that grows annually. As forests dwindle, wood becomes scarce and expensive, adding to the misery of the poor, while the deforestation itself seriously diminishes wildlife values, contributes to the greenhouse effect, and generates erosion and downstream flooding. (Devastating floods in Bangladesh have become commonplace, periodically killing tens of thousands and making hundreds of thousands of people homeless, due to the destruction of forests in the foothills of the Himalayas, above that country.)

Another significant consequence of the demographic-economic-environmental trap is the production of large numbers of so-called eco-refugees, people who are forced to leave their ancestral homes because of environmental degradation. Land-hungry farmers are increasingly driven onto wildlife preserves and marginal land that is highly erodable and easily destroyed. The result is *desertification*, a process that is distinct from drought. In this case, overgrazing, overplowing, and deforestation destroys the productivity of the soil, on which whole ecosystems depend. The process is accentuated by natural drought, to which weakened and overcrowded people are especially susceptible. The increasing numbers of eco-refugees congregate in cities and refugee centers, where they rely on government assistance and are highly susceptible to disease and—as has occurred in drought-stricken sub-Saharan Africa—massive starvation when and if relief efforts run into political, economic, or logistic difficulties.

Uncontrolled population growth in subsistence economies threatens not only the country's environment but also its social and economic system. Universal public education becomes virtually impossible when school systems are drowned beneath a tidal wave of youngsters. When population is constant or declining slightly (as in Germany or Switzerland), a 2% increase in economic growth results in increased overall per capita prosperity; when the population increases by 3% or 4%, that same 2% economic growth results in painfully *declining* living standards for most people. Environmental activist Lester Brown notes,

> The world is dividing largely into countries where population growth is slow or nonexistent and where living conditions are improving, and those where population growth is rapid and living conditions are deteriorating or in imminent danger of doing so.[1]

It is difficult to make a cogent case that more people are needed, in any part of the world. Those regions that we generally consider to be "unpopulated" usually possess few people because in fact the land and its climate can support only small populations. Deserts, high mountain slopes, or low-lying marshland or swampland that is regularly inundated by floods cannot—and should not—be heavily populated. There are no Shangri-las on the planet Earth: regions that are currently unpopulated, but that could provide idyllic, well-balanced lives for substantial numbers of people. Moreover, as we have seen, Third World countries are already dangerously overextended in their ability to care for their current population.

On the other hand, it must be pointed out that overpopulation can easily be exaggerated as a cause of human misery. Some of the most horribly impoverished regions of the earth—such as Sudan, Chad in Africa, or northeastern Brazil—are among the most sparsely populated. (Ecologists would note that such regions, because of their environmental limitations, should not be heavily populated in the first place; given the extreme susceptibility of tropical soils to destruction, and the dryness of northern Africa, it seems likely that the natural "carrying capacity" of such regions for human population is necessarily low.) The extreme poverty of India, Pakistan, and Indonesia is often blamed on their high birthrates and population density, yet they have fewer people per square mile than England, Japan, Holland,

West Germany, and Italy, among others. During the 1950s, Cuba—with a population of five million—suffered devastating poverty and widespread starvation; today, with more than twice the population, the Cuban people are well nourished. Clearly, then, although population can be a problem, and can add to existing problems, it is not the entire problem.

The Demographic Transition

Many European states, as well as those formerly comprising the Soviet Union, and the United States as well, have virtually attained zero population growth, whereas in Latin America, Africa, and Asia, the population growth rate is about 2%. There is some reason to hope, however, that the DEE (demographic-economic-environmental) trap may be avoidable and that these high rates of population increase will decline in the future, as many women experience an improvement in their social and economic status, and when (and if) developing countries experience general social and economic improvements more generally. This expectation is based on one of the most important trends in human population, known as the *demographic transition*: Birthrates consistently decline as a result of industrialization, urbanization, and a general improvement in economic conditions.

In nonindustrial, rural societies experiencing the first stage of this demographic process, birthrates and death rates both tend to be high, and the population therefore remains relatively stable. Then, with public health measures, immunizations, widespread food distribution, and so on, death rates decline while birthrates remain high. In this second demographic stage, population levels increase dramatically. But in the final stage of the demographic transition, social and economic conditions improve, and this, along with lowered infant mortality, produces a desire for smaller families, as growing numbers of parents realize that they do not need large numbers of children to serve as field hands, to compensate for high mortality, or as social security in their old age. Moreover, many parents recognize that to provide their children with such benefits as a higher education, they must have fewer of them. As a result, in the final stage of the demographic transition, populations eventually level off.

Many countries have successfully made this transition, notably much of Europe, Oceania, and increasingly, the United States and the western republics of the former Soviet Union. Fertility has also gone down impressively among those Asian countries that have experienced substantially improved economic conditions, notably South Korea, Singapore, Taiwan, and Japan.

Efforts at Birth Control

Successful birth control requires more than just appropriate technology; as a matter of public policy, it also requires understanding the social causes and effects of population growth. There are four basic theories correlating population growth with socioeconomic situations

1. *Reproduction leads to poverty*: People have too many children, forcing them to try to feed too many mouths, to divide their land and resources across too many individuals.

2. *Poverty leads to reproduction*: People have children because they are needed to work hard, to help support their families, and moreover, children don't cost very much if you don't buy VCRs and computers for them or send them to college. In addition, under conditions of poverty, a relatively small number of children survive, which generates pressure for having large numbers of children.

3. *Oppression of women leads to reproduction*: Women would have fewer children if they had greater control over their lives, especially an increase in status and access to inexpensive, reliable family planning techniques. Fundamentalist religious traditions also contribute to the suppression of women.

4. (actually a variant of theory 3) *Male pig-headedness leads to reproduction*: Population growth is due to the influence of men, who equate large families with sexual virility and other "macho" characteristics.

To some extent, all of these theories seem to be true; they are not mutually exclusive. Large families are often a result of poverty and low status of women, but they also generally lead to a vicious circle of yet more poverty and sexism.

At present, about two thirds of all birth control users live in the industrialized world. In some cases, hesitation regarding birth control can be attributed to cultural factors: the "macho" tradition in Latin America, which equates manhood with the production of children, and opposition by the Catholic Church in Mexico, the Philippines, and Kenya and by Islamic fundamentalists in Egypt, Iran, Pakistan, and India. However, there is reason to believe that birth control technology, if widely available, would be used: UN surveys, for example, have found that one half of all married women do not want *any* more children. And yet funding for contraceptive research and population assistance has declined in recent decades, in part because conservative politicians in the United States—long antagonistic to family planning, contraceptives, and abortions—have become increasingly influential, both domestically and globally. The World Bank estimated that it would cost $8 billion (about 10 days' worth of U.S. military spending) to make birth control easily available worldwide.

Breast-feeding is a moderately effective means of birth control, or at least, of birth spacing: Lactation tends to inhibit ovulation. (This is one reason why Western corporate campaigns to convince mothers in poorer nations to

substitute artificial infant formula for breast-feeding are especially pernicious.) Sterilization is also becoming increasingly popular. It is cheaply
available, and with relatively little risk for both sexes. Approximately 28
million abortions are performed annually in developing countries, and
about 26 million in industrialized countries—of these, roughly one half are
illegal, and thus, likely to be performed by unskilled people and under
unsafe conditions. Abortion is a highly charged issue for many people; even
its supporters concede that it is a relatively intrusive means of family planning, and thus, less desirable than contraception. Nonetheless, when other
means of birth control have failed, access to safe abortions would seem
preferable to enforced childbearing.

Reproductive Rights for Women

Perhaps the most effective way to reduce population growth is to improve
the status of women. For example, when the government of Bangladesh
initiated a program of financial loans to rural women, for developing their
own small businesses, contraceptive use among the recipients increased
from an average of 35% to 75%. The relatively low social and economic
status of women worldwide contributes to high birthrates, in several ways.
Thus, married women—typically subordinated to their husbands—are often
denied social permission to say no to their husband's demands for more children. In much of Africa, for example, social pressures are especially strong,
since at marriage, the husband essentially purchases his wife's labor as well
as her future children; each additional child solidifies the mother's place
within the household.

When large numbers of women are denied access to education and other
forms of advancement, childbearing may become the only accepted rite of
passage to adulthood. As a result, widespread female education is likely to
help reduce fertility, thereby diminishing poverty and also helping to prevent
further environmental degradation.

It is also noteworthy that birth control and family planning are strongly
indicated as matters of public health alone. For example, complications arising from pregnancy and childbirth are the leading killers of Third World
women in their 20s and 30s. More than 3,000 maternal deaths occur per
100,000 live births in regions of Ethiopia and Bangladesh, as compared with
10 in the United States and only 2 in Norway. This all adds up to a cogent
argument in favor of enhanced reproductive rights for women. The case
would be very strong simply as a matter of human rights alone. With the
addition of economic and ecological arguments, it becomes overwhelming.

Government Policies

China began its "one-family, one-child" program in 1979. The goal—no
more than 1.2 billion people by the year 2000—was essentially achieved.

Violators were punished by fines and dismissal from government jobs, while better housing and stipends were available to one-child households. The complete results have been mixed: There is some reason to believe that female infanticide increased, as parents sought to make their one child a boy. Moreover, only 19% of Chinese families have just one child. Chinese population policy has been concentrated among urban, ethnic (Han) Chinese, whereas ethnic minorities and rural people have been to some extent exempted. Population growth in China, however, has decreased, from nearly 3% to 1.4%, largely because of a recent Chinese tendency to marry and bear children at a later age and because of the active efforts of the Chinese government. (One very effective way of slowing population growth is for women to delay reproduction until later in life—for example, age 32 instead of 17—a cultural tradition that has reduced the population growth of Ireland, for example, a country that is strongly Roman Catholic and where contraception was frowned upon and where abortion has long been illegal.)

It seems clear that although population policies are necessary, they must be based on voluntary compliance rather than compulsion; that is, they should educate, provide incentives and technology, and minister to existing demand, without being heavy-handed.

Unmet Need

There is, in fact, a very large unmet need with respect to family size limitation. For example, women of reproductive age were surveyed in four developing countries: India, Egypt, Peru, and Ghana. The percentages of women who indicated that they did not want any more children were, respectively, 50, 56, 70, and 90, whereas the percentages using contraception were, respectively, 28, 30, 25, and 10. Subtracting the latter from the former, we get the proportion of women who wish to limit their family size but are not employing any form of birth control: 22%, 26%, 45%, and a staggering 80% in Ghana. Thus, the unmet need for contraception is clearly enormous, and whereas it can be seen as a personal, family, national, and world tragedy, it also provides population planners with an immense opportunity—a chance to reduce the catastrophic increase in human population while at the same time satisfying the desires of the people involved.

In the past 20 years, average fertility in developing countries has dropped from six children per woman to four; use of contraceptives by potentially reproductive, married women has increased from 9% to 43%, and as a result, the rate of world population increase has slowed from 2.1% per year to 1.7%. But this is a reduction in the *rate of increase*, not in world population itself. (Analogously, consider a bus hurtling toward a cliff and accelerating as it goes: Even though the *rate* of acceleration may eventually decline, this is likely to convey little comfort to the occupants!) Also note that population growth is not evenly spread: Typically, states that are already pressing hard on their economic and ecological resource base—and that accordingly are most threatened by increasing numbers of people—are likely to be experiencing the most rapid population growth.

An enlightened population policy commends itself on financial grounds alone. Mexican studies, for example, indicate that for every peso spent on family planning, nine pesos are saved (from maternal and infant health care, not even counting education). Although birth control programs are no substitute for investment in education, health care, or economic and environmental betterment, it is clear that fertility reduction is essential if the foregoing are to be meaningful and to have any significant chance of succeeding.

The Developed Countries

As we have seen, poor countries tend to reduce their rate of population growth as they become wealthier, and wealthy countries (like the United States and Western Europe) have relatively low rates of population increase. However, this is no reason to be complacent or self-righteous, because the wealthy countries use far more resources per capita than do the poor ones, and they also produce proportionately more pollution as well. The United States is about twice as wasteful as the other developed states—with about 5% of the world's population, the United States consumes more than 30% of the world's resources, six times its "rightful" share. Or look at it this way: The average U.S. citizen is about 20 times as hurtful to the world's supply of resources as is the average Third Worlder.

Clearly, population growth in the world's poorest countries is a serious social, environmental, and economic problem for the residents of these countries. However, when considering the planetary costs of overpopulation, population growth in economically developed states such as the United States is far more serious. Americans, in short, have no justification for blaming others for the effects of their fertility on the world's environmental plight; the United States is a disproportionately large part of the problem.

Future Directions _____

If we don't change our direction, states an ancient Chinese proverb, we shall end up where we are headed. An overcrowded, overarmed world, increasingly divided between haves and have-nots, is not a desirable prospect, either in terms of basic morality or its more practical consequences: misery, disruption, and perhaps, increased probability of violence. Writing in 1974, economist Robert Heilbroner predicted possible "wars of redistribution," driven by the rage of the impoverished, subsisting in a world of obscene luxury. But poor people are unlikely to march aggressively into the rich countries, especially so long as the latter are guarded by abundant lethal weaponry. Unlike a ghetto riot, in which people's poverty and frustration erupt into looting a local department store, poverty is more apt to continue generating its own kind of structural violence, eroding the quality of human life. It may also continue to generate political instability, especially in the poor countries themselves.

As with so many other issues in peace studies, the problem of poverty is easier to diagnose than to cure. It is a major accomplishment just to appreciate the problem, since—like human rights and environmental degradation—it is vast and multidimensional. The plight of the poor is not just temporary, but it need not necessarily be eternal. One of the greatest impediments to effective action in this respect is the inclination of powerful governments—representing people who are essentially satisfied with the status quo—to ignore the problem, minimize it, blame it on its victims, and if pressed, give only lip service to its urgency. There is a near-universal tendency, especially among the relatively wealthy and self-satisfied, to opt for the easiest and most short-sighted, temporary palliatives, such as narrowly targeted foreign aid or improved terms of trade in specific cases. Among the more general and widespread suggestions for reducing global poverty, the following may have particular merit:

- Recognizing that whereas economic growth is to some degree desirable, growth in itself does not necessarily lead to a greater sharing of prosperity, either between states or within them.
- Establishing an internationally accepted floor below which poverty shall not be permitted, analogous to the "safety net" currently in place in most Western democracies.
- Making birth control universally available, either free or at minimal cost.
- Developing and implementing a worldwide literacy program, plus upgrading of educational facilities and opportunities, especially in the developing world.
- Enhancing the role and effectiveness of local, grassroots activities that promote economic growth along with environmental protection.
- Providing massive debt relief for the poorest states, coupled with reorientation of their economies from being export oriented to satisfying domestic needs.
- Making serious efforts toward achieving self-reliant "ecodevelopment," which is neither stagnation nor ecological exploitation, but rather a differentiated and autonomous development, respecting the cultural heterogeneity of the local inhabitants as well as their need to work with nature rather than against it.
- Recognizing that resource-guzzling technologies will likely be hurtful for many if not most developing countries as well as for the industri-

alized world; in addition, realizing that high-technology procedures put relatively few people to work, whereas unemployment is a major contributor to poverty. It should be emphasized, however, that even though technology has often been misused, the real barriers to human betterment are not technological but social, political, and economic. "Alternative technology," based on the notion that "small is beautiful," can be helpful, but alternative social and political forms are likely to be even more important, and indeed, a prerequisite for sustainable and meaningful development.

- Redirecting a large proportion of planetary resources, currently eaten up by military spending, to upgrading the living conditions of the world's people. For example, for a painful example of misplaced priorities, consider that with the Cold War merely a bad dream, and in a time of horrifying poverty and dreadful environmental abuse, military spending by the United States seems unlikely to diminish. Thus, even if, as seems probable, the United States and Russia reduce their nuclear stockpiles to roughly one third of their year 2000 levels, it appears that U.S. insistence on some form of Ballistic Missile Defense ("Star Wars") as well as the newly initiated "war on global terrorism" will keep military spending in the United States at somewhat more than $300 billion dollars per year.

The Case of Costa Rica

A hope—thus far, largely frustrated—is that with the apparent cessation of East-West military competition, resources previously consumed by the military could be released for desperately needed civilian purposes. The experience of Costa Rica may be instructive. This small Central American state has no army, and just a small national police force. Whereas Guatemala and Honduras, by contrast, spend 15% of their GNP on their military, Costa Rica spends only about 3% of its GNP on its police. These savings permit Costa Rica to devote 11% of its GNP to health and education, more than twice the proportional expenditure of Honduras and three times that of Guatemala. As a result, polio and diphtheria have been eradicated in Costa Rica, and whooping cough, tetanus, and measles are nearly gone. Infant mortality has plummeted, as has the birthrate, which declined nearly 40% from 1960 to 2000. During the 1980s, the U.S. government regularly pressured Costa Rica to reverse its priorities, and invest in national armed forces, ostensibly as defense against communism (but, in fact, as part of the Reagan administration's desire to put military pressure on nearby Nicaragua). It seems clear, however, that the demilitarized, prosocial policy of Costa Rica is a surer path to stability and security. Costa Rica may represent the wave of the future.

_____ A Final Note on Economic Well-Being

During the final decade of the 20th century, the United States experienced the longest and most powerful peacetime economic boom in its history, achieving previously unheard-of, and for many, undreamed-of, levels of prosperity. Nonetheless, many people within the United States have not benefited from these developments, and outside the United States, even more persons have been left out. In fact, most of the world's people are poor, some of them so poor that their lives are shortened or made miserable; even more are prevented from experiencing their full potential. Only a small number enjoy substantial material advantages. Indirect or structural violence is thus widespread and, despite advances in science and technology, in many areas it is increasing. Overpopulation exacerbates this problem as well as the disparity between the haves and the have-nots (who, not surprisingly, are also "want-mores"). Solutions, however, do exist, including various redistribution strategies, programs of genuine development, and family planning. The problem of poverty—like that of human rights, the environment, and war itself—is ancient, but not necessarily intractable. Enough resources exist on the planet Earth to provide a decent material life for everyone, especially if human population is eventually controlled. The greatest obstacle to economic well-being appears to be the social and political inclinations of some human beings themselves, but whether this leads to optimism or pessimism is best left to the reader. Substantial, long-term changes are morally, economically, and environmentally necessary; the question is whether the world's wealthy and powerful nations and their leaders will acknowledge this, and respond in time.

Note _____

1.   Lester Brown. 1987. "Analyzing the Demographic Trap." In L. Brown et al., eds., _State of the World, 1987_. New York: Norton.

20 Nonviolence

No army can withstand the force of an idea whose time has come.

—Victor Hugo

Nonviolence is intimately associated with certain ethical and religious traditions, notably Buddhism, Hinduism, and Christian pacifism. However, it has achieved such stature, both as a goal and as a practical strategy in the struggle for peace—both positive peace and the avoidance of war—that it deserves a separate treatment. Because Mohandas Gandhi is the major teacher of nonviolence in modern times, we begin this chapter with a brief consideration of his life.

Mohandas K. Gandhi

Mohandas Gandhi is revered by most Indians as the founder of their nation, and also by millions of others as the leading exponent of nonviolence and as a virtual modern-day saint. He pioneered the modern use of nonviolent resistance as both a spiritual/philosophical approach to life and an intensely practical technique of achieving political and social change. Gandhi was widely known among Indians as "Mahatma" (Great Soul), for his courage, simplicity, penetrating insight, and the extraordinary impact of his teachings and his life.

Central to Gandhi's worldview was the search for truth, and indeed, he titled his autobiography *My Experiments With Truth*. Gandhi considered that nonviolent love (*ahimsa*, in Sanskrit) was achievable only through compassion and tolerance for other people; moreover, it required continual testing, experimentation, occasional errors, and constant, unstinting effort. His teachings emphasized courage, directness, friendly civility, absolute honesty, nonviolence, and adherence to the truth. Perhaps the most important Gandhian concept is *satyagraha*, literally translated as "soul-force" or "soul-truth." *Satyagraha* requires a clearheaded adherence to goals of love and mutual respect, and it demands a willingness to suffer, if need be, to achieve these goals.

Early Years

Gandhi was born in India, in 1869; his parents were merchant-caste Hindus. He remained a devout Hindu throughout his life, although he made room for numerous other religious and ethical traditions and was strongly influenced by pacifist Christianity, as well as the writings of Thoreau and Tolstoy on the rights and duties of individuals to practice civil disobedience when government authorities intrude on civil rights and political liberties. He married very young (he and his wife were both 13), and studied law in London. After a brief time in India, the young barrister went to South Africa, where he was outraged by that country's system of racial discrimination (there was, and still is, a large Asian—especially Indian—population in South Africa). He remained there for 21 years, leading numerous campaigns for Indian rights, editing a newspaper, and developing his philosophy of nonviolent action as well as specific techniques for implementing it. He was physically abused and arrested many times by British authorities, but he also served courageously on the British side when he agreed with their positions; for example, he organized an Indian Ambulance Corps during the Boer War (1899–1902) and the Zulu Rebellion (1906), for which he was decorated by the government.

Gandhi's Return to India

After achieving some notable reforms, Gandhi returned to India in 1915, and within a few years became the leader of the Indian nationalist movement, seeking independence from colonial Britain. When the British government made it illegal to organize political opposition, Gandhi led a successful *satyagraha* campaign against these laws. In 1919, British troops fired into a crowd of unarmed Indian men, women, and children, who had been demonstrating peacefully; nearly 400 were killed in what became known as the Amritsar Massacre. This served to highlight the difference between the steadfast nonviolence of Gandhi's followers and the relative brutality of the colonial government; it also moved Gandhi to refine his techniques of *satyagraha*. In particular, he took the great Sanskrit epic, the *Bhagavad Gita*, to be an allegory not about war but about the human soul, and the need for all people to devote themselves, unselfishly, to the attainment of their goals. He urged that for real success, it is necessary to "reduce yourself to zero," that is, to remove the self-will and striving for personal aggrandizement that so often leads to arrogance or even tyranny.

Gandhi was a small, slight man with indomitable moral certitude and remarkable physical stamina. He frequently employed fasts to emphasize the importance of personal self-denial and to protest the violence that periodically broke out as less disciplined Indian nationalists rioted against British rule, notably during the Bombay riots in 1921 and the Chauri-Chaura riots in 1922. Following these painful experiences, Gandhi temporarily called off his struggle for Indian independence. During the 1920s, Gandhi continued to fight for the rights of the lowest Hindu caste, the Untouchables—which he renamed the *Harijan*, children of God—and for miners, factory workers, and poor peasants. He urged Indians to develop cottage industries, notably spinning and weaving, so as to deprive Britain of their major economic advantage in occupying India: markets for English textile products. In addition, hand weaving contributed to the potential of national self-sufficiency (*swaraj*) in India, while also emphasizing the dignity of labor.

When Britain introduced the Salt Acts, requiring that all salt must be purchased from the government, Gandhi led a massive march, 320 kilometers to the sea, where he and his followers made salt from seawater, in defiance of the law. In all, Gandhi spent about seven years in various jails for his numerous acts of nonviolent resistance, making it respectable—indeed, honorable—for protesters to be imprisoned for their beliefs. Gandhi was an ascetic and intensely frugal, possessing a biting sense of humor: Once, when he visited the British king in London, the half-naked Gandhi was asked whether he felt a bit underdressed for the occasion, to which he replied, "His Majesty wore enough for the two of us." Another time, when asked what he thought of Western civilization, he replied, "I think it would be a good idea."

Gandhi was deeply grieved by the intense periodic violence between Hindus and Muslims, and he opposed the partition of British colonial India into an independent Muslim Pakistan and Hindu India. He was assassinated (by a fanatical Hindu who opposed his insistence on religious tolerance) in 1948, the year after India won its independence from Britain. However, Gandhi had accomplished what many thought impossible: He gained independence for his country of 400 million people, without firing a shot. He also showed that a highly spiritual concept—nonviolence—can be an intensely practical tool in the quest for peace, even in the 20th-century world of *Realpolitik*, power, and violence.

Nonviolence in Theory

Unfortunately, Gandhian *satyagraha* has often been translated into English as "passive resistance." This is like translating *light* as "nondarkness," or defining *good* as "absence of evil." It omits the positive, creative component of its subject. *Satyagraha* is passive only insofar as it espouses self-restraint rather than the active injuring of others. In all other respects, it is active and assertive, requiring great energy and outright courage.

Nonviolent Love and Suffering

A key to understanding Gandhi's efforts at nonviolence is embodied in the concept of nonviolent love, *ahimsa*, the bedrock of *satyagraha*. As Gandhi expressed it, "Ahimsa and Truth are so intertwined that it is practically impossible to disentangle and separate them. . . . Nevertheless, ahimsa is the means; truth is the end." As with the term *passive resistance*, however, defining *ahimsa* as nonviolence does a disservice to the concept, which instead implies active love. It is closer to Albert Schweitzer's principle of "reverence for life," a concept that is not only negative (determination not to destroy living things unnecessarily) but also positive (a commitment in favor of life, especially the life of other human beings). *Ahimsa* requires deep respect for the opponent's humanity, an insistence upon meeting the other with sympathy and kindness—but also with absolute, unwavering firmness. It is not meek or mild or retiring. It implies nothing less than the willingness of each individual to take unto herself or himself the responsibility for reforming the planet, and necessarily, to suffer in the process. Gandhi emphasized that

> ahimsa in its dynamic condition means conscious suffering. It does not mean meek submission to the will of the evil-doer, but it means pitting of one's whole soul against the will of the tyrant. Working under this law of our being, it is possible for a single individual to defy the whole might of an unjust empire to save his honor, his religion, his soul, and lay the foundation for that empire's fall or its regeneration.[1]

And again,

> Suffering is the law of human beings; war is the law of the jungle. But suffering is infinitely more powerful than the law of the jungle for converting the opponent and opening his ears, which are otherwise shut, to the voice of reason. . . . Suffering, not the sword, is the badge of the human race.[2]

The basis for this suffering (termed *tapasya*, by Gandhi) is several-fold. For one thing, unless one is prepared to suffer, the depth of one's commitment can be questioned. Moreover, since any serious conflict must lead to suffering, the nonviolent resister's devotion to justice will almost certainly precipitate suffering. *Tapasya* therefore indicates willingness to undergo this suffering oneself, and not to shift its burden onto anyone else—including the opponent—as a consequence of one's commitment to the truth of nonviolence.

Gandhi's emphasis on suffering is especially difficult for many people to understand or accept. It tends—probably more than any other aspect of his thought and practice—to make Gandhian nonviolence relatively inaccessible to many Westerners. And yet *tapasya* should not be altogether foreign, especially to Christian tradition, given the central importance attributed to Christ's redeeming agony on the cross. In addition, it is not stretching Gandhi's concept too greatly to substitute "courage" for "willingness to suffer." This has the added benefit of helping dispel the frequent misunderstanding that practitioners of nonviolence are cowards, seeking an easy way out of conflict.

Nonviolence as Active Force

Gandhi strongly emphasized that *satyagraha* must be distinguished from passive acquiescence or the desire to avoid conflict—even pain or death—at any price. The middle class in particular has often been scorned as having an excessive fear of conflict and a corresponding desire to be comfortable at all costs. "The inability of the bourgeois to dream great dreams and ambition noble deeds," according to a biographer of Martin Luther King, Jr.,

> is revealed in their timidity in the face of violence and conflict. . . . This cowardice also shows itself in what may be called the mercenary impulse, the impulse to hire others to fight one's own battles. This impulse has such concrete manifestations as hiring additional police to suppress domestic unrest or in spending money for a so-called all volunteer army, rather than personally accepting the obligations of citizenship. . . . [T]hey represent what Gandhi called the nonviolence of the weak. Such nonviolence he took to be counterfeit, a cloak for passivity and cowardice.[3]

Gandhian nonviolence, by contrast, is the nonviolence of the strong, the courageous, the outraged—not merely passive acquiescence by the weak, the cowardly, or the comfortable. "My creed of nonviolence is an extremely active force," wrote Gandhi. "It has no room for cowardice or even weakness. There is hope for a violent man to be some day nonviolent, but there is none for a coward."[4]

Gandhian nonviolence suggests answers to some fundamental questions. For example, what is the more important measure of worth, the individual or society? It can be a prescription for anarchy to make individuals the supreme measure of moral action; alternatively, when the community is rendered supreme, the door is opened to despotism. Nonviolent civil disobedience seeks (uniquely, perhaps) to recognize both aspects of humanity: the right of individual choice and also the obligation of each individual to experience the consequence of that choice, as judged and determined by the society of which he or she is a part.

But the nonviolent answer is not an easy one. Beatings, imprisonment, even death can all be part of the nonviolent struggle. Individuals are called upon to function, and to suffer, for the good of all. The *satyagrahi* (practitioner of *satyagraha*) must be prepared to accept such suffering. Because of the clarity it evokes in the *satyagrahi*, as well as the confusion, self-doubt, and empathy it evokes in the opponent, nonviolence unleashes a remarkable kind of power, a "force" with which most people are unaccustomed.

Satyagraha, the means whereby *ahimsa* is expressed and nonviolent victory attained, also requires respect for the opponent and perseverance in weaning the other from error, rather than trying to injure or annihilate him or her. It must be conducted without hate, aimed at policies, not persons. It must be based on absolute truthfulness. It must take the opponent seriously and seek to engage him or her in dialogue and self-examination. It must respect the opponents and permit them to change direction without loss of face.

Traditionally, when conflicts are resolved by violence, they simply involve the triumph of one protagonist over the other. Such a "resolution" may occur via threat, persuasion, or naked force, but in any event the presumption is that one side wins and the other loses: This is what mathematicians call a *zero-sum game* (as in most competitive sports, where for every winner there is a loser, so that the sum total of wins and losses equals zero). Even when overtly seeking a compromise—hence, a win-win or positive-sum game solution—each side typically attempts to profit at the other's expense and to compromise only when it has no alternative. By contrast, *satyagraha* aims to resolve the source of the conflict rather than to defeat or annihilate the opponent. In *satyagraha*, the goal is to persuade the adversary that all parties have more to gain by acting in harmony and love than by persevering in discord and violence. Rather than viewing the adversary as an enemy to be overcome, the *satyagrahi* considers him or her a participant in a shared search for a just (i.e., "truthful") solution to the problem at hand.

Ends Versus Means

Not surprisingly, since he attributed so much importance to the process of attaining truth and justice, Gandhi was unalterably opposed to any doctrine in which the ends justify the means. He maintained that there was "the same inviolable connection between the means and the end as there is between the seed and the tree." Of course, a seed can be distinguished from a tree, but nonetheless, the two are inseparably linked; French philosopher Jacques Maritain wrote that the means of achieving a goal is "in a sense the end in the process of becoming." When the means are pure, the end will be desirable; if the route to political protest is sullied with violence or hatred, the end also will be spoiled. Philosopher Hannah Arendt seconded this, adding that "the practise of violence, like all action, changes the world, but the most probable change is to a more violent world."

For pacifists in the Gandhian mold, violence is reactionary: The more violence, the less revolution. By using violent methods, revolutions and antiwar movements can build up reservoirs of resentment and hatred, as well as possibly laying the foundations for additional injustice and yet more violence. This stands not only as a warning against violence but also as a caution against letting frustration drive peaceful protest into violent and often self-destructive avenues. In the late 1960s, for example, Thomas Merton, one of the towering figures of nonviolence in the United States, warned that the peace movement "may be escalating beyond peaceful protest. In which case it would also be escalating into self-contradiction."

By contrast, political activists of the extreme left and right are often prone to make moral compromises, convinced that their vision of the world-as-it-should-be justifies almost any means of attaining it. Lenin, for instance, announced that "to achieve our ends, we will unite even with the Devil." For Lenin, any tendency to moralize about the evil of using violent means to achieve revolutionary ends was "the petty hypocrisy of sentimentalists drawn from the dominant but doomed class." In his poem "To Posterity," Bertolt Brecht, playwright and Marxist, warned about how violence has corrupted and perverted the noblest intentions:

> Even anger against injustice
> Makes the voice grow harsh. Alas, we
> Who wished to lay the foundations of kindness
> Could not ourselves be kind.[5]

Neither the extreme left nor the far right has shared Gandhi's acute sensitivity to the relationship between means and ends. And whereas everyone would agree that it is desirable to avoid aggression and international intimidation, a Gandhian would also question the legitimacy of employing (i.e., deploying) nuclear weapons or any other instruments of violence as means toward those ends.

Nonviolence in Practice

Cicero, in *The Letters to His Friends*, asks, "What can be done against force, without force?" Students of nonviolence would answer, "Plenty." Moreover, they would question whether anything effective, lasting, or worthwhile can be done against force, *with* force. The Reverend Martin

Luther King, Jr., nonviolent leader of the civil rights movement in the United States during the late 1950s and 1960s, and a visionary who, like Gandhi, was also intensely practical and result oriented, wrote that "returning violence for violence multiplies violence, adding deeper darkness to a night already devoid of stars. Darkness cannot drive out darkness; only light can do that. Hate cannot drive out hate; only love can do that."

As Gandhi put it,

> Noncooperation with evil is as much a duty as is cooperation with good. But in the past, noncooperation has been deliberately expressed in violence to the evil-doer. I am endeavoring to show to my countrymen that violent noncooperation only multiplies evil, and that as evil can only be sustained by violence, withdrawal of support of evil requires complete abstention from violence.[6]

This did not mean, however, that the *satyagrahi* was forbidden anger, even hatred; rather, these feelings were carefully directed toward the various *systems* of evil, rather than toward individuals. Gandhi wrote that

> I can and do hate evil wherever it exists. . . . I hate the ruthless exploitation of India even as I hate from the bottom of my heart the hideous system of untouchability for which millions of Hindus have made themselves responsible. But I do not hate the domineering Englishman as I refuse to hate the domineering Hindus. I seek to reform them in all the loving ways that are open to me. My noncooperation has its roots not in hatred, but in love.[7]

For Gandhi and his followers, it was impossible to elevate oneself by debasing others, just as it debases others by permitting them to dominate oneself.

Nonviolent Action and Government Reaction

In practice, Gandhi's *satyagraha* and King's nonviolent actions took many forms: marches, boycotts, picketing, leafleting, strikes, civil disobedience, the nonviolent occupation of various government facilities, vigils and fasts, mass imprisonments, refusals to pay taxes, and a willingness at all times to be abused by the authorities and yet to respond nonviolently, with politeness, courage, and determination. This, as Gandhi was fond of pointing out, demanded far more strength than is required to pull a trigger, far more courage than is needed to fight, or to fight back.

But the practitioner of nonviolence does not cease struggling; indeed, the nonviolent struggle is if anything more intense than its violent counterpart. Gandhian techniques do not offer an alternative to fighting; rather, they provide other, nonviolent ways of doing so. During the famous "salt *satyagraha*" of 1930, for example, Gandhi arrived at the Dharasana Salt Works with 2,500 marchers. According to a Western eyewitness, the men arrived at a police stockade in complete silence, then approached and were in turn battered on the head with steel-shod clubs, while no one so much as even raised an arm in self-protection:

> From where I stood I heard the sickening whack of the clubs on unprotected skulls. The waiting crowd of marchers groaned and sucked in their breath in sympathetic pain at every blow. . . . The survivors, without breaking ranks, silently and doggedly marched on until struck down.[8]

This event, like the Amritsar Massacre, not only underscored the courage and humaneness of the Indian *satyagrahis*, it also contrasted dramatically with the ugly violence of the government, thereby helping to sway world opinion as well as the British electorate—which became increasingly sympathetic to Gandhi's cause.

Violent governmental overreaction to nonviolent protest historically has had the effect of transforming victims into martyrs, who become symbols of their regime's callous wrong-headedness. For example, in 1819, a nonviolent crowd in Manchester, England, was attacked by soldiers while peacefully listening to speeches calling for the repeal of the Corn Laws. This so-called Peterloo Massacre became a rallying cry for radicals who eventually succeeded in their demands. The slaughter of participants in the Paris Commune of 1871 led to greater solidarity among the French working class. Violence and brutality directed toward U.S. civil rights workers in the 1960s led to widespread revulsion and moral indignation against the system of racial segregation in the South. The Kent State University killings in 1970 galvanized sentiment opposed to the Vietnam War, just as the "police riot" at the Democratic Party Convention in Chicago in 1968 led to widespread condemnation of the political system. The Israeli policy of beating Palestinian protesters who have sought an end to Israeli occupation of the West Bank led to solidification of Palestinian sentiment and an outpouring of condemnation against the Israeli government, including protests from many in the U.S. Jewish community. (It is interesting to note that in this case, a Palestinian, Mubarak Awad, was expelled from the Israeli-occupied West Bank for advocating Gandhian nonviolence, including refusal to cooperate with Israeli authorities as well as nonpayment of taxes. Some observers suggest that the Israeli authorities considered Awad's nonviolent tactics a greater threat than the prospects of Palestinian violence, because violence can readily be countered with yet more violence, whereas nonviolence leaves the authorities in a much more difficult quandary.)

Living With and Transforming Violence

For nonviolent campaigns to be successful, the campaigners must have immense determination, self-respect, and also (Gandhi would add) respect for the opponent. A popular phrase among radical U.S. activists during the 1960s was "power to the people." Followers of nonviolence believe that the people are most powerful when they have sufficient moral courage that they are immune not only to the threat of violence directed toward them but also to the inclination to employ violence themselves. The latter comes from having sufficient clarity of purpose (Gandhi would call it "selflessness"). As Gandhi saw it, this does not involve a purging of anger, but rather a transforming of it: "I have learnt through bitter experience the one supreme lesson to conserve my anger and as heat conserved is transmuted into energy, even so our anger controlled can be transmuted into a power which can move the world."[9]

When a victim responds to violence with yet more violence, he or she is responding in predictable, perhaps even instinctive, ways, which tend to confirm the original attacker and even, in a way, to vindicate the original violence, at least in the attacker's mind: Since the "victim" is so violent, then presumably he or she deserved it. Moreover, there is a widespread expectation of countervailing power analogous in the social sphere to Newton's First Law, which states that for every action there is an equal and opposite reaction. In most aspects of life, from the personal to the international, the exercise of power usually produces a symmetric and countervailing response: Abused children often become abusing adults, laissez-faire capitalism gave rise to communism, European liberal democracy helped spawn fascism, and so forth.

If A hits B, and then B hits back, this nearly always encourages A to strike yet again. Gandhi was not fond of the Biblical injunction "an eye for an eye, a tooth for a tooth," pointing out that if we all behaved that way, soon the whole world would be blind and toothless. Instead, if B responds with nonviolence, this not only breaks the chain of anger and hatred (analogous to the Hindu chain of birth and rebirth), it also puts A in an unexpected position. "I seek entirely to blunt the edge of the tyrant's sword," wrote Gandhi, "not by putting up against it a sharper-edged weapon, but by disappointing his expectation that I would be offering physical resistance."[10] Accustomed to counterviolence—and even, perhaps, hoping for it—the violent person who encounters a nonviolent opponent who is also courageous as well as respectful, even loving, becomes a "victim" of a kind of moral judo, in which the attacker's own energy is redirected, placing him off balance. "It would at first dazzle him and at last compel recognition from him," wrote Gandhi, "which recognition would not humiliate him but would uplift him." And in fact, Gandhi's most bitter opponents were almost inevitably won over.

Consider this account of a meeting between the young Gandhi and the legendary General Jan Smuts of South Africa. Gandhi spoke first:

"I have come to tell you that I am going to fight against your government."

Smuts must have thought he was hearing things. "You mean you have come here to tell me that?" he laughs. "Is there anything more you want to say?"

"Yes," says Gandhi. "I am going to win."

Smuts is astonished. "Well," he says as last, "and how are you going to do that?"

Gandhi smiles. "With your help."[11]

Years later, Smuts recounted this meeting, noting—with humor—that Gandhi was correct.

Nonviolence as a Proactive Force

Nonviolence is often described as nonviolent *resistance*, implying that it is a reaction, a response to some initial force. But in fact, nonviolence as practiced by Gandhi and his followers (including, notably, Martin Luther King, Jr., in the United States) was *pro*active much more than *re*active. These very successful practitioners of politically active nonviolence became masters at initiating their struggles, keeping their opponents off balance. Their tactics were unpredictable, spontaneous, radical, experimental—and not surprisingly, government authorities found them baffling and exasperating in the extreme. It is said—of some people and some nations—that "they only understand force" and therefore they cannot be moved by anything other than force or the threat of force. The truth, however, may be precisely the opposite: Those who understand and expect force can generally deal effectively with it. *Satyagraha*—soul-force rather than physical force—may be more likely to disconcert and move those who understand violence, but have had little experience with Gandhi's truth-force.

Part of the goal of *satyagraha* is to make the oppressor reflect on his or her unity with the resister, and to change, internally. Consider the analogy of an iceberg: In warm water, an iceberg melts below the water line, invisibly, until suddenly, as the weight shifts, it may flip over. In this way, the consciousness of the oppressor may be changed suddenly and dramatically. "If my soldiers began to think," wrote Frederick the Great, "not one would remain in the ranks." Nonviolence, adroitly and persistently practiced, has the power of inducing soldiers—and government leaders—to think.

Martin Luther King, Jr., and the U.S. Civil Rights Movement _____

Second to Gandhi, the most influential modern exponent and practitioner of nonviolence was the Reverend Martin Luther King, Jr., who consciously adapted *satyagraha* for use in the American South. King studied Gandhi's philosophy and methods, traveled to India, and emerged as the chief spokesperson, architect, and spiritual leader of the nonviolent civil rights campaign in the United States. Like Gandhi, King spent much time behind bars for his nonviolent defiance of unjust laws supporting racial discrimination. His "Letter From Birmingham Jail" is one of the classic statements of the philosophy of nonviolent civil disobedience, and the evils of racial intolerance. In it, King also expressed a sense of courage and urgency:

> We know from painful experience that freedom is never voluntarily given by the oppressor; it must be demanded by the oppressed.... I guess it is easy for those who have never felt the stinging darts of segregation to say "wait." But when you have seen vicious mobs lynch your mothers and fathers at will . . . then you will understand why we find it difficult to wait.[12]

During the 1950s and 1960s, transportation, restaurants, sports events, restrooms, libraries, and schools were often racially segregated in the South, with superior facilities reserved for "whites only." Voting rights were often denied or severely restricted by poll taxes, literacy tests, and outright intimidation. Lynching of African Americans was relatively common, and racial violence was widespread, led especially by the Ku Klux Klan, a semisecret band of white supremacists.

Perhaps the seminal event in King's leadership of the civil rights movement was the Montgomery (Alabama) bus boycott, which started in December 1955, when Rosa Parks refused to take a seat in the back of a public bus. After thousands of African Americans walked miles to work rather than ride on segregated buses, public facilities were eventually integrated. Later, Freedom Riders, seeking to desegregate interstate bus transportation (in accord with a 1960 Supreme Court decision), endured frequent beatings and mob violence, while the state police often failed to provide protection, and typically arrested the Riders instead. Sit-ins began at segregated lunch counters on February 1, 1960, in Greensboro, North Carolina, at the soda fountain of a five-and-ten-cent store. With King's encouragement, these nonviolent sit-ins, boycotts, and marches quickly spread to more than 100 cities, and succeeded in integrating restaurants throughout the South.

These were the years when Governor George Wallace stood in the doorway of the University of Alabama, to deny admission to black students, and when electric cattle prods, police dogs, and high-pressure water hoses were used against peaceful demonstrators in Birmingham, Alabama. Peaceful civil rights marchers were herded to jail in Jackson, Mississippi, with the police harassing the marchers and offering them no protection against abusive crowds. Four young black girls were killed by a bomb blast while at Sunday school in Birmingham Baptist Church. Through all this, King maintained a steadfast devotion to nonviolence, based on his perception of

Christian principles. "Let no man pull you so low," he was fond of saying, "as to make you hate him."

It is no small task, though, to separate hatred of offenses—or of offending institutions—from hatred of the offenders: to hate murder but love the murderer, to hate oppression but not the oppressor, to hate torture but not the torturer. In this, King once again showed himself to be a disciple of Gandhi, showing uncompromising respect, even love, for his opponents, while being equally uncompromising in pursuit of the Truth as he saw it. And of course, Martin Luther King, Jr., was himself assassinated—just as Gandhi had been.

But like Gandhi, King also mobilized a nonviolent army of followers, captured the conscience of millions, and achieved monumental reforms. He founded the Southern Christian Leadership Conference, which emphasized nonviolence and grassroots, community action, and in 1963, he organized the March on Washington for Jobs and Freedom, also known as the Poor People's March, which brought about 500,000 people to the U.S. capital. This effort represented a new dimension of King's nonviolent campaign: extending it from integration and civil rights to a broader concern with social justice for all people. His campaign in favor of the Voting Rights Act also helped lead to its passage in 1965. The year before, King had been awarded the Nobel Peace Prize.

Shortly before his death, King also started speaking out in opposition to the Vietnam War and the nuclear arms race. "If we assume that humankind has a right to survive," he once wrote,

> then we must find an alternative to war and destruction. In a day when sputniks dash through outer space and guided ballistic missiles are carving highways of death through the stratosphere, nobody can win a war. The choice today is no longer between violence or nonviolence. It is between nonviolence or nonexistence.[13]

Nonviolent Successes

Nonviolence has relatively few dramatic political successes that can be celebrated. By contrast, there have been far more examples of "successful violence," if we measure "success" by the achievement of immediate goals: conquest of territory, booty, and people; the imposition of a particular social system; or the forcible defeat of would-be aggressors and imposers. But it can also be argued that violence, by its nature, inhibits lasting success and sows the seeds for its own overthrow. When "peace" is imposed by violence or the threat of violence, it is not really peace but rather, a temporary disequilibrium maintained by the constant input of energy and fear. It is violence that is temporarily suppressed, held in abeyance, not eliminated. The situation in apartheid South Africa was a good example: A kind of "peace" was maintained for decades, but only through massive structural violence and much direct violence as well. It is not surprising that this was not only destructive of human values but also unstable. (The only surprise is that the demise of South African apartheid was, in the end, so nonviolent!) Indeed, the turmoil of human history—some of which has been chronicled in this text, and the horrors of which have motivated its writing—can itself be seen as a monument to the *failure* of violence, not to its success.

In any event, there have been cases of successful nonviolent actions, beyond the best-known examples of Indian independence and the American civil rights movement. Gandhi himself pointed out that, in fact, nonviolence is far more pervasive in ordinary human life than most of us realize, and far more frequent (and successful) than violence:

> The fact that there are so many men still alive in the world shows that it is based not on the force of arms but on the force of truth or love. Therefore, the greatest and most unimpeachable evidence of the success of this force is to be found in the fact that, in spite of the wars of the world, it still lives on. Thousands, indeed tens of thousands, depend for their existence on a very active working of this force. Little quarrels of millions of families in their daily lives disappear before the exercise of this force.[14]

The Third World

As to major political events in the realm of states, one of the most notable example of the recent triumph of nonviolence was the toppling of Philippine dictator Ferdinand Marcos by the "people power" of Corazon Aquino's followers, in February 1986. This virtually bloodless coup occurred after Marcos loyalists attempted to rig an election in the dictator's favor. The ensuing protest revolved around persistent nonviolence by Filipino civilians, who at one point interposed themselves between armed forces loyal to Marcos and a small band of dissidents who had declared themselves in support of Aquino and her followers. Newspapers worldwide printed remarkable photographs showing Catholic nuns inserting flowers in the barrels of automatic rifles carried by Philippine Army soldiers. Marcos relinquished power and went into exile in the United States when it became evident that his own military would not fire on the unarmed Filipino populace. (And also after the Reagan administration, which had propped up the Marcos regime, indicated that it was withdrawing support.)

Within a few months, a similar popular expression of discontent drove Jean-Claude Duvalier, son of long-time Haitian dictator "Papa Doc" Duvalier, from power. Regrettably, the departure of Duvalier did not immediately restore democracy to impoverished Haiti, which has the highest illiteracy rate and lowest per capita income in the Western Hemisphere, as well as a long tradition of autocratic governments. (A military junta overthrew the popularly elected leftist government of Jean-Bertrand Aristide; this junta was eventually forced from power by military threats from the United States, which, for a time, stationed troops in Haiti.) In any event, in the case of Haiti and the Philippines, spontaneous nonviolent movements succeeded in deposing military dictatorships that appeared deeply entrenched and that had received substantial assistance (military as well as economic) from the United States. In both cases, it seems likely that traditional violent revolution would have led to an enormous number of casualties.

In 1987, popular discontent in South Korea led to a series of largely nonviolent demonstrations, which in turn caused the military dictatorship to relinquish power and permit the first democratic elections ever held in that country. It is noteworthy that in the cases of Haiti, the Philippines, and South Korea, violent repression of popular resistance—often several or more years earlier—on the part of these dictatorships contributed heavily to the nonviolent, popular discontent that ultimately toppled their governments.

Eastern Europe

Under reformist leader Alexander Dubcek, the Czechoslovak government in 1968 began granting a range of political and economic freedoms, seeking to establish "socialism with a human face." The USSR apparently felt threatened by these developments, and organized an invasion of Czechoslovakia later that summer, crushing the brief and ill-fated "Prague spring." Most Americans think of that Soviet-led invasion as an overwhelming victory for the forces of Soviet repression. In fact, however, the people of Czechoslovakia mounted a remarkable program of nonviolent opposition at that time. Although essentially no military resistance was offered to the invading force of nearly 500,000 troops, the Czech people prevented the installation of a collaborationist government for eight months, using general strikes, work slowdowns, clandestine radio broadcasts, and noncooperation on the part of government employees. A compromise (the so-called Moscow Protocols) was even reached, which allowed most of the reform leaders to remain in authority; only when riots occurred at Aeroflot offices in Prague—that is, when nonviolent discipline broke down—did Soviet occupying forces remove the reformists, and subdue the country.

Twenty-one years later, in the autumn of 1989, massive peaceful demonstrations finally drove the Communist Party from its preeminent place in Czechoslovakia. It may be significant that this occurred within days after Czech security forces brutally suppressed one of the initial prodemocracy demonstrations; outrage at this "police violence" appears to have fueled Czech determination to replace the discredited government. In contrast to the Czech experience, the overthrow of Romanian dictator Nicolae Ceausescu involved violence. Significantly, however, it was public outrage at the brutal military response to a nonviolent, citizens' protest in the city of Timisoara that ignited the countrywide revolt.

The Polish trade union movement Solidarity followed a more strenuously nonviolent path, one that was ultimately successful in forcing dramatic political change in Poland and that served in many ways as a model for the electrifying events in Eastern Europe during 1989, whereby an array of unrepresentative, Soviet-backed governments were replaced by others, all of them proclaiming democracy—and some of them actually practicing it. After being banned in a Soviet-inspired government crackdown in 1981—which included the imposition of martial law—continued nonviolent agitation, including boycotts and strikes, led to official government recognition of Solidarity and its affiliates. By 1989, Solidarity leaders, some of whom had been in prison shortly before, were elected to positions in a democratic Polish government. In the words of Polish Solidarity leader Lech Walesa, these formidable events, some of the most remarkable in modern times, were accomplished without "so much as breaking a single window-pane." (It must be acknowledged, however, that nonviolent protest campaigns in Eastern Europe were not always successful, at least not immediately. Despite numerous opposition rallies, Serbian dictator Slobodan Milosevic was able to cling to power throughout the 1990s, largely because opposition to his regime remained bitterly divided.)

Apparent Failures

Also in 1989, the world witnessed the spectacle of China—the world's most populous country, and one that was in the grip of a rigidly authoritarian government since 1949—convulsed by demands for reform and democratization. For several weeks, nonviolent protesters, led by college students but including a wide cross section of the population, occupied Tiananmen Square in the heart of Beijing, with popular demonstrations of more than one million people. Prodemocracy protesters also made themselves heard in Shanghai, Nanking, Hunan, and Hong Kong, and even after martial law was declared and the protesters ordered to disperse, "people power" nonviolently persuaded Chinese troops to refrain from moving against the students.

Then, the Chinese government cracked down, with a brutal military assault; the precise number of casualties is not known, but probably thousands were killed. The government survived these incidents, although it seems likely that the final word on this process has not yet been spoken. Moreover, the bitterness sown by the government's violent repression—which in many ways resembles the British Army's Amritsar Massacre in colonial India—will almost certainly have consequences for the future of China and other governments that practice brutality against nonviolent protesters.

There is, as Gandhi noted, a special outrage associated with such one-sided uses of lethal force. The "Tiananmen Massacre," occurring on a Sunday in June, was not the first "Bloody Sunday" in history: In 1905, a mass of nonviolent Russian peasants in St. Petersburg, led by Father Gapon, attempted to submit a petition to Czar Nicholas. His troops responded by slaughtering hundreds of unarmed people. This led to a general strike, which ushered in some limited democratic reforms on the part of the government, but which also signaled the beginning of the end for czarist tyranny, culminating ultimately in the Russian Revolution.

A similar case can be made for the "Kent State Massacre," in the United States, although the numbers involved were far smaller, and the public response was far short of revolution. In this incident, Ohio National Guardsmen shot four students who were part of a crowd peacefully demonstrating in opposition to the U.S. bombing of Cambodia in 1970. It generated widespread outrage in the United States and marked a turning point in citizen respect for the federal government and its prosecution of the Vietnam War.

The point is that nonviolence, especially when contrasted with a brutal government response, has an extraordinary power to influence the human mind. Hence, it may well have a profound role to play in practical politics, even—and perhaps especially—against violent, heavily armed, repressive regimes. In China, just as in Russia 84 years before, the populace, as well as many military leaders themselves, were shocked and infuriated in the heavy-handed use of violence against peaceful demonstrators: "The People's Army," exhorted one communiqué from the Chinese military itself, "absolutely must not attack the people!" When it does so, it is likely that such a regime will quickly lose its legitimacy, its popular support, and ultimately, its power.

Interstate Examples

The above examples of nonviolent successes and near-successes all occurred in conflicts taking place within a given state, rather than between states. Examples of the successful use of nonviolent tactics between states are harder to come by, although there are some historical examples. During the mid-19th century, for example, imperial Austria was seeking to dominate its partner in union, Hungary. The Hungarians were militarily weaker than the Austrians, and they recognized that physical resistance would be useless and probably counterproductive. Instead, Hungarians responded by boycotting Austrian goods, refusing to recognize or cooperate with Austrian authorities, and establishing independent Hungarian industrial, agricultural, and educational systems. Noncompliance proved a powerful tool. For example, Hungarians refused to pay taxes to Austrian collectors. When the resisters' property was seized, no Hungarian auctioneers would sell them, so Austrian auctioneers were imported. But then, no Hungarian would buy the property, so Austrian purchasers had to be imported as well. In the end, the process proved to be a net financial cost to the Austrian authorities. Austria also sought to enforce compulsory military service and the billeting of Austrian soldiers in Hungarian homes, but the noncompliance was such that in 1867 the Austrian emperor consented to a constitution giving Hungary full rights within the Austro-Hungarian union.

Many people associate successful independence movements with war and armed rebellion, such as the American Revolution, the liberation of the Netherlands from Spanish control, the independence of Algeria from France and of Kenya from Britain. But in fact, there have been numerous examples of independence achieved by nonviolent means: Canada from Great Britain in the 19th century, many colonies from Western powers in the decades following World War II, and so on. In 1905, Norway was granted its independence from Sweden, with no violence whatever. Shortly before, Norwegian nationalists had declared their country to be a free and independent state, almost precipitating a war, but in a subsequent plebiscite, all but 184 Norwegians voted for independence, and the Swedish government, seeing itself isolated in this respect, relented.

Several decades later, Norway again became a notable site of nonviolent resistance, during the Second World War. Germany invaded Norway in April 1940, quickly overcoming Norwegian military resistance. Overcoming the people, however, was much more difficult. A pro-Nazi Norwegian, Vidkun Quisling, was made dictator (since then, a *quisling* has entered the lexicon as a collaborator who helps form a puppet government). Norwegian society spontaneously and persistently undermined the Quisling government, with solidarity on the part of students, the clergy, and especially, public school teachers, who refused to participate in mandated pro-Nazi indoctrination programs for their students. The Nazis responded by imprisoning and killing many, but the refusals continued and the country gradually became increasingly ungovernable. As President Franklin Roosevelt put it, Norway became "at once conquered and unconquerable."

During the autumn of 1943, when Denmark was occupied by German armed forces, large numbers of Danes prevented Nazi authorities from seizing 94% of the 8,000 Danish Jews and deporting them to concentration camps. Using improvised methods of communication and transportation, the outnumbered and vastly outgunned Danish citizens succeeded in smuggling most of these would-be victims to safety in Sweden. Another successful resistance tactic was for large numbers of Danes to defy the German authorities by wearing the Star of David, which supposedly was used to identify Jews. Virtually the entire country—government, religious leadership, trade unions, and professionals—opposed the Nazi efforts at liquidating the Jewish population, and they were largely successful.

Abundant evidence suggests that military force has its political and social limits, even when (as in the modern world) such force is technologically almost unlimited. The United States, for example, dropped eight million tons of bombs on Indochina—the equivalent of about 300 Hiroshima bombs, and 80 times the amount of bombs that Germany dropped on Britain during World War II—but the United States nonetheless lost the Vietnam War. It remains to be seen if a military mailed fist can successfully oppress a resistant population over the long haul; most public opinion—at least in the West—holds that it cannot. Nonetheless, it is questionable whether governments will move in the near future to de-emphasize significantly the use of violence or the threat of violence in their internal and international affairs.

Civilian-Based Defense

Advocates of nonviolence are not limited to religious zealots and high-minded moralists. More and more, people are questioning fundamental assumptions about peace, defense, and security, as the limitations and dangers of traditional military "solutions" become increasingly clear. A classic case, epitomizing what for many is the paradox of reliance on military means of defense, was the Vietnamese village of Ben Tre, which according to a U.S. major, had to be destroyed "in order for us to save it." The notion of being defended with nuclear, biological, or chemical weapons leaves many people incredulous.

If nonviolence is to have any practical effect on international affairs, however, it needs to be seen as something more than the divine idiosyncrasy of uniquely empowered saints and martyrs, or an impractical tactic proposed by marginal figures, but rather a hardheaded approach, feasible and practical for use by the great majority of people, who are no more than human. Among the practical suggestions for applying nonviolence to national defense, the most organized and—possibly—realistic involve so-called civilian-based defense, or CBD. (This must be distinguished from "civil defense," the much less realistic government plans for protecting citizenry in the aftermath of a nuclear war.) CBD embraces a variety of nonviolent techniques intended to make it very difficult if not impossible for a conquering state to govern another and to gain any benefit from its "victory."

The major theorist of CBD, Gene Sharp, has identified more than 146 specific techniques of nonviolent action, ranging from general strikes, boycotts, and nonpayment of taxes to removal of street signs and sabotage of electrical services. Civilian defenders would not violently resist the occupation of their country, and substantial hardship, suffering, and even death may well result. But military defenders must also anticipate great amounts of hardship, suffering, and death, even in a "successful" war. Advocates of CBD emphasize that to be successful, substantial training would be required, as well as a populace willing to commit itself to the success of their enterprise. But there is nothing new in this: Military training also requires time, effort, and sacrifice, as well as committed participants. (One important distinction is that CBD demands that the public, not just the military, be the participants.) Moreover, most efforts at nonviolent resistance—for example, Hungary in the mid-19th century, Norway in the early 1940s, and Czechoslovakia in 1968—were spontaneous, unprepared, and largely leaderless. Widespread CBD, well-rehearsed and planned in advance, has never seriously been tried. Given its impressive track record when it was essentially extemporized on the spot, the future of CBD might well be bright indeed if it were ever carried out by a populace that had been well trained and prepared. Furthermore, the prospects of having one's soldiers face such a populace, who were committed to denying the invader virtually all fruits of conquest, just might serve to deter invasion no less effectively than the amassing of military forces—and at substantially less cost and risk.

Even beyond its possible deterrent value, CBD—based on an organized determination never to surrender, even if overrun by an adversary—could well have even greater prospects for "victory" than more traditional military tactics and strategies. This is because as weapons become ever more destructive, doctrines of national security based on traditional military techniques offer less and less prospect of defense, or even of narrowly defined battlefield success.

Sharp argued persuasively that under traditional military doctrines, "the capacity to defend in order to deter has been replaced by the capability to destroy massively without the ability to defend." By contrast, CBD would aim to

> deny the attackers their objectives and to make society politically indigestible and ungovernable by the attackers. . . . Potential attackers are deterred when they see that their objectives will be denied them, political consolidation prevented, and that as a consequence of these struggles unacceptable costs will be imposed on them politically, economically, and internationally.[15]

Rather than focusing on moral considerations, Sharp has emphasized the merits of CBD relying on "hardheaded" strategic and cost-effectiveness grounds. He also pointed out that if nuclear deterrence fails, the results are going to be utterly catastrophic. By contrast, if deterrence based on CBD fails, the result will be the first opportunity to attempt to implement a truly nonviolent defense.

A national policy of nonviolent CBD would require that a state largely renounce its interventionist goals in other countries, or at least, it would have to forgo the prospect of direct military intervention in support of economic and political "neo imperialism." States such as the United States, Britain, and France have long deployed military forces capable of "projecting power" far from their shores. These forces—including aircraft carriers, long-range fighter-bombers, mobile artillery, and amphibious assault units—are not normally used for defending a nation's own borders; rather, their purpose is overwhelmingly to intervene (or threaten to intervene) in other countries, generally far from home, and most often in the Third World. A populace trained and organized for civilian defense might or might not be able to deter an aggressor. But it assuredly could not invade or intimidate a distant country. For some people, this is an added advantage of CBD; for others, a liability.

There is presently little chance that CBD will soon be adopted as the defense strategy of any major state. However, it need not be initiated in an all-or-nothing manner. There is no reason why CBD training could not be gradually integrated into existing military doctrine, after which it will be available to assume a more significant role as part of a transition from offensively oriented forces to those concerned—at first primarily, and then exclusively—with defense. Highly respected military and political planners in several European states have been studying the prospects for such a transition. It represents a revolution in security policy, one that is currently bubbling just below the level of official policy but that might well emerge in the 21st century, especially with the end of the Cold War and with it, most justification for the existence of large, offensive standing armies.

Paradoxically, there is some danger that in de-emphasizing the role of traditional military forces, and placing the primary burden of defense on the shoulders of the civilian population, CBD could contribute to a kind of militarizing of national cultures, as civilians find themselves forced to confront the nitty-gritty of national security. The greatest problem, however, is probably a deeply ingrained distrust—on the part of the public as well as the military—of nonviolence as a workable strategy, combined with a widespread fascination with violence and a tendency to rely on it as a last resort, when—in a revealing phrase—"push comes to shove."

Prospects for Nonviolence

Despite the appeals of nonviolence, it seems unlikely that states will soon give over their defense to such strategies—whether Gandhian *satyagraha* or CBD. In the long run, however, it can be argued that nonviolence, in whatever form, offers hope whereas violence does not. Nonviolence, in fact, is not limited to tactics of defending a given people; rather, it is directed toward overthrowing an entire system of relationships that is fundamentally based on violence, oppression, and the unfair dominance of some by others. Thus, nonviolence is directly relevant not only to the prevention of war but also to the establishment of social justice, environmental protection, and the defense of human rights. It does not aim at merely achieving a more effective national defense, but rather a defense of all humanity and of the planet against destructiveness and violence, by seeking to change the terms within which individuals and groups interact.

It can be argued, for example, that the destructive patterns whereby people and states interact violently with each other are also reflected in the destructive style that characterizes the interaction of people with their environment. The destruction of rain forests, the clear-cutting of temperate zone woodlands, the gouging of the earth in the course of strip-mining, the pollution of water and air, the extinction of plant and animal species, even according to some people, the eating of meat and the use of internal combustion engines: All these may be considered forms of violence, and all result, in a sense, from a lack of *ahimsa*, in Gandhian terms. As former black power leader H. Rap Brown once pointed out, violence is as American as cherry pie. Sometimes this is presented as reassuring; that is, violence in the United States is nothing new and therefore nothing to get alarmed about. More appropriately, however, it is a warning: Violence is widely considered inimical to humanistic values. Accordingly, it has become commonplace to decry the prevalence of violence in American life, applied not only to international affairs but also to interpersonal patterns, including homicide and abuse of children and spouses, as well as to the wider, deeper patterns of structural violence including homelessness, drug abuse, environmental destruction, unemployment, poverty, unequal career options, inadequate medical care, and low-quality education.

Among some persons deeply committed to nonviolence, the legitimate outrage against violence is sometimes carried to excess; some would claim, for example, that education is violence, child rearing is violence, marriage is violence. If so, then perhaps even eating, sleeping, and breathing are violent (consider the destructive action of our molars, not to mention digestive acids). By this point, however, a serious distinction has been trivialized, leaving no alternatives than passivity and eventually, death, or else indifference and business-as-usual. But this is a minority and extreme view; as we have seen, nonviolence is, if nothing else, hardheaded and realistic, demanding that we become immersed, albeit with high ideals, in the actual world.

The leading advocates of nonviolence in the 20th century, Mohandas Gandhi and Martin Luther King, Jr., derived the core of their philosophy and the wellsprings of their activism from deeply felt religious faith: Gandhi was a devout Hindu, King was an ordained Southern Baptist minister. Others, by contrast, have emphasized the practical aspects of nonviolence as a tactic for achieving results in the social sphere. For example, Gene Sharp bases his commitment to nonviolence largely on the utilitarian need for alternatives to violence in meeting social injustice, as well as domestic tyranny and international aggression.

Advocates of nonviolence have been accused by many conservatives of being unpatriotic, not only because in the past they recommended a less bellicose attitude toward the Soviet Union (among others) but also because their efforts are in some ways subversive of accepted American values. Thus, in an invited memorandum to the Kerner Commission (convened by President Lyndon Johnson to investigate the causes of violence in American life, following the inner-city riots of the mid-1960s), Thomas Merton warned that the sources of violence can be found "not in esoteric groups but in the very culture itself, its mass media, its extreme individualism and competitiveness, its inflated myths of virility and toughness, and its overwhelming preoccupation" with various means of destruction.

Nonviolence, Merton emphasized, is likely to be resisted because it will be seen as weakening the position of the world's great powers. There will be other problems. Some government leaders find it much easier, for example, to preside over the rape and pillage of national resources, reaping short-term advantage (including election and reelection) rather than facing the daunting task of working toward a self-sustaining natural ecology that might remain viable indefinitely. A domestic society purged of structural societal violence might also require a deep rearrangement of current attitudes toward wealth, property, and privilege. And imagine a state whose military forces are dismantled, which is prepared to defend itself only nonviolently. Wouldn't it be vulnerable to coercion and attack, leading to loss of freedom and very high casualties? On the other hand, Costa Rica abolished its army in 1948 (after the military supported an unpopular dictator who was subsequently overthrown). It has persisted as a model democracy and has never been invaded, even though Costa Rica's neighbors have long been dictatorships and Central America has hardly been a peaceful region.

Pacifism is largely tolerated in the United States and many other countries, so long as it is practiced only by small and relatively uninfluential groups. But as Merton has pointed out,

> There is also an implication that any minority stand against war on ground of conscience is ipso facto a kind of deviant and morally eccentric position, to be tolerated only because there are always a few religious half-wits around in any case, and one has to humor them in order to preserve the nation's reputation for respecting individual liberty.[16]

Would it ever be practical to rest a state's defense on nonviolent, civilian-based tactics and strategies? Some claim that Gandhi only succeeded in India and King in the United States because both Britain and the United States had a long tradition of humane, civilized treatment of others. In fact, the opposite can also be argued: British responses to colonial insurrections (such as the "Sepoy Mutiny" of the mid-19th century) were often extraordinarily brutal, and the U.S. government did not exactly treat its Native Americans with forbearance, at least not at Wounded Knee and during numerous other massacres. It is certainly questionable whether even a Gandhi could have prevailed against a Stalin or a Hitler. CBD, for that matter, would be helpless against bombardment attacks, especially using nuclear weapons—but of course, military defense would be equally helpless. Opponents of nonviolence as a national strategy often point to the slaughter that might take place if a nonviolent country were invaded by a violent opponent. Supporters can point out, however, that in this case the casualties might very well be lower than if such an invasion were met with countervailing military force.

The question remains: Beyond nonviolence as a theoretical ideal, or as a profound personal witness, or even as it may someday inform domestic policy and contribute to positive peace, what about the realistic prospects of nonviolence in the realm of military affairs? Will the avoidance of war ever rest on a studied, collective refusal to engage in violence?

Admittedly, it is neither psychologically nor politically appealing to contemplate a strategy that "allows" an aggressor to take over one's country. But neither is it pleasant to contemplate military defense. It may be that military force is something with which we are considerably more familiar, not that it is necessarily more effective, especially if the billions of dollars now expended on the military were to be redirected toward nonviolent means. It may also be that governments would be vigorously opposed to instituting widespread nonviolent training, not only because it would compete with traditional military efforts but also because such training would empower the population to resist the government, thereby posing a threat—even to democracies, which, like most governments, are more comfortable responding in kind to violent provocations and armed resistance than to unarmed, nonviolent protest.

A Final Note on Nonviolence

Practical and efficacious nonviolence, not as an ideal but as an immediate policy—personal as well as national—seems foreign to most Westerners, including most professed Christians. "Christianity has not been tried and found wanting," noted the English writer G. K. Chesterton, "rather, it has been difficult and left untried." What, we may ask, is the future of nonviolence? That is for you, the readers of this book, to determine. Or, alternatively, we might ask: Does the world have a future *without* nonviolence? In his masterpiece, *Leaves of Grass*, the 19th-century American poet Walt Whitman gives this simple answer:

> Were you looking to be held together by lawyers?
> Or by an agreement on a paper? Or by arms?
> Nay, nor the world, nor any living thing, will so cohere.
> Only those who love each other shall become indivisible.[17]

Notes

1. Quoted in E. Easwaran. 1978. *Gandhi the Man*. Petaluma, CA: Nilgiri Press.

2. Quoted in N. K. Bose, ed., 1957. *Selections From Gandhi*. Ahmedabad, India: Navajivan.

3. James P. Hanigan. 1984. *Martin Luther King, Jr., and the Foundations of Nonviolence*. New York: University Press of America.

4. Mohandas K. Gandhi. 1940. *An Autobiography: The Story of My Experiments With Truth*. Ahmedabad, India: Navajivan.

5. Bertolt Brecht. 1976. *Poems*. London: Methuen.

6. Mohandas K. Gandhi. 1968. *Selected Works*. S. Narayan, ed. Ahmedabad, India: Navajivan.

7. Gandhi, *An Autobiography*.

8. Quoted in Erik Erikson. 1969. *Gandhi's Truth*. New York: Norton.

9. Quoted in Joan Bondurant. 1971. *Conflict: Violence and Nonviolence*. Chicago: Aldine Atherton.

10. Quoted in Bose, *Selections*.

11. Easwaran, *Gandhi*.

12. Martin Luther King, Jr. 1964. *Why We Can't Wait*. New York: New American Library.

13. Martin Luther King, Jr. 1983. "My Pilgrimage to Nonviolence." Reprinted in *The Catholic Worker*, January/February.

14. Mohandas K. Gandhi. 1951. *Non-Violent Resistance*. New York: Schocken.

15. Gene Sharp. 1985. *Making Europe Unconquerable: The Potential of Civilian-Based Deterrence and Defense*. Cambridge, MA: Ballinger.

16. Thomas Merton. 1980. *The Non-Violent Alternative*. New York: Farrar, Straus & Giroux.

17. Walt Whitman. 1968. *Leaves of Grass*. New York: Norton.

21 Personal Transformation and the Future

There are moments when things go well and one feels encouraged. There are difficult moments and one feels overwhelmed. But it's senseless to speak of optimism or pessimism. The only important thing is to know that if one works well in a potato field, the potatoes will grow. If one works well among men, they will grow—that's reality. The rest is smoke. It's important to know that words don't move mountains. Work, exacting work, moves mountains.

—Danillo Dolci, renowned social activist

This will be a brief chapter, not because there isn't much to say but because personal transformation is fundamentally, well, personal. Concern with peace works in different ways for each of us. Some of you, reading this book in a course like any other, will simply obtain a grade and file it—along with whatever you may have learned along the way—someplace in your academic repertoire, to be variously forgotten or half-remembered. For others, exposure to peace and conflict studies may expand your consciousness in some significant way, influencing your subsequent behavior and perceptions. This book will have been successful in proportion as most readers find themselves in the latter category.

Transformations of Self and Society

When exposed to issues that are particularly relevant, or arguments that are especially cogent, or simply when emotions and other unconscious factors "click" in a mysterious and little-known manner, people may suddenly see the world in a different way. Individuals who have undergone a religious "conversion experience," for example, often speak of having been "born again," after which everything seems new and different. Peace studies does not necessarily aim for a comparable conversion experience, although it sometimes happens. There are many varieties of personal transformation, from the intense and mystical, to a practical determination to vote differently, give money to or get directly involved in a particular cause, read another book, take another course, or develop a lifelong vocation.

There are many people now working in various ways to help establish a world at peace. Richard Falk calls them "citizen/pilgrims," and they typically focus on specific goals, such as economic conversion; the abolition of nuclear weapons; an end to military interventionism; the abolition of poverty, malnutrition, political oppression, or environmental destruction; the defense of human rights; and a more life-affirming relationship of people and their planet as well as each other. The route of such citizen/pilgrims, like that of the earlier pilgrims hundreds of years ago, is likely to be long and difficult, but not impossible.

It has widely been claimed that peace must start within each individual, then spread outward: "Peace begins with me." This implies not only examining one's own life and making changes that seem consistent with one's beliefs but also identifying those personal patterns that may reinforce societywide systems of oppression. Such self-examination may in turn lead to some painful recognitions and decisions: recognizing how one's life may have at times involved the oppression of others, questioning what balance is desirable (and feasible) between relative personal privilege and selfless devotion to a cause. For some people, fighting oppression requires breaking out of their own oppression. "A liberal," goes the saying, "fights for other people's liberation; a radical fights for his or her own." Minimizing oppressive personal relationships may well be a prerequisite for helping alleviate the oppression of others.

To some degree, the world will be a better and less violent place if each individual makes peace in his or her own life. Important as it is, however, the personal transformation involved in making one's own inner peace is only part of the necessary equation; peace must be made not only internally but also externally, out "there" in the real and sometimes nasty world. No amount of "centeredness," "organic living," "alternative lifestyles," or personal peace will solve the problems of surrogate war in the developing world, of poverty, of the denial of human rights, and of environmental abuse, to say nothing of the danger of nuclear war. One can think pure thoughts, eat only organic foods, and never think ill of another, but this won't prevent destruction of the rain forests, provide a decent education for a little girl in Mozambique, or prevent the next episode of genocide and "ethnic cleansing." Peace may begin with each of us, but war, at least, is likely to begin elsewhere, and peace must entail significant changes in the world at large. It may be satisfying—and even necessary—to "liberate" one-self, but it is not sufficient.

In the course of becoming involved in the struggle for peace, an awkward collision may be unavoidable, between a personal, ethical commitment to nonviolence and some of the harsh realities of a world in which "freedom," "equality," and "liberation" may require conflict—preferably nonviolent—with existing authorities if any meaningful change is to occur.

Stumbling Blocks to Personal Transformation

These are deeply personal challenges that everyone will confront in his or her unique way. For some people, the decision to become involved in solving the world's problems derives from ethical/religious conviction. For others, a sense of outraged humanism opens their eyes to the injustices and dangers afflicting this planet. Sometimes a commitment to peace derives from a kind of transformative experience, perhaps a sudden crash of insight, what has been called a moment of "epiphany," when things are seen with a unique and breathtaking clarity. At other times, it comes slowly and gradually, with the progressive realization that something long suspected is in fact true, as fact, ideas, and personal experiences fit into a coherent whole. Sometimes the appeal is primarily logical, at other times emotional and apparently beyond reason.

For others, of course, it doesn't come at all. The thrust of this final chapter is that personal transformation is a prerequisite for the achievement of a just and enduring peace, but not its only precondition. (Not that everyone must be transformed; for most successful social movements, it is only necessary that a critical number—perhaps fewer than 10% of the population—become sincerely committed to the outcome. For a major restructuring of any large industrial society, perhaps 40% to 50% will be needed.) In any event, it may well be that the greatest barrier to peace is less the intractability of world problems than the fact that those problems are psychologically, and thus politically, invisible. Moreover, many of those in the affluent West who do perceive these problems tend to respond either with hopelessness or self-defeating violence.

Violence generally evokes its own response, comparably violent. As to hopelessness, there are several avenues. One is to point out some hopeful possibilities, as we have tried to do in this book. Another is to adopt the existential view that hopelessness is itself fundamental to the human condition, which in turn necessitates that we struggle—without hope—because that is what it *means* to be human. And yet another is to embrace despair as an indication of our fundamental love for the planet and its living creatures. After all, if we did not care, we would not grieve. And, paradoxically, out of that recognition can come renewed strength.

Hopelessness, in turn, can result from two different sources. On the one hand, there is the literal lack of hope, a denial that solutions even exist, or could ever be implemented. On the other, there is a frustration that derives from facing life as a small, isolated individual in a very large and complicated world. The issue in this case is not so much an absence of hope as a lack of power, or rather, a perception of one's powerlessness. One purpose of peace studies is to provide some empowerment, on both levels.

There are those who refuse to see the world's plight, possibly worrying that the problem of peace is so vast that if they open themselves to its immensity, they would be sucked in, irresistibly, as into a black hole. To these people, we point out that insofar as they see the problem this way, they have already been engulfed, whether they recognize it or not. Admitting their concerns and anxieties, and allowing themselves to act on them, will be refreshing in the extreme, even exhilarating. And of course, they do not really have to devote themselves to planetary betterment 100%, body, mind, and soul. They can support peace, with their votes, some volunteer time, occasional financial contributions, and so forth, without disrupting their entire lives. To be sure, they can also make a deeper commitment; there is no objective right or wrong in such cases.

Those who fail to see the planetary plight, on the other hand, tend to be reacting to one of three circumstances:

1. A sense that the world's ills are inevitable, part of the natural landscape, like many people once imagined slavery to be

2. A refusal to admit that which is discomfiting—that is, possibly practicing denial—because of an understandable inclination to spare themselves emotional pain

3. A feeling of being victims of inadequate public and private attention to the problems

In a society that in some ways does not really *want* to confront the world's difficulties and especially, its own complicity in creating them (such as the situation of the United States today), it is relatively easy to avoid thinking very much about nuclear weapons, environmental deterioration, and world poverty, not to mention genocide against what are (for affluent Westerners) obscure populations in, say, Brazil or the Philippines.

But what is "easy" may not be what is right. And since the world is small and getting smaller, as the problems begin to mount, no one will long be insulated from their effects. We are rapidly approaching the situation when only an ostrich, head determinedly buried in the sand, will be able to avoid the fundamental issues of avoiding war and establishing peace.

The Brazilian social activist Paulo Freire has coined the term *conscientization* to denote the achievement of, first, personal and then group awareness. Freire is primarily concerned with the establishment of social justice, and he calls, accordingly, for "humanization," which is "thwarted by injustice, exploitation, oppression, and the violence of the oppressors; it is affirmed by the yearning of the oppressed for freedom and justice, and by their struggle to recover their lost humanity."

As Freire emphasizes, one of the most important components of personal transformation is empowerment. In some cases, to be sure, individuals commit themselves to a cause despite a certainty that they will ultimately fail; the most notable example is that of the French existentialists, such as Albert Camus, who argued that death makes life absurd, and who emphasized that as a result, it is fundamental to the human condition that we each define ourselves by our struggle against so uncaring a universe—even though, like Sisyphus, we are necessarily doomed to repeated failure. But for most people, commitment and action are not forthcoming without a sense of ability, and of hope. The image of ultimate failure is not usually considered a reassuring one, likely to recruit a large number of enthusiastic followers. "In order for the oppressed to wage the struggle for their liberation," writes Freire,

> they must perceive the reality of oppression not as a closed world from which there is no exit, but as a limiting situation which they can transform. This perception is a necessary but not a sufficient condition for liberation; it must become the motivating force for liberating action.[1]

_____ Motivating Factors in Personal Transformation

Although oppression is most blatant in the *favelas* (slums) of São Paolo, the grinding rural poverty of Chad and Ethiopia, or in the treatment of political prisoners in Cuba, Israel, Iraq, or China, it should be clear even to relatively fortunate college students in the United States that they, too, are both contributors to, and victims of, what has been called "invisible oppression." This includes environmental abuse, economic maldistribution, and the state-sponsored terrorism of nuclear weapons.

This is a large part of our personal motivation in writing this text: to contribute to the awakening and empowering of peace and conflict studies students. But even knowledge and information, taken alone, are not enough. Also needed is a sense of personal responsibility and, in most cases, of realistic prospects for success.

Helen Caldicott, Australian physician and influential peace worker, used to recruit antinuclear activists by urging each individual in her audience to "take the world upon your shoulders, like Atlas." It may be a heavy load, but it is somewhat lighter when shared. And furthermore, if each of us doesn't do it, who will? Law professor Roger Fisher once made an especially effective plea for personal involvement, when he was speaking at an antiwar symposium. He began by recounting a friend's reaction to the title of his presentation, "Preventing Nuclear War." His friend's response was "Boy, have *you* got a problem!" Here are Fisher's own words:

> That reaction a few minutes ago to the title of these remarks reminded me of an incident when during World War II, I was a B-17 weather reconnaissance officer. One fine day we were in Newfoundland test-flying a new engine that replaced one we had lost. Our pilot's rank was only that of flight officer because he had been court-martialed so frequently for his wild activities; but he was highly skillful.
>
> He got us up to about 14,000 feet and then, to give the new engine a rigorous test, he stopped the other three and feathered their propellers into the wind. It is rather impressive to see what a B-17 can do on one engine. But then, just for a lark, the pilot feathered the fourth propeller and turned off that fourth engine. With all four propellers stationary, we glided, somewhat like a stone, toward the rocks and forests of Newfoundland.
>
> After a minute or so the pilot pushed the button to unfeather. Only then did he remember: In order to unfeather the propeller you had to have electric power, and in order to have electric power you had to have at least one engine going. As we were buckling on our parachutes, the co-pilot burst out laughing. Turning to the pilot he said, "Boy, have *you* got a problem!"

Fisher then went on to discuss some of the difficulties as well as the prospects of preventing global war. At the end of his talk, he returned to the hapless B-17, with himself inside, without power and about to crash:

> Well, we didn't crash; we weren't all killed. On that plane we had a buck sergeant who remembered that back behind the bomb bay we had a putt-putt generator for use in case we had to land at some emergency air field that did not have any electric power to start the engines. The sergeant found it. He fiddled with the carburetor; wrapped a rope around the flywheel a few times; pulled it and pulled it; got the generator going and before we were down to 3,000 feet we had electricity. The pilot restarted the engines, and we were all safe. Now saving that plane was not the sergeant's job in the sense that he created the risk. The danger we were in was not his fault or his responsibility. But it was his job in the sense that he had an opportunity to do something about it.[2]

It can be argued that each of us has a duty to contribute to world peace, if only because—like the crew in Roger Fisher's stricken B-17—we are all in this world together, and it is definitely at risk. There aren't even any parachutes. At least as important, however, is the fact that each of us can make a contribution.

Social psychologists have determined that of the various factors that seem likely to motivate people to change their behavior, the most powerful is the simple message "You can do it," that is, evidence that individual behavior will be effective in generating some desirable effect. For example, in a psychological experiment, participants were given three different kinds of information about cigarette smoking, automobile injuries, and sexually transmitted disease. The purpose was to determine which information was most effective in changing the behavior of the participants: (1) details about the noxious consequences of the events (interviews with lung cancer patients, gruesome photos of automobile and sexually transmitted disease victims); (2) statistical data about the probability of experiencing or contracting these outcomes if behavior remains unchanged; and (3) information specifying what preventive measures can be taken and emphasizing their likely effectiveness. The results showed clearly that the third factor, the "efficacy of coping responses," was the most influential in inducing people to change their behavior. Moreover, the first consideration—appeals to fear by emphasizing the noxiousness of the threat—actually served to *reduce* the likelihood that people would engage in adaptive behavior, apparently because such appeals evoked powerful psychological resistances in the participants.[3]

The implications for peace studies may be important. If significant numbers of people are to change, to break through their crust of denial and indifference, it may be most effective to appeal to their sense of efficacy rather than to their rational evaluation of danger, or to their raw fear. The latter, in fact, may even be counterproductive.

An additional motivating factor deserves mention in this context: fun. The ironic truth is that it can be great fun trying to bring peace to the world. For Roger Fisher, it is:

> an exciting venture. It is a glorious world outside. There are people to be loved and pleasures to share. We should not let details of past wars and threat of the future take away the fun and joy we can have working together on a challenging task. I see no reason to be gloomy about trying to save the world. There is more exhilaration, more challenge, more zest in tilting at windmills than in any routine job. Be involved, not just intellectually but emotionally. Here is a chance to work together with affection, with caring, with feeling. Feel some of your emotions. Don't be uptight. You don't have to be simply a doctor, a lawyer, or a merchant. We are human beings. Be human.
>
> People have struggled all of their lives to clear ten acres of ground or simply to maintain themselves and their family. Look at the oppor-

tunity we have. Few people in history have been given such a chance—
a chance to apply our convictions, our values, our highest moral goals
with such competence as our skills may give us. A chance to work with
others—to have the satisfaction that comes from playing a role, however small, in a constructive enterprise. It's not compulsory. So much
the better. But what challenge could be greater? We have an opportunity to improve the chance of human survival.[4]

The Social Efficacy of Individual Action

No one can accurately assess the prospects of establishing peace in the
world. Certainly, the problems can be identified, and some of the proposed
solutions can be discussed. This we have attempted to do. Many of them
may be feasible, especially if initiated in combination rather than alone: a
switch to nonprovocative defense, substantially reduced and de-alerted
nuclear arsenals, redistribution of global expenditures from the military to
social needs, protection of the environment and human rights, strengthening
of various world peacekeeping systems in the context of establishing global
rather than national security, a widespread shift toward nonviolence, and a
conscientious collective effort to address inequities in wealth.

As to the efficacy of individual action, it cannot be stated too strongly
that individuals *can* make a difference, and not only larger-than-life figures
such as Mother Teresa or Martin Luther King, Jr. In a democracy, individuals count. Each one of us. Moreover, powerlessness is often a self-fulfilling
prophecy, but so is empowerment. When people are convinced that they are
helpless and that their behavior is insignificant, then in fact they will behave
helplessly and without significance. But the opposite can also be true. "It
is within our power," wrote Thomas Paine more than 200 years ago, "to
begin the world anew." To some degree, that is exactly what happened
when a country was formed based on the principle of democracy and self-
government. And the prospect of major, transformative change—not only
within individuals but in their society as well—is no less true in our time
than it was in his. (Interestingly, Edmund Burke, writing at about the same
time as Paine, but espousing a very different view of what the world should
be like, noted that "the only thing necessary for the triumph of evil is for
good men[5] to do nothing.")

In addition, there is some reason for optimism. The Cold War is over, and
nuclear weapons are becoming increasingly delegitimized in the minds of
some leaders and citizens alike. War itself may be headed in a similar direction. Next might come the elimination of major violent conflicts, and eventually, progress toward positive peace. For this process to continue (to some
degree it has already begun), at least three things are needed: (1) belief in the
possibility of peace, (2) belief in one's personal power and efficacy, and (3)

motivation to proceed, whether individually or collectively. We emphasize the first of these.

A primary block to the establishment of peace is not so much the actual difficulty of achieving it, but rather the *feeling* that it is impossible, the inability or refusal of many people to imagine peace as a realistic prospect. The widespread disbelief that peace is possible is a major hindrance to its ever becoming real. Before anything can be done, it must first be imagined, and the importance of effective imagery and of visualizing one's goal cannot be overestimated:

> It is a way of thinking that raises up images of what might be—should be—and thereby helps people to see potential that otherwise might not be understood and evokes action that might not otherwise occur. These images generate energy and forestall early compromise with lesser results. Such images are often dismissed as visionary and impractical. And the state of mind that often evokes that response is one of the burdens of our society. It is a state of mind that inhibits movement towards goals that may be widely accepted as valid and important by discounting them in advance as unachievable.[6]

Athletics coaches, business leaders, and many actors on the world stage have come to recognize the value of visualization: imagining one's body perfectly coordinated during a gymnastics exercise, or envisioning oneself achieving a new sales record, and so forth. Subtly, unconsciously, the mind can be essentially "reprogrammed," releasing new potentials and facilitating the accomplishment of things previously thought out of reach. Personal transformation does occur, but only after people believe in the possibility of themselves changing, have a positive image of the kind of change they desire, and are positively reinforced by others seeking to accomplish similar goals.

At the same time, for the world to be transformed toward peace, people must believe in the *possibility* of peace, or their efforts are liable to be half-hearted, if they make any at all. They must begin imagining a world at peace. Such an image need not be finished in all its fine points and details. But it must be realistic and feasible. It must not project so far into the future that it seems irrelevant to the present, and it must not make excessive demands on human capacities as we know them. At the same time, it must be idealistic enough to be inspirational, to be worth striving for.

There are many people who believe that the world today stands at the brink of a major transformation. In less than a decade, the Internet has changed many personal habits, not to mention world commerce for millions, with effects that are just being glimpsed. National barriers have fallen, not only with the demise of the Soviet Union but also with the growth of continentwide identity (political, economic, social) in Europe particularly. South African apartheid is now a bad memory. The very idea that society may change profoundly may itself be the most profound of all social ideas, capable of midwifing remarkable changes.

Toward the Future

It has been said that the only constant throughout history is change. The future is not optional. This is to say that there will be some sort of future; the question is, what sort? In a representative democracy, people who do not vote are not in the strongest position to complain if they do not get the outcome they want. This is also true for people who do not work toward a preferred future.

There is nothing necessarily fixed and immutable about the world as it exists today. A world system based on nation-states could give way to one based on local, semiautonomous communities, just as reliance on nuclear weapons may be replaced by widespread revulsion toward them. Nonviolence could swell and violence could shrink in human affairs. Many aspects of a world at peace, discussed in the preceding chapters, could be instituted with only minimal alteration in the basic face of human society as it now exists. As progress is made and new systems are institutionalized, social change could then be evolutionary rather then revolutionary. It may also be lasting.

Among recent exciting developments has been the emergence of connections among social activists who used to work in relative isolation. The worldwide women's movement, for example, has gradually emerged from being primarily a concern of middle- and upper-class white women to embrace "sisters" of many different races and economic classes (and even large numbers of men). Similarly, environmental concerns are increasingly seen as issues that transcend the interests of people who are economically and socially privileged. There is growing recognition that, if anything, "environmental racism" tends to be particularly a burden for the poor and dispossessed. At the anti-World Trade Organization protests in Seattle in late 1999, for example, shared interests were identified and relationships forged among labor, environmentalists, and peace and human rights activists, reflecting a kind of cross-connecting solidarity that has rarely been seen before in the United States. Particularly striking was a poster reading, "Turtles and Teamsters, together at last." Such "togetherness" would have been an oxymoron in the recent past, since U.S. environmentalists and labor unions—although basically sharing a progressive agenda—have been more likely to quarrel than to agree: Loggers and miners, for example, used to side with industry in opposition to environmental protection. A new recognition of shared interests may augur an exciting future of unforeseen empowerment. To the above must also be added the unique opportunity provided by the Internet. This technological milestone is not only a convenience for many and a source of immense wealth for a privileged few: It also offers a previously unavailable opportunity for the low-cost sharing of information, worldwide, with the further prospect of mobilizing opinion and political action.

This is a heady time to be alive. Soviet communism and South African apartheid have both collapsed, and essentially without a shot being fired. In such a world of unprecedented interconnections and increasing democratization, who is to say that other monumental achievements are impossible?

A Final Note on Personal Transformation

The achievement of peace is only secondarily a problem of "hardware," to be solved by the manipulation of structures, whether biological or social. Primarily, it is a problem in human "software," in the ways we think, and often stubbornly refuse to do so. And herein lies the hope, because there is enormous potential within the human species, not only to remove the "bugs" from our own program but also to re-create our lives as we rebuild our world. "Every transformation of man," wrote Lewis Mumford,

> has rested on a new metaphysical and ideological base; or rather, upon a new picture of the cosmos and the nature of man. . . . We stand on the brink of a new age. . . . In carrying man's self-transformation to this further stage, world culture may bring about a fresh release of spiritual energy that will unveil new potentialities, no more visible in the human self today than radium was in the physical world a century ago, though always present.[7]

Mumford's exhortation is not simply a softheaded appeal to quasi-mysticism and "feel-good" pop psychology; it is the stuff of which conceptual revolutions (and sometimes, flesh-and-blood revolutions) are made. Social organizer Saul Alinsky coined a valuable phrase for would-be activists: "Think globally, act locally." There are many avenues for personal involvement, additional training to acquire, and numerous organizations to join, a large number of which are active at the local as well as at the national and global levels. Most people find it difficult to persevere alone, and education is empowering; this is why peace and conflict studies is taught, and why various action groups are also so important.

If a little knowledge is a dangerous thing, try getting a lot of knowledge, either through additional coursework or on your own. On an applied level, groups tend to have a larger voice than a solitary individual. If you are a "joiner," join. If not, consider acting alone. Either way, when was the last time you stood up for something you believed in, and that had such enormous implications for your own future—not to mention the future of the world? Do you *really* have anything more important to do?

Notes

1. Paulo Freire. 1970. *Pedagogy of the Oppressed*. New York: Continuum.

2. Roger Fisher. 1981. "Preventing Nuclear War." In R. Adams and S. Cullen, eds., *The Final Epidemic*. Chicago: Educational Foundation for Nuclear Science.

3. R. W. Rodgers and C. R. Mewborn. 1976. "Fear Appeals and Attitude Change: Effects of a Threat's Noxiousness, Probability of Occurrence, and the Efficacy of Coping Responses." *Journal of Personality and Social Psychology* 34: 54–67.

4. Fisher, "Preventing."

5. Make that, "good *people*."

6. James Rouse, in a commencement address at Johns Hopkins University in 1985. Quoted in H. B. Hollins, A. L. Powers, and M. Sommer. 1989. *The Conquest of War*. Boulder, CO: Westview.

7. Lewis Mumford. 1956. *The Transformation of Man*. New York: Harper & Row.

Name Index

Subject Index

About the Authors _____

David P. Barash (PhD, 1970, University of Wisconsin) is Professor of Psychology at the University of Washington, Seattle, and is cofounder and codirector of the Peace and Strategic Studies program there. He is a Fellow of the American Association for the Advancement of Science (Washington, D.C.) and of the Center for Advanced Study in the Behavioral Sciences (Stanford University), and he has also been a Fellow at the Bellagio Study Center at Lake Como (Rockefeller Foundation). He has written nearly 200 technical articles and 21 books and has lectured—and protested—widely throughout the world. His original training was in evolutionary biology; since 1979 he has turned much of his professional attention to the question of peace. His books include *Stop Nuclear War! A Handbook*—nominated for the 1982 National Book Award—and *The Caveman and the Bomb* (1985), both coauthored with his wife, Judith Eve Lipton, MD, as well as *Beloved Enemies: Our Need for Opponents* (1994). He is also author of the following peace-related textbooks: *The Arms Race and Nuclear War* (1986), *Approaches to Peace: A Reader in Peace Studies* (2000), and *Understanding Violence* (2001).

Charles P. Webel (PhD, University of California at Berkeley) is currently a member of the Executive Faculty at Saybrook Graduate School in San Francisco and is also a faculty member at Walden University. He has also taught at the University of California at Berkeley, California State University at Chico, and Harvard University. He was a Fulbright Scholar at the University of Frankfurt, Germany, and has received grants from the National Endowment for the Humanities and the Social Science Research Council. He is author of many articles in philosophy, psychology, psychoanalysis, and social science; coeditor of *Marcuse: Critical Theory and the Promise of Utopia* (1988); and general editor of the scholarly book series Twenty-First Century Perspectives on War, Peace, and Human Conflict. He is a member of many professional and peace-related organizations, including TRANSCEND and International Philosophers for the Prevention of Nuclear War.